Praise for *The Apocryphal Sunday*

Uta Heil and the team of scholars around her have produced a remarkable and singular piece of scholarship, and they are to be heartily commended. The place of Sunday as a feast in the Christian tradition is a core object of Christian theology and biblical exegesis, and this monograph brings into the light a lesser-known but incredibly influential text, the so-called Letter from Heaven. Weaving together the weighty work of a critical edition of the document's various recensions with a wide-ranging exploration of how Sunday has been understood, *The Apocryphal Sunday* is now *the* place where all scholars will have to begin.

—Matthew S. C. Olver, Nashotah House Theological Seminary and Durham University

Sunday is central to Christian tradition, yet little is known about its origins. Uta Heil and her colleagues open our eyes to a fascinating body of texts from Late Antiquity, which they rigorously analyze, edit, and translate, revealing new perspectives from the margins of mainstream Christianity on the early observance and meanings of Sunday.

—Sacha Stern, FBA, University College London

This careful introduction to and collection of the popular literature on the observance of Sunday in Christian practice establishes the significance of the issue for both clergy and laity. By providing both an analysis and translations of the surviving documents, it appeals for and invites further investigation and evaluation of the startling means which some Christians dared to employ to urge their preferred practices on their fellows.

—J. Patout Burns Jr., University of Notre Dame

THE APOCRYPHAL SUNDAY

History and Texts from Late Antiquity

Uta Heil

Fortress Press
Minneapolis

THE APOCRYPHAL SUNDAY
History and Texts from Late Antiquity

Library of Congress Cataloging-in-Publication Data

Names: Heil, Uta, author.
Title: The apocryphal Sunday : history and texts from late antiquity / Uta Heil.
Description: Minneapolis : Fortress Press, [2023] | Includes bibliographical references and index. | English and Greek.
Identifiers: LCCN 2023008286 (print) | LCCN 2023008287 (ebook) | ISBN 9781506491073 (paperback) | ISBN 9781506491080 (ebook)
Subjects: LCSH: Sunday—History—Sources. | Apocryphal books—Criticism, interpretation, etc. | Church history—Primitive and early church, ca. 30-600—Sources.
Classification: LCC BV111.3 .H45 2023 (print) | LCC BV111.3 (ebook) | DDC 263/.3—dc23/eng/20230503
LC record available at https://lccn.loc.gov/2023008286
LC ebook record available at https://lccn.loc.gov/2023008287

Cover image: Cupola of Creation (or of Genesis), c.1230, - Byzantine, (13th century) Bridgeman Images
Cover design: Laurie Ingram

Print ISBN: 978-1-5064-9107-3
eBook ISBN: 978-1-5064-9108-0

Contents

Preface *(Uta Heil, with Canan Arıkan-Caba, Philip Polcar, Christoph Scheerer, and Angela Zielinski Kinney)* vii

A Introduction 1

1 Contexts *(Uta Heil)* 3

2 Texts in Addition to the Letter from Heaven *(Uta Heil)* 24

2.1. The Pseudepigraphal Acts of the Council of Caesarea 24

2.2. A New Fragment of the Dialogue between Jason and Papiscus (CPG 1101) from Sophronius of Jerusalem, *Oratio de circumcisione Christi* 25

2.3. *Visio Pauli* 34 or Apocalypse of Paul 44 (BHG 1460; BHL 6580–82) 25

2.4. A Homily: "Today, My Beloved, I'd Like to Praise the Day of the Lord" (CPG 2955 and CPG 4869) 26

2.5. A "Question and Answer about Sunday" (CPG 5525) 27

2.6. A Homily: "Hear, All Brothers Christians, What the Prophets Say" (CPG 4848) 28

2.7. An Anonymous Fragment on Four Sunday Names (Codex Vaticanus graecus 2392) 28

2.8. The *Diataxis* of the Holy Apostles (BHG 812a–e) 28

2.9. A Passage from the Apocalypsis Iohannis Apocrypha Altera (BHG 922i; CANT 332) 29

2.10. A Passage from the Apocalypse of Anastasia or *Visio Anastasiae Monialis* (BHG 1868-1870) 30

3 Letter from Heaven 31

3.1 Introduction and Research History *(Uta Heil)* 31

3.2 Latin Manuscripts *(Angela Zielinski Kinney)* 39

3.3 Manuscript Studies (Latin) *(Angela Zielinski Kinney)* 45

3.3.1 Methodology 45

3.3.2 Additional Manuscripts of the Latin Letter from Heaven (Up to 1500 CE) 46

3.3.3 Results: Latin Recension I 48
3.3.4 Results: Latin Recension II 52
3.3.5 Preliminary Conclusions 79
3.4 Greek Manuscripts *(Canan Arıkan-Caba)* 80
3.5 History *(Uta Heil)* 84
4 Considerations *(Uta Heil)* 134
4.1 Framing, Structure, and Discovery Legends *(Uta Heil)* 134
4.2 Rest or Work *(Uta Heil)* 143
4.2.1 The Sabbath Commandment in the Greek Sunday Apocrypha 144
4.2.2 Legacy of Eusebius of Caesarea? 153
4.2.3 Sunday Rest in the Latin Letter from Heaven 161
4.2.4 A Day of Reconciliation 168
4.2.5 Ecclesiastical Canons and Punitive Miracles 172
4.2.6 Duration of Sunday until Monday Morning 182
4.3 Threats and Punishments *(Uta Heil)* 184
4.4 Punishment of Women *(Uta Heil)* 195
5 Evaluation *(Uta Heil)* 201

B Texts and Translations 207
1 The Letter of Licinianus of Cartagena *(Philip Polcar)* 209
2 Letter from Heaven—Latin Recension II *(Philip Polcar and Christoph Scheerer)* 221
3 Letter from Heaven—Stone Inscription *(Michel-Yves Perrin)* 239
4 Letter from Heaven—Latin Recension I *(Philip Polcar)* 245
5 Letter from Heaven—Greek Recension Alpha *(Canan Arıkan-Caba)* 291
6 Letter from Heaven—Greek Recension Beta *(Angela Zielinski Kinney)* 329
7 Letter from Heaven—Greek Recension Beta (London) *(Canan Arıkan-Caba)* 383
8 The So-Called Acts of the Council of Caesarea *(Uta Heil and Christoph Scheerer)* 387
9 Sophronius of Jerusalem and Dialogue of Jason and Papiscus *(Uta Heil)* 411
10 *Visio Pauli* 34 or Apocalypse of Paul 44 *(Uta Heil)* 419
11 Three Pseudepigraphal Sunday Homilies *(Annette von Stockhausen)* 435
A Homily "Today, My Beloved, I'd Like to Praise the Day of the Lord" 435

A "Question and Answer about Sunday" 444
A Homily "Hear, All Brothers Christians, What the Prophets Say" 460
12 Four Names for Sunday (from Codex Vaticanus Graecus 2392) *(Renate Burri)* 467
13 *Diataxis*—Instructions of the Twelve Apostles *(Uta Heil and Ioannis Grossmann)* 475
14 The Second Apocryphal Apocalypse of John *(Uta Heil)* 491
15 The Apocalypse of Anastasia *(Uta Heil)* 497

C Literature 505
Selected Bibliography 507

Indexes 515

Preface

This book is produced as part of the research project on the Apocryphal Sunday funded by the Austrian Science Fund FWF (P 31428-G32). The volume is committed to various anonymous pseudepigraphal writings about Sunday, first and foremost the so-called Letter from Heaven, and thus combines research on the cultural history of Sunday with recent research on pseudepigraphal writings, whose significance is increasingly coming into focus. Therefore, the title was chosen because the importance of apocryphal and pseudepigraphal texts of late antiquity, which call for a clear Sunday worship, should be emphasized. In addition, it is intended to express that Sunday led a rather shadowy existence for many centuries in Christianity as well and was therefore in a sense equally apocryphal.

The volume is a collaborative work, on the one hand by members of the research project (Canan Arıkan-Caba, Philip Polcar, Christoph Scheerer, and Angela Zielinski Kinney) and on the other hand by colleagues working on texts that are also relevant. Angela Zielinski Kinney would also like to thank the Israel Institute for Advanced Studies, its director Yitzhak Hen, and her research group leader Yaniv Fox (as well as all the fellows in the group); a sizable portion of this research was conducted during her IIAS fellowship in the group "Purity and Pollution in Late Antique and Early Medieval Culture and Society."

Michel-Yves Perrin is to be thanked for his willingness to present the inscription with the Letter from Heaven here. Furthermore, I thank Renate Burri for her text find, which fits wonderfully into this text collection. Great thanks are also due to Annette von Stockhausen, who has worked on three pseudepigraphal sermons and has even created a new edition of these texts. I also thank Christoph Scheerer for his commitment to transfer the so-called Acts of the Synod of Caesarea into a new edition. In addition, I would like to thank Ioannis Grossmann, who together with me some time ago prepared the Greek *Didascalia* or *Diataxis* of the Twelve Apostles for a new edition. Study assistant Kathrin Breimayer is generally to be thanked for her assistance! And last but not least, I wish to show my gratitude to Angela Zielinski Kinney for her proofreading and for correcting our English—thanks a lot!

We are very pleased that this book, which is divided into two parts with a longer introduction and text presentations, has been accepted by Fortress Press. We thank you very much for the editorial support!

Uta Heil,
with Canan Arıkan-Caba, Philip Polcar, Christoph Scheerer,
and Angela Zielinski Kinney
Vienna, September 2022

A INTRODUCTION

1
CONTEXTS

Uta Heil

The cultural history of Sunday as a day of rest in late antiquity and the early Middle Ages is complex. The previously proposed outline of its development has been repeatedly challenged by scholars of history and religion, and the story of Sunday has been revealed as far more variegated than is apparent at first glance. For example, Sunday did not simply replace the Jewish Sabbath, nor was the Sabbath commandment directly transferred to Sunday.[1] Furthermore, the various Sunday laws enacted by the emperor Constantine officially gave the inhabitants of the Roman Empire a day of rest from work, but the effect and reception of these laws are hard to ascertain, even among Christian authors. Moreover, the commandment of rest in Constantine's legislation is not even referenced in later imperial legislation.[2] In addition, Sunday was by no means a central theme in the history of late antique Christianity, so the scattered extant references must be interpreted carefully. Even the origins of the weekly gatherings of Christians on the first day of the week or on the Lord's Day can only be roughly and indirectly deduced, although much detailed research has been conducted on this topic.[3] For the further

1. See on this below, 4.2 "Rest or Work" at pp. 143–200.

2. See Mitthof, "Christianization of the Empire," 27–74, on Constantine's law, discussing the sources and further literature; and Heil and Mitthof, "Missachtung der Sonntagsruhe," 75–92, on a recently found inscription with a law on Sunday of the *Codex Theodosianus*.

3. Early NT evidence does not provide a clear picture: the collection on the first day of the week mentioned by Paul in 1 Cor 16:2 does not necessarily presuppose an assembly; neither does the assembly at Troas when Paul preached there, according to the account in Acts 20:7; and the Lord's Day of Rev 1:10 could also be meant as an eschatological day. However, the evidence from the second and third centuries taken together (Barn. 15.8; Ign. *Magn.* 9.1; Gos. Pet. 35; 50; Justin Martyr, *1 Apol.* 67; *Dial.* 24.1; 41.4; 138.1; Did. 14.1; Dionysius of Corinth, *Letter to Soter of Rome* [in Eusebius of Caesarea, *Hist. eccl.* 4.23.11], the practice of the Ebionites [according to Eusebius of Caesarea, *Hist. eccl.* 3.27]; Melito of

development from the fourth century on, after the Sunday laws of Constantine, there are rather rough overviews[4] and some specific studies, but they do not do justice to the diversity of practice and regional differences. Christian life looked different in the city from its manifestation in the countryside, different in Asia Minor from North Africa, and different again in monastic circles, which were themselves diverse.[5] Beyond that, there are a handful of source texts that are repeatedly referenced, especially since Willy Rordorf so conveniently compiled them into a bilingual edition.[6] The focus of this volume, however, is on other texts that have so far received only secondary attention, especially certain important apocryphal and pseudepigraphal writings that were nevertheless widespread and made an impact. They must not be neglected as an important supplement. In essence, the history of Sunday can be viewed from three angles.

First, of course, one can take a look at the liturgical development of the church service,[7] but this will be considered only marginally here. However, one interesting text is included, the so-called pseudepigraphal Acts of the Synod of Caesarea, based on a new edition of the text. Here one can see how the growing importance of the Lord's Day flows into the justification of the Easter date calculation, especially in order to prevent Easter from being celebrated on a fixed date with a changing day of the week.

Second, Sunday as a regularly recurring day of the week can be considered a special temporal category. Obviously, Sunday gained significance as a

---

Sardis [according to Eusebius, *Hist. eccl.* 4.26.2]; Clement of Alexandria, *Exc.* 63; *Strom.* 5.14.106.2–4; Tertullian, *Idol.* 14.7; *Cor.* 3.3f.; *Jejun.* 15.2; *Fug.* 14.1; *Nat.* 1.13; *Apol.* 16.11; 39; Minucius Felix, *Oct.* 9; 31) suggests that the "certain day" (*stato die*) on which Christians met, referred to by Pliny in his famous letter on the persecution of Christians (*Ep.* 10.96.7), was indeed a Sunday. See especially Alikin, *Earliest History*; Bacchiocchi, *Du Sabbat au Dimanche*, with the review by Allen, "How Did the Jewish Sabbath," 337–53; Bradshaw and Johnson, *Origins of Feasts*; Carson, *From Sabbath to Lord's Day*, here especially the contributions of Bauckham: "The Lord's Day," 222-50, "Sabbath and Sunday in the Post-apostolic Church," 252-98, and "Sabbath and Sunday in the Medieval Church," 300-309; Heil, "Ignatios von Antiochia," 201–27; Durst, "Sonntag"; Durst, "Remarks on Sunday," 373–400; Rordorf, *Der Sonntag*; ET: *Sunday*.

4. See the general overview by González, *Brief History of Sunday*, and the literature above, n. 3 and below n. 8. A still worthwhile study that extends to the high Middle Ages, although it often includes problematic evaluations, is Huber, *Geist und Buchstabe*. Outdated is Thomas, *Der Sonntag*. See on problematic views on the early Middle Ages Meier, "Christian Sunday," 251-72, esp. 254-57.

5. See Müller, "Sunday in Palestinian Monasticism," 233-49.

6. Rordorf, *Sabbat und Sonntag in der Alten Kirche*.

7. See now Buchinger, "Sunday Celebration," 401-33; Drecoll, "Not Every Sunday Is the Same," 435-52, both with additional bibliography.

calendrical and computational fixed point for the structuring of time in weekly rhythms and for dates with weekday designations.[8] The understanding of time and its manifestation in calendrical form are not natural; rather, they are based on a social agreement. Living together in a community is not merely shaped by a common urban space, for example, but also by various temporal activities influenced by or associated with the time of the day, the day of the month, or the month of the year.[9]

Therefore, in every society there is something like a matrix, an invisible map of time that coordinates temporal activities. The presupposed calendar in which these events and appointments are found is a temporal topography, so to speak, within which each person must locate oneself. This temporal location reveals how an individual or group makes use of time and (in part) what is important to a person: what is worth one's time.

If one could synthesize the individual calendars of everyone in a community or city, the impact of religion in everyday life would become visible. Accordingly, religious experiences and religious identity are highly influenced by temporal categories. Of course, these can also change; some items can increase in importance, others can decrease. The growing importance of Sunday within this temporal matrix, as it is promoted by several apocryphal and pseudepigraphal texts, provides the topic of this volume.[10]

It is obvious that a common identity of a special group, a social milieu, or a specific religion can be established very effectively through temporal practices such as a common festival calendar, just as the process of othering occurs in reverse through a different temporal rhythm. That is a consistent concern of these texts presented here: Christians observe Sunday. So the reverse is also

8. Mark Anderson's article ("Christianizing the Planetary Week," 128–91) is one of the latest contributions on the names of the weekdays, with many Greek and Latin sources in the appendices, along with Bultrighini and Stern, "Seven-Day-Week," 10–79; but see also Michele Renée Salzman on their gradual development ("Pagan and Christian Notions"). See also n. 3. The thorough article by Henri Dumaine ("Dimanche") is still worth consulting, as well as Pietri, "Le temps de la semaine"; Dölger, "Die Planetenwoche," 228–38; and Schürer, "Die siebentägige Woche," 1–66. See in general Rüpke, *Roman Calendar*.

9. On the concept of social time, see the inspiring essay by Norbert Elias, *Über die Zeit* (Frankfurt am Main: Suhrkamp, 1984). See on Elias's concept Simonetta Tabboni, "The Idea of Social Time in Norbert Elias," *Time & Society* 10 (2001): 5–27; in addition, Barbara Adam, *Time and Social Theory* (Cambridge: Polity Press, 1990). These are important reflections on the impact of the social construction of time and temporal rhythms in addition to natural (e.g., solar, lunar) and biological (e.g., aging) influences.

10. On Sunday and the weekly structures of life, see Remijsen, "Business as Usual?," 143–86; Graumann, "In Search for Synodical Activities," 187–206; and Müller, "Sunday in Palestinian Monasticism."

true: only those who behave properly on Sunday as Lord's Day and honor this day are true Christians. Otherwise, there is the threat of ecclesiastical exclusion or divine judgment. Therefore, apart from a more or less peaceful coexistence of different religious, economic, political, and family activities, there exists of course also an element of competition in the case of simultaneity or in the case of different estimations of a special day.

In addition, one has to take into consideration that not all days are equal. This means that time is not regarded as a neutral continuum but as qualified in many aspects: through astrology (good/bad days, lucky/unlucky days), through imperial feasts, through ecclesiastical calendars, through birth and death of individuals, and so on. The seven-day week as a planetary week is itself connected with astrological-astronomical thinking.[11] As is widely known, it was common to use a plug-in calendar to determine the day of the week, the so-called *parapegmata*; and even the Calendar of Philocalus from 354 CE provides corresponding astrological information.[12] Here one oriented oneself to the character of the day in order to secure its activities, namely, whether they should be undertaken or postponed. Thus, it is important to recognize that not all days are monochromatic—meaning quotidian religious experience actually differs from day to day. This is especially true of Sunday: this day stands out from the crowd of weekdays and has been ordained by God to play a special role in the course of salvation history, as these texts in this volume claim. One finds fluent transitions between what is vehemently criticized as (unchristian) astrology and what is accepted as Christian theology and piety.

Third—a topic in the foreground of this volume—Sunday acquires prominent importance among cultural-historical questions concerning the celebration of the day as a whole. How did one arrange the day? What was allowed to be done on it, and what was not allowed? How was this justified? How was any agreement reached on this at all? Of course, these three aspects (liturgy, chronology, culture) are interrelated and influence one another. And relevant to all aspects are interreligious relations such as the relationship with Judaism, as well as other cross-cultural issues such as public bathing culture,

11. See the latest contribution on this topic by Bultrighini, "Theōn Hemerai," 217–39; and Bultrighini and Stern, "Seven-Day-Week."

12. See the recommendation and prognostic for Sunday in the Calendar of Philocalus: "Good for travel start, for land and especially for ship voyages. Those born on this day are fit to live. Recovery of missing persons is possible. Those who fall ill on this day will recover, a theft will be solved, stolen goods will be recovered." See Johannes Divjak and Wolfgang Wischmeyer, eds., *Das Kalenderhandbuch von 354. Der Chronograph des Filocalus*, vol. 1, *Der Bildteil des Chronographen*; vol. 2, *Der Textteil—Listen der Verwaltung* (Vienna: Holzhausen, 2014), here 1:112.

theater culture,[13] aspects of economic life (How does Sunday legislation influence the rhythm and form of weekly markets?) and of the military (Was there Sunday rest in the army?), in addition to persisting astrological conceptions.[14] To put it another way, addressing these temporal aspects helps one understand lived religious experience. The competition between Sabbath and Sunday is just one example of this effect. In addition, the rivalry between Sunday and other Christian feasts (e.g., martyr festivals), as well as between Sunday and non-Christian holidays, is relevant.

Against this background, it becomes understandable that the cultural history of Sunday depicts a multilayered process. Even though it was already a matter of course in the second century for Christians to meet and worship together on Sunday,[15] there was actually no consensus on how the day as a whole should be organized and what significance should be given to it: Should people still conduct business and work on this day if it did not make too much noise? Could one go shopping? Were stores open? What about a visit to the thermal baths (which then must also be in operation), the theater, chariot races, other games?[16] Could one go on trips or visit relatives? Or was it all beside the point? Was the main thing whether one attended a church service or not?

Moreover, it should be pointed out once again that Constantine had indeed issued laws on Sunday rest, first for the army and the imperial court

13. On the widespread Christian critique of going to the theater and on complaints that Christians prefer to go to the theater rather than to church services, see Puk, *Das römische Spielewesen*, 21–50; concerning the theological discussion see also Winrich Löhr, "Christliche Bischöfe und die klassische Mythologie in der Spätantike," in *Antike Mythologie in christlichen Kontexten der Spätantike*, ed. Hartmut Leppin, Millennium Studies 54 (Berlin: de Gruyter, 2015), 115–37.

14. Unfortunately, there is only one inscription from Pannonia from the time of Emperor Constantine that refers to the theme of the market on Sunday. This building inscription (314/316 CE) at the *thermae* of the springs of Aquae Iasae (in modern-day Croatia) shows that the weekly market *nundinae*, which actually took place according to an eight-day rhythm, was also allowed to be held on Sundays. However, it is not clear whether this was a special concession or whether this was the rule elsewhere (*CIL* 4121, in *CIL* 3.2:523 Mommsen, or HD064415).

On the Christianization of the military in general, see John Helgeland, "Christians and the Roman Army from Marcus Aurelius to Constantine," *ANRW* 23.1:724-834; Karl L. Noethlichs, "Krieg," *RAC* 22:1–75; Manfred Clauss, "Heerwesen," *RAC* 13:1074–1113. Emperor Constantine's first laws on Sunday apparently concerned allowing Christians in the army and at the imperial court to practice their faith and attend worship on Sundays. See n. 2 above. However, the Christianization of the army with all the rites and oaths was a longer process.

15. See n. 3 above.

16. On the laws against games on Sunday, see the discussion of Puk, *Das römische Spielewesen*, especially 53–84, and below, n. 42.

and then also for the entire society of the Roman Empire.[17] But both the effect and the reception of the requirement of rest from work remain hardly verifiable, just as little consensus is discernible as to what this temporal free space should be filled with. A few quotes may illustrate the different views on Sunday or the Lord's Day as a special day—or as an unremarkable one.

On the occasion of an Epiphany celebration (387? 390? CE[18]), the famous preacher John Chrysostom complains in *De baptismo Christi et de epiphania* 1 that many Christians go to church only on major holidays, writing:

> The week has seven days, and God has allotted these seven days for our benefit, and he has not given the larger portion to himself and the lesser to us; furthermore, nor has he divided it in half, taking three [days] for himself and giving us three, but he allotted six to you and left only one for himself. But you do not dare on this one whole day to avoid everyday matters, but just as those do who divest themselves of holy matters, so also you dare to do, seizing this day and using it for everyday matters, although it is holy and dedicated to hearing spiritual words. What shall I say about the perfect day? What a widow did for mercy, you also should do in like manner on this day. Just as she gives two *oboloi* and obtains much love from God, so in like manner you too should give two hours to God and you will bring the benefit of countless days upon your own house.[19]

---

17. See above, n. 2.

18. Chrysostom possibly presupposed here that Epiphany was on a Sunday this time, since he argues using the weekly rhythm; thus, the sermon could have been held in 390 CE, since January 6, 390 CE, was a Sunday. See the famous sermon delivered in 386 for the inauguration of the Christmas feast—here consequently "only" the baptism of Jesus is part of the feast of Epiphany, no longer the birth of Jesus (text in PG 49:351–62). On Chrysostom in general, see Rudolf Brändle, *Johannes Chrysostomus. Bischof, Reformer, Märtyrer* (Stuttgart: Kohlhammer, 1999); J. H. W. G. Liebeschuetz, *Ambrose and John Chrysostom: Clerics between Desert and Empire* (Oxford: Oxford University Press, 2011).

19. John Chrysostom, *Bapt.* 1 (PG 49:364; CPG 4335): Ἑπτὰ ἡμέρας ἡ ἑβδομὰς ἔχει· τὰς ἑπτὰ ταύτας ἐμερίσατο πρὸς ἡμᾶς ὁ Θεός· καὶ οὐχ ἑαυτῷ μὲν τὸ πλέον, ἡμῖν δὲ τὸ ἔλαττον ἔδωκε, μᾶλλον δὲ οὐδὲ ἐξ ἡμισείας αὐτὰς διενείματο, οὐκ ἔλαβε τρεῖς καὶ ἔδωκε τρεῖς, ἀλλὰ σοὶ μὲν ἀπένειμεν ἕξ, ἑαυτῷ δὲ κατέλιπε μίαν. Καὶ οὐδὲ ἐν ταύτῃ τῇ ὅλῃ ἀνέχῃ τῶν βιωτικῶν ἀπηλλάχθαι πραγμάτων, ἀλλ' ὅπερ οἱ τὰ ἱερὰ συλῶντες χρήματα ποιοῦσι, τοῦτο καὶ σὺ ἐπὶ τῆς ἡμέρας ταύτης τολμᾷς, αὐτὴν οὖσαν ἱερὰν καὶ ἀνακειμένην τῇ τῶν πνευματικῶν ἀκροάσει λογίων ἁρπάζων καὶ καταχρώμενος εἰς βιωτικὰς φροντίδας. Τί δὲ λέγω περὶ ἡμέρας ὁλοκλήρου; ὅπερ ἐπὶ τῆς ἐλεημοσύνης ἐποίησεν ἡ χήρα, τοῦτο ποίησον ἐπὶ τοῦ καιροῦ καὶ σὺ τῆς ἡμέρας· καθάπερ ἐκείνη δύο κατέβαλεν ὀβολούς, καὶ πολλὴν παρὰ τοῦ Θεοῦ ἐπεσπάσατο τὴν εὔνοιαν· οὕτω καὶ σὺ δύο δάνεισον ὥρας τῷ Θεῷ, καὶ μυρίων ἡμερῶν κέρδος εἰς τὴν οἰκίαν εἰσάξεις τὴν σήν. See SOLA database, https://sola-preview.acdh-dev.oeaw.ac.at/dataset?id=2003&type=Passage with the translation by Canan Arıkan-Caba (accessed February 11, 2022).

As is so often the case, a complex picture emerges here as well: Chrysostom's complaint shows that most Christians in his congregation were busy with normal, everyday affairs on Sunday as well, so they were not heeding a general commandment to set the day aside as a day of rest. In contrast to the alleged practice of his congregation, Chrysostom wishes to dedicate the day to God's word and therefore complains that his congregation uses the day for everyday concerns, so to speak. However, although a whole day of the seven-day week is to be set aside for God, Chrysostom exhorts his congregation to devote just two hours to worship. Thus, he rhetorically emphasizes the sanctity of the whole day, although he admits here and elsewhere that Christians can spend only part of the day in worship.[20] He does not himself seem to presuppose a general rest from work, and he mentions the worries of a day laborer (*Tagelöhner*) about not being able to go to church and rest the whole day because of his poverty.[21]

The famous presbyter Jerome wrote his commentary on Galatians around the same time as Chrysostom, namely, in 386 CE. Inspired by the Scripture passage, "You observe days and months and times and years! I fear for you, that I may have labored over you in vain" (Gal 4:10–11), he composed an even more restrained statement against the special status of particular days than Chrysostom:

> Someone may say: If it is not permissible to observe special days, months, seasons, and years, then we run into a similar problem by observing the fourth day of the week, the day before the weekly Sabbath, the Lord's day,

20. See John Chrysostom, *Hom. Matt.* 5.1 (on Matt 1:22–25 [PG 57:55]): Οὐ γὰρ ἐχρῆν ἀπὸ τῆς συνάξεως ἀναχωροῦντας, εἰς τὰ μὴ προσήκοντα τῇ συνάξει ἐμβάλλειν ἑαυτοὺς πράγματα· ἀλλ᾽ εὐθέως οἴκαδε ἐλθόντας τὸ βιβλίον μεταχειρίζεσθαι, καὶ τὴν γυναῖκα καὶ τὰ παιδία πρὸς τὴν κοινωνίαν τῆς τῶν εἰρημένων καλεῖν συλλογῆς, καὶ τότε τῶν βιωτικῶν ἅπτεσθαι πραγμάτων. Εἰ γὰρ ἀπὸ βαλανείου οὐκ ἂν ἕλοιο εἰς ἀγορὰν ἐμβάλλειν, ὥστε μὴ τὴν ἐκεῖθεν ἄνεσιν λυμήνασθαι τοῖς ἐν ἀγορᾷ πράγμασι· πολλῷ μᾶλλον ἀπὸ συνάξεως τοῦτο ποιεῖν ἐχρῆν. "For we ought not as soon as we retire from the Communion, to plunge into business unsuited to the Communion, but as soon as ever we get home, to take our Bible into our hands, and call our wife and children to join us in putting together what we have heard, and then, not before, engage in the business of life. For if after the bath you would not choose to hurry into the market place, lest by the business in the market you should destroy the refreshment thence derived; much more ought we to act on this principle after the Communion." See SOLA database, https://sola-preview.acdh-dev.oeaw.ac.at/dataset?id=2113&type=Passage (accessed February 11, 2022), with translation by George Prevost and M. B. Riddle, *Saint Chrysostom: Homilies on the Gospel of Saint Matthew*, *NPNF*[1] 10:31.

21. Introducing the quoted passage, he states in diatribe style, Πάντως μοι τὴν πενίαν ἐρεῖς κώλυμά σοι γίνεσθαι τοῦ καλοῦ τοῦδε συλλόγου· "Of course, you will say your poverty prevents you from attending this pleasant gathering." See also n. 37.

> Lenten fasting, the Paschal feast, Pentecost, and feast days established in honor of martyrs that reflect diverse local traditions. A simple answer to this objection is that the days observed by the Jews are not the same as those that we observe. . . . Certain days have been designated for all of us to come together as one, to insure that a poorly organized gathering does not compromise the people's faith in Christ. This does not mean that the day on which we congregate is more festive, but instead that a greater joy arises from the fellowship we share with one another, on whatever day we must congregate. A more pointed answer to the question at hand is that all days are equal and that Christ not only is crucified throughout the day before the Sabbath and raised [from the dead] on the Lord's day, but for the saint every day is the day of Christ's Resurrection and he always feeds on the Lord's flesh. But days for fasting and gathering together for worship were instituted by prudent men for the sake of those who leave more time for the world than for God and are unable, or rather unwilling, to congregate in church every moment of their lives or to put the offering of the sacrifice of their prayers to God ahead of their human activities.[22]

Jerome emphasizes that all days are equal; there is no day that is in itself somehow more festive. Sunday was chosen for purely practical reasons, since it was simply necessary to agree when to meet. Jerome's phrase "introduced by wise men" remains vague; unfortunately, he does not specify more in detail when and by whom he thinks this was introduced. However, since he mentions days

---

22. Jerome, *Comm. Gal.* 2.4.10–11 (CCSL 77A:118.46–120.90 Raspanti): *Dicat aliquis: si dies obseruare non licet et menses et tempora et annos, nos quoque simile crimen incurrimus quartam Sabbati obseruantes et Parasceuen et diem dominicam et ieiunium quadragesimae et paschae festiuitatem et pentecostes laetitiam et pro uarietate regionum diuersa in honorem martyrum tempora constituta. Ad quod qui simpliciter respondebit dicet non eosdem Iudaicae obseruationis dies esse quos nostros; . . . Et ne inordinata congregatio populi fidem minueret in Christo, propterea dies aliqui constituti sunt ut in unum omnes pariter ueniremus; non quo celebrior sit dies illa qua conuenimus, sed quo quacumque die conueniendum sit et ex conspectu mutuo laetitia maior oriatur. Qui uero oppositae quaestioni acutius respondere conatur illud adfirmat omnes dies aequales esse nec per Parasceuen tantum Christum crucifigi et die dominica resurgere, sed semper sancto resurrectionis esse diem et semper eum carne uesci dominica; ieiunia autem et congregationes inter dies propter eos a uiris prudentibus constituta qui magis saeculo uacant quam Deo nec possunt, immo nolunt, toto in ecclesia uitae suae tempore congregari et ante humanos actus Deo orationum suarum offerre sacrificium.* See SOLA database, https://sola-preview.acdh-dev.oeaw.ac.at/dataset?id=1614&type=Passage (accessed February 11, 2022), with translation by Andrew Cain, *St. Jerome Commentary on Galatians*, FC 121 (Washington, DC: Catholic University of America Press, 2010), 166f. See on Jerome in general Stefan Rebenich, *Jerome*, ECF (New York: Routledge, 2002).

of fasting and assembly in general, probably Constantine and his advisers are not meant. For Christians, of course, there is a common calendar with its own holidays, but these are based on a necessary agreement and not on a scheme of fundamentally holy or unholy days, as he states. In contrast to monks and nuns, who are able "to assemble in church every moment of their lives or to put the offering of their prayers to God above their human activities," other Christians should use at least one day per week for this.

This sober assessment, however, was not shared by all. A few decades after Jerome and Chrysostom, Leo, the bishop of Rome between 440 and 461,[23] wrote a series of letters to several episcopal sees in which he tried to enforce his special concern that presbyters and deacons, like bishops, should be ordained only on Sundays. Here a papal claim to power is combined with new ideas of canonical law, which go hand in hand with a justification of the special theological and salvific significance of Sunday. Three letters have survived, sent in different geographic directions: to Illyricum, to Egypt, and to Gaul. Taken together, they present a picture of the growing importance of the Lord's Day, but at the same time they depict a plurality of opinions. Here Leo tries to introduce something new, although he describes it as an old custom.[24]

In 444 CE, Leo sent a letter (*Ep.* 6) to Anastasius of Thessalonica (bishop ca. 431–452 CE). This letter is also important with respect to papal authority in this province and the western orientation of Illyricum: after Gratian had handed the province over to Theodosius in 379 CE, Dacia, Macedonia, and Thrace belonged to the eastern part of the empire and formed the so-called Eastern Illyricum. However, in 412 CE, Pope Innocent (402–427 CE) appointed the bishop of Thessalonica as *vicarius Romanus* (papal vicar), resulting in

---

23. On Leo the Great, see Susan Wessel, *Leo the Great and the Spiritual Rebuilding of a Universal Rome*, VCSup 93 (Leiden: Brill, 2008). See also p. 17, 138n3.

24. See on clerics and their ordination Paul F. Bradshaw, *Ordination Rites of the Ancient Churches of East and West* (New York: Pueblo, 1990); Bradshaw, *Rites of Ordination: Their History and Theology* (Collegeville, MN: Liturgical Press, 2013); see also Gregor Predel, *Vom Presbyter zum Sacerdos: Historische und theologische Aspekte der Entwicklung der Leitungsverantwortung und Sacerdotalisierung des Presbyterates im spätantiken Gallien*, Dogma und Geschichte 4 (Münster: LIT, 2005). Most studies deal with bishops; see Johan Leemans et al., eds., *Episcopal Elections in Late Antiquity*, Arbeiten zur Kirchengeschichte 119 (Berlin: de Gruyter, 2011), however, without reflection on the day of ordination. See also Willy Rordorf, "L'ordination de l'évêque selon la Tradition apostolique d'Hippolyte de Rome," *QLP* 55 (1975): 137–50; Thomas Michels, *Beiträge zur Geschichte des Bischofsweihetages im christlichen Altertum und im Mittelalter*, Liturgiegeschichtliche Forschungen 10 (Münster: Aschendorff, 1927), despite outdated evaluations of the sources. See also n. 28.

these provinces coming under papal jurisdiction.[25] Obviously, Anastasius of Thessalonica was willing to act in this role and exercised his privilege by ordaining the metropolitan bishops of Illyricum.[26] It is not the place to go into the ecclesiastical entanglements in Illyricum. Of interest here is the request of Leo that the ordinations of presbyters and deacons should occur on Sunday. He writes:

> We hear, indeed, and we cannot pass it over in silence, that only bishops are ordained by certain brethren on Sundays only; but presbyters and deacons, whose consecration should be equally solemn, receive the dignity of the priestly office indiscriminately on any day, which is a reprehensible practice contrary to the canons and tradition of the Fathers, since the custom ought by all means to be kept by those who have received it with respect to all the sacred orders: so that after a proper lapse of time he who is to be ordained a priest or deacon may be advanced through all the ranks of the clerical office, and thus a man may have time to learn that of which he himself also is one day to be a teacher.[27]

---

25. See Stanley L. Greenslade, "The Illyrian Churches and the Vicariate of Thessalonica," *JTS* 46 (1945): 17–29; Josef Rist, "Das apostolische Vikariat von Thessalonike als Beispiel der Begegnung zwischen Rom und Konstantinopel in der Spätantike," in *Frühes Christentum zwischen Rom und Konstantinopel: Akten des 14. int. Kongresses für Christliche Archäologie 1999*, ed. Reinhardt Harreither, Archäologische Forschungen 14 (Vienna: Österreichische Akademie der Wissenschaften, 2006), 649–62. The papal vicariate ended in 732 CE.

26. See Diego A. Arfuch, "Anastasius of Thessalonica," in *Brill Encyclopedia of Early Christianity Online*, gen. ed. David G. Hunter, Paul J. J. van Geest, and Bert Jan Lietaert Peerbolte, 2018: "From the time of Pope Damasus, the metropolitan of Thessalonica was the vicar of the bishop of Rome with jurisdiction over the region of eastern Illyricum (this region was civilly dependent on Constantinople but, in religious matters, dependent on the bishop of Rome). . . . The exchange of letters between Pope Leo and Anastasius shows us that the privilege that Anastasius enjoyed in ordaining the metropolitan bishops of Illyricum was at times resisted by the bishops of the territory. In July of 444 CE Leo specified in various letters Anastasius' powers, and he renewed his faculties."

27. Leo of Rome, *Ep.* 6.6 (PL 54:616–20, here 620A, or Textus et Documenta 23:57 Silva-Tarouca): *cognovimus sane, quod non potuimus silentio praeterire, a quibusdam fratribus solos episcopos tantum diebus Dominicis ordinari; presbyteros vero et diaconos, circa quos par consecratio fieri debet, passim quolibet die dignitatem officii sacerdotalis accipere; quod contra canones et traditionem Patrum usurpatio corrigenda committit, cum mos quibus est traditus circa omnes sacros ordines debeat omnimodis custodiri. Ita ut per longa temporum curricula, qui sacerdos vel levita ordinandus est, per omnes clericalis officii ordines provebatur, ut diuturno discat tempore, cuius et doctor ipse futurus est.* English translation by Charles L. Feltoe, *The Letters and Sermons of Leo the Great, NPNF*[2] 12 (Edinburgh: T&T Clark, 1895), 6. See also SOLA database, https://sola.acdh.oeaw.ac.at/de/dataset?id=94&type=Passage (accessed February 11, 2022).

Interestingly, Leo criticizes the practice in Illyricum of presbyters and deacons being ordained on any day of the week. It is not clear whether consecrating only bishops on Sunday was an old tradition in Illyricum—the scanty evidence does not help answer this question. It is also unclear to which canons Leo is referring.[28] Leo is possibly establishing a new practice here, or perhaps applying regulations from Rome to matters handled differently elsewhere. This latter option is supported by two other letters, which make the same demand but were written by Leo to other regions: one to Dioscurus in Alexandria in June 445 and one to the bishops in Gaul, also in 445.

In the letter written by Leo to Dioscurus in Alexandria in June 445 (*Ep.* 9), which demands ordinations of presbyters on Sundays, two concerns apparently overlap. First, Leo wants to see practices of the church of Rome implemented in other places as well, thus asserting his claim to power as the bishop of Rome. Second, within this letter it becomes obvious that Leo indeed

---

28. For episcopal (but not priestly) ordinations on Sunday, there are two earlier sources, namely, *Trad. ap.* 2: *Episcopus ordinetur electus ab omni populo, quique cum nominatus fuerit et placuerit omnibus, conueniet populum una cum praesbyterio et his qui praesentes fuerint episcopi, die dominica. Consentientibus omnibus, inponant super eum manus, et praesbyterium adstet quiescens.* See Bernard Botte, ed., *Hippolyte de Rome: La Tradition apostolique*, 2nd ed., SC 11 (Paris: Éditions du Cerf, 1984), 40, Latin version. The text of *The Apostolic Tradition* is a hypothetical reconstruction of a church order with material from the third century (Greek), which is only available through later translations (a Latin source from the fourth century and a Coptic one in the Synodus of Alexandria from the fifth century) and adaptions (Arabic in the *Canones Hippolyti*, Greek in the *Testamentum Domini*, Greek in the Apostolic Constitutions). See introduction to *Traditio Apostolica*, trans. Wilhelm Geerlings, Fontes Christiani 1 (Freiburg im Breisgau: Herder, 1991), 143–57; Christoph Markschies, "Wer schrieb die sogenannte *Traditio Apostolica*?," in *Tauffragen und Bekenntnis: Studien zur sogenannten "Traditio Apostolica, zu den "Interrogationes de fide" und zum "Römischen Glaubensbekenntnis,"* ed. Wolfram Kinzig, Christoph Markschies, and Markus Vinzent, Arbeiten zur Kirchengeschichte 74 (Berlin: de Gruyter, 1999), 1–74; and Paul F. Bradshaw, Maxwell F. Johnson, and L. Edward Phillips, *The Apostolic Tradition: A Commentary*, ed. Harold W. Attridge, Hermeneia (Philadelphia: Fortress, 2002), 1–18. The versions vary significantly in this passage, especially concerning the participation and role of the presbyters and of the other bishops. Bradshaw (*Rites of Ordination*, 59–61) argues that at first the presbyterate conducted the proceedings, but in later versions they were silent and the bishops claimed the responsibility. Geerlings is tentative (*Traditio Apostolica*, 163n46). The second source is Ap. Const. 8.4.3: οὗ ὀνομασθέντος καὶ ἀρέσαντος συνελθὼν ὁ λαὸς ἅμα τῷ πρεσβυτερίῳ καὶ τοῖς παροῦσιν ἐπισκόποις ἐν ἡμέρᾳ κυριακῇ, ὁ πρόκριτος τῶν λοιπῶν ἐρωτάτω τὸ πρεσβυτέριον καὶ τὸν λαόν, εἰ αὐτός ἐστιν, ὃν αἰτοῦνται εἴς ἄρχοντα. See Marcel Metzger, ed., *Les Constitutions apostoliques*, SC 336 (Paris: Éditions du Cerf, 1987), 3:140.10–142.14. In these church orders, the ordination of presbyters is described without any hint regarding the day of the week.

introduces an innovation, which he tries to justify at length by referring to the importance of Sunday. He writes:

> That therefore which we know to have been very carefully observed by our fathers, we wish kept by you also, viz. that the ordination of priests or deacons should not be performed at random on any day; but after Saturday, the commencement of that night which precedes the dawn of the first day of the week should be chosen on which the sacred benediction should be bestowed on those who are to be consecrated, ordainer and ordained alike fasting. This observance will not be violated, if actually on the morning of the Lord's Day it be celebrated without breaking the Saturday fast. For the beginning of the preceding night forms part of that period, and undoubtedly belongs to the day of resurrection as is clearly laid down with regard to the feast of Easter.[29]

After this general demand, he supports his view with a reference to the dispatch of Paul and Barnabas after a period of fasting, which he interprets as a hint regarding the day of the week:

> For besides the weight of custom, which we know rests upon the apostles' teaching, the sacred Scripture also makes this clear, because when the apostles sent Paul and Barnabas at the bidding of the Holy Ghost to preach the gospel to the nations, they laid hands on them fasting and praying: that we may know with what devotion both giver and receiver must be on their guard lest so blessed a sacrament should seem to be carelessly performed.[30]

---

29. Leo of Rome, *Ep.* 9 (PL 54:625): *Quod ergo a patribus nostris propensiore cura novimus esse servatum, a vobis quoque volumus custodiri, ut non passim diebus omnibus sacerdotalis vel levitica ordinatio celebretur; sed post diem sabbati, eius noctis quae in prima sabbati lucescit, exordia deligantur, in quibus his qui consecrandi sunt ieiunis, et a ieiunantibus sacra benedictio conferatur. Quod eiusdem observantiae erit, si mane ipso Dominico die, continuato sabbati ieiunio, celebretur, a quo tempore praecedentis noctis initia non recedunt, quam ad diem resurrectionis, sicut etiam in Pascha Domini declaratur, pertinere non dubium est.* English translation by Feltoe, *Letters and Sermons of Leo the Great*, 7f. See also SOLA database, https://sola-preview.acdh-dev.oeaw.ac.at/dataset?id=96&type=Passage (accessed February 11, 2022).

30. Leo of Rome, *Ep.* 9 (PL 54:625f.): *Nam praeter auctoritatem consuetudinis, quam ex apostolica novimus venire doctrina, etiam sacra Scriptura manifestat, quod cum apostoli Paulum et Barnabam ex praecepto Spiritus sancti ad Evangelium gentibus mitterent praedicandum, ieiunantes et orantes imposuerunt eis manus: ut intelligamus quanta et dantium et accipientium devotione curandum sit, ne tantae benedictionis sacramentum negligenter videatur impletum.* The biblical reference is Acts 13:2f.

Leo proceeds to demonstrate the special salvific quality of Sunday—it is, according to him, a heavenly pattern that various blessings are granted on Sunday, and this day is reserved for the bestowal of divine grace:

> And therefore you will piously and laudably follow apostolic precedents if you yourself also maintain this form of ordaining priests throughout the churches over which the Lord has called you to preside, viz. that those who are to be consecrated should never receive the blessing except on the day of the Lord's resurrection, which is commonly held to begin on the evening of Saturday, and which has been so often hallowed in the mysterious dispensations of God that all of the more notable institutions of the Lord were accomplished on that high day. On it the world took its beginning. On it through the resurrection of Christ death received its destruction, and life its commencement. On it the apostles take from the Lord's hands the trumpet of the gospel, which is to be preached to all nations, and receive the sacrament of regeneration which they are to bear to the whole world. On it, as blessed John the Evangelist bears witness when all the disciples were gathered together in one place, and when, the doors being shut, the Lord entered to them, he breathed on them and said: "Receive the Holy Ghost: Whose sins you have remitted they are remitted to them; and whose you have retained, they shall be retained" [John 20:22f.]. On it lastly the Holy Spirit that had been promised to the apostles by the Lord came; and so we know it to have been suggested and handed down by a kind of heavenly rule, that on that day we ought to celebrate the mysteries of the blessing of priests on which all these gracious gifts were conferred.[31]

---

31. Leo of Rome, *Ep.* 9 (PL 54:626): *Et ideo pie et laudabiliter apostolicis morem gesseris institutis, si hanc ordinandorum sacerdotum formam per Ecclesias quibus Dominus praeesse te voluit, etiam ipse servaveris: ut his qui consecrandi sunt numquam benedictio nisi in die resurrectionis Dominicae tribuatur, cui a vespera sabbati initium constat ascribi, et quae tantis divinarum dispositionum mysteriis est consecrata, ut quidquid est a Domino insignius constitutum, in huius diei dignitate sit gestum. In hac mundus sumpsit exordium. In hac per resurrectionem Christi, et mors interitum, et vita accepit initium. In hac apostoli a Domino praedicandi omnibus gentibus Evangelii tubam sumunt, et inferendum universo mundo sacramentum regenerationis accipiunt. In hac, sicut beatus Ioannes evangelista testatur, congregatis in unum discipulis, ianuis clausis, cum ad eos Dominus introisset, insufflavit, et dixit: Accipite Spiritum sanctum; quorum remiseritis peccata remittuntur eis; et quorum detinueritis, detenta erunt. In hac denique promissus a Domino apostolis Spiritus sanctus advenit; ut coelesti quadam regula insinuatum et traditum noverimus, in illa die celebranda nobis esse mysteria sacerdotalium benedictionum, in qua collata sunt omnia dona gratiarum.*

This list is indicative of a new conviction: Sunday is a special divine day, chosen by God for the distribution of his benedictions. Therefore, all ordinations have to occur on this holy day as well. The idea that all the great acts of God's salvific work took place on Sunday underscores the dignity of the day and makes the occurrence of these events on Sunday anything but random. The letters of Leo constitute one of the earliest examples of a longer list of these so-called Sunday benedictions.[32] In his *Epistula* 9, Leo collects Sunday benedictions that are in some way relevant for ordinations. He wants to emphasize the importance of Sunday, which in turn heightens the importance of the presbyter, who is to be ordained on this special day.[33]

His third letter on Sunday ordinations, *Epistula* 10 (written in 445 CE), is addressed to the bishops in the province of Vienne in Gaul; in the background are ongoing quarrels about the metropolitan status of Hilary, the bishop of Arles. Within the context of the disputed ordination of Proiectus, Leo gives a general command concerning ordination. He restates briefly his opinion that Sunday is a special day within salvation history and that it should be appointed for ordinations, which are otherwise invalid:

> The ordination should be performed not at random but on the proper day. And it should be known that anyone who has not been ordained on the evening of Saturday, which precedes the dawn of the first day of the week, or actually on the Lord's Day, cannot be sure of his status. For our forefathers judged the day of the Lord's resurrection as alone worthy of the

32. Justin Martyr (*1 Apol.* 67.8 [PTS 38:130.24–36 Marcovich]) already connects the creation of the world and the resurrection of Christ with Sunday as the first day of the week, and Origen demonstrates that the dispensation of manna (Exod 16) also occurred on a Sunday (*Hom. Exod.* 7.5 on Exod 16:4f. [SC 321:220–26 Borret]). However, later the so-called *Ambrosiaster* (between 366 and 384 CE) presents more examples: Sunday or the Lord's Day is the day of creation, of circumcision, of manna distribution, of handing over of the law on Mount Sinai, of incarnation, of resurrection, and of Pentecost. See *Liber quaestionum Veteris et Novi Testamenti, quaestio* 29, 84, 95, 112 (CSEL 50:57; 144f.; 166–70; 238f. Souter). The author states in *quaestio* 29 (CSEL 50:57.16f. Souter): *quia enim salus futura per Christum in primo die erat praedestinata, qui dominicus ideo dicitur, quia in eo resurrexit dominus*; and in *quaestio* 95 (167 Souter): *totum, quod ad salutem humanam pertinet, dominico die et inchoatum et adimpletum noscatur*. See SOLA database https://sola.acdh.oeaw.ac.at/de/dataset?id=1263&type=Person (accessed February 11, 2022).

33. The preference for Sunday, including Saturday evening vigil, as the day for priestly ordinations also is confirmed by Gelasius of Rome (492–496 CE), *Ep.* 14.11; 15.3; 16.3. See Andreas Thiel, ed., *Epistolae Romanorum pontificum genuinae et quae ad eos scriptae sunt a S. Hilario usque ad Pelagium II,1* (Braunsberg: E. Peter, 1868), 368f., 380–81. See Gelasius, *Ep.* 41 (Thiel, *Epistolae Romanorum pontificum genuinae*, 454), as an exception to the rule.

> honour of being the occasion on which those who are to be made priests are given to God.[34]

It is obvious that a change occurred in Rome during the fifth century: Pope Leo demanded that presbyters be ordained only on Sundays, even though this had apparently not yet become common in other regions. He wanted a custom that perhaps had emerged in Rome to be enforced in Illyricum, Egypt, and Gaul, and thus also to establish the alignment of these regions with Rome. In the course of time, more and more events of Christian salvation history are connected with Sunday, so that it finally becomes God's special day: God singled out that day to accomplish his good deeds throughout history. Leo emphasized this to support his estimation that ecclesiastical blessings—the ordinations—should also occur only on Sundays. Even though Leo emphasized the special significance of the Lord's Day in these letters, he wrote them only to place a special liturgical act, ordination, on this day. There are no other statements in his writings about the sanctity of the day, nor about admonitions concerning Sunday. Even if, of course, in a sermon in which he once exhorts Christians to take the feast days as an occasion to adorn themselves inwardly and outwardly, Sunday might also be meant:

> If it seems reasonable and in some way devotional to appear in more elaborate clothes on a festival, and to show a joyful spirit by the clothing of the body, and if we decorate the house of prayer at that time as far as we can with more attentive care and greater ritual, then it is not right that a Christian soul, which is the true and living temple of God, should prepare its appearance carefully, and when it is going to celebrate the mystery of its redemption, take every precaution that no spot of sin cloud it, nor any wrinkle of doublemindedness mar it.[35]

---

34. Leo of Rome, *Ep.* 10 (PL 54:634B): *Non passim, sed die legitimo ordinatio celebretur; nec sibi constare status sui noverit firmitatem qui non die sabbati vespere, quod lucescit in prima sabbati, vel ipso Dominico die fuerit ordinatus. Solum enim maiores nostri resurrectionis Dominicae diem hoc honore dignum judicaverunt, ut sacerdotes qui sumuntur hoc die potissimum tribuantur.* Trans. Feltoe, *Letters and Sermons of Leo the Great*, 13. On the background and the dispute, see Georg Langgärtner, *Die Gallienpolitik der Päpste im 5. und 6. Jahrhundert: Eine Studie über den apostolischen Vikariat von Arles*, Theophaneia 16 (Bonn: Hanstein, 1964); Martin Heinzelmann, "The 'Affair' of Hilary of Arles (445) and Gallo-Roman Identity in the Fifth Century," in *Fifth-Century Gaul: A Crisis of Identity?*, ed. John Drinkwater and Hugh Elton (Cambridge: Cambridge University Press, 1992), 239–51.

35. Leo of Rome, *Sermo* 41.1 (CCSL 138A:232f. Chavasse): *Si enim rationabile et quodammodo religiosum uidetur per diem festum in uestitu nitidiore prodire, et habitu corporali hilaritatem mentis ostendere, si ipsam quoque orationis domum propensiore tunc cura et ampliore cultu, quantum possumus, adornamus, nonne dignum est ut anima*

In this way, the divine blessing of the day will also be visible, so to speak.

This image of divine blessings corresponds with the idea that Sunday is a privileged day for good deeds in general. The Lord's Day is thus also the day of charity and *diakonia*. There are indications of this from the earliest days of Christianity, such as in the writings of Justin Martyr (see *1 Apol.* 67).[36] The aforementioned preacher John Chrysostom also expresses his recommendations for charitable deeds in connection with the Lord's Day, as the opportunity arises.[37] Chrysostom, who urged his congregation to love their neighbors and denounced social ills in many sermons, also regarded Sunday as a special day that should remind Christians of their social duties. Regarding the occasion of the apostle Paul's exhortation in his letter to the Corinthians on taking up collections, he reminds his congregation that Sunday is a good day to take care of the poor and to put aside one's own business. According to Chrysostom, the reason the Lord's Day was assigned by Paul for almsgiving is not only related to the greatness of the day (as the day of resurrection), but it is also practical: one can dedicate oneself to benevolence, having been released from daily toil:

> See how he [Paul] even uses the time for exhortation: For this was precisely the day fit for bestowing benevolent gifts. For consider, he will say, what ye have received this day! Unspeakable goods and the origin and beginning of our life happened on this day. But not only for this reason is the moment favorable for tuning us to willingness and joyfulness in doing good, but also because it gives rest and relief from toil. For a carefree soul is more skillful and lively in doing good.[38]

Christiana, quae uerum uiuumque dei templum est, speciem suam prudenter exornet, et redemptionis suae celebratura sacramentum omni circumspectione praecaueat ne ulla eam macula iniquitatis obfuscet, aut duplicis cordis ruga dedecoret? Translation by Jane Patricia Freeland and Agnes Josephine Conway, *St. Leo the Great: Sermons*, FC 93 (Washington, DC: Catholic University of America Press, 1996), 176.

36. See nn. 3, 32.

37. See in general Michael Theobald, *Eucharistie als Quelle sozialen Handelns. Eine biblisch-frühkirchliche Besinnung* (Neukirchen-Vluyn: Neukirchener, 2012), 229–53, on Justin Martyr; Blake Leyerle, "John Chrysostom on Almsgiving and the Use of Money," *HTR* 87 (1994): 29–48; Adolf Martin Ritter, "Zwischen 'Gottesherrschaft' und 'einfachem Leben'. Dio Chrysostomus, Johannes Chrysostomus und das Problem einer Humanisierung der Gesellschaft," in *Studia Chrysostomica. Aufsätze zu Weg, Werk und Wirkung des Johannes Chrysostomus (349–407)*, STAC 71 (Tübingen: Mohr Siebeck, 2012), 34–67. But the contributions to the social welfare do not take into account the day of the week.

38. John Chrysostom, *Hom. 1 Cor.* 43.1 (on 1 Cor 16:2 [PG 61:368]): Ὅρα πῶς καὶ ἀπὸ τοῦ καιροῦ προτρέπει· καὶ γὰρ ἡ ἡμέρα ἱκανὴ ἦν ἀγαγεῖν εἰς ἐλεημοσύνην. Ἀναμνήσθητε γάρ, φησί, τίνων ἐτύχετε ἐν τῇ ἡμέρᾳ ταύτῃ. Τὰ γὰρ ἀπόρρητα ἀγαθά, καὶ ἡ ῥίζα καὶ ἡ ἀρχὴ τῆς ζωῆς τῆς ἡμετέρας ἐν ταύτῃ γέγονεν. Οὐ ταύτῃ δὲ μόνον ἐπιτήδειος ὁ καιρὸς

This same sentiment can also be read in his treatise *De eleemosyna*. This sermon was delivered in Antioch, where Chrysostom observed the poor begging in the marketplace during the winter. In this passage Chrysostom encourages his listeners to consider the Lord's Day as an opportune time for philanthropy by saving some of their income and donating it to the poor, referencing Paul. The day is characterized by happiness and reminds Christians of the blessings of God. They should give thanks for these gifts from God to humankind by doing their own good deeds on behalf of the needy.[39]

That Sunday was a day for good deeds is also confirmed in an interesting law, which has been heretofore neglected—namely, *Codex Theodosianus* 9.3.7, issued by Honorius in Ravenna on January 25, 409:

> Emperors Honorius and Theodosius, both Augustus, to Caecilianus, Praetorian Prefect. [After other matters:] On every Lord's Day, judges shall inspect and question the accused persons who have been led forth from the confinement of prison, lest human needs be denied these prisoners by corrupt prison guards. They shall cause food to be supplied to those prisoners who do not have it, since two or three *libellae* a day, or whatever the prison registrars estimate, are decreed, by the expenditure of which they shall provide sustenance for the poor. Prisoners must be conducted to the bath under trustworthy guard. Fines have been established, fixed at twenty pounds of gold for the judges and the same weight of gold for their office staffs, and for the high-ranking members of the office staffs fines of three pounds of gold have been set, if they should scorn these very salutary statutes. For there shall not be lacking the laudable care by the bishops of the Christian religion, who shall suggest this admonition for observance by the judge.[40]

εἰς προθυμίαν φιλανθρωπίας, ἀλλ' ὅτι καὶ ἄνεσιν ἔχει καὶ πόνων ἀτέλειαν. Ψυχὴ γὰρ ἀφιεμένη μόχθων, εὐκολωτέρα καὶ ἐπιτηδειοτέρα πρὸς τὸ ἐλεεῖν γίνεται. English translation by Talbot W. Chambers, *Chrysostom: Homilies on the Epistles of Paul to the Corinthians*, *NPNF*[1] 12 (Grand Rapids: Eerdmans, 1979), 259.

39. John Chrysostom, *Eleem.* 3 (PG 51:264.53–265.47). See SOLA database, https://sola-preview.acdh-dev.oeaw.ac.at/dataset?id=1998&type=Passage (accessed February 11, 2022).

40. Cod. theod. 9.3.7: *Iudices omnibus dominicis diebus productos reos e custodia carcerali videant interrogent, ne his humanitas clausis per corruptos carcerum custodies negetur. Victualem substantiam non habentibus faciant ministrari, libellis duobus aut tribus diurnis vel quot existimaverint commentarienses decretis, quorum sumptibus proficient alimoniae pauperum. Quos ad lavacrum sub fida custodia duci oportet. multa iudicibus viginti librarum auri et officiis eorum eiusdem ponderis constituta, ordinibus quoque trium librarum auri multa proposita, si saluberrime statuta contempserint. Nec deerit antistitum Christianae religionis cura laudabilis, quae ad observationem constituti iudicis hanc ingerat monitionem.* See Theodor Mommsen, ed., *Theodosiani libri XVI cum constitutionibus Sirmondianis et leges novellae ad Theodosianum pertinentes*, vol. 1,

According to this law, on Sunday there is to be detention relief for prisoners. Their conditions of confinement are to be inspected, and they are to be provided with the most basic necessities, including a trip to the baths. Unfortunately, it is difficult to say anything specific about whether and how this law was actually applied; there are no relevant reports. Since this law explicitly orders the alleviation of imprisonment for the Lord's Day and refers to Sunday, it is interpreted religiously.[41] The verse from the Gospel chapter on the last judgment (Matt 25:16), where visiting prisoners is mentioned among the works of mercy, may have served as a biblical inspiration. Since the prisoners are to be escorted to the thermal baths, this confirms that they must have been open to everyone on Sundays as well. While imperial Sunday legislation increasingly forbade chariot races, gladiator games, and theatrical performances,[42] there are no extant prohibitions for the thermae, which apparently continued to operate without weekly pauses.[43] Therefore, the information represented in a singular legal inscription from the second century was probably still valid to a large extent in later times, even if details about the opening for women and men differed:

Theodosiani libri XVI cum constitutionibus Sirmondianis. Pars prior: Prolegomena; Pars posterior: Textus cum apparatu (Berlin: Weidmann, 1904–1905), 442f. English translation by Clyde Pharr, ed., *The Theodosian Code and Novels and the Sirmondian Constitutions: A Translation with Commentary, Glossary, and Bibliography* (Princeton: Princeton University Press, 1952), 229.

41. A parallel exists in Cod. justin. 1.4.9. According to Cod. justin. 1.4.22 (529 CE), this episcopal visitation should take place once a week, but either on Wednesdays or Fridays, apparently to keep Sunday free from litigation. There is also a law that provides for prisoners to be brought out and led to worship on holidays such as Easter (Cod. justin. 1.4.3 [385 CE]). Of interest is one parallel, namely, in canon 20 of the Council of Orléans (Aurelianense) V from 549 CE (CCSL 148A:155.197–203 de Clercq): *id etiam miserationis intuitu aequum duximus custodiri, ut, qui pro quibuscumque culpis in carceribus deputantur, ab arcidiacono seu praepositu eclesiae singulis diebus dominicis requirantur, ut necessitas uinctorum secundum praeceptum diuinum misericorditer subleuetur adque a pontifice instituta fideli et diligenti persona, quae necessaria prouideat, competens uictus de domo eclesiae tribuatur.* "For the sake of mercy, we thought it appropriate to ensure that those who are sent to prison for any crime should be visited on every Lord's Day by the archdeacon or by the head of the Church, so that the plight of the prisoners may be mercifully alleviated according to divine prescriptions; furthermore, an honest and conscientious person should be appointed by the bishop to provide necessities and distribute the food provided by the episcopal see in sufficient quantities." See SOLA database, https://sola-preview.acdh-dev.oeaw.ac.at/dataset?id=372&type=Passage (accessed February 11, 2022); see also the *Visio Pauli* (see pp. 419–33).

42. See the laws in Cod. theod. 2.8.20 (392 CE); 2.8.25 (409 CE); 15.5.2 (394 CE); 15.5.5 (425 CE), and in Cod. justin. 3.12.9 (469 CE).

43. See also Harry J. Magoulias, "Bathhouse, Inn, Tavern, Prostitution, and the Stage as Seen in the Lives of the Saints in the Sixth and Seventh Centuries," *Epeteris Hetaireias Byzantinon Spoudon* 38 (1971): 233–52, on baths in early Byzantine times.

> Regulations for operating the baths. The *conductor* of the bath or his partner is to heat the bath every day [*omnibus diebus calfacere*] and keep it open for use, entirely at his own expense, as stipulated in the lease for the bath that runs until 30 June next, for women from first light to the seventh hour of day, and for men form the eighth hour to the second hour night, in accordance with the decision of the procurator who runs the mines.[44]

This text of the law about the prisoners is also quoted here in the introduction because it is relevant for the interpretation of a passage from the *Visio Pauli*, which is included in this volume: here a Sunday relief from the torments in hell is granted.[45] Against this background, Sunday does not appear primarily as a day of rest but as a special day for good deeds. However, if one examines the law more closely, the judges and prison guards were certainly well occupied on Sundays, as were other staff who handled finances. In addition, there were supervisors who led the prisoners to the thermal baths and those who kept these very thermal baths in operation. The law does not seem to provide for a general day of rest.

A clear indication of the special significance of Sunday also appears in a completely different area—namely, the good deeds of healing. The cult sites of the pagan healing god Asclepius in Epidaurus, Athens, Kos, and other places found themselves confronted, despite great successes, with Christian healing sites, which, like them, treated diseases through spiritual cleansing and healing sleep. Interestingly, we learn from the seventh-century collection of the miracle narratives of Artemios, alleged martyr of Alexandria under Emperor Julian (*BHG* 173), regarding miracles the saint performed in the St. Johannis church in Constantinople, that incubation sleep in the crypt near the saint's tomb was permissible only on Sunday night (*Miracle* 17: μὴ ἐξὸν εἶναί τινι ἐκτὸς Κυριακῆς διαφαυούσης κοιμηθῆναι κάτω; see also *Miracle* 33, 41).[46] The incubatory healing cult narratives emphasize proper rites, which include special observance of the day of the week. Unfortunately, the ideas associated with this are not elaborated. Is it simply because of the greater sanctity of Sunday, or does it reveal astrological thinking similar to that of the planetary

44. The so-called Lex Metalli Vipascensis from Aljustrel, Portugal, is a bronze plate about mining regulations (CIL 2.5181 = ILS 6891). See on the part about bathing of this inscription Garrett G. Fagan, *Bathing in Public in the Roman World* (Ann Arbor: University of Michigan Press, 1999), 324–26.

45. See below, p. 421.

46. Athanasios Papadopoulos-Kerameus, "Miracula xlv sancti Artemii," in *Varia graeca sacra*, Subsidia Byzantina 6 (St. Petersburg: Kirschbaum, 1909), 1–75. English translation: Virgil S. Crisafulli and John W. Nesbitt, *The Miracles of St. Artemios: A Collection of Miracle Stories by an Anonymous Author of Seventh Century Byzantium*, The Medieval Mediterranean 13 (Leiden: Brill, 1997), 108f.

week, or is illness as something demonic more likely to be exorcised on the Lord's Day? On the other hand, this narrative is again exceptional, because the day of the week is not known from other healing miracles, nor can it be seen that the observance of a day of the week played any role at all.[47] At this point, however, one can only point to a need for further research.

It becomes clear from these exemplary source quotations how different the assessments turn out and how much Christian, Jewish, astrological, practical, apologetic, and pastoral concerns overlap. Moreover, it must be taken into account, of course, that these prescriptive or protreptic texts only describe how the Lord's Day should be structured according to various authors, not how the day was actually spent. This is precisely the background for the production of the apocryphal and pseudepigraphic texts on Sunday presented in this volume.

At the center of this volume is the so-called Letter from Heaven, written by Christ, which employs massive threats to exhort people to honor Sunday, to rest from work on that day, and to attend Sunday church services. However, it is placed here in the context of other revelatory writings and apocalypses, as well as pseudepigraphal exhortative sermons, dialogues, and visionary literature in order to broaden the scope. What all these texts have in common is the interest in giving the Lord's Day a unique quality and assigning greater urgency to the subject of what should be done on this day. But this is not the only issue—these texts all also insist that people honor the day itself and observe the commandment to rest and not to work. Interestingly, it is not Constantine's legislation in the background as a point of reference here, but the Sabbath rest transferred to Sunday—if it is mentioned at all.

These texts want to achieve, albeit differently, something that even Gregory the Great fiercely rejects around 600 CE: that some want to keep Christians off work on both the Sabbath and Sunday; they would even want to prohibit body cleansing on Sunday. These people Gregory even calls preachers of the antichrist. He states:

> Gregory, by the grace of God bishop to his very beloved sons and citizens of the city of Rome. I have been informed that certain people with a perverted mind spread among you some wrongs which are against the holy faith, with

47. See in general the special issue of *ZAC* 17 (2013), ed. Christoph Markschies, *Heil und Heilung, Inkubation, Heilung im Schlaf: heidnischer Kult und christliche Praxis*. Here included is also a contribution of Thomas Pratsch, "'. . . erwachte und war geheilt': Inkubationsdarstellungen in byzantinischen Heiligenviten," *ZAC* 17 (2013): 68–86, who also deals with Artemios but does not go into the relevance of the weekdays. See also Wolfgang Häfele, *Krankheit und ihre Behandlung. Studien zu Sophronios von Jerusalems Wundern der Heilige Kyros und Johannes*, STAC 118 (Tübingen: Mohr Siebeck, 2020), who also presents the latest research on healing miracles on 1–13 and 55–57.

> the result that they prohibit undertaking anything on Sabbath. How shall I call them other than preachers of Antichrist who will come and cause that Sabbath and Sunday will be kept without any work. Namely, because he pretends that he died and resurrected he wants Sunday to be kept in veneration, and because he compels the people to live like Jews in order to bring back the external rite of the law and subject the perfidiousness of the Jews himself, he wants Sabbath to be celebrated. This scilicet which is said by the prophet: "Do not carry burdens through your gates on Sabbath" [Jer 17:24] could be kept as long as it was allowed to keep the law according to the letter. But after the grace of Almighty God our Lord Jesus Christ has appeared, the precepts of the law which are said figuratively cannot be observed according to the letter.[48]

Of course, on the Lord's Day, in keeping with its name, he states that one must devote oneself above all to spiritual things,[49] but he rejects rigid restrictions beyond that. He does not refer to the Letter from Heaven but rather to currents in Christianity that might have subscribed to the contents of this letter. The subject obviously remained controversial, despite the earnest unambiguity presented by some of the apocryphal and pseudepigraphal texts presented in this volume.

---

48. Gregory the Great, *Registrum epistulae* 13.1 (CCSL 140A:991.1–15 Norberg): *Gregorius gratia dei episcopus dilectissimis filiis suis ciuibus romae. Peruenit ad me quosdam peruersi spiritus homines praua inter uos aliqua et sanctae fidei aduersa seminasse, ita ut die sabbato aliquid operari prohiberent. Quos quid aliud nisi antichristi praedicatores dixerim, qui ueniens diem sabbatum atque dominicum ab omni faciet opere custodiri? Quia enim mori se et resurgere simulat, haberi in ueneratione uult dominicum diem et, quia iudaizare populum compellit, ut exteriorem ritum legis reuocet et sibi Iudaeorum perfidiam subdat, coli uult sabbatum. Hoc enim quod per prophetam dicitur: Ne inferatis onera per portas uestras die sabbati tam diu teneri potuit, quamdiu legem licuit iuxta litteram custodiri. At postquam gratia omnipotentis Dei Domini nostri Iesu Christi apparuit, praecepta legis, quae per figuram dicta sunt, iuxta litteram seruari non possunt.* Translation by Christoph Scheerer.

49. Gregory the Great, *Registrum epistulae* 13.1 (CCSL 140A:992.46–49 Norberg): *Dominicorum uero die a labore terreno cessandum est atque omnimodo orationibus insistendum, ut, si quid neglegentiae per sex dies agitur, per diem resurrectionis dominicae precibus expietur.* "On Sunday one must in fact desist from terrestrial work and abide in prayers in every way, for if he did something negligent in the course of the six days, he may expiate this on the day of the resurrection of the Lord by means of prayers." See on this idea also the sermons presented here at pp. 435–65. See also his letter to Ianuarius of Cagliari (*Reg. Ep.* 9.1 [CCSL 140A:562f. Norberg]), where he criticizes how Ianuarius, before celebrating the Mass, set off to reap someone else's harvest and afterward celebrated Mass. The point in dispute is not the harvest work on Sunday but the stealing of the crop and moving of the property line.

2

TEXTS IN ADDITION TO THE LETTER FROM HEAVEN

Uta Heil

The following list of texts are presented in this volume in addition to the Letter from Heaven. For a more detailed introduction, see the second part of the book. Many of these writings are apocryphal, pseudepigraphal, or apocalyptic texts that claim authority from Christ, the apostles, or famous theologians.

The pseudepigraphal Acts of the Council of Caesarea
Sophronius of Jerusalem, *Oratio de circumcisione Christi*, with a fragment of the Dialogue between Jason and Papiscus *(CPG 1101)*
A passage from the Greek Apocalypse of Paul, also known as the Latin *Visio Pauli* (BHG 1460; BHL 6580–82)
A homily: "Today, My Beloved, I'd Like to Praise the Day of the Lord" (CPG 2955 and 4869)
A "Question and Answer about Sunday" (CPG 5525)
A homily: "Hear, All Brothers Christians, What the Prophets Say" (CPG 4848)
An anonymous fragment on four Sunday names (Codex Vaticanus gr. 2392)
Passages from the *Diataxis* or Instructions of the Apostles (BHG 812a–e)
A passage from the Second Apocryphal Apocalypse of John (CPG 4755)
A passage from the Apocalypse of Anastasia (BHG 1868–70)

2.1. The Pseudepigraphal Acts of the Council of Caesarea

In the computistic works of Isidore of Seville, Bede, and Hrabanus Maurus, there is a reference to an early Council of Caesarea at the end of the second century, which was already mentioned by Eusebius in his *Church History* (5.23-25). The reason for the council was a dispute about the length of Lent and the end of the pre-Easter fast, that is, a dispute about the date of Easter. Since the issue was whether Easter should be celebrated on a fixed date (14th of Nisan) with a changing day of the week, or on a changing date with a fixed day of the week (Sunday), the importance of Sunday was also discussed. However, the Acta as contained in many Latin manuscripts are pseudepigraphal and were written at a later date, since they presuppose subsequent debates about the date of Easter and the fixed celebration of Christmas on December 25.

The acts have survived in two recensions. Excerpts of both are presented here, namely, the passages that deal with the importance of Sunday. They offer a multilayered revised history of the Synod of Caesarea—a memory that acquired "updates" at different times as needed. The text is based on a new edition of these acts by Christoph Scheerer and Uta Heil.

2.2. A New Fragment of the Dialogue between Jason and Papiscus (CPG 1101) from Sophronius of Jerusalem, *Oratio de circumcisione Christi*

Sophronius of Jerusalem became bishop at an advanced age (roughly eight years old) in 634 CE; he served in this position until he was forced to hand over the city to Caliph Omar in 638 CE. In a sermon delivered on January 1, 635, Sophronius addresses the subject of the day of the week, since the Feast of the Circumcision of Christ fell on a Sunday that year. This sermon, which was discovered only recently by John M. Duffy and François Bovon, is preserved in Codex Sinaiticus graecus 1807. Because of the preceding quotation from his Christmas sermon, it can be attributed without doubt to Sophronius.

Sophronius claims in this sermon that the birth and circumcision of Jesus actually occurred on a Sunday. To prove this, he quotes from the Dialogue between Jason and Papiscus (CPG 1101), which he attributes to the apostle Luke. Actually, this dialogue is to be dated to the second century and was probably written by a person named Ariston of Pella. However, the text has survived only in small fragments and later references. Because of the advanced form of the referred creed and the significance of Sunday, however, this passage certainly seems to have undergone later editing.

2.3. *Visio Pauli* 34 or Apocalypse of Paul 44 (BHG 1460; BHL 6580–82)

The (Greek) Apocalypse of Paul or (Latin) *Visio Pauli* (see also ECCA 818; CANT 325[1]), probably written at the end of the fourth century CE, gives an

1. The further Armenian, Arabic, Church Slavonic, Coptic, Ethiopic, and Syriac versions underscore the wide distribution of this text. See the entry in North American Society for the Study of Christian Apocryphal Literature: https://tinyurl.com/3patcay7.

account of a vision experienced by the apostle Paul (possibly referencing 2 Cor 12:2f.) and describes in detail the afterlife, especially the punishment and torment of sinners. The longer version of the Latin text begins with the legendary discovery of a book: An angel appears at night to a respected man who lives in Tarsus in the house where Paul formerly lived. The angel orders him to break open the foundations of the house and publish what he finds there. The man obeys and discovers a codex in a marble box; he gives it to a judge, who sends it to Emperor Theodosius, in whose possession it is finally published.

Through the intercession of the archangel Michael, other angels, and Paul, the damned are granted relief from torment on the Lord's Day—not so much so that the torturers have a day of rest, but so that the tortured can at least experience a certain holiday on Sundays. In the narrative, this weekly relief forms the conclusion of the description of the punishments of hell, prior to the description of paradise. The passage presented here is taken from three shorter and one longer Latin versions.

2.4. A Homily: "Today, My Beloved, I'd Like to Praise the Day of the Lord" (CPG 2955 and CPG 4869)

Among the many pseudepigraphal sermons, there is one text dedicated to the veneration of Sunday that has apparently been handed down in two different versions, one attributed to Basil of Caesarea and the other to John Chrysostom. Annette von Stockhausen presents one version of this hitherto unpublished pseudepigraphal sermon based on a new critical edition.

As stated, this eulogy of the Lord's Day became necessary because only some honor the day, but many slander or disdain it. On this day, one should not work for one's "belly" but rather devote oneself to the service of God; under this condition one is justified, healed, and inspired. Sunday, therefore, is the one day of the week on which Christians can "work" for their salvation, with hymns and with prayers. The Jews have a Sabbath for this purpose, the pagans a Thursday, but Christians celebrate Sunday. So one should not work seven days without break—this is justified with reference to the decalogue (Deut 5:13). Servants are also to be granted a day of rest on the day of resurrection. There follows an extraordinary exegesis of the Balaam story (Num 22:25-28): the donkey's protest is interpreted as a warning not to force working on Sunday! Therefore, God's commandment must not be transgressed by labor on Sunday. On Sunday, God stretched out the heavens and the earth. It is only a small commandment, but nevertheless transgression of it will be followed by serious punishments. Corresponding punitive miracles are mentioned (Gen 3; 2 Sam 6 [ark]; Josh 7:16–26; Num 16), and the preacher also reminds the congregation of the fates of Dathan and Abiram. All should respect and observe Sunday, including disciples, soldiers, and rulers. All should offer on this day a living sacrifice: works of righteousness, fruits of poverty, prayer, and praise to God.

2.5. A "Question and Answer about Sunday" (CPG 5525)

A total of twenty-two sermons in various manuscripts are attributed to a certain Eusebius of Alexandria, a fictitious bishop who is said to have followed Cyril of Alexandria († 444 CE). One of these sermons is dedicated to the Lord's Day. The tradition is very broad and complicated but seems to be attributable to four different versions of the text. The text on Sunday might not even originally be a homily but rather part of a text corresponding to the genre of *Quaestiones et responsiones* or *Erotapokriseis*.[2] For this collection of texts, Annette von Stockhausen decided to offer the version according to a manuscript that probably represents the oldest version well.

The "Sunday Sermon" of this Eusebius takes the form of a dialogue. A certain Alexander asks why Sunday is to be honored and why one should not work on this day—what is the reward for this behavior? In his answer, Eusebius first recalls Jesus's words of the Last Supper, "Do this in memory of me!" (Luke 22:19), stating that Sunday exists in memory of Jesus (as the Eucharist is celebrated on Sundays). Sunday, as the lord of the days, reigns over the other days and is also called the first day, because on this day creation began and Christ rose from the dead. This makes the day important in triple respects: the beginning of creation, the beginning of the resurrection, the beginning of the week is like a "Trinity" of Sunday. Therefore, work is done on six days, but the seventh day serves for prayer and rest—and as a result, liberation from evil and guilt. After all, sins are confessed in the divine service, and one should participate in the Lord's Supper only with a clear conscience. Of course, one should not leave the church service before it is concluded. Judas also left early, and then Satan entered him. In addition, Eusebius addresses the problem that some people like to use the day off from work for other things than worship; these people receive no benefit from this day. They sin on their day off and devote themselves to other pleasures, such as theater and music. Additional admonitions are given: on Sunday no legal arguments should be made in court, especially not after the church service. Woe is pronounced against judging clerics on Sunday. One may also have pity on the day laborers who longed for a day of rest. The text closes with the quotation of Psalm 118:24.

2. See p. 444.

2.6. A Homily: "Hear, All Brothers Christians, What the Prophets Say" (CPG 4848)

John Chrysostom was admired for his excellent sermons, which led to many spurious sermons being attributed to him. It is therefore not surprising that yet another sermon on Sunday was credited to him. This also hitherto unpublished sermon is presented here on the basis of fresh insight into the manuscript evidence by Annette von Stockhausen. Here, too, there are apparently two versions, one of which, which can be described as the more original, is presented here.

This admonition begins with a call to honor the day, since the Lord himself honored it—quoting Psalm 45:11 and 117:24 LXX. On Sunday, Gabriel appeared, God showed himself to Moses at Sinai, Christ was resurrected, and he will come again. Although Moses had delivered the Sabbath commandment, Christ brought a new law, since he had fulfilled the old one. Just as Christ is the Lord of creation, now Sunday is the lord of the days of the week. There follows a long series of "he who reverences the day . . ." describing benefits for the one who obeys the commandment. The subsequent series of negations blame "who does not honor the day . . ." along with a "quotation" from the Epistle to the Galatians by the apostle Paul, which cannot be proven. What follows is a series of instructions for behavior on Sunday, such as avoiding quarrels, going to church, and so on. The second version mainly enlarges the series with further items.

2.7. An Anonymous Fragment on Four Sunday Names (Codex Vaticanus graecus 2392)

In the Codex Vaticanus graecus 2392, there is a fragment of text on the last two pages (fols. 88v–89v) that deals with the Lord's Day. On the basis of the various names for this day, the special nature of Sunday is described. It seems to be a fragment of a previously unknown sermon. Renate Burri discovered this text and presents it in this volume with a transcription and translation.

2.8. The *Diataxis* of the Holy Apostles (BHG 812a–e)

The *Diataxis* of the Holy Apostles consists of questions from the twelve disciples, including Paul, and answers from Christ. The first part (§§1–29) deals with fasting and praying on Wednesday and Friday, as well as honoring Sunday through communion and sexual abstinence, all of which is necessary to attain salvation. In the second part (§§31–55), Christ speaks about the seven heavens (§§32–34), the creation of Adam and the fall of the devil (§§37–41), the sins of men (§§43–45), and their punishments in hell, to which he transports the apostles temporarily (§§47–53). The text ends with the apostolic charge to teach all nations (§55).

The days of the week form a central theme of the *Diataxis*. Andrew, as the third apostle, asks about the power of the seven days of the week. In Christ's answer, the different value of the days of the week is justified using details from the history of creation. The Lord's Day surpasses all other days; it is the first day, since God created heaven and earth on it (Gen 1:1). God set it at the head of his works and days. Therefore, Sunday is to be kept from the ninth hour of the Sabbath. This is followed by a prohibition of work on the Lord's Day. The next question, from James, also ties in with the days of the week: he asks about the reward for fasting on Wednesday and Friday. The answer describes again the special days Wednesday, Friday, and the Lord's Day, but this time referencing heavenly mysteries: the soul will meet the aforementioned days in heaven in person (!), who will greet them with joy. The Lord's Day will be magnificently adorned with eight brightly robed angels, and he (or she) himself will be like the daughter of Zion surrounded by these angels. However, the anonymous author does not give further details as to how Sunday should be observed, aside from prohibiting work.

This text was probably written at the end of the sixth century. The text offered here is based on a new edition by Uta Heil and Jannis Grossmann, which replaces the old edition by Francois Nau, "Une Didascalie de notre-Seigneur Jésus-Christ (ou: Constitutions des saints apôtres)," *ROC* 12 (1907): 230–54.

2.9. A Passage from the Apocalypsis Iohannis Apocrypha Altera (BHG 922i; CANT 332)

The Second Apocryphal Apocalypse of John presents questions from John of Patmos to Christ. The Lord answers his inquiries about sins, including the sin of disrespecting Sunday, followed by questions about the church liturgy. The text ends with a call to show respect for priests, to respect baptism, and to practice mercy. The disrespect of Sunday as the second sin discussed thus leads into an explanation of the liturgy and its symbolism. Here an excerpt on the appropriate observance of the Lord's Day is presented.

In genre the text resembles the *Diataxis* of the Apostles or the *Testamentum Domini* (this late church order in dialogue form, however, does not have Sunday as an independent theme) and, just as the *Diataxis* of the Apostles, probably dates to the end of the sixth century.

2.10. A Passage from the Apocalypse of Anastasia or *Visio Anastasiae Monialis* (BHG 1868–1870)

The anonymous Apocalypse of Anastasia was compiled between the tenth and twelfth centuries, although the text is attributed to a sixth-century nun named Anastasia. In the account, the archangel Michael leads her—barely alive—through heaven and hell to see the consequences of the morality of individuals during their lives on earth. Anastasia is resurrected after her heavenly journey and records her experience so that future generations might be saved.

Here (§14), just as in the *Diataxis* of the Apostles, the days of the week appear as female celestial figures around the heavenly throne. Another paragraph (§25) deals with the commandment to worship on Sunday, an act these very personifications also supervise. "Holy Sunday" and "Holy Wednesday and Friday" implore God to wipe defiled humanity from the face of the earth, because no one obeys the commandments of their days. There even follows a loud curse on those who work on Sunday, eat meat and cheese on fast days, and disregard fasting. But Mary acts as an intercessor so that the whole of humanity is not destroyed at this time. Thus, this text also incorporates aspects encountered in the Letter from Heaven.

It is likely that future research, especially the ongoing digitization of the manuscripts, will bring further texts to light. Both the sermon of Sophronius and the fragment on the four Sunday names are recent discoveries, and the new editorial considerations presented here on already known texts provide a textual basis for further research. These texts broaden our view of the cultural history of Sunday and show the diversity of theological argumentation. They are to be added to the understanding of the Letter from Heaven, which is presented in more detail in the following chapter.

3

LETTER FROM HEAVEN

3.1. Introduction and Research History

Uta Heil

The Letter from Heaven or Letter of Jesus Christ about the Lord's Day is an anonymous invention that can be dated to the end of the sixth century, since at this time the Spanish bishop Licinianus of Cartagena criticizes a colleague for having taken this letter seriously and read it publicly.[1] Through this external attestation, a Latin Letter from Heaven is verified, but whether it was originally written in Latin or originated in Greek remains controversial. In addition to the primary Greek and Latin traditions of the letter, in the meantime classified in Latin Recension I–III and Greek Recensions Alpha, Beta, and Gamma, translations into the Oriental and European languages are extant, testifying to the broad tradition of this Letter from Heaven in diverse versions that hardly allow for tidy, stemmatic classification.

According to the self-presentation of the letter, the frame narrative,[2] the following impression emerges: The letter appears either in Rome or Jerusalem/Bethlehem—the discovery is embellished with various fantastic elements in most versions—and presents itself as a letter of Christ or of God the Father, is read publicly, and admonishes above all the observance of the Lord's Day. A threatening setting is displayed in front of the eyes to lend emphasis—either with diverse tribulations predicted in the style of biblical plagues or other catastrophes such as the fate of the cities Sodom and Gomorrah, sometimes painted with various apocalyptic motifs.[3] But this short characterization cannot begin to elucidate the variety of motifs and versions, which are displayed in the sections below.[4]

1. See below, pp. 209–19.
2. For further details, see below, pp. 134–42.
3. For further details, see below, pp. 184–95.
4. See below, chapter 4, "Considerations."

According to the genre, it is a *letter* in the very general sense that a document is sent from A to B and is read. Of course, it is not a letter as part of a correspondence; no answer is expected, nor is there a formula for greeting framing the text. The letter lacks any polite form of address.[5] Therefore, it is clear that with "letter" the genre is only inaccurately described. Actually, it is a court speech or an *indictment*:[6] Christians are accused of not worshipping Sunday and also of committing other misdeeds, and so they have incurred divine judgment or condemnation. The letter serves to announce this. On the other hand, it is also clear that the letter actually wants to change the behavior of the Christians addressed. Therefore, it is not pure judgment but is to be read in the sense of a *sermon*.[7] This also explains why the letter is often transmitted in the context of sermons.[8]

When reading the letter, however, it also becomes clear that it does not only address an individual or a congregation but the whole of humankind: it is threatened with destruction by God. This is especially the tendency of the Greek recensions. Therefore, this Letter from Heaven also has features that connect it with apocalyptic in the sense of a description of the last judgment at the end of time. The Letter from Heaven is therefore similar to a *prophetic judgment speech*, as it can be studied in Amos or other prophets, but also takes elements from the so-called little apocalypse from the Gospels (Matt 24 parr.). A recurring verse in the Greek recensions is therefore Matthew 24:35, "Heaven and earth will pass away, but my words will not pass away!" from this same little apocalypse;[9] also elements from the subsequent chapter of the

5. On letters in antiquity, their form and functions, see Schneider, "Brief"; Divjak, "Epistulae," esp. 893–99 on letters in general.

6. On indictment as court speech / *genus iudicale*, see Hohmann, "Gerichtsreden," esp. 787–91 on late antiquity and the early Middle Ages. The Letter from Heaven, however, is not a rhetorically elaborated indictment but a patchwork of accusations, admonitions, and threats.

7. On sermons, see Sachot, "Homilie B. christlich." See also Stanley E. Porter, ed., *Handbook of Classical Rhetoric in Hellenistic Period (300 B.C.–400 A.D.)* (Leiden: Brill, 1997), s.v. See also the introductory chapters in Alexander Deeg et al., eds., *Preaching in Judaism and Christianity: Encounters and Developments from Biblical Times to Modernity*, SJ 41 (Berlin: de Gruyter, 2008); Mary B. Cunningham and Pauline Allen, eds., *Preacher and Audience: Studies in Early Christian and Byzantine Homiletics*, A New History of the Sermon 1 (Leiden: Brill, 1998); and Anthony Dupont et al., eds., *Preaching in the Patristic Era: Sermons, Preachers, and Audiences in the Latin West*, A New History of the Sermon 6 (Leiden: Brill, 2018)—all, however, not mentioning the Letter from Heaven.

8. See below, pp. 48–79.

9. At least in the Greek traditions—the Latin version is more regionalized and does not announce the destruction of the whole of humankind. Regardless, hell is envisaged only rarely.

last judgment from Matthew 25 are encountered. Of course, in these biblical texts Sunday is not in the foreground, but in general the approaching end of the world and in Matthew 25 the care of the needy, such as the hungry, the thirsty, foreigners, the sick, and prisoners. If one has not shown mercy to these during one's lifetime, then eternal fire threatens. The Letter from Heaven was written on the basis of this biblical tradition—thus the letter places itself in the biblical tradition, which is read by Christians as the word of Christ. Thus, reading the letter evokes a recognition of biblical language but is alienated by the threat of catastrophe and the radical nature of the letter: Can it really be true that God announces destruction of humankind just because Sunday has not been observed sufficiently? It is not surprising, then, that the history of the Letter from Heaven is accompanied by its critique, as will be shown below. Yet despite all the criticism, the letter was not lost but was copied and circulated again and again. In addition, the manuscript tradition shows how differently the letter could be read, so that it could be interpreted as an anti-Jewish text, as a text for church consecrations, as an example of visionary literature, as an apocalyptic text, as an exhortation for repentance as well as a computistic text.

Also in modern times, the knowledge of this Letter from Heaven was never lost, because vernacular versions were in circulation from the late Middle Ages and the letter enjoyed great popularity as an amulet and protective sign that could even protect against wounding in wars.[10] However, it only gradually came to light what a broad distribution this letter has had since late antiquity. The following overview describes the path of discovery of the ancient versions of the letter, about which knowledge grew steadily, but this has also made the stemmatic and historical classification increasingly complicated. What is completely missing from previous scholarship, however, is the attempt to consider West and East or Latin and Greek versions together in detail. Nevertheless, the Letter from Heaven is presented in many collections of apocryphal texts as well as in encyclopedias.[11] However,

10. See Baechtold-Stäubli, "Sonntagsbrief"; Dieterich, "Himmelsbriefe"; Dieterich, "Weitere Beobachtungen zu den Himmelsbriefen"; Otto Weinreich, "Antike Himmelsbriefe," *AR* 10 (1907): 566–67; Edgar J. Goodspeed, *Strange New Gospels* (Chicago: University of Chicago Press, 1931), 96–107, about an American version.

11. Articles about the letter: Renoir, "Christ (Lettre du) tombée du ciel"; Speyer, *Bücherfunde in der Glaubenswerbung der Antike*, 27–28; Schnell, "Himmelsbrief"; Palmer, "Himmelsbrief." The letter is included in collections: Beskow, *Strange Tales about Jesus*, 25–30; de Santos Otero, "La carte del Domingo," 664–76 (with translation of the Greek Recension Alpha 1); Santos Otero, "Der apokryphe sogenannte Sonntagsbrief"; Santos Otero, "Epistola de die dominica"; Erbetta, *Gli Apocrifi del Nuovo Testamento* 3:113–18 (with translation of Greek Recension Alpha 1); Backus, "Lettre du Jésus-Christ

the following overview clearly shows that the main studies on this text were done in the nineteenth and early twentieth centuries. Only in 2010 was a new turn introduced by Dorothy Haines, as she once again took a more thorough look at the Latin tradition in order to open up the background of the Letter from Heaven in the Anglo-Saxon world. In more recent publications, the state of research is usually summarized briefly or even only in excerpts, and the letter is presented according to one or at most two versions. Further research into the dissemination of this text in other languages can only be recommended here.

1677—Étienne Baluzius, a famous French historian,[12] brought attention to the Letter from Heaven in a Latin version according to a now-lost manuscript from Tarragona from the twelfth century and described the letter as written between the seventh and ninth century, that is, during the Carolingian period; this text presented by him is now one exemplar of Latin Recension I.[13] He includes the text in his collection as an appendix, "Actorum veterum."

1719—Johannes Alberto Fabricius, a philologist and theologian in Hamburg,[14] was the first to design in short notes the Latin tradition of the Letter from Heaven through the Middle Ages, including the already mentioned letter of Licinianus, with a reprint of the Letter from Heaven from Baluzius in his collection of apocryphal texts. In volume 3, he also presents the beginning of a Greek version, namely, from Codex Huntington 583 in the library of the Bodleian, now assigned to Greek Recension Beta 2.

1727—Nicolaus Staphorst, church historian in Hamburg,[15] was the first to present another Latin version of the Letter from Heaven, namely, from a manuscript in Hamburg (Bibliothek der Hansestadt, St. Petri-Kirche 30b), an exemplar from Latin Recension II.

1773—Johannes Christoph Amaduzzi, Italian philologist at La Sapienzia in Rome,[16] was able to present a transcription of another Latin version of a now-lost manuscript in Todi from Perugia in the twelfth century, now assigned to Latin Recension II.

---

sur le Dimanche" (with translation of Latin Recension II according to the Codex Munich 9550, and also Greek Recension Alpha 1); Miceli, "Epistle of Christ from Heaven" (with translation of Greek Recension Alpha 1).

12. Baluzius, *Capitularia regum Francorum II*, 1396–99.

13. Presented below, pp. 270–89.

14. Fabricius, *Codex apocryphus Noui Testamenti* 1:308–13; 3:511–12.

15. Staphorst, *Hamburgische Kirchengeschichte* 1.3:345–47.

16. Amaduzzi, *Anecdota litteraria ex mss codicibus eruta I*, 69–74; repr. in Jacques-Paul Migne, *Dictionnaire des Apocryphes* (Paris, 1858), vol. 2, cols. 367–69.

1890—Reinhold Röhricht, a teacher in Berlin and historian mainly of the Crusader period,[17] broadened the view of the wide distribution of the letter in the East as well. He was able to hint at further versions in other languages, namely, Ethiopic, Syriac,[18] Arabic, Greek, Latin, Spanish, and German versions, of which he lists some manuscripts, and he was the first to print a transcription of a Greek version from a manuscript in Carpentras (BM 103; Omont 36), which is now assigned to Greek Recension Beta 1, and added also a Latin version according to the *Chronicle* of Roger de Hoveden about the sermon tour to England conducted by Eustachius of Fly in 1201 (see the quotation below, pp. 121–24; this is actually one exemplar of the Latin Recension III), and he reprints the version from Staphorst in Hamburg.

1893—Athanasius Vassiliev[19] continued on the path of Röhricht and enriched the known Greek versions with a transcription and edition of two versions, namely, Greek Recension Alpha: Codex Vaticanus Barber. gr. 284; Codex Venetianus Marc. vii 38, Codex Parisinus gr. 947 and 929, and Greek Recension Beta: Codex Roman. Casanatense 481, and Codex Turin. 148 b. II,1.

1899—Hippolyte Delehaye, Jesuit and Belgian church historian, well-known for his studies on hagiographic literature,[20] presented the first thorough study about the Latin Letter from Heaven, including more manuscripts within a description of the history of the letter, therefore taking up the line of Fabricius and presenting a continuation up to modern times. It was his idea to differentiate between a Latin "Rome Recension" and a Latin "Jerusalem Recension." He was also able to present further examples, namely, from Munich the Codex BSB clm 9550, now assigned to the Latin Recension II, and Codex Parisinus lat. 12270, Codex Vaticanus Regius lat. 852 (mostly erased), both now assigned to Latin Recension I. Furthermore, he detected more manuscripts now assigned to Latin Recension III that belong to the high Middle Ages, namely, the period of the Crusades and the Flagellants (see below, pp. 118–20). He included also remarks on the Greek versions of Vassiliev and Eastern versions (namely, Ethiopic, Arabic, and Syriac).

1906—Maximilian Bittner, Orientalist in Vienna,[21] deserves the credit for having delved into the Eastern versions and, following Vassiliev, presenting

17. Röhricht, "Ein 'Brief Christi.'"

18. Hall, "Letter of Holy Sunday" (he presents a Syriac version [Second Syr. Recension] with English translation).

19. Vassiliev, *Anecdota graeco-byzantina I*, 23–32.

20. Delehaye, "Note sur la légende."

21. Bittner, *Der vom Himmel gefallene Brief Christi.*

Greek Letters from Heaven, as well as Armenian, Syrian, Carjunian [= Arabic in Syrian script], Arabic, and Ethiopian versions. His study is therefore the starting point for all further work on the letters. He confirmed the two versions of Vassiliev,[22] detected a late third one (Greek Recension Gamma), and determined that the Armenian and Syrian versions stem from Greek Recension Alpha, on which the other Eastern versions depend.

1906—Ernest-Maria Rivière[23] detected and published an additional Latin Letter from Heaven, to be attributed now to Latin Recension III.

1918—Rudolf Stübe, teacher in Leipzig and historian of religions,[24] presented a summary of the state of research, which extends to the later vernacular versions. In a second part, as the subtitle, "Ein Beitrag zur allgemeinen Religionsgeschichte," states, the phenomenon of heavenly letters is classified with respect to corresponding phenomena in other religions.

1928—Georg Graf, Orientalist in Munich, editor of the Arabic series of the Corpus Scriptorum Christianorum Orientalium and the journal *Oriens Christianus*,[25] presented, in addition to the material of Bittner, another Arabic version of the letter, including a German translation.

1928—Hippolyte Delehaye[26] provided yet another interesting manuscript from London, namely, Codex BL Add. 30853, which contains a homiliary, that is, a collection of exemplary sermons on the church year, wherein among an appendix of various sermons the Epistle from Heaven can also be found. This represents an example of Latin Recension II.

1936—Robert Priebsch, professor of Germanic studies in London,[27] presented anew a history of this letter, beginning with the first reference in the letter of Licinianus of Cartagena up to the Middle Ages. (This study was posthumously published.) He deals mainly with the various witnesses for Latin Recension I, which he considers the earlier one; he traces this recension back to the letter of Licinianus and the Synod of Macon in 585 via the version of the Letter in the lost manuscript from Tarragona, which Baluzius had transcribed. He had already handled this letter as the basis for Anglo-Saxon versions in "The Chief Sources of Some Anglo-Saxon

22. See, however, the confusion of the manuscripts below, p. 80n1.

23. Rivière, "La Lettre du Christ tombée du ciel."

24. Stübe, *Der Himmelsbrief*.

25. Graf, "Der vom Himmel gefallene Brief Christi."

26. Delehaye, "Un exemplaire de la letter tombée du ciel."

27. Priebsch, *Letter from Heaven*.

Homilies" (1899) and for early German translations in *Diu vrône botschaft ze der Christenheit* (1895).[28]

1966—Réginald Grégoire, Italian theologian and historian,[29] expands knowledge of the homiliary that Delehaye had already presented (1928) with a precise listing of the texts it contains, and places its origin in the seventh century in the Visigothic Empire.

1989—Michel van Esbroeck, Belgian Jesuit and Orientalist,[30] argues for locating the text in the Greek East. Delehaye only cautiously raises the possibility that the letter could also have originated in the East, and most previous authors looked for its origin mainly in the Latin West. More precisely, Esbroeck tries to locate its origin in Jerusalem in the time directly after the Council of Chalcedon in 451. According to his estimation, the text is directed against a group of Miaphysites who opposed the decisions made at Chalcedon and who prefer to take Wednesday as the day of creation as well as the day of the Annunciation of Mary. In this context, therefore, the Letter pleads clearly for the preeminent importance of Sunday. However, he falls prey to an overinterpretation of some aspects of the Letter from Heaven and actually cannot present any resilient sources for a "Wednesday group," so to speak, among the Miaphysites.[31] Reserved remarks can also be found in Backus.[32]

2010—Dorothy Haines[33] presents the latest thorough analysis of the Latin versions of the Letter from Heaven. She assigns the letters to three recensions, building on earlier research, and is able to provide evidence of many more manuscripts. Furthermore, she determines further subgroups, Latin Recension IIa as well as Latin Recension IIIa; presents once again in a transcription the letter from Codex Parisinus lat. 12270, Codex Vienna ÖNB 1355, Codex London BL Add. 19725, and Codex Basel UB B VII 7 (all Latin Recension I) as well as Codex Vienna Dominikanerkloster 133 (Latin Recension IIa); and presents a thorough list of the Latin manuscripts at pp. 211–14. Her interest lies in presenting the Latin

28. Priebsch, "Chief Sources of Some Anglo-Saxon Homilies"; Priebsch, *Diu vrône botschaft ze der Christenheit.*

29. Grégoire, *Les homéliaires du moyen âge*, 161–85, with the text at 226f.

30. Van Esbroeck, "La lettre sur le Dimanche."

31. Actually, he mainly refers to himself: Michel van Esbroeck, "Un court traité pseudo-Basilien de mouvance aaronite conserve en Armánien," *Le Muséon* 100 (1987): 385–95; and reiterates his thesis in "Deux homélies pseudo-basiliennes sur le dimanche et le vendredi," *Parole de l'Orient* 16 (1990/91): 49–71.

32. See above, note 11.

33. Haines, *Sunday Observance.*

versions on which the Letters from Heaven are based in the Anglo-Saxon context. She also presents these in six versions with commentary.

It becomes clear that the focus of previous research on the Letter from Heaven lies on the Latin West. Consequently, the clearest overview of the manuscript tradition has been achieved here. This is certainly because secondary evidence for the Letter from Heaven is found in the Latin West, not in the East. The difficulty is not only that the origin of the letter lies in the dark but also that it is hard to determine a context and background for the different versions. With traditional means of textual criticism, no original letter can be reconstructed. It is particularly problematic when either only the Latin or only the Greek tradition is considered. Possible interactions and regional transfers should be taken into account. A special feature is of course that this letter is accompanied from the beginning by a clear criticism of it—it is therefore a letter often read and copied and yet rejected (see "History of the Letter from Heaven" below).

Methodologically, there are three ways to sort and assign the tradition of the different versions: On the one hand, one can try to identify references, dependencies, and further developments by an internal textual comparison between the Letters from Heaven. This approach has been applied in research so far and will be built on here.

On the other hand, it is worthwhile to consider the manuscript tradition as a whole and thus to look at the context of the tradition, which reflects the reading comprehension of the scribe or copyist at the time. This second approach, which has not been applied in this way before, expands previous access to the Letters from Heaven and is presented in 3.3, "Manuscript Studies," by Angela Zielinski Kinney, including some remarks on methodology.

Third, of course, external attestation is relevant, as the reference to the criticism of Licinianus already showed. Here, at least for the Latin West, four waves of the spread of the letter can indeed be observed for the Middle Ages: at the end of the sixth century—attested by Licinianus; in the Carolingian period—attested by Boniface, a Roman synod, and the *Admonitio generalis*, as well as in a chronistic note also for the Holy Land; in the time of the Crusades—attested in some chronicles; in the time of the plague epidemic in the late Middle Ages—attested mainly in sources related to the so-called Flagellants. This will be demonstrated in the chapter below on the history of the Letter from Heaven that extends and refines the previous observations.

3.2. Latin Manuscripts

Angela Zielinski Kinney

Research to date, as well as our own research, has yielded the following manuscripts for the Letter from Heaven (CANT 311; BHG 812i–s). The manuscripts in bold are new discoveries and additions to the list (seventeen in total) by Angela Zielinski Kinney. The manuscripts underlined are presented in this volume.[1]

Latin Recension I

[Vatican City, Biblioteca Apostolica Vaticana, Reg. lat. 49 (s. ix/x), 53r, *extract*[2]]
[Vatican City, Biblioteca Apostolica Vaticana, Reg. la. 852 (s. x), 6v[3]]
Basel, Universitätsbibliothek B VII 7 (s. x), 1r[4]
London, British Library Add. 19725 (s. x/xi), 87v–88r[5]
Tarragona (Spain), Cathedral Library (s. xii?), *transcript of a lost manuscript*[6]
Paris, Bibliothèque nationale lat. 12270 (s. xii), 31vb–32vb[7]
Vienna, Österreichische Nationalbibliothek 1355 (s. xiv/xv), 89r–90v, *1 of 2 letters*[8]
Graz, Universitätsbibliothek 248 (s. xv), 133rb–133va, *1 of 2 letters*[9]

1. The list uses as a basis the manuscript index in Haines, *Sunday Observance*, 211–14. Additional manuscripts and information are found in Jiroušková, *Die Visio Pauli*. All the manuscripts she describes combine the Letter from Heaven with the *Visio Pauli*, sometimes even merged together.

2. Edited by Robert E. McNally in *Scriptores Hiberniae minores*, CCSL 108B (Turnhout: Brepols, 1973), 186.42-56. On these short extracts see the discussion in Haines, *Sunday Observance*, 49.

3. Only the title *Incipit epistola Salvatoris Domini nostri* is transmitted. See Schmitz, "Tironische Miscellen," and Schmitz, "Nochmals ein vom Himmel gefallener Brief."

4. Edited in Haines, *Sunday Observance*, 206f. (appendix IIc).

5. Edited in Haines, *Sunday Observance*, 204f. (appendix IIb).

6. The manuscript is now lost but was transcribed by Baluzius, *Capitularia regum Francorum*, vol. 2, cols. 1396–99 (see above, p. 34), and reprinted by Priebsch, *Letter from Heaven*, 35–37 (see above, p. 36f.) with remarks at p. 3: "Petrus de Marca, Archbishop of Paris (†1164) discovered it in a MS. of the Cathedral library of Tarragona." Priebsch (33) believes this to be the earliest form of the Sunday letter; see, however, the history of the letter, pp. 84–133, and see the presentation, pp. 121–24.

7. Edited by Delehaye, "Note sur la légende," 181–84. Haines, *Sunday Observance*, reprints this on 199-201 (appendix I). See p. 37.

8. Edited by Priebsch, "Chief Sources of Some Anglo-Saxon Homilies," 130–34. Haines, *Sunday Observance*, reprints this on 201-3 (appendix IIa). See the presentation, pp. 245–67.

9. See the presentation, p. 268f.

Latin Recension II

Paris, Bibliothèque nationale lat. 8508 (s. x^{1}), 57v–63r, *in margin*
Munich, Bayerische Staatsbibliothek clm 9550 (s. xi), 1r[10]
Brussels, Bibliothèque Royale Albert Ier II 1053 (s. xi/xii), 4r[11]
London, British Library Add. 30853 (s. xi/xii), 231r–232v[12]
London, Lambeth Palace Library 539 (s. xii), 141r–141v[13]
Cambridge, Pembroke College, MS 103 (s. xii), 73v–75r[14]
Todi, Perugia (s. xii?), *transcript of a lost manuscript*[15]
Vienna, Österreichische Nationalbibliothek 1878 (s. xii), 35v–36v
Munich, Bayerische Staatsbibliothek clm 14673 (s. xii/xiii), 119v–120r, *1 of 2 letters*
Innsbruck, Universitäts- und Landesbibliothek Tirol Cod. 409 (s. xiii/xiv), 100r–102r
Göttweig, Benediktinerstift Cod. 199 (s. xiv), 38r–39r
Prague, National Library III. D. 13. (Y. 1. 4. n. 79) (s. xiv), 213r–214r[16]
Uppsala, Universitetsbibliotek C 212 (s. xiv) 1v–2v[17]
Vienna, Österreichische Nationalbibliothek lat. 1629 (s. xiv), 102r–103v[18]
Budapest, University Library lat. 39 (s. xiv/xv), 86vb–88r
Einsiedeln, Stiftsbibliothek 726 (s. xiv/xv) 124r
Kremsmünster, Stiftsbibliothek 283 (s. xiv/xv), 92v–93r
London, British Library Royal 11 B x (s. xiv/xv), 184r[19]

---

10. Edited by Delehaye also in "Note sur la légende," 179–81. See p. 35. See the presentation, p. 236f.

11. Described in Jiroušková, *Visio Pauli*, 45.

12. Edited by Grégoire, *Les homéliaires du moyen âge*, 161–85, with the text at 226f. (see below, p. 92f.). See also Delehaye, "Un exemplaire de la lettre tombée du ciel." See in introduction, p. 36f.

13. See the description of the manuscript at the Lambeth Palace Library online at https://archives.lambethpalacelibrary.org.uk/calmview/Record.aspx?src=CalmView.Catalog&id=MSS%2f539 (accessed September 1, 2022).

14. Described in Jiroušková, *Visio Pauli*, 50f.

15. Edited by Amaduzzi, *Anecdota litteraria*, 69–74; reprinted by Jacques-Paul Migne, *Dictionnaire des apocryphes, ou collection de tous les livres apocryphes relatifs à l'Ancien et au Nouveau Testament* (Paris, 1856–1858), cols. 367–69. See above, p. 34.

16. Described in Jiroušková, *Visio Pauli*, 118-19. Here the *Visio Pauli* is part of the Letter from Heaven.

17. Described in Jiroušková, *Visio Pauli*, 131f. The Letter from Heaven is only partially transmitted; the *Visio Pauli* is part of the Letter from Heaven.

18. Described in Jiroušková, *Visio Pauli*, 135f. The Letter from Heaven is part of the *Visio Pauli*.

19. Described in Jiroušková, *Visio Pauli*, 83f.

Oxford, Merton College 13 (s. xiv/xv), 64v–65v[20]
Vienna, Österreichische Nationalbibliothek 1355 (s. xiv/xv), 91r–92r, *1 of 2 letters*
Berlin, Staatsbibliothek zu Berlin—Preußischer Kulturbesitz, Magdeburg 21 (s. xv), 162va–162vb
Berlin, Staatsbibliothek zu Berlin—Preußischer Kulturbesitz, Magdeburg 196 (s. xv), 381r–381v
Bernkastel-Kues, Bibliothek des St. Nikolaus-Hospitals 128 (s. xv), 129r, *fragment*
Fritzlar, Dombibliothek 37 (s. xv), 178v–181v
Hamburg, Bibliothek der Hansestadt, S. Petri-Kirche 30b (s. xv), 35r–36v[21]
Innsbruck, Stiftsbibliothek Wilten (s.n.) (s. xv), 153rb–154ra
Jena, Thüringer Universitäts- und Landesbibliothek, Ms. Klosterbibl. 5 (s. xv), 246va
London, British Library Royal 8 F.vi (s. xv), 24rv[22]
Lucca, Biblioteca Statale di Lucca 3540 (s. xv), 134r–134v[23]
Mainz, Stadtbibliothek I 227 (s. xv), 143r–143v
Mattsee, Stiftsbibliothek 49 (s. xv), 182ra–184rb
Munich, Universitätsbibliothek 2° 120 (s. xv), 33rb–34rb
Munich, Bayerische Staatsbibliothek clm 3433 (s. xv), 209vb–210rb
Munich, Bayerische Staatsbibliothek clm 3766 (s. xv), 177va–178ra

20. Described in Jiroušková, *Visio Pauli*, 106–8. In the explicit, the transmission of the letter to "Petrus of Antioch" is mentioned.

21. Edited by Staphorst, *Hamburgische Kirchengeschichte* 1.3:345–47, repr. in Thilo Brandis, ed., *Die Handschriften der S. Petri-Kirche Hamburg* (Hamburg: Hauswedell, 1967), 345–47; repr. in Röhricht, "Ein 'Brief Christi,'" 440–42. See above, p. 35.

22. Described in Jiroušková, *Visio Pauli*, 81f.; edited by Priebsch, "John Audelay's Poem," 400–406.

23. For the contents of this manuscript, see Susan Powell, "Biblioteca Statale di Lucca, ms 3540: The Manuscript and Its Provenance," in *Middle English Manuscripts and Their Legacies: A Volume in Honour of Ian Doyle*, ed. C. Saunders, R. Marshall, A. R. Lawrie, and L. Atkinson (Leiden: Brill, 2021), 26–54. Incipit and explicit, p. 48: *Incipit epistola de die dominica quem homines minime tenent nec volunt custodire. O homines, quare hoc facitis propter hec, enim venit ira die super vos et super filios vestros et super omnes possessiones vestras . . .* [134v] *Sed sciatis vere quod dei est transmissa et digitis suis instructa qualiter diem dominicum custodire debeatis. Explicit epistola quomodo observaremus diem dominicum per revelacionem inventa.* The original catalogue has "observantiam diem dominicam" instead of "observaremus diem dominicum" (Leone Del Prete, *Repertorio generale ossia Catalogo descrittivo di tutti i manoscritti della Pubblica Biblioteca di Lucca con Indice tripartito, Appendice* [Lucca, 1883], ms. 3540, 158v).

[Munich, Bayerische Staatsbibliothek clm 12005 (s. xv), 91r (s. xv), *extract*[24]]
Munich, Bayerische Staatsbibliothek clm 22377 (s. xv), 82va–83ra
Paris, Bibliothèque nationale lat. 3343 (s. xv), 153v–154r[25]
Paris, Bibliothèque Sainte-Geneviève Ms 1424 (s. xv), 71v–72r[26]
Prague, National Library XIII G 18 (s. xv), 119v–120v[27]
Rostock, Universitätsbibliothek, theol. 37a (s. xv), 47va–48rb
Uppsala, Universitetsbibliotek C47 (s. xv), 277rv
Uppsala, Universitetsbibliotek C133 (s. xv), 145r
Uppsala, Universitetsbibliotek C226 (s. xv), 52v–53r
Uppsala, Universitetsbibliotek C364 (s. xv), 183v, 195r
Vienna, Österreichische Nationalbibliothek 3496 (s. xv), 4r–5r
Wilhering, Stiftsbibliothek IX 162 (s. xv), 105rb–106va

Latin Recension IIa

Kassel, Murhardsche Bibliothek der Stadt Kassel und Landesbibliothek, theol. 39 (s. xiv), 158r[28]
Vienna, Dominikanerkloster 133 (102) (s. xv), 134vb–135vb[29]

Latin Recension III

Berlin, Staatsbibliothek zu Berlin—Preussischer Kulturbesitz, Ms. Theol. Lat. Fol. 589 (s. xi/xii), 156r–157v
Oxford, Bodl. MS. Canon. Liturg. 366 (s. xi/xii), 36v–38r[30]
Cambridge, Pembroke College 67 (s. xii), f. 88r–88v
Munich, Bayerische Staatsbibliothek clm 21518 (s. xii), 1r–1v[31]
Munich, Bayerische Staatsbibliothek clm 14673 (s. xii–xiii), 117r–119r, *1 of 2 letters*[32]

24. Described in Jiroušková, *Visio Pauli*, 94f. The fragment is transmitted as part of the *Visio Pauli*; it has been edited by Theodore Silverstein, *Visio sancti Pauli* (see below, p. 432f.), 194.

25. Described in Jiroušková, *Visio Pauli*, 112-13.

26. See the description of the manuscript online at http://www.calames.abes.fr/pub/#details?id=BSGB10407 (accessed September 1, 2022).

27. Described in Jiroušková, *Visio Pauli*, 121f. Here the *Visio Pauli* is part of the Letter from Heaven.

28. The text is written on a smaller leaf bound with this manuscript. Haines has edited this in *Sunday Observance*, 207-11 (appendix III).

29. Haines has edited this in *Sunday Observance*, 207-11 (appendix III).

30. See the description of the manuscript online at https://medieval.bodleian.ox.ac.uk/catalog/manuscript_3048 (accessed September 1, 2022).

31. Edited by Priebsch, *Diu vrône botschaft*, 40–71.

32. Listed in Priebsch, *Diu vrône botschaft*, 23.

Paris, Bibliothèque nationale lat. 12315 (s. xii^2), 37vb–40rb
Vienna, Österreichische Nationalbibliothek lat. 510 (s. xii), 134r–141v[33]
Munich, Bayerische Staatsbibliothek clm 2625 (xiii), 39r–47v[34]
Paris, Bibliothèque nationale lat. 5302 (s. xiii), 52va–53rb
Klosterneuburg, Bibliothek des Chorherrenstifts 918 (s. xiii), 1ra–3ra
Toulouse, Bibliothèque Publique 208 (III, 135) (s. xiii), 101r–104r[35]
Klosterneuburg, Bibliothek des Chorherrenstifts 79 (s. xiii/xiv), 57r
Erlangen, Universitätsbibliothek 306 (444) (s. xiv), 1r–4r[36]
London, British Library Add. 16587 (s. xiv), 184r–186r
London, British Library Add. 23930 (s. xiv), 93va–94va
Venice, Biblioteca Nazionale Marciana lat. Z. 507 (s. xiv), 80r–83r[37]
Jena, Thüringer Universitäts- und Landesbibliothek, Ms. El f. 22 (s. xiv/xv), 137rb–138ra
Prague, Archi Pražského Hradu, N 42 (s. xiv/xv), 49v–50r[38]
Dresden, Sächsische Landesbibliothek App. 2300 (s. xv), 292rb–294vb
Leipzig, Universitätsbibliothek 537 (s. xv), 215r
Leipzig, Universitätsbibliothek 594 (s. xv2), 345r–345v
Mainz, Stadtbibliothek I 469 (s. xv), 195r–197r
Michaelbeuern, Stiftsbibliothek 82 (s. xv), 264va–266va
Michaelbeuern, Stiftsbibliothek 97 (s. xv), 172v–174v
Padua, Biblioteca Civica, C.M. 226 (s. xv), 3r–3v[39]
Wrocław, Ms I Q 143 (s. xv) [parchment tucked into manuscript]
Wolfenbüttel, Cod. Guelf. 11 Aug. 4° (Heinemann-Nr. 3006) (s. xv), 210r–212v[40]

Latin Recension IIIa

[Roger of Hoveden, ed. Stubbs, letter used by Eustace de Flay (s. xiii?)[41]]
Oxford, Bodl. Lat. th. f. 19 (s. xiv), 24r–26r

33. Collated with Munich 21518 as variant text W in Priebsch's *Diu vrône botschaft.*

34. Described in Jiroušková, *Visio Pauli*, 92f.

35. Edited by Rivière, "La lettre du Christ tombée du ciel"; see p. 36.

36. Collated with Munich 21518 as variant text E in Priebsch's *Diu vrône botschaft.*

37. Described in Jiroušková, *Visio Pauli*, 133f.

38. Described in Jiroušková, *Visio Pauli*, 117f. Here the *Visio Pauli* is part of the Letter from Heaven.

39. I suspect this text is Latin Recension III; however, the catalogue lacks a full incipit, and I was unable to view the manuscript before the publication of this volume.

40. See the description of the manuscript online at https://diglib.hab.de/?db=mss&list=ms&id=11-aug-4f&catalog=Heinemann (accessed September 1, 2022).

41. William Stubbs, ed., *Chronica Magistri Rogeri de Houden*, Chronicles and Memorials of Great Britain and Ireland during the Middle Ages 4 (London: Longman & Trübner, 1871), 167–69, repr. in Röhricht, "Ein 'Brief Christi,'" 438–40. See p. 35.

Oxford, Bodl. Lyell 12 (s. xiv), 263r–264r
Oxford, Bodl. Douce 54 (s. xv/xvi), 1r–3v
London, British Library Add. 6716 (s. xv), 72rb–73vb
Dublin, Trinity College Library 516 (s. xv), 37r–38v
Graz, Universitätsbibliothek 248 (s. xv), 133va–134ra, *1 of 2 letters*
Trier, Stadtbibliothek 530 (s. xv), 121r[42]

We present Latin Recension II as the oldest and most widely used version; the text printed in this volume stems from a manuscript from Vienna (ÖNB 1355) that seems to record an early version related to the now-lost version (Todi) transcribed by Amaduzzi. A postscript discusses deviations from the other version, the Munich manuscript (BSB Clm 9550), which is otherwise often cited in scholarship on the Letter from Heaven. In addition, we offer the two earlier versions of the Latin Recension I: the text of the now-lost manuscript from Tarragona, transcribed by Baluzius, and the version of Recension I from the manuscript from Vienna mentioned above, as it preserves letters from both Recension I and II (ÖNB 1355). The manuscripts from Basel and London offer only excerpts and are therefore not included separately. Examples of the later Latin Recensions III (Toulouse 208) and IIIa (Hoveden) are presented in the introduction to the history of the Letter from Heaven.

42. Three members of this list also contain portions of Latin Recension II. These are Bodl. Lyell 12, Lat. th. f. 19, and BL Add. 6716.

3.3. Manuscript Studies (Latin)

Angela Zielinski Kinney

3.3.1. Methodology

In the section of this volume devoted to the history of the Letter from Heaven, Uta Heil has given a summary of previous work on the tangled transmission of the Letter from Heaven and has hypothesized new relationships and dating for the various recensions, both Greek and Latin.[1] To complement this work, a new method of examining the Latin recensions of the Letter from Heaven in its manuscript contexts has been undertaken. An analysis of the texts that surrounded or traveled with the Letter from Heaven may give insight on the various purposes for the letter and what functions various recensions may have served.

To accomplish this work, spreadsheets were assembled for each individual manuscript known to contain the Letter from Heaven. Each spreadsheet was filled with the full table of contents as listed in its respective manuscript catalogue. Often the accuracy of these catalogues was checked by viewing scans of the manuscripts. The spreadsheets contained the name of each text in the manuscript, the folios each text spans, and some simple notation concerning where the text is placed in relationship to the Letter from Heaven (immediately before the Letter, immediately after the Letter, concurrent [marginal text or marginal Letter], or no direct connection). If the Letter from Heaven begins or ends the codex (or a section), this was noted. In the case of composite manuscripts, notes were made concerning the beginning and end of each composite part. These spreadsheets were then combined into a master file, which could be queried using a Python script.

Originally this analysis was intended to be done using *clavis* numbers; however, the large number of anonymous, unidentified, or untitled works required a different and more time-consuming solution. I examined the spreadsheet, and keywords were assigned to each individual text manually. The keywords could then be used to sort and identify similar groupings of texts, as well as identify which texts tended to abut the Letter from Heaven. In some way, the process of assigning keywords was a beneficial burden; not only did I become acquainted with the various titles and texts, but I also realized just how many unstudied, intriguing works hide in composite volumes, including marginal notes and prayers. In the future, I intend to write a

1. See Heil, pp. 84–133.

methodological article regarding this type of manuscript analysis and offer the code for public use. From the beginning of this endeavor, there was always the intention to analyze the proximity of certain texts to the Letter from Heaven. This goal quickly became too onerous but will provide a challenge for future work using this methodology.

In the following chapter, I will discuss new discoveries made in the course of carrying out this work, and a working analysis of the types of texts transmitted with and alongside the Letter from Heaven in Latin Recensions I and II. The study below will fill in some background regarding how the Latin Letter from Heaven was perceived, used, and read prior to 1500 CE. Notably, the clusters of texts that tend to be transmitted together with the Letter from Heaven often give the impression that the Letter may have served a practical purpose for clergy—namely, that it provided exciting parabiblical material that could be used in sermons or at dedication rites for churches. The texts in Latin Recension III (the latest of the three recensions) are not discussed in this contribution but may be discussed in a future publication; the data on Latin Recension III largely adheres to trends established for Latin Recension II.

3.3.2. Additional Manuscripts of the Latin Letter from Heaven (Up to 1500 CE)

A list of all previously noted manuscripts of the Latin Letter from Heaven was compiled using the work of Dorothy Haines and Lenka Jiroušková.[2] In the process of examining the contents of these known manuscripts, I discovered seventeen additional manuscripts containing the Letter from Heaven. These codices had been catalogued (some, however, poorly), but they are for the first time presented here as a list sorted according to recension. Notably, one early copy (s. xii) belonging to Latin Recension II and three early copies (s. xi–xii) belonging to Latin Recension III were discovered. These early copies should not be overlooked in future studies. The newly added twelfth-century (incomplete) copy of Latin Recension II (in London, Lambeth Palace Library 539) is unavailable in digital format and may be worth a look in situ.

A previously unstudied piece of parchment folded in fourths and tucked into a fifteenth-century Wrocław manuscript (Wrocław, Ms I Q 143) provides the earliest—and thus far, only—piece of evidence that the Latin Letter from Heaven was used as a personal apotropaic amulet. The version of the Latin Letter from Heaven in this folded parchment belongs to Latin Recension III but has distinctive features that may reward further study. At this time, only the vernacular versions of the Letter from Heaven have been examined as

2. Haines, *Sunday Observance*, 211–14; Jiroušková, *Visio Pauli*.

protective amulets (*Schutzbriefe*), but the popularity of other heavenly letters as textual amulets suggests that this Letter from Heaven may also have been used occasionally for this purpose. In the future, I wish to undertake a closer examination of amuletic features in the various Letters from Heaven, including the use of popular biblical verses associated with protective prayers/charms; time has not permitted a full study of these components prior to the publication of this volume.

List of Newly "Discovered" Manuscripts Containing the Latin Letter from Heaven

Recension II

London, Lambeth Palace Library 539 (s. xii), 141r–141v[3]
Innsbruck, Universitäts- und Landesbibliothek Tirol Cod. 409 (s. xiii/xiv), 100r–102r
Göttweig, Benediktinerstift Cod. 199 (s. xiv), 38r–39r
Berlin, Staatsbibliothek zu Berlin—Preußischer Kulturbesitz, Magdeburg 21 (s. xv), 162va–162vb[4]
Berlin, Staatsbibliothek zu Berlin—Preußischer Kulturbesitz, Magdeburg 196 (s. xv), 381r–381v
Jena, Thüringer Universitäts- und Landesbibliothek, Ms. Klosterbibl. 5 (s. xv), 246va
Lucca, Biblioteca Statale di Lucca 3540 (s. xv), 134r–134v[5]
Munich, Bayerische Staatsbibliothek clm 3766 (s. xv), 177va–178ra[6]
Paris, Bibliothèque Sainte-Geneviève Ms 1424 (s. xv), 71v–72r[7]

---

3. https://archives.lambethpalacelibrary.org.uk/calmview/Record.aspx?src=CalmView.Catalog&id=MSS%2f539.

4. *[Epistola Jesu Christi de die dominica] Quia nescitis deum timere nec diem dominicum seruare . . . — . . . Juro ego Petrus per dei potestatem, per Christum . . . vobis omnibus quod ista epistola non est formata manu hominum sed de trono dei et digitis suis quanta vice transmissa est de septimo trono.*

5. For the contents of this manuscript, see Powell, "Biblioteca Statale di Lucca," 26–54. Incipit and explicit, p. 48: *Incipit epistola de die dominica quem homines minime tenent nec volunt custodire. O homines, quare hoc facitis propter hec, enim venit ira die super vos et super filios vestros et super omnes possessiones vestras . . . [134v]. Sed sciatis vere quod dei est transmissa et digitis suis instructa qualiter diem dominicum custodire debeatis. Explicit epistola quomodo obseruaremus diem dominicum per reuelacionem inuenta.* The original cataloguer wrote "observantiam diem dominicam" instead of "obseruaremus diem dominicum" (Del Prete, *Catalogo descrittivo di tutti*, Ms. 3540, 158v).

6. http://bilder.manuscripta-mediaevalia.de/hs//projekt-Muenchen-Augsburg-pdfs/Clm%203766.pdf.

7. http://www.calames.abes.fr/pub/#details?id=BSGB10407.

Recension III

Berlin, Staatsbibliothek zu Berlin—Preußischer Kulturbesitz, Ms. Theol. Lat. Fol. 589 (s. xi/xii), 156r–157v
Oxford, Bodl. MS. Canon. Liturg. 366 (s. xi/xii), 36v–38r[8]
Cambridge, Pembroke College 67 (s. xii), 88r–88v
Jena, Thüringer Universitäts- und Landesbibliothek, Ms. El f. 22 (s. xiv/xv), 137rb–138ra
Leipzig, Universitätsbibliothek 594 (s. xv^2), 345r–345v
Padua, Biblioteca Civica, C.M. 226 (s. xv), 3r–3v[9]
Wolfenbüttel, Cod. Guelf. 11 Aug. 4° (Heinemann-Nr. 3006) (s. xv), 210r–212v[10]
Wrocław, Ms I Q 143 (s. xv) [parchment tucked into manuscript]

3.3.3. Results: Latin Recension I

Latin Recension I contains the fewest number of manuscripts, with a large chronological gap in the central medieval period. There are two fragments in ninth- to tenth-century manuscripts; of the complete surviving copies, two appear in tenth- to eleventh-century manuscripts, one in a twelfth-century manuscript, and two in manuscripts from the fourteenth to fifteenth centuries. The paucity of manuscripts makes it difficult to establish any strong patterns in the content, but some thematic trends can nonetheless be established. Two of the earliest manuscripts include Hiberno-Latin works either immediately before or after the Letter from Heaven,[11] demonstrating potential insular influence on (or context for) the transmission. Vatican, BAV Reg. lat. 49 is a late ninth-century manuscript most likely produced in Brittany; it is the sole witness to the *Catechesis Celtica*, an extremely influential collection of homilies, Gospel passages for Sunday liturgies, and various exegetical material.[12] Extracts from the Letter from Heaven are placed immediately after the *Catechesis Celtica* (together with a Sunday list), suggesting that the compiler of the codex saw a thematic link between the Letter from Heaven and the

8. https://medieval.bodleian.ox.ac.uk/catalog/manuscript_3048.

9. This is suspected to be Latin Recension III, but without the text or incipit, it is difficult to say for sure.

10. https://diglib.hab.de/?db=mss&list=ms&id=11-aug-4f&catalog=Heinemann.

11. Vatican, BAV Reg. lat. 49 (s. ix/x) and Paris, BN lat. 12270 (s. xii).

12. See André Wilmart, *Analecta reginensia: extraits des manuscrits latins de la Reine Christine conservés au Vatican*, Studi e testi 59 (Vatican City: Biblioteca Apostolica Vaticana, 1933), 29–112. The title *Catechesis Celtica* is assigned by modern scholars, based on Wilmart's edition of the material under the title "Catéchèses celtiques."

preceding florilegium.[13] In Paris, BN lat. 12270, the Letter from Heaven follows an eschatological text, the *Prognosticorum futuri saeculi libri tres* by Julian of Toledo,[14] and immediately precedes the *Liber de XII abusionibus seculi* ("A Book on the Twelve Abuses of the World"),[15] a seventh-century Hiberno-Latin treatise. Both the *Catechesis Celtica* and the *Liber de XII abusionibus seculi* treat problems of morality and eschatology similar to those in the Letter from Heaven. The inclusion of the Letter from Heaven in codices alongside these Hiberno-Latin texts suggests that Latin Recension I may have been influenced by insular contexts or concerns. The framing of apocalyptical punishments and eschatology in Latin Recension I is easy to situate (theoretically) within the insular fascination concerning heaven and hell, but the Letter from Heaven in Latin Recension I does not travel alongside the more descriptive accounts of hell popular in late antique and medieval Ireland and England.[16]

Another early manuscript (London, BL Add. 19725 [s. x/xi]) includes the Letter from Heaven as a later addition, spilling into the margin of

---

13. See Haines, *Sunday Observance*, 49.

14. CPL 1258. Edition: Jocelyn Nigel Hillgarth, ed., Julian of Toledo, *Prognosticorum futuri saeculi libri tres*, CCSL 115 (Turnhout: Brepols, 1976), 11–126.

15. CPL 1106. Edition: Siegmund Hellmann, ed., *Ps.-Cyprianus. De xii abusiuis saeculi*, TUGAL 34 (Leipzig: Hinrichs, 1909), 32–60.

16. Such as the *Visio Pauli* (ECCA 818; CANT 325; see pp. 419–33), the anonymous *Liber de ordine creaturarum* (CPL 1189), or other apocalyptic visions of hell. There is considerable documentation of insular interest in eschatological, apocalyptic, and apocryphal works in the medieval period. New editions of apocrypha circulating in medieval Ireland have been published by Martin McNamara, MSC, Caoimhín Breatnach, Pádraig A. Breatnach, John Carey, Uáitéar Mac Gearailt, Máire Herbert, Caitríona Ó Dochartaigh, Erich Poppe, and Charles D. Wright, eds., *Apocrypha Hiberniae II, Apocalyptica 2*, CCSA 21 (Turnhout: Brepols, 2019). On Irish interest in apocrypha, see Martin McNamara, *The Apocrypha in the Early Irish Church* (Dublin: Institute of Advanced Studies, 1975), and McNamara, *The Bible and the Apocrypha in the Early Irish Church (A.D. 600–1200)*, Instrumenta Patristica et Mediaevalia 66 (Turnhout: Brepols, 2015). On English interest in apocryphal texts, see Kathryn Powell and Donald Scragg, eds., *Apocryphal Texts and Traditions in Anglo-Saxon England* (Cambridge: D. S. Brewer, 2003). On the "insular vision of hell," see the discussion by Charles D. Wright, *The Irish Tradition in Old English Literature*, Cambridge Studies in Anglo-Saxon England 6 (Cambridge: Cambridge University Press, 1993), 106–74. See also Richard Bauckham, *The Fate of the Dead: Studies on the Jewish and Christian Apocalypses*, NovTSup 93 (Leiden: Brill, 1998); though the entire volume is useful, the chapter "The Apocalypse of the Seven Heavens: The Latin Version" (304–31) is relevant in relation to insular apocalyptic. One should, however, note that Bauckham's discussion of the sources for the Seven Heavens Apocryphon does not concur with a consensus of scholars who argue for gnostic sources.

another text, the *Liber de gestis sanctorum patrum miracula* ("A Book on the Deeds and Miracles of the Holy Fathers").[17] A large number of the preceding folios are devoted to a text listed as *Regulae et instructiones ecclesiastice sacerdotum* on the paper pastedown (s. xiv/xv hand) listing the contents of the manuscript (f. 1r) and in the British Library online manuscript catalogue entry.[18] In fact, this is an extract from the *Epistola de baptismo*, a text attributed to the Carolingian bishop Jesse of Amiens.[19] The section copied begins by discussing the biblical canon: *Prima enim adnotatione percunctare curavimus quid sit canon, vel quid contineatur in canone* ("For in the first record we have undertaken to ascertain what the canon is, or rather, what is contained within the canon"). It is delightfully ironic that this otherwise orthodox codex, which treats the nature of scriptural canon seriously and contains standard doctrinal works (such as Gennadius of Massilia, *De ecclesiasticis dogmatibus*, "Concerning Church Doctrine"[20]) includes an early version of the apocryphal Letter from Heaven inked just before the miracles of the holy fathers.

The late manuscripts of Latin Recension I include more than one recension of the Letter from Heaven, and this radically alters the "cohorts" of the letter (by this I mean the types of works transmitted alongside and with the Letter from Heaven). Here one glimpses some concerns that will dominate the other two recensions: the Letter from Heaven is set amid texts that focus overwhelmingly on confession, penance, and sin. Vienna, ÖNB 1355 places the Letters from Heaven (Recensions I and II) after a series of short sermons with rubricated titles and a series of anonymous brief theological texts (*Tractatus breves argumenti theologici*). But immediately following the Letters from Heaven is the apocryphal *De expulsione Ade et Eve de paradiso* ("On the Expulsion of Adam and Eve from Paradise," or more frequently, "The Life of Adam and Eve").[21] The Letters from Heaven—themselves noncanonical works, however

17. An anonymous text on the works of the holy fathers.

18. http://www.bl.uk/manuscripts/FullDisplay.aspx?ref=Add_MS_19725.

19. PL 105:781–96.

20. CPL 958. PL 42:1213–42.

21. There are various titles and versions of this popular OT apocryphon. It has a tangled transmission much like the Letter from Heaven, such that to speak of a single text is impossible. It was sometimes called the Apocalypse of Moses (referring to the Greek version), and some recensions interpolate or tack on other stories, especially legends of the "Holy Rood" (describing the history of the cross for Jesus's crucifixion prior to this event). Edition and discussion of the primary Latin recensions, as well as the Greek, Armenian, and Georgian versions, may be found in Jean-Pierre Pettorelli, Jean-Daniel Kaestli, Alfred Frey, and Bernard Outtier, eds., *Vita latina Adae et Evae*, 2 vols., CCSA 18-19 (Turnhout: Brepols, 2012). The version transmitted in this manuscript belongs to the oldest attested

useful they may have been for influencing Sunday activities—are set (literally) in a space between orthodoxy and overt apocrypha. After *De expulsione Ade et Eve*, the manuscript returns more or less to orthodox concerns, especially with regard to confession and penance. The subsequent folios include an anonymous *Libellus de peccatorum agnitione, seu inquisitione, seu facienda confessione* ("A Small Book on the Admission and Inquisition of Sins, and the Confession That Should Be Made") and the *Summa de poenitentia* ("Compendium on Penance") by Raymond of Penyafort (ca. 1175–January 6, 1275 CE).[22]

Another manuscript provides even more material on confession and penance. Graz, UB 248 includes no fewer than six works on sin and penance, some of unknown authorship: an anonymous *Tractatus de indulgenciis* ("Tractate on Indulgences"), an anonymous *Tractatus de peccato* ("Tractate on Sin"), Jean Gerson's *Tractatus de condicionibus confessionis, absolucionis, excommunicacionis et penitencie iniunccionis* ("Tractate on the Conditions for Confession, for Absolution, for Excommunication, and for the Command to Perform Penance"),[23] Nicolaus von Dinkelsbühl's *De confessione* ("On Confession"),[24] Heinrich von Langenstein's *Tractatus de confessione* ("Tractate on Confession"), a work called *Collatio copiosa de indulgentiis* ("Extensive Collection of Material on Indulgences"), and even some verse lines about

form of the text, the form called the "southern German redaction" by Jean-Pierre Pettorelli, "La Vie latine d'Adam et Eve: analyse de la tradition manuscrite," *Apocrypha* 10 (1999): 195–296. A discussion of "Adam texts" in medieval Europe is the focus of Brian Murdoch, *The Apocryphal Adam and Eve in Medieval Europe: Vernacular Translations and Adaptations of the "Vita Adae et Evae"* (Oxford: Oxford University Press, 2009), but he also summarizes the history of scholarship on the Vita. See also the presentation of the Letter from Heaven from this manuscript below, pp. 221–35, 245–67, and 476.

22. This work often bears the title *Summa de casibus poenitentiae*; it is a handbook for clergy and monks who heard confessions and prescribed penance. Edition: Xaviero Ochoa and Aloisio Diez, eds., *S. Raimundus de Pennaforte, Summa de paenitentia*, Universa Bibliotheca Iuris I B (Rome: Editiones Institutum Iuridicum Claretianum, 1976).

23. The standard edition for Gerson's work remains that of Palémon Glorieux, ed., *Jean Gerson: Oeuvres complètes*, 10 vols. (Paris: Desclée et Cie, 1960–73). Gerson was a prolific author and wrote several works on confession. It is difficult to ascertain from which work this extract has been pulled without more research.

24. This work by Nicolaus von Dinkelsbühl shows up with various titles, for example, *Tractatus de septem viciis, Tractatus parvus de modo confitendi septem peccata mortalia, De septem vitiis capitalibus et de virtutibus iisdem oppositis*, and *Confessionale de septem peccatis mortalibus*. Edition: Alois Madre, *Nikolaus von Dinkelsbühl. Leben und Schriften*, Beiträge zur Geschichte der Philosophie und Theologie des Mittelalters 40/4 (Münster: Aschendorff, 1965), 192–99. Madre's edition should be used with care, as it does contain mistakes; see the discussion by Christopher Ocker, "German Theologians and the Jews in the Fifteenth Century," in *Jews, Judaism, and the Reformation in Sixteenth-Century Germany*, ed. Dean Phillip Bell and Stephen G. Burnett (Leiden: Brill, 2006), 42–43 and 42n38.

how to make confession.[25] But the two Letters from Heaven (Recensions I and IIIa) precede a different sort of text, the eschatological *Versus de signis iudicii ultimi* ("Verses on the Signs of the Last Judgment"), which in conjunction with the Letters of Heaven serves to warn the sinner what awaits the sinner should the sinner not be reconciled to God. Just a couple folios after the Letters from Heaven is an anti-Jewish text, a Latin translation of Anastasius Sinaita's *Disputatio adversus Judaeos* ("Argument against the Jews," originally written in Greek).[26] Analysis of Latin Recension II will identify anti-Jewish material as an additional thematic strand among the manuscripts containing the Letter from Heaven.

3.3.4. Results: Latin Recension II

As Uta Heil has convincingly argued,[27] Latin Recension II is chronologically the earliest of the Latin recensions and served as a blueprint or model for Latin Recension I and (along with the Greek recensions) Latin Recension III. Latin Recension II is contained in forty-seven extant medieval manuscripts, plus a transcript from a (now lost) manuscript in Todi, Perugia.[28] Two analyses of the manuscript context for Latin Recension II are offered here: first, the texts that stand directly adjacent to the Letter from Heaven, and second, the texts that travel in the same codices as the Letter but are not directly adjacent.

3.3.4a. Texts Adjacent to the Letter from Heaven

This discussion begins by examining which texts are transmitted as direct neighbors (before, after, or concurrent with the Letter). Of all the Latin recensions of the Letter from Heaven, Latin Recension II is transmitted in the greatest number of manuscripts. This recension thus provides sufficient material for analyzing which texts and which kinds of texts were copied adjacent to the Letter from Heaven.

Two of the earliest manuscripts, Paris, BN lat. 8508 (s. x/xi) and London, BL Add. 30853 (s. xi/xii) transmit the Letter from Heaven in the margin of other texts: in the case of the former, an anonymous *Summa poenitentiae* in six books; in the case of the latter, the famous Toledo Homiliary. As both of these marginal insertions were added later by a new hand, not much can be

25. Folio 242r: *Qualiter debeat esse confessio. Sit simplex humilis confessio* . . . See the presentation of the Letter from Heaven from this manuscript at p. 268f.

26. CPG 7772.

27. See Heil, p. 86.

28. Amaduzzi, *Anecdota litteraria*, 69–74.

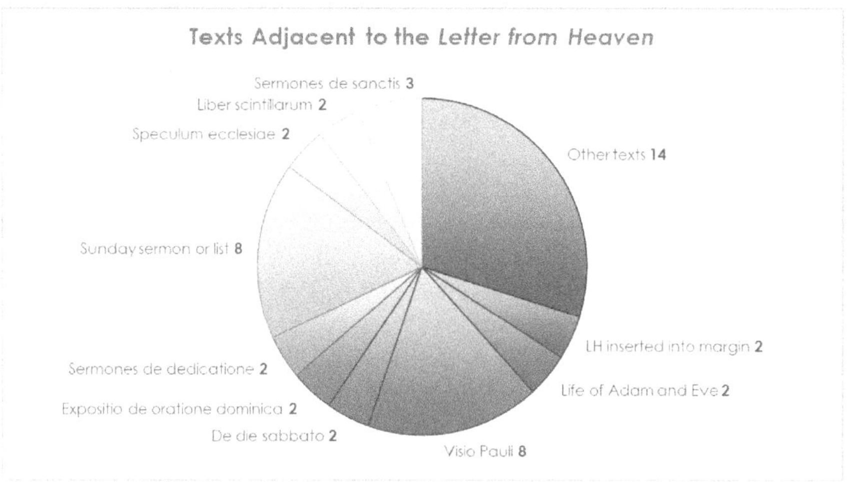

Figure 3.1. Texts adjacent to the Letter from Heaven.

said about them. There was space enough in those margins to copy the Letter from Heaven, and someone did so.

The texts abutting the Letter from Heaven in the remaining forty-five codices demonstrate some patterns. Some involve a larger group of manuscripts, while some only include two; yet in the absence of a stemma, minor similarities may prove useful for future study of the transmission. These patterns also may suggest how the Letter from Heaven may have been contextualized, viewed, or used by the people who copied it and read it. Eight manuscripts contain the *Visio Pauli* ("Vision of Paul") either immediately before or after the Letter from Heaven, a phenomenon documented in Lenka Jiroušková's work on the *Visio*.[29] In six manuscripts, the Letter from Heaven has been copied after the *Visio Pauli*, whereas the Letter from Heaven is placed before the *Visio Pauli* in only two manuscripts.[30] The Letter seems to have functioned better as an epilogue to the apocalyptic vision of Paul than as a prologue.

Seven manuscripts contain an anonymous sermon concerning Sunday (beginning *Veneranda/o nobis est dies*, or similarly) either before or after the

29. Jiroušková, *Die Visio Pauli*, 377–85.

30. *Visio Pauli* immediately before the Letter from Heaven: Brussels, Bibliothèque Royale Albert Ier, II 1053; Cambridge, St John's College F.22 (159); London, BL Royal 11 B.x; London, BL Royal 8 F.vi; Munich, Bayerische Staatsbibliothek clm 12005; Vienna, ÖNB 1629. *Visio Pauli* immediately after the Letter from Heaven: Paris, Bibliothèque nationale lat. 3343, and Prague, National Library III.D.13 (Y.1.4. n. 79).

Letter from Heaven.[31] This sermon is sometimes called a *sermo* in a title or rubric; at other times it is called a *nota* or even *alia epistola*. One manuscript adds a "Sunday list" immediately after the Letter from Heaven, although this is listed in the manuscript catalogue incorrectly as the Letter itself (i.e., *Epistola de die dominica*).[32]

Three manuscripts include the Letter from Heaven adjacent to a collection of sermons on saints;[33] notably, two transmit it in the middle of such a collection,[34] although not as an afterthought. The first, lengthy portion of an anonymous sermon collection organized by feast days of the saints (*Sermones de sanctis*) is written by single scribe in the codex Bernkastel-Kues, Bibliothek des St. Nikolaus-Hospitals 128. A second scribe then copies the Letter from Heaven before continuing the *Sermones*. In Paris, Bibliothèque Sainte-Geneviève Ms 1424, the text of Peregrinus de Oppeln's *Sermones de tempore et sanctis* ("Sermons according to the Season and to the Feasts of the Saints")[35] is divided into two sections, both written by the same scribe. A contemporary second hand has written the Letter from Heaven in the ample space between the *Sermones de sanctis* and before the *Sermones de tempore*. The addition is not marginal, and one cannot rule out the possibility that extra space was indeed left specifically for the Letter from Heaven. Another manuscript, Wilhering, Stiftsbibliothek IX 162, is devoted primarily to Peregrinus de Oppeln's *Sermones de sanctis*, which directly precede the Letter from Heaven. The remaining similarities involve pairs of manuscripts.

31. *Sermo de die dominica* immediately before the Letter from Heaven: Einsiedeln, Stiftsbibliothek 726; Munich, Bayerische Staatsbibliothek clm 3766; Munich, Universitätsbibliothek 2° 120. After the Letter from Heaven: Innsbruck, Stiftsbibliothek Wilton (s.n.); Innsbruck, Universitäts- und Landesbibliothek Tirol (ULBT), Cod. 409; Mainz, Stadtbibliothek I 227; Vienna, ÖNB 3496. Sometimes this sermon is wrongly attributed to Augustine of Hippo.

32. Göttweig, Benediktinerstift Cod. 199. For more on the anonymous Sunday sermon and the Sunday list tradition see Clare Lees, "The 'Sunday Letter' and the 'Sunday Lists,'" *Anglo-Saxon England* 14 (1985): 129–51; Haines, *Sunday Observance*, 59; and Linder, "*De plaga*" (throughout). Stephen Pelle, "Source Studies in the Lambeth Homilies," *The Journal of English and Germanic Philology* 113 (2014): 34–72, suggests that the Sunday sermon was written in the tenth century in an insular context.

33. Bernkastel-Kues, Bibliothek des St. Nikolaus-Hospitals 128; Paris, Bibliothèque Sainte-Geneviève Ms 1424; Wilhering, Stiftsbibliothek IX 162.

34. Bernkastel-Kues, Bibliothek des St. Nikolaus-Hospitals 128, and Paris, Bibliothèque Sainte-Geneviève Ms 1424.

35. Edition: Richardus Tatarzyński, *Peregrini de Opole. Sermones de tempore et de sanctis*, Studia "Przeglądu Tomistycznego" 1 (Warsaw: Instytut Tomistyczny, 1997).

Expositio de oratione dominica

Treatises on the Lord's prayer are included after the Letter from Heaven in two manuscripts; these texts bear similar names but are by different authors. The Berlin *Expositio de oratione dominica* ("Exposition on the Lord's Prayer") is the work of Nicolaus of Dinkelsbühl.[36] The text in Budapest, University Library, lat. 39 is attributed to Thomas of Aquinas but may be a patchwork of interpretations. If indeed the Budapest *Expositio* is a patchwork, it would not be out of place, as the manuscript also transmits a popular florilegium (the *Liber scintillarum*) immediately before the Letter from Heaven.

Berlin, Staatsbibliothek zu Berlin—Preußischer Kulturbesitz, Magdeburg 196	*Expositio de oratione dominica*
Budapest, University Library, lat. 39	*Expositio super oratione dominicali*

Liber Scintillarum

Defensor of Ligugé's *Liber scintillarum* ("Book of Sparks"),[37] a late seventh- or early eighth-century compilation of biblical and patristic sayings, precedes the Letter from Heaven in two manuscripts. In these cases, the Letter may have been included out of a sense of tradition (if one existed), or perhaps as a curiosity. The Letter from Heaven is rather unproblematic in the context of an encyclopedic compilation, and perhaps it adjoins the *Liber scintillarum* precisely for that reason.

Munich, Bayerische Staatsbibliothek, clm 22377	*Liber scintillorum [sic]*
Budapest, University Library, lat. 39	*Liber scintillarum*

Speculum Ecclesiae

Hugh of Saint Cher's *Speculum ecclesiae* ("The Mirror of the Church")[38] is an exposition or commentary on the order of the Mass; the author gives both practical explanations (what is and isn't said during Lent, Advent, etc.) and an

36. Edition: Madre, *Dinkelsbühl*, 175–80.

37. Edition: Hénri-Marie Rochais, ed., *Liber Scintillarum*, CCSL 117 (Turnholt: Brepols, 1957). See Yitzhak Hen, "Defensor of Ligugé's *Liber Scintillarum* and the Migration of Knowledge," in *East and West in the Early Middle Ages: The Merovingian Kingdoms in Mediterranean Perspective*, ed. Stefan Esders, Yaniv Fox, Yitzhak Hen, and Laury Sarti (Cambridge: Cambridge University Press, 2019), 218–29.

38. Edition: Gisbert Sölch, ed., *Hugonis a St. Charo tractatus super missam seu speculum ecclesiae* (Münster: Aschendorff, 1940), 8–52 and appendix 53–55.

explanation of how each action and word in the service has a biblical foundation and a spiritual meaning. This text follows the Letter from Heaven in an Uppsala manuscript; the apocryphal Letter becomes a kind of preface for a wildly popular and strictly orthodox piece of exegesis.

The *Speculum* precedes the Letter from Heaven in Göttweig, Benediktinerstift Cod. 199. Its *explicit* links the work to the Letter from Heaven with the words *Explicit expositio missae et incipitur epystola* ("Here the exposition of the Mass is ended and the letter begins"). This conjunction is a small detail, but one indicating that the Letter from Heaven is deliberately placed after the *Speculum*.[39]

Uppsala, Universitätsbiblithek C133	*Speculum ecclesiae*
Göttweig, Benediktinerstift Cod. 199	*Speculum ecclesiae*

De die sabbato

An anonymous note on Saturday precedes the Letter from Heaven in a Berlin manuscript and follows the Letter from Heaven in Rostock, Universitätsbibliothek, theol. 37a. It is notable that neither of these texts contrasts Saturday (or the Jewish Sabbath) with Sunday; rather, they discuss the function of Saturday and appropriate activities a Christian should undertake on this day. The Rostock text seems to function more as an extension of the Letter from Heaven, giving further instructions not just for Saturday but for Friday as well.

Berlin, Staatsbibliothek zu Berlin—Preußischer Kulturbesitz, Magdeburg 21	*De die sabbato*
Rostock, Universitätsbibliothek, theol. 37a	*De die sabbato*

Sermones de dedicatione

Two manuscripts record sermons and readings for the dedication of churches (or for the anniversary of a dedication) immediately after the Letter from Heaven. These two collections seem to be unattributed to a particular author.

Munich, Bayerische Staatsbibliothek, clm 12005	*Sermones de dedicatione et alii*
Uppsala, Universitätsbiblithek C226	*Lectiones de dedicatione ecclesiae*

A public reading of the Letter from Heaven during ecclesial dedication ceremonies or at commemorations of the dedication cannot be ruled out. The connection between the Letter from Heaven and dedication/consecration of

39. Göttweig, Benediktinerstift Cod. 199, 38r.

churches is explored in more detail in the respective category below, as several codices transmit numerous dedicatory materials with the Letter from Heaven, even if these are not immediately adjacent to it in the codex.

Vita Adae et Evae

Apocryphal accounts of the Life of Adam and Eve follow the Letter from Heaven in two manuscripts.

Vienna, ÖNB 1355	*De expulsione Ade et Eve de paradiso*
Munich, Bayerische Staatsbibliothek clm 3433	*De Adam et Eva*

The Vienna manuscript is notable for transmitting two different recensions of the Letter from Heaven, followed by *De expulsione Ade et Eve de paradiso* (as discussed in the section on Latin Recension I). The text ends prematurely, however, at a point in the narrative when the archangel Michael orders Seth not to mourn the death of his mother longer than six days because the Lord rested on the seventh day. Seth then makes tablets of stone and tablets of earth (as Eve, his mother, had instructed him) and records the life of his parents on them.

> "*Homo Dei, ne amplius lugeas mortuos tuos quam sex dies, quia septimo die signum resurrectionis est futuri seculi requies, et in die septimo requievit Dominus ab omnibus operibus suis.*" *Tunc Seth fecit tabulas lapideas et luteas et scripsit in eis omnem vitam patris et matris.* (Vita Adae et Evae 51.2)[40]
>
> "Man of God, do not mourn your dead longer than six days, because in the seventh day is the sign of resurrection and the respite for the age to come, and on the seventh day the Lord rested from all his labors." Then Seth made the tablets of stone and those of clay, and he wrote upon them the entire life of his father and mother.

That Vienna, ÖNB 1355, records two separate Letters from Heaven concerning Sunday, followed by a truncated Life of Adam and Eve, cannot be purely coincidental. Perhaps it is overreading to see in the two versions of the Letter from Heaven parallels to the double set of tablets created and inscribed by Seth (which are themselves allusions to the tablets received by Moses [Exod 31:18], smashed by him [Exod 32:19], and then rewritten [Exod 34:1] by God). But surely the premature ending of the Life of Adam and Eve (with the command to honor the Lord's day of rest) intentionally amplifies the content of

40. According to the new edition by Pettorelli et al., *Vita Latina Adae et Evae*.

the apocryphal Letters from Heaven by means of a further miraculous, apocryphal text. Sunday binds these three texts together.

Other Texts

The remaining manuscripts transmitting Latin Recension II have various other texts adjacent to the Letter from Heaven. These texts tend to belong to the broader categories discussed in the next section.

3.3.4b. Texts Transmitted with the Letter from Heaven

Calendars and Computistical Texts

The practical and eschatological importance of time in the Letter from Heaven[41] meant that in some cases, the letter was transmitted in the same codex as computistical and calendrical texts. The texts noted below do not correspond to known edited texts.

Munich, Bayerische Staatsbibliothek, clm 22377	*Tabula intervallorum inter nativitatem et quadragesimam annorum 1372–1406*	158v–159v
Innsbruck, Universitäts- und Landesbibliothek Tirol (ULBT), Cod. 409	*Computistical instructions for calculating the moon and sun cycles, the indiction and epact*	82r–83r
Innsbruck, Universitäts- und Landesbibliothek Tirol (ULBT), Cod. 409	*On the number of weeks between Christmas and Lent*	177v
Munich, Bayerische Staatsbibliothek clm 3433	*Tabulae ad inveniendum numerum aureum*	64r–65r
Cambridge, Pembroke College 103	*Prognostics of weather, etc., and divinations, such as are often attributed to Esdras*	77v
Vienna, ÖNB 3496	*Cisiojanus germanicus [calendar, incomplete]*	10r

Additional texts that pertain to time, such as *Sermones de tempore* (which are actually liturgical texts keyed to seasons, but one may understand the liturgy as an ordering of ecclesiastical calendrical time) and rites for specific feast days likewise occur in the transmission, but are so common as to perhaps not be of much use in interpreting the status of the Letter from Heaven. Moreover, these are primarily sermons, not primarily works about time itself. One may, however, mention some other types of "technical" texts relevant to this

41. See Heil on the length of Sunday, p. 182f.

category by reason of their practicality, such as glossaries, miscellaneous recipes, medical and anatomical notes, and an alphabetical list used for interpreting dreams. The dream book *Somniale Danielis* ("The Dreams of Daniel")[42] in particular appears in two manuscripts of the Letter from Heaven, and a third manuscript includes a verse interpretation of a biblical dream:

Cambridge, Pembroke College 103	*Sompniale Danielis*	75r–77r
Vienna, ÖNB 1878	*Somniale Danielis [fragment]*	162r
London, BL Royal 8 F.vi	*Interpretation of Nebuchadnezzar's vision (verse)*	25v–27r

Dream interpretation was not only a practical concern but also a hermeneutical one in the context of understanding apocalyptic literature, a topic that will be discussed below.

Anti-Jewish Literature

The Letter from Heaven appears in several codices alongside collections of anti-Jewish polemical texts produced in the fourteenth and fifteenth centuries. Although none of these texts directly abuts the Letter from Heaven, they are nonetheless important contextual threads for understanding its transmission.

Oxford, Merton College 13	*Contra Iudaeos, paganos et Arianos. Sermo de symbolo.*	117v-119r
Mattsee, Stiftsbibliothek 49	*Pharetra fidei contra Iudaeos*	246rb–257ra
Mattsee, Stiftsbibliothek 49	*Responsio ad quendam Iudaeum*	257ra–273vb
Mattsee, Stiftsbibliothek 49	*Vindicta salvatoris*	274ra–274vb
Munich, Bayerische Staatsbibliothek, clm 22377	*Denariis triginta deum vendidit Galilaeus*	199r-199v
Munich, Bayerische Staatsbibliothek, clm 22377	*Pharetra fidei contra Judaeos*	209r-210v
Munich, Bayerische Staatsbibliothek, clm 22377	*Excerpta de erroribus Judaeorum in Thalmut quos transtulit Theobaldus supprior ord. praedicat.*	211r

(*Continued*)

42. See Valerio Cappozzo, *Dizionario dei sogni nel Medioevo. Il Somniale Danielis in manoscritti letterari*, Biblioteca dell' "Archivum Romanicum"—Serie I: Storia, Letteratura, Paleografia (Florence: Leo S. Olschki, 2018), including previous scholarship on this medieval dream book.

(Continued)

Munich, Bayerische Staatsbibliothek, clm 22377	*Disputatio Christiani cum Judaeo*	211r–211v
Vienna, ÖNB 3496	*Epistola ad Rabbi Isaac de religione judaica et christiana*	72r–92v
Vienna, ÖNB 3496	*Pharetra fidei contra versucias haereticorum ad infideles judaeos*	93r–101r
Vienna, ÖNB 3496	*Responsio ad quemdam judaeum ex verbis evangelii secundum Matthaeum contra Christum nequitur arguentem*	101v–128v
Vienna, ÖNB 3496	*Disputatio facta per Christianum fidelem contra judaeum, interprete Paschasio de Roma*	163r–167r
Vienna, ÖNB 3496	*Reprobatio Talmot iudeorum*	167v–172v

Common texts in this strand include the *Pharetra fidei contra Iudaeos* by Theobald of Sézanne ("Quiver of Faith against the Jews," three manuscripts),[43] the *Responsio ad quendam Iudaeum* by Nicholas of Lyra ("Response to a Certain Jew," two manuscripts),[44] the *Disputatio Christiani cum Iudaeo* ("Disputation of a Christian with a Jew," two manuscripts), translated from Greek into Latin by Pascalis Romanus in the twelfth century, and a refutation of Talmudic excerpts translated into Latin by the Dominican prior of Paris, Theobald de Sézanne (two manuscripts).[45] Vienna, ÖNB 3496 includes all four of these anti-Jewish works, prefaced by a polemical text, the *Epistola ad Rabbi Isaac* ("Epistle to Rabbi Isaac"). The epistle pretends to be Alfonso Buenhombre's Latin translation of an eleventh-century Arabic letter written by Samuel of Fes, a Moroccan rabbi who had converted to Christianity, to his contemporary, Rabbi Isaac of Sijilmasa. Yet Buenhombre is certainly the author of the fictitious letter, the purpose of which was to persuade Jews to

43. On this work, see Carmen Cardelle de Hartmann, "Drei Schriften mit dem Titel *Pharetra fidei*," *Aschkenas* 11 (2001): 327–51.

44. For editions and further manuscript history of this text, see Johann Albert Fabricius, *Bibliotheca latina mediae et infimae aetatis V* (Florence, 1858), 114–17; Palémon Glorieux, *Répertoire des maîtres en théologie de Paris au XIII*[e] siècle (Paris, 1934), vol. 2, n. 345; Edward A. Gosselin, "A Listing of the Printed Editions of Nicolaus de Lyra," *Traditio* 26 (1960): 399–426; and Klaus Reinhardt, "Das Werk des Nicolaus von Lyra im mittelalterlichen Spanien," *Traditio* 43 (1987): 321–58.

45. The Paris Talmud trial (1240–1242) spurred the translation and circulation of Latin translations of the Talmud; afterward dissemination of tractates concerning the "errors" of the Talmud often appeared in conjunction with other anti-Jewish works. See Deeana Copeland Klepper, *The Insight of Unbelievers: Nicholas of Lyra and Christian Reading of Jewish Text in the Later Middle Ages*, Jewish Culture and Contexts (Philadelphia: University of Pennsylvania Press, 2007), 25–26.

convert to Christianity. The collection of texts in Vienna, ÖNB 3496 bears a closer look, given the bounty of anti-Jewish material this manuscript contains. Anti-Jewish texts have been bolded in the following table, and material concerning Sunday has been italicized:

Vienna, ÖNB 3496	
Certa miracula de dedicatione ecclesiae	2r–4r
Notula de dignitate diei dominicae	4r
Ut dies dominicus districte custodiatur, hanc epistolam scripsit Christus	4r–4v
Homilia: "Venerando est nobis . . ." [Sunday homily]	5r–5v
Bulla de anno jubilaei . . . 1473	6r–8v
Cisiojanus germanicus [calendar, incomplete]	10r
[Blank]	10v–12v
De victoria Christi contra Antichristum	13r–64r
Sibylle: Vaticinantes de Christo	64v–65r
[Blank]	65v–71v
Epistola ad Rabbi Isaac de religione judaica et christiana	72r–92v
Pharetra fidei contra versucias haereticorum ad infideles judaeos	93r–101r
Responsio ad quemdam judaeum ex verbis evangelii secundum Matthaeum contra Christum nequitur arguentem	101v–128v
Examinatio haereticorum atque infidelium et rebellium contra fidem	128v–129r
[Blank]	129v–131v
Homilia: "De misera vita seculi"	132r–132v
Duo loci notabiles ex S. Augustino et Alberto Magno	132v
Nicolaus von Dinkelsbühl, Sermones super passione Christi	133r–163r
Disputatio facta per Christianum fidelem contra judaeum, interprete Paschasio de Roma	163r–167r
Reprobatio Talmot iudeorum	167v–172v
De iudicio extremo bonus tractatulus	172v–173r
Iohannes Geuss, Sermo de igne conflagrationis	173r–176v
Notulae et sententiae variae praesertim e s. Scriptura depromptae	176v–178r
Nota salutares effectus, quos operatur paenitentia	178r–179v
Tractatus de christiana religione	180r–191v
De custodia et studio conscientiae	192r–199r
Homilia: "De vanitate saeculi"	199r–201v
Anselmus Cantuariensis, *De miseria humanae conditionis*	202r–203v
Thomas à Kempis, *De imitatione Christi*	204r–215v

(*Continued*)

(*Continued*)

Vienna, ÖNB 3496	
Bernardus Claravallensis, *Locus ex "De perfectione vitae contemplativae"*	215v
[Blank]	216r–216v
Godefridus Viterbiensis, Speculum regum.	217r–267v
Iohannes prior Carthusiae in Mauerbach, Diploma a. 1471 Carthusiam Mauerbacensem concernens.	Addition to end

Vienna, ÖNB 3496 seems to have been designed as an anthology of texts useful for converting Jews to Christianity or for arguing against beliefs considered "judaizing." The codex begins with a legend concerning the consecration of a church, then segues to the importance of Sunday, including a *Notula* on Sunday, the Letter from Heaven, and the anonymous sermon on Sunday (*Venerando/a est nobis*). The "Sunday cluster" is followed by the *Bulla de anno jubilaei* (1473), a text that makes explicit reference to Jewish practices:

Si populus israeliticus, qui sub legis umbra vivebat, frequenter accedens oraturus ad locum, quem elegit dominus, ut ibi poneret nomen suum, vota et donaria plurima offerebat, tanto fortius populus christianus, cui apparuit benignitas et humanitas salvatoris, tenetur basilicas, presertim devota religione conspicuas, in quibus, ad honorem et sub vocabulo precelse dei genetricis fundatas Christus ad abolendam nostrorum criminum corruptelam immortaliter et incorruptibiliter vivens quotidie immolatur, congruis honoribus frequentare ac ibidem offerre munera cum animi puritate, quanto certiora sunt experimenta quam enigmata figurarum.

If the people of Israel, who lived under the shadow of the law, often used to go to pray at the place the Lord had chosen, that his name would dwell there, and used to offer there very many gifts and donations, then all the more should the Christian people, for whom the benevolence and human kindness of the savior appeared, continue to go frequently with all due reverence to the churches, especially those distinguished by their faithful piety and dedicated to the honor and in the name of the exalted mother of God, where Christ, who is alive immortally and imperishably, is daily sacrificed to blot out the corruption of our transgressions; and there they should keep offering up gifts in spiritual purity, since knowledge by experience is so much more certain than obscure symbols.[46]

46. Translation by Angela Zielinski Kinney.

This papal bull, issued by Sixtus IV in 1473, pertains to an indulgence granted for the benefit of the churches of Maria and Severus at Erfurt, which were rebuilt after their destruction by a fire in 1472. The Israelites serve as a negative foil for the right behavior of Christians: if the people of Israel regularly went to the temple to offer sacrifices, Christians—who have benefited from God's kindness through the sacrifice of the Savior, Christ—should all the more eagerly attend churches, especially those devoted to Mary, the mother of God. The devotion of Christians should be all the more zealous, because they know their Savior and reap the benefits of a faith proven to be true, whereas the religion of the Jewish people was performed without this surety. Bolstering this negative portrait of the Jewish religion as confusing and without clear hope are two images of darkness: the beginning of the bull states that the people of Israel lived *sub legis umbra*, which provides a key for the end of the sentence. The *enigmata figurarum* (obscure signs) are inferior to the *experimenta* (proven knowledge) enjoyed by Christians.

After a fragmentary calendar, Vienna, ÖNB 3496 transmits a long apocalyptic treatise on the triumph of Christ over the antichrist. The first part of the work handles the antichrist's name, origin, and reign on earth. The second treats the return of Enoch and Elijah, Christ's triumph, and the last judgment. Such a work complements the apocalyptic themes in the Letter from Heaven and situates Christ's purpose within Old Testament prophecies. This text is followed by Sibylline prophecies concerning Christ. Later in the codex are two sections of overtly anti-Jewish material, augmented by additional apocalyptic and theological texts. Among all the manuscripts with an anti-Jewish focus, the purpose of the Letter from Heaven seems clearest here: it is meant to serve as an apocalyptic tool in the conversion of Jews. The inclusion of another pseudepigraphical letter (*Epistola ad Rabbi Isaac*) for precisely the same purpose is a noteworthy feature of this codex.

The other manuscripts using anti-Jewish texts are more diverse; one could argue that their collections are more representative of subsequent categories (apocryphal works and apocalyptic writings). Yet it would be remiss not to mention their additional anti-Jewish texts. Munich, Bayerische Staatsbibliothek clm 22377 adds a poem by Godfrey of Viterbo about Judas's betrayal of Jesus in exchange for thirty shekels of silver (likened to thirty denarii), a work with distinctly anti-Jewish themes.[47] To the Mattsee manuscript is added part of the *Vindicta salvatoris* ("The Vengeance of the Savior"), a work that condemns the Jewish people for Jesus's crucifixion and envisions them murdered in horrific ways.

47. There is a curious connection between this legend (which stars an Armenian hero) and another story about Abgar, king of Edessa. See George Francis Hill, "The Thirty Pieces of Silver," *Archaeologia* 59 (1905): 235–54.

Quodvultdeus's *Contra Iudaeos, paganos et Arianos* ("Against the Jews, Pagans, and Arians"),[48] a work included in Oxford, Merton College 13, can be viewed not only as anti-Jewish literature but as part of a collection of apocryphal and apocalyptic works. Using a quotation from the Sibylline Prophecies, Quodvultdeus depicts the earth as consumed by flames but reinterprets this to symbolize the resurrection of Christ. This treatise is often transmitted with the *Evangelium Nicodemi* ("Gospel of Nicodemus"),[49] which likewise appears in Oxford, Merton College 13, alongside other apocryphal gospels.

Apocrypha

The Letter from Heaven sometimes appears with other apocryphal texts, such as the *Evangelium Nicodemi*, noncanonical gospels, and versions of the *Vita Adae et Evae*.

Vienna, ÖNB 1878	De signis diei novissimi (=Apocalypse of Thomas, fragment)	161v–162r
Prague, National Library III. D. 13. (Y. 1. 4. n. 79)	**Evangelium Nicodemi**	19r–25r
Vienna, ÖNB 1629	**Poenitentiale Adae et Evae, et de vita et morte eorundem**	98v–101v, 104r
Oxford, Merton College 13	Gospel of Ps.-Matthew, Gospel of Ps.-Thomas	26r–31v
Oxford, Merton College 13	**Evangelium Nicodemi**	186r–191r
Vienna, ÖNB 1355	**De expulsione Ade et Eve de paradiso**	92r–97v
Munich, Bayerische Staatsbibliothek clm 3433	**De Adam et Eva**	211r–213r

This list of works demonstrates that the Letter from Heaven was transmitted with specific apocrypha (the *Evangelium Nicodemi* and *Vita Adae et Evae*). The *Vita Adae et Evae* is a Jewish apocryphon elaborating on the fall of Adam and Eve. The Vita, like the Letter from Heaven, was transmitted in multiple languages (Greek, Latin, Old Church Slavonic, Armenian, Georgian, and Coptic). These versions vary in their vocabulary, length, and emphases; each version is unique in that it omits or alters material in other versions. However,

48. Edition: René Braun, ed., *Contra Iudaeos, Paganos et Arrianos*, CCSL 60 (Turnhout: Brepols, 1976).

49. Montague Rhodes James, *A Descriptive Catalogue of the Manuscripts in the Library of Corpus Christi College* (Cambridge: Cambridge University Press, 1912), 60. The description of Oxford, Corpus Christi ms. 288 bears some similarities to Oxford, Merton College ms. 13, including the selection of apocrypha.

all of the texts transmitted seem to ultimately stem from a Hebrew source that is no longer extant.[50] Connections to the Letter from Heaven may be found in the themes of creation, sin, penance, judgment, and mercy, all of which are recounted in the Vita. Yet perhaps two of the strongest links between the various versions of the Vita and the Letter from Heaven are the exegesis of the number seven in the context of creation and human activity, and the tablets on which Seth, at Eve's behest, records the Vita of his parents. As mentioned earlier, the Letter from Heaven's divine, pseudepigraphical nature is not unlike the story of how the Vita allegedly was written down by Seth on a double set of tablets.

The *Evangelium Nicodemi* belongs to a group of texts known as the Pilate Cycle: early Christian pseudepigrapha attributed to Pontius Pilate or accounts of his life. The Pilate Cycle also includes the *Vindicta salvatoris*, which was discussed in the previous category ("Anti-Jewish Literature"). Although the Pilate Cycle does not appear to be a driving theme in the transmission of the Letter from Heaven, it is worth noting that one manuscript (Prague, Národní knihovna ČR XIII.G.18) includes the rhyming hexameter poem by Peter Pictor, *De vita Pilati* ("On the Life of Pilate"), immediately after the Letter from Heaven.

Yet among the manuscripts containing Recension II of the Letter from Heaven, only Oxford, Merton College 13, with its inclusion of infancy gospels, represents anything approaching a true curiosity shop of apocrypha. The Letter from Heaven seems to have been viewed as a different type of genre—polemic or apocalyptic, for example—and thus grouped with different sorts of texts. Regardless, certain apocrypha retained undeniable influence or usefulness within the context of edification; they could be adapted or paraphrased in homiletic form (e.g., the *Transitus Mariae* and the Gospel of Pseudo-Matthew—both of which appear in a Carolingian homiliary).[51]

One may also note an apocryphon that does *not* appear alongside the Letter from Heaven: the other famous letter of Christ (the correspondence with Abgar)[52] is never transmitted in the same codex as the Letter from Heaven. Some thought may be given to this in future studies of both letters—since codices exist with more than one recension of the Letter from Heaven, which later acquired apotropaic properties, why is the correspondence with Abgar, an earlier type of apotropaic Christ-letter, missing from

50. M. D. Johnson, "Life of Adam and Eve, a New Translation and Introduction," *OTP* 2:251.

51. Henri Barré, *Les Homéliaires carolingiens de l'école d'Auxerre*, Studi e testi 225 (Vatican City: BAV, 1962), 22–24.

52. *Epistula Abgari cum Christi responso*: ECCA 489; CANT 88. The correspondence circulated in many languages, including Greek, Latin, Syriac, and Coptic.

the manuscripts? This is a question that requires a thorough study of that text's transmission as well.

Apocalyptic

A considerable number of instances of the Letter from Heaven occur immediately before or after an apocalyptic text, and an even greater number appear within a manuscript containing several apocalyptic works. As discussed previously, eight manuscripts transmit the Letter from Heaven immediately adjacent to the *Visio Pauli*. An additional four manuscripts include the *Visio Pauli* within the same codex, for a total of twelve manuscripts transmitting the Visio with the Letter from Heaven. The *Visio Pauli*[53] is a fourth-century work that is both apocryphal and apocalyptic; it purports to be a vision of heaven and hell experienced by the apostle Paul. The (now lost) original text was written in Greek and translated into Latin sometime between the fourth and sixth centuries;[54] it subsequently enjoyed a healthy transmission in Latin and a variety of vernacular languages throughout the medieval and early modern periods. The interplay between the Letter from Heaven and the *Visio Pauli*, as well as the related text *De xv signis ante diem iudicii*, has been studied at length by Lenka Jiroušková. The apocalyptic threats of the Letter from Heaven dovetail with the punishments of hell detailed by Paul, and a considerable amount of attention is given to wayward or unfaithful clergy in both the *Visio* and the Letter from Heaven. The *Visio Pauli* also contains an intercession by Paul (or the Virgin Mary, depending on the recension) on behalf of the sinners in hell: Jesus ultimately agrees to temporarily pause the torments of hell on the day of his resurrection, that is, each Sunday.[55]

Apocalyptic Texts Transmitted in Codices with the Letter from Heaven

Mainz, Stadtbibliothek I 227	De septem seris	156vb–159vb
Cambridge, Pembroke College 103	**De xv signis ante diem iudicii**	69r
Innsbruck, Universitäts- und Landesbibliothek Tirol (ULBT), Cod. 409	**De quindecim signis diem iudicii praecedentibus**	107v–108r
Mainz, Stadtbibliothek I 227	**De Antichristo**	148r–149v
Munich, Bayerische Staatsbibliothek, clm 22377	**De extremo tempore**	158r–159r

53. Also known as the *Apocalypsis Pauli*.
54. Silverstein, *Visio sancti Pauli*, 5–6.
55. See this passage of the *Visio Pauli* below, pp. 419–33.

Rostock, Universitätsbibliothek, theol. 37a	**Exemplum de Antichristo**	38vb
Uppsala, Universitätsbibliothek C226	**Quindecim signa [finis mundi]**	3r–4v
Berlin, Staatsbibliothek—Preußischer Kulturbesitz, Ms. theol. lat. qu. 61	**De Antichristo**	58v
Berlin, Staatsbibliothek—Preußischer Kulturbesitz, Ms. theol. lat. qu. 61	**De inicio annorum ante tempora Christi. De iudicio Antichristi**	58r
Berlin, Staatsbibliothek—Preußischer Kulturbesitz, Ms. theol. lat. qu. 61	**De XV signis ante diem iudicii**	59r
Innsbruck, Universitäts- und Landesbibliothek Tirol (ULBT), Cod. 409	Aufzählung von Guten und Bösen in der Heilsgeschichte	111v–112r
Berlin, Staatsbibliothek—Preußischer Kulturbesitz, Ms. theol. lat. qu. 61	**Signa quindecim. Hec sunt quindecim signa quindecim dierum ante diem iudicii**	225v
Berlin, Staatsbibliothek—Preußischer Kulturbesitz, Ms. theol. lat. qu. 61	**Post hec erit dies iudicii.** Dies domini sicut fur ita in docte veniet . . .	225v
Paris, Bibliothèque nationale lat. 3343	Apocalipsis Goliae	160r–165r
Munich, Bayerische Staatsbibliothek, clm 14673	Commentarius in Apocalypsim	57v–116v
Uppsala, Universitätsbibliothek C212	**Epistola Luciferi**	10r–11r
Rostock, Universitätsbiblithek, theol. 37a	**Epistola Luciferi**	39ra–40rb
Oxford, Merton College 13	**Revelationes [Ps.-Methodius]**	53v–55r
Prague, Národní knihovna ČR XIII.G.18	**Visio Philiberti**	119r–119v
Prague, Národní knihovna ČR XIII.G.18	**Revelationes [Ps.-Methodius]**	123v–124v
Bruxelles, Bibliothèque Royale Albert Ier, II 1053	**Visio Pauli**	3r–4r
Cambridge, Pembroke College 103	**Visio Pauli (shortened form)**	124r–124v, 126r–126v
Prague, National Library III. D. 13. (Y. 1. 4. n. 79)	**Visio Pauli**	213va–214rb
Vienna, ÖNB 1629	**Visio Pauli**	102r–103v
Einsiedeln, Stiftsbibliothek 726	**Visio Pauli**	125v

(Continued)

(*Continued*)

London, BL Royal 11 B x	**Visio Pauli**	2r–2v, 184r
Berlin, Staatsbibliothek—Preußischer Kulturbesitz, Ms. theol. lat. qu. 61	**Visio Pauli**	226r–226v
Oxford, Merton College 13	**Visio Pauli**	65v–66v
London, BL Royal 8 F.vi	**Visio Pauli**	23r–23v
Munich, Bayerische Staatsbibliothek, clm 12005	**Visiones Pauli (de inferno et paradiso)**	190r–191r
Cambridge, St John's College F.22 (159)	**Visio Pauli**	24v–25v
Paris, Bibliothèque nationale lat. 3343	**Visio Pauli**	153v–154

Some of the texts containing apocalyptic visions and descriptions of the impending last judgment are composed of multiple genres, mixing serious threats and punishments with satirical or polemical critique. One such example is the twelfth-century *Apocalipsis Goliae*, a poetic, parodic apocalypse (addressed to "seven churches," just as the NT book of Revelation).[56] A fictional bishop, Golias, receives a vision, in which Pythagoras serves as his guide. An angel then delivers an invective against all types of clergy (the pope, bishops, priests, deacons, and others), who are envisioned as various animals. Monks are depicted as excessively depraved; the poet describes their greed and lust at length. A second example is the fourteenth-century *Epistola Luciferi*: a satirical letter from Satan to the clergy, in which Satan applauds the corruption of the church and promises them choice seats in hell.[57] This epistle provided entertainment with a moral varnish, accusing church officials of being comrades of the devil and pillorying their excesses. Yet all of this takes place within an eschatological reality wherein the torment of hell is a real threat. That a letter from Satan is transmitted alongside the Letter from Heaven is fitting not only because of its apocalyptic flair but also because clerical sins and corruption feature prominently in both. This epistle and its relationship to clerical matters in the transmission of the Letter from Heaven will be discussed in the next section.

Clerical Life

The category "Clerical Life" encompasses not only works applicable solely to priests and monks but also expositions of church order written for the use of clergy. Many works could well be added here, as these *Sammelbände* contain

56. See Frederic James Edward Raby, "The *Apocalypse of Golias* and Other Poems," in *A History of Secular Latin Poetry in the Middle Ages* (Oxford: Clarendon, 1934), 2:214–27.

57. On this work, see Chris Schabel, "*Lucifer princeps tenebrarum* . . . The *Epistola Luciferi* and Other Correspondence of the Cistercian Pierre Ceffons (fl. 1348–1353)," *Vivarium* 56 (2018): 126–75.

many such expositions, but the following list includes (at the very least) any works appearing more than once among the manuscripts containing the Letter from Heaven; the list thus attempts to provide a representative account of works pertaining to clerical life and education. The presence of the Letter from Heaven among texts written specifically for the education and practical use of clergy is perhaps unsurprising, but it nonetheless lends a sense of legitimacy to the Letter. Although there is no concrete evidence that the Letter from Heaven was read aloud regularly in churches, its inclusion alongside monastic rules, liturgical commentaries, materials for sermon preparation, and the like suggests it may have been a piece of evidence useful for answering the question, "Why do we worship on Sunday?" or for warning clergy who did not take the Sunday service seriously. With respect to the latter, the Letter from Heaven includes several admonitions specifically for unbelieving and disobedient monks and priests.

Cambridge, Pembroke College 103	De clericis	62r
Munich, Bayerische Staatsbibliothek, clm 14673	Sermo de communi vita clericorum	127v–132v
Munich, Bayerische Staatsbibliothek, clm 14673	De vita et moribus clericorum suorum	132v–139v
Göttweig, Benediktinerstift Cod. 199	**Stella clericorum**	7r–21r
Göttweig, Benediktinerstift Cod. 199	**Tractatus super missam sive Speculum ecclesiae**	21r–38r
Uppsala, Universitätsbibliothek C212	**De dignitate sacerdotum**	50r–56r
Berlin, Staatsbibliothek—Preußischer Kulturbesitz, Ms. theol. lat. qu. 61	Monastic rule	181r–184r
London, BL Royal 11 B x	Pupilla oculi	3ra–173va
Oxford, Merton College 13	De institutione novitiorum	123r–131r
Bernkastel-Kues, Bibliothek des St. Nikolaus-Hospitals 128	Speculum sacerdotum	156r–163r
Hamburg, Bibliothek der Hansestadt, S. Petri-Kirche 30b	**Stella clericorum**	30r–33r
Hamburg, Bibliothek der Hansestadt, S. Petri-Kirche 30b	Manipulus curatorum	58r–187r
Innsbruck, Stiftsbibliothek Wilton (s.n.)	**De novo sacerdote**	271ra
Munich, Bayerische Staatsbibliothek, clm 12005	Quaestiones super officium missae	195r–201v
Munich, Bayerische Staatsbibliothek, clm 22,377	Liber Pastoralis	1r–42v

(Continued)

(*Continued*)

Rostock, Universitätsbibliothek, theol. 37a	**Stella clericorum**	33ra–38vb
Rostock, Universitätsbiblitohek, theol. 37a	Quattuor incommoda in servitio dei	256vb–257va
Rostock, Universitätsbibliothek, theol. 37a	**De dignitate sacerdotum**	257vb–258ra
Uppsala, Universitätsbibliothek C133	**Speculum ecclesiae**	146r–150v
Uppsala, Universitätsbibliothek C226	**Speculum ecclesiae**	38r–48v
Oxford, Merton College 13	**Elucidarium**	31v–41r
Jena, Thüringer Universitäts- und Landesbibliothek, Ms. Klosterbibl. 5	**Elucidarium**	151ra–171vb
Berlin, Staatsbibliothek—Preußischer Kulturbesitz, Ms. theol. lat. qu. 61	**Elucidarium**	61r–117v
Uppsala, Universitätsbibliothek C212	Sermo Synodalis de emendatione morum et cleri	42r–49v
Rostock, Universitätsbibliothek, theol. 37a	**Sermones de novo sacerdote**, de sanctis, de diversis cum notis	219va–285rb
Rostock, Universitätsbibliothek, theol. 37a	Versus de recto servitio Christi	259ra
Uppsala, Universitätsbibliothek C212	**Epistola Luciferi**	10r–11r
Rostock, Universitätsbibliothek, theol. 37a	**Epistola Luciferi**	39ra–40rb

Two manuscripts in this category include the Letter from Heaven either immediately before Hugo de Sancto Caro's *Speculum ecclesiae* (Göttweig, Benediktinerstift Cod. 199) or after it (Uppsala, Universitätsbibliothek C133). This treatise on the order of the Mass was a popular work in the central and late Middle Ages; more than 240 copies survive in manuscripts and printed editions. Moreover, it is a thoroughly orthodox work, written specifically for a clerical audience. The work starts by discussing priestly vestments and their significance, then proceeds to discuss each portion of the church service and its meaning. The arguments are supported by biblical verses explaining the liturgy. That the Letter from Heaven should be appended either before or after this work suggests that it may have been used as a piece of evidence for the veneration of Sunday, despite its apocryphal status. Indeed, the Letter from Heaven supports its own argument by linking biblical passages in the same way many liturgical commentaries did: the narrator mentions the actions God performed on Sunday and the commandments to honor the Lord's Day.

The *Stella clericorum*,[58] an anonymous manual for pastoral care and theology, appears in three manuscripts. This thirteenth-century work, written after the Gregorian reforms, underscores the moral responsibilities borne by the clergy and the solemn dignity of the priesthood. This work, like the *Speculum ecclesiae*, aims to explain the moral and theological grounding of clerical service and is not merely a practical guidebook. Rostock, Universitätsbibliothek, theol. 37a contains both the *Stella clericorum* and a text related to it, the pseudo-Augustinian *De dignitate sacerdotum*. This short tractate on the merit of priests and their role in the eucharistic mystery starts with the statement that priests must be worthy because Christ is born in their hands via the Eucharist, just as he was born in the virgin's womb. This popular text is also found in Uppsala, Universitätsbibliothek C133.

In three different manuscripts, the Letter from Heaven is transmitted with the *Elucidarium* of Honorius of Autun.[59] While the *Speculum ecclesiae* and *Stella clericorum* could be considered works aimed at more educated clergy, the *Elucidarium* is an encyclopedic summary of medieval theology and folk beliefs composed for less educated clergy. The three books of the *Elucidarium* are written in the form of a dialogue between a teacher and his disciple. The first discusses God, creation, and Christ's life on earth; the second discusses Christ's divinity and the foundation of the church; the third focuses on Christian eschatology, with vivid descriptions of the antichrist, return of Christ, judgment day, purgatory, hell, and heaven. The Letter from Heaven, itself a work pertaining to "folk belief," connects nicely to this final eschatological section.

One final clerical text of interest is the *Epistola Luciferi*, which was discussed briefly in the section on Apocalyptic Texts.[60] That an anticlerical medieval letter from Lucifer should be transmitted in two manuscripts along with the Letter from Heaven is an interesting occurrence, as it provides the "letter from heaven" with a contrasting "letter from hell." The *Epistola Luciferi*, attributed to Peter Ceffons of Clairvaux, is a mid-fourteenth-century satirical attack on the secular clergy. Although the Letter from Heaven and the *Epistola Luciferi* are not immediately conjacent in the manuscripts, both letters are transmitted in what may be considered a block of texts focusing on apocalyptic matters, threats, punishments, and the end of the world. Uppsala, Universitätsbibliothek C212 begins with the Letter from Heaven; two folios later, one

58. Edition: Eric Reitner, ed., *Stella clericorum*, Toronto Medieval Latin Texts 23 (Turnhout: Brepols, 1997).

59. Edition with French translation: Yves Lefèvre, ed. and trans., *L'Elucidarium et les Lucidaires*, Bibliothèque des écoles Françaises d'Athènes et de Rome 180 (Paris: E. de Boccard, 1954).

60. See reference in previous section.

finds a text on original sin and the end of the world, and then the *Epistola Luciferi*. In Rostock, theol. 37a, apocalyptic material is transmitted alongside some practical notes regarding fasting, Friday, and Saturday. The Letter from Heaven is sandwiched between a text on the Ten Commandments and plagues of Egypt (*De decem praeceptis et plagis Aegyptiacis*)[61] and remarks on Friday and Saturday (*De sexta feria . . . De sabbato*).

Uppsala, Universitätsbibliothek C212 (s. xiv)

Epistula Jesu de die dominica	1v–3r
Compendium theologiae veritatis (excerpts from Lib. II, cap. 42–56: De potencia racionali)	3v–4v
Auctoritates	5v
De originali peccato et de fine mundi	5v–9v
Epistola Luciferi	10r–11r

Rostock, Universitätsbibliothek, theol. 37a (s. xv)

Exemplum de Antichristo	38vb
Epistola Luciferi	39ra–40rb
[Nota ad ieiunium]	40rb
De arte loquendi et tacendi	40va–46vb
De miraculis faciendis [discerning who performed a miracle—angels or demons]	46vb
De decem praeceptis et plagis Aegyptiacis	47ra–47va
Epistula Jesu de die dominica	**47va–48rb**
De sexta feria ... De sabbato	48rb–vb

Of all the manuscripts focusing on clerical duties, Rostock, theol. 37a may be worth a more comprehensive examination, as the codex seems to have been put together specifically as a handbook for priests. Some of the other codices containing the Letter from Heaven have a similar assortment of material intended for practical use and sermon preparation.

Rostock, Universitätsbibliothek, theol. 37a

De matrimonio	1va–1vb
[Commentary on the twenty-first chapter of the Fourth Lateran Council: “On yearly confession to one’s priest, yearly communion, the confessional seal”]	2ra–32vb
Stella clericorum	33ra–38vb

(*Continued*)

61. See Heil on *De plaga*, pp. 104–108.

(*Continued*)

Exemplum de Antichristo	38vb
Epistola Luciferi	39ra–40rb
[Nota ad ieiunium]	40rb
De arte loquendi et tacendi	40va–46vb
De miraculis faciendis [discerning who performed a miracle—angels or demons]	46vb
De decem praeceptis et plagis Aegyptiacis	47ra–47va
Epistula Jesu de die dominica	**47va–48rb**
De sexta feria . . . De sabbato	48rb–vb
[Medical and dietetic verse proverb(s?): Nota homines sani de mane habent urinam albam, ante prandium rubeam, post prandium candidam, ante cenam calidam]	48vb
[Collectio exemplorum fabularumque]	49ra–67vb
Exemplum de miraculo de corpore Christi	68ra–69ra
[Sermones de tempore]	71ra–219rb
[Sermones de novo sacerdote, de sanctis, de diversis cum notis et quaestionibus variis]	219va–285rb

Rostock, theol. 37a begins with a short tract about conditions that can invalidate or prevent a marriage. This is followed by a long commentary on the section of the Lateran Council pertaining to confession, the privacy of confession, and the necessity of confession for participation in communion. The next text is the *Stella clericorum*, a manual for pastoral care. The apocalyptic *Exemplum Antichristi* and the satirical *Epistola Luciferi* (addressed to clergy) follow. Then a mixture of practical and theoretical texts: notes on fasting, a treatise on when to speak and when to stay silent, a tract on how to determine whether a miracle is angelic or demonic in nature, an exposition on the commandments and plagues of Egypt, the Letter from Heaven, and short texts on Friday and Saturday. A verse proverb about healthy urine is then followed by a long collection of exempla and fables, presumably material that could be easily worked into sermons. The codex is rounded off by a large number of sermons for various occasions. That the Letter from Heaven is considered a useful piece of material within this collection is clear: it follows a treatise on the commandments and fits nicely alongside material complementing its content, namely, the notes on fasting, Friday, and Saturday. Its apocalyptic and eschatological significance dovetails with the notes on the antichrist and the concern about miracles.

Confession, Penance, Sin

A considerable number of manuscripts transmit the Letter from Heaven with a collection of materials relating to sin, confession, and penance. In three manuscripts, texts on penance precede or coincide with the Letter from Heaven. The earliest manuscript in Recension II (Paris, BN lat. 8508) transmits the Letter from Heaven written in the margin of the *Summa poenitentiae*. The Letter from Heaven precedes a penitential in another early manuscript, London, BL Add. 30853, and a text on confession (*De confessione*) in a later codex, Prague, Archiv Pražského Hradu, N 42. The connection between the Letter from Heaven and notions of sin and penance can be explained in a number of ways. The Letter from Heaven contains a great deal of explicit and implicit instructions and prohibitions, both for clergy and laypersons. One should honor Sunday in a particular way (namely, attending church), but one could violate it in a variety of different ways. Such violations must be confessed and penance performed in order to atone for the violations. The eschatological framework of the Letter from Heaven establishes that repeated violation of Sunday will bring a variety of apocalyptic punishments reminiscent of both Old Testament plagues (such as water turning to blood) and those that portend the judgment day to come. Within this framework, the importance of confession and penance takes on a greater role. As the copying of penitential handbooks (lists of sins with recommended penance for each) dwindled in the eleventh century, other tractates and manuals for penance took over the role of the pentential in the central and late medieval period, including texts instructing priests in the proper formulae to use for confession and texts on indulgences.

More texts could be added to this list of materials, as there are numerous anonymous notes and tractates on penance and confession transmitted in the codices of the Letter from Heaven. However, this list provides the primary named texts that circulated with the Letter from Heaven. The relationships between each of these texts and the aims of the Letter from Heaven could be a topic for future study.

Paris, BN lat. 8508	Summa poenitentiae, sex libris	57r–164v
London, BL Add. 30853	Penitential and Gloses Silenses	309r–324v
Innsbruck, Universitäts- und Landesbibliothek Tirol (ULBT), Cod. 409	Tractatus de confessione	112r–114v
Innsbruck, Universitäts- und Landesbibliothek Tirol (ULBT), Cod. 409	Sermones de diversis. Sermo 104: De quatuor impedimentis confessionis.	130v–131v
Innsbruck, Universitäts- und Landesbibliothek Tirol (ULBT), Cod. 409	Confessio	176r–176v

(Continued)

(*Continued*)

Innsbruck, Universitäts- und Landesbibliothek Tirol (ULBT), Cod. 409	De confessione (Verse)	177v
Innsbruck, Universitäts- und Landesbibliothek Tirol (ULBT), Cod. 409	De poenitentia	228r
Göttweig, Benediktinerstift Cod. 199	De confessione (Summa confessionis, De paenitentia)	57v–64r
Oxford, Merton College 13	De paenitentibus (Serm. 393)	121v–122r
Prague, Archiv Pražského Hradu, N 42	Formula confessionis	120r–145r
Prague, Archiv Pražského Hradu, N 42	De confessione	50v–68r
Prague, National Library III. D. 13. (Y. 1. 4. n. 79)	Summa poenitentialis	37r–?
Vienna, ÖNB 1355	Libellus de peccatorum agnitione, seu inquisitione, seu facienda confessione	104r–119v
Vienna, ÖNB 1355	Summa de poenitentia	120v–137v
Berlin, Staatsbibliothek zu Berlin—Preußischer Kulturbesitz, Magdeburg 196	Manuale confessorum	299r–303v, 314v–340v
Berlin, Staatsbibliothek zu Berlin—Preußischer Kulturbesitz, Magdeburg 21	Lumen confessorum	261va–293ra
Berlin, Staatsbibliothek zu Berlin—Preußischer Kulturbesitz, Magdeburg 21	Modus confitendi	293rb–295va
Jena, Thüringer Universitäts- und Landesbibliothek, Ms. Klosterbibl. 5	Quaestio de sollemniter paenitentibus	138ra–138vb
London, BL Royal 8 F.vi	Miracle story in English how a curate saw the devil dancing on a woman's neck who made an imperfect confession	28v–29r
Mattsee, Stiftsbibliothek 49	De septem peccatis capitalibus	203va–213ra
Mattsee, Stiftsbibliothek 49	Sermo app. 254 [Ps.-Aug. excerpt]	301rb–301vb
Mattsee, Stiftsbibliothek 49	Sermo app. 393 [Ps.-Aug. excerpt]	302ra–303ra
Munich, Bayerische Staatsbibliothek clm 3766	Formula confitendi	104ra–147vb

(*Continued*)

(Continued)

Munich, Bayerische Staatsbibliothek, clm 12005	De indulgentiis	193r
Munich, Universitätsbibliothek 2° 120	Tractatulus de confessione	311ra–324vb
Rostock, Universitätsbibliothek, theol. 37a	Augustinus de sera penitencia	285rb
Uppsala, Universitätsbibliothek C133	De confessione	99v
Uppsala, Universitätsbibliothek C226	Sermones. Formula confessionis	151r–158v
Uppsala, Universitätsbibliothek C47	Sermo de uno confessore	234r
Wilhering, Stiftsbibliothek IX 162	Tractatus de poenitentia et confessione	1r–9v
Hamburg, Bibliothek der Hansestadt, S. Petri-Kirche 30b	Ablassgebete	29r–29v
Hamburg, Bibliothek der Hansestadt, S. Petri-Kirche 30b	Ablassgebete	42r–42v

Consecration of Churches

The number of manuscripts transmitting sermons or readings for the dedication of churches or altars (or the anniversaries of such dedications) was one of the most surprising and interesting results of this study. As discussed elsewhere in this volume, the Letter from Heaven exists in a single inscription in Liguria commemorating the dedication of a church.[62] In the manuscript history of the Letter from Heaven, one may see evidence that the Letter from Heaven played some kind of role in ceremonies for the dedication of churches. Perhaps it was read aloud at the dedication of a new church and on the anniversary of the dedication. This theory is speculative, but it helps explain why the Letter from Heaven is found in codices with numerous texts for the consecration of churches. In the absence of concrete evidence that the Letter from Heaven was read out loud every Sunday, one plausible theory is that it was read once a year, to remind the congregation and clergy alike of the sanctity of Sunday and the place of the church service within the weekly rhythm.

62. See Heil, pp. 91–95, and Michel-Yves Perrin, pp. 239–43.

Texts concerning the Consecration of Churches		
Berlin, Staatsbibliothek—Preußischer Kulturbesitz, Ms. theol. lat. qu. 61	Item duo sermones de dedicacione	245r–254r
Wien, ÖNB 3496	Bulla de anno jubilaei. . . 1473	6r–8v
Innsbruck, Stiftsbibliothek Wilton (s.n.)	De dedicatione	273ra
Innsbruck, Stiftsbibliothek Wilton (s.n.)	In dedicatione ecclesiae	292va
Uppsala, Universitätsbibliothek C226	Lectiones de dedicatione ecclesiae	53r–53v
Innsbruck, ULBT Cod. 409	Sermo in dedicatione ecclesiae.	88r–90r
Uppsala, Universitätsbibliothek C212	Sermones de dedicatione ecclesiae	60r–83v
Mainz, Stadtbibliothek I 227	Sermones de dedicatione	1ra–25va
Mainz, Stadtbibliothek I 227	Sermones de dedicatione	50r–73v
Mainz, Stadtbibliothek I 227	Sermones de dedicatione	99r–123v
Mainz, Stadtbibliothek I 227	Sermones tres de dedicatione	124r–127r
Mainz, Stadtbibliothek I 227	Sermo de dedicatione	127v–128r
Mainz, Stadtbibliothek I 227	Sermo de dedicatione	150r–150v
Kremsmünster, Stiftsbibliothek 283	Sermones quinque: de dedicatione ecclesiae; super Misit servum suum hora cene dicere invitatis ut veniant; super Reddet Deus mercedem laborum sanctorum suorum; de passione Domini; super Gloriosa dicta sunt de te civitas Dei.	1r–54r
Innsbruck, ULBT, Cod. 409	Sermo in dedicatione ecclesiae	231r–231v
Innsbruck, ULBT, Cod. 409	Sermo in dedicatione ecclesiae	231v–233v
Innsbruck, Stiftsbibliothek Wilton (s.n.)	Sequitur sermo de dedicacione	272rb–272vb
Munich, Bayerische Staatsbibliothek, clm 12005	Sermones de dedicatione et alii	173r–178v
Munich, Bayerische Staatsbibliothek, clm 12005	Sermones de dedicatione et alii	191r–192v

Several of these codices transmit lengthy materials that could be used to compose sermons for church dedications or anniversaries: Mainz, Stadtbibliothek I 227 is an extreme example, where practically the entire codex comprises material for dedications.

Mary

A final category of interest is the connection between the Letter from Heaven and a large amount of Marian material. The role of the Virgin Mary in the Letter from Heaven cannot be understated: she is overtly stated to be the advocate for humankind, and Christ states that he stayed his anger because of his mother's tears. In this vein, various sermons commemorating Mary and establishing her sanctity (as well as her family's sanctity) are transmitted alongside the Letter from Heaven.[63] Some of these texts, such as the "Geistliches ABC auf Maria," were actually sung hymns.

Signatur	Text	Folios
Innsbruck, Universitäts- und Landesbibliothek Tirol (ULBT), Cod. 409	Sermo in purificatione BMV	97v–98r
Innsbruck, Universitäts- und Landesbibliothek Tirol (ULBT), Cod. 409	Geistliches ABC auf Maria	99v
Innsbruck, Universitäts- und Landesbibliothek Tirol (ULBT), Cod. 409	Trinubium sanctae Annae	174r–174v
Budapest, University Library, lat. 39	Sermones "Opus Mariae virginis"	1r–83r
Berlin, Staatsbibliothek—Preußischer Kulturbesitz, Ms. theol. lat. qu. 61	Explanation of the Ave Maria	141r–157r
Berlin, Staatsbibliothek—Preußischer Kulturbesitz, Ms. theol. lat. qu. 61	Nomen virginis Maria	228r
Berlin, Staatsbibliothek—Preußischer Kulturbesitz, Ms. theol. lat. qu. 61	Ave gratie plena	230r–240r
Einsiedeln, Stiftsbibliothek 726	Miraculorum beatae virginis	125r
Einsiedeln, Stiftsbibliothek 726	De annunciatione	125r
Einsiedeln, Stiftsbibliothek 726	Nota: beata virgo	125r
Oxford, Merton College 13	Draft sermon: Corona est Maria	13r–13v
Oxford, Merton College 13	De Beatae Mariae Virginitate	149r–154r
Oxford, Merton College 13	Dialogus Beatae Mariae et Anselmi de Passione Domini	191r–194v
Hamburg, Bibliothek der Hansestadt, S. Petri-Kirche 30b	Sermones de BMV. Concept. BMV	1r–13r
Hamburg, Bibliothek der Hansestadt, S. Petri-Kirche 30b	Sermo de conceptione BMV	15r–26v

63. See also the intercession of Mary in the Letter from Heaven.

Signatur	Text	Folios
Hamburg, Bibliothek der Hansestadt, S. Petri-Kirche 30b	Item de concepcione	26v–28v
Hamburg, Bibliothek der Hansestadt, S. Petri-Kirche 30b	Sermo de visitatione BMV	44r–48v
Jena, Thüringer Universitäts- und Landesbibliothek, Ms. Klosterbibl. 5	De nomine et humilitate BMV	243va–245vb
Jena, Thüringer Universitäts- und Landesbibliothek, Ms. Klosterbibl. 5	Sermo de assumptione BMV	246vb–247rb
Munich, Bayerische Staatsbibliothek clm 3766	Sermo: De nativitate Marie	178rb–178vb
Berlin, Staatsbibliothek zu Berlin—Preußischer Kulturbesitz, Magdeburg 21	Tractatus super Magnificat	203ra–224rb
Innsbruck, Stiftsbibliothek Wilton (s.n.)	Mary material	276ra–291rb
Mainz, Stadtbibliothek I 227	De septem virtutibus turturis sive beatae virginis	127r–127v
Uppsala, Universitätsbibliothek C133	Expositio de Ave Maria	2r–8r
Uppsala, Universitätsbibliothek C133	[Aufzeichnungen über Maria und Jesus]	10v–11r
London, BL Royal 8 F.vi	Miracle (clerk dissuaded from marriage by Mary)	22v
London, BL Royal 8 F.vi	Five miracles of the Virgin	24v–25r
Mattsee, Stiftsbibliothek 49	Carmen de tribus Mariabus	316vb–317ra
Uppsala, Universitätsbibliothek C226	Gebet an Maria	2r–v

3.3.5. Preliminary Conclusions

Research of this sort is almost never completed to satisfaction, as new manuscripts and connections surface the more one examines the material. However, the manuscripts of Latin Recensions I and II have elicited bountiful fruit for the study of the Latin Letter from Heaven. In addition to texts that were expected to be found—those pertaining to clerical and eschatological concerns—texts pertaining to the dedication of churches, anti-Jewish diatribes, and Marian material were also noted. The texts pertaining to dedication are especially important in light of the inscription in the church at Liguria, as it suggests that the Latin Letter from Heaven may have played a role—either overtly or in the background—at church dedication ceremonies or anniversaries thereof.

3.4. Greek Manuscripts

Canan Arıkan-Caba

This list compiles the manuscripts that transmit Greek versions of the Letter from Heaven, based on the study by Maximilian Bittner, supplemented by entries in the Pinakes database by the Bollandists. The versions presented here in this volume are underlined.

Greek Recension Alpha (Rome Recension)

BHG 812m; Bittner Alpha 1:

Codex Parisinus gr. 947, s. xvi, fols. 21v-26[1]
Maximilian Bittner, *Der vom Himmel gefallene Brief Christi*, 16–21

BHG 812k; Bittner Alpha 2:

Codex Parisinus gr. 929, s. xv, pp. 548-61
Codex Athos (Koutloumousiou) 176 (Lambros 3249), s. xv, fol. 25r–v
Codex Venet. Marc. vii 38, s. xvi, fols. 339–42
Bittner, *Der vom Himmel gefallene Brief Christi*, 21–25

BHG 812i; Bittner Alpha:

Codex Vatic. Barber. gr. 284 (olim iii, 3), an. 1497, fols. 55–65[2]
Codex Meteora (Hagiou Stephanou) 119, 1771 CE, fols. 35ff.
Cod. Jerusalem, Patriarchike bibliotheke (Hagiou Saba) 57, s. xv, fols. 173–194r

1. This manuscript Codex. Paris. gr. 947 includes also Ps.-Eusebius of Alexandria, Sermo 16 *De dominica die* (see above pp. 27, 444–47), the Apocalypse of Pseudo-Methodius (CAVT 259), and the First Apocryphal Apocalypse of John (CANT 331). It is therefore a collection of texts dealing with death, apocalypse, and threatening hell for disbelievers. Bittner mixed up his two Greek manuscripts as Alpha 1 = Paris 925 (instead of 929!) and Alpha 2 = Paris 947 at p. 8. In addition, in his transcriptions, at pp. 16-21 is Alpha 1 (but this is Paris 947), and pp. 21-25 is Alpha 2 (but this is Paris 929); this caused some confusion in secondary literature. This Greek version of Alpha 1 is translated by Miceli, "Epistle of Christ," 460–63; by Backus, *Lettre du Jésus-Christ*, 1109–16; by Santos Otero, *La Carta del Domingo*, 362–66; and by Stern, *La Salette*, 375–92.

2. Transcribed in Vassiliev, *Anecdota graeco-byzantina*, 23–28, who (p. XIII) already points to Codex Parisinus gr. 929; Codex Parisinus gr. 947; and Codex Venet. Marc. vii 38 for this version.

Codex Parisinus gr. 1313, s. xv, fols. 1–5
Bittner, *Der vom Himmel gefallene Brief Christi*, 11–16

BHG 812p (not in Bittner); Alpha?:

Codex Panorm. (Palermo, Biblioteca centrale) II D 26, s. xv-xvi, fols. 36v–39

Greek Recension Beta (Jerusalem Recension)

BHG 812n; Bittner Beta:

Codex Roman. Casanatense 481 (olim G. vi. 7), s. xvi, fols. 27–37[3]
Codex Athos (Philotheou) 98 (Lambros 1862), s. xv, fol. ?
Codex Rom, Biblioteca Nazionale Centrale Vittore Emanuele II (S.A. Valle) 102, s. xvii, fols. 168–170
Codex Taurinensi 148, B. II. 1, s. xv; fols. 103-106[4] (not found)
Bittner, *Der vom Himmel gefallene Brief Christi* 25–33[5] (right column)

BHG 812n; Bittner Beta 1:

Codex Carpentras (BM) 103 (Omont 36), s. xvi, fols. 1–20
Codex Tübingen Mb 33, saec. xvi, fols. 131–137 (former BHG 812q, but belongs to Beta Recension)
Bittner, *Der vom Himmel gefallene Brief*, 25–33 (left column)

BHG 812n; Bittner Beta 2:

Codex. Oxford, Bodleiana (olim Huntington 583) Auct. E. 5.17[6]
Bittner, *Der vom Himmel gefallene Brief Christi*, 8–9 and 26 (initium)

BHG 812n; Bittner Beta 3:

Cod. Collegii graeci (Romae) 18, s. xvi
Bittner, *Der vom Himmel gefallene Brief Christi*, 8–9 and 26 (initium)

---

3. Transcribed in Vassiliev, *Anecdota graeco-byzantina* (Mosquae, 1893), 1:28–32.
4. Already mentioned by Vassiliev, *Anecdota graeco-byzantina*, XIII, but not further used by Bittner, probably lost or indiscernible.
5. According to Fabricius, *Codex apocryphus Noui Testamenti* XIII.
6. Its beginning was transcribed in Fabricius, *Codex apocryphus Noui Testamenti* 511f.

BHG 812r; Bittner Beta 4:

Codex Ambrosianus B 146 sup., anni 1629 CE., fols. 5–6
Bittner, *Der vom Himmel gefallene Brief Christi*, 8–9 and 26 (initium)

BHG 812j (not in Bittner); Beta 5:

Codex London. Highgate School II 29 (cod. 488), saec. xv, fols. 120v–124v
Codex Sinaiticus gr. 1670, saec. xvi, fols. 130v–136 (online)
Codex Atheniensis gr. (EBE) 838, saec. xvi, fols. 198–201v
Codex Vaticanus gr. 2235, s. xvi, fols. 222–229 (online)

BHG 812s (not in Bittner); Beta 6?

Codex Lond. (British Library) Add. 10073, saec. xv, fols. 307–318

Greek Recension Gamma (Jerusalem Recension)

no BHG number; Bittner Gamma:

Cod. Pyrghi (Chios)—manuscript from Monastery of Pyrghi, current location unknown
Bittner, *Der vom Himmel gefallene Brief Christi*, 9 and 33–36[7]

7. This was apparently contained in a codex containing texts in modern Greek that included also a version of the Apocalypse of Maria; see Hubert Pernot, "Descente de la Vierge aux Enfers d'après les manuscrits grecs de Paris," *Revue des Études Grecques* 13.53–54 (1900): 233–57. Remarkably, according to Pernot's note the Apocalypse of Maria of the Pyrghi manuscript included a description of sinners such as those not loyal to their wives (see in this volume Alpha 1, 7.12), those who encroach their neighbors' ground by plowing their furrows (Alpha 1, 7.7), those who have done injustice to widows or orphans (Alpha 1, 2.7), and those who fornicate with priests' wives or with nuns ("La nomenclature du manuscrit de Pyrghi comprend aussi ceux qui ont eu des relations avec la femme d'autrui, qui ont empiété sur le champ du voisin en traçant leur sillon, qui ont fait injustice à des veuves ou à des orphelins, les impies, ceux qui ont péché avec des femmes de prêtres ou avec des religieuses"; see Pernot, "Descente de la Vierge," 236n1), which reminds of the similar moral concern that we encounter in the Letter from Heaven. Bittner does not inform on the current location of the manuscript. It is noteworthy to mention that the eighteenth-century manuscript Codex Meteora 119 contains also the Letter from Heaven and the Apocalypse of Maria. This text, however, is grouped along with other Alpha texts under 812i, whereas the one from Pyrgi, according to Bittner, belonged to the modern Greek version of the Jerusalem recension, namely, Gamma.

no BHG; Bittner Gamma 1:

from a modern publication (Athens, 1894), bought in Jerusalem by Bittner
Bittner, *Der vom Himmel gefallene Brief Christi*, 9 and 36–40[8]

In this volume we present with translation the Greek Recension Alpha 1 as the oldest, but also the Greek Recension Alpha 2, since it, as a further development of Greek Recension Alpha 1, is probably related to the Latin Recension III and possibly served in a version available at that time as its Greek template. Furthermore, a new version of the Greek Recension Beta 1 and 2 is offered, since with the manuscript from Tübingen another important witness is available, which was unknown to Bittner and is able to fill in gaps. In addition, a later version based on a codex from London (British Library, Add. 10073, saec. XV, fols. 307-318; BHG 812s) is presented with extensions that point to the reception, among other things, also in the liturgy.

8. Already printed in a similar version by Vassiliev, *Anecdota graeco-byzantina* 1:xiii–xx, introduced with (p. XIII): *Atque hoc exemplum paucis mutatis prelo subiectum Hierosolymis nunc ad loca veneranda migrantibus datur cum titulo in involucro impresso.* This recension thus covers the modern printings of the Letter from Heaven and points to the continuous presence of the letter, especially in Jerusalem, where it had been sighted according to this version.

3.5. History

Uta Heil

The Letter of Christ or the Letter from Heaven, which demands the observance and sanctification of Sunday, was never lost. From the end of the sixth century until modern times, it was repeatedly found, copied, and disseminated in several waves. Interestingly, the letter was accompanied from the beginning by fierce criticism, so that the path of its dissemination can be roughly traced. Even though criticism and rejection of the Letter was voiced from the beginning, the tradition of the Letter from Heaven shows that it was widely distributed and even handed down together with works on clerical life, church dedications, and collections of sermons or works on repentance, sin, and forgiveness[1] and was understood here as a valuable text.

The crucial question is, of course, which versions of the Letter from Heaven or which manuscripts can be linked to which of these waves? However, since the manuscript tradition begins much later (in the tenth century for the Latin recensions, in the fifteenth century for the Greek), any historical references to the earlier period can only be approximated, and these earlier versions can only be inferred indirectly.

Another central question is that of the transfer of the texts between East and West (from West to East? from East to West? or both?). Certainly, in the Carolingian period the text moved between East and West, likewise at the time of the Crusades. The congruences between Latin Recension I and Greek Recension Alpha 1 as well as between Latin Recension III and Greek Recension Alpha 2 prove the exchange, but without clearly determining the historical location and direction.

Several questions remain unclear. Was the first Letter from Heaven a purely Latin invention? Was this the letter to which Licinianus referred? Consequently, did the letter originate in the Latin West and reach the East only later? With respect to the surviving Latin versions, Latin Recensions I–III, further concrete questions arise. Is the short version of the Latin Heavenly Letter—that is, the so-called Latin Recension II, which is a recension concerned with domestic activities and regulations for the family and household—a later, condensed, and more moderate redaction of an older, longer letter? Namely, is it a redaction of Latin Recension I, which is clearly a more apocalyptic Letter from Heaven referring to the downfall of the whole world? Or,

1. See the manuscript studies by Angela Zielinski Kinney, pp. 45–79.

conversely, is Latin Recension II an earlier, shorter version that was later expanded, universalized, and dramatized into Latin Recension I? This second hypothesis is the one proposed here. Congruencies between Latin Recensions I and II, especially in the latter part of Latin Recension I, indicate a connection, which, however, could theoretically be explained in both directions.

In the Greek sphere, with its three recensions (Alpha, Beta, and Gamma), the Alpha group provides the oldest version, since this is the version on which the Armenian and Syriac translations were based. The Beta and the Gamma versions based on it came later. However, the manuscript tradition for Recension Alpha begins quite late, making any assessments subject to reservation. Was a former Greek letter the model for Greek Recension Alpha and the starting point of the various Letters from Heaven? Or was it a previous version of Latin Recension I or II?

The following is an attempt to approach the history and context of the Letter from Heaven taking into account both the Greek and Latin versions. Previous research on this text has focused too narrowly on only one version of the language, without considering the overall context and interaction.

The respective creative adaptations of the Letters from Heaven each have their own profile, so to speak. Even if all the versions contain the command that the letter is to be read publicly, copied, and distributed, this did not prevent the recipients from rearranging, expanding, and embellishing the material (see chapter 4, "Considerations").

The first reference to the Letter from Heaven comes from Spain. Already at the end of the sixth century, Licinianus, the bishop of Cartagena, expressed outrage about a so-called Letter from Heaven, which allegedly was found floating above the altar of Christ in St. Peter's Church in Rome, and his indignation fortuitously provides the first datable testimonium of the letter. Licinianus implores his addressee, the bishop Vincentius of Ibiza, to tear up immediately the Letter from Heaven, which he had read aloud in church; he warns Vincentius that it is utter nonsense and, moreover, written in poor Latin. Licinianus proceeds to state that there cannot exist such thing as a Letter from Heaven, nor is there any need for such an exhortation concerning the sanctification of Sunday; moreover, a radical rest from work should be rejected. If someone does not go to church, it is better that s/he works rather than indulging in other pleasures. On account of the great importance of Licinianus's letter, it is presented in this volume with translation and commentary.[2]

2. See the letter presented below, pp. 209–19.

From Licinianus's letter, it is clear that the Letter from Heaven claims to have been written in the name of Christ (*sub nomine Christi*), that it supposedly fell from heaven (*de coelo*) onto the altar of Christ (*super altare Christi*) in the memorial chapel of the holy apostle Peter (*in memoria sancti Petri apostoli descendit*), that the letter begins by saying that the Lord's Day should be observed (*ut dies Dominicus colatur*), and additionally that on this day no one should prepare necessary food (*necessaria victus praeparet*) or travel long distances (*viam ambulet*). It may also have mentioned gardening (*hortum facere*), traveling (*iter agere*), and/or working the distaff (*colum tenere*). Rome is not mentioned but is suggested on account of the memorial chapel of the apostle Peter.

Unfortunately, this characterization cannot be clearly connected with a single transmitted version. Greek Recension Alpha tells of its discovery in Rome, floating directly above the altar. The profile of Sunday rest in the Licinianus letter, however, fits better with the domestic and manual labor mentioned in Latin Recension II, which also contains the description "from the (seventh) heaven." Here, however, there is no story of discovery; Rome is referenced only indirectly, insofar as at the end a certain Peter swears to the letter's authenticity. Since Licinianus does not mention Jerusalem, nor does the letter show signs of a universal apocalyptic perspective, the other Latin Recension I is rather out of the question as a source.[3] Thus, it can probably be concluded that Licinianus's correspondence partner had in his hands an earlier version of Latin Recension II, a version that offered a discovery narrative similar to that of Greek Recension Alpha 1. Moreover, this Greek version, due to its explicit Petrine theology,[4] more likely originated in the Latin West, anyway. Thus, one may assume the existence of earlier versions of Latin Recension II and Greek Recension Alpha 1 that have not survived.

The profile of Sunday sanctification from Latin Recension II also corresponds better to the punitive miracle narratives associated with Sunday; these begin to appear in other literature in Gaul at this time, for example, in the work of Gregory of Tours.[5] These accounts typically pertained to domestic or manual labor; the punishment for violation of Sunday is limited to the offender—by no means is the demise of the whole world threatened.

Perhaps a Greek transformation of this previous version reached the vicinity of Jerusalem around 600 CE, especially since Cartagena, the episcopal see

---

3. Differently Haines, *Sunday Observance*, 38 and 44, which treats Latin Recension I. However, she connects the Letter from Heaven criticized by Licinianus in the sixth century with the Roman synod of 754 (see pp. 95–99 below), but these should probably be differentiated.

4. See Greek Recensions Alpha 1, 1.3–5 and also pp. 135–39.

5. See below on punitive miracles and their connection to the Letter from Heaven, pp. 172–82.

of Licinianus, was then under Byzantine rule after the wars of conquest under Emperor Justinian.[6] This may have promoted contact and exchange between East and West. However, there is no comparable testimonium for the existence of the Letter from Heaven from Byzantine territory. A passage from Sophronius of Jerusalem, likewise included in this volume, does not refer to the Letter from Heaven but instead draws on a passage from the second-century Dialogue between Jason and Papiscus; in this respect it represents only a general testimony to the high esteem in which Sunday was held as a feast day.

The term *transformation* was chosen because the Greek versions of the Letter from Heaven, despite some congruencies, have a different profile from the Latin ones. In particular, details concerning the main theme, Sunday sanctification, differ: while the Greek texts confine themselves to exhortation of a general rest from work and attendance at church services, the Latin versions list various activities to be done or avoided on Sundays. In contrast, the Greek versions expand the spectrum of other moral demands in various catalogues of vices (see below). In the Latin versions, the imperatives are expanded to include injunctions to pay tithes and not to swear, which the Greek versions lack. Then again, only the Greek texts prophesy impending distress, such that people will long to escape tribulations, namely, to hide themselves in opened graves. Also characteristic of the Greek texts is the expansion of the so-called Sunday benedictions, as well as the quotation from Matthew 24:35: "Heaven and earth will pass away, but my words remain unchanged!" This "Sunday profile" can be linked to the ideas of the other Greek texts presented in this volume, especially the *Diataxis of Jesus Christ* and the three pseudepigraphal sermons (see chapter 4, "Considerations," below). Obviously, there are differences between East and West with regard to the design of the Lord's Day, so it was natural for the person who drafted the Greek version of the Letter from Heaven to make adjustments here. These regional changes include the addition of remarks about Friday as well as other saints' days, which occur only in Greek versions.[7] In view of these great differences between the Letters from Heaven in

6. Between 552 (in the course of the rebellion of Athanagild with support of Byzantine troops) and 625 CE, the south of Spain belonged to the Byzantine Empire. See Dietrich Claude, "Die diplomatischen Beziehungen zwischen dem Westgotenreich und Ostrom (475–615)," *MIÖG* 104 (1996): 13-25; John Moorhead, "Western Approaches," in *The Cambridge History of the Byzantine Empire c. 500–1492*, ed. Jonathan Shepard (Cambridge: Cambridge University Press, 2019), 196-220. But see on the low interest in Sunday under Emperor Justinian and in the *Codex Justinianus* below, p. 127.

7. See, however, the section on Latin Recension III, which is probably a Latin version of Greek Recension Alpha 2 (pp. 112–16).

their respective manuscript traditions, it is not possible to compile a critical edition in the classical sense. Only rough references, that is, cluster formations, can be shown. This is an interesting observation insofar as one may assume that scribes would have copied this letter with special care—after all, it is a Letter from Heaven from Christ himself. But the opposite is the case; the temptation in each case to adapt the letter somewhat to local concerns was obviously too great.

The broader history of the Letter from Heaven can, on the other hand, be better contextualized in the Latin West, namely, from the early Carolingian period. Indeed, a remarkable witness to the Letter from Heaven is offered by an inscription.[8] The inscription was found at the small church Santa Maria Assunta in the little village of Piazza, which belongs to the municipality of Deiva, located in Liguria, south of Genoa halfway to Pisa, not far from the coast. The inscription resembles a stela. It consists of forty-nine lines carved on a marble plaque about 0.425 meters wide by 1.20 meters high and is divided into two parts separated by a line. The first part, in much larger characters, sets May 29 as the anniversary of the *dedicatio* of a church to the Savior, St. Michael, St. Martin, and St. George the Martyr, and the second part contains the Letter from Heaven. The inscription is thus a good example of how the Letter from Heaven was associated with church consecrations.[9] The original place at the church is not known, as the stone was already removed and placed within the church in 1869 by Pietro Merzarolus, dean of the church, then placed within the vestry.[10]

Tosi would like to attribute the inscription to a monk,[11] since the writing is more like handwriting, and places it in the context of the missionary movement of the famous monastery of Bobbio.[12] That the monks of Bobbio knew of

8. A big thank-you is due to Michel-Yves Perrin, who brought this inscription to my attention and will also publish an essay in the journal *Apocrypha* on it: "Entre apocryphicité, épigraphie et philologie: les plus anciens témoins de la Lettre tombée du ciel sur le dimanche (CANT 311)." He presents below the inscription, pp. 239–43.

9. See p. 76f.

10. The stone is now housed in the Museo Diocesano in Brugnato. The inscription was published by Remondini, *Iscrizioni medioevali*, 2-4 with plate 2; then analyzed again with a partial correction of the transcription by Patetta, "Una pretesa lettera di Gesù Cristo," 282-308; presented also by Rugo, *Le iscrizioni*, 137f., and analyzed again by Tosi, "I monaci colombaniani," 36-42. The publications of Patetta and Tosi are reprinted in Benente, *Santa Maria*, 10-24 and 25-32. While Remondini suggested a dating in the eleventh century, Patetta gave plausible typographical arguments for an earlier dating, around 700 CE, which have been accepted by Tosi and by Perrin.

11. Tosi, "I monaci colombaniani," 40 [repr., p. 26].

12. Tosi, "I monaci colombaniani," 41 [repr., p. 27].

this Letter from Heaven he deduces from the condemnation of this letter in the *Admonitio generalis* under Charlemagne of 789.[13] However, his suggestions remains speculative, since the *Admonitio generalis* does not refer to the authors or the place of distribution of the Letter from Heaven, and neither does it mention an inscription. Moreover, the singularity of this inscription must be emphasized, so that the Letter from Heaven can hardly be a standard element of "missionary preaching" from Bobbio. Tosi refers to a penitential of Bobbio—this is now edited as *Poenitentiale Merseburgensea* (CPL 1893f.).[14] Canon 83 or 92 (depending on the recension), which treats Sunday observance (*Si quis in dominica per neglegentiam opera facit aut se balneat aut se tondit aut caput lauat, VII dies peniteat, et si iterum facit, XL dies peniteat. Et si pro dampnatione diei hoc facit aut non emendat, expellatur ab aecclesia catholica sicut iudeus*), is of course in line with the general aim of the Letter from Heaven; however, it does not refer to the letter and includes the possibility of penance, which the letter does not offer likewise. Thus, a general impulse to live according to Christian ideas, including Sunday rest, can perhaps be attributed to the popular spirituality of monastic asceticism associated with insular monks and their communities. But to actually enforce this with an inscription of the Letter from Heaven is probably a special local initiative.[15]

13. See on this the text below, pp. 101–104.

14. *Poenitentiale Merseburgensea* (CCSL 156:126–68 Kottje).

15. In sum, in the insular penitential books, Sunday rest plays a subordinate role overall. See the only passage in the penitential of Theodore of Canterbury (11.1): "Those who labor on the Lord's day, the Greeks reprove the first time; the second, they take something from them; the third time, [they take] the third part of their possessions, or flog them; or they shall do penance for seven days" (*Medieval Handbooks on Penance: A Translation of the Principal "Libri Poenitentiales" and Selections from Related Documents*, ed. John T. McNeill and Helena M. Gamer [New York: Octagon Books, 1965], 104). Other passages deal with fasting or abstinence. On Sunday in the *Libri poenitentiale* see also Kinzig, "Sunday Observance," 333-39. See, however, on the connections of the other, more apocalyptic Recension I to the insular context above, p. 49. One must also take into account that research has since corrected the image of missionary Irish: they appeared more as monastic founders in remote places (*locus deserti*), and understood the *peregrinatio* as part of monastic asceticism, not as a missionary journey. See Knut Schäferdiek, "Die irische Mission des siebten Jahrhunderts. Historisches Geschehen oder historiographische Legende?," in *Schwellenzeit. Beiträge zur Geschichte des Christentums in Spätantike und Frühmittelalter*, ed. Winrich A. Löhr and Hanns Christof Brennecke, AKG 64 (Berlin: de Gruyter, 1996), 438-58; Schäferdiek, "Columbans Wirken im Frankenreich (591-612)," in *Die Iren und Europa im früheren Mittelalter*, ed. Heinz Löwe, Veröffentlichungen des Europa Zentrums (Tübingen: Klett-Cotta, 1982), 171-201. Thus, the inscription is an important early witness of the Latin Letter from Heaven, but the connections to the monastery of Bobbio may not be so close as suggested by Tosi. See also the remarks on Boniface and on Pirmin's *Scarapsus* below.

This inscription threatens various calamities to those who do not observe the Lord's Day (*observare, custodire*) or do not devote themselves to it (*convertere*). Aside from general rest (*requiescere*), the only concrete details mentioned are engaging in legal or business disputes (*causam/negotium/intentionem facere/agere, iure*), and washing and cutting the hair (*caput lavare, coma tondere*); and, in contrast, a general compassion for the poor, widows, and orphans is demanded. Calamity is threatened in various forms: insects and locusts (*brucus et locustas*) that will destroy all harvests, rashes (*pustellas*, twice), suffering under a pagan people (*gentes paganas*), famine and death (*famen et mortaletatem*), God turning his face away (*avertam facie[m] meam*), and a threat of being lead into the depths of the sea (*producam vos ad profundum maris*; see Ps 68:3 LXX).

In terms of its profile, the inscription therefore resembles again the shorter Latin Recension II, with which there is some overlap; moreover, here individual families or households are explicitly addressed and threatened (*in domo sua; in domo eius, ante domus vestras*). Interestingly, the text of the inscription is in many passages (highlighted in gray below) identical with the letter as found in the Codex London Add. 30853 (s. xi/xii). This is the manuscript with the so-called homilary of Toledo that Delehaye had already presented in 1928 and Grégoire described in more detail in 1966.[16] In this manuscript, the Letter from Heaven appears after one homiliary that can probably be traced back to the seventh century, and it is followed by another homiliary. It is thus inserted at a junction, so to speak, as a stand-alone text, but is thereby classified within the framework of two sermon series, as it were, as another exhortation sermon. In this version of the letter, it is connected with a Peter of Nîmes, who had found the letter in St. Bauduli and testified to its authenticity.[17] If this is Peter Ermengaud, bishop of Nîmes between 1080 and 1090,[18] the rediscovery of the letter would have to be dated to the end of the eleventh century, just as the manuscript itself is dated. But it might be another otherwise unknown Peter as well. The similarities of this version of the Letter from Heaven with the inscription definitely speak for an older text from the seventh century, as suggested for the rest of the homiliary of which Spain is the origin. In that period, Nîmes also belonged to the Visigothic Empire. This, in addition to the first known reference in the letter of Licinianus, would be another hint to Spain as probably the earliest area of a circulation of the Letter of Heaven.

16. See above, pp. 35–37.

17. See below, n. 23 and pp. 138f.

18. This is suggested by Morin, "A propos du travail," 217, with the conclusion that this exemplar "is therefore closely linked, by its origin, to the region where the apocryphal letter was reported from the sixth century by Licinianus."

Remarkably, the second homiliary, which follows the Letter from Heaven, contains another Sunday text, namely, a passage from a Latin version of the Sunday sermon of Pseudo-Eusebius of Alexandria (*Sermo* 16). Germain Morin hinted at this passage and suggested a Latin translation of Pseudo-Eusebius.[19]

Both letters (from Codex London Add. 30853 and from the inscription) have a similar composition and a parallel structure, and there are many congruencies in general with Latin Recension II, as the following table shows. Although Haines understands this version in London Add. 30853 rather as an "outlier" and believes it to be a summary or paraphrase of Latin Recension II with minor elements from Latin Recension I,[20] the inscription in Liguria indicates that such a version of Latin Recension II was in circulation. Thus, in light of these witnesses, the core of the Letter from Heaven can be surmised. This core text in an early version served as a template for Greek Recension Alpha 1. It was also expanded and supplemented in later versions of Latin Recension II as well as to Latin Recension I.

19. Morin, "Sermo de dominica," 530–34. On the original Greek version, see the study of Annette von Stockhausen below, pp. 444–59.

Christoph Scheerer made the following preliminary observations to be presented here: Morin observed a longer insertion: his lines 16–44, which he was not able to identify but which are from Isidore of Seville, *De ecclesiasticis officiis* 1.24.1–25.4, in an individual order of single passages of this section starting with 25.3. Just the connection to the following section of Ps.-Eusebius of Alexandrias homily (Morin's lines 45–52) might show the hand of the redactor himself insofar as the mention of the *resurrectio corporis* or the *mysterium corporis et sanguinis* is not to be found in any Greek version known to us until yet. The manuscript London, BL Add. 30853 provides texts of authors not older than Isidore of Seville and Ildefons of Toledo. It is highly speculative, but as Julian of Toledo revised the Toletanian liturgy and also dealt with the *resurrectio corporis* (see, e.g., Julian of Toledo, *Prognosticorum futuri saeculi libri tres* 3.14 [CPL 1258]), it is conceivable that he was the redactor who gathered the passages from Ps.-Eusebius of Alexandria and Isidore of Seville.

20. Haines, *Sunday Observance*, 47. However, she only mentions the *brucos et locustas* from the first sentence (which, however, can also be interpreted as an ecphrasis of the plagues [*flagellas*] mentioned in Latin Recension II as, e.g., Munich 9550 [see below, p. 236f.]), and the hint at the arrival on an altar, which is, however, a feature of Greek Recension Alpha (see below, p. 135) and not Latin Recension I (where the letter arrived at the *sepulchum* of St. Peter in Rome, not the *altar*). This hints, actually, at a connection between this Latin Recension II and Greek Recension Alpha. Further parallels can be explained by the fact that one version of the text of Latin Recension II was probably the template for the extension to Latin Recension I, as suggested here. This is shown by the underlined text in the table on p. 94. Already Tosi observed connections between the inscription and the Codex London Add. 30853 (p. 26), but he also suggested other manuscripts. However, there are more parallels to Codex London Add. 30853, which are demonstrated in this overview.

Inscription (around 700 CE)[21]	Latin Recension II, according to Codex London Add. 30853 (eleventh/twelfth century)
Amen dico uobis: misi uobis **brucus et locustas** qui omnes **labores uestrus** subduxerunt; **misi pustellas** et omnes langoris et **non** conuersi estis ad diem **sanctum dominicum; misi super uos gentes** paganas **qui** corpora **uestra et filius uestrus** vel omnes **labores uestrus** possedeant et sub pedis eorum estis cottidie et non agnuscitis; **ideo** producam **uos** ad profundum maris **quia non** obseruastis diem **sanctum dominicum; auertam facie meam a uobis** et a tabernaculis quibus fecit manus mea; et si cufugeretis **in eclesia mea** et ego uos indecabo **et trada in manus** gentium quia non **obseruastis** diem **sanctum dominecum** et omnium animalium quatropedium clamantium uoces ad me et ego eas exaudia quia non permisistis **requiescere in die sancto dominico** nisi ad eclesia cum ueneritis, si quis causam ad **negutium in domo sua fecerit,** aut si **caput lauauirit,** aut **coma toderit, anatima** erit illi in **generationem** et progenie;	**Amen dico uobis** quia **misi** super **populum brucos et locustas** et non cognouerunt me et **misi super uos gentes** malas **qui** ducunt **filios** et filias **uestras** in captibitate **et labores uestros** in exterminatione quia **sanctum dominicum non** coluistis et **aeclesias meas** non honorastis. **Ideo inmittam** super **uos** serpentes pinnatas et canes rauidos et **auferam faciem meam a uobis, quia non** coluistis **sanctum dominicum** et estis increduli et non honorastis **aeclesias meas** et **tradam** uos **in manibus** inimicorum. Set **obserbate** praecepta mea quae mando uobis et sollerter custodite ea in **diem sabbati ab ora <nona> usque** ad secunda feria ora prima nullum laborem faciatis, neque **caput tondatis** nec **labetis** in die dominico neque **aliquo negotio** in eo die **faciatis.** Si quis non obserbaberit quae praecipio uobis uidebitis iram super iram quem subportare non potest nec ipsi montes et colles sustinere non ualebunt **et anathemabo eos anathema** marathenata que est super septuaginta et duas **generationes** usque in seculum seculi.

21. For a translation, see below the presentation of Perrin, p. 243.

Inscription (around 700 CE)	Latin Recension II, according to Codex London Add. 30853 (eleventh/twelfth century)
super eus qui non costodirent die sanctum dominicum **mittam in domo eius famem et mortaletatem** invisibilem **glandola** cetatam. **Si quis** autem in die sancto dominico **causa** agere uoluerit aut intentionem **mitta in** ipsis **pustellas in** oculus dolorem ut ceci fiant. Amen dico uobis **populous** imgredibilis, **generatio praua** et peruersa, ut quit non uultis cunuerti ad die sancto dominicum, **nescitis quia multum pacies sum** super vos propter **electus meus;** obdurati estis haec non intellegentes, pauperis uoces clamantium ante domus vestras haec non intellegetis nec exaudiebatis facire misericordiam et persecuti estis eos bene facientes; super uiduas et orfanus opremere nolite. Nullus iuret in die sancto dominico. Amen dico uobis: requiescite **ab ora nona sabati usque** et in tertio die luciscentem. Amen dico uobis: crucefixus sum et **resurrexi die** sanctum **dominicum** in **celis ascinsi sederem ad dexteram dei patris et requieui ab omnibus operibus** ad quod **fici celum et terram et santefecaui** hunc die ut omnes **requiem** abeant sibe ad superus sibe ad inferus.[22]	**Inmittam in domos eorum famem et** egritudinem et **mortalitatem** et <in> labores eorum grandinem et ustulationem. **Si quis** tamen auditas **causas** diiudicauerit aut exactiones fecerit **mittam in** eos latrones et tribulationes et **pustellas** in corporibus eorum. Audite ergo **gens praba** et amara et increduli. **Non scitis quia multum paciens sum** et misericors ego **super electos meos? Surrexi in diem dominicum** et omnes **requiescere** debent in eo diae. **In caelis ascendi ad dexteram patris mei requiebi ab omnibus operibus meis. Faeci caelum et terram** et omnia quae in eis sunt et **sanctificabi** sanctum dominicum. Et si quis non coluerit eum suscitabo tonitrua et tempestates et disperdent omnes fruges uestras et uineas uestras et ostendent oculis uestris fruges et non colligetis eas. Et si obseruaueritis praecepta mea et feceritis ea, multiplicabo messes uestras et uineas uestras fructificabunt et auferam a uobis omnem malitiam, quia ego sum dominus Deus uester et non est alius praeter me. Si quis uero acceperit hanc epistolam et non obseruauerit ea et notam eam non fecerit universis, anathema sit in perpetuum.[23]

(*Continued*)

22. Does this short ending mean that all rest also in hell on Sunday? See on rest of punishment in hell below the passage of the *Visio Pauli*, p. 421.

23. After this, there follows a subscription like a historical note and certification testimony: *Nam iuro ego Petrus episcopus de civitate Nimaso omnibus legentibus hanc epistolam per crucifixum Dominum nostrum Iesum Christum filius Dei et patrem omnipotentem et Trinitatem inseparabilem et sancta quattor aevangelia quia non est hac epistola ab homine abtata nec subtracta sed a domino Deo directa in sacrosanto altare sancto Baudoli in civitate Nimaso, et dum essem vigilans media noctis ora pro facinora mala mea audivi hanc vocem et inveni hanc epistolam.* Text from Réginald Grégoire (see above, p. 37).

(Continued)

Inscription (around 700 CE)	**Latin Recension II, according to Codex London Add. 30853 (eleventh/twelfth century)**
Latin Recension I, according to Codex from Tarragona (Amaduzzi; see below, pp. 282–85):	
… 9.1 Amen dico vobis, si non corrigeritis vosmet ipsos, mittam super vos brucus et locustas, qui comedant fructus vestros, et lupos rapaces qui comedant vos, quia non custodistis diem sanctum dominicum. 9.2 qui istum non custodierit, maledictus erit. 9.3 die dominico non lavare vestimenta non caput neque capillos tondere. 9.4 qui haec fecerit, anathema sit. 9.5 si custodieritis mandata mea, <non> avertam faciem meam a vobis, et <non> mittam in domibus vestris omnem malitiam et amaritudinem et infirmitatem. 9.6 si quis tamen in die dominico aut causas voluerit committere vel intentiones facere, aut rixas commiserit, mittam in eis pustellas, accessiones et langores, et omne genus infirmitates. 9.7 et pro eo quod non concurritis ad ecclesias meas, sed magis ad mercimonia vel ad silvam vel otiium, et per plateas sedere, fabulas vanas loquere, et me non timere, et ecclesias meas non venerare, propter hoc tradam vos in fame et in manus gentium (et non pluam super vos) incredulorum paganorum, qui epistolam istam non custodiunt.	
10.1 Iam enim vobis ante legem meam mandavi, sed minime custodistis diem sanctum dominicum. 10.2 propterea mittam gladium meum super vos, quia non custodistis haec omnia. 10.3 amen dico vobis: crucifixus fui propter vos, et resurrexi die dominica, ascendi ad dextram dei, et requiem dedi omnibus die dominico. 10.4 in ipso feci coelum et terram, solem et lunam, mare et omnia quae in eis sunt. 10.5 et postea Adam de limo terrae plasmavi, et die dominico sanctificavi, et dedi requiem in ipso ut bene agant, et sine pressure sint, et requiescant per omnia. [underlined are the parallels with the inscription in the left column above]	

The added testimony from the now-lost manuscript from Tarragona also shows parallels with the inscription, especially with regard to the underlined words, which reveal a further adaptation of the text of Latin Recension II. The comparison gives the impression that Latin Recension I of the Letter from Heaven is an extended version of an exemplar from Latin Recension II. The following expansions have been added to Latin Recension II: a prefatory legend detailing the discovery and forwarding of the letter from Jerusalem via other places to Rome; an apocalyptic warning concerning the impending demise of the whole world (Latin Recension II is focused on household and family, and does not indicate that the whole world will perish); a warning not to doubt the letter; reference to preceding letters (this being already the third one); a narration that a previous threat of destruction was averted only due to the intercession of Mary, the archangel Michael, Peter, the apostles and the saints; and additional moral criticism.

Against this background, it is probable that an earlier version of the shorter Latin Recension II is the starting point of the Letters from Heaven. Both the Licinianus letter and the inscription attest to a shorter Latin Recension II. The short Latin Recension II seems to have been revised and expanded into a longer Latin Recension II on the one hand, and on the other hand, it was more heavily revised and altered to form the basis of Latin Recension I. Nevertheless, an extended Latin Recension II also remained in circulation independently, besides the enlarged Latin Recension I, as evidenced by the much broader manuscript tradition. The shorter Latin Recension II was perhaps also the starting point for the Greek Recension Alpha.[24]

The extension of the Letter from Heaven into Latin Recension I apparently happened in the Carolingian period, for which there are several indications, namely, the correspondence of Boniface, the *Admonitio generalis* of Charlemagne, and a short Latin text about plagues in Jerusalem (*De plaga que facta est in Hierusalem*).

The next reference to the letter, again in the context of a fierce rejection, is attested in the letters of Boniface (d. 754), the famous archbishop who worked to eradicate paganism in Thuringia and the Hessian region and was commissioned by the pope to restructure the church in the Frankish Empire. A certain quarrel is relevant to his involvement: he advocated for Pope Zacharias's condemnation of the Gallic bishop Aldebertus,[25] after his imprisonment at the Synod of Soissons (March 2, 744) had no effect, although this synod rejected his heresy (canon 2), as well as "field crosses" that he had erected (canon 7). The following attestations to this conflict have survived: a letter from Zacharias to Boniface (*Ep.* 57, June 22, 744) about Aldebertus as a pseudo-prophet and false priest who leads people astray with his sermons, spreads false doctrines, erects crosses and prayer houses in the fields, and allows himself to be venerated (a corresponding earlier letter from Boniface to Zacharias is not extant); another letter from Zacharias to Boniface on the matter (*Ep.* 60; October 31, 745), following a Roman synod of October 25, 745; a further letter from a Roman deacon named Gemmulus to Boniface (*Ep.* 62), to which the report of the Roman synod (745 CE, *Ep.* 59) was probably attached; this report also cites a preceding letter from Boniface on the subject. A later papal letter (*Ep.* 77, January 5, 747) also inquires again about the status of Aldebertus in Gaul. The enterprising bishop aroused enthusiasm in

24. See below, p. 108.

25. The letters of Boniface are published in Michael Tangl, *S. Bonifatii et Lulli Epistolae*, MGH Epp. sel. 1 (Berlin: Weidmann, 1916). See Jan Berger, "Aldebert und Clemens: Ein Blick in die Quellen," *Aventinus medievalia* 15 (2011): 6–31; John Laux, "Two Early Medieval Heretics: An Episode in the Life of Boniface," *CHR* 21 (1935/36): 190–95; Jeffrey B. Russel, "Saint Boniface and the Eccentrics," *CH* 33 (1964): 235–47; Nicole Zeddies, "Bonifatius und zwei nützliche Rebellen: Die Häretiker Aldebert und Clemens," in *Ordnung und Aufruhr im Mittelalter: Historische und juristische Studien zur Rebellion*, ed. Marie Rheres Fögen (Frankfurt am Main: Klostermann, 1995), 217–63.

his congregation via his sermons and attacked pagan rites, just as Boniface did, but with unusual methods. Yet he resisted the ideas of Boniface. He apparently not only erected the aforementioned "field crosses," where he held large prayer services,[26] but he also circulated a kind of autobiographical hagiographic *vita* for himself, composed new prayers, dealt in relics including his own hair and nails, allowed himself to be honored as a miracle worker, and pronounced forgiveness of sins to the people without their prior confession and penance. In addition, he promoted Sunday rest with the assistance of the Letter from Heaven, which he claimed was written by Jesus, fell from heaven over Jerusalem (*divulgabat esse Iesu et de caelo cecidisse*), was found at the gate of Ephraim, and was brought to Rome by intermediaries. After this Letter from Heaven was read at the synod in Rome—the beginning is quoted in the synodal report below—an indignant rejection followed:

> Of a truth, beloved brethren, this Aldebert is mad, and all who make use of this wickedly invented letter are lacking in mind and memory like children or senseless women.[27]

Even if the pronounced condemnation did not refer chiefly to the Letter from Heaven but to the other accusations against the bishop, it is clear that the letter was both circulated and rejected by some clergy at this time. In the letter of Pope Zacharias to Boniface (*Ep.* 60), Aldebertus's schismatic teachings (*schismatica dogmata*) are condemned, and the members of the Roman synod were allegedly eager to burn his biography immediately. Zacharias, however, arranged for the archiving of the text—whether the Letter from Heaven was archived with it unfortunately remains unclear, but this may be assumed.

As far as the manuscript tradition can be surveyed, the witnesses of Latin Recension I can be linked to these events. This is indicated by the record of

---

26. Boniface, *Ep.* 59 = report of the Roman synod of 745, which includes a letter of Boniface quoted at that synod (MGH Epp. sel. 1, 111.32–112.2 Tangl): *Fecit cruciculas et oratoriola in campis et ad fontes vel ubicumque sibi visum fuit et iussit ibi publicas orationes celebrare, donec multitudines populorum spretis ceteris episcopis et dimissis antiquis ecclesiis in talibus locis conventus celebrant dicentes: Merita sancti Aldeberti adiuvabunt nos.* "He had little crosses and prayer-houses erected in the fields and by the springs and wherever it seemed good to him, and had public prayer meetings held there, until great masses of people, who despised the other bishops and abandoned the old churches, gathered in such places, saying, 'The merits of St. Aldebert will help us.'" See also p. 270.

27. Boniface, *Ep.* 59 (MGH Epp. sel. 1, 115.30–116.2 Tangl): *Pro certo, karissimi fratres, et predictus in insaniam conversus Aldebertus et omnis, qui hanc utitur scelere commentatam epistolam, parvulorum more absque memoria mentium esse possunt et quibusdam mulieris insaniunt sensibus.* Translation by Ephraim Emerton, *The Letters of Saint Boniface Translated* (New York: Columbia University Press, 1940), 140.

the Roman synod, which includes an opening of the Letter from Heaven that can be reconciled with this recension:

Presentation of the Letter from Heaven at Roman synod 754 CE (Boniface, *Ep.* 59)[28]	Latin Recension I according to Codex Vienna lat. 1355[29]
. . . In the name of God. Here begins the letter of our Lord Jesus Christ, the Son of God, which fell to **Jerusalem**, and by Archangel Michael this letter was found at the gate of **Ephraim**. And by the hand of a priest named Ichor this letter was read and given as an example; and he sent this letter to the city of **Jeremiah** to another priest Talasius. And this Talasius sent this letter to the region of **Arabia** to another priest Leoban. And this Leoban sent the letter to the city of **Betania**, and this letter was received by Macrius, priest of God, and he sent this letter to the **mountain of saint archangel Michael**. And this letter came through the hand of an angel to the city of **Rome** to the place of the tomb of Saint Peter, where the keys to the kingdom of heaven are stored. And the twelve bishops who are in the city of Rome watched and fasted for three days, praying day and night. . . . . . . And other things were read through to the end. . . .	It begins the letter, in the name of the trinity of the savior Lord Jesus Christ, that fell down from heaven in **Jerusalem** by [the action of] the archangel Michael. (2) The letter was found at the gate **Ephraim** by the great priest called Ichor. (3) The same letter was left there and copied and sent to the city **Ermia** to another priest called Talasius. (4) Talasius sent it from the city **Ebrea** to another priest whose name is Lebonius. (5) And Lebonius sent it to the province **Cappadocia** to another priest called Juras. (6) And Juras sent it to the city **Bethania** to another priest called Marchabeus. (7) And the priest Marchabeus sent the letter to the **mountain of the archangel saint Michael**. (8) And the letter came to the city of **Rome** through the will of our Lord Jesus Christ to its predestined place, to the chapel of saint Peter and Paul. (9) Those who were in the city held vigils and fasted and prayed for three days that the good God may gift them help and understanding in their hearts; for through his help the letter had already come to Jerusalem and to other cities. (10) And through the arrangement of our Lord, Jesus Christ, they found that it had come because of the holy Lord's Day.

28. Boniface, *Ep.* 59 (MGH Epp. sel. 1, 115.13–29 Tangl): *In Dei nomine. Incipit epistola domini nostri Iesu Christi filii Dei, qui in Hierosolima cecidit, et per Michael archangelum ipsa epistola inventa est ad portam Effrem. Et per manus sacerdotis nomine Icore epistola ista fuit relecta ipsa exemplata; et transmisit ipsam epistolam ad Geremiam civitatem ad alio sacerdoti Talasio. Et ipse Talasius transmisit ipsam epistolam ad Arabiam civitatem ad alio sacerdote Leoban. Et ipse Leobanus transmisit epistolam istam ad Uetfaniam civitatem; et recepit epistolam istam Macrius sacerdos Dei et transmisit ipsam epistolam in monte sancto archangelo Michael. Et ipsa epistola per manus angeli Domini pervenit ad Romanam civitatem ad locum sepulcri sancti Petri, ubi claves regni caelorum constitute sunt. Et XII papati, qui sunt in Romana civitate, triduanas fecerunt vigilias in ieiuniis, in orationibus per diebus et noctibus . . . et cetera usque ad finem perlecta* (my translation).

29. Cod. Vienna lat. 1355: 1.1 *Incipit epistola in nomine trinitatis salvatoris domini Iesu Christi quae de celo in Ierusalem cecidit per Michahelem archangelum.* (2) *ista epistola*

So even if the manuscript evidence does not begin until two hundred years later in the tenth century, the letter handed down here is probably connected with the disputes about the enterprising Aldebertus. In particular, the passage in the text from now-lost codex from Tarragona (Cathedral Library, described by Baluzius), which preaches against pagan rites performed at springs, trees, and stones, fits the antipagan engagement of Aldebertus. Here, in fact, it states:[30]

> 7.2 See, reliably I say to you again, come often to my churches with offerings. 7.3 Listen to the divine readings with intent hearts, so that you may be redeemed. 8.1 Who secretly goes to the springs or to the trees or stones and is found making sacrifices, or who dares to chant by the graves of the dead or rubs [trees or stones] in any of these places,[31] I will curse them, and they

est inventa ad portam Effrem per magnum sacerdotem cui nomen Ichor. (3) *ipsa epistola fuit relicta ibi et ipsam exemplavit et transmisit ad Ermiam civitatem ad alium sacerdotem nomine Talasium.* (4) *ipse Talasius transmisit eam de Ebrea civitate ad alium sacerdotem cui nomen Lebonius.* (5) *et ipse Lebonius transmisit eam ad Capadociam civitatem ad alium sacerdotem nomine Iuram.* (6) *et ipse Iuras transmisit eam ad Bethaniam civitatem ad alium sacerdotem nomine Marchabeus.* (7) *et ipse Marchabeus sacerdos transmisit illam epistolam ad montem sancti Michahelis archangeli.* (8) *et ipsa epistola per voluntatem domini nostri Iesu Christi pervenit ad Romam civitatem ad locum praedestinatum ad sepulcrum sancti Petri et Pauli.* (9) *qui erant in civitate, triduanas fecerunt in vigiliis et ieiuniis <et> in orationibus, ut pius deus perdonasset eis auxilium et sensum in corda eorum, pro quali iam ista epistola in Ierusalem et in alias civitates venisset,* (10) *et per ordinationem domini nostri Iesu Christi invenerunt, quia propter diem sanctum dominicum advenisset.* See also below, pp. 250–53.

30. Latin Recension I (Codex from Tarragona): (7.2) *ecce, fideliter iterum dico vobis, ad ecclesias meas cum oblationes frequenter venite.* (3) *lectiones divinas intento corde audite, ut salvi esse possitis.* (8.1) *qui dissimulaverit ad fontes aut ad arboribus aut ad petra fuerit inventus sacrificare, aut ad sepulcra mortuorum praesumpserit incantare aut in quolibet locis tergere, anathemabo eum, et peribit in inferno inferiori, quia omnis incantator non habebit partem in regno meo.* (2) *ille tamen qui dimiserit sanctum diem dominicum et non coluerit eum sicut oportet, anathemabo eum.* (3) *maleficos, divinos, incantatores, auguriatores fugite.* See below, p. 280.

31. It is not easy to evaluate this description in terms of religious history. Is it indeed a Germanic natural religion or an ancestral cult that is being described here? Or are there clichés of a "paganism" mixed in here, as it has been handed down in Christian sources since the apologetic writings of the second century? See Bernhard Maier, *Die Religion der Germanen. Götter—Mythen—Weltbild* (München: Beck, 2003), esp. 142-54; Alexander Rubel, *Religion und Kult der Germanen* (Stuttgart: Kohlhammer, 2016). However, James C. Russell, *The Germanization of Early Medieval Christianity. A Sociohistorical Approach to Religious Transformation* (Oxford: Oxford University Press, 1994), esp. 183-208, stresses this point very strongly. On the problem that a stricter demand for Sunday rest was also associated with Germanic "taboo" thinking, see below, p. 176.

> will go down into the deepest hell, because no soothsayer will have a place in my kingdom. (2) But he who neglects the holy Lord's day and does not worship it as required, I will curse them. (3) Stay away from witches, divinators, soothsayers, bird watchers.

Perhaps the complaint in the Letter from Heaven that the addressees do not go to church on Sundays, but instead hang around the marketplaces or in the woods, are idle, loiter in open spaces, and tell each other empty fables[32] could be interpreted as antipagan, but it could also apply generally to other Sunday amusements.

Since Latin Recension I exists in three versions—one based on the lost manuscript from Tarragona transcribed by Baluzius; a second based on the Codex Vienna, ÖNB 1355 (fourteenth/fifteenth century);[33] and a later, third one based on a manuscript from Paris, BN lat. 12270 (twelfth century)—it is clear that this recension of the Letter from Heaven itself not only is an expansion of the Latin Recension II but had already undergone changes and possessed its own history. While the letter according to the manuscript from Tarragona/Baluzius threatens that there will be no further letter and that the disaster will come in November (perhaps as in Aldebert's version?), the Codex Vienna, ÖNB 1355 includes a revision, namely, that the disaster almost came last November but will now come *next* November. Codex Vienna, ÖNB 1355 declares that it is already the third letter and that no further letter will follow. The letter according to Codex Paris, BN lat. 12270 also claims to be the third letter, but it does not mention any date of an impending disaster. Moreover, this Parisian version seems to reflect a further stage of editing, since it inserts extra passages on three topics: tithing, prohibition of swearing, and criticism of unchaste and finely dressed women.[34]

Unfortunately, no statements on Sunday have survived in the corpus of Boniface. However, a passage from a work of his contemporary Pirmin (d. 753), the *Dicta Pirmini*, also called *Scarapsus*, is worth examining. Pirmin compiles a small history of the world in the first part of this work, and in the

---

32. Latin Recension I (Codex from Tarragona): (9.7) *et pro eo quod non concurritis ad ecclesias meas, sed magis ad mercimonia vel ad silvam vel otiium, et per plateas sedere, fabulas vanas loquere, et me non timere, et ecclesias meas non venerare, propter hoc tradam vos in fame et in manus gentium (et non pluam super vos) incredulorum paganorum, qui epistolam istam non custodiunt.* See the quotation above, p. 94, and below, pp. 282–85.

33. As are also the manuscripts from Basel (UB B VII 7, tenth century), London (BL Add. 19725, tenth/eleventh century), and Graz (UB 248, fifteenth century, somewhat shorter, therefore perhaps even older; see p. 268f.).

34. See below, pp. 195–200.

second part, he gives an introduction to the Christian faith.[35] It is therefore a protreptic text for catechesis. Within this work, chapter 23 is devoted to a discussion of Sunday. Aldebert may have preached something similar along with the help of the Letter from Heaven to enhance the urgency of the instruction. The *Scarapsus* includes the following passage after an exhortation to go to church and follows it with a passage about tithing:[36]

> Do not disdain the Lord's Day, but keep it with reverence. Servile work, that is, work in the fields, meadows and vineyards, and other hard labor, do not do on this day. Nor should you announce legal affairs or complaints against each other on the Lord's day, with the exception of preparing the necessary food to strengthen the body. Indeed, the Lord's Day was created first. On it the darkness disappeared and light appeared, and the elements of the world were formed, and the angels were created. On this day the people went out of the land of the Egyptians, as it were out of the darkness of sin, through the Red Sea as through a baptismal fountain into deliverance. On that day, the food of heaven, the manna, was given to the people for the first time. For that day Moses commanded the people, "Keep the first and the last day" [see Exod 12:16f.]. On this day the prophet says, "This is the day the Lord has made; let us rejoice and be glad in it" [see Ps 117:24 LXX]. On this day also

35. About the *Scarapsus*, see Owen M. Phelan, "Catechising the Wild: The Continuity and Innovation of Missionary Catechesis under the Carolingians," *JEH* 61 (2010): 455–74, esp. 460–63; and Eckhard Hauswald, "Quellenrezeption und sprachliche Dynamik in Pirmins Scarapsus," in *Language of Religion—Language of the People. Medieval Judaism, Christianity and Islam*, ed. Michael Richter et al., MittelalterStudien 11 (München: Wilhelm Fink, 2006), 275-96.

36. Pirmin, *Scarapsus* 23 (MGH QQ zur Geistesgeschichte 25, 83.1–87.3 Hauswald): *Die dominico nolite comdemnere, sed com reverencia colite. Opus servile, id est agrum, pratum, vineam, vel si qua gravia sunt, in eo non faciatis, nec causas, nec calomnias inter vos nolite dicere die dominico, preter tantum quod ad necessitatem reficiendi corpusculi pro exquoquenda pertenit cibo; quia ipsi dies dominicos primus creatus est, et in ipso tenebre remuti sunt, et lux apparuit, et in eo formata sunt elimenta mundi, et creati sunt angeli. In eo die terra Aegypti velut ex tenebras peccatorum quasi per fontem babtismi per mare rubro populus fuit liberatus. In eodem die celesti cibo, ut est manna, hominibus primo data est. De ipso mandavit Moysis ad populo: OBSERVABETIS VOBIS DIEM PRIMUM ET NOVISSIMUM. Et de ipso dicit profeta: HEC EST ‹DIES, QUEM FECIT DOMINUS; EXULTEMUS ET LETEMUR IN EO. In ipso quoque a mortuis resurrexit Christus; in ipso de celis super apostulus sanctus discendit spiritus; quia ideo dominicus appellatur, ut in eo, ab terrenis operibus vel a mundi inlecebris abstenentes, tantum devinis cultibus serviamus. Ideo rogamus vobis, dum tanta et talea sancta testimonia de ipso die proferuntur, ut ipso die, sicut dicit Christianus, iuxta quod supra scriptum est, cum magna honore et diligentiam in amore Christi pro retributione aeterna custodiatis* (my translation).

> Christ rose from the dead and the Holy Spirit descended from heaven upon the apostles.[37] That is why this day is called Lord's Day, so that on it we may keep away from the earthly works and temptations of the world and devote ourselves only to the service of God. Since so many and holy testimonies are testified about this day, we ask you to keep it as befits Christians and as is written, with great reverence and conscientiousness, in the love of Christ and for your eternal reward.

Even though the topic is the same, the tone is different from the Letter from Heaven. A rest from work should be observed, but there are exceptions. Sunday is an important day for Christians, but its observance is urged with a heavenly reward, not enforced with divine punishments. Pirmin thus offers in his catechetical treatise a little Sunday theology that forbids heavy menial labor for that day, by now a standard recommendation,[38] as well as quarrels or disputes in court, also an expected recommendation already found in Constantine's law on Sunday rest and recurring in Christian sermons as well.[39] Strict rest from work is not demanded, however, as food preparation is permitted. This is justified with a longer series of Sunday benedictions.[40] Perhaps Boniface would have been quite comfortable with such a Sunday sermon contrary to the Letter from Heaven, which claims divine offspring and, so to say, canonical status. This passage is yet another testimony to the growing importance of Sunday in the Carolingian period.

Only some forty years later, discussion of the Letter from Heaven was renewed. Perhaps stimulated by the horror of a solar eclipse on Sunday, September 16, 787, in the Frankish Empire, from the first to the third hour (i.e., at the time of the departure for Sunday service), the topics of Sunday sanctification and Sunday rest came to attention. The memory of Aldebert's Letter from Heaven had not yet faded and apparently for some received a quasi-heavenly confirmation through this solar eclipse.[41] In any case, it has been handed down in the

37. On this list of Sunday benedictions, see above, pp. 13–16, the letters of Leo the Great.

38. See below, pp. 172–82.

39. See below, pp. 168–72.

40. See on these benedictions the introduction above, pp. 13–16.

41. See the introduction in *Die Admonitio generalis Karls des Großen*, ed. Hubert Mordek, Klaus Zechiel-Eckes, and Michael Glatthaar, MGH. Fontes iuris Germanici antiqui in usum scholarum separatim editi 16 (Wiesbaden: Harrassowitz, 2013), 1–160, here 8f.: "Neben der bloßen Sonnenfinsternis mussten 787 aber auch Tag und Stunde zu denken geben. Zum einen war der 16. September ein Sonntag, was selten genug vorkam und vom Reichskalender wie den Lorscher Annalen eigens vermerkt wurde. Zum anderen soll die Verfinsterung von der ersten bis zur dritten Stunde gedauert oder wenigstens die

Admonitio generalis (March 789) that Charlemagne forbade the reading of a Letter from Heaven and ordered its burning (§76 [78]):

> Likewise, spurious writings and doubtful narratives—or that which runs counter to the Catholic faith in general, such as the utterly evil and false letter that last year some claimed fell from heaven, erring themselves and leading others astray—should neither be believed nor read, but burned, lest the people be led astray by such writings.[42]

The Letter from Heaven was therefore known and circulated, which is the only way to explain why this paragraph was added to the *Admonitio*. At the same time, this *Admonitio* confirms, despite all the criticism of the Letter from Heaven, a wave of intensification pertaining to Sunday sanctification, since in the final paragraph 79 [81] such measures are expressly specified: for men, menial labor (*opera servilia*) is not permitted, be it in the form of agricultural work such as tilling vineyards, plowing, harvesting, haymaking, fencing, clearing forests, stone work, building houses, or gardening. Court proceedings are barred; hunting is forbidden. Only in case of war is movement of goods permitted as well as food transport, or for funerals. Women are forbidden to weave, tailor clothes, sew, knit, spin, prepare flax, wash clothes, and shear sheep—*ut omnimodis honor et requies diei dominicae servetur.*[43] Subsequent Carolingian synods at Frankfurt in 794 (canon 21), and at Friuli in 796 (canon 13) confirmed the increased efforts for Sunday sanctification; these efforts were continued at the five reform synods of 813, as well as at Rome 826 (canon 9) and at Paris 829 (canon 50).[44] Other collections of laws

zweite Stunde ausgefüllt haben. Damit traf das himmlische Schauspiel höchst eindrucksvoll jene Morgenzeit, da man sich zum Gang in die Sonntagsmesse anschickte, die kanonisch der dritten Stunde zugewiesen war. . . . Auf die Sonntagssonnenfinsternis dürfte zuerst freilich jener Himmelsbrief reagiert haben." Probably, the expanding of Latin Recension I to apocalyptic dimensions is caused by this experience.

42. *Admonitio generalis* 76 [78] (228.357–361 Mordeck/Zechiel-Eckes/Glatthaar): *Item et pseudografia et dubiae narrationes, vel quae omnino contra fidem catholicam sunt et epistola pessima et falsissima, quam transacto anno dicebant aliqui errantes et in errorum alios mittentes quod de celo cecidisset, nec credantur nec legantur sed conburentur, ne in errorem per talia scripta populus mittatur* (my translation).

43. *Admonitio generalis* 79/81 (228.388 Mordeck/Zechiel-Eckes/Glatthaar).

44. Frankfurt 794, canon 21 (MGH.Conc. 2.1 Concilia Aevi Karolini, 168.21 Werminghoff): *ut dies dominica a vespera usque ad vesperam servetur*; Friaul 796, canon 13 (MGH.Conc. 2.1 Concilia Aevi Karolini, 194.21–25 Werminghoff); Arles 813, canon 16 (MGH Conc. 2.1 Concilia Aevi Karolini, 252.16–18 Werminghoff): *publica mercata neque causationes disceptationesque exerceantur et penitus a rurali servili opera cessetur*; Reims 813, canon 35 (MGH Conc. 2.1 Concilia Aevi Karolini, 256.31–33 Werminghoff): *nec ad*

from this time also reflect this tendency. It is evident that it was not until the time of the Carolingians that consistent legislation on Sunday was implemented to set uniform standards for all Christians.[45]

If one considers these legal provisions, far more prohibitions are enacted than are even included in the Latin Letter from Heaven. Thus, none of the surviving versions of Latin Recension I can be directly associated with them. Latin Recension II, which lists even fewer prohibitions and has already been described above as an earlier version, certainly has no connection to these provisions, let alone Latin Recension III, which is in the tradition of the Greek Letter from Heaven [Recension Alpha 2; see p. 112 below] and is even less detailed with regard to Sunday activities.

Against this background, the question naturally arises as to where the error of the Letter from Heaven is supposed to lie: on the one hand, certainly, in the assertion that it fell from heaven and is a letter from Christ; on the other hand, perhaps, in the duration of Sunday rest from Sabbath eve up to Monday morning. This is a common feature in all versions of the Letter from Heaven but cannot be found anywhere else independently.[46]

Another point of critique was, perhaps, the threat of the end of the world, which did not occur. If this latter error is the one meant, then the version of the letter announcing corresponding catastrophes for November (Tarragona/ Baluzius) or for the next November (Vienna 1355) could be connected with

---

placita conveniat nec etiam donationes in publico facere; Mainz 813, canon 37 (MGH Conc. 2.1 Concilia Aevi Karolini, 270.14-16 Werminghoff); Tours 813, canon 40 (MGH Conc. 2.1 Concilia Aevi Karolini, 292.1-3 Werminghoff); Chalôn 813, canon 50 (MGH Conc. 2.1 Concilia Aevi Karolini, 283.29-31 Werminghoff); Paris 829, canon 50 (MGH Conc. 2.2 Concilia Aevi Karolini, 643.6–644.2 Werminghoff), a long text, more like a sermon, see below, p. 111; Rome 826, canon 9 and 30 (MGH Conc. 2.2 Concilia Aevi Karolini, 557.34–558.4 and 580.1–6 Werminghoff). See about the synod of Friaul Uta Heil, "Ein Sonntag in Cividale," 91-109; on the synods in general, see Wilfried Hartmann, *Die Synoden der Karolingerzeit im Frankenreich und in Italien*, Konziliengeschichte, Reihe A: Darstellungen (Paderborn: Schöningh, 1989).

45. Laws against *opera servilia* on Sunday: Lex Alamannorum 38 (MGH LL nat. Germ. 5.1, 98.1-20 Lehmann/Eckhardt) from the beginning of the eighth century; similar to Lex Baiuvariorum 7.4 (MGH LL nat. Germ. 5.2, 349.1–351.4 E. von Schwind) composed before 754; Lex Frisonum 18 (MGH Fontes iuris 12, 62.24–27 K. A. Eckhardt/ A. Eckhardt), composed around 802, very short. See Rosamund McKitterick, *The Carolingians and the Written Word* (Cambridge: Cambridge University Press, 1989), 23–76; Theodore J. Rivers, "Contributions to the Criticism and Interpretation of the Lex Baiuvariorum: A Comparative Study of the Alamannic and Bavarian Codes" (PhD diss., Fordham University, 1973), 184–87; Rivers, *Laws of the Alamans and Bavarians* (Philadelphia: University of Pennsylvania Press, 1977), with translations of the laws.

46. See n. 44 above, on canon 21 of the Council of Frankfurt 794, and below, p. 182f.

the *Admonitio*, since these had just failed to occur.[47] The demand for payment of tithes, which is handed down in these versions, can also be easily connected with the Carolingian period (see below).

Another Latin text about misfortunes in Jerusalem is also significant for this era. Although it does not directly refer to the Letter from Heaven, it provides a historical context that suggests an interest in this letter and argues similarly: *De plaga, quae facta fuit in Hierusalem, eo quod dominicum diem non servaverunt*. In 2007 [[per CMS 6.31]] Amnon Linder published a new edition of this short, quasi-chronistic text on the basis of nine Latin manuscripts (tenth/eleventh century to fifteenth century);[48] to be added is a manuscript with a homiliary by the bishop of Prague (eleventh century): Prague, National Library III F.6. It reports a series of calamities, interpreted as plagues (*magna plaga*), over a period of five years, that afflicted the inhabitants of Jerusalem, namely, Christians, Jews, and Muslims: earthquakes (*terrae motus*) from Easter to Pentecost (even three per day = 150 earthquakes) in the first year; locusts and insects (*lucusta et brucus*) in the second year; high mortality rate (*mortalitas*, an epidemic?) in Jerusalem in the third year; many deaths in Jerusalem's environs because of a watermelon or pumpkin (*cucurbitam*) in the fourth year; raiding by the Saracens along the Jordan River, also affecting the Sabas monastery, in the fifth year, combined with a drought (*siccitas magna*). The attempts of the Jews and Muslims to appease God failed or even aggravated the situation because the prayer of the Jews for rain prolonged the drought, and the prayer of the Saracens for rain led to a great hailstorm (*grando atque tempestas*). Thus, the five plagues now became seven. Only the three days of penance and fasting (*triduanum ieiuniam*) by the Christians brought the longed-for rain; and the insight, mediated by an angel, into the reason for the misery, namely, that the Lord's Day had not been observed (*ista*

47. See introduction in Mordek, Zechiel-Eckes, and Glatthaar, *Die Admonitio generalis Karls des Großen*, 10: "Die genannte Novemberfrist indiziert folgende Chronologie: Entstanden unter dem Eindruck des 16. September, wurde der Himmelsbrief nach November 787 in Umlauf gebracht . . . so dass in der Tat 'vergangenes Jahr,' wie die Admonitio am 23. März 789 sagt, einige Irrende und andere in die Irre Führende behaupten konnten, der Brief sei vom Himmel gefallen. Von Irren und Irrtum aber spricht die *Admonitio* zu Recht, da es keine Anzeichen gibt, irgendwelche der angekündigten Strafen seien im November 788 eingetreten."

48. Amnon Linder, "De Plaga que facta est in Hierusalem eo quod Dominicum diem non Custodiebant. History into Fable?," in *In laudem Hierosolymitani: Studies in Crusades and Medieval Culture in Honour of Benjamin Z. Kedar*, ed. Iris Shagir, Ronnie Ellenblum, Jonathan Riley-Smith, and Christopher Simon; Crusades—Subsidia 1 (Aldershot, UK: Ashgate, 2007), 3–29.

tribulatio et ista plaga venit super homines eo quod diem dominicum non custodierunt), put an end to the horrors. God's blessing (*abundantia*) turned again to the land. The text reads:

> During the time of our most holy father Georgios, a great plague among the Christians, Saracens, and Jews occurred in Jerusalem. In the first year, an earthquake struck from the paschal feast until Pentecost, and every day the earth shook three times; for this reason, the earthquake caused great distress. In the second year came locusts and grasshoppers in a countless swarm, and they ate up the whole crop from the earth and all the bark of the trees, as well as their leaves and roots. In the third year came a plague, such that through one gate of the city of Jerusalem eighty-six human corpses were taken out, among them men, women, and infants. In the fourth year, on account of one watermelon/pumpkin, people were slaughtered in the area of Jerusalem, on one side eighty, and on the other side sixty. In the fifth year the Saracens pillaged settlements and monasteries, and they spoiled both the one on the Jordan and three other monasteries, and they injured one hundred monks in the monastery of Saint Sabas, and they cremated twenty-eight in fire. And in that year, there was a great drought, and on account of that drought the Jews began to make prayers of supplication and asked for rain. As the Saracens saw that the Jews were unable to obtain their request, they began to make their own supplicatory prayers, and a hailstorm came. But as a third attempt, the Christians undertook a three-day fast, and God sent them rain. After this one servant of God saw in a vision an angel of the Lord coming to him, and the angel said to him, "This tribulation and this plague comes upon mankind, because they do not keep the Lord's day." Then the servant of God went to Georgios, the patriarch, and made known the revelation, just as it was shown to him. And then the lord patriarch went up into the lectern and commanded that the Lord's day be kept from evening until evening, and let he who did not keep the Lord's day be anathematized, and afterwards they began to keep the Lord's day, and abundance came upon the earth.
>
> *In diebus Georgii patris sanctissimi fuit magna plaga facta in Hierusalem super Christianos et Sarracenos et Iudaeos. Primo anno venit terraemotus a pascha usque in pentecosten, cotidie tribus vicibus, et ex ipso terraemotu fuit tribulatio magna. Secundo anno venit locusta et brucus innumerabilis multitudo, et comederunt omne foenum terrae et omnes cortices arborum et folia usque ad radices earum. Tertio anno venit mortalitas, ita ut per unam portam civitatis Hierusalem exierunt corpora hominum inter viros et mulieres et parvulos LXXXVI. Quarto anno fuerunt interfecti circa Hierusalem propter unam cucurbitam, de una parte LXXX, de alia vero parte LX hominum. Quinto vero anno fecerunt Sarraceni predas per villas et per monasteria, et*

predaverunt Iordanem et tria alia monasteria, et Sancto Saba monasterio C monachos plagaverunt, et XXVIII igne cremaverunt. Et ipso anno fuit siccitas magna, et pro ipsa siccitate coeperunt Iudei facere laetaniam et pluviam postulaverunt. Ut viderunt Sarraceni quod Iudei impetrare non potuerunt, coeperunt et ipsi eorum facere laetaniam, et venit grando et tempestas. Tertia autem vice fecerunt Christiani triduanum ieiunium, et misit illis deus pluviam. Post hec vidit unus servus dei per visionem angelum domini ad se venientem, qui dixit ei: Ista tribulatio et ista plaga venit super homines, eo quod diem dominicum non custodiunt. Deinde ipse servus dei venit ad Georgium patriarcham, et indicavit ei sicut revelatum illi fuerat, et tunc dominus patriarcha ascendit in ambonem, et iussit custodire diem dominicum a vespera usque ad vesperam, et qui non custodisset diem dominicum, anathematizaretur, et coeperunt postea observare diem dominicum, et venit habundantia super terram.[49]

This short story follows the same theological interpretation of history as the Letter from Heaven, only in reverse order. While the Letter threatens disasters and plagues as consequences for the failure to observe the Lord's Day, here similar disasters and plagues have already afflicted the inhabitants of Jerusalem and its surroundings because they have not observed the Lord's Day. Thus, *De plaga* presents an exemplary narrative in which good and bad times are interpreted as blessings or as curses (or divine punishments) for ignoring the Lord's Day. As in the Letter from Heaven, a three-day fasting and prayer prepared the divine relevation.[50] In addition, another motif is associated with this narrative, namely, a contest or quasi-theomachy among the religions of Judaism, Christianity, and Islam (Saracens), all three of which were (and are) practiced in Jerusalem and surrounding areas. Strikingly, the Saracens have a double, actually contradictory role here. On one hand, they cause part of the misery in the fifth year, in addition to the general drought; on the other hand, they appear at the beginning of the story as well as at the end of the competition, along with Christians and Jews, as merely a third religious group. This indicates that here a historical memory is combined with a theological interpretation, although this combination is not entirely free of contradictions.

The merit of Linder's study is his analysis of these historical backgrounds, especially the extraordinary events of the "Melon War" and the martyrdom of the monks of Sabas, which retain greater historicity in the narrative than the theological-hagiographic interpretation would initially suggest:[51]

49. Text from Linder, "*De Plaga*," 9–12. English translation: Angela Zielinski Kinney.

50. About the *triduum*, see p. 140.

51. See Linder, "*De Plaga*," 22–28, with the sources.

In 792/793 and 796 there was indeed a "watermelon war" between hostile Bedouin tribes, which began precisely as a conflict over watermelons and led to high death tolls.[52]

The *passio* of the martyrs of Sabas, *Passio XX monachorum Sabaitarum*, by Stephen the Younger[53] confirms a Muslim raid through the Jordan Valley that led to the destruction of towns and monasteries, affecting the well-known monasteries of Euthymios and Chariton, and to the martyrdom of the monks of Sabas on 19 March 797. The detail of the burning of eighteen monks is also reported. This *passio* also mentions epidemics and a great drought—which ended miraculously.

An earthquake is more difficult to determine; for the spring of 796 a strong earthquake is recorded for Crete, Alexandria, and Constantinople, but none for Jerusalem.

A plague of locusts is actually documented for 784.

Against this background, it is likely that the narrative *De Plaga que facta est in Hierusalem* is based on reports sent to the Latin West soon after the events themselves; moreover, four delegations between Jerusalem and the Carolingian court between 799 and 807 are known.[54] The patriarch George mentioned in the narrative replaced the patriarch Elias II in 797 and was himself replaced by Thomas in 807.

In addition to information from Linder should be added the support of the Latin Christians in Palestine by Charlemagne, which can be detected

52. Michel le Syrien, *Chronique* 12.3, ed. and trans. Jean-Baptiste Chabot (Paris, 1905), 3: 8.

53. BHG 1200; surviving in Cod. Paris. Coislin 303 and 309; in ASS Mart. III (1668), 2–14; and A. Papadopoulos-Kerameus, *Συλλογὴ παλαιστινῆς καὶ συριακῆς ἁγιολογίας*, Pravoslavnyj Palestinskij Sbornik XIX. 3 [= 57] (Petropoli: Venumdat C. Ricker, 1907), 1:1–41; Robert P. Blake, "Deux lacunes complées dans la Passio XX monachorum Sabaitarum," *AnBoll* 68 (1950): 32–37.

54. Linder, "*De Plaga*," 27. The Frankish imperial annals mention (ad a. 799/800, also for later dates) the various gifts he sent to holy sites in the East, and in 810 a capitulary is recorded about the sending of alms to Jerusalem for the restoration of various churches. In sum, Charlemagne had established intense diplomatic relations with the Abbasid Empire. Multiple delegations, gifts, and elephants were sent to Aachen confirming Charlemagne as patron of Christians in the East, and a symbolic presentation of the key was made (Einhard, *Vita Caroli* 16; 27 [MGH Ss rer. germ. 25, 19, and 31f. Holder-Egger]). See Klaus Bieberstein, "Der Gesandtenaustausch zwischen Karl dem Großen und Harun al-Raschid und seine Bedeutung für die Kirchen Jerusalems," *ZDPV* 109 (1993): 152–73; Michael Borgolte, *Der Gesandtenaustausch der Karolinger mit den Abbasiden und mit den Patriarchen von Jerusalem* (München: Arbeo Gesellschaft, 1976), and Anne Latowsky, "Foreign Embassies and Roman Universality in Einhard's Life of Charlemagne," *Florilegium* 22 (2005): 25–57.

through the *Commonitorium de casis die vel monasteriis* (808).[55] This highly interesting survey of the ecclesiastical structures in the Holy Land at the beginning of the ninth century was the basis for his financial support of the Latin Christians and pilgrims there. It is based on the procurement and transmission of information from the Holy Land to Charlemagne's court and thus illuminates the picture of the communication connections between the Frankish Empire and the eastern Mediterranean region. It was most likely Charlemagne himself who sent several *missi* to the Holy Land to investigate the situation of the churches in and around Jerusalem on the basis of a predetermined catalogue of questions. The emissaries returned via Rome to Charlemagne's court in 808, where two years later the information they had compiled served the emperor as a guide for decisions on financial support for the churches in the eastern Mediterranean. Against this background, intimate contact between East and West can be assumed, which could also have provided for the dissemination of the Letter from Heaven.[56]

Perhaps related to this is one reference in the discovery and transmission legend of the Letter from Heaven, namely, to Mont Saint Michele on Mount Garganus, a popular pilgrimage center on the Italian coast and starting point for voyages across the Mediterranean.[57] Such a place is easily suitable for the transfer or dissemination of such texts for those interested in religion. Moreover, in the Carolingian period, this place was developed as a major pilgrimage center. So, if there should be a historical core behind the mention in the itinerary of the Letter in Latin Recension I, this is another indication for the relevance of the eighth and ninth centuries in the dissemination of the Letter from Heaven.

This lively exchange between East and West certainly also made the dissemination of the Letter from Heaven possible. As already made plausible above, an early form of the short Latin Recension II may also have reached the Greek East and may have been the template for the version that has been developed into Greek Recension Alpha. Perhaps even an early (bilingual?) form that contained an opening similar to the finding narrative of Rome in the Greek recension Alpha was the starting point. But of course, this remains speculative and cannot be proven. In the meantime, however, the Letter from Heaven was expanded or recast into the longer Latin Recension I—and seems to have appeared in a similar form in the Greek East. Greek Recension Alpha 1 shows congruencies with

55. This text is presented and commented on by Michael McCormick, *Charlemagne's Survey of the Holy Land: Wealth, Personnel, and Buildings of a Mediterranean Church between Antiquity and the Middle Age*, Dumbarton Oaks Medieval Humanities (Washington, DC: Dumbarton Oaks Research Library and Collection, 2011).

56. See n. 54 above.

57. See p. 250f. with n. 25.

Latin Recension I. If one considers that according to the Syriac version, which is based on Greek Recension Alpha 1, a dating is provided[58] that fits here, then the development of Greek Recension Alpha 1 in this time frame is confirmed. The following table gives an overview of parallel elements of these two recensions:

Latin Recension I according to Vienna 1355	Greek Recension Alpha 1
Discovery legend Jerusalem—Rome (*sepulchrum sancto Petri et Pauli*) three days' prayer	**Discovery legend** Rome (at the temple of the holy apostle and chief leader Peter), three days' prayer
Too many activities on Lord's Day	"You do not observe the Lord's Day!"
Warning: The world perishes the world perishes, the judgment of the Lord comes over his entire people present	**Warning**: barbaric tribes, storms, frost, plagues, earthquakes, hailstorms, grasshoppers, worms, locusts "I decided to destroy all of mankind!"
Sunday: creation in six days; rest on Lord's Day	
call for penance last November you almost perished	
compassion because of intercession of Mary, archangel Michael, Peter, Paul	**compassion** because of intercession of Mary, angels, apostles, martyrs, John the Baptist
call for penance, amend your ways, e.g., helping **widows and orphans**	show compassion **widows and orphans** cry aloud
	pagans show compassion Jews (law of Moses) observe law
divine covenant: divine regulations, **baptism**, sacraments, Scripture: you did not follow nor believe it	Christians have gospel, law, **baptism**: you violate it
	Sunday and Friday: creation in six days, resurrection Friday: creation of Adam and Eve, crucifixion Sunday: visit of Abraham (Gen 18), Moses on Mount Sinai, annunciation to Mary, baptism of Christ, final judgment observe Friday and Sunday

(*Continued*)

58. Bittner: in the Syrian redaction, two letters claiming to be first/second or second/third, dated after the Seleucid era: (1) 1042 = 731 CE; (2) 1057 = 746 CE; (3) 1094 = 783 CE.

(*Continued*)

Threats (see Latin Recension II): diverse plagues	**Threats**: natural catastrophes, Ishmaelites
Observe Sunday from the ninth hour of the Sabbath until the morning of Monday.	Observe Sunday from the ninth hour of the Sabbath until dawn of the second day (= Monday).
Women: "Truly I say to you, if women collect vegetables on the Lord's Day, I will send over you feathered snakes that will mangle your breasts until you die. I say to you, if you do not observe the Lord's Day, children will be born who neither hear nor see nor walk and thus they die."	**Women**: "I will send poisonous beasts to eat the breasts of women who will not nurse the infants left without the milk of their own mothers, and wild wolves will snatch your children."
Give the tithe!	List of diverse sins woes against many sins (also against priests and monks)
no further letter	no further letter
clerics must announce this letter	clerics must announce this letter
	final announcement of bishop of Rome (see Latin Recension II)

Despite the fundamental differences between the Latin and Greek versions described above,[59] there is a similarity in content and structure here. A discovery legend is expanded and prefixed, albeit differently. The warning that the Lord's Day is being disregarded leads to the threat of disaster for all humankind. Once in the past, however, respite was granted due to the intercession of Mary and the saints. John the Baptist is a prominent figure within both versions. Through baptism, Christians have entered into a new covenant with God, which they must also keep, in addition to associated regulations such as observance of the Lord's Day.[60] Both versions have a separate passage on women,[61] and both exhort the clergy to read the letter. Criticism of its authenticity is repudiated; no further letter will follow. This synoptic view of the different Latin and Greek versions of the Letter from Heaven is therefore necessary and important, and deepens our knowledge about the history of the Letter from Heaven. Unfortunately, it has been neglected so far. This is all the more regrettable since a relationship between Greek Recension Alpha 2 and Latin Recension III can also be shown (see below).

In comparison to the short description of *De plaga* presented above, however, there are interesting differences. While in the Greek version the gentiles

59. See p. 87.

60. See below, p. 152, 248.

61. See below, p. 195–200.

and Hebrews can be used as a model for comparison (in the Latin, gentiles are encountered only as those who do not tithe), *De plaga* clearly demarcates the Christians from the Jews and Saracens. Although the Ishmaelites also appear in the Greek recensions of the Letter from Heaven as one of the plagues that sweeps across the land, using other peoples or religions as a model for argumentation seems to have been far from the author's mind.

Another difference is the duration of Sunday. While in the Letter from Heaven Sunday lasts from the evening before until the morning following, the narrative *De plaga* limits the Lord's Day to the period from evening to evening, which corresponds to the normal liturgical understanding (based on Lev 23:32).[62] Therefore, despite the identical theological approach, there might also be an indirect criticism embedded in the Letter—if the Greek Letter from Heaven was available to the author of the narrative *De plaga* in a version similar to the Greek Recension Alpha 1. This, indeed, is probably to be assumed, for here an interpretation of historical misfortunes as plagues, that is, divine punishments for a very specific sin (disregarding the Lord's Day), is clear.

This connection of divine punishments for disrespecting Sunday seems to have been widespread also in the Carolingian reign—perhaps also due to the very Letter from Heaven and such texts as *De plaga*. At a synod in Paris in 829, not only the longest canon on the Lord's Day is found (canon 50),[63] but also an echo of this thinking: it is reported almost as a fact that one could see farmworkers being struck by lightning on Sunday, and others suffering damage to their limbs or even burned with blazing fire. These are horrors demonstrating how God is offended by the disrespect of the Lord's Day.[64] So even though the Letter from Heaven was officially forbidden, this canon may belie

62. See below, p. 182f.

63. Synod of Paris 829, canon 50 (MGH Conc. 2.2 Concilia Aevi Karolini, 643.6–644.2 Werminghoff).

64. See Synod of Paris 829, canon 50 (MGH Conc. 2.2 Concilia Aevi Karolini, 643.23–28 Werminghoff): *Multi namque nostrorum visu, multi etiam quorundam relatu didicimus quosdam in hac die ruralia opera exercentes fulmine interemptos, quosdam artuum contractione multatos, quosdam etiam, visibili igne corporibus ossibusque simul sub momento absumptis, in cinerem de subito resolutis, poenaliter occubuisse. Et multa alia terribilia indicia extiterunt et hactenus existunt, quibus declaratur, quod Deus in tanti diei dehonoratione offendatur.* "In fact, many of us have seen with our own eyes, and many have learned from factual accounts, how some were doing land work on that day and were struck by lightning as punishment, how others were punished by crippling of the limbs, and still others were carried off and incinerated by blazing fire, skin and bones in an instant. Many other horrors existed and still exist today, showing how God is offended by the defilement of such a day." See the stories about the punishment miracles from the sixth century below, pp. 172–82.

its effect. Moreover, as in the Letter from Heaven, the gentiles and Jews are cited as positive examples for contrast: they adhere to their worship more consistently. The veneration of different days is a distinguishing mark of identity between gentiles, Jews, and Christians.

A further distribution of the Letter from Heaven, namely, to and within the Anglo-Saxon realm at the beginning of the ninth century, is likewise documented with an immediate condemnation. The Letter from Heaven elicited considerable criticism by Ecgred of Lindisfarne in a letter to Wulfsige of York from the 830s. Ecgred rejects the claim of a certain Pehtred that this Letter from Heaven, along with other heretical writings, is authentic and also criticizes the transfer of the Jewish Sabbath rest to Sunday. However, the history of the Letter from Heaven in Britain is beyond this study and has already been thoroughly analyzed by Dorothy Haines.[65]

While until now the transfer or the stimulus for the dissemination of the Letter from Heaven came predominantly from the Latin West, it is obviously the other way around with Latin Recension III. This is, namely, a transmission of the Greek Recension Alpha 2, which in turn is to be understood as a further development or new edition of the Letter from Heaven from Greek Recension Alpha 1. The following elements in Latin Recension III derive from the Greek tradition of the Letter from Heaven, following Alpha 2:

the exhortation to observe the other saints' days in addition to the Lord's Day (*festivitates sanctorum meorum*),
the injunction to observe Friday as well as the Lord's Day (*in die veneris letanias facientes ieiunando et orando*),
the biblical quotation from Matthew 24:35 (*celum et terra transibunt, verba autem mea non preteribunt vel non transibunt*),
the comparison with the Hebrews or with the law of Moses, which is to be observed.

65. Haines, *Sunday Observance*, with 39f. on Ecgred, and further references for Ireland (42). This was already the focus of Robert Priebsch (see above, p. 36f.); see also Dorothy Whitelock, "Bishop Ecgred, Pehtred and Niall," in *Ireland in Early Medieval Europe: Studies in Memory of Kathleen Hughes*, ed. Dorothy Whitelock, Rosamund McKitterick, and David N. Dumville (Cambridge: Cambridge University Press, 1982), 47–68; Jordan Zweck, *Epistolary Acts: Anglo-Saxon Letters and Early English Media* (Toronto: University of Toronto Press, 2018), 63–105. See also the relevant manuscript studies by Angela Zielinski Kinney, pp. 48–52.

Furthermore—despite all the differences—the legend of discovery includes an angel's cry, as well as the exclamation "Kyrie eleison." There is a comparable structure, even if rearrangements and extensions are recognizable; this is especially noteworthy because the manuscript tradition for Greek Recension Alpha 2 dates only from the fifteenth century, and therefore uncertainties in the tradition must be assumed. That these parallels can nevertheless be identified indicates a clear connection. And since with this recension, foreign elements appear in the Latin tradition, elements that are more likely to have been derived from the Greek tradition, this speaks for a transfer from East to West in this case. The table below compares four passages for illustration:

Latin Recension III (according to Codex Toulouse, Bibliothèque publique 208)[66]	**Greek Recension Alpha 2**[67]
Quia vidisti[s], **filii hominum,** quod prius mandavi vobis et **non credidistis,** et ideo quia increduli exstitistis omnes et **diem meum sanctum dominicum** non custodistis, **nec etiam de aliis peccatis vos (non) penituit,** que innumerabilia perpetrastis; nam **celum et terra(m) transibunt,** verba autem mea non preteribunt, vel non transibunt. [Matt 24:35] **Ego adimplevi vos frumento et vino,** et vos cum abstulistis ab oculis vestris propter peccata vestra et **diem meum sanctum dominicum non custodiendo. Quare mandavi super vos Saracenos et alias gentes que vestrum sanguinem [effuderunt]** et in captivitatem quamplures vestrum duxerunt, et **terremotus,** et **fames, bruscos** *(sic)*, **serpentes, locustas,** murices et omnia mala ostendi vobis **propter diem meum sanctum dominicum,** quem non custodistis. (Rivière 602.6-17)	2.1 Οὐκ οἴδατε, ὦ υἱοὶ τῶν ἀνθρώπων, ὅτι ἐγώ εἰμι ὁ ποιήσας τὸν οὐρανὸν καὶ τὴν γῆν καὶ ὑμᾶς πάντας. 2.2 Οὐκ οἴδατε τὴν πρώτην ἐπιστολήν, ἣν ἐπέστειλα πρὸς ὑμᾶς καὶ οὐκ ἐπιστεύσατε, ἵνα ἁγιάσω ὑμᾶς διὰ τὴν ἡμέραν τῆς ἁγίας κυριακῆς. 2.3 καὶ οὐκ ἀπέχετε τῶν πονηρῶν ὑμῶν πράξεων. 2.4 Καὶ οὐ νοεῖτε τὰ γεγραμμένα, ὅτι ὁ οὐρανὸς καὶ ἡ γῆ οὐ μὴ παρέλθωσι; 3.1 ἔδωκά σας καρπό, σῖτον, οἶνον καὶ ἔλαιον. 3.2 Καὶ διὰ τὴν ἀπιστίαν, τὴν ἔχετε εἰς τὴν ἁγίαν κυριακήν, ἀπέστειλα ὑμᾶς βαρβάρων ἐπιδρομὰς καὶ ἐξέχεαν τὸ αἷμα ὑμῶν καὶ οὐδὲ οὕτως ἐμετανοήσατε. 3.3 Σεισμοὺς καὶ λιμοὺς καὶ συμπτώματα (οὐκ) ὀλίγα ἐποιήσας ὑμᾶς. 3.4 ἀλλὰ καὶ σκότος καὶ χάλαζα, ἀκρίδας καὶ ἑρπετὰ ἀπέστειλα ὑμᾶς διὰ τὴν ἁγία μου κυριακὴν καὶ οὐ μὴ μετανοήσατε καὶ οὐκ ἐπιστρέψατε ἐκ τῶν πονηρῶν ὑμῶν πράξεων, ἀλλὰ πωρώθησαν αἱ καρδίαι ὑμῶν, τοῦ μὴ εἰσακοῦσαι τῆς φωνῆς μου.

(*Continued*)

66. Text from Rivière, "La Lettre du Christ," 602–5. See above, p. 36.
67. See below, p. 318.

(*Continued*)

Latin Recension III (according to Codex Toulouse, Bibliothèque publique 208)	Greek Recension Alpha 2
Proinde cogitavi **ut disperderem corpora vestra de terra, et tamen me penituit, non propter vos tamen, sed propter multitudinem angelorum meorum, qui ceciderunt sub pedibus meis, rogantes pro vobis, ut averterem iram meam a vobis, et sicut placatus misericordiam feci super vos, et vos, contra, malum operari non destitistis.**	3.5 Καὶ ἠβουλήθην ἀπολέσαι ὑμᾶς ἐκ τῆς γῆς καὶ πάλιν ἐμετεμελήθην, οὐ διὰ ὑμᾶς, ἀλλὰ τὰ πλήθη τῶν ἀγγέλων μου, οἵ προσέπεσαν ὑποπόδιον τῶν ποδῶν μου καὶ ἐδυσώπησαν ὑπὲρ ὑμῶν, τοῦ ἀποστρέψαι τὴν ὀργήν μου ἀφ' ὑμῶν· καὶ ἐλέησα ὑμᾶς· καὶ πάλιν εἰς τὸ χεῖρον προεκόψατε.
O miseri, ge[ni]mina viperarum, torpissime generatio prava et incredula, dedi legem in montem Sinai per Moysem, et tenuerunt diem sabbati, et non dimiserunt usque adhuc: vobis dedi baptismum meum per memetipsum, et non tenuistis, nec mandatis meis obedistis, nec diem sanctum dominicum, qui est resurrectio mea, observastis, neque festivitates sanctorum meorum honorastis. **Ideo iuro vobis** per desteram meam et brachium meum excelsum, **si vos non penituerit, et diem meum sanctum non observaveritis et etiam festivitatem sanctorum meorum,** mittere habeo super vos iram meam, bestias et lupos, ut manducent infantes vestros, et **faciam ut moriamini sub pedibus equorum <u>Saracinorum</u> et gladio barbarorum** propter sanctam resurrectionem meam, quam cotidie violatis. (Rivière 603.8-24)	4.1 Οὐαὶ ὑμᾶς, ἄθλιοι καὶ ἄφρονες· ὅτι τοὺς Ἑβραίους ἔδωκα ἔνταλμα ἐν τῷ ὄρει τῷ Σινὰ διὰ Μωσέως τῷ σαββάτῳ καὶ φυλάττουσιν καὶ οὐ παραβαίνουσιν. 4.2 ὑμεῖς δὲ διὰ τὸ βάπτισμά μου, ὃ ἔχετε, οὐκ ἐπιβλέπετε τὸν νόμον μου καὶ οὐκ ἐμνήσθητε μίαν ἐντολήν, ἵνα φυλάττετε τὴν ἁγίαν κυριακήν. 4.3 ὅτι ἐν αὐτῇ τῇ ἡμέρᾳ μέλλω κρῖναι ζῶντας καὶ νεκροὺς καὶ κατακαύσειν αὐτοὺς ὡς κονιορτὸν ὑπὸ ἅλωνος θερινῆς. 4.4 ἐγὼ λέγω ὑμᾶς· εἴ τις οὐ τιμᾷ τὴν ἁγίαν κυριακὴν καὶ τὰς λοιπάς μου ἑορτὰς καὶ τὰ γεγγραμμένα οὐ φυλάξετε, ἐξαποστελῶ τὸ Ἰσμαηλιτῶν γένος καὶ κακῷ θανάτῳ ἀποθανεῖτε διὰ τὴν ἁγίαν κυριακὴν καὶ τὰς λοιπάς μου ἑορτάς· μὰ τὸν βραχίονά μου τὸν ὑψηλὸν τὸν ἐπισκιάζοντα τὴν κεφαλήν μου τὴν ἄχραντον.

Latin Recension III (according to Codex Toulouse, Bibliothèque publique 208)	Greek Recension Alpha 2
Amen, amen dico vobis, quia si non custodieritis diem sanctum dominicum ab hora nona sabbati usque in diem lune luce clara coruscant[i] et sancti cumpatres et fratres qui ponunt manum in Christi crucem, sed non observantes; **et in die veneris letanias facientes ieiunando et orando, credite quia si ista et mea precepta [non] observaveritis, mittere habeo super vos lapides igneos et desuper aquam ferventem.** Cogitavi etiam in decimo die mensis Septembris, ut disperderem **desuper terram** omnes animas viventes, **sed per intercessionem matris mee et sanctorum cherubin** et seraphin, qui die ac nocte me **rogarent** *(sic)* **pro vobis** et non cessant, **vobis spatium y[n]dulsi et misericordia[m] feci vobis.**	10.1 ἀμὴν ἀμὴν λέγω ὑμῖν, ὅτι, (ἐὰν) οὐ φυλάξητε τὴν ἁγίαν κυριακὴν καὶ τὰς λοιπάς μου ἑορτάς, καὶ ἀπὸ ὥρας ἐννάτης τοῦ σαββάτου νὰ ἀφήνετε τὸ ἐργόχειρον ἕως τῆς δευτέρας ἐπιφαυσκούσης ἡλίου, καὶ τετράδας καὶ παρασκευὰς μετὰ νηστειῶν καὶ λιτανειῶν οὐ ποιῆτε, 10.2 ἀμὴν λέγω ὑμῖν, ἐὰν οὐ πιστεύσητε τὰ γεγραμμένα, βρέξω ἔχω λίθους πύρινους καὶ πῦρ καὶ χάλαζα, Ἰουνίῳ μηνί, καὶ ὕδωρ πικρὸν εἰς ὅλον τὸν κόσμον καὶ εἰς τὴν ἐνδεκάτην τοῦ Ὀκτωβρίου μηνός, ἵνα καὶ τοὺς ἀγροὺς ὑμῶν ἀφανίσω παντελῶς· 10.3 ἀλλὰ διὰ τὰ ἄχραντά μου Χερουβίμ, ὅπου ἐδυσώπησαν ὑπὲρ ὑμῶν, ἐμετεμελήθην καὶ ἐφύλαξα ὑμᾶς καὶ ἐγενόμην ἵλεως·
Nunc autem iuro vobis per sanctos angelos meos atque archangelos, si non custodieritis sanctum diem meum dominicum, perdam vos de terra, ut non fiat amplius de vobis memoria super terram. (Rivière 603.24–36)	10.4 καὶ πάλιν ὀμνύω εἰς ὑμᾶς κατὰ τὸν ἁγίων μου ἀγγέλων, ἐὰν μὴ φυλάξητε τὴν ἁγίαν κυριακήν, ἀποστρέψω ἔχω τὸ πρόσωπόν μου ἀφ' ὑμῶν 10.5 καὶ οὐ μὴ ἐλεήσω ὑμᾶς καὶ ποιήσω ἔχω τὸ φῶς σκότος, ἵνα καταφάγετε ἀλλήλους διὰ τὴν ἁγίαν μου κυριακήν· 10.6 καὶ ἀποστρέψω τὸ πρόσωπόν μου ἀφ' ὑμῶν καὶ γένηται κλαυθμὸς καὶ ὀδυρμὸς καὶ θρῆνος καὶ πῦρ καὶ συνοχὴ ἐθνῶν, καὶ οὐ μὴ ἐλεήσω ὑμᾶς.

(*Continued*)

(*Continued*)

Latin Recension III (according to Codex Toulouse, Bibliothèque publique 208)	**Greek Recension Alpha 2**
Et cum **lecta fuisset epistola** ab angelo, qui eam tenebat in manibus, **venit vox de celo dicens:**	7.1 Καὶ μετὰ τὸ ἀναγνωσθῆναι τὴν ἁγίαν ἐπιστολὴν φωνὴ ἐκ τοῦ οὐρανοῦ ἦλθε λέγουσα·
Credite, credite, impii et duro corde, creatorem vestrum, qui **istam epistolam** mandavit vobis; ad quem speratis fugere? Certe nullus se abscondere posset ante faciem meam. Tunc erexit se patriarcha cum omni clero suo et cum omni populo qui erant ibi. Et ait angelus: Audite, populi, et intelligite, quia vobis iuro per virtutem Domini nostri Ihesu Christi, et **per genitricem eius Mariam,** et per omnes choros angelorum, et per virtutes sanctorum, et per coronas martirum, quoniam **ista epistola non est de manu hominum scripta, sed a** summis celorum venit **de manu Domini nostri Ihesu Christi,** et qui non crediderit eam, **anathema sit,** et ira Dei veniat super eum, et pereat cum tota domo eius, et indulgentiam non habebit in vitam eternam; et qui eam scripserit et transmiserit, habebit vitam eternam. (Rivière 605.15-27)	πιστεύσατε τὴν ἁγίαν ἐπιστολὴν ταύτην· 7.2 καὶ ἐφοβήθημεν πάντες φόβον μέγαν. 7.3 Καὶ πάλιν λέγω ὑμῶν ὅτι μὰ τὴν μητέρα μου τὴν ἄχραντον καὶ τοὺς ἁγίους μου ἀποστόλους οὐκ ἐγράφη ἡ ἐπιστολὴ αὕτη παρὰ χειρὸς ἀνθρώπου, οὐδὲ πρόσταξις ἀνθρώπου ἐγένετο, ἀλλ᾽ ἔστι ὁλόγραφος ὑπὸ τοῦ ἀοράτου πατρός· 7.4 καὶ εἴ τις εὑρεθῇ φλύαρος, ὢν κακοῦργος ἢ θεομάχος, καὶ εἴπῃ ὅτι ἡ ἐπιστολὴ αὕτη οὐκ ἔστιν τοῦ κυρίου ἡμῶν Ἰησοῦ Χριστοῦ, ἀλλὰ προστασίαις ἀνθρώπου ἐγένετο, ὅτι οὗτος κληρονομήσει τὸ ἀνάθεμα εἰς τοὺς αἰῶνας ἀμήν. 8.1 ὁ δὲ ἀρχιεπίσκοπος Ῥώμης εἶπεν, ὅτι μὰ τὴν δύναμιν τοῦ θεοῦ καὶ τῶν ἁγίων ἀγγέλων καὶ τῆς κυρίας τοῦ κόσμου καὶ τῶν ἁγίων ἀποστόλων καὶ εἰς τοὺς στεφάνους τῶν ἁγίων μαρτύρων οὐκ ἐγράφη ἡ ἐπιστολὴ αὕτη ὑπὸ χειρὸς ἀνθρώπου, ἀλλ᾽ ἔστι ὁλόγραφος ὑπὸ τοῦ ἀοράτου πατρός· 8.2 καὶ εἴ τις οὐ μὴ πιστεύσῃ αὐτῇ καὶ πέμψῃ εἰς ἕτεραις ἐκκλησίας, ἡ ὀργὴ τοῦ θεοῦ ἔλθῃ ἐπ᾽ αὐτὸν καὶ ἐξολοθρευθείη ἐκ γῆς τὸ μνημόσυνον αὐτοῦ· 8.3 καὶ εἴ τις ἴδῃ τὴν ἐπιστολὴν ταύτην καὶ οὐ μὴ ἀντιγράψῃ αὐτήν, ἡ ὀργὴ τοῦ θεοῦ εἰς αὐτούς· 8.4 παρακαλῶ οὖν ὑμᾶς, ἀδελφοί μου, μηδεὶς ἀπιστήσῃ, ἀλλὰ ἐπιστρέψῃ· 8.5 εἴ τις δὲ παρακούσῃ, παραχρῆμα ἀπολεῖται. 8.6 ἀλλ᾽ ἐπακούσετε τοῦ κυρίου ἀληθῶς, ἵνα ἐξαλείψῃ ὁ θεὸς πᾶν ἁμάρτημα αὐτῶν, καὶ τύχητε ἐν ἡμέρᾳ κρίσεως.

The version of Latin Recension III according to the Toulouse manuscript is shorter than the other witnesses (see the overview above, p. 48); however, the extension seems to consist mostly of repetition. Indeed, Greek Recension Alpha 2 restarts after the celestial attestation as well. Therefore, there are analogies even beyond the material presented in the table above.

Unfortunately, it is difficult to determine when, where, and under what circumstances this further version of the Letter from Heaven was written. Perhaps it is also and already a reaction to the series of catastrophes reported in *De plaga* and thus originated around 800. The opening series of threats from the Latin Recension III could fit the eschatological and apocryphal concerns of this time period:[68]

> For this reason, I sent upon you the Saracens and other foreign peoples to spill your blood and lead very many of you into captivity; and earthquakes, and famine, locusts, serpents, mice, and everything evil I revealed to you because of my holy Lord's day, which you did not keep. In addition, I revealed hailstorms, flashes of lightning and serious illnesses, and many other evils because of your sins and the holy Lord's day; but you hardened your hearts, and you did not want to heed the voice of your redemption. For this reason, I sent upon you many tribulations and very horrible wild beasts, which devoured your sons. Then I gave you intense droughts, and then floods, so that the rivers went forth from their places and swallowed up the whole earth. Then I sent evil peoples against you to spill your blood, by taking many into captivity; I spread upon you many tribulations and much lamentation, and I made you eat dry wood on account of your iniquities and the holy Lord's day, which you did not keep as I admonished you: and therefore, you, faithless and unbelieving, are not mindful that the wrath of God is

68. Letter from Heaven according to Toulouse 208 (in Rivière, "La Lettre du Christ," 602.13–603.5): *Quare mandavi super vos Saracenos et alias gentes que vestrum sanguinem [effuderunt] et in captivitatem quamplures vestrum duxerunt, et terremotus, et fames, bruscos (sic), serpentes, locustas, murices et omnia mala ostendi vobis propter diem meum sanctum dominicum, quem non custodistis. Ostendi insuper vobis grandines, coruscationes et infirmitates validas et multa alia mala propter peccata vestra et diem sanctum dominicum; sed obdurastis corda vestra, et noluistis audire vocem redemptionis vestre. Propterea misi super vos multas tribulationes et fer(r)as pessimas, que devoraverunt filios vestros. Deinde dedi vobis siccitates validas, et iterum pluvias multas, ita ut flumina exirent de locis suis et totam terram obsorberent. Deinde misi super vos gentes malas, que vestrum sanguinem effuderunt, multos captivando; tribulationes et plorationes multas induxi super vos, et feci vos comedere lignum aridum propter iniquitates vestras et diem sanctum dominicum, quem non observastis, sicut vobis precepi: et ideo, perfidi et increduli, non memoramini quod ira Dei venit super vos propter iniquitates, quas fecistis super terram. Propterea cogitavi vos delere desuper terram propter incredulitatem vestram, et tamen vos noluistis intelligere verba mea sancta, sicut in euangelio locutus sum, quod celum et terra transibunt, verba autem mea non preteribunt vel non transibunt* [Matt 24:35]*; ideo verba et precepta mea mandavi vobis, etc., et tamen vos non creditis neque custoditis diem sanctum dominicum.* English translation by Angela Zielinski Kinney. The passage before and afterward is given in the table above.

> coming upon you because of the iniquities that you have committed upon the earth. For this reason I thought to destroy you from the face of the earth on account of your unbelief, and nevertheless you refused to understand my holy words, which I spoke in the gospel, that heaven and earth will pass away, but my words will not perish or pass away [Matt 24:35]; so I delivered to you my words and commandments, etc., and still you do not believe, nor do you keep the holy Lord's day.

This connection, however, remains speculative; later events (or even no specific events at all) could have prompted a new edition of the Letter from Heaven. The order to copy and distribute the letter invites this.

Meanwhile, in the eleventh century, under Bishop Joannicius, the Greek Recension Beta seems to have emerged or been in circulation. The discovery of the letter in Jerusalem, or more precisely in Bethlehem, is reported here, and if Angela Zielinski Kinney's reflections on Bishop Joannicius[69] are correct, this would provide further historical evidence for the history of the Letter from Heaven. Actually, it would be the first historical anchorage of the Letter from Heaven for the Greek East.

In addition, at the latest during the high Middle Ages,[70] perhaps as an effect of increased pilgrimage during the eleventh century,[71] or at the time of the Crusades, Latin Recension III circulated in the Latin West. This can be deduced from chronistic works of the period.

---

69. See on pp. 331–35.

70. The *Chronica sive chronographia universalis* of Sigebert of Gembloux report for the year 1033 about *celitus delatas litteras*, ed. Ludwig C. Bethmann, MGH, Scriptores in Folio [= SS] 6 (Hannover: Hahn, 1844), 300–374, here at 357.9), by which, however, the Letter from Heaven on Sunday is probably not meant, since the reference is to fasting on Saturday, as well as keeping the peace. The Crusader preacher Peter of Amiens, according to North German chronicles, also refers to a special Letter from Heaven, which, however, also had different content: Christians everywhere should set forth to drive the pagans out of Jerusalem. See *Annales Roselveldensis* ad a. 1096, ed. Georg H. Pertz, MGH SS 16 (Hannover: Hahn, 1859), 99–104, here at 101.43–46: *circumferens cartulam, quam de celo asserebat lapsam, quaque continebatur universam de cuntis mundi partibus christianitatem Iherusalem armis instructam migrare debere, indeque paganos propulsantem, eam cum finibus suis in perpetuum possidere*. Also mentioned in the *Annales Magdeburgenses* ad a. 1096 (ed. G. H. Pertz, MGH SS 16, 179); *Annalista Saxo* ad a. 1096 (ed. D. Georg Waitz and P. Kilon, MGH SS 6, 728f.); *Annales Disibodi* ad a. 1096 (ed. D. Georg Waitz, MGH SS 17, 16); Helmoldus, *Chronica Slavorum* ad a. 1096 (ed. Bernhard Schmeidler, MGH SrG 32, 59).

71. See also the suggested dating of the Greek Recension Beta during the middle of the eleventh century by Angela Zielinski Kinney, including references to the pilgrimage in those times, at pp. 333–35.

The chronicler Eckehard (d. after 1125), abbot of the monastery Aura near Bad Kissingen in Germany, wrote a chronicle (*Chronicon universale* ab o.c. ad a. 1116–1117), which he dedicated to the abbot Erkembert of Corvey in 1116/17 on the occasion of his upcoming pilgrimage to the Holy Land. This work contains in the form of an appendix under the title *Hierosolymita* a special report on the First Crusade to the Holy Land.[72] There he relates in chapter 36.4 that he came in contact with a Letter from Heaven:

> There has also come into our hands a copy of a certain letter, which we believe has already been disseminated throughout the whole world; it is reported that the archangel Gabriel brought that letter to this church from the person of our savior and through that [church] it was sent to all churches. Just as it raises many alarming, menacing threats for transgressors, so also are the typical consolations of divine clemency not denied to those who have changed their ways.

With this detail, Eckehard hoped to prove the sanctity of the city of Jerusalem and encourage pilgrimage to this holy city. Earlier, he had informed the reader about the heavenly fire that was lit every Holy Saturday.[73] The letter he mentions probably also fell into his hands in Jerusalem, though he wrote that it had spread all over the world. This could refer simply to the final passage of the letter, which calls for its dissemination. Of course, it can also be interpreted as an indication that someone—precisely who remains unclear—in Jerusalem knew about the Letter from Heaven, which is meant to have been found in Jerusalem according to Latin Recension I (also reported by Greek Recension Beta), and made use of this knowledge to demonstrate the sanctity of the city in situ. Perhaps, in fact, in Jerusalem these letters were read by clerics or monks or sold to pilgrims.

---

72. Ekkehardi Uraugiensis Abbatis, *Hierosolymita*, based on the recension by Waitz, with commentary and an appendix by Heinrich Hagemeyer (Tübingen: Franz Fues, 1877), 313–15: *Venit etiam in manus nostras, quod iam per totum orbem disseminatum credimus, exemplar cuiusdam epistolae, quam Gabrielem archangelum ex persona Salvatoris nostri ipsi aecclesiae et per illam omnibus aecclesiis missam referunt attulisse, quae sicut multos prevaricatoribus intentat minarum terrores, ita conversis solitas divinae clementiae non denegat consolationes.* English translation by Angela Zielinski Kinney. See also Priebsch, *Letter from Heaven*, 18.

73. This miraculously lit Easter fire on Holy Saturday has been liturgically celebrated since the time of Charlemagne and is described in many pilgrim accounts, even after the destruction and rebuilding of the Church of the Holy Sepulchre in the eleventh century. See Jürgen Krüger, *Die Grabeskirche zu Jerusalem. Geschichte—Gestalt—Bedeutung* (Regensburg: Schnell & Steiner, 2000), 150–53.

Unfortunately, nothing more is reported about the letter's contents. However, the reference to an archangel (Gabriel, not Michael) and the announcement of heavenly punishments or divine blessings could indeed indicate the Letter from Heaven. If so, it may have been a version of Latin Recension III, which begins exactly that way:

> The letter of our Lord Jesus Christ, which descended from heaven in marble tablets above the altar of Saint Peter in Jerusalem, and a brightness like unto lightning was being emitted from it. And an angel of the Lord was holding it in his hands, and all the people, as they saw him, fell down upon their faces from fear, and they were crying aloud, saying: "Kyrie, Kyrie, Kyrie,"[74]

Another brief statement in the thirteenth-century chronicle of the Benedictine monastery of St. Maxentius in Poitiers states for the year 1110 CE: *Epistolam ferunt descendisse in Jerusalem de caelo, de die Dominica et observatione eius* ("they report that a letter concerning the Lord's day and its observation has descended in Jerusalem").[75] The Letter from Heaven could indeed have been meant. In connection with the emerging manuscript transmission, which begins in the tenth and eleventh centuries, these two references from chronicles about the First Crusade and the time thereafter confirm another wave of distribution of the Letter from Heaven at the beginning of the high Middle Ages. Probably the composition or the redistribution of Greek Recension Alpha 2 and Latin Recension III can be united with this period. However, other, former versions may have circulated simultaneously as well. And, in addition, Greek Recension Beta also originated in the eleventh century, as mentioned already.

Latin Recension IIa of the Letter from Heaven may also have been written at this time. Here the conquest of Jerusalem during the Jewish War is recalled—perhaps this represents an updating of the letter on account of the Crusades or because of the conquest by the Seljuks. But this cannot be proved and thus remains speculative.

---

74. Rivière, "Lettre du Christ," 602.1–5: *Epistola Domini nostri Ihesu Christi descendens de celo super altare sancti Petri in Ierusalem in tabelis marmoreis, et lumen de ea egrediebatur sicut fulgur. Angelus autem Domini eam tenebat in manibus, et omnis populus cum videret eum, prae timore ceciderunt in facies suas, et clamantes dicebant: Kirie, Kirie, Kirie.* English translation by Angela Zielinski Kinney.

75. Jean Verdon, ed. and trans., *La chronique de Saint-Maixent (751–1140)*, Les Classiques de l'histoire de France au Moyen Âge 33 (Paris: Société d'édition es Belles Lettres, 1979). Old edition: Paul Marchegay and Emile Mabille, eds., *Chronicon Sancti-Maxentii Pictavensis, Chroniques des églises d'Anjou*, Société de l'histoire de France (Paris: Renouard, 1869), 349–433. English translation by Angela Zielinski Kinney.

> Why does this wicked and depraved people not remember that they dwell in the end times of this world, and how I ordered the kings of the Roman people to the city of Jerusalem, which was loved by me above all other cities? And I ordered them to lead on the holy day of Easter eleven times one hundred thousand into captivity, and they killed and struck down one hundred thousand from that city, because they scorned me and my teachers and they did not keep the Lord's day as I commanded them.[76]

Another recension of the Letter from Heaven of the high Middle Ages—according to Haines,[77] Latin Recension IIIa—can be connected with the work of the Cistercians. The chronicle of the history of England by Roger de Hoveden (†1201 CE)[78] states regarding one Eustachius, abbot of Flay/Fly (Cistercian,[79] Normandy; †1211 CE), that during a journey to England in 1201 he preached with the help of a heavenly mandate or Letter from Heaven and advocated Sunday sanctification (*praedicans in ea verbum Domini de civitate in civitatem, et de loco in locum, prohibuit ne quis forum rerum venalium in diebus Dominicus exerceret*). Roger even quotes the text in his chronicle, which allows the version of the Letter from Heaven to be verified; it is actually a variation of Latin Recension III (IIIa):

> The holy commandment concerning the Lord's day, which came down from heaven in Jerusalem, and was found above the altar of Saint Symeon, which is in Golgatha, where Christ was crucified for the sins of the world. And the Lord sent this letter, which was received above the altar of Saint Symeon, and for three days and three nights people beheld it and fell to the ground while praying to God for mercy. And after the third hour, the patriarch

76. Latin Recension IIa, from Haines, *Sunday Observance*, 209.50–55, according to the manuscript from Vienna, Dominikanerkloster 133 (102): *Quare non recordat gens prava et perversa quod moratur in ultimo tempore huius mundi quo iussi reges Romanorum Ierusalimam civitatem que mihi pre omnibus civitatibus dilectissima fuit quod deduxerunt in die pasce sancto undecies centum milia in captivitatem et centum milia occisa et prostrata de illa civitate eo quod spreverunt me et meos doctores et non custodierunt diem dominicum sicut precepi eis.* English translation by Angela Zielinski Kinney.

77. Haines, *Sunday Observance*, 52–54; Röhricht, 438–40; Delehaye, 161f.

78. Stubbs, *Chronica Magistri Rogeri de Houdene*, 167–69.

79. On the Cistercians in general, see Jörg Oberste, *Geschichte der christlichen Orden: Die Zisterzienser* (Stuttgart: Kohlhammer, 2014); Georg Mölich, Norbert Nußbaum, and Harald Wolter-von dem Knesebeck, eds., *Die Zisterzienser im Mittelalter* (Cologne: Böhlau, 2017). However, these studies mention neither the Letter from Heaven nor a special interest of the Cistercians in Sunday rest beyond Benedictine monastic tradition. There is still a need for research here to find out the connection of the Cistercians to the Letter from Heaven and Sunday worship.

stood up, and Akarias the archbishop, and they spread out the mitre, and they received the holy epistle of God: I, the Lord, who commanded you to keep the holy Lord's day, and you did not keep it, and you did not repent of your sins as I told you through my gospel: "Heaven and earth will pass away, but my words will not pass away." (Mark 13:31) And I also caused that you would be exhorted to penance for life, and you did not believe, and I sent pagan peoples upon you to spill your blood upon the earth, and yet you still did not believe, and because you did not keep the holy Lord's day, you had a famine for a few days; but I quickly gave you your fill, and later you did worse again. Again, I want no one to undertake any work, aside from that which is good, from the ninth hour of Saturday until the sun rises on Monday. But if anyone should do work, let him reform himself with penance, and if you do not obey this commandment, Amen I say to you and I swear by my seat and my throne and the cherubim, who guard my holy seat, that I will not command you anything by means of another letter, but I will open the heavens, and instead of rain I will send down upon you stones and wood and hot water during the nights, so that no one can prevent me from destroying all the wicked people. I say this to you: you will die because of the holy Lord's day and the other feast days of my saints, which you did not observe. I will send you beasts with the heads of lions, the hair of women, the tails of camels, and they will be so famished that they will devour your flesh, and you will wish to flee to the tomb of the dead and to hide yourselves for fear of the beasts; and I will take away the light of the sun from your eyes, and I will send upon you darkness, so that you do not see and that you kill each other, and I will take away my face from you, and I will not show you mercy. For I will burn up your bodies and the hearts of those who do not observe the holy Lord's day. Heed my voice, lest you perish upon the earth on account of the holy Lord's day. Withdraw from evil, and do penance for your wicked acts. But if you do not, you will perish like Sodom and Gomorrah. Now know that you have been saved through the prayers of my most holy mother, Mary, and of my holy angels, who pray each day for you. I gave you wheat and wine in abundance, and then you did not obey me. For widows and orphans cry out to you every day, but you show them no mercy. The pagans have mercy, but you do not. I will make the fruit-bearing trees dry up on account of your sins; rivers and springs will not give forth water. I gave you the law on Mount Sinai, and you did not keep it. For your benefit I was born in the world, and you failed to acknowledge my feast day. Wicked people, you did not keep the Sunday of my resurrection. I swear to you by my right hand, unless you keep the Lord's day and the feast days of my saints, I will send pagan nations to kill you. Yet you take up other matters, and about this you have no consideration. Because of this, I will send worse beasts upon you to devour the breasts of your women. I will curse those who have done anything evil on the Lord's day. I will curse those who act unjustly toward their brothers. I will curse those who judge wickedly the poor and the orphans whom the earth bears. But you abandon me and follow the leader of the current age. Heed my voice, and you will enjoy good compassion. But you do not leave off from evil works, nor from the works of the devil, since you commit perjury, adulteries; therefore, the nations will surround you and devour you like beasts.[80]

Mandatum sanctum Dominicae diei, quod de coelo venit in Jerusalem, et inventum est super altare Sancti Symeonis, quod est in Golgatha, ubi Christus crucifixus est pro peccatis mundi. Et mandavit Dominus hanc epistolam, quae apprehensa super altare Sancti Simeonis, quam per tres dies et tres noctes homines aspicientes corruerunt in terram, rogantes Dei misericordiam, et post horam tertiam erexit se patriarcha, et Akarias archiepiscopus, et expanderunt infulam, et sanctam acceperunt epistolam Dei: Ego Dominus, qui praecepi vobis, ut observaretis diem sanctum Dominicum, et non custodistis eum, et de peccatis vestris non poenituistis, sicut dixi per Evangelium meum: Coelum et terra transibunt, verba autem mea non transient. Feci autem praedicare vobis poenitentiam vitae, et non credidistis, et misi super vos paganos gentes, qui effuderunt sanguinem vestrum in terra, nec tamen credidistis, et quia sanctum diem Dominicum non custodistis, per paucos dies habuistis famem; sed cito dedi vobis saturitatem, et postea peius fecistis. Volo iterum, ut nemo ab hora nona Sabbati usque ad solem surgentem diei Lunae aliquid operetur, nisi quod bonum sit. Quod si quis fecerit, cum poenitentia emendet; et si huic mandato non obedieritis, Amen dico vobis, et iuro vobis per sedem Meam, et thronum Meum, et Cherubin qui custodiunt sanctam sedem Meam, quia non mandabo vobis aliquid per aliam epistolam: sed aperiam coelos, et pro pluviam pluam super vos lapides et ligna et aquam calidam per noctes, ut nemo praecavere possit, quin destruam omnes malos homines. Hoc dico vobis, Morte moriemini propter diem Dominicum sanctum, et alias festivitates sanctorum Meorum, quas non custodistis; mittam vobis bestias habentes capita leonum, capillos mulierum, caudas camelorum, et ita erunt famelicae quod carnes vestras devorabunt; et vos desiderabitis fugere ad sepulcrum mortuorum, et abscondere vos propter metum bestiarum; et tollam lumen solis ab oculis vestris, et mittam super vos tenebras, ut occidatis vos invicem non videntes; et auferam a vobis faciem Meam, et non faciam vobiscum misericordiam. Incendam enim corpora vestra, et corda illorum qui non custodiunt diem sanctum Dominicum. Audite vocem Meam, ne pereatis in terra propter diem Dominicum sanctum. Recedite a malo, et

80. English translation by Angela Zielinski Kinney.

poenitentiam agite de malis vestris. Quod si non feceritis, quasi Sodoma et Gomorra peribitis. Nunc scitote quod salvi estis per orationes sanctissimae Genitricis Meae Mariae, et sanctorum angelorum Meorum, qui orant pro vobis quotidie. Dedi vobis triticum et vinum abundanter, et inde non obedistis Mihi. Nam viduae et orphani clamant ad vos quotidie, quibus nullam facitis misericordiam. Pagani habent misericordiam, vos autem non habetis. Arbores, quae fructificant, siccari faciam pro peccatis; flumina et fontes non dabunt aquam. Dedi vobis legem in monte Synai, quam non custodistis. Dedi per Me legem, quam non observastis. Pro vobis natus fui in mundo, et festivitatem Meam nescivistis. Pravi homines diem Dominicum resurrectionis Meae non custodistis. Juro vobis per dextram Meam, nisi Dominicum diem et festivitates sanctorum Meorum custodieritis, mittam vobis paganos gentes, ut occidant vos. Tollitis tamen res alterius, et de hoc nullam considerationem habetis. Propter hoc mittam super vos bestias pejores, quae devorent mulierum vestrarum mamillas. Maledicam illis qui in die Dominica aliquid mali operati fuerint. Maledicam illis qui injuste agunt versus fratres suos. Maledicam illis qui male pauperes et orphanos judicant, quos terra portat. Me autem derelinquitis, et principem huius saeculi sequimini. Audite vocem Meam et hebebitis misericordiam bonam. Vos autem non cessatis ab operibus malis, nec ab operibus diaboli, quia facitis perjuria, adulteria, ideo circumdabunt vos gentes, et devorabunt ut bestiae.

Along with this special recension, however, Latin Recension III remains dominant in the late Middle Ages. It is of paramount importance for the movement of the Flagellants, who, with the help of the Letter from Heaven, called for repentance and announced impending doom. After the plague reached Europe in 1348, the so-called Flagellants not only publicly staged penance but also preached in public. In some places, they apparently also resorted to the Letter from Heaven, which allowed them to interpret the disaster of the plague religiously as God's punishment for immorality and disrespect of Sunday.[81] The following sources indicate this possibility:

81. Delehaye, "Note sur la légende," 162f.; Stübe, *Himmelsbrief*, 21f. See Jiroušková, *Die Visio Pauli*; Ingrid Würth, *Geißler in Thüringen: Die Entstehung einer spätmittelalterlichen Häresie* (Berlin: de Gruyter, 2012), 73-77; August Closs, "Himmelsbriefe: Beitrag zur Entwicklung der Sonntagsepistel," in *Festschrift für Wolfgang Stammler* (Berlin: Schmidt, 1953), 25–28. See Klaus Bergdolt, *Der schwarze Tod in Europa. Die große Pest und das Ende des Mittelalters* (München: C. H. Beck, 1994), 82–84; Frantisek Graus, *Pest —Geißler—Judenmorde. Das 14. Jahrhundert als Krisenzeit*, 2nd ed., Veröffentlichungen des Max-Planck-Instituts für Geschichte (Göttingen: Vandenhoeck & Ruprecht, 1988); Arthur Hübner, *Die deutschen Geißlerlieder. Studien zum geistlichen Volksliede des Mittelalters* (Berlin: de Gruyter, 1931).

A study on the *Historia Flagellantium* in Thuringia by Augustinus Stumpf from 1780 refers to a Letter from Heaven, which he knew from a manuscript in Erfurt and attributed to the Flagellants.[82] Since the Flagellants did not preach in Latin but in the vernacular, corresponding vernacular translations of the Letter from Heaven can be connected with this movement. An additional indication of this is given by the so-called *Chronicle of Fritsche Closener* about the city of Strasbourg; this work reports about the Flagellants there, that they had publicly read out such a letter. This letter is then even quoted in its entire length.[83] This is confirmed by the critique of Hugo of Reutlingen, who declares that the Letter from Heaven is a false document and full of ill-conceived doctrines, and the altar of St. Peter, on which the Letter from Heaven is to have descended, never existed in Jerusalem.[84]

---

82. Augustinus Stumpf, *Historia flagellantium praecipue in Thuringa, zum Druck gebracht 1835 von Henrico Augusto Erhard*, Neue Mitteilungen aus dem Gebiete historisch-antiquarischer Forschungen III (Halle: Thüringisch-Sächsischer Verein, 1835), with quotation of the letter at pp. 9–15 according to Codex H.96 from Erfurt with the beginning words: *Haec est Epistola Domini nostri Jhesu Christi descendens super altare Sancti Petri in Jerusalem scripta in tabulis marmoreis, et lumen de ipsa sicut fulgur erat. Angelus autem Domini tenebat eam in manibus, et omnis populus, cum videret eam, prae timore acciderunt super facies suas clamantes Kyrie eleyson.* This is obviously a version of Latin Recension III. See also the condemnation of this letter in the articuli against the Flagellants of Sundershausen (fifteenth century), at p. 32 in Stumpf.

83. *Fritsche (Friedrich) Closener's Chronik 1362*, in *Die Chroniken der Oberrheinischen Städte: Strassburg*, ed. Karl Hegel, Die Chroniken der deutschen Städte vom 14. bis ins 16. Jahrhundert, tom. 8 (Leipzig, 1870; repr., Göttingen, 1961), 1:3–151, here 111–16. The German prose version is also based on the Latin Recension III. See, however, Würth, *Geißler*, 73–77: she does not see a strong connection between the Flagellants and this letter. Her caution is justified insofar as not all Flagellants everywhere resorted to the Letter from Heaven; but a regional recourse to this letter can be clearly proven and may have given a boost to its spread. See, however, also above the considerations on the manuscript transmission, according to which the witnesses for the Letter from Heaven cannot be unambiguously connected with Flagellant property. The letter was more widespread than just in Flagellant circles, if only because of its antecedents.

84. Hugo of Reutlingen, *Chronica metrificata* (a chronicle that ends with a description of the Flagellants of 1349 CE). See Eberhard Stiefel, ed., "Hugo Spechtshart von Reutlingen. Die Lehrwerke," *Reutlinger Geschichtsblatter*, n.s. 24 (1985): 7-169, here 110–69; Würth, *Geißler*, 97. See also the hint at the Letter from Heaven in the passage about the Flagellants in Flandern and Brabant, in *Les Grandes Chroniques de France selon que elles sont conservees en l'eglise de Saint-Denis en France*, ed. M. Paulin Pari (Paris: Techener Libraire, 1837), 5:493f.; and in the *Corpus documentorum inquisitionis haereticae pravitatis Neerlandicae*, ed. Paul Fredericq (Gent and 's Gravenhage: Nijhoff, 1906), vol. 3, no. 71 at pp. 119f. the Letter from Heaven is mentioned (with a quotation that confirms that it is Latin Recension III), after the edict of Philip IV Valois against the Flagellants.

Interestingly, the Letter from Heaven is in some manuscripts transmitted together with the *Visio Pauli*, a text that was also used by the Flagellants.[85] Remarkably, however, this connection mainly concerns Latin Recension II. The two sources together, the secondary attestation in the chronicles and the manuscript tradition, confirm the late medieval interest (not only) of the Flagellants in the Letter from Heaven. During this time, also the vernacular transmission of the Letter from Heaven begins, but this is beyond the scope of the current study.

The Letter from Heaven thus left a clear trace in the Latin West. This looks different in the Byzantine Empire. Here only the Greek version itself and the Oriental and Slavic translations emanating from it testify to a dissemination and reception of the letter. There is no external reference to or comparable explicit criticism of the Letter from Heaven.[86] Perhaps the Letter from Heaven fell on more fertile ground in the West, since after a first regional wave in Spain and in the Merovingian Empire in the sixth century,[87] stricter Sunday legislation became standard, especially after the Carolingian reforms[88]—but there was also more explicit criticism of this alleged letter of Christ. In the East, the reception remained rather marginal, as comparable Sunday legislation was also lacking. Nevertheless, the texts included in this volume, which adds other texts to the Greek versions of the Letter from Heaven, show that the issue of Sunday sanctification apparently continued to arise and more radical positions were formulated from time to time. Also, of course, it must be taken into account that there were contacts between East and West, as explained above, and therefore not too much of a dividing line should be drawn. Likewise, for example, Latin people also lived in the East, especially in the Holy Land. The text *De plaga* has drawn attention to this exchange as well as the connections between Latin and Greek versions of the Letters to the Lord. Nevertheless, the cultural history of Sunday in the Greek East looks somewhat different from that in the West.

The starting point for the Byzantine development was, on the one hand, the imperial laws on Sunday, which articulated not only judicial peace but also the prohibition of tax collection and, around 400 CE, also prohibited amusements such as theater and chariot races on Sundays.[89] Compared to the *Codex Theodosianus*, however, Sunday plays only a minor role in the *Codex*

85. See on this pp. 66–68 and p. 423.

86. Only the mention of Bishop Johannicius may be historically relevant; see pp. 84–88, 95–104, 331–35.

87. See pp. 172–82.

88. See p. 102f.

89. See above, pp. 3, 19f., 168, with references.

Justinianus. As Mischa Meier stated recently: "The legislation of Justinian does not explicitly deal with Sunday, and only part of the Constantinian or post-Constantinian Sunday laws found their way into the *Codex Justinianus.*"[90] Only summarizing constitutions within the context of general feast days, not within the book on religious laws, are taken up. "The emperors in the East during the sixth century evidently showed no interest in Sunday."[91]

Only much later, around 900 CE, is a new legal development detectable. This is to be connected with the one verifiable imperial initiative of Emperor Leo VI (886–912 CE), who actually issued a new canon on Sunday (*Novel* 54).[92] Here one can read:

> A law was in force among the disciples of these distinguished men which directed that every kind of labor shall be suspended on the day of the Resurrection. There is, however, another which contradicts this, and provides that all persons shall not be prevented from working upon that day, but that some should be indulged in this respect; for it declares that judges, the inhabitants of cities, and all artisans should rest on this venerated day, but that persons residing in the country can freely engage in the cultivation of their fields, which exception is not founded upon reason.
>
> For although, in this instance, the pretext that the crops must be saved can be alleged, this excuse is of no weight, and indeed is futile, as when God gave us the fruits of the earth he intended that they should be preserved by the effect of the sun, to which, rather than to the industry of the cultivators of the soil, is due the abundance of the crops, and should be so attributed; and as the existence of a law of this kind dishonors the worship of the Lord, and is contrary to what was prescribed by those who, with the assistance of the Holy Spirit, obtained a victory over all their adversaries, We hereby decree, in accordance with the wishes of the Holy Spirit, as proclaimed by Jesus Christ and His Apostles, that, during the sacred day when our redemption is celebrated, everyone shall desist from labor, and neither farmers nor anyone else shall be allowed to perform any unlawful work. For if those who

90. Meier, "Christian Sunday," 251f.

91. Meier, "Christian Sunday," 252. Meier also points to Severus of Antioch, Romanus Melodus, John Lydus, and John Malalas, where Sunday does not form a discernible theme.

92. Pierre Noailles and Alphonse Dain, eds., *Les Novelles de Leon VI le Sage*, Nouvelle Collection de Textes et Documents (Paris: Les Belles Lettres, 1944), 205–9. See on Leon in general Theodora Antonopoulou, "Emperor Leo VI the Wise and the 'First Byzantine Humanism': On the Quest for Renovation and Cultural Sythesis," in *Autour du Premier humanisme byzantin & des Cinq études sur le xie siècle, quarante ans après Paul Lemerle*, ed. Bernard Flusin and Jean-Claude Cheynet, Traveaux et Memoires 21.2 (Paris: Sorbonne, 2017), 187–233.

> observed only the shadow and semblance of the laws had so much respect for the Sabbath as to strictly abstain from every kind of labor, how can those who are enlightened by divine grace, and cultivate the truth, fail to exhibit the same reverence for the one day out of seven which has been consecrated to the glory of God, and on which he has honored us, and delivered us from death? And when one day of the seven has been dedicated to Our Lord, does it not evince contempt for religion to refuse to be satisfied with working during the other days and not preserve this one sacred and inviolate for God, nor make a distinction between it and the others by using it for the same purpose?[93]

Leo appears here as a legislator who, like Constantine and Theodosius, legislated on the topic of Sunday and tightened the preceding regulations. The previously granted exceptions of harvest work are now declared excuses, since God as Creator will also take care of the harvest. A comparison with the Sabbath is also made, in contrast to which Sunday should be distinguished by an even greater veneration. Moreover, six days of the week should be enough for work.

The Letter from Heaven is not mentioned, neither positively nor negatively. Also, no violent punishments are announced for lawbreakers. Nevertheless, a new tendency is recognizable, one that is especially consistent with the other pseudepigraphal sermons included in this volume.[94] Of course, it remains difficult to judge where Leo took the impulse for this law—from a general tendency of the time? Or from texts such as the sermon of Eusebius of Alexandria? Or the circulating Letter from Heaven? Or was he even inspired by Carolingian Western legislation—even if this would of course not be explicitly addressed? However, after all, contacts with the West were restored after the end of Photius's schism.[95]

Of course, it is difficult to measure what effect or consequence this law had. In any case, the ecclesiastical canonical tradition does not address this rest from work but deals with questions concerning worship. Of relevance are some ecclesiastical canons that deal with Sunday and actually refer to kneeling as a posture of prayer and to fasting: both are forbidden on

93. Translation by S. P. Scott, https://tinyurl.com/2p9y5kr6.

94. See pp. 435–65. Baun, "Taboo or Gift?," is probably too courteous about this law.

95. Milton V. Anastos, *Aspects of the Mind of Byzantium: Political Theory, Theology, and Ecclesiastical Relations with the See of Rome*, Variorum Collected Studies Series 717 (Aldershot: Routledge, 2001), here no. VIII, his article "Constantinople and Rome: A Survey of the Relations between the Byzantine and the Roman Churches," esp. 39–44.

Sundays.[96] The later Byzantine legislation was also influenced by a larger collection of North African canons, translated into Greek, which in one canon (canon 64/61) also included the imperial prohibition of games.[97] Taken together, however, they confirm the impression that little attention

96. See Council of Nicaea (325 CE), canon 20 (Fonti IX.2.1.1, 41.11–17 Ioannou): Ἐπειδή τινές εἰσιν ἐν κυριακῇ γόνυ κλίνοντες καὶ ἐν ταῖς τῆς πεντηκοστῆς ἡμέραις, ὑπὲρ τοῦ πάντα ἐν πάσῃ παροικίᾳ ὁμοίως παραφυλάττεσθαι, ἑστῶτας ἔδοξε τῇ ἁγίᾳ συνόδῳ τὰς εὐχὰς ἀποδιδόναι τῷ κυρίῳ. "As there are some persons who kneel on the Lord's Day and during the days of Pentecost, because all things should be uniformly observed in every parish, it seems appropriate to the holy synod that prayer be given to God standing." Council of Gangra (fourth century), canon 18 (Lauchert, *Kanones*, 82): εἴ τις διὰ νομιζομένην ἄσκησιν ἐν τῇ κυριακῇ νηστεύοι, ἀνάθεμα ἔστω. "If someone, because he is of the opinion to live ascetically on the Lord's day is fasting (on this day), he should be condemned." Apostolic Canons (= Constitutiones Apostolorum 8.47, fourth century), §64 (SC 336:298.297–299 Metzger): Εἴ τις κληρικὸς εὑρεθῇ τὴν κυριακὴν ἡμέραν ἢ τὸ σάββατον νηστεύων πλὴν τοῦ ἑνὸς σαββάτου, καθαιρείσθω· ἐὰν δὲ λαϊκός, ἀφοριζέσθω. "If a cleric is found to fast on Sunday or Sabbath, except from one Sabbath, he should be deposed; a layperson should be condemned." Petrus of Alexandria (I.), *De paschate ad Tricentium* 15 (Fonti IX II.2 58 Ioannou): Τὴν γὰρ κυριακὴν χαρμοσύνης ἡμέραν ἄγομεν διὰ τὸν ἀναστάντα ἐν αὐτῇ, ἐν ᾗ οὐδὲ γόνατα κλίνειν παρειλήφαμεν. "Because we celebrate the day of the Lord as a day of joy because of the resurrection on this day, on which we do not kneel." Council of Trullo (691/2 CE), canon 55 (repeats Apostolic Canons §64) and canon 90 (repeats Nicaea 325, canon 20, with additional remarks; ACO ser. sec. 2.4, 56.11–21 Flogaus/Kraus/Ohme): Ταῖς κυριακαῖς μὴ γόνυ κλίνειν ἐκ τῶν θεοφόρων ἡμῶν πατέρων κανονικῶς παρελάβομεν, τὴν τοῦ Χριστοῦ τιμῶντες ἀνάστασιν. ὡς ἂν οὖν μὴ ἀγνοῶμεν τὸ σαφὲς τῆς ἐπὶ τοῦτο παρατηρήσεως, δῆλον τοῖς πιστοῖς καθιστῶμεν, ὥστε μετὰ τὴν ἐν τῷ σαββάτῳ ἑσπερινὴν τῶν ἱερωμένων πρὸς τὸ θυσιαστήριον εἴσοδον κατὰ τὸ κρατοῦν ἔθος μηδένα γόνυ κλίνειν μέχρι τῆς ἐφεξῆς κατὰ τὴν κυριακὴν ἑσπέρας· καθ' ἣν μετὰ τὴν ἐν τῷ λυχνικῷ εἴσοδον αὖθις τὰ γόνατα κάμπτοντες, οὕτω τὰς εὐχὰς κυρίῳ προσάγομεν· τῆς γὰρ τοῦ σωτῆρος ἡμῶν ἐγέρσεως πρόδρομον τὴν μετὰ τὸ σάββατον νύκτα παραλαμβάνοντες τῶν ὕμνων ἐντεῦθεν πνευματικῶς ἀπαρχόμεθα, εἰς φῶς ἐκ σκότους τὴν ἑορτὴν καταλήγοντες ὡς ἐν ὁλοκλήρῳ ἐντεῦθεν νυκτὶ καὶ ἡμέρᾳ πανηγυρίζειν ἡμᾶς τὴν ἀνάστασιν. "We have been taught canonically by our inspired fathers that in honour of Christ's resurrection we should not kneel on Sundays. Therefore, to provide clear knowledge of how this practice is to be observed, we inform the faithful that, according to the custom in force, after the entry into the sanctuary of the sacred ministers on Saturday evening no one is to genuflect until the following evening on the Sunday, when after the entry for the lighting of the lamps we again bend the knee and so offer the prayers to the Lord. For we consider Saturday night to be a forerunner of the resurrection of our Saviour and begin our spiritual hymnody then, while we complete the festival from darkness into light in such a way that we celebrate the resurrection for a whole night and day." Translation by Richard Price, *The Canons of the Quinisext Council (691/2)*, TTH 74 (Liverpool: University Press, 2020), 163.

97. Council of Carthage 419 (= *Causa Apiarii*), canon 64 (Greek) = canon 61 (Latin; see PL 67:202 [Dionysius Exiguus] and see Greek in PG 138:247f.): "In concern of the spectacles, that on Sunday and the other festvivals of the saints they should not at all be

has been paid to the issue. Sunday, as the Lord's Day, is, moreover, a feast day, a day of joy, on which Christ's resurrection is celebrated. The continuous theme remained fasting and kneeling as a posture of prayer.

The observation that Sunday was not such a central theme probably accounts for the research situation—there are hardly any studies on this topic from the field of Byzantine studies. However, perhaps the Greek Recension Beta itself gives a historical indication of a renewed circulation of the Letter from Heaven, since its finding legend is associated with a Bishop Iohannicius. Linking this name can be linked to a patriarch of Jerusalem from the eleventh century would provide a first historical date that points to a distribution of this recension in the period after the rebuilding of the Church of the Holy Sepulchre but before the Crusades. This would in turn strengthen the assumption that the preceding Greek Recension Alpha was actually distributed earlier, probably in the eighth and ninth centuries.[98]

In one essay, Jane Baun outlines the developments with reference to the Apocalypse of Anastasia.[99] Here she also refers to the Byzantine jurists of the twelfth century who comment on the canons mentioned above: John Zonaras (†1159 CE, canonist), Theodore Balsamon (†1195 CE, canonist and patriarch of Antioch), and Nicholas III Grammatikos (†1111 CE), who still show the same tendency as the late antique canons. This can be detected in their commentaries to these relevant canons.[100]

However, a few new accents can be seen here as well. One example will be introduced: besides his just-mentioned commentary on the ecclesiastical canons, Theodor Balsamon composed a work in the form of "question-and answer"

---

performed: That is yet truly necessary to demand that the spectacles of the theatrical games be forbidden on Sunday and the other festive days of the Christian faith, especially seeing that on the eighth day of holy Easter the people gather rather at the circus than at church. It behoves to transfer the appointed days of them [i.e., the spectacles], when it will happen, and it does not behove that anyone of the Christians is forced to the spectacles." Translation by Christoph Scheerer.

98. See the introduction to the Greek Recension Beta by Angela Zielinski Kinney, pp. 329–35.

99. Baun, "Taboo or Gift?," 45–56. The article by Maroula Perisandi, however, does not deal with the days of the week at all: "Entertainment in the Twelfth-Century Canonical Commentaries: Were Standards the Same for Byzantine Clerics and Laymen?," *Byzantine and Modern Greek Studies* 38 (2014): 185–200. On the Apocalypse of Anastasia, see pp. 497–503.

100. See the passages in PL 137:169–72; 308f.; 708f.; 744f.; 821–25; 1265f.; and PL 138:247–50; 516; 940. See Baun, "Taboo or Gift?," 47 with nn. 2–3. See on these canonists Wilfried Hartmann and Kenneth Pennington, eds., *The History of Byzantine and Eastern Canon Law to 1500*, History of Medieval Canon Law (Washington, DC: Catholic University of America Press, 2012), with 176–78 on Zonoras and 180–83 on John Balsamon.

literature,[101] *Responsa ad interrogationes canonicae Marci*. It was Mark of Alexandria (III, 1180-1209 CE) who posed these questions while staying at Constantinople, and provoked several queries on differences between Alexandrian and Constantinopolitanian ecclesiastical and liturgical practices and their differences. Here one of the sixty-four (sixty-six) questions, namely, question 51 (53), was posed by Mark of Alexandria about bathing[102] on Sunday: "Is it without danger on the day that bears the name of the Lord to go to the baths and to cleanse oneself with warm water, or not?"[103] Theodore's response begins with the general comment that it is necessary for Christians to abstain from work on Sundays. Interestingly, this is now directly justified with the *Novella* of Leo VI (καὶ οἱ θεῖοι Πατέρες ἐδίδαξεν καὶ ἡ νδ Νεαρὰ τοῦ βασιλέως κυρίου Λέοντος τοῦ Σοφοῦ δικαίως ἐθεσπεῴδητα), which is even quoted. He draws from this amendment the conclusion that going to the bath on Sunday is also forbidden, because then one is no longer occupied with spiritual things such as praying, singing hymns, and listening to the Word of God, but with waiting for the warm water.[104]

---

101. See on this genre Heinrich Dörries, "Eratapokriseis," *RAC* 6:342-70. See also p. 444.

102. In addition to other questions, related to Sunday, about sexual abstinence (questions 5, 10, 13, and 49).

103. Baun, "Taboo or Gift?," 48. Text in PG 138:997–1000, here 997: ἀκίνδυνόν ἐστι κατὰ τὴν κυριώνυμον ἡμέραν εἰς βαλανεῖον ἀπέρχεσθαι καὶ θερμοῖς λουτροῖς ἀπονίπτεσθαι ἢ οὔ; An English translation is presented by Patrick Demetrios Viscuso, *Guide for a Church under Islām: The Sixty-Six Canonical Questions Attributed to Theodōros Balsamōn. A Translation of the Ecumenical Patriarchate's Twelfth-Century Guidance to the Patriarchate of Alexandria* (Brookline, MA: Holy Cross Orthodox Press, 2014), 62 (question), 120f. (answer).

However, there are two versions of this *Responsiones*, one perhaps by John Kastamonites of Chalcedon (edition by M. Gedeon in *Ekklesiastike Aletheia* 35 [1915]: 169–89); see Viktor Grumel, "Les résponses canoniques à Marc d'Alexandrie: Leur caractère officiel, leur double rédaction," *Échos d'Orient* 38 (1939): 321–33, and Hartmann and Pennington, *History of Byzantine and Eastern Canon Law*, 201-2, however, without difference in this question.

104. Theodor Balsamon, *Responsio* 51 (53) (PG 138:1000; translation Viscuso, 121): "On account of which we also say that all the activity of merchants and indeed farmers cease, as is stated, and all of them are compelled to be occupied in the churches, and rather to glorify God on this day that bears the name of the Lord, in order, that on it we the faithful see the shining sun of righteousness. Therefore, the ones working in the baths' furnaces, waters, and the rest shall neither serve them not might any faithful man be deemed worthy of pardon when abstaining from prayer, standing away from the greatly praised worship and teachings of the Lord's day, and being devoted and occupied with warm waters, but he shall be corrected according to episcopal discretion through penances" (οὔτε οὖν οἱ τὰ τῶν βαλανείων προκαυστήρια, λουτήριά τε καὶ λοιπὰ ἐνεργοῦντες τούτοις ὑπερετήσουσιν, οὔτε τις πιστὸς συγγνώμης ἀξιωθείη· τῆς μὲν προσευχῆς ἀποσχόμενος καὶ τῶν πολυυμνήτων δοξολογιῶν καὶ διδασκαλιῶν τῆς κυριωνύμου ἀφιστάμενος, καὶ θερμοῖς ὕδασι προσανέχων καὶ ἀσχολούμενος· ἀλλὰ διὰ ἐπιτιμίων κατὰ τὴν ἐπισκοπικὴν διάκρισιν διορθωθήσεται).

So the answer draws a conclusion from the new novella of emperor Leo in relation to the attendance of the thermae. Visiting the baths was not generally forbidden but would stand in the way of a service, as one would be occupied with it too long. Interestingly, this canon confirms the assumption already formulated above that the thermal baths were in operation on Sundays.[105] On the other hand, this is a topic that does not occur in the Letter from Heaven and therefore could not have drawn its inspiration from there.

Against this background it can be summarized that the path of the Greek Letter from Heaven can only be grasped through its manuscript distribution. This also corresponds to the observation that the Letter from Heaven in its Greek versions tends to address far more general ethical issues and, for example, denounces misconduct by clerics, monks, and nuns.[106] Thus, as much as Sunday remains the central theme of the Letter from Heaven, the Greek Letter from Heaven bears a different character from the Latin one.[107] But here further research on the Oriental and also Slavic versions must be undertaken—a task beyond the scope of the present monograph.

105. See above, p. 20f.

106. See pp. 144–52.

107. See also the observations in the next chapter "Considerations".

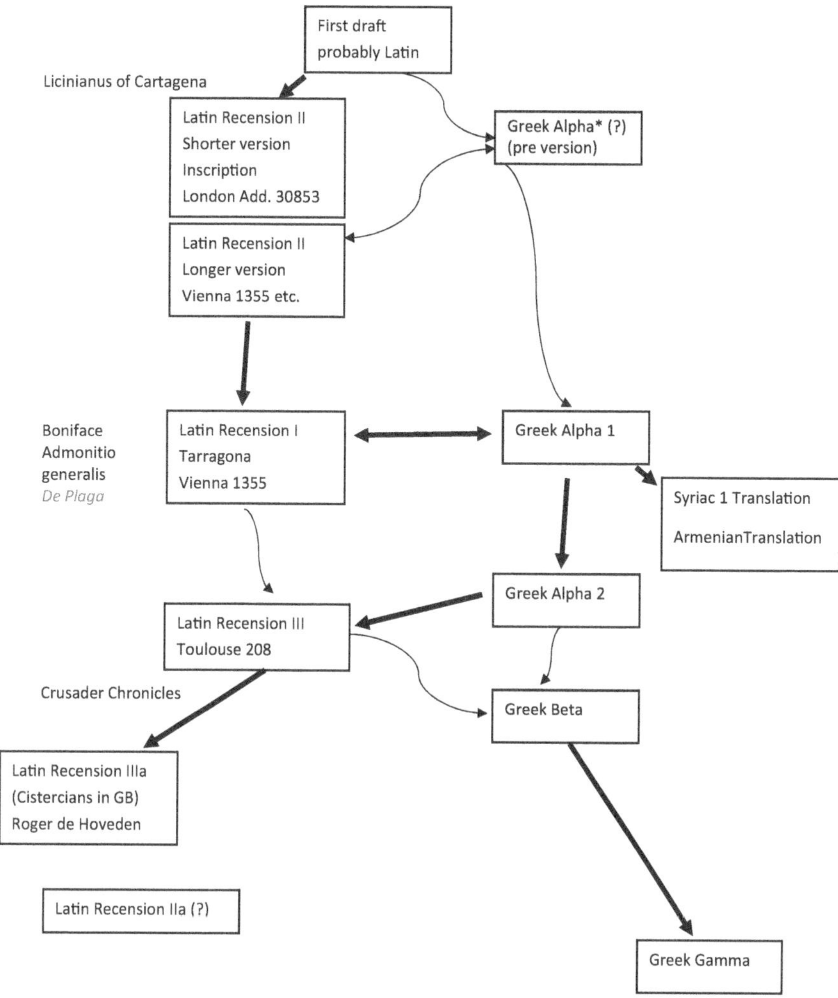

Figure 3.2. Overview of the stages of the Letter from Heaven.

4

CONSIDERATIONS

4.1. Framing, Structure, and Discovery Legends

Uta Heil

The versions of the Letter from Heaven differ in their respective framing narratives. These are paratexts, so to speak, to the actual Letter from Heaven. First, they report the discovery of the letter; second, they relate under which circumstances the letters were opened and read; third, they provide attestations of authenticity; and fourth, they order the reading and dissemination of the letter. In addition, some versions mention that such letters had been sent before, meaning that the letter in question was the second or even the third one. Furthermore, temporal details are also repeatedly given, either to the time when the letter was found or to the impending calamity. The following overview gives an impression of the various framings and some relevant structural elements:

Latin Recension II	Latin Recension I (mainly Vienna 1355)	Greek Recension Alpha 1 and 2	Greek Recension Beta (and London Add. 10073)
	Discovery of the letter in **Jerusalem,** Ephraim Gate, Priest Ichor / Achor / Eros		Discovery of the letter in **Jerusalem,** Bethlehem, hidden in a heavy stone 4 September (Beta); 12 September (Gamma) Bishop Johannicius
	Ermia / Erim / Armenia, Priest Talasius / Jora / Leopas		
	Ebrea, Priest Lebonius		
	Cappadocia, Priest Juras	letter sent to **Rome** to Peter's shrine (α1 quotes Matt 16:18f.), letter suspended above the altar Peter (α1: 1.5) or angel (α2: 1.3) appeared to the bishop of Rome (dream, voice)	
	Bethania, Priest Marchbeus		
	Garganus, Mont-Saint-Michel (C. Paris. 12270)		
[see the "Peter" below"]	**Rome**, tomb of Peter (and Paul), predestined place		
"In the name of our Lord, Jesus Christ: the letter begins about the Lord's day"	1.9 three days of preparation	α1: 1.7; α2: 1.4 three days of preparation	1.5 three days of preparation **1.5f. voice from heaven**
(first) Letter from Heaven	(third) Letter from Heaven	(first α1 / second α2) Letter from Heaven (see α2: 2.2; 4.6)	(first) Letter from Heaven

(*Continued*)

(*Continued*)

Latin Recension II	Latin Recension I (mainly Vienna 1355)	Greek Recension Alpha 1 and 2	Greek Recension Beta (and London Add. 10073)
	4.1; 7.6 letter is genuine, not suspect it 11.6 letter from the **seventh throne**, from the hand / word of God	**Christ swears** (α1: 6.1); **voice from heaven** (α2: 7.1.3f.): letter is genuine, from the Father	8.1 **voice from heaven** (Beta; London): Christ swears: letter is genuine, from the Father
	4.4 calamity almost occurred last November		
	8.6 two previous letters; this is the third letter	α2: 2.2 You did not acknowledge the first letter!	2.4 one previous letter
	11.1 no further letter	α1: 4.6; α2: 4.6 no further letter	3.1; 5.1 no further letter
7.3f. bishops should read the letter publicly, letter is genuine, from Jesus Christ	11.3 priests are to disseminate the letter	priests (α1: 7.1f.13f.), everyone (a2: 5.2; 8.2f.; 12.2, 6) should disseminate the letter. curse on reluctant priests (α1) / critics (α2) blessing for priests (α1) / disseminators (α2)	6.17 curse upon priests as critics of the letter 7.1 blessing for disseminators and listeners
			8.5f. buying and selling of letter (Beta and London)
	11.8 calamity next November	α1: 4.6 calamity in April α2: 10.2 calamity in June; October 11	3.1 calamity on April 5, and 3.2 calamity on June 14 (B)
8.1f. **Peter** (bishop of [?] Gaza, Nimes, Antioch, Cassiana) swears: letter from God, not from human hand, from the **seventh heaven from the throne of God**		**bishop of Rome** (α1: 9.1–4): appeal to observe the Lord's Day, then peace, but God's judgment threatens **bishop of Rome** (α2: 8.1–6; see 12.1–6): swears that the letter is genuine	8.4 Bishop Johannicius: appeal (London: with **voice from heaven**)

The reports of the discovery of the letters are legendary texts that can neither be confirmed by other sources nor evaluated historically. They are part of the legitimation of the Letter from Heaven and can be compared with frame tales, a popular literary genre of the medieval period that was widely adopted in both Eastern and Western cultures. Defined by Bonnie D. Irwin, a frame tale is "a fictional narrative composed primarily for the purpose of presenting other narratives."[1] From the beginning, the reading and dissemination of the Letter from Heaven was accompanied by criticism, which can be detected again and again in the Latin reception history as presented above; hence the writers resorted to these legendary materials all the more to demonstrate the authenticity and necessity of this new Letter from Heaven. These legends vary, so they stand at the crossroads between written and oral transmission—since the letter is to be transcribed and also read out in public.

This frame narrative also has the function of presenting the reader or listener an appropriate response to this Letter from Heaven. It demonstrates, with the help of the text's internal handling of this Letter from Heaven, how other, text-external recipients should behave: to humble themselves in the face of the heavenly exhortation in reverence to God and Christ, to change their behavior and to forward the letter.

While Latin Recension II of the Letter from Heaven does not offer a discovery legend at all (only an oath of authenticity at the end), the special feature of the smaller group of manuscripts, grouped as Latin Recension I, is a travelogue of the letter, so to speak, from Jerusalem via intermediate stations to Rome. A chain of priests pass the letter on. While the other versions of the Latin Recension I only inform about the places, Codex Vienna 1355 states that the letter was deposited in Jerusalem and a copy was sent on. The procedure thus corresponds to the desired dissemination of the letter, modeling what the letter itself urges its readers to do. Likewise, it gives the impression of an already wide distribution of the letter.

However, a special emphasis is recognizable at the last station, Rome. In Codex Paris 12270, it is said that the letter came to Rome by the will of God (*per voluntatem Dei*); in Codex Vienna 1355 it is formulated even more strongly: "This letter came through the will of our Lord Jesus Christ to the predestined place [*ad locum predestinatum*]." However, this sentence ends the travelogue of the letter somewhat abruptly. This reinsertion within the text shows that the stations between Jerusalem and Rome are variable but that the

1. Bonnie D. Irwin, "What's in a Frame? The Medieval Textualization of Traditional Storytelling," *Oral Tradition* 10 (1995): 27–53, here 28f. See also below, pp. 291–93. The *Visio Pauli* also offers such a comparable frame narrative with the finding legend in Paul's former house in Tarsus (in some versions); see p. 420.

destination of Rome is a fixed point in this recension. As stated already, in the other Latin Recension II, no location is mentioned, but interestingly, at the end, a testimony of authenticity is pronounced by a certain Peter—and this name is of course indirectly connected with Rome as well. Perhaps, then, an original "Peter version" of the Letter from Heaven was expanded with a stronger emphasis on Rome and then underwent a revision including a prelude to connect a finding story from Jerusalem to it.[2]

Rome is also the place where the letter was found according to Greek Recension Alpha. This recension is parallel to Latin Recension II, insofar as here (at the end, in Alpha 2 in the middle) the letter is commended to all Christians by means of a plea from the bishop of Rome. Interestingly, Greek Recension Alpha 1 offers the strongest "papal theology," with Peter and his successors addressed as the leaders of the church, quoting Matthew 16:18f.:

> 1.3 Epistle of our Lord, God, and Saviour Jesus Christ, sent to ancient Rome to the shrine of the holy apostle and first leader Peter, to whom Christ said, *"You are Peter, and on this rock I will build my church, and the gates of Hades will not prevail against it and I will give you the keys of the kingdom of heaven, and whatever you bind on earth will be bound in heaven, and whatever you loose on earth will be loosed in heaven"* [Matt 16:18f.]. 1.4 This epistle was suspended in the middle of the shrine at the sanctuary. 1.5 Peter, the great apostle of the Lord, appeared to the bishop of Rome in a dream saying, "Wake up, bishop, and behold the undefiled letter of our Lord Jesus Christ." 1.6 The archpriest woke up trembling and went to the altar, and seeing the undefiled letter in the middle of the shrine in the air, he cried out with tears: "Great are you, Lord, and so are your miraculous works that revealed this letter to the whole universe." (see Ps 85:10 LXX)[3]

---

2. See above on the history of the letter, pp. 68f., 94.

3. See the whole letter below, pp. 302–17. Since the fifth century, the Roman claim to primacy has been developed, and Leo I (440–461) played an especially decisive role in this. He created the foundations on which the confidence of the bishop of Rome as a *vicarius Petri* is built from then on. This is substantiated with this passage from Matthew and increasingly legally secured. On the importance of these verses from Matthew for claiming papal authority above and within the church, see Ferdinand Hahn, "Die Petrusverheißung Mt 16,18f. Eine exegetische Skizze," in *Das kirchliche Amt im NT*, ed. Karl Kertelge, WdF 189 (Darmstadt: Wissenschaft Buchgesellschaft, 1977), 543–63; Paul Hoffmann, "Der Petrus-Primat im Matthäusevangelium," in *Studien zur Frühgeschichte der Jesus-Bewegung*, SBAB 17 (Stuttgart: Katholisches Bibelwerk, 1994), 326–49. See, on Leo the Great, Susan Wessel, *Leo the Great and the Spiritual Rebuilding of a Universal Rome*, VCSup 93 (Leiden: Brill, 2008), here 285–321, and Bronwen Neil, *Leo the Great*, ECF (London: Routledge, 2009), and above, pp. 11–18, on some of Leo's letters of relevance here. On the development of papacy,

The bishop of Rome, who is here personally instructed by Peter to accept the letter, is seen as the central and universal authority for the church. Addressing a letter to him guarantees that it is relevant for all Christians and can be communicated to the whole church. These claims suggest that there are probably Latin or Roman conceptions behind this Greek version (possibly Alpha 1 and Latin Recension II have a common Latin antecedent; see above). In the transmitted version of Alpha 2, however, this papal theology is somewhat retracted: the letter is found in Rome, but it is an angel, not Peter, who appears to the bishop there, and the quotation from Matthew 16:18f. is missing.

The Greek Recensions Beta and Gamma offer a different localization. Here the letter is found in Jerusalem, more precisely in Bethlehem, and it is not a bishop of Rome but rather a bishop Johannicius who finds the letter,[4] and here even the date of September 4 (Beta) or September 12 (Gamma), a Wednesday, is given. A Wednesday is of course convenient, in that it is followed by three days of preparation with fasting and prayers before the letter can be opened, allowing enough time before the coming Sunday to prepare properly. Jerusalem was, as already said, also the starting point of the journey of the Letter from Heaven in Latin Recension I.

How the genesis of these different localizations can be explained historically remains speculative. It is conceivable, of course, that the itinerary of Latin Recension I seeks to connect both places that were associated with the Letter from Heaven, Rome and Jerusalem, to create one tradition from several. However, it is also possible that the itinerary of Latin Recension I was intended from the outset. It connects the location of the incarnation of Jesus Christ—where Christ now once again communicates to the people, this time through the Letter from Heaven—with the central episcopal see of the church in the Latin West. The composers of the Letter from Heaven thus expanded the stations to include the place that was central in Christian perception: Jerusalem. This is where Christ was born—this is where Christ's letter now comes to earth.[5] The sky above Jerusalem is, so to speak, open for divine

see Peter Gemeinhardt, "'Ecclesia Romana semper habuit primatum.' Die Entwicklung des päpstlichen Primats im ersten Jahrtausend," in *Papstamt—pro und contra. Geschichtliche Entwicklungen und ökumenische Perspektiven*, ed. Walter Fleischmann-Bisten, Bensheimer Hefte 97 (Göttingen: Vandenhoeck & Ruprecht, 2001), 9–38.

4. See, about the possibility that in this case a historical person can be identified, pp. 331–34. Therefore, the Letter from Heaven, so to speak, invites the local bishops, in this case Johannicius of Jerusalem, to "refind" and use this letter.

5. See also the connection of the finding legend in the Greek Recension Beta in a stone, which could then be opened, with the opened tomb of Christ, p. 336f.

messages. The fact that parallel to this (or in competition with it) a discovery narrative was fashioned for Jerusalem alone (in Greek Recensions Beta and Gamma) is therefore not surprising. Moreover, these two places, Jerusalem and Rome, were the most important pilgrimage centers for Christianity. Thus, the discovery legends of course plainly underscore the importance of the Letter from Heaven.

The origin of the letter is described in the Latin recensions as from the seventh throne or from the seventh heaven. The Greek recensions do not specify this so precisely, but they do incorporate, sometimes several times over, a voice from heaven that accompanies the act of reading the letter. Here it is also Christ personally who swears to the authenticity of the letter. In Latin Recension II, as well as in Greek Recension Alpha, it is the bishop of Rome who makes this oath, as already observed—thus in Greek Recension Alpha, we find both Christ and a bishop swearing to its authenticity.

It is interesting in this context that this very oath on the authenticity of the letter contradicts the injunction within that letter not to swear. The contradiction was probably quite clearly seen, such that in the Latin Recension I of Codex Paris. lat. 12270, where the injunction not to swear was expanded and extended, the attestation of authenticity is made without the word *swear*.[6]

All of the reports about the letter have in common a three-day preparation before the letter is to be read.[7] However, while in the Latin recensions the letter is easy to open and to read, in the Greek ones the sense of the miraculous is heightened. In Greek Recension Alpha, the letter hovers above the altar in Rome, and in the Beta and Gamma versions, the letter is hidden in a very small but exceedingly heavy stone that fell from the

6. Swearing authenticity of the letter in Latin Recensions II (Vienna 1355) 8.4; (Tarragona) 14.1; Greek Recensions Alpha 1, 4.4; 6.1; Alpha 2, 4.5; 7.3; 8.1; 10.4. Critique of swearing in Latin Recension I (Vienna 1355), 2.1; extended in Codex Paris. Lat. 12270 (200.54-60 Haines); see Matt 5:33-37.

7. Comparable to the *triduum sacrum*, the three days of preparation before Easter (see, however, on the pure evidence in this liturgical rite: Harald Buchinger, "Was There Ever a Liturgical Triduum in Antiquity?," *Ecclesia orans* 27 [2010]: 257-70]), and especially to the three days of *rogationes* introduced by bishop Mamertus in Gaul in the fifth century for three days before ascension of Christ; see also the Council of Orléans 511 on *rogationes*, canon 27. See Geoffrey S. Nathan, "The Rogation Ceremonies of Late Antique Gaul: Creation, Transmission, and the Role of the Bishop," *Classica et Mediaevalia* 49 (1998): 275-303. See already Paul in Acts 9:9–19. On biblical references, especially in the OT, see David Lambert, "Fasting as a Penitential Rite: A Biblical Phenomenon?," *HTR* 96 (2003): 477–512. *Rogationes* as a communally practiced penitential exercise with an attitude of humility is certainly the parallel here.

sky—apparently somewhere in the open field—and that no one was able to lift. Only after these three days of preparation did the letter fall from the sky or was it possible to lift and break the stone in which the letter was hidden.[8] These miracles, associated with an experience of divine threat and fear in the congregation, increase the importance of the letter and thereby serve as testimonies to its heavenly origin.

A special feature of this Letter from Heaven is the appeal for its dissemination. Either there is a direct appeal to send the letter or it is cast in a blessing and curse formula, which can affect both the senders and the addressees. It is mainly the clergy who are called on, but in the Greek recensions laypeople are also included. Thus, the Latin tradition is more clerical, so to speak, while in the Greek recensions, clerics are also criticized for failing to take care of the letter or the liturgy or the church. The Letter from Heaven is therefore an early form of a chain letter.[9] This command for dissemination is structurally similar to the so-called canon formula (as in Deut 4:2 and 13:1)—only this time the text is not to be kept unchanged (oddly enough) but is to be spread. It is, after all, an interesting phenomenon of tradition that the Letter from Heaven has come down to us in so many different versions that no text-critical edition can be produced. One would actually have to assume that a heavenly letter from Christ himself would be copied especially carefully so as not to make any mistakes, but the opposite is the case. The text itself is actually not treated with special reverence but creatively adapted to one's own needs. In this respect, the situation of transmission rather resembles that of a sermon. So there is actually a paradox: one could assert that a text personally sent from Christ needs no textual criticism at all, as this is necessary only to correct human transcription errors. What has been handed down, however, is an overgrown epistle that can only be presented in several versions.

---

8. See Speyer, *Bücherfunde in der Glaubenswerbung der Antike*, also with a chapter on "Bücher vom Himmel," including heavenly letters within stones/meteors (23-42). He also deals with books found in graves, under the earth, in temples, archives, and libraries. See the finding story of the Apocalypse of Paul / *Visio Pauli*, p. 420. Speyer (31) states (translated): "There can be no doubt that meteors contributed significantly to the creation and shaping of the religious concept of the Letter from Heaven. Their sudden fall startled people and made them inclined to see in them a revelation of God's will. The surface of the stone, moreover, might remind scribes of familiar letters."

9. See the literature in note 11, and also Andreas Rauchegger, "Himmelsbriefe und Kettengebete. Ein kulturwissenschaftlich-ethnologischer Beitrag zum Phänomen der magisch-religiösen Kettenbriefe," *Zobodat* 6 (2013): 245-55.

The Letter from Heaven thus combines three elements that are also encountered in other apocryphal texts: (1) a letter from Christ (see the correspondence between Jesus and Abgar[10]), (2) a letter from heaven,[11] and (3) a legend of discovery. All the stops are pulled out, so to speak, to authenticate the letter and prove its importance. The letter is found in a prominent place, induces a fear of God, can only be read after three days' repentance, and threatens disaster. Sacred places, sacred times, and sacred texts come together in this letter. This perhaps also explains the distribution despite all the criticism: even if someone had doubts about the authenticity, one did not dare to ignore the letter or throw it away.

10. ECCA 489; CANT 88; see https://tinyurl.com/5hc9bch3.

11. This is a common feature in antiquity: the Decalogue can be described as a letter from God (Exod 20; see 2 Kgs 22f.); the calling of the prophet Ezekiel happens through a heavenly letter that the prophet eats (Ezek 3:1–3); the Odes of Solomon are to be understood as a Letter from Heaven, in the Apocalypse of John 10:1–11 the prophet eats a heavenly book handed over by the angel; also the epistles in chapters 2 and 3 are to be read as heavenly letters; the Shepherd of Hermas (visio 2) also knows a Letter from Heaven; the Jewish-Christian group of the Elkasaites invoked a Letter from Heaven (see Eusebius, *Hist. eccl.* 6.38; Hippolytus, *Philosophumena* 9.13). For further examples from Pausanias to Aelius Aristides, Epicurus, Lucian of Samosata, and the Qur'an, also the Jewish tradition in the book Sohar (Adam already received a book from heaven), see already Stübe, *Himmelsbrief*, 31–41; Weinreich, "Antike Himmelsbriefe"; Dietrich, "Himmelsbriefe."

4.2. Rest or Work

Uta Heil

The central theme of the Letter from Heaven is Sunday rest. This aspect, however, should not be treated in isolation, considering only the Letter from Heaven, but together with the other texts of this volume as well. As demonstrated in the introduction, observing rest from work on Sunday gained importance only in the course of time. And it has already been pointed out that this rest was apparently neither self-evident nor uniform. It is precisely here that the apocryphal texts of this book intervene and plead with greater emphasis for the observance of Sunday rest—not, however, with recourse to Constantine's imperial Sunday law but rather based on the Jewish Sabbath.

The Christian interpretation of the Sabbath is a very broad field. One reason lies in the several different biblical passages on the Sabbath, whose interpretation and reception could be addressed.[1] In addition, there were different attitudes toward the Sabbath itself within the Christian communities. As is known, in some places the Sabbath continued to be observed. Here, therefore, Sunday joined the Sabbath as a new, additional feast day—both days were

1. There is not only the Sabbath commandment in the Decalogue in its two versions, already each with its own justification, but also Sabbath commandments in the various collections of laws. The oldest are probably from the so-called Book of the Covenant (Exod 23:12) and the so-called private law of Yahweh (Exod 34:21). Furthermore, there are the famous passages from the prophetic books, such as Hosea (Hos 2:13), Amos (Amos 8:5), and Isaiah (Isa 1:13), which criticize Sabbath practice. From exilic and postexilic times then probably come the more stringent Sabbath laws in the so-called Priestly Source (Exod 35:2f.; 31:13–17; Decalogue version Exod 20:8–11; Exod 16:5, 29 manna narrative; Gen 2:1–3), which even threaten to impose the death penalty, and the law in Lev 16–26 (Lev 19:3, 30; 23:7f., 21, 25, 35f.; 24:8f.), which, in addition to the prohibition of work, prescribes an assembly and the exhortation to keep the Sabbath, picked up in Jer 17:17–29. This postexilic tightening is also reflected in the account of Nehemiah (Neh 9:14; 10:32; 13:15–22), who ordered the city gates of Jerusalem to be closed during the Sabbath. In addition, there are the psalm headings that designate some psalms for the Sabbath day (Ps 37; 91), the day after the Sabbath (Ps 23), the day before the Sabbath (Ps 92), the second day after the Sabbath (Ps 47), and the fourth day after the Sabbath (Ps 93; see also Ps 6 and Ps 11 about the "eighth"). Last but not least, of course, the NT discussions about the Sabbath from the Gospels are relevant (Mark 2:23–28 plucking heads of grain on the Sabbath; Mark 3:1–5 healing on the Sabbath; Matt 12:11f.; Luke 14:5; 13:15f. saving animals on the Sabbath; John 7:22f. circumcision on the Sabbath; Matt 12:5–7 priests in the temple breaking the Sabbath; Matt 12:8; Mark 2:28; Luke 6:5 "the Son of Man is Lord over the Sabbath"). On Jewish evidence and history, see the recent work by Lutz Doering, "Sabbat"; see also Bultrighini and Stern, "Seven-Day-Week," 10-79, esp. 11-18, for the seven-day week as rhythm of time.

solemnly celebrated.[2] In other texts, the Sabbath was explicitly rejected as a relevant day of rest for Christians (see the Epistle of Barnabas; Justin Martyr).[3] Other texts show a purely spiritual exegesis of the Sabbath commandment.[4] Therefore, the discussion about the Sabbath was also part of the growing separation of Christianity from Judaism and further development of anti-Jewish sentiment within Christianity. In the following, however, the question is not whether Christians kept the Jewish Sabbath, or, if they did, how they kept it, but rather which conceptions of rest on the Lord's Day the texts developed and how the Jewish Sabbath was transferred to the Christian Sunday.[5] Unfortunately, anti-Jewish attitudes associated with this topic can be found even in recent research literature, which likes to speak sweepingly of a Sabbatization of Sunday and describes this "judaizing tendency" as an erroneous development toward legalization or casuistry. Apart from whether this general judgment is accurate at all, such resentments would be better overcome by more recent research.[6]

To place the Letter from Heaven in the context of other relevant texts, I will present the texts from the Greek region first. I will supplement this with a discussion of the thesis that the *Commentary on the Psalms* by Eusebius of Caesarea played a proactive role here. Subsequently, I will present the traditions of the Latin Letter from Heaven. Furthermore, I will address specific aspects individually: judicial recess, good deeds on the Lord's Day, prohibition of work, and punitive miracles.

4.2.1. The Sabbath Commandment in the Greek Sunday Apocrypha

What is known today as the sixteenth "sermon" of Pseudo-Eusebius of Alexandria—however, better titled as a Question and Answer about Sunday[7]—

---

2. See Rouwhorst, "Reception of the Jewish Sabbath"; see also Bauckham, "Sabbath and Sunday in the Post-apostolic Church," esp. 255–69. See also the quotation from Gregory the Great above, p. 22f.

3. See on this Stemberger, "Sabbath or Sunday." See also p. 3, n. 3.

4. See Rakotoniaina, "Redefining the Sabbath Rest," 113–41. See also below on Eusebius of Caesarea, p. 153.

5. See also the analysis above by Angela Zielinski Kinney about the transmission of the Letter from Heaven within the context of other anti-Jewish literature, pp. 59–64.

6. See the critical remarks in Rouwhorst, "Reception of the Jewish Sabbath," esp. 226–36. The emergence of Christian anti-Judaism and hatred of Jews cannot be discussed in detail here; see Peter Schäfer, *Kurze Geschichte des Antisemitismus* (München: Beck, 2020); David Nirenberg, *Anti-Judaism: The Western Tradition* (New York: Norton, 2013), both including chapters on Christianity in late antiquity.

7. See p. 27 and p. 444.

has the Lord's Day as its sole theme. The catalyst is a conversation after a Sunday service in which a certain Alexander asks Eusebius: "I beg you, my Lord, why is it necessary to keep the day of the Lord and not to work? And what kind of gain do we have, if we do not work?"[8] The author builds the answer to this question on the biblical quotation from the words of the Lord's Supper (Matt 26:26): Sunday is the day of remembrance of the Lord and the day of forgiveness of sins. Sunday has long been known as the beginning of creation and the week, but since Christ it has been above all the day of resurrection. Thus the question of the interlocutor Alexander about the reward for resting gives the preacher Eusebius an opportunity to transform the earthly reward (which is lost in the case of a day of rest) into a heavenly reward—that is, the possible forgiveness of sins if one attends church in memory of Christ's resurrection.[9] So even if no tangible reward, such as money or payment in kind, can be earned on the Lord's Day because of the commandment to rest, nevertheless, by attending church and praying, one obtains a spiritual reward: reconciliation with God. Eusebius states:

> Well, seven days has the week, God gave us six days to work and he gave us one for prayer, rest, and deliverance from evil and that we may make atonement for them before God on the day of the Lord, if we did sinful actions during the six days. . . . We keep the day of the Lord only to stay away from work and to have opportunity to pray. But if you stay away from work and do not go to church, you gain nothing. . . . Do not transgress the commandment of the Lord, do not steal his day, do not deprive your slaves and your hired labourers from their rest, do not get separated from the prayer, do not stay away from the church![10]

8. Question and Answer about Sunday (formerly Eusebius of Alexandria, *Homily* 16; PG 86:416A; see below, p. 448f.): Δέομαί σου, κύριέ μου, τίνος ἕνεκεν ἡμῖν ἐστιν ἀναγκαῖον φυλάττειν τὴν κυριακήν, καὶ μὴ ἐργάζεσθαι, καὶ ποῖον κέρδος ἔχομεν μὴ ἐργαζόμενοι;

9. Interestingly, the text mentions here (see PG 86:416D–417A) the duration of the service of about one hour, a rare time specification! The context is to exhort the congregation not to leave the service prematurely. If they did, they would act like Judas, who got up from the Lord's Supper and then betrayed Jesus. Christians who leave the service prematurely are equated with Judas, into whom Satan fell, and who thus sin even more and deprive themselves of the chance of forgiveness of sins. See also pp. 299, 362, 450, 464, 492.

10. Question and Answer about Sunday 2 (see PG 86:416C): Ἑπτὰ τοίνυν ἡμέρας ἡ ἑβδομὰς ἔχουσα, τὰς ἓξ δέδωκεν ἡμῖν ὁ Θεός, ἐργάζεσθαι, καὶ τὴν μίαν δέδωκεν ἡμῖν, εἰς εὐχὴν καὶ ἀνάπαυσιν, καὶ λύσιν κακῶν, καὶ ἵνα, εἴτε ἐν ταῖς ἓξ ἡμέραις ἁμαρτήματα πεποιήκαμεν, ὑπὲρ τούτων ἐν τῇ τῆς Κυριακῆς ἡμέρᾳ τῷ Θεῷ ἐξιλασκώμεθα. . . . 3 (see 417A) Δι' οὐδὲν δ' ἕτερον φυλάττομεν τὴν ἡμέραν τῆς κυριακῆς, ἀλλ' ἵνα τοῦ ἔργου ἀπεχόμεθα, καὶ τῇ εὐχῇ σχολάσωμεν· εἰ δὲ τοῦ ἔργου ἀπέχεις, εἰς τὴν ἐκκλησίαν δὲ οὐκ

The argument is based on an axiomatic transfer of the Sabbath commandment to the Lord's Day, which is justified exegetically in the final part of the sermon. Namely, Eusebius states, it is true that God gave the law to Moses and commanded the Hebrews to observe a rest from all work on the Sabbath. But since they broke the law, Christ issued a new law and introduced a new day as a day of rest, that is, the first day on which he began to create heaven and earth: the Lord's Day. So, on the one hand, the author argues with the Sabbath commandment of the Decalogue from Exodus 20:12, where the Sabbath is also justified by the creation week described in Genesis 1, but now he does not refer the Sabbath to the seventh day but as the first day, the beginning of creation. On the other hand, with Christ as the new lawgiver, so to speak, the old law is declared abolished and a new one is enacted—a "supersessionist"[11] argument. Indeed, the version of the sermon according to the Codex Parisinus graecus 1468, folio 232r, reads thus:

> On the seventh day rest was given to man. Therefore, when God gave the law to Moses, he commanded the Hebrews to rest on the Sabbath day, for on that very day God rested from all his works. Thus, he also commanded them to cease from their work and to take a rest. But because they angered him and did not persevere in his commandments, he swore to them through the prophet, "They shall not enter into my rest!" [Ps 95:11; Heb 4:3]. For the Sabbath he called rest. Now when the Lord came to the earth, born of the holy virgin, he renewed the whole law, since he was also the lawgiver. Because he saw that the law was hard and that no one could keep it, he cast out the law and introduced grace, giving us all things new according to the testimony of the apostle: "If anyone is in Christ, he is a new creature; old things have passed away; behold, all things have become new" [2 Cor 5:17]. Now that all things were made new, he also had to abolish the law of the Sabbath and establish another day for us instead. Thus, for rest and worship he gave us the first day on which he began to create the world, calling it the Lord's Day.[12]

εἰσέρχῃ, οὐδὲν ἐκέρδανας. . . . (remarks are inserted [417-20] that on Sundays one should refrain from sinful activities such as dancing, music and theatre, litigating, fighting and insulting each other) . . . 5 (see 421A) μὴ παρέλθῃς τὴν ἐντολὴν τοῦ κυρίου, μὴ κλέψῃς τὴν ἡμέραν αὐτοῦ, μὴ ἀποστερήσῃς τοῖς δούλοις, καὶ τοῖς μισθίοις σου τὴν ἀνάπαυσιν, μὴ χωρισθῇς τῆς εὐχῆς, μὴ ἀποστῇς τῆς ἐκκλησίας. On the text, see pp. 448–59 below.

11. This means the idea that the church has taken the place of the Jewish people as the people of God, and God's former covenant with Israel is now discarded or discontinued. R. Kendall Soulen, "Supersessionism," in *Encyclopedia of Jewish-Christian Relations Online*, ed. Kathy Ehrensperger (Berlin: de Gruyter, 2020).

12. Question and Answer about Sunday, according to Codex Parisinus gr. 1468, fol. 232r (Version B5, transcribed by Annette von Stockhausen): τῇ δὲ ἑβδομῇ ἡμέρᾳ ἀνάπαυσις ἐδόθη τοῖς ἀνθρώποις· ὅτε οὖν ἐδίδου ὁ θεὸς τὸν νόμον τῷ Μωυσῇ· προσέταξεν

With the new covenant or law, therefore, also another day for rest and worship and prayer (πρὸς τὸ οὖν ἀναπαύεσθαι καὶ εὔχεσθαι) was introduced as a distinguishing feature.

This is similarly expressed in the homily "Hear, All Brothers Christians, What the Prophet Says" (Ps.-Chrysostom, CPG 4848): Christ fulfilled the old covenant and established a new covenant, to which belongs a new day, the Lord's Day, in place of the Sabbath.[13] Only in contrast to the previous text, the new day of worship is justified by the coming of Jesus as a sign of the new law, without accusing Israel or the Jews as transgressors of the law. The benefits of observing and worshipping the Lord's Day are manifested in a long series of divine blessings (ὁ τιμῶν τὴν ἁγίαν κυριακήν [15x]), followed by a series of disadvantages for those who ignore the Lord's Day (ὁ μὴ τιμῶν τὴν ἁγίαν κυριακήν [21x]). The commandment to rest on Sundays is then even reinforced with a quotation said to be from the epistle of the apostle Paul (though nothing of the sort is in the biblical text):[14] "Whatever work he does, it is cursed. On the holy Day of the Lord, man has no permission not even to go for a walk, as the apostle says: nobody should walk around cunningly (see Rom 13:13), nobody should go to law, nobody should bear malice, but go to

---

τοῖς ἑβραίοις ἐν τῇ ἡμέρᾳ τοῦ σαββάτου ἔχειν ἀνάπαυσιν· ἐν αὐτῇ γὰρ τῇ ἡμέρᾳ κατέπαυσεν ὁ θεὸς ἀπὸ πάντων τῶν ἔργων αὐτοῦ· διὰ τοῦτο καὶ τούτοις ἐκέλευσεν καταπαύσαι τὰ ἔργα καὶ ἀναπαυεῖναι· ἀλλ' ἐπειδὴ παρόργησαν αὐτὸν καὶ οὐκ ἐνέμειναν τοῖς προστάγμασιν αὐτοῦ, ὤμωσεν αὐτοῖς διὰ τοῦ προφήτου λέγων· εἰ εἰσελεύσονται εἰς τὴν κατάπαυσίν μου· τὸ σάββατον γὰρ ἀνάπαυσιν ἐκάλεσεν· ὅτε οὖν ἦλθεν ὁ κύριος ἐπὶ τῆς γῆς, γεννηθῆς ἐκ τῆς ἁγίας παρθένου· ἀνεκαινοποίησεν ὅλον τὸν νόμον· αὐτὸς γὰρ ἦν καὶ τοῦ νόμου ποιητής· εἶδεν γὰρ ὅτι βαρὺς ὁ νόμος καὶ οὐδεὶς δύναται φυλάξαι· ἐξῆβαλεν τὸν νόμον, καὶ εἰσήγαγε τὴν χάριν· καὶ πάντα ἡμῖν καινᾶ ἔδωκεν· καθὼς μαρτυρεῖ ὁ ἀπόστολος· εἴ τις ἐν χριστῷ καινὴ κτίσις· τὰ ἀρχαῖα παρῆλθεν ἰδοὺ γέγονε τὰ πάντα καινά· ἐπεὶ οὖν γέγονε τὰ πάντα καινά, ἔδει καὶ τὴν τοῦ σαββάτου νομωθεσίαν καταλῦσαι· καὶ ἀντεισενεγκεῖν ἡμῖν ἄλλην ἡμέραν· πρὸς τὸ οὖν ἀναπαύεσθαι καὶ εὔχεσθαι ἔδωκεν ἡμῖν τὴν πρώτην ἡμέραν, ἐν ᾗ ἤρξατο ποιεῖν τὸν κόσμον· καὶ ὀνόμασεν αὐτὴν κυριακήν.

13. Homily "Hear, All Brothers Christians, What the Prophet Says" 1 (CPG 4848) according to Codex Parisinus gr. 1034, fol. 296v (see p. 462f.): ὁ Μωυσῆς παρέδωκεν τοῖς ἑβραίοις τὸ σάββατον καὶ φυλάττουσιν αὐτὸ καὶ οὐ παραβαίνουσιν· ἀφ' οὗ δὲ κατέβη ὁ κύριος ἐπὶ τῆς γῆς, ἐπλήρωσε τὸν παλαιὸν νόμον ‹καὶ παρέδωκε ἡμᾶς τὴν νέαν διαθήκην, ἵνα› φυλάττομεν αὐτήν· ὥσπερ οὖν ἔστιν ὁ κύριος ἐν τῷ κόσμῳ, οὕτως καὶ ἡ ἁγία κυριακὴ εἰς τὰς ἡμέρας ὅλας τῆς ἑβδομάδος. "Moses gave the Hebrews the Sabbath and they keep it and do not transgress it. But since the Lord came down to earth, he fulfilled the old law and gave us the new testament that we keep it; therefore, as the Lord is in the world, so the holy day of the Lord in regard to all days of the week." On the text, see pp. 460f. below.

14. In the version of this sermon in Codex Vaticanus graecus 659 (fol. 206v), this quotation is ascribed to Paul's letter to the Galatians, but this is not true. Perhaps this was incorrectly taken from a sermon on Galatians? Or the association with Paul's exhortation from Gal 1:8f. was drawn?

church with a clean conscience, so that he may receive reward by God and eternal life."[15]

The question of reward for Sunday rest is also the central topic in the *Diataxis* of Jesus (around 600 CE). Here, in answer to the question about the reward for fasting on Wednesday and Friday, the text includes a remark on Sunday: those who observe the day of the Lord are promised a life in paradise as a heavenly reward. The woes add that this also includes rest:

> 13. Woe to those who despise the divine Scriptures! Woe to those who work on the holy Lord's Day! Woe to those who disobey the laws, for they have no forgiveness! . . . 14. James also came near and asked the following question: "Lord, what is the reward for Wednesday and Friday?" 15. The Savior says: "Blessed is he who keeps them in faith, for immediately after he is cast out of this perverse life and goes away with the help of angels to the worship of the undefiled throne, the fourth and the sixth days meet him as his soul enters heaven and say delightedly: 'Greetings, our friend, who labored much on earth, praying to God with fasting and watchfulness, and keeping all thy house from all occupation with earthly things. But now be glad and rejoice in paradise.' 16 And while they are speaking, the holy Lord's Day also comes, together with eight brightly robed angels, and he in the midst adorned like the daughter of Zion. He bears witness to the soul and salutes it, saying to the eight angels with him, 'Come, behold a righteous soul which has no blemish, which has fought well on earth and has kept itself from all activity of the devil.' Then the angels and all the powers of heaven rejoice over it and greet the soul that has walked well. This, then, is the reward for those who have kept the holy Lord's Day and fasted on Wednesday and Friday."[16]

A distinctive feature of this text is Sunday personified as a woman who meets and welcomes the resurrected soul in heaven. This conception ties in with the fact that the days of the week were substantiated in the feminine form[17] and here now "Sunday" is elevated to a heavenly figure who appears in paradise

15. Ps.-Chrysostom, "Hear, All Brothers Christians" 4 (see p. 464f.): ὅσα ἔργα ἐργάζεται, ἐπικατάρατα εἰσίν· ἐν γὰρ τῇ ἁγίᾳ κυριακῇ οὐκ ἔχει ἄνθρωπος ἐξουσίαν κἂν τοῦ περιπατεῖν, καθὼς λέγει ὁ ἀπόστολος· μηδεὶς περιπατεῖ ἐν δόλῳ, μηδεὶς δικάζεται, μηδεὶς μνησικακεῖται· ἀλλὰ εἰσέρχεσθαι εἰς τὴν ἐκκλησίαν μετὰ καθαροῦ συνειδότος, ἵνα λάβῃ μισθὸν ἐκ θεοῦ καὶ ζωὴν αἰώνιον.

16. On the text, see pp. 484–87 below.

17. Behind this, of course, is the association of the days of the week with the seven planets, which were personified as gods, though of course not all in feminine form. See Anderson, "Christianizing the Planetary Week," 128–91.

like an angel. The *Diataxis* seems to be the first text to offer this personification of Sunday as a heavenly woman.[18]

In the pseudepigraphal sermons attributed to Eusebius and Chrysostom, a replacement of the Sabbath by the Lord's Day is explicitly described and even exegetically justified, but in the *Diataxis* a rest from work is simply demanded without further justification. There are also other texts in which no exegetical difficulty is perceived, and the Sabbath is implicitly identified with the Lord's Day. In the pseudepigraphal homily "Today, My Beloved, I'd Like to Praise the Day of the Lord" (Ps.-Basilius of Caesarea CPG 2955 / Ps.-Chrysostom CPG 4869), rest from work becomes a characteristic feature that distinguishes Jews, Greeks, and Christians from one another: Jews refrain from work on the Sabbath, Greeks on Thursday, and Christians on Sunday.[19] One day a week, one should "work" spiritual work (§2: ἔργα πνευματικά) on one's salvation (§2: μίαν ἡμέραν ὀφείλεις ἀργῆσαι διὰ τὸν θεὸν κατὰ πᾶσαν ἑβδομάδα); anything else would be against the law of God. Here (§4), the Sabbath commandment from Deuteronomy 5:13 is quoted; without problematizing the fact that the Sabbath is a different day of the week from the Lord's Day, the commandment is applied directly to the Lord's Day. This is underscored by an interesting reference to the Balaam narrative (Num

18. See Apocalypse of Anastasia 1 (6.1f. below Homburg), 2 (12.5; 13.4f.11f.; 15.5 above; 13.6.10f.; 15.4f. below Homburg); see Baun, *Tales from Another Byzantium*, 139-41, 196f., and below, p. 498f. See also Kretzenbacher, "Sveta Nedelja." In the late Middle Ages, analogous to the suffering Christ, the female Sunday is depicted with tools from the world of work, which, disregarding the commandment to rest, inflict suffering on Sunday, so to speak. See also the interesting depiction of the days of the week as angels in the mosaic of the creation in the narthex of S. Marco, Venice (see the cover of this book), where God blesses the seventh angel on the seventh day (a unique depiction, probably inspired by the so-called Cotton Genesis). See Karin Krause, "Venedigs Sitz im Paradies. Zur Schöpfungskuppel in der Vorhalle von San Marco," *Mitteilungen des kunsthistorischen Instituts Florenz* 48 (2004): 9-54; Arne Effenberger, "Die Weltschöpfungskuppel in der westlichen Vorhalle der Markuskirche zu Venedig," in *Atlas der Weltbilder*, ed. Christoph Markschies and Peter Deuflhard (Berlin: de Gruyter, 2011), 78-89; Marcello Angheben, *Les strategies de la narration dans la peinture médievale. Le représentation de l'Ancien Testament aux ive-xiie siècles* (Turnhout: Brepols, 2020), with the conclusion of Herbert L. Kessler at 373-402.

19. On the text, see pp. 435–37 below. Accordingly, three orders or groups (τάγματα) are in the world: the Jews, the pagans (who worship idols), and the Christians (§3). While the Greek and Jews practice their rest from work, Christians do not, as the author criticizes. Actually, Thursday seems to have been honored as a special pagan feast day since the time of Diocletian; see Bultrighini, "Thursday (*Dies Iovis*) in the Later Roman Empire." This passage is an interesting additional testimony to the papyri analyzed by Bultrighini. See *De Plaga*, pp. 104–107.

22:25–28): the donkey complained that he was beaten unjustly (§4). The author states: "Do not beat your cattle that works on the day of the Lord, that it may not turn around and then say to you: Why do you beat me? You are not allowed to work today!"[20]

Comparable opinions can be found in the several Greek versions of the Letter from Heaven. With reference to the creation story, the Sabbath as a day of rest is related to the Lord's Day, even if the details of the commands for Sunday rest are formulated differently. It is also noticeable that although the Lord's Day is the central topic, the demand for observance of the day is given in very general terms (with the verbs τιμήσατε, "to reverence"; ἑορτήσατε, "to celebrate"; φυλάξετε, "to keep") without further details. Rest from work and attendance at religious services are the main focus.[21] After six days of worldly labor, the Lord's Day as the seventh day gives people the opportunity to purify themselves from the sins committed on the other days—an idea that is also encountered in the sermons presented above. The following table gives an overview of the imperatives that are directly related to the Lord's Day (for the picture presented in the Latin Letter from Heaven, see pp. 163–65 below).

Sunday Observance in Greek Letters from Heaven			
Alpha 1	Alpha 2	Beta	Gamma (Bittner, p. 9)
1.2 λόγος περὶ τῆς ἁγίας καὶ κυρίας κυριακῆς τῶν ἡμερῶν, ἐν ᾗ Χριστὸς ἀνέστη ἐκ νεκρῶν. / Teaching concerning the holy Sunday, the lord of the days, on which Christ, our Lord and God Jesus Christ, rose from the dead.	1.1 Ἐπιστολὴ καὶ πρόσταγμα τοῦ κυρίου ἡμῶν Ἰησοῦ Χριστοῦ ἐμφανισθεῖσα ἐν Ῥώμῃ περὶ τῆς ἁγίας κυριακῆς. / Epistle and command of our Lord Jesus Christ concerning the holy Lord's Day, which was manifested in Rome.	1.1 Ἐπιστολὴ τοῦ κυρίου ἡμῶν Ἰησοῦ Χριστοῦ / Letter of our Lord Jesus Christ	Ἐπιστολὴ τοῦ κυρίου ἡμῶν Ἰησοῦ Χριστοῦ / Letter of our Lord Jesus Christ

(*Continued*)

20. §4: μὴ τυπτήσῃς τὸν βοῦν σου ἐργαζόμενον ἐν τῇ κυριακῇ, ἵνα μὴ στραφεὶς εἴπῃ πρός σέ· τί με τύπτεις; οὐκ ἔξεστί σοι ἐργάζεσθαι σήμερον. See below, p. 440f. See "The Cow That Observed the Sabbath," in the Midrash Aseret Hadibrot, Pesiq. Rab. 14. The text has a certain radicalism, as Sunday rest is also demanded for schools and the military (§6). On the command to observe the Lord's Day depend heaven and earth (§5).

21. This is not the case in the Latin versions; see p. 154f. below.

(Continued)

Sunday Observance in Greek Letters from Heaven			
Alpha 1	Alpha 2	Beta	Gamma (Bittner, p. 9)
ἐτιμήσατε / honor (2.1; also 3.2; 4.5; 8.4) ἑορτάσατε / celebrate (2.1; also 3.2) φυλάξετε / keep (4.4; also 9.1) τὴν ἁγίαν κυριακὴν / the holy Lord's Day	τιμᾷ / honor (4.4) φυλάξητε / keep (10.1.4) τὴν ἁγίαν κυριακὴν / the holy Lord's Day	φυλάξετε / keep (5.5) τὴν ἁγίαν κυριακὴν / the holy Lord's Day	φυλάξετε / keep τὴν ἁγίαν κυριακὴν / the holy Lord's Day
Going to Church on the Lord's Day			
3.2 (see 7.3f.16) Each baptized human being is obliged to esteem and celebrate [the Sunday] and come to the holy church of God.	5.1 Cursed is anyone who does not come to the holy church together with his whole household.	8.2 Blessed is the one who goes to church on Sunday with his family and partakes in the mysteries.	Woe to those who leave my holy church during the reading and go to stand in the vineyards of the fields. Woe to the people who sleep on the holy Lord's Day.
No Working on the Lord's Day			
[no details are given]	5.4 Do you not know that I appointed six days for you to work, and the holy Lord's Day so that you come to the holy church of God and pray to wash away the sins of the six days? 10.1 quit your handwork	7.3 Do you not know, people, that I have granted six days for you to work and the holy Lord's day to pray and be redeemed from your sins of the six days? 7.8 Accursed is the man who works . . .	. . . that you would work six days of the week and that you would keep my holy Lord's Day free of work, in order to praise your creator. . . . I have given you six days that you may work and that you may preserve my holy Lord's Day. Woe to those who leave my holy church during the reading and go to stand in the vineyards of the fields.
2.7 compassion for widows, orphans, poor (see 5.1)	6.6 receive guests, give food to the poor, clothe the naked		no dances no games

While the Greek Recension Alpha 1 only admonishes the veneration and keeping of Sunday, and going to the church, the Greek Recension Alpha 2 and Beta illustrate this with a reference to rest from work and a reminder to go to church in order to be delivered from sin—as in the two sermons above. The only concessions in Greek Recension Alpha 2 are hosting guests and providing for the needy—these are good works that also atone for sins committed. The Greek Recension Gamma adds to the rest from work the prohibition of participating in amusements.[22] Some woes against those who oversleep on Sunday or leave church services early supplement the picture. These texts thus mark a clear replacement of the Sabbath or a transfer of the commandment of a day of rest to Sunday, justified with explicit exegesis or in terms of salvation history, or simply implicitly presupposed. This is also confirmed by the Armenian tradition,[23] which is probably based on an earlier version of the Greek Recension Alpha and to which reference should be made here. Here, too, the celebration of the mysteries on Sunday is placed in the center; Sunday is therefore praised as a gift from Christ so that one may atone for sins. A curse is pronounced against those who work from the ninth hour of the Sabbath until Monday morning[24]—and people are accused of contrary behavior: they work on Sunday and commit even more sins and immoderate feasting on that day.

The Letter from Heaven thus presents the observance of Sunday as a sign of the new covenant—each baptized Christian is obliged to observe it. So says the Greek Recension Alpha 1, 2.10: "to you I gave the holy Gospel, my law and baptism," and 3.2, "Because of this, each baptized human being is obliged to esteem and celebrate and come to the holy church of God." With baptism, therefore, every Christian has entered this "Sunday covenant," and Sunday becomes the identity marker of a Christian existence.[25] In the Letter from Heaven, however, this is simply stated without further exegesis or reflection on the old and new covenants, on the Sabbath of the Decalogue and Sunday of the new covenant. Although it presupposes the transfer of the old to the

22. This is a long tradition generally: on the one hand, there are ecclesiastical authors who rail against theater attendance and other amusements on the Lord's Day; on the other hand, since Theodosian times, imperial laws prohibited theatrical performances and games, as well as chariot races, on Sundays. See Puk, *Das römische Spielewesen*, 21–50, and above, p. 126f.

23. Bittner, *Brief Christi*, with a German translation of Armenian Recension Alpha at 49–87; see esp. 57, 61, 75, 81, 85. A claim that work on Sunday is necessary for subsistence is also rejected (85).

24. See, about this unique time span for Sunday in the Letter from Heaven, p. 182f.

25. As this is also written in the Armenian version, this seems to be a consistent and old feature of Greek Recension Alpha.

new covenant, it is too simplistic to describe it as "Sabbatarization" of Sunday; the rest from work itself is not further specified.

4.2.2. Legacy of Eusebius of Caesarea?

Was this transfer of the Sabbath to Sunday self-evident, since the Sabbath was observed in some Christian circles anyway, since Sabbath and Sunday were adjacent days in the seven-day week, and since the idea of rest from work had already been in the air since Constantine? One encounters in scholarship again and again, however, the notion that one church father was especially influential and prepared the way for the idea of transferring the Sabbath to Sunday, namely, Eusebius of Caesarea (†339/40). The famous bishop of Caesarea, known for his *Church History* and his *Vita* of Emperor Constantine, is said to have been innovative with regard to this matter, as he was the first to explicitly argue for a transfer of the Sabbath to Sunday. The alleged evidence is his *Commentary on Psalm* 91 LXX.[26] Eusebius was therefore called the founder or originator of the Sabbatization of Sunday. In his latest contribution, Michael Durst states, for example:

> The parallel and analogous consideration of Sabbath and Sunday soon led to the transfer of aspects of the Old Testament Sabbath rest to Sunday rest and thus to a "Sabbatisation" of Sunday. For the first time, Eusebius of Caesarea († 339) says that Christ "by the New Covenant transferred the feast day of the Sabbath to the rising of the light (i.e. to the following day, Sunday) and handed over to us an image of true rest, namely the wholesome Lord's Day"; everything that was prescribed for the Sabbath, the Christians transferred to the Lord's Day, which was more precious than the Jewish Sabbath.[27]

---

26. A preliminary Greek text of the new critical edition by Barbara Villani: https://tinyurl.com/y96thbyy.

27. Durst, "Remarks on Sunday," 379. This goes back to Willy Rordorf, who states: "This is the decisive sentence. The indefinite 'all other things' can actually only mean the laws which were enacted to observe the Sabbath rest and which since Constantine have again gained importance in the Church." *Sabbat und Sonntag*, 45 (translated). See also Haines, *Sunday Observance*, 4 with n. 18; Mitthof, "Christianization of the Empire," 39 ("Sabbath celebration to be transferred to the day of the Lord"); Rakotoniaina, "Redefining the Sabbath," 114 with n. 7; also Grund, *Die Entstehung des Sabbats*, 315: "Doch erst nach der konstantinischen Bestimmung des Sonntags zum Ruhetag 321 n.Chr. wird eine Theorie der Ersetzung des Sabbats durch den Sonntag bei Eusebios manifest." Also Doering, "Sabbat," 278; and Bradshaw and Johnson, *Origins of Feasts*, 25f.; see also Casey Carmichael, *A Continental View: Johannes Cocceius's Federal Theology of the Sabbath* (Göttingen: Vandenhoeck & Ruprecht, 2019), 34–36. Critical to this estimation, however, was already Bauckham, "Sabbath and Sunday in the Post-apostolic Church," 282–84.

Eusebius probably worked on this psalm commentary in the 330s CE. It is the first Christian commentary on the Psalms that goes through the entire Psalter verse by verse. Therefore, it is a voluminous work, partly preserved in direct tradition, but also partly only in catenae.[28] Eusebius wrote this commentary after Constantine's Sunday legislation,[29] which he mentions in other writings quite extensively, although not in this commentary. But why was a single passage from a commentary on the Psalms relevant for the Sabbath? It is because of the headings of the Psalms, some of which begin with a time specification, namely, a day of the week. Psalm 91 is said to be a psalm song for the Sabbath day (ΨΑΛΜΟΣ ΩιΔΗΣ, ΕΙΣ ΤΗΝ ΗΜΕΡΑΝ ΤΟΥ ΣΑΒΒΑΤΟΥ). This was the reason for Eusebius engaging with the Sabbath in his commentary. However, one has to question this standard assumption about Eusebius as a promoter of the transfer of the Sabbath to Sunday after a closer look at Eusebius's commentary on the Psalms.

Eusebius begins with the statement that all righteous and God-beloved people before Moses did not know the (literal) Sabbath.[30] By contrast, those "from the circumcision" (i.e., Jewish people), who believe that by observing the Sabbath they are doing something admirable, do not fulfill the true meaning of the law.[31] *Sabbath* means "rest" (see Gen 2:2f.), and Psalm 94:10f. LXX states that impious men will never enter God's eternal rest. Therefore, Sabbath

28. Michael J. Hollerich, "Eusebius' Commentary on the Psalms and Its Place in the Origins of Christian Biblical Scholarship," in *Eusebius of Caesarea: Tradition and Innovations*, ed. Aaron Johnson and Jeremy Schott, Hellenic Studies Series 60 (Washington, DC: Center for Hellenic Studies, 2013), 265: "The CPs is a late work of Eusebius, as proven by the mention in his commentary on Ps 87:11 of the *mnêma* (tomb) and *martyrion* of the Savior in Jerusalem, where, he says, miracles were being performed among the faithful. This is a reference to the buildings constructed by Constantine over the alleged site of Christ's burial, sometime between 326 and 333." See also Carmelo Curti, *Eusebiana I: Commentarii in Psalmos*, Saggi e testi classici, cristiani e medievali 1 (Catania, Sicily: Università di Catania 1989), 196 with n. 7. See also now the just-published edition of the third part of the commentary on Ps 101–150 by Franz Xaver Risch, *Eusebius von Cäsarea: Der Psalmenkommentar*, GCS Eusebius Werke 10.3 (Berlin: de Gruyter, 2022), with the praefatio, pp. vii–lxii, however, concentrating on the transmission of the text, not the dating and tendencies of this commentary.

29. See above, p. 3.

30. Eusebius, *Comm. Ps.* 91 (PG 23:1165D): Τὰς τῶν Σαββάτων ἡμέρας οἱ πρὸ Μωσέως δίκαιοι καὶ θεοφιλεῖς ἄνδρες οὔτ' ᾔδεσαν οὔτε ἐφύλαττον.

31. Eusebius, *Comm. Ps.* 91 (PG 23:1165D): Ἐπεὶ τοίνυν οἱ ἐκ περιτομῆς ὡς μέγα τι κατορθοῦντες τὰ Σάββατα φυλάττειν ἡγοῦνται, ἃ οὐδὲ φυλάττουσι κατὰ τὸ βούλημα τοῦ νόμου, παραθετέον αὐτοῖς τὰ εἰρημένα. "Because those out of circumcision think that in observing the Sabbath they do something great, although they do not observe it according to the will of the law, these verses are presented to them."

and rest must be interpreted according to their true meaning (κατὰ διάνοιαν), and it was precisely this true Sabbath that those before Moses nevertheless observed—for God's rest means dwelling with the spiritual and the otherworldly.[32] The perfect Sabbath, however, and the triple-blessed rest exist only in the kingdom of God, in the hereafter and outside the perceptible world.[33] The spiritual, earthly Sabbath is only an image of this divine, eternal, Sabbath. Now what is to be done on this Sabbath, the image of the heavenly Sabbath? Exactly what the psalm lists: thanksgiving to the Lord, singing to his name, proclaiming his mercy, speaking his truth, certainly also with music. Afterward, there follows the relevant passage in which Eusebius transfers the Sabbath interpreted in this spiritual way to Sunday, the day of resurrection.[34] He does not do this in passing but follows up on his previous criticism that those "from the circumcision" do not keep the Sabbath properly. Citing the prophetic criticism of the Sabbath (Amos 6:3 and Isa 1:13), he then writes:

> Therefore, the Logos, spurning those, by the new covenant transposed and transferred the feast of the Sabbath to the rising of the light, and delivered to us the image of true rest, the first day of light, which belongs to the Lord and brings salvation.[35]

He continues that on this day, which is the "day of light," the first day, and the day of the true sun, gentile Christians, who have been redeemed by Christ from the nations throughout the world, also come together after the interval of six days to celebrate the holy and spiritual Sabbaths.[36] All things, as much as had to be accomplished on the Sabbath in its original meaning, Christians

32. Eusebius, *Comm. Ps.* 91 (PG 23:1168BC): πρὸς τοῖς νοητοῖς καὶ ὑπερκοσμίοις διαγωγῆς . . . πρὸς τοῖς ἀσωμάτοις καὶ ὑπερκοσμίοις . . . πρὸς τῷ θεῷ καὶ πρὸς τῇ τῶν θείων καὶ νοητῶν σχολῇ τε καὶ θεωρίᾳ.

33. Eusebius, *Comm. Ps.* 91 (PG 23:1168C): τὸ γὰρ τέλειον σάββατον καὶ ἡ τελεία καὶ ἡ τρισμακαρία κατάπαυσις ἐν τῇ τοῦ θεοῦ βασιλείᾳ τυγχάνει ὑπὲρ τὴν ἑξαήμερον δημιουργίαν καὶ τῶν αἰσθητῶν ἁπάντων ἐκτὸς ἐν ἀσωμάτοις καὶ ὑπερκοσμίοις.

34. Eusebius, *Comm. Ps.* 91 (PG 23:1169B): Ὁρᾷς οὖν, ὅσα πράττειν ὁ παρὼν λόγος παραινεῖ κατὰ τὴν τῆς ἀναστάσεως ἡμέραν.

35. Eusebius, *Comm. Ps.* 91 (PG 23:1169C): διὸ δὴ παρητημένων ἐκείνων διὰ τῆς καινῆς διαθήκης λόγος μετήγαγε καὶ μετατέθεικε τὴν τοῦ Σαββάτου ἑορτὴν ἐπὶ τὴν τοῦ φωτὸς ἀνατολὴν καὶ παρέδωκεν ἡμῖν ἀληθινῆς ἀναπαύσεως εἰκόνα τὴν σωτήριον καὶ κυριακὴν καὶ πρώτην τοῦ φωτὸς ἡμέραν.

36. Eusebius, *Comm. Ps.* 91 (PG 23:1169D): Ἐν ᾗ φωτὸς οὔσῃ καὶ πρώτῃ καὶ τοῦ ἀληθοῦς ἡλίου ἡμέρᾳ καὶ ἡμεῖς αὐτοὶ συνερχόμενοι διὰ μέσων ἓξ ἡμερῶν ἅγιά τε Σάββατα καὶ πνευματικὰ ἑορτάζοντες, οἱ ἐξ ἐθνῶν δι' αὐτοῦ λελυτρωμένοι καθ' ὅλης τῆς οἰκουμένης.

have transferred to the Lord's Day, inasmuch as it is more significant and has precedence, and inasmuch as it is the first and more precious than the Jewish Sabbath.[37] The Sabbath is replaced by Sunday as the day of the Lord, the day of resurrection, the day of creation and new creation. The transfer of the day explicitly occurs within the context of the replacement of the Jewish people, the dissolution of the old covenant and the founding of the new covenant. Therefore, the anti-Jewish tendency of this passage is obvious.[38] Indeed, Eusebius goes a step further than previous exegetes who had either interpreted the Sabbath spiritually, saying that Christians are not to attend to earthly affairs but to their souls or to God, or that Christians are to turn away from sin, or who had referred to the afterlife and eschaton as God's eternal rest.[39] All this can also be read in Eusebius, but he additionally transfers the Sabbath to Sunday.

This interpretation fits very well with Eusebius's understanding of the Psalter as a whole. Of course, this extensive work cannot be briefly presented here, but there is a very interesting text that quickly demonstrates his understanding of the Psalms: the so-called *Periochai*. These are psalm headings newly composed by Eusebius, which provide the entire Psalter with both a Christian and an anti-Jewish meaning. They replace or supplement the headings handed down in the Septuagint and give the Psalms a Christian designation. Thus, for example, Psalm 5 is a prayer of the church, Psalms 11–13 prophesy the coming of Christ, Psalm 45 the calling of the apostles, Psalm 47 the end of the persecution of Christians. Psalms 41–43, 58–59, and 68 thematize the persecution of the Jews, Psalm 73 the siege of Jerusalem under Vespasian. Psalm 89 also deals with the persecution of the Jews, Psalm 90 with Christ's victory, Psalm 91 with godly rest, Psalm 92 with Christ's kingship, Psalm 93 with the persecution of the church, and Psalm 94 with the calling and rejection of the Jews.[40] This anti-Jewish hostility also runs throughout the commentary on Isaiah, which he wrote at this time, where he transfers the prophetic criticism of Israel to the Jews of the present or to the Jews at the time of Jesus. An example is his exegesis of the criticism of the sacrificial system and feast day practice from Isaiah

37. Eusebius, *Comm. Ps.* 91 (PG 23:1172A): καὶ πάντα δή, ὅσα ἄλλα χρῆν ἐν Σαββάτῳ τελεῖν, ταῦτα ἡμεῖς ἐν τῇ κυριακῇ μετατεθείκαμεν, ὡς ἂν κυριωτέρας οὔσης αὐτῆς καὶ ἡγουμένης καὶ πρώτης καὶ τοῦ Ἰουδαϊκοῦ Σαββάτου τιμιωτέρας. Eusebius uses two verbs here to express the transfer, both constructed with "μετα . . .".

38. See above, p. 144.

39. See the literature above in n. 27.

40. See Cordula Bandt, "Periochae," in *Die Prologtexte zu den Psalmen von Origenes und Eusebius*, ed. Cordula Bandt, TU 183 (Berlin: de Gruyter, 2019), 122–42, with introduction, text, and commentary.

1:11–15.[41] This anti-Jewish attitude apparently inspired Eusebius not only to comment on the Psalter in a christianized way but also to reject the Jewish Sabbath and at the same time to imbue it with Christian meaning. Sunday is the new Sabbath.

A similar strategy can be seen in his description of church buildings. Here Eusebius is also the first to refer to the Christian assembly room as a temple: the Jewish temple has been destroyed, and since Constantine there has been increased Christian church-building activity. Thus, according to Eusebius, the church is the new, true temple of the true worship of God. Against this background, it is understandable that not only the building (place) but also the day of the week for assembly (time) is described with Jewish sacral language. The church building is the temple; Sunday—when Christians gather in church—is the true Sabbath.[42]

Nevertheless, it must of course be considered that Eusebius is not transferring the literal Sabbath rest to Sunday. Of course, he keeps to the level of the spiritual interpretation of the Sabbath here, the Sabbath in the true, original sense, as he has elaborated before this quotation and will continue to do afterward. For he then describes how the various parts of Christian worship correspond to this psalm: on Sundays Christians come together, confess their sins, offer a prayer of praise, sing hymns, and hear a sermon, which in turn exhorts them to practice this spiritual worship. Interestingly, Eusebius describes here the Christian service on Sunday, which takes place first in the early morning hours and then again at dusk—as if Constantine's law on Sunday rest did not exist.

It would not be in keeping with God's original intention to observe the Sabbath commandments literally—accordingly, in former times, the Jews themselves actually broke a "literal" Sabbath commandment with their psalm singing.[43] But now it is finally possible for Christians to fulfill the Sabbath according to the spiritual law (τὰ τῷ σαββάτῳ πράττειν . . . κατὰ τὸν πνευματικὸν νόμον ἐπιτελοῦμεν) and sing hymns in a spiritual way

---

41. See Eusebius, *Comm. Isa.* I.16 (GCS Euseb 9.8.12–33 Ziegler).

42. Sources are Eusebius, *Enkomion* on the new church of Tyrus (between 314 and 320 CE) in Eusebius, *Hist. eccl.* 10.4; Eusebius, *Vit. Const.* 3.25; 3.35–43; 4.41.2; 4.44.2; 4.59; 4.60.4; 4.70.2. See Hanns Christof Brennecke, "*Templa et busta despiciunt*: Das Fehlen von Tempeln im vorkonstantinischen Christentum als Argument der antichristlichen Polemik," in *Kulträume: Studien zum Verhältnis von Kult und Raum in alten Kulturen*, ed. Hans-Ulrich Wiemer, Potsdamer Altertumswissenschaftliche Beiträge 60 (Stuttgart: Steiner, 2017), 247–66.

43. Eusebius, *Comm. Ps.* 91 (PG 23:1172D): Πάλαι μὲν οὖν, ὁπηνίκα διὰ συμβόλων καὶ τύπων ἐλάτρευον οἱ ἐκ περιτομῆς, οὐκ ἀπεικὸς ἦν διὰ ψαλτηρίων καὶ κιθάρας ἀναπέμπειν τινὰς τῷ θεῷ τοὺς ὕμνους, καὶ τοῦτο ποιεῖν ταῖς ἡμέραις τοῦ Σαββάτου, παραλύοντας δηλαδὴ τὴν ἀργίαν καὶ παραβαίνοντας τὸν νόμον τὸν περὶ τοῦ Σαββάτου.

(πνευματικαῖς). Therefore, resting—ἀργεῖν—does not mean doing nothing but abstaining from worldly affairs, and being at leisure—σχολάζειν—also means devoting oneself to works pleasing to God.

In summary, Eusebius in his commentary actually speaks of the Sabbath being moved to Sunday, but of course in a spiritual sense. It is the day for true Christian worship, that is, what those he calls the "men of God" also practiced before Moses. One looks in vain for precise rules on rest from work. Moreover, one searches in vain for a reception or an effect of this passage from Eusebius. It is by no means the case that, since his Psalms commentary, Psalm 91 has been interpreted in the same way as Eusebius did or that a Sabbatization of Sunday actually begins with this text. On the contrary, it is only in the sixth century that the various apocryphal texts presented here in this volume appear, texts calling for a stricter rest from work on Sundays—so about 250 years in between. Therefore, in my opinion, one should not describe this as a line of development, and one should avoid understanding this text as a turning point. A look at other commentaries on the Psalms can confirm this observation:

> The pseudo-Athanasian commentary on the Psalms, *Expositiones in Psalmos*, written probably around 400 CE, states simply that this psalm is a song for the Sabbath and that the Sabbath means the future rest at the end of time.[44]
>
> Another introduction to Psalm 91, attributed variously to Cyril of Alexandria or Diodorus of Tarsus, considers the Sabbath rightly understood as a picture of life in Christ, for Christ has transformed the shadow of the law into a spiritual service.[45]
>
> Gregory of Nyssa († end of fourth century), in his work on the superscriptions of the Psalms, relates the Sabbath to the burial rest of Christ. This, however, was not a rest in the grave but a struggle against death in order to conquer it and achieve the resurrection.[46]
>
> Theodoret of Cyrus (†466 CE) states that the Sabbath prescribed leisure, but not complete leisure; it involved much greater spiritual activity. Similar to Eusebius, he states that the Sabbath law prescribed abstinence from bodily exertion. In sum, the rest refers to the life to come, which is free from all

44. Athanasius of Alexandria, *Expositiones in Psalmos* (PG 27:404). A new edition of this commentary is prepared by me and my team.

45. Cyril of Alexandria or Diodorus of Tarsus, *In Psalmum* 91 (PG 69:1225).

46. Gregory of Nyssa, *In inscriptiones Psalmorum* 43 (Gregorii Nysseni Opera 5:97–99 McDonough).

care. The psalm therefore foretells honor for the righteous and punishment of the wicked, which will be bestowed in this eternal rest.[47]

Arnobius the Younger († after 455 CE), like Gregory of Nyssa, also refers the Sabbath rest to the burial rest of Christ—so on this day the enemies of God pass away (*inimici domini pereunt*), and the friends of God rejoice in the Lord on Sunday. Despite this interpretation, Arnobius does not declare Sunday to be the new Sabbath. On the contrary, he emphasizes that Christians have to confess their sins daily (*cotidie*).[48]

Hilary of Poitiers (†367/68 CE; he translated the commentary of Origen on the Psalms) presents a longer sermon on this psalm. He emphasizes that the law is a mirror of the future and a shadow of the truth. So here, too, it is necessary to look at what is meant by the Sabbath. Since nothing about rest is mentioned in this Psalm, the actual rest in the eschaton must be meant—which the Jews will never reach (see Ps 94:11 LXX). Rest from work cannot be meant, since God never rests—no day with God is without work. This perfect and true rest can only be attained in Christ—for which one prepares oneself with watchfulness and prayer, Scripture reading, fasting, humility, good works, and chastity. Therefore, in Hilarius, one can read an interpretation that is also clearly anti-Jewish, but without finding Eusebius's shifting of the Sabbath to Sunday.[49]

Augustine († 430 CE) includes in his *Exposition* on Psalm 91 a similar anti-Jewish remark in his interpretation of this psalm verse: "We rest from wrongdoing. . . . They take a rest from good behaviour" (*vacatio nostra a malis operibus—vacatio illorum a bonis operibus est*). Then follows his interpretation, which also appears elsewhere in his writings: "God formally appoints the Sabbath for us, but what kind of Sabbath? Consider above all where it is to be kept. Our Sabbath is within, in our hearts." (*Nobis sabbatum indicit Dcus. Qualc? Primo ubi sit vidctc. Intus cst, in cordc cst sabbatum nostrum.*) This is "freedom and tranquillity and serenity of conscience" (*in vacatione et tranquillitate et serenitate conscientiae suae*).[50]

Cassiodorus († around 580 CE), in his *Expositio Psalmorum* on Psalm 91, states that we must give thanks to the Godhead in all our actions, because the psalm denotes spiritual work. The Sabbath day means the rest to come

47. Theodoret of Cyrus, *Commentarii in Psalmorum* (PG 86:1616f.).

48. Arnobius Iunior, *Commentarii in Psalmos* 91 (CCSL 25:136.1-13 Daur; PL 53:459).

49. Hilary of Poitiers, *Tractatus super Psalmos* 91 (CCSL 61:322–330 Doignon).

50. Augustine, *Enarrat. Ps.* 91.2 (CCSL 39:1280.6f.9f.21f. Dekkers and Fraipont). See Rakotoniaina, "Redefining the Sabbath."

> for those who give their minds a holiday from vices. The Jews do not observe the Sabbath properly, for they have imposed a literal observance.[51]
>
> Only one text stands out here, and that is a homily by Jerome (†419 CE; *Homily* 21 on Ps 91). He applies the Sabbath commandment to Christians and says that no one should work and do menial labor (*opus servile*; see Lev 23:3) on the Sabbath. However, he understands this in a figurative sense: when one is not pursuing worldly matters but spiritual matters such as singing and meditating on this psalm, it is the Sabbath. It becomes clear that he is referring to the whole monastic existence, which means leaving the world and going over to a new sphere of life. The whole monastic existence becomes, so to speak, life in the spiritual Sabbath.[52]

After this overview on other commentaries on this psalm, it is obvious that the commentary of Eusebius of Caesarea on Psalm 91 is an exception. He emphasizes the replacement of the Sabbath by Sunday in the history of salvation. With the rejection of the Jews as the chosen people, the Lord transferred the Sabbath to Sunday. This is part of his anti-Jewish argumentation, which on the one hand includes a rejection of all Jewishness, and on the other hand appropriation of Jewish traditions. This does not mean, however, that a literal observance of rest from work is meant—a spiritual interpretation of the Sabbath is also the consensus in Eusebius. There are, as demonstrated, no commentators on the Psalms who have followed Eusebius in this, neither in the surviving Greek commentaries nor in the Latin ones.

So far I am aware of only one pseudepigraphal homily of Athanasius, namely *De semente*, in which the idea of shifting the Sabbath to the Lord's

51. Cassiodorus, *Expositio in Psalm* 91.1 (CCSL 98:836.1–18 Adriaen): *Psalmus cantici commonet nos ut in uniuersis actibus nostris diuinitati gratias referre debeamus. Psalmus enim (sicut saepe dictum est) significat operas spiritales, quae sursum tendunt ad dominum christum. In his enim cantare debemus et gratias semper agere, quando eius beneficio reddimur liberi, qui per nos sumus peccatorum nexibus obligati. Ipse enim cantat in psalmo, qui omnem uitam suam in gratiarum actione constituit. Dies autem sabbati requies interpretatur, per quam commonemur ab omni praua actione cessare et feriatos animos a uitiis reddere operum caelestium sanctitate. Hanc recte iudaei non colunt, cum obseruantiam eius ad intellectum litterae transtulerunt. Sed illis est in die sabbati requies, qui praecepta domini ad noui testamenti significantiam ducunt et ueraciter intellegunt quod in praefiguratione dictum esse cognoscunt. Et ideo uerba ecclesiae in hoc psalmo debemus accipere, quae nobis per diem sabbati futuram requiem cognoscitur intimare. Primo ingressu ecclesia loquitur, bonum esse commemorans laudes domino dicere, quod insipientem et irreligiosum profitetur modis omnibus ignorare.*

52. Jerome, *Tract. Ps.* 91.1 (CCSL 78:133.1–24 Morin).

Day is taken up. It is a sermon on the disputes about the sanctification of the Sabbath in the Gospels (Luke 6:1–5 and 6:6–11), handed down among the writings of Athanasius.[53] Unfortunately, it is not known by whom the text was composed, nor when, nor how it made its way into the corpus of writings attributed to Athanasius. The sermon opens with the remark that although the community has just gathered on the Sabbath, they do not hold to Judaism, for the point is to worship Christ, the Lord of the Sabbath. Even though the Jews once honored the Sabbath, now the Lord has changed the Sabbath into Sunday. The Jews had themselves disregarded the Sabbath, and the law has now been abrogated by Christ.[54] Also, in a later section of the sermon (9.1), the Jews' custom of honoring the Sabbath is contrasted with the Christians' custom of honoring the Lord's Day. However, since the sermon focuses more on the Sabbath, it does not elaborate on how the author believes the Lord's Day should be honored. He preaches that the Jews were forbidden to work on the Sabbath, but that Christians are also allowed to work on the Sabbath, since it was already allowed for the priests (14.5f.). Whether from this statement the conclusion can be drawn that the Lord's Day is free of work, however, remains an open question.

This survey of various interpretations of Psalm 91 in Greek and Latin authors of late antiquity shows how the apocryphal texts of this volume differ from them. Here, an attempt is made to justify or at least demand a rest from work on Sunday, which was not so tangible in the previous exegesis.

4.2.3. Sunday Rest in the Latin Letter from Heaven

Back to the Letter from Heaven. In contrast to the Greek texts and Greek versions of the Letter from Heaven considered so far, the Latin versions

---

53. Ps-Athanasius of Alexandria, *Homilia de semente*, by Annette von Stockhausen, "Die pseud-athanasianische *Homilia de semente*: Einleitung, Text und Übersetzung," in *Von Arius zum Athanasianum: Studien zur Edition der "Athanasius-Werke,"* ed. Annette von Stockhausen and Hanns Christof Brennecke, TU 163 (Berlin: de Gruyter, 2010), 157–205.

54. Ps-Athanasius of Alexandria, *Homilia de semente* 1.1–3 (171.9–24 von Stockhausen): πάλαι μὲν γὰρ ἦν ἐν τοῖς ἀρχαίοις τίμιον τὸ σάββατον, μετέθηκε δὲ ὁ κύριος τὴν τοῦ σαββάτου ἡμέραν εἰς κυριακήν· καὶ οὐχ ἡμεῖς ἐσμεν οἱ ἀφ᾽ ἑαυτῶν τοῦ σαββάτου καταφρονήσαντες, ἀλλ᾽ ὁ προφήτης ἐστὶν ὁ ἀποβαλὼν καὶ εἰπών· "τὰς νεομηνίας ὑμῶν καὶ τὰ σάββατα μισεῖ ἡ ψυχή μου." μέχρι μὲν γὰρ ὅτε ἄξια ἐπράττετο τῶν πραγμάτων τῆς νομοθεσίας ἢ μέχρις ὅτε μὴ ἦν παραγενόμενος ὁ διδάσκαλος, ἐνήργει τὰ τοῦ παιδαγωγοῦ, *ἐλθόντος δὲ τοῦ διδασκάλου κατηργήθη ὁ παιδαγωγὸς* καὶ ἡλίου ἀνατείλαντος ὁ λύχνος ἐπαύσατο.

emphasize other things. This is shown by the various recensions of the Latin Letter from Heaven despite their differences. These recensions state, very often without further detail, as in the Greek Recensions, that Sunday is to be observed or kept (*custodire, observare, colere, celebrare*). That said, short lists of concrete activities to be performed or avoided on the Lord's Day can also be found. Forbidden activities include (court) disputes, housework, fieldwork, and hunting, as well as drunkenness and murder.[55] Permitted activities on the Lord's Day, besides church attendance and prayer, include visitation of the sick, funerals, almsgiving, and care for widows and orphans.

Of course, foundational also in the Latin versions is that the Sabbath commandment is directly applied to the Lord's Day, with reference to the creation narrative. In the Latin Letter from Heaven version in Codex Vienna 1355 (Latin Recension II), the Sabbath commandment is applied directly to the Lord's Day, as if the seventh day were actually Sunday: "Within six days the Lord created everything and on the seventh day he rested from all work. Thus, you shall rest as well from all your work, be it slave or free man,"[56] So also in the Latin Recension I, according to Codex Vienna 1355, God's rest on the seventh day is the reason for work rest on Sunday:

> Understand, miserable souls, that in six days God made heaven and earth, sun and moon, the four evangelists, the sea, and everything that dwells there; apart from that he formed the human Adam from the earth. Because he rested on the holy Lord's Day, now sinners and righteous men alike must rest as the angels rest in heaven.[57]

---

55. Probably not only on Sunday—this demonstrates that the list is enlarged with further issues.

56. Codex Vienna 1355, 4.2. See the Latin Recension II, according to Munich 9550 (also Hamburg St. Petri-Kirche 30b): *septio autem requievi ab omni opere. Ita et vos requiescite ab omnibus operibus et laboribus vestris, tam servi quam liberi, si vultis vitam aut requiem habere mecum*. See also Codex London, Add. 19725, where the seventh day, following six days of creation activity, is directly referred to as the Lord's Day (204.19f. Haines): *et in diem <dominicum> ab universe opera requievit, et nunc sic debent peccatores et iusti sicut angeli requiescunt in coelo*. See also the brief reference in Codex London, Add. 30854 (Delehaye 169): *Faeci caelum et terram et omnia quae in eis sunt et sanctificabi sanctum dominicum*.

57. Codex Vienna 1355, 2.2f.: *Cognoscite, miserae animae, quia in sex diebus fecit deus coelum et terram, solem et lunam, quattuor evangelistas, mare et omnia quae in eis sunt* [see Exod 20:11]; *praeterea hominem Adam plasmavit de terra. quia in die sancto dominico requievit, et nunc sic debent peccatores et iusti sicut angeli requiescunt in celo*. Rather differently in the Tarragona manuscript (transmitted only in the transcription of Baluzius) 10.3 and 5: *et requiem dedi omnibus die dominico . . . et die dominico sanctificavi, et dedi requiem in ipso ut bene agant, et sine pressure sint, et requiescant per omnia*. Here, the explicit decree of a new day of rest could also be meant, rather than the tacit transfer of the Sabbath to Sunday.

However, in addition to this proclamation, the Latin versions present more details about what to do and to avoid on the Lord's Day. This tendency of the Latin Letter from Heaven to offer concrete lists of Sunday morality is also mirrored by the first reference to the Letter from Heaven, namely, the letter of Licinianus of Cartagena: here the alleged letter of Christ forbids preparation of necessary food, gardening, spinning, and walking or traveling on a road on the Lord's Day.[58] Traveling (*viam ambulet*; *iter agere*) is found in the Letter from Heaven only insofar as the letters emphasize that one may set out only to go to church, unless one must visit the sick. The following overview may illustrate these items—but the table lists only those activities that are directly associated with Sunday. General topics—which are also mentioned, since the text lent itself to addressing various moral topics, often in the form of a catalogue of vices—are not listed here.[59]

Recension II,[60] acc. to Vienna ÖNB 1355 (Munich, clm 9550 Munich, clm 14673 Hamburg, S. Petri 30b Todi / Amaduzzi)	**Recension I, acc. to Tarragona (Baluzius)**[61] (with an expanded call to repentance with antipagan passages in 8f.)	**Recension I, acc. to Vienna ÖNB 1355**[62] **(London, Add. 19725 Basel, UB B VII 7)**	**Recension I, acc. to C. Parisinus lat. 12270** (Rec. I with expansions on tithing, swearing, and women)[63]
What to Refrain from Doing on the Lord's Day			
2.1 do not walk around (*ambulare*)	3.1 do not go hunting	2.1 do not go hunting	do not go hunting

(*Continued*)

58. See the text, pp. 214–19.

59. In Latin Recension III, comparable to the Greek recensions, the admonitions are limited to observing Sunday, practicing compassion (for example, almsgiving), and abstaining from disputes (see manuscript Toulouse 208 above pp. 113–17). This confirms the close connection between this recension and the Greek versions.

60. See below, pp. 221–37. In the Latin Recension IIa, according to Codex Vienna, Dominikanerkloster 133, the "list of Sunday morals" at the beginning of the letter is extended to a long catalogue of vices (208.23–209.27 Haines) and a catalogue of virtues (209.27–31 Haines), with the following explanation (209.31–32 Haines): *Ecce opera digna coram deo omni tempore, maxime vero custodiendus est dies dominicus, quia dies domini prima est omnium dierum et ultima*. Referring specifically to Sunday, the following is mentioned in a later section (209.43–46 Haines): *quicumque negotium seculare in die dominico fecerit vel vestimenta abluerit, artificium aliquod egerit vel capillos totonderit vel panem coxerit vel aliquam tam illicitam perpetraverit exterminabo eum et eius fautores suosque adiutores de regno meo.*

61. See below, pp. 272–89.

62. See below, pp. 250–67.

63. See Haines, *Sunday Observance*, 199–201.

(*Continued*)

Recension II, acc. to Vienna ÖNB 1355 (Munich, clm 9550 Munich, clm 14673 Hamburg, S. Petri 30b Todi / Amaduzzi)	**Recension I, acc. to Tarragona (Baluzius)** (with an expanded call to repentance with antipagan passages in 8f.)	**Recension I, acc. to Vienna ÖNB 1355 (London, Add. 19725 Basel, UB B VII 7)**	**Recension I, acc. to C. Parisinus lat. 12270** (Rec. I with expansions on tithing, swearing, and women)
2.2 do not conduct business (*negotium facere*)	3.1 do not judge idle cases		do not conduct business do not make purchases do not conduct sales do not implement contracts do not dispense legal judgments
2.2 do not bake bread (*panem coquere*)	12.1 do not collect vegetables 3.1 do not milk cattle	2.1; 10.1 do not collect vegetables 2.1 do not turn a millstone 2.1 do not milk cattle	do not gather herbs do not mill
2.2 do not cut / wash hair (*capillos tondere / lavare*) 2.2 do not wash clothes (*vestimenta lavare*)	9.3 do not wash head 9.3 do not cut hair 9.3 do not wash clothes	8.3 do not wash head 8.3 do not cut hair	
3.5[64] do not swear (*iurari*)		2.1 do not swear, lie	do not swear
2.3 do not accuse a neighbor (*proximum causari*)[65] 2.3 do not instigate slander (*detractationem, contentionem*)	9.6 do not commit causes or make intentions or start fights		do not slander

(*Continued*)

64. Only in Codex Munich 9550. See above, pp. 87, 99, 136, 140, on swearing.
65. Only in Codex Munich 9550.

(*Continued*)

Recension II, acc. to Vienna ÖNB 1355 (Munich, clm 9550 Munich, clm 14673 Hamburg, S. Petri 30b Todi / Amaduzzi)	**Recension I, acc. to Tarragona (Baluzius)** (with an expanded call to repentance with antipagan passages in 8f.)	**Recension I, acc. to Vienna ÖNB 1355 (London, Add. 19725 Basel, UB B VII 7)**	**Recension I, acc. to C. Parisinus lat. 12270** (Rec. I with expansions on tithing, swearing, and women)
2.3 do not instigate anger (*ira perpetrare*)[66]			remain chaste (women)
2.3 do not laugh illicitly (*inlicitum / inhonestum / immoderatum risum*)	6.1 cease from evil deeds 6.1 do not murder	5.2 cease from evil deeds 5.2 do not murder 6.2 avoid drunkenness 6.2 avoid greed	
What to Do on the Lord's Day			
2.1 *ad ecclesiam ambulare / equitare*	6.1 give alms 4.1; 7.2 go to church 4.2 venerate the cross	5.2 give alms 3.2; 6.2 8.2 go to church 3.2 venerate the cross	give alms go to church
2.1 support widows, orphans, pilgrims (*viduis et orphanis et peregrinantibus subvenire*)[67]	6.1 help widows and orphans	5.2 help widows and orphans	
2.1 visit the sick (*infirmos visitare*)	4.2 visit the sick		visit the sick
2.1 bury the dead (*mortuo sepellire*)[68]	4.2 bury the dead		bury the dead seek out places for prayer
2.1 bring disputants back into harmony (*discordes ad concordiam revocare*)	4.2 settle disputes		

66. Only in manuscript Todi / Amaduzzi; see p. 40.
67. Only in manuscript Todi / Amaduzzi.
68. Only in manuscript Todi / Amaduzzi.

This overview shows how more detailed activities are listed in the Latin versions than in the Greek ones. But even here there are clear differences. Latin Recension II lists fewer actions by comparison: besides aspects of quarreling (do not quarrel, do not accuse your neighbor, do not slander or engage in disputes), which, so to speak, do not abide by the commandment of peace on the Lord's Day, one reads of only three domestic activities that are forbidden (baking bread, cutting hair, washing clothes). This recension concentrates on the household, the family, or the clan group, as reflected also in the threatened punishments, which correspondingly affect work, the harvest yield, and livestock *in domo*. This is also attested by the letter of Licinianus.

Latin Recension I, on the other hand, expands the catalogue to include activities outside the home (working with livestock, working in the mill, going hunting, gathering vegetables or herbs) and is more general (not murdering, which is certainly forbidden not only on the Lord's Day; giving alms; caring for widows and orphans). This is also reflected here in the threat to the entire people or the whole world (2.1):

> Because of this the world is perishing and because of this the judgment of the Lord is coming over the whole present populace.
> *proper hoc perit mundus et propter hoc venit iudicium die super populum cunctum praesentem.*

That statement comes right at the beginning of Latin Recension I, according to Codex Wien, ÖNB 1355, which ends correspondingly (11.9): "the whole world is put to ruin" / *totus mundus in ruina est positus.*[69] Despite this universal apocalyptic aspect in Latin Recension I, in contrast to the local-familial perspective in Latin Recension II, the Latin Recension I also lists many activities from the domestic and agricultural spheres that are forbidden on the Lord's Day.[70]

The difference between the Latin Letter from Heaven and the Greek recensions is striking. While in all versions, of course, visiting the church for the service and also caring for the needy are admonished, the prohibition of manual labor activities in the Latin versions stands out. This profile of Sunday rest cannot be derived from the late antique imperial legislation following Emperor Constantine, which was based on holiday conceptions in the Roman Empire, with the concession of an exception for necessary agricultural work.

---

69. On the threatened punishments, see pp. 184–95 below. Here also a universal perspective is discernible, a common feature of Latin Recension I and the Greek recensions.

70. See also below on punishments, p. 186f.

The lack of reception of this rest from work by Christian authors and also in later imperial legislation has already been pointed out (see p. 3f. above), indicating that the prohibition of manual labor in the Letters from Heaven cannot be explained as a late reception of Constantine's legislation.[71] The texts display an innovation that transfers biblical Sabbath legislation to the Lord's Day and demands its observance.

Stylistically, too, the Letter from Heaven is comparable to the biblical texts here. Apart from the occasional vague use of the term *opera* or *labor*, there is no more precise definition of labor. The texts rather give illustrative examples of activities that are to be refrained from on Sundays, as shown above. This is also the case, for example, in Exodus 34:21; 35:3; Numbers 15:32; Isaiah 58:13.[72] Also in *Jubilees* (second century BCE), one finds lists of activities to describe Sabbath rest (Jubilees 2:29f. and 50:8–12[73]). The book claims to be a heavenly revelation to Moses on Mount Sinai and retells in precise chronology the events from creation to the present day of Moses. Central are the commandments to be observed by Israel, which secure its existence. The narrative culminates in the Sabbath commandment, which Israel is chosen by God to observe on the seventh day of creation. This book, which was originally written in Hebrew, translated into Greek and into Ethiopian, also has found a Latin translation (probably fifth century CE) that has survived in a palimpsest manuscript.[74] Since this manuscript also contained a commentary to Luke, a Christian tradition can be assumed. Perhaps a writing such as Jubilees was also inspirational for the author of the Letter from Heaven. Of course, this cannot be substantiated; also, the list of forbidden activities is far shorter in the Letter from Heaven or even missing in the Greek

71. See Heil, introduction to *From Sun-Day to the Lord's Day*.

72. See above, n. 1.

73. Sabbath prohibitions mentioned are (in Ethiopic transmission): not preparing something for eating or drinking (see Exod 16:5), not drawing water, not carrying (see Jer 17:21f.) anything (Jubilees 2:29); also not being with one's wife, making a journey for the purpose of buying or selling, drawing water, walking a path, tending one's property at home or elsewhere, kindling a fire, packing an animal, traveling by ship on the sea, striking or killing someone, slaughtering an animal or bird, hunting or fighting (50:8–12).

74. James C. VanderKam, *The Book of Jubilees: A Critical Text and Translation*, 2 vols., CSCO 510–11 (Leuven: Peeters, 1989). See also his thorough commentary in the Hermeneia series: *Jubilees: A Commentary in Two Volumes* (Minneapolis: Fortress, 2018), here 1:14 on the Latin text, 1:202f. and 2:1202–14 on the prohibitions. See also Doering, "Notion of *mela'khah*," 94f. The palimpsest manuscript is Codex Ambrosianus C 73 inf.; the website of the transcription project of Todd R. Hanneken is https://tinyurl.com/45857e8u (accessed September 14, 2022). However, the relevant chapters on Sabbath restriction are missing in Codex. Ambros. C 73 inf.

recensions. A clear example is the lighting of a fire, which does not occur here in the letter.[75] So the Sabbath is transferred to Sunday, but the Sabbath rest associated with it is by no means identical. The direct call to other good deeds, for example, also accompanies the commandment to observe Sunday. Therefore, the emphasis is not on work rest per se but on such activities that prevent a person from spending the day doing spiritual things and going to church.

An interpretation that places the prohibitions of activities in a context with the prohibition of fasting and kneeling as a posture of prayer[76] might be helpful. These two practices have a character of penance and call into question the joyful and festive character of Sunday, as do the activities described as servitude. Not only do they prevent attendance at worship; they also contradict the character of the day. In the Greek texts the celebration of the Christians in communion with the angels and saints is an act that also has the power to absolve sins, so that an absence or preoccupation with other things defiles the community and attracts heavenly punishment. In the Latin texts the character of the holiday itself is more in the foreground, and the determination as to what behavior is appropriate or not. Common to all texts is the prohibition of disputes and other quarrels, which of course generally contradict a Sunday as a holiday and a day of reconciliation, which will be briefly explained below.

4.2.4. A Day of Reconciliation

The pausing of court proceedings is the only area of actual overlap between imperial legislation and Christian conceptions, as handed down in the church orders and as offered by the Letter from Heaven in its general admonitions to avoid strife. In Constantine's law about Sunday rest in 321, one can read that "all judges [*iudices*] and urban peoples [*urbanaeque plebes*] and artisans of all crafts [*atrium official cunctarum*] should rest on the venerable day of the sun."[77] Interestingly, the effect of this law on legal proceedings is documented in two extant papyri from the 320s CE, which mention the pause of negotiations until Monday.[78] Later imperial legislation also repeats this judicial recess, which thus forms the most distinctive aspect of Sunday legislation.

---

75. Jubilees 50:12.

76. For the references, see p. 129.

77. See p. 19f. and p. 3 above with n. 2. Especially in this aspect Constantine's law is based on the general Roman understanding of a holiday (*feriae*). Still worth reading is Nicolai, "Feiertage und Werktage," esp. 202-7.

78. Stephen R. Llewelyn, *New Documents Illustrating Early Christianity*, vol. 9, *A Review of the Greek Inscriptions and Papyri Published in 1986–87* (Grand Rapids: Eerdmans, 2002): Papyrus Oxyrhynchos LIV 3759 and Papyrus Oxyrhynchos XLVIII 3407 on pp. 106–18.

This has obviously also been the practice in ecclesiastical trials. Evidence of this is a passage in the Apostolic Constitutions 2.47 (probably from the fourth century), where one can read that Monday should be the day for lawsuits, in order to keep Sunday free from legal disputes:

> Your courts are to be held on the second day of the week, so that if your judgment is contested, you may have time until the Sabbath to consider the appeal and to bring peace among those who quarrel with each other until the Day of the Lord.[79]

This is confirmed to some extent at the Spanish Council of Tarragona in 516 CE, canon 4, which shows that this conviction is not limited to the Greek East of the fourth century:

> No bishop or presbyter or cleric shall dare to sit in judgment on Sunday, whatever the case, but they shall celebrate only the sacrifices due to God. On other days, however, they have the freedom to judge what is just to settle quarrels, with the exception of criminal cases.[80]

Interestingly, clerics are also responsible for judging cases in which someone has not respected Sunday rest by performing some work—for example, according to canon 31 of the Council of Orléans in 538 CE.[81] This congruence

---

79. Const. Ap. 2.47:1–2 (SC 320:288:1–6 Metzger): Τὰ δικαστήρια ὑμῶν γινέσθω δευτέρᾳ σαββάτων, ὅπως, ἐὰν ἀντιλογία τῇ ἀποφάσει ὑμῶν γένηται, ἕως σαββάτου ἔχοντες ἄδειαν δυνηθείητε εὐθῦναι τὴν ἀντιλογίαν καὶ εἰρηνεῦσαι εἰς τὴν κυριακὴν τοὺς διαφερομένους πρὸς ἀλλήλους (my translation). See also *Syriac Didaskalia* 11.

80. Gonzalo Martínez Díez and Félix Rodríguez, eds., *La colección canónica Hispana IV: Concilios Galos: Concilios Hispanos: primera parte* (Madrid: Consejo Superior de Investigaciones Científicas, 1984), 274:61–65: *Ut nullus episcoporum aut presbyterorum vel clericorum die Dominico propositum cuiuscumque causae negotium audeat iudicare, nisi hoc tantum, ut Deo statuta sollemnia peragant; ceteris vero diebus, conibentibus personis, illa quae iusta sunt, habeant licentiam iudicandi, excepto criminalia negotia* (translation by Nadine Pirringer). This seems to exclude even manumission, which Constantine had conceded as a possible exception from Sunday rest (*emancipandi* and *manumittendi*; see Mitthof, "Christianization of the Empire"). Interestingly, also presbyters are responsible for legal proceedings, not only the bishop. See the laws on *iudicium episcopale* or *audientia episcopalis* in Cod. theod. 1.27.1 (Constantine declared that if parties in a lawsuit wanted to defer their case to a bishop as arbitrator, the secular judge had to be in agreement and must pronounce the bishop's decision as his verdict); 1.27.2; 1.4.7–8 (Arcadius/Honorius/Theodosius). On disputed matters regarding the bishop's legal jurisdiction and duties, see Caroline Humfress, *Orthodoxy and the Courts in Late Antiquity* (Oxford: Oxford University Press, 2007); Adriaan J. B. Sirks, "The *episcopalis audientia* in Late Antiquity," *Droit et cultures* 65 (2013): 79–88.

81. See below, p. 177f.

between imperial and ecclesiastical conceptions is probably the background for the fact that an inscription with an imperial law of 386 CE confirming these judicial vacations on Sunday was placed on a wall of a church. It has recently been excavated in Anaia, south of Ephesus, and the Greek text of the law even threatens capital punishment.[82] In addition, as far as the sources indicate, it can also be assumed that ecclesiastical synods began on Monday rather than on Sunday. At most, a solemn final declaration may have been read during a Sunday service.[83]

This judicial recess for Sundays, formulated in imperial as well as ecclesiastical laws, is not cited in the Letters from Heaven, to be sure. But the general idea that Sunday is a day of peace, on which one should not approach the altar in strife and hatred, is always cited. This is thus formulated along the lines of the Sermon on the Mount, where Matthew 5:23f. says: "Therefore, if you are offering your gift at the altar and there remember that your brother or sister has something against you, leave your gift there in front of the altar. First go and be reconciled to them; then come and offer your gift." The texts consider Sunday as a day of reconciliation with God, a day of forgiveness of sins. Therefore, all Christians are invited to go to church and seek forgiveness for their sins, as the above-presented sermons explicitly state. Parallel to reconciliation with God, quarrels on earth should be avoided, and therefore debates about legal issues should be suspended for the time of this day.

In addition to the call to reconcile and avoid strife, readers or listeners of the Letter from Heaven are urged to care for the poor, the sick, orphans, and widows, and also to welcome guests and pilgrims and bury the deceased (Latin recensions). This confirms the aspect already mentioned in the introduction, that the Lord's Day is a day of good deeds. In this respect, despite all

82. See Heil and Mitthof, "Missachtung der Sonntagsruhe," 75–92. This concerns the law in Cod. theod. 2.8.18 from 386 CE: "Emperors Flavii Theodosius and Valentinian, Augustuses, to Principius, Praetorian Prefect. On the bright day, which our ancestors properly called the Lord's Day, the prosecution of all litigation, court business, and lawsuits shall be entirely suspended. No person shall demand the payment of a public or a private debt, nor shall there be any acknowledgment of controversies before arbitrators, whether they have been requested or chosen voluntarily. Such a person shall be adjudged not only as infamous and sacrilegious, but shall also be subject to sentence of capital punishment." ☦ Φλ(άουιοι) Θεοδόσιος καὶ Οὐαλλεντινιανὸς Αὔγουστοι πρὸς Πρινκήπιον ἔπαρχον πό(λεως). ἐν τῇ φαιδρᾷ ἡμέρᾳ, ἣν κυριακὴν κυρίως οἱ πρόγονοι εἰρήκασιν, πασῶν τὸ καθόλου δικῶν, πραγμάτων τε καὶ μεθοδιῶν ἐπίτασις ἡσυχαζέτω· ὄφλημα δημόσιον ἢ ἰδιωτικὸν μηδεὶς ἀνυέτω, μήτε δὲ ἐπὶ μεσιτῶν αὐτῶν, αἰτηθέντων ἢ ἑκουσίως αἱρηθέντων, ἐπίτασις ἀψιμαχιῶν τις συνκροτίσθω·οὐ μόνον γὰρ ἄτιμος καὶ ἱερόσυλος κληθήσεται ὁ τοιοῦτος, ἀλλὰ καὶ κεφαλικὴν ὑποστήσεται τιμωρίαν. ☦. See also Malay, "Inscription from Anaia," 175f.

83. See Graumann, "Synodical Activities."

restrictions, the Letter from Heaven remains within a Christian tradition of designating the Lord's Day as a feast day for good deeds. As an early example, we can refer to Justin Martyr, who writes in his *First Apology* (chap. 67) about Sunday activities:

> And there is a distribution and partaking of the eucharistic elements to each one, and they are sent by means of the deacons to those who are not present. (6) But those who are well-off and are willing give—each what he wishes, according to his own choice—and what is gathered together is deposited with the supervisor. (7) And he assists orphans and widows and those who are in need because of illness or some other cause, and those who are in chains, and the foreigners who are staying with us. And he is generally the protector of all who are in need.[84]

The text speaks for itself: even if Justin here in his apologetic text wants to show the behavior of the Christians in a more than positive light, other texts also indicate that especially Sunday was used to distribute the donated gifts and to take care of the needy. In the introduction, examples from John Chrysostom are quoted, as well as the interesting law to take care of prisoners on Sunday.[85] Therefore, it is not only a day for worship but also one for charity. Thus, one was admonished in the sermon to donate from one's abundance to the needy, either by presenting contributions to the deacon for distribution or by delivering contributions to the needy oneself. There are many studies on how care for the poor and sick was organized and how important it was,[86]

---

84. Justin, *1 Apol.* 67.5–7 (260.4–11 Minns and Parvis with translation p. 261, slightly altered): καὶ ἡ διάδοσις καὶ ἡ μετάληψις ἀπὸ τῶν εὐχαριστηθέντων ἑκάστῳ γίνεται, καὶ τοῖς οὐ παροῦσι διὰ τῶν διακόνων πέμπεται. (6) οἱ εὐποροῦντες δὲ καὶ βουλόμενοι, κατὰ προαίρεσιν ἕκαστος τὴν ἑαυτοῦ, ὃ βούλεται δίδωσι, καὶ τὸ συλλεγόμενον παρὰ τῷ προεστῶτι ἀποτίθεται. (7) καὶ αὐτὸς ἐπικουρεῖ ὀρφανοῖς τε καὶ χήραις καὶ τοῖς διὰ νόσον ἢ δι' ἄλλην αἰτίαν λειπομένοις καὶ τοῖς ἐν δεσμοῖς οὖσι καὶ τοῖς παρεπιδήμοις οὖσι ξένοις, καὶ ἁπλῶς πᾶσι τοῖς ἐν χρείᾳ οὖσι κηδεμὼν γίνεται. See above, p. 18, and Jörg Ulrich, "Ethik als Ausweis christlicher Identität bei Justin Martyr," *ZEE* 50 (2006): 21–28.

85. See pp. 8f. and 19f.

86. Tobias Georges, "Das Gemeindemahl bei Tertullian in Apologeticum 39—eine nichtsakramentale Agapefeier?," *ZAC* 16 (2012): 279–91; Becky Walker, "The Salvific Effects of Almsgiving and the Moral Status of the Poor in Talmudic Judaism and Late Antique Christianity," *JSQ* 27 (2020): 1–21; Blake Leyerle, "John Chrysostom on Almsgiving and the Use of Money," *HTR* 87 (1994): 29–48; Gary B. Fengren, *Medicine and Health Care in Early Christianity* (Baltimore: Johns Hopkins University Press, 2009); Paul Allen and Wendy Meyer, "Through a Bishop's Eyes: Towards a Definition of Pastoral Care in Late Antiquity," *Augustinianum* 40 (2000): 345–97.

ever since Adolf von Harnack included a large chapter in his standard work on mission and spread of Christianity during the first three centuries under the keyword "Gospel of Love."[87] Unfortunately, the temporal aspect is not taken into account here, even if the texts addressed suggest that such actions were organized especially on the Lord's Day. This is a desideratum for further research.

4.2.5. Ecclesiastical Canons and Punitive Miracles

While the Letter from Heaven opens up the possibility of being out and about on Sunday "for charitable purposes," so to speak, the list of activities that are forbidden is much longer and shapes the character of the letters especially in the Latin recensions. This is underscored by a backdrop of weighty threats, which are outlined in various passages of the letters (see below). In this respect, it has often been stated that the Letter from Heaven is to be interpreted in the context of other texts, especially from Gaul in the late sixth century, even if the interpretation of the phenomenon varies.[88] These texts can be sorted into three groups: (1) sermons and *vitae*, containing Sunday punitive miracle stories; (2) ecclesiastical canons; and (3) royal laws. Overall, they show that a specific regional development in the northern area of Gaul, beginning in the sixth century, is reflected in punitive miracle narratives about people who worked on Sunday.[89] This then finds its way into ecclesiastical canons, and finally into

---

87. Adolf von Harnack, *Mission und Ausbreitung des Christentums in den ersten drei Jahrhunderten, 4. verbesserte und vermehrte Auflage mit elf Karten* (Leipzig, 1924). See Jan M. Bremmer, *The Rise of Christianity through the Eyes of Gibbon, Harnack, and Rodney Stark: A Valedictory Lecture on the Occasion of His Retirement from the Chair of Religious Studies, in the Faculty of Theology and Religious Studies, Delivered in Abbreviated Form before the University of Groningen on 29 January 2010* (Groningen: Barkhuis, 2010). See also Andreas Müller, ed., *Wohltätigkeit im antiken und spätantiken Christentum*, Studien der Patristischen Arbeitsgemeinschaft 16 (Leuven: Peeters, 2021), and Müller, "Caritas im Neuen Testament und in der Alten Kirche," in *Caritas—Barmherzigkeit—Diakonie. Studien zu Begriffen und Konzepten des Helfens in der Geschichte des Christentums vom Neuen Testament bis ins späte 20. Jahrhundert*, ed. Michaela Collinet, Religion—Kultur—Gesellschaft 2 (Münster: LIT, 2014), 17–47 (a good overview).

88. See Meier, "Christian Sunday," and Wood, "Hagiography and the Canons," and Kinzig, "Sunday Observance," 251-72, 273-92, 319-72; see also my introduction to this volume, at pp. 22–24. See also next note and note 98.

89. Duard Grounds, *Miracles of Punishment and the Religion of Gregory of Tours and Bede*, Theologie 110 (Vienna: LIT, 2015), with his research history at 3-19 on different previous interpretations of these miracles (phenomenon of decline, pagan magical thinking, mirror of violence and crime in society, means to strengthen episcopal authority, their juridical might, to enforce attending Sunday church service).

royal legislation. Even though all these texts do not mention the Letter from Heaven, they are probably to be understood as background music.

Of course, punitive miracles in themselves are not unique to the sixth century, and neither are they alien to Christianity, as we have some examples also in the New Testament (e.g., the punishment of the skeptical Zechariah in Luke 1; the penalty of death for Ananias and Sapphira in Acts 5; the cursing of the fig tree in Mark 11; Acts 13), and many in the apocryphal Acts of the Apostles—pseudepigraphal texts that are widespread and often read (e.g., Acts of John 44; 86; Acts of Philip 133–136). One can also consider the Acts of the Martyrs, which sometimes contain a malediction of the martyr on his tormentor.[90] What is new, of course, is the theme of Sunday.

The very special character of the punitive miracles related to Sunday[91] is obvious. They all have a common scheme quite different from other stories about divine punishments: someone is doing some sort of work on Sunday. The context is rural labor or housework, as in the Letter from Heaven, and both men and women are affected. Then an accident with serious injury occurs, and the injury is related to the previous deeds as a symbolic punishment. The one affected searches for help either from a living saint or at a saint's grave, sometimes immediately, sometimes years later. An admonition often concludes the story. Therefore, the stories have two foci, the misdeed and the healing, such that the term "punishment miracle" is actually

90. Protomartyr Stephen asks God for forgiveness for his persecutors (Acts 7:58f.), but see, e.g., the *Passio Perpetua et Felicitas* 18.8 (ed. Thomas J. Heffernan, *The Passion of Perpetua and Felicitas* [Oxford: Oxford University Press, 2012], 120): *tu nos, inquiunt, te autem Deus.* See also Tertullian's threats with divine punishment (*Scap.* 3.4f.); also Mart. Pol. 9.2; Justin Martyr, *1 Apol.* 45.

91. Most can be found in Gregory of Tours (538-594 CE): his *Liber vitae patrum* (twenty *Lives* of the Fathers) contain thirteen punitive miracles, of which two are related to Sunday (§7.5—Gregory of Langres; §15.3—Abbas Senoch from Tours); *Liber in Gloria martyrum*, with forty-three punitive miracles, one related to Sunday (§15); *Vita Juliani*: one out of sixteen punishment miracles (§11); *Vita Martini*: ten out of thirty punishment miracles (2.13; 2.24; 3.3; 3.7; 3.29; 3.31; 3.45; 3.55; 3.56; 4.45); *Historia Francorum*: one out of fifty-four punishment miracles (10.30). Another example is Venantius Fortunatus (540–610 CE) and his *vita* of Germanus of Paris. He presents seven punishment miracles related to Sunday labor (§§14, 16, 35, 49, 50, 51, 58), but his focus is on the healing activities of Germanus, mainly via oil, to show Germanus as a medical expert (*mirificus medicus*). Afterward there are only rare examples (*Vita beati Maurilii; Vita Audoini episcopi Rotomagensis* 9; *Vita sancti Arnulfi* 28; Rimbert, *Vita Ansgarii* 37). See also Hans-Werner Goetz, "Wunderberichte im 9. Jahrhundert. Ein Beitrag zum Genus der frühmittelalterlichen Mirakelsammlungen," in *Mirakel im Mittelalter: Konzeptionen —Erscheinungsformen—Deutungen*, ed. Martin Heinzelmann et al. (Stuttgart: Steiner, 2002), 180-226.

misleading—they are at the same time healing stories. They are examples of rebuke, but with good endings. This is interesting insofar as other punishment stories on theft, heresy, stealing relics, and so on may even result in death—but this is not the case with Sunday miracles.[92]

In addition, the story as a whole is a public event. It presents a kind of public penance, sometimes concluding with admonishing words by the one affected, like in the *Vita Martini* (3.7), "He praised the bishop's [Saint Martin] power and warned that no one else attempt what he had dared,"[93] or in the *Vita Juliani* (11): the affected person "presented to the people an important lesson, because what had been done on a Sunday was also forgiven on a Sunday. The man extolled the glory of the martyr and departed in good health. Never again did he dare to do any work on the day of the Lord's resurrection."[94] Usually, a bishop or another cleric is lacking, and the interpretation of the misdeed is given by the affected individual, who is a layperson. The reports therefore tend to reflect stories told among laypeople, even if they are handed down in *vitae* written by bishops.

This upcoming regional movement (Gaul) of telling Sunday miracles can be detected first in the *Vita Genovefae*, written in the 520s, which contains two punitive miracles related to Sunday.[95] In chapter 37 we read:

> In that town [Troyesin the province of Lyon], a man was brought to her who had been blinded by divine vengeance for working on the Lord's Day, as well as a girl of nearly twelve years who had similarly been blinded. She illuminated their eyes by making the sign of the cross, invoking each person of the Trinity.

And in chapter 55:

---

92. See also the above-mentioned incubation miracle on Sunday, p. 21f.

93. Gregory of Tours, *Libri de virtutibus sancti Martini* 3.7 (MGH SRM 1.2, 184.1f. Krusch): *conlaudans virtutem antistitis, et, ut nullus adgrederetur, quod ipse praesumpserat, praedicabat.*

94. Gregory of Tours, *Liber de virtutibus sancti Juliani* 11 (MGH SRM 1.2, 119.14–18 Krusch): *Statim in ipsa die dominica reserata manus lignum, quod invitus tenebat, amisit; magnam inferens populo disciplinam, ut quod die dominica fuerat perpetratum ipsa quoque die dominica purgaretur. At ille magnificans gloriam martyris, recessit incolomis, nec ultra die resurrectionis dominicae quicquam ausus est operare.* Translation by Raymond Van Dam, *Saints and Their Miracles in Late Antique Gaul* (Princeton: Princeton University Press, 1993), 171.

95. *Vita Genovefae* (MGH SRM 3, 204–38 Krusch); see on the *vita* Martin Heinzelmann, "L'hagiographie mérovingienne: Panorama des document potentiels," in *L'hagiographie mérovingienne à travers ses réécritures*, ed. Monique Goullet et al., Beihefte der Francia 71 (Ostfildern: Thorbecke, 2010), 27–82.

> Both hands of a certain Goth who was working on the Lord's Day became contracted. All night he lay at Genovefa's tomb, imploring that his health be restored. The next day his hands were healed and he went forth cured from the oratory above the wooden sepulcher.[96]

Therefore, in the *vita* there are already two similar Sunday miracles, one by the living Genovefa, one by the deceased Genovefa. In contrast, nothing comparable is mentioned in the *vita* of Rusticola of Arles in Southern Gaul, for example, or of Caesarius of Arles. And in the *vitae* of saints in Spain in those days, this theme is completely missing as well.[97]

Of course, the punishment stories present an interpreted reality, not reality itself. This is obvious in the recurrent feature of a time span between injury and healing. Injuries are later interpreted as the consequence of working on Sunday—this is also a kind of elucidation. Thus, on the one hand, these stories have a "desupernaturalizing" effect: the cause of an injury is now clear (Sunday violation). Therefore, these punishment miracles relating to Sunday are actually not divine punishment stories including a woe or prophetic warning or a curse; instead, all of these stories are healing stories, as stated above. The healing power of a saint is the focus of these stories, and the goal is the public (!) repentance of the sinner, who sees and confesses his failure.

Interestingly, Ian Wood states that the stories can also be read as directed against any doubt or skepticism regarding Christian saints and feasts. The stories, therefore, are not only examples of strong belief in miracles but also indicate the contrary and present an "index of the limits of popular devotion."[98] In those times, it was still not obvious for everybody that this kind of Sunday labor may have had such an impact—it was a debated issue met with

---

96. *Vita Genovefae* 37 (MGH SRM 3, 230.19–231.4 Krusch): *Cumque ad civitatem Trecassium pervenisset, occurrit ei multitudo populi offerentes infirmus, quos illa signans et benedicens incolomis reddebat. Oblatus est ei in eadem urbem homo, quem dominico die operantem ultio divina damnavit in lumine, nec non et puella annorum fere XII similiter ceca. Quorum illa oculos, facto crucis signaculo, invocata individua Trinitate, inluminavit.* *Vita Genovefae* 55 (MGH SRM 3, 237.12–15 Krusch): *Cuidam Goto die dominico operanti manus utraque contraxerunt. Hic cum ad sepulcrum Genuvefe sanitatem sibi reddi nocte tota inplorasset, in crastinum ab oraturio super sepulcrum de ligno contextum, recepta manuum suarum sanitatem incolomis egressus est.* Translation by Jo Anne McNamara, *Sainted Women of the Dark Ages* (Durham, NC: Duke University Press, 1992), 31 and 26. See Wood, "Hagiography," 281f.

97. As also in the Spanish councils of Toledo. On Martin of Brage, see n. 101.

98. Last sentence in Ian Wood, "How Popular Was Early Medieval Devotion?," Essays in Medieval Studies 14 (1997), online, https://tinyurl.com/m43jdpv8 (accessed September 19, 2022). See also Wood, "Early Merovingian Devotion in Town and Country," *Studies in Church History* 16 (1979): 61–76.

much skepticism. This explains the inclusion of admonishing remarks, as well as the involvement of laypeople.

On the other hand, the stories demonstrate a new tendency toward a sacralization of time. The whole day demands special behavior, not only the time given to a Sunday service. As the society changed and certain elements lost importance, including the traditional Roman calendar with its feasts, offerings, processions, and games, the new Christian festal calendar became more important than in previous decades. Therefore, the growing importance of not working on Sunday replaced other activities or omissions from earlier times as identity markers of a Christian life, such as not going to a temple and refusing to make offerings to gods or to the emperor. This interpretation refutes, therefore, other evaluations of these stories as part of a pre-Christian pagan heritage, pagan magical thinking, or even pre-animistic thinking or Germanic taboos intruding into Christianity.[99]

Another common explanation is simply to see a higher degree of necessary disciplinary measures here, with recourse to the Old Testament. The newly converted "Germanic tribes" were only superficially Christians and would have had to be painstakingly taught a Christian way of life by means of laws and punishments. This explanation erroneously assumes an unbroken Christian acceptance of Sunday rest since Constantine's law and overlooks the fact that something new begins here, a Christian sacralization of time, which expresses itself in the sanctification of Sunday and the prohibition of "unholy" activities.[100] It is by no means the case that a proven practice only

---

99. This was emphasized above all by Thomas, to whom reference is made again and again: *Der Sonntag*, 22: "spätantiker Tagesgötterglaube [wird] von der ungebrochenen Primitivität germanischer Religiosität aufgegriffen und aus einem Winkel-Aberglauben zur sittenbildende Kraft gesteigert," 26: "primitive Tabu-Religiosität," "Germanisierung (oder Keltisierung) des Sonntags," 27: "ein Zugeständnis an tabuistische Strömungen dunklen Ursprungs"; see also 34, 37f., 48f.; see, e.g., McReavy, "Sunday Repose," 310 (who calls Gregory of Tours and the Letter from Heaven "Sabbatarian extremist" [314]); see Jungmann, "Die Heiligung des Sonntags," 65f.; also Haines, *Sunday Observance*, 36: "a popular belief in taboo-like restrictions." Apart from the aspect of rest from work, this refers above all to the references to a venerated Thursday, as attested by Caesarius of Arles. But today this is unanimously attributed to late antique heritage since Diocletian and not to a special Gallic or Celtic practice. See the contributions of Ilaria Bultrighini, "Thursday". On sacralization, see p. 192f.

100. See the critique with references also by Meier, "Christian Sunday," 254–57. Add Scheibelreiter, "Sonntagsarbeit," 176f., the problematic statement: "Diese wiederholten Bestimmungen verraten, dass das Christentum in den germanisch dominierten Gebieten überwiegend kultisch-rituell aufgefasst wurde und den neubekehrten, oberflächlich christianisiserten Menschen am ehesten auf dieser Ebene eingeschärft werden konnte. . . . Man musste dem Volk das Gebot des Sonntags gleichsam von der negativen Seite her

needs to be enforced with more harshness on the new converts. It is just that two historical lines of development overlap, that of the Christianization of time and the calendar and that of the Christianization of new groups since the fifth century.

Therefore, one can estimate that at the beginning of the sixth century, there emerged a special regional development in northern Gaul of telling such punishment stories against Sunday work—stories that are taken up later especially by Gregory, who finds in them a means to promote his favorite saint, Martin of Tours. They are likewise taken up by Venantius Fortunatus in his *vita* of Germanus of Paris to demonstrate his healing competence.[101] But as the decreed punishments in ecclesiastical canons or royal decrees do not correspond to the related miracle stories above, these stories therefore belong more to a popular movement regarding Sunday veneration occurring at this time. One text is of special importance, as it mirrors a new tendency and mentions a new popular belief, but at the same time displays some hesitation to go further. This is canon 31 from the third Council of Orléans under Merovingian rule in 538 CE:

---

einprägen, und das in seiner handfesten, derb-anschaulichen Art: durch den sichtbaren strafenden Eingriff Gottes." Also Bauckham, "Sabbath and Sunday in the Medieval Church," 303f. ("legalistic Sabbatarianism").

101. See n. 91. Venantius Fortunatus was a good friend of Gregory of Tours, Martin of Braga a good friend of Venantius; all three were engaged in promoting the saint Martin of Tours. These contacts probably led to the fact that also Martin of Braga gave a certain emphasis to Sunday; see *De correctione rusticorum* 18 (Barlow, *Opera omnia*, 202:11–22): *Diem dominicum, qui propterea dominicus dicitur, quia filius dei, dominus noster Iesus Christus, in ipso resurrexit a mortuis, nolite contemnere, sed cum reverentia colite. Opus servile, id est agrum, pratum, vineam, vel si qua gravia sunt, non faciatis in die dominico, praeter tantum quod ad necessitatem reficiendi corpusculi pro exquoquendo pertinet cibo et necessitate longinqui itineris. Et in locis proximis licet viam die dominico facere, non tamen pro occasionibus malis, sed magis pro bonis, id est aut ad loca sancta ambulare, aut fratrem vel amicum visitare, vel infirmum consolare, aut tribulanti consilium vel adiutorium pro bona causa portare. Sic ergo decet Christianum hominem diem dominicum venerare.* "Do not neglect the Lord's Day, but hold it in reverence, because on it the Son of God, our Lord Jesus Christ, arose from the dead. Do not perform servile work on the Lord's Day in field, meadow, vineyard, or any such important place, except only what pertains to cooking food to refresh the body or what is necessary for a long journey. You may make a journey on the Lord's Day to places nearby, but not for evil reasons, rather for good reasons, such as walking to holy places, visiting a brother or a friend, consoling the sick, or carrying counsel or aid for a good cause to one in trouble. Thus the Christian should honor the Lord's Day" (Barlow, *Iberian Fathers* 1:84). See Wood, "Hagiography and the Canons," 282–84 (with further literature).

> Because the opinion is spreading among the people that they are not allowed to cover a distance by horse or ox or with a wheelbarrow, nor to prepare any food, nor to do anything to ornament the house or the person on the Lord's Day, which are things known to belong more to Jewish than to Christian observance, we decree that that which was allowed on the Lord's Day in former times is still allowed. Nevertheless, regarding agricultural labor, namely plowing, (working in) vineyards, cutting, harvesting, winnowing and cultivation or hedging, we decree that they ought to be laid aside, in order that the people may come more easily to the church and may be free for thanksgiving and prayer. However, if someone is found doing such work as just mentioned, which is forbidden, he must be cleansed, but this is not in the competence of the layman, rather in that of episcopal penal power.[102]

This canon is an interesting mixture, for it also criticizes as a dispensable precaution and Jewish attitude people's avoidance of traveling, cooking, and adorning themselves—of course, people are still allowed to do these things on a Sunday. Nevertheless, lengthy, exhausting agricultural work is forbidden because it hinders people from attending church services. Interestingly, the canon takes up a popular opinion among common people in its first sentence. One must take this statement seriously; the other punitive miracle stories can be read as the background for the remark in canon 31: *quia persuasum est populos die domineco agi . . . non debere*. It is exactly this conviction of the common people that can be observed in the punishment miracles.[103]

Of importance here is to take a look at the mentioned cities or villages in the punitive miracle stories: the places where the miracles occur are Tours (5x); Langeais, eight miles west of Tours (1x); Angers (3x); Bourges (3xs); Limoges (1x); Brioude (1x); and Langres (1x). These are all in the province of

102. Concilii Aurelianensis (538 CE), canon 31 (CCSL 148A:125.281–92 de Clercq): *Quia persuasum est populis die domineco agi cum caballis aut bubus et ueiculis itinera non debere neque ullam rem ad uictum praeparari uel ad nectorem domus uel hominis pertenentem ullatenus exerciri, quae res ad iudaicam magis quam ad christeanam obseruantiam pertenere probatur, id statuimus, ut die dominico, quod ante fieri licuit, liceat. De opere tamen rurali, id est arata uel uinea uel sectione, messione, excussione, exarto uel saepe, censuimus abstenendum, quo facilius ad ecclesiam uenientes orationis gratiae uacent. Quod si inuentus fuerit quis in operibus supra scriptis, quae interdicta sunt, exercere, qualiter emundari debeat, non in laici districtione, sed in sacerdotis castigatione consistat* (my translation).

103. This conviction is also mirrored in the commentary presented by Gregory in five of his stories, in each of which the person healed offered something like a small sermon of admonishment (v. Jul. 11; v. Mart. 2.24; 3.7; 3.29; and Hist. Franc. 10.30; see above, n. 91).

Lyon and in the area of *Aquitania prima*. By far the majority of them belong to the region between Angers, Tours, and Bourges. Interestingly, all these cities were also represented at the Council of Orléans in 538. This council was called by Childebert I and Theodebert; therefore, the bishops of the other regions of Gaul, namely, those of Chlothar I, were not present. This observation supports the assessment that there is a regional trend here.

In contrast to these miracle stories, however, the canon states in its last sentence that it is not the task of laymen to judge here but of the bishops—they have the power of punishment. In later canons, penalty rates differentiated according to social status are established. In the miracle reports, it was a direct intervention of the punishing God with the transgressor; also in the healing or release from punishment, the episcopal authority does not occur, as described above. Also the Letter from Heaven (authorized by the highest Christian authority and publicly disseminated by the clergy) threatens immediate heavenly punishments—this is perhaps also a background for the ecclesiastical criticism of this letter.[104]

Some decades later, as a preliminary culmination of this development, bishops subscribed canon 1 of the Synod of Macon from the year 585, which states:

> For we see that the Christians, through inconsiderate habit, treat the Lord's Day with contempt and devote themselves to continuous work just as on non-festive days. Therefore, we determine with this synodal letter that each one of us should admonish those who are subordinate to him in the most sacred churches; if they receive the admonition willingly, it will serve them well, but if not, they will be subject to the punishment established by us according to divine will. Thus, all you Christians who do not delight in this name in vain, listen to our admonition, knowing that it is our duty to make provision for your well-being and to keep you from wrongdoing. Preserve the Lord's Day, which has given us new birth and freed us from all sins. None of you should use his time to instigate litigations, none of you should appear in court, nobody should put himself in the sort of predicament which forces him to place a yoke upon the neck of cattle. All of you, focus intently with body and soul on prayers and praise to God. If someone has a church nearby, he shall rush to it and devote himself to the Lord's Day with prayers and tears. Your eyes and hands shall be upraised to God this whole day. For this is the everlasting day of rest, it is that which is foretold to us through the figure of the seventh day and recognized by laws and prophets. Thus, it is right that we celebrate this day in peace, through which we have been made

104. See above the chapter on the history of the letter, p. 84.

what we were not before; for before we were servants of sin, but through it we have been made children of righteousness. Therefore, let us render willing service to the Lord, through whose love we know ourselves to be liberated from the prison of error—not because the Lord requires that we celebrate the Lord's Day with bodily abstinence, but because he demands obedience, through which, when we have relinquished worldly affairs, he guides us mercifully to heaven. Therefore, if any of you considers this healthful injunction unimportant or treats it with contempt, he shall know that he will be punished first by God and then will also be mercilessly subjected to priestly wrath, according to his respective status. If he is a lawyer, he shall irrecoverably lose his case; if he is a farmer or a servant, he shall suffer hard blows with a rod; if he is a cleric or a monk, he shall be banned from the community of the brothers for six months. For all this propitiates God towards us and drives away the torments of disease and barrenness and keeps them away. And let us spend that night which restores us to the divine and unapproachable light in spiritual watching and not sleep like those who are Christians in name only; but let us pray and watch with sacred occupations, so that we are considered worthy to become heirs of the kingdom of the Saviour.[105]

105. Macon, canon 1 (CCSL 148A:239.31–240.73 de Clercq): *Videmus enim populum christianum temerario more die dominica contemtui tradere et sicut in priuatis diebus operibus continuis indulgere. Propterea per hanc sinodalem nostram epistolam decernimus, ut unusquisque nostrum in sacrosanctis ecclesiis admoneat sibi subditam plebem; et si quidem admonitioni consensum praebuerint, suis proderunt utilitatibus, sin autem, subiacebunt poenis a nobis diuinitus definitis. Omnes itaque christiani, qui non incassum hoc nomine fruimini nostrae admonitione aurem accomodate, scientes, quoniam nostrae est auctoritatis utilitate uestrae prospicere et a malis operibus cohercere. Custodite diem dominicam, quae nos denuo peperit et a peccatis omnibus liberauit. Nullus uestrum litium fomitibus uacet, nullus ex uobis causarum actionis exerceat, nemo sibi talem necessitatem exibeat, quae iugum ceruicibus iuuencorum imponere cogat. Estote omnes in himnis et laudibus dei animo corpore que intenti. Si quis uestrum proximam habet ecclesiam, properet ad eandem et ibi dominico die semetipsum precibus lacrymis que afficiat. Sint oculi manus que uestrae toto illo diem ad deum expanse. Ipse est igitur dies requietionis perpetuus, ipse nobis per septimi diei umbram insinuatus noscitur legibus et profetis. Iustum igitur est, ut hanc diem unanimiter celebremus, per quam facti sumus, quod non fuimus; fuimus enim ante serui peccati, sed per eam facti sumus filii iustitiae. Exhibeamus dominum liberam seruitutem, cuius nos nouimus pietate de ergastulis liberatus errores, non quia hoc dominus noster a nobis expetit, ut corporali abstinentia die dominica celebremus, sed querit obedientiam, per quam nos calcatis terrenis actibus coelum usque misericorditer proueat. Si quis itaque uestrum hanc salubrem exortationem parui penderit aut contemtui tradiderit, sciat se pro qualitatis merito principaliter a deo punire et deinceps sacerdotali quoque irae implacabiliter subiacere; si causedecus fuerit, irreparabiliter causam amittat; si rusticus aut seruus, grauioribus fustium ictibus uerberabitur; si clericus aut monachus,*

This canon takes up the idea of divine punishment, but also the episcopal right to set up an episcopal penal roll. Mentioned is a "punishment established by us according to divine will." Likewise, the sentence "Therefore, if any of you considers this healthful injunction unimportant or treats it with contempt, he shall know that he will be punished first by God and then will also be mercilessly subjected to priestly wrath, according to his respective status," also combines divine punishment with episcopal might. Criticized is the fact that Christians devote themselves to continuous work, just as on non-festive days, and to personal business (e.g., they instigate litigation, appear in court, or place a yoke on the neck of cattle); these critiques are comparable to aforementioned texts. This is not the place to list all of the following synodical provisions.[106] It should only be noted that some of them were also incorporated into royal law collections. In the sixth and seventh centuries, this theme both strengthened episcopal power in the church and demarcated ecclesiastical and secular spheres of power, as it was quite arguable who determined and also enforced the measures. It is only in the Carolingian period that we find a resumption of this topic and corresponding heaps of synodal decisions. This has already been discussed in the context of the history of the Letter from Heaven.

These texts discussed here have a congruence in time and content with the Letter from Heaven, whose existence is also first attested at the end of the sixth century. It is possible, therefore, that a cleric saw himself called on to resort to yet another means, in addition to the tales of punitive miracles, in order to impress on the population the importance of the Lord's Day, not to miss church services, and to cease completing their daily chores on Sundays. Of course, this cannot be proven. The differences between the various versions, especially between the Latin and Greek traditions, could also indicate that in the Latin area an already existing Greek letter was adapted. The Greek texts in this volume, especially the three sermons and the *Diataxis*, show an interest in the subject in the Greek-speaking world around 600 CE. The tradition and external testimonia, however, argue for a Latin origin of the Letter from Heaven. We would like to know from where the bishop of

mensibus sex a consortio suspendatur fratrum. Haec namque omnia et placabilem erga nos dei animum reddunt et plagas morborum uel sterelitatum amouent atque repellunt. Noctem quoque ipsam, quae nos inspiratae luci inaccessibili reddit, spiritalibus exigamus excubiis nec dormiamus in ea, quemadmodum dormitant, qui nomine tenus christiani esse noscuntur, sed oremus et uigilemus operibus sacris, ut digni habeamur in regno haeredes fieri saluatoris. Translation by Kathrin Breimayer; see https://sola.acdh.oeaw.ac.at/dataset?id=385&type=Passage.

106. See Kinzig, "Sunday Observance," 319–72.

Ibiza had obtained his letter—Licinianus does not give any information about this.[107]

Nevertheless, the Letters from Heaven also have a tendency somewhat different from the punitive miracles: the Letters are more ecclesiastical, so to speak, since they clearly demand church attendance, issue a reminder for the payment of tithes, and require their content to be read publicly by the clergy, as mentioned in the letter of Licianus. After all, the letters are found by priests or bishops who attest to the authenticity of the Letter from Heaven. Thus, it would appear that a resourceful cleric seized on this new regional movement, evidenced in the punitive miracles, and with this Letter from Heaven gave it a slant of its own.

4.2.6. Duration of Sunday until Monday Morning

An extraordinary feature within the Letter from Heaven is the determination of the length of Sunday from Sabbath evening to Monday morning. The ninth hour of the Sabbath is always mentioned (that is, about 3:00 p.m.);[108] the end is given either as dawn or the first hour of the second day.[109] This is found not only in the Greek versions but also in the Latin ones.[110]

---

107. See pp. 85–88 and 209–12. It also remains a riddle because, although Martin of Braga offers comparable statements about Sunday work (see above, n. 101), there are no punitive miracle narratives about Sunday there.

108. The ninth hour can mean the time between 2 and 3 p.m., exactly 3 p.m., or even some time after that, because we must not apply a modern standard of punctuality to the ancient texts. It was widespread in antiquity to divide the day of light into four parts by *terz*, *sext*, and *non*. See Anja Wolkenhauser, *Sonne und Mond, Kalender und Uhr. Studien zur Darstellung und poetischen Reflexion der Zeitordnung in der römischen Literatur*, Untersuchungen zur antiken Literatur und Geschichte 103 (Berlin: de Gruyter, 2010), esp. 68-148.

109. See Latin Recension II (Vienna 1355) 5.1: *ab hora nona sabbati usque in horam primam secundae feriae*; Latin Recension I (Vienna 1355) 9.4: *in die sabbati de hora nona usque lucescente die lune feriatis*; Latin Recension I (Graz 248): *in die sabbato de hora nona usque lucescente die lunae*; Latin Recension III (Toulouse 208, see p. 115): *ab hora nona sabbati usque in diem lune luce clara coruscant*; Greek Recension Alpha 1, 4.5: ἀπὸ ὥρας ἐννάτης τοῦ σαββάτου ἕως δευτέρας ἐπιφαυσκούσης; Greek Recension Alpha 2, 10.1: ἀπὸ ὥρας ἐννάτης τοῦ σαββάτου νὰ ἀφήνετε τὸ ἐργόχειρον ἕως τῆς δευτέρας ἐπιφαυσκούσης ἡλίου; Greek Recension Beta 7.8 (as a woe, also in Gamma): ἀπὸ ὥρας ἐννάτης τοῦ σαββάτου ἕως δευτέρας ἐπιφωσκόυσης ἡλίου. It is only missing in Latin Recension I in the manuscripts Paris 12270 and London 19725, probably left out by intention.

110. It is also found in some versions of the *Visio Pauli*—probably owing to the influence of the Letter from Heaven; see p. 426 (Version B: *de hora nona sabbati usque ad secundam feriam hora prima*), and in the Apocalypse of Anastasia; see p. 500 (ἀπὸ ὥρας ἐννάτης τοῦ σαββάτου ἕως δευτέρας ἐπιφωσκούσης).

It is common and in line with traditional liturgical thinking, including the Jewish tradition, to have the day begin and end on the eve (see Lev 23:32 on Sabbath: from evening to evening).[111] Several texts in late antiquity and the early Middle Ages confirm this understanding *a vespere ad vesperam*.[112] What is unusual here is to extend the day to Monday morning. Is the intention here simply to protect Sunday by an additional temporal buffer? So that the following night does not desecrate the Sunday again?

Another explanation might be that this extended period for Sunday unites different understandings of the beginning and end of the day. While in Judaism the day begins from the evening before, which is also common in Christianity in liturgical traditions, in Egypt the day ends only on the next morning, so the night still belongs to it.[113] Furthermore, as is well known, when counting the hours of the day, the day begins at sunrise, and the bright time of day is divided into twelve hours (light hours). This is also the basis for the indication of the ninth hour in the Letter from Heaven.

This seems to be a more reasonable explanation than assuming that the author simply wanted to extend Sunday as long as possible. The letter does not explain this in more detail, but it is simply demanded. Perhaps this detail was even one of the reasons for writing the Letter from Heaven. It is conspicuous, however, and not specifically explained. Even in the criticism of the Letter from Heaven, as far as it is tangible, this point is not addressed. Therefore the explanation of this unique feature of the Letter from Heaven remains speculative.

---

111. Therefore, the liturgy of some festivals has the feast day begin the evening before, although a beginning of a day in the morning is also transmitted in the Hebrew Bible (see Gen 1:3–5). See Jack Belzer, "Tagesbeginn," in *Neues Bibel-Lexikon* (Zürich: Benziger, 2001), 3:770f.

112. See Dumaine, "Dimanche," 961–63.

113. See Beckerath, "Zeiteinteilung, -messung, " 1371f.; Kadish, "Time"; Victor Grumel, *La chronologie*, Traité d'études byzantines 1 (Paris: Presses Universitaires, 1958), 163-65. Also Harald Buchinger confirms (by email) this extraordinary feature and suspects that two different ways of thinking have come together here: one, in the cultural context of the source, common counting of days from morning to morning, and one (as a relic of a more archaic reckoning) counting from evening to evening on highlighted feast days.

4.3. Threats and Punishments

Uta Heil

As described already, the Letter from Heaven is first of all a letter in the general sense that a document is sent from A to B and is read. However, a reply is not expected, nor is there a polite greeting, because it is actually an indictment. The Letter from Heaven is therefore also similar to a prophetic judgment speech, as in Amos or other prophets, but also takes elements from the so-called little apocalypse from the Gospels. A recurring verse (only in the Greek recensions) is therefore Matthew 24:35: "Heaven and earth will pass away, but my words will not pass away!" From this same little apocalypse,[1] elements from the subsequent chapter of the last judgment from Matthew 25 are also incorporated. Of course, in these biblical texts Sunday is not in the foreground, but the focus is in general the approaching end of the world and in Matthew 25 the necessary care of the needy, such as hungry, thirsty, or sick persons, foreigners, and prisoners. If one has not shown mercy to these during one's lifetime, then eternal fire threatens. In addition, one has to add threats against those who reject the letter and refuse to read and distribute it. The Letter from Heaven was written on the basis of this biblical tradition—thus the letter places itself in the biblical tradition, which is read by Christians as the word of Christ. In this way, reading the letter imitates biblical language, but this is alienated by the threat of catastrophe and the radical nature of the letter.

The general tendency of the Greek recensions is that the letter pertains not only to an individual or a congregation but to the whole of humankind, which is threatened with destruction by God. The Latin Recension II is more individual and does not announce the destruction of all humankind. Rather, it threatens individual punishments and is in this respect comparable to the punitive miracles described above.[2] The following tables provide an overview, first of the Latin recensions:

1. At least in the Greek traditions; see pp. 87, 295.
2. See pp. 172–82.

Recension II, acc. to Vienne ÖNB 1355 (also Munich clm 9550, Hamburg, S. Petri 30b, Todi / Amaduzzi)	**Recension I, acc. to Tarragona (Baluzius)**	**Recension I, acc. to Vienne ÖNB 1355** (also Graz 248, London, Add. 19725, Basel, UB B VII 7)
house	**world**	
2.1.2 *conturbationem malam in domos vestras / maledictionem*—a bad disturbance / curse into your houses	14.3 *mundus iste iudicatus est in grandi ruina*	2.1 *propter hoc perit mundus*—because of this the world is perishing (see 4.4) 2.1 *iudicium dei super populum cunctum praesentem*—the judgment of God over all people alive 11.9 *totus mundus in ruina est positus*—the whole world was put to ruin
1.2 *flagella*—plagues 2.1 *diversis flagellis*—various plagues 2.1 *plagam*—plague	no terminology of "plague"	
1.4 *caligines*—darkness 1.4 *in profundum maris*—into the depths of the sea 2.2 *infirmitates*—illnesses	9.4f. *malitiam, amaritudinem, informitatem, accesiones, langores*	11.9 *malitiam et amaritudinem*—evil and bitterness
	9.6 *pustellas*	8.7 *pustulas in faciem*—blisters in face 9.5 *vermes*—worms
	9.1 *brucus et locustas*	8.1 *locustas et brucos*—locusts and insects
1.4 *lupi rapaces*—ravenous wolves	9.1 *lupos rapaces*	8.1 *lupos rapaces et canes malignos*—ravenous wolves and evil dogs
5.2 *grandinem*—hail	11.2 *grandines*	9.5 *grandinem*—hail 4.3 *lapides pendentes ponderibus*—rocky hail 4.3 *aquas calidas*—hot water
5.2 *ignem*—fire 5.2 *fulgura*—lightning 5.2 *coruscationes*—lightning 5.2 *tempestates*—storms	5.2 *lapides calidos ignem et flammam producentes* 11.2 *tempestates*	11.9 *flammam ignis ardentis*—flame of burning fire
5.3 *non habundantia*—no abundance	11.2 *siccitatem* 11.3 *fame, frigore* 11.3 *aestum gravem*	8.5 *famem et tribulationem*—hunger and tribulation
5.1 *anathematizabo*—curse	8.4–5 *anathimati eristis*	8.6 *anathemata erit*

(*Continued*)

(*Continued*)

Recension II, acc. to Vienne ÖNB 1355 (also Munich clm 9550, Hamburg, S. Petri 30b, Todi / Amaduzzi)	**Recension I, acc. to Tarragona (Baluzius)**	**Recension I, acc. to Vienne ÖNB 1355** (also Graz 248, London, Add. 19725, Basel, UB B VII 7)
	punishment of women	
	12.2 *serpentes pinnatas qui comedant et percutiant mamillas vestras*	10.1 *serpentes pinnatos qui lacerant mamillas*—feathered snakes that will mangle your breasts
1.3 *gens pagana*—pagan people 1.5 *in manus alienas*—into foreign hands 1.5 *submergam sicut submersi Sodomam et Gomorram*—bury like Sodom and Gomorrah	9.7 *in manus gentium paganorum*	8.2 *in malignantium manus*—into the hands of evildoers
	3.2 *in infernum* 4.5 *in gehenna ignis* 8.1 *in inferno inferiori* (see Paris 12270: *magnam penam in inferno; descendent ad infernos ubi vermis eorum non morietur et ignis non extinguitur*) 14.1 *ad poenam mense Novembrio*	6.1 *igne ardente*—burning fire 11.8 *iram grandissimam*—grandest wrath 4.4; 11.8 *in isto mense Novembre proxime . . .*

According to Latin Recension I, the threatened punishments concern all humankind and the whole world; individual calamities are conceived as universal. Epidemics such as smallpox or other plagues are mentioned as well; the letter also depicts disasters such as earthquakes and volcanic eruptions. In Latin Recension II, however, individual punishments are listed, for example, Vienna 1335, 2.2: "If somebody conducts any business on the holy Lord's Day, and wherever they do any work, whether they wash their hair or clothes, or bake bread, whatever they do, I will banish them and they will not find any blessing, neither by day or by night, but I will send curses upon their houses and all kinds of illness upon them and upon their children." The same applies to someone who files a lawsuit or starts a quarrel on the Lord's Day. In Latin Recension II—this has already been pointed out above—the threatened calamities are bad weather and forces of nature such as storms, drought, fire, or hail. Here, a rural environment is more in view and the threatened existence of a peasant; accordingly, the punishments visit a house or come over a house but do not affect the whole world or all humankind. In Latin Recension I, collective punishments dominate, being pronounced with urgency and a certain sense of imminence. Forces of nature such as thunderstorms, hail, storms, frost, lightning, fire, or even volcanic eruptions are mentioned, as well as dangerous animals or diseases. In addition, besides general curses and condemnation, punishments in hell are threatened. The earlier and more widespread Latin Recension II thus shows a different profile from the extended Latin Recension I, which can probably be dated to the Carolingian period[3] and which demands Sunday rest with greater dramatization.

While Codex München BSB clm 9550 states generally that there are only a few days left and that the end is approaching (*pauci enim sunt vestri dies, cotidie appropinquat finis vester*), and Codex Paris. lat 12270 states that God's wrath will soon come upon humankind (but as long as there is still time, the kingdom of God can still be attained by fasting and prayer, etc.), God's earthly blessings are nevertheless held out to those who observe the Lord's Day. In other versions, however, a greater urgency is aroused—on the one hand, by the threat that this is the third and last letter, thus it offers the last warning (so Codex Paris. lat. 12270; Codex Vienna 1355) and, on the other hand, by specification of dates. According to the transcription of the now-lost Tarragona manuscript, the calamity is announced for November; according to the codices from Vienna 1355, London, BL Add. 19725, and Basel UB B VII 7, it was postponed due to the intercession of Mary, the archangel Michael, the apostle Peter, and the saints, and is now announced for next November. Without a date but with the same supplication, Codex Paris. lat. 12270 mentions a postponement of the destruction.[4]

The threat to humankind is described in the Greek recensions of the Letter from Heaven as follows:

3. See above in the chapter about the history of the letter, pp. 95–104.

4. See also above, p. 99.

Alpha 1	Alpha 2	Beta
destruction of the whole world		
2.6 I decided to destroy the whole mankind (ἀπολέσαι πάντα ἄνθρωπον).	3.5 I decided to destroy you from the earth. 9.4 I wanted to destroy the whole mankind.	2.6 I will burn up every human being. 2.7 I wanted to destroy every human being. 5.4; 5.5 all will die, be destroyed
foreign troops		
2.2 I sent barbaric tribes (βάρβαρα ἔθνη) and poured out your blood. 4.9 I will send the Ishmaelites so that they enslave you and kill you by the sword.	3.2 I sent you barbaric raids and poured forth your blood. 4.4 I will send you the tribe of Ishmaelites so that you die with a bad death. 4.7 barbarians 10.6 conflict of nations	5.6 Ishmaelites
plagues and natural disasters		
2.4 I sent storms (χειμῶνας) and frost (παγετούς) and plagues (λοιμούς; Exod 9:13–35) and earthquakes (σεισμούς) . . . and hail (χάλαζα), locusts (ἀκρίδας), grasshoppers (κάμπας), and larvae (βροῦχον; see Exod 10:1–20). 4.6 I will open the heavens and I will pour fire, hail, boiling water, . . . and I will make dreadful earthquakes and will pour out blood and ash. 4.6 I will wipe away all seeds, vineyards and trees and will destroy your sheep, flocks and herds 4.7 and I will send winged beasts to devour your bodies.	3.3; 9.5 I made earthquakes, famine and disasters. 3.4 I sent you darkness and hail, locusts and reptiles. 9.2 lions 4.6 I will open the skies and throw fire stones. 9.1 earthquakes, earth opens up 10.2 fiery stones, fire, hail, bitter water 10.2 destroy your fields	2.5 storms, frosts, fire, hail, locusts and larvae of locusts, wild rivers 5.1 sun into darkness, moon into blood 5.2 noises from the heavens, lightning and thunder, 3.1 open the trapdoors of heavens and rain down boiling water. 3.2 rain down blood and ash 3.3 turn rivers into blood, destroy your herds, vineyards, grain

(*Continued*)

(Continued)

Alpha 1	Alpha 2	Beta
women[5]		
4.4 I will send poisonous wild beasts (θηρία ἰοβόλα) so that they devour the breasts of women.	4.7 I will send on you wild beasts which have eagle wings, but with women's hair instead of feathers, to snatch the breasts of women and your infants.	
day of divine judgment		
4.3; 5.2; 9.1 day of judgment curse of Satan, anathema, woes (4.1; 7.1–17)	4.3 judge the living and the dead (see 8.6) curse, anathema, woes (4.1; 6.1–3)	4.5 day of judgment anathema, woes (5.12; 6.1-17)
6.2 curse of Sodom and Gomorrah		5.13f. Sodom and Gomorrah 5.12; 9.2 curse of Judas
7.15 burn in fire	4.3 I will burn you up	2.6; 3.1 burn up everyone 5.6 evil death

Obviously, the impending universal catastrophe and the end of the world is common to all Greek versions—which can also be found in Latin Recension I. In addition to natural disasters such as earthquakes or hail storms, the image of a fire or world conflagration is central: everything will be destroyed by fire. The special feature of the Greek recension is the additional threat of being conquered and annihilated by foreign peoples—this is parallel to Latin Recension II, but now these threats are concretely identified with the Ishmaelites.

In sum, therefore, three biblical patterns are obvious:

First, the destruction of Sodom and Gomorrah—God rained fire and brimstone from heaven on Sodom and Gomorrah (Gen 19:24; see 2 Pet 2:6; see p. 364).

Second, the ten Egyptian plagues (Exod 7–10: waters transformed into blood, frogs, mosquitoes, biting flies, cattle plague, leaves, hail, locusts, darkness) are in the background. There is also explicit mention of plagues in the Letter from Heaven. But Amos also sees locusts and fire sent against Israel (Amos 7:1–6; see Ezek 38:22); and Revelation 8:7–9, 15 (announcement of disasters of the first six trumpets) about several disasters that herald the end of the world.

5. See below, pp. 195–200.

Third, the foreign peoples sent against Israel from the prophetic judgment speeches (such as Isaiah's conquest of Israel by the Assyrians in Isa 8; 29). This is encountered in the Letter from Heaven in an updated form, either barbarians (a typical Roman perspective on other peoples) or Ishmaelites—that is, Arabs. Therefore, the text already takes up experiences from the seventh century.[6]

These biblical models are somewhat expanded to include other natural disasters, which can be linked to weather and volcanic eruptions, and the fight against dangerous animals such as wolves. What is missing[7] in the Letter from Heaven, on the other hand, are descriptions of punishments in hell as found in apocalyptic texts: eternal fire, red-hot iron, sleepless worms, and so on. Although reference is made to the day of judgment—which, by the way, will also be a Sunday—the threatened calamities refer to events here on earth. After all, the whole scenario is also under the threat of wiping out the whole of humanity, thus to turn the whole world into Sodom and Gomorrah. Here, therefore, the punishments of hell are not threatened, but the warning pertains to misery and ruin on earth—though this is not less terrible.

An interesting observation is the different valuation of the open sky: while the Latin versions, if they mention this description, associate it with the transmission of divine blessing and, for example, announce a good harvest—if Christians convert and observe Sunday—in the Greek versions the open sky becomes a threat and introduces the punishment. See, for example, the Latin Recension I according to the Codex Paris. Lat. 12270: *Si vos emendaveritis, aperiam vobis ianuam celi et dabo vobis ad tempus fructus terre et omnem habundantiam*; or the Latin Recension II according to the Codex Vienna 1355 (7.1): *Si custodieritis dominicum diem, aperiam vobis cataractas caeli in omni bono, et multiplicabo labores vestros.*[8] In contrast, one can read in the Greek Recension Alpha 1 (4.6): εἰ δὲ καὶ ταῦτα οὐ μὴ ποιήσετε, οὐ μὴ πέμψω ἄλλην ἐπιστολήν, ἀλλὰ ἀνόξει θέλω τοὺς οὐρανοὺς καὶ βρέξει θέλω πῦρ, χάλαζαν, ὕδωρ καχλάζον, ὅτι οὐ γινώσκει ἄνθρωπος, καὶ ποιήσω σεισμοὺς φοβερούς; or in the Greek Recension Alpha 2 (4.6): οὐ μὴ πέμψω ἄλλην ἐπιστολὴν ἐπὶ τῆς γῆς, ἀλλὰ ἀνοίξω ἔχω τοὺς οὐρανοὺς καὶ βρέξω λίθους πυρίνους; or in the Greek Recension Beta (3.1): καὶ διὰ τοῦτο λέγω ὑμῖν· οὐ μὴ ἀποστείλω ἄλλην ἐπιστολὴν ἐπὶ τῆς γῆς, ἀλλὰ ἀνοίξειν ἔχω τοὺς καταράκτας τοῦ οὐρανοῦ καὶ

6. See below, p. 297.

7. Almost: in Latin Recension I (see the overview above), here the threat is reinforced by apocalyptic motifs; the fire is painted as hell (*inferno*, *gehenna*). See also the later Greek version, Greek Recension Gamma.

8. The biblical allusion is to Mal 3:10.

βρέξειν ἔχω ὕδωρ καχλάζον.[9] This observation supports the assessment that the Greek versions are more likely to express a universal threat to humanity, unlike the Latin versions, even if this classification cannot explain the phenomenon.

Why did someone resort to such means and write this letter? Can the text be understood as the product of a frustrated cleric[10] who pulled out all the stops to drive his congregation to worship? According to the strategy that threats are more effective than friendly invitations? That might resonate, but since there were certainly frustrated clerics at all times and in all places, it doesn't actually explain the tactics of this letter. Or does the Letter from Heaven benefit a cleric—namely, could he make himself particularly prominent and important by means of it, or earn money with it, or promote a pilgrimage site—a means of advertising, so to speak, for a congregation that is in possession of this very letter? That, too, may be true in general. It has already been alluded to in the section above on the Gallic tales of punishment miracles that the Letter from Heaven may have resonated there around 600 CE and may have served the clergy's interest in encouraging Christians to attend Sunday services. However, these two aspects seem to be relevant only to explain the distribution of the letter, not its origin. Probably two further aspects are more important, namely, crisis and time.

Crisis: Even if the Letter from Heaven is not to be described as an apocalypse, as it lacks a horror scenario of hell, one aspect known to provoke the production of apocalyptic texts may still be relevant: the experience of a crisis. This cannot explain the wide distribution of the text, otherwise one would have to assume an everlasting crisis. But crises seem to explain at least in part the writing and also the waves of dissemination of the text. The exact crisis at the end of the sixth century, when the first testimonium of the Letter from Heaven appears, can no longer be determined. Was it the plague during the reign of Justinian? Together with the consequences of the so-called little ice age in the sixth century?[11] The many threatened harvest damages and also the pustules or rashes (in the Latin Letter from Heaven) could point to this. The above

9. Biblical parallels: Gen 7:11 (the flood); 8:2 (end of flood); Isa 24:18 (announced punishment). See also 2 Kgs 7:2; Ps 41:8; Rev 11:19. In addition, the "open sky" is mentioned for introducing a vision (e.g., Ezek 1:1; Acts 10:11) or a divine message (e.g., John 1:51; Rev 19:11), also within the story about the baptism of Christ (Matt 3:16).

10. Baun, "Taboo or Gift?," 56.

11. See on plagues in antiquity in general: Mischa Meier, "Seuche," *RAC* 30:421–56. Two issues have brought this plague into the focus of research: first, the question of whether this plague was one of the triggers for the fall of the Roman Empire, and second, the question of previous pandemics on account of the current one, COVID-19. The Justinian plague started in 541 CE, spread up to Ireland, and actually lasted until the eighth century. Former plagues

mentioned text *De plaga, quae facta fuit in Hierusalem, eo quod dominicum diem non servaverunt*[12] (around 800 CE) supports this estimation. It presents an exemplary narrative in which good and bad times are interpreted as blessings or as divine punishment for ignoring the Lord's Day. Also, the Greek recension Beta may be connected to the experience of crises and an apocalyptic atmosphere.[13] The Letter from Heaven is therefore a text that wants to clarify theologically the causes for the catastrophes experienced.[14] So it is also remarkable that in the Letter from Heaven both future and past disasters are listed—always introduced with the phrase, "I have sent to you . . ." and continued by "but you have not repented." The letter frames previous disasters—barbarian invasions and weather variations, as well as plagues of locusts—as God's punishments for neglecting Sunday and threatens even worse disasters that could wipe out humankind.

The Letter from Heaven also avoids (mostly) the historical-theological problem of apocalyptic literature that the predicted end of the world and end times do not come to pass—so the many earthly, nonapocalyptic horrors mentioned in the Letter from Heaven can undoubtedly always be named, such as failing harvests, storms, or earthquakes. Nevertheless, the versions of the Letter from Heaven that include announced dates actually demonstrate

---

known to have occurred include the Antonine plague of the second century CE and the mid-third-century CE plague described by Cyprian of Carthage. See the discussion about the plague of Justinian in light of modern experiences: Mischa Meier, "Die Justinianische Pest—im Spiegel der Covid-19-Pandemie betrachtet," *Forum: Zeiterfahrung online*, https://tinyurl.com/3j7bjx8u (accessed September 21, 2022). Kyle Harper (*The Fate of Rome: Climate, Disease, and the End of an Empire*, The Princeton History of the Ancient World [Princeton: Princeton University Press, 2017]) places the pandemic at the center of his decadent narrative of the Roman Empire and incipient "dark age of Byzantium" and points to a connection with emerging apocalyptic discourse.

12. See p. 104.

13. See the observations of Angela Zielinski Kinney on this recension, pp. 334f., 364.

14. Christian authors offer different models for interpreting disasters theologically. Besides interpretation as divine punishment, there is also an interpretation of them as divine admonitions or warnings, so that the call to repentance is more in the foreground. Both are recognizable in the Letter from Heaven. In addition, catastrophes can also be interpreted apocalyptically as harbingers of the end of the world. But they are also interpreted in a different way, namely, as divine tests and a phases of probation. Occasionally, however, there are also references to natural interpretations. Another model is to understand catastrophes as being caused by demons (which can again be connected with divine trials). See on this the contribution of Wolfram Kinzig, "Kommen Katastrophen von Gott? Antworten aus der christlichen Antike," *TRu* 86 (2021): 311–30, with further literature. See also Marco Frenschkowski, "Seuchengötter, Heilungsgötter. Konkurrierende Deutungen epidemischer Krankheiten in spätantiken Religionen und im antiken Christentum," *EvT* 81 (2021): 350–61. See also above on the punitive miracles, pp. 172–82.

the dilemma of nonfulfillment: the date is postponed; reference is made to previous letters; the current letter is declared to be the second or third.

Time: The crisis as the background of the letter is of course relevant, but it does not at all explain the particular theme of the letter: Sunday. Here the second aspect comes into play, namely, time. Much of the letter is concerned with bringing the importance of Sunday to the attention of the reader or listener. In sum, the picture that emerges is that this day from the beginning of creation is the day chosen by the Lord; it structures the entire history of salvation and has always been the day on which outstanding events occurred. It is not only the first day of creation but will also be the last; it is the day blessed by the Lord himself, the day of the resurrection, the day of Jesus's baptism, the day of Mary's annunciation, the day of the visit to Abraham, the day when he appeared to Moses on Mount Sinai, the day of divine rest,[15] and the appointed day of judgment. Sunday is envisaged as a temporal grit—a fundamental part of God's plan for this world. The day is thus separated from the timeline, just as a holy place is separated from its surroundings. The rising importance of Sunday belongs, therefore, to the general tendency of Christianization and sacralization[16] of the calendar. As stated above,[17] in late antiquity the

---

15. See above on the transfer of the Sabbath to Sunday, pp. 144–53.

16. *Sacralization* is, of course, a broad and disputed term; see the thorough article by Albrecht Dihle, "Heilig," *RAC* 14:1-63, here 1: sacred refers "auf Erscheinungsformen unverfügbarer Macht, von deren Wirken sich der Mensch in der Endlichkeit u. Unvollkommenheit seiner Erfahrungswelt gerade hinsichtlich der fundamentalen Gegebenheiten seiner Existenz als abhängig erlebt"; see also Peter Gemeinhardt: "sacred means, oriented towards an ultimate reality, the divine, or which is thought to come from the divine. Thus, it refers to areas of human praxis and reflection that are directed towards the divine, initiate and govern contact with the divine, and regulate the subsequent consequences, behaviors, and patterns of thought for people—as individuals or in groups" (in Peter Gemeinhardt and Katharina Heyden, eds., *Heilige, Heiliges und Heiligkeit in spätantiken Religionskulturen*, RVV 61 [Berlin: de Gruyter, 2012], 421); see also Auffarth, "Wie kann man von Heiligkeit sprechen"; and Rüpke, "Sakralisierung von Zeit," who states (232): "Die Universalkategorie des Heiligen ist einem genaueren Blick auf Prozesse von Sakralisierung und Desakralisierung gewichen." See also Jörg Rüpke, *Ritual als Resonanzerfahrung*, Religionswissenschaft heute 15 (Stuttgart: Kohlhammer, 2021), with 149-62 on "Sakralisierung von Zeit." An object or a space can be delimited from something profane by a visible distinction; it is a different matter with virtual temporal categories. Here a social agreement and media are needed on which this can be made visible, such as public calendars or visible rites that introduce a day or a festival. The Letter from Heaven attempts to establish precisely this social consensus. The latest book of Goldhill, *Christian Invention of Time*, does not deal with this topic, nor with Sunday, but it poses more philosophical questions about time.

17. See p. 176.

traditional Roman calendar with its feasts, offerings, processions, and games lost importance,[18] and the new Christian festal calendar became more important than in previous centuries. Therefore, the growing importance of what to do and not to do on Sunday replaced other activities or omissions from earlier times as identity markers of a Christian life: not going to a temple and refusing to make offerings to other gods or to the emperor.

Sunday became the feast day for worshipping together with the angels in heaven—on that day, heaven is open over the altar, so to speak. Therefore, each Christian is obliged to be part of this common celebration.[19] If one connects this with the aspect of crisis discussed above, then one can see: the sacred conveys order and structure in a fundamentally disordered, contingent world. As temporal units such as days, weeks, months, and years were given Christian meaning, ultimately a more suprapersonal sacred emerged as a new structure or pattern of order. But whoever violates this order will also suffer the corresponding divine punishment.

Sunday has also penitential might in itself: for those who go to church and venerate the day, the day is an offer to atone for the sins committed during the week. However, the ones who stay away from church and scorn Sunday remain stuck in their sins. Thus, they are actually already condemned, but in the letter the divine condemnation is pronounced extra, since, according to the authors of the letter, the disrespect of Sunday not only harms the individual but also damages the entire Christian community, which is affected by this behavior. Obviously, this view is more explicit in the Greek recensions. This also explains why they add criticism of clerics and explicitly denounce clerical misconduct when good communal worship does not take place. This does not only concern the cleric but the whole Christian community. The Latin recensions basically emphasize that behavior on Sunday determines heavenly grants: benediction or malediction. Behavior on Sunday determines whether one is in Christ or out of Christ,

18. See for a convenient overview about the Roman festival calendar Graf, *Der Lauf des rollenden Jahres*. See also (ordered by months) Fowler, *Roman Festivals*, and Scullard, *Festivals and Ceremonies*.

19. On sacralization and also liturgization in the Greek East, see Mischa Meier, "'Sind wir nicht alle heilig?' Zum Konzept des 'Heiligen' (*sacrum*) in spätjustinianischer Zeit," *Millennium* 1 (2003): 133–64, especially about Mariology, emperors, and icons from the sixth century CE; he unites this sacralization with the crises of that era: "Die Zunahme der Marienverehrung, die Ausbreitung des Bilderkultes und die Sakralisierung des Kaisers—letztere als Reaktion auf die aus den Katastrophen resultierende Kaiserkritik—lassen sich als äußere Indizien des Liturgisierungsprozesses unmittelbar mit den Ereignissen der frühen 40er Jahre in Beziehung setzen" (139), however, only dealing with the liturgical year (159f.) and not with Sunday (see also note 16 and p. 366).

whether one belongs to the Christian community or is excommunicated. Working on Sunday, even doing heavy physical labor, not only prevents one from attending religious services but also goes against the character of the day as a holiday, as do fasting and kneeling as an attitude of prayer. Thus, it is not only important how someone behaves but also when someone is performing certain actions.

Of course, the Letter from Heaven aims at improving Christian attitude and changing the behavior of the Christian community. This is probably how the order came about not only to read the letter publicly but also to copy and distribute it—the first chain letter in history was created, and an extraordinary history of the letter's distribution began, a circulation that has still not been fully researched.

4.4. Punishment of Women

Uta Heil

Christians who do not care about Sunday are threatened with severe punishments. In contrast to Latin Recension II, where punishment is meted out to individual persons or households, in Latin Recension I punishment is extended to the whole of humanity, which is threatened with destruction.

In this recension, one punishment stands out—the punishment of women (which lacks a clear counterpart for men). In this matter, there is a parallel with Greek Recension Alpha.[1] However, in Latin Recension II and in Greek recensions Beta and Gamma (as well as in the Armenian version) this theme is missing. The other recensions threaten women with flying snakes (Latin) or poisonous wild beasts (Greek), which will either suck at or bite and eat their breasts. The relevant passages are:

> Latin Recension I according to Vienna 1355—*serpentes pinnatos qui lacerant mamillas*
>
> [10] (1) *amen dico vobis, <si> colligent mulieres holera in die dominico, mittam super eas serpentes pinnatos qui lacerant mamillas usque in finem. (2) dico vobis, si non custodieritis diem dominicum, erunt infantes nati qui non audiunt neque vident neque ambulant et sic pereunt.* / [10] (1) Truly I say to you, if women collect vegetables on the Lord's day, I will send over you feathered snakes that will mangle your breasts until the end. (2) I say to you,

1. This confirms the relationship between these two recensions.

if you do not observe the Lord's day, children will be born who cannot hear nor see nor walk and so they die.

Comparable is Tarragona—*serpentes pinnatas qui comedant et percutiant mamillas*:

[12] (1) *Amen dico vobis: die dominico observate cum omni diligentia, sicut nec ipsas oleras in hortibus vestris die dominico colligatis.* (2) *si haec feceritis, vos mulieres, mittam super vos serpentes pinnatas qui comedant et percutiant mamillas vestras.* / [12] (1) Verily I say to you, observe the Lord's day with all diligence, so that you do not collect vegetables in your gardens on the Lord's day. (2) If you do that, you women, I will send over you flying snakes who eat you and pierce through your breasts.[2]

Similar is Greek Recension Alpha 1:[3]

[4] 4 ὀμνύω κατὰ τοῦ θρόνου μου τοῦ ὑψηλοῦ, ὅτι, ἐὰν μὴ φυλάξετε τὴν ἁγίαν κυριακὴν καὶ τετράδη(ν) καὶ παρασκευὴν καὶ τὰς ἁγίας ἐπισήμους ἑορτάς, πέμψειν ἔχω θηρία ἰοβόλα, ἵνα καταφάγωσι τοὺς μασθοὺς τῶν γυναικῶν, αἵτινες οὐ θηλάζουσι βρέφη μὴ ἔχοντα μητέρων γάλα, καὶ ἁρπάζουσι λύκοι ἄγριοι τὰ τέκνα ὑμῶν. / [4] 4 I swear down from my lofty throne, should you not observe the holy Lord's day, Wednesday, and Friday and other notable feasts as well, I will send poisonous wild beasts so that they devour the breasts of women, who will not be able to nurse their infants left without the milk of their mothers, and wild wolves to snatch your children.

Compare also Greek Recension Alpha 2:[4]

[4] (6) οὐ μὴ πέμψω ἄλλην ἐπιστολὴν ἐπὶ τῆς γῆς, ἀλλὰ ἀνοίξω ἔχω τοὺς οὐρανοὺς καὶ βρέξω λίθους πυρίνους (7) καὶ πάλιν (πέμψει) ἔχω ἐφ᾽ ὑμᾶς θηρία ἰοβόλα ἔχοντ᾽ ἀετῶν πτέρυγας καὶ ἀντὶ πτερύγων τρίχας γυναικῶν, ἵνα καταφάγωσιν τοὺς μαστοὺς τῶν γυναικῶν καὶ τὰ νήπια (διὰ) τὴν παρακοὴν ὑμῶν [4] (6) I will not send another letter to the earth, but will open the skies and throw fire stones, (7) and I will send upon you again wild

2. See p. 286 and Bas1 (ed. Haines, *Sunday Observance*, 207.21–23): *Mulieres si colligerent olera diem sanctum dominicum mittam super illas serpentes pennatas qui lacerant mamillas eorum usque ad mortem.* Graz1 8.1 (see below, p. 269): *cum se colligunt mulieres holera in horto in die dominico, mittam super eas serpentes pennatas, ut lacerent mamillas earum usque ad mortem*; in Lon1 this passage is missing.

3. See below, p. 308.

4. See below, p. 320.

> beasts which have eagle wings but with women's hair instead of feathers to snatch the breasts of women and your infants because of your disobedience.

Punishment is given for disrespecting Sunday in general (Greek recensions) or for gathering products (Latin recensions). This corresponds to the general tendency of the versions, because in the Greek versions Sunday worship is admonished in principle without further details, whereas the Latin versions also address concrete deeds.

But why are women addressed as a special group at all? In the Letter from Heaven, it remains unclear whether women are especially punished for something, or whether the text just paints a detail of the horrors. Perhaps this ties in with a verse in the little apocalypse of the Gospels, where it says (Matt 24:19): "But woe to those who are pregnant and to those who are nursing at that time!" Another inspiration may be a verse of the apostle Paul, who sees all sinners punished by beatings (1 Cor 10:9, remembering Num 21:6). Here, however, only their special misery is emphasized, whether they are just pregnant or nursing when the end time breaks in. In contrast, in the Letter from Heaven, an explicit attack on women is pronounced. The context is not the particular misery of women in the end times but their particular punishment during their life for disregarding Sunday.

This image is striking. Of course, one is also reminded that in paradise Eve was seduced by a snake, and of the fight between the snake and the women in Revelation 12:13–19.[5] Interestingly, the seventh-century Apocalypse of Pseudo-Methodius states that the Ishmaelites, like wild beasts of the desert, will attack pregnant women and infants (11.17)—taking up the idea of the biblical apocalypse that women suffer more than men: "And when the time comes, when they begin to leave the desert they will stab the pregnant women with a sword and snatch babies from their mother's arms and smash them, and they [sc. the babies] will be meat for the beasts."[6]

---

5. See also the flying or biting serpents as means of divine punishment in Isa 14:29 (against the Philistines); Isa 30:6 (against Egypt); Num 21:6 (against Israel in the desert—God then instructs Moses to make a bronze serpent as a sign of God's protection [Num 21:8; see 2 Kgs 18:4 for its name "Nehuschtan"]). See further Notker Baumann, "Schlange," *RAC* 29:885–912, but also Reinhold Merkelbach, "Drache," *RAC* 4:226–50, with many references to the fight of dragon-like snakes against men.

6. Benjamin Garstad, ed. and trans., *Apocalypse of Pseudo-Methodius, An Alexandrian World Chronicle*, Dumbarton Oaks Medieval Library 14 (Cambridge: Harvard University Press, 2012), 46f. (with English translation): καὶ ἐν τῇ ἀρχῇ τοῦ καιροῦ τῆς ἐξόδου αὐτῶν τῆς ἐξ ἐρήμου γενομένης ῥομφαίᾳ τὰς ἐν γαστρὶ ἐχούσας κεντήσωσι, καὶ τὰ βρέφη ἐκ τῶν μητρικῶν ἀγκαλῶν ἁρπάζοντες πατάξωσι, καὶ ἔσονται τοῖς θηρίοις εἰς βρῶσιν.

Perhaps one author of the Letter from Heaven takes up an idea that is known from the Apocalypse of Peter from the second century (8.4—Ethiopic version), where one can find a special condemnation against abortion. Here we encounter the image of wild animals that have been formed from the mother's milk sucking back on the women's breasts: "The milk of women that flows from their beasts and coagulates will produce small carnivorous animals that will return to her and consume her," a sentence quoted already by Clement of Alexandria, *Eclogae propheticae* 48.1–49.1.[7] The Apocalypse of Peter also contains a passage on women who have made an effort to have beautiful hair in order to seduce men into fornication—they will be hanged in their place of punishment in hell by that same hair and thrown into the pit.[8] Of interest is also the Greek Apocalypse of Ezra 5.2f. (second century CE or later), where a condemnation of infanticide is expressed with the following words: "And I saw a woman hanged, and four beasts sucking at her breasts. And the angels said to me, 'This one refused to give milk; indeed, she threw the children into the rivers.'"[9] The later Latin *Visio beati Esdrae* 53f. (fourth century CE or later) presents this topic in a comparable way:

> And I saw other women hanging in the fire, and serpents were suckling on their breasts. And I said to the angels: "Who are those?" And they told me: "These are those, who killed their children and gave not their breasts to other orphans."[10]

---

7. See Thomas J. Kraus and Tobias Niklas, eds., *Das Petrusevangelium und die Petrusapokalypse. Die griechischen Fragmente mit deutscher und englischer Übersetzung*, GCS 11.1 (Berlin: de Gruyter, 2004), 91. See the Ethiopic version: Dennis D. Buchholz, ed., *Your Eyes Will Be Opened: A Study of the Greek (Ethiopic) Apocalypse of Peter*, SBLDS 97 (Atlanta: Scholars Press, 1988).

8. First published by Hugo Duensing, "Ein Stück der urchristlichen Petrusapokalypse enthaltender Traktat der äthiopischen pseudo-clementinischen Literatur," *ZNW* 14 (1913): 65–78, here 70.

9. Text in *Apocalypsis apocryphae Mosis, Esdrae, Iohannis, item Mariae dormitio*, ed. Konstantin Tischendorf (Leipzig: Mendelssohn, 1866), 1:29.23–29: 5.2. Καὶ ἴδον γυναῖκα κρεμαμένην, καὶ τέσσαρα θηρία θηλάζοντα τοὺς μαστοὺς αὐτῆς. 5.3 Καὶ εἶπόν μοι οἱ ἄγγελοι· αὕτη τὸ γάλα ἐφθόνησεν τοῦ δοῦναι, ἀλλὰ καὶ τὰ νήπια ἐν τοῖς ποταμοῖς ἔρριψεν. See also Thomas Hieke, "Esra-Schriften, außerbiblische (AT)," *Das Wissenschaftliche Bibellexikon im Internet* (2005), 4.2.

10. *Apocalypsis Esdrae, Apocalypsis Sedrach, Visio beati Esdrae*, ed. Otto Wahl, PVTG (Leiden: Brill, 1977), 58: *53 Et vidi alias mulieres per ignes pendentes, et serpentes mamillas earum suggentes. 54 Et dixi ad angelos: Quae sunt istae? Et dixerunt mihi: Istae sunt, quae suos parvulos necaverunt et aliis orphanis mamillas non dederunt.* Angela Zielinski Kinney has thankfully pointed out this parallel. Interestingly, here (10 [50 Wahl]), men are punished for sex on Sunday: *Isti sunt, qui Dominum negaverunt et in die dominica ante missam cum mulieribus peccaverunt.* "These are those who denied the Lord and sinned with women on the Lord's day before mass."

The Letter from Heaven thus takes up images from apocalyptic literature without, however, creating explicit depictions of the afterlife or images of hell.[11] The scenario of punishment in the Letter from Heaven is here on earth, not in the afterlife. In addition, abortion, infanticide, and fornication are not connected themes in the context of women's punishment in the Letter from Heaven.[12] Greek Recension Alpha includes this threat concerning Sunday observance in general; Latin Recension I unites it with collecting vegetables on Sunday. Nevertheless, the author takes up this terrible image to make the

---

11. It is also well-known in some depictions of the last judgment, either on portals of the church or in the book cover, for example, of the famous Bamberger Perikopenbuch (tenth century, now Munich, Codex Clm 4452, but the ivory table is from the ninth century), one can find the personified earth / *terra* or *luxuria* as a woman with snakes feeding on her breasts. In the high Middle Ages, this is a common motive to visualize *luxuria* and unchastity. In its Latin meaning, *luxuria* denotes luxuriance, both in connection with the fertility of the earth and in the sense of licentiousness, ostentation, hedonism, and lust. The term thus refers to a dissolute lifestyle, of which sexual lust and fornication are only partial aspects—as described in the Paris Codex; see the following footnote. Snakes explicitly punishing women in hell can be found at wall paintings on Crete (St. Pelagia in Anno Vianos, Herakleion, with descriptions: "abandoner of children," "procuress," "witch," and "slanderer"; St. Paraskive in Kithrios, Chania, with descriptions: "who refuses to nourish her children," "prostitute," "promiscuous male"; St. Athanasios in Kisamos, a prostitute); see Mati Meyer, *An Obscure Portrait: Imaging Women's Reality in Byzantine Art* (London: Oindar, 2009), plates 66, 67, 152.

12. One exception is the one manuscript of Latin Recension I: Paris 12270 (see the list at p. 39). The relevant passage starts in a similar way: *Mulieres autem non colentes diem dominicum et festivitates sanctorum, transmittam super vos serpentes pendentes ad mamillas, sucgentes quasi filius, et puniemini propter castitatem quam non habuistis.* "But you women who do not observe the Lord's Day and the feasts of the saints, I will send over you snakes that will hang on your breasts, suckling like a child, and you will be punished" (Haines, *Sunday Observance*, 200.60–63; her suggestion at 179f. to change *pendentes* into *pinnatos* as in the other versions, also *lacerant* into *lacterent*, is not necessary; the writer rewrote and enlarged the whole passage and was probably inspired by the picture of the hanging women in the Apocalypse of Peter and the flying snakes in the *Visio beati Esdrae*, quoted above [comment of Angela Zielinski Kinney]), but continues with blaming women who are not chaste but have sexual intercourse the night before Sunday, do not bridle their tongues, who swear and worry about jewelry. This passage is in all likelihood an embellishment of the textual record by an author who took the opportunity to express general criticism of women's behavior, which is only loosely connected to Sunday. In the same version, a passage on paying tithes and also on swearing has been expanded. Here one can see how the letter was also used to creatively adapt moral criticism to one's own needs. The lack of chastity is a broad topic, not only in apocalyptic literature (see above) but also in tractates or sermons of several bishops; see Caesarius of Arles, *Sermones* 44.7 (CCSL 103, 199–200 Morin). See also Kinzig on the demand of being chaste with respect to Sunday in "Sunday Observance," 332f., 344f., but also 334–38 (on penitential books).

threat more intense. The Letter from Heaven is not specifically misogynistic and does not emphasize any special sinfulness of women,[13] nor does it explicitly link Sunday worship with a call to chastity, as can certainly be found in other texts treating Sunday.[14] The gathering of fruits and products is probably *pars pro toto* for agricultural work or activities in the household that women do. The threat of punishment with an extra comment on women thus picks up on the tendency of apocalyptic texts to depict misery and horror with the particular suffering that women have to bear.

13. This is a huge topic, and literature on this is abundant. The juxtaposition of the sinning Eve and the sin-dissolving Mary (already in the second century; see Justin Martyr, *Dial.* 100; Irenaeus, *Haer.* 3.22.4; Tertullian, *Carn. Chr.* 17; *Cult. fem.* 1) was especially influential. See Gary A. Anderson, *The Genesis of Perfection: Adam and Eve in Jewish and Christian Imagination* (Louisville: John Knox, 2001); Kari E. Borresen and Emanuela Prinzivalli, eds., *Christliche Autoren der Antike*, Die Bibel und die Frauen. Eine exegetisch-kulturgeschichtliche Enzyklopädie 5.1 (Stuttgart: Kohlhammer, 2016); Agnethe Siquans, ed., *Biblische Frauenfiguren in der Spätantike*, Die Bibel und die Frauen. Eine exegetisch-kulturgeschichtliche Enzyklopädie 5.2 (Stuttgart: Kohlhammer, 2022). The veneration of Mary as God-bearer (*theotokos*; established as doctrine at the Council of Ephesus in 431 CE) and as perpetual virgin promoted the demand for women to live in chastity to overcome their own sinfulness. See also Vladimir Tumanov, "Mary versus Eve: Paternal Uncertainty and the Christian View of Women," *Neophilologus* 95 (2011): 507–21.

14. And in the one version of the Letter from Heaven in Paris 12270; see n. 12 above.

5
EVALUATION

Uta Heil

The Letter from Heaven is an extraordinary apocryphal text, the entire distribution of which has not yet been researched. The present investigation may inspire further studies, especially with regard to versions transmitted in other languages. In this book, more versions of the Letter from Heaven, with English translations and commentaries, are made accessible than have been heretofore available. In general, research has passed over the Letter from Heaven since the innovative studies of the nineteenth and early twentieth centuries; not even the revived interest in apocrypha and pseudepigrapha in recent decades has changed this. Dorothy Haines's study from 2010 is an important exception and has primarily explored the reception of the Letter from Heaven in the English-speaking world. In works on the history of Sunday, the letter is usually only worthy of a footnote.

The Letter from Heaven was accompanied by criticism from the beginning, but this did not prevent its distribution. Perhaps a cautious attitude (since after all it could potentially be a letter from Christ) overlapped with an intention to use the letter to exhort attendance at the church service and to sanctify Sunday as a Christian day. Transcribers of the letter have expanded its frame tale, which is not only to authenticate the letter but at the same time to demonstrate the desired way of dealing with it: venerate, read out, and disseminate. The letter assigns itself redemptive power, a power accessible not only by following its precepts but by reading, copying, and distributing the text. Apparently enough people complied with this, which explains the wide distribution and creation of the first-known phenomenon of a chain letter.

The Letter from Heaven is at the same time a letter, a heavenly revelation, an exhortation, a sermon, a judgment speech, and a threatening missive. Therefore, the contexts of its transmission are varied. It was transmitted alongside many different kinds of texts, ranging from sermons to apocalyptic literature, to anti-Jewish texts, to liturgical texts, church dedications, and clerical life as well as in anthologies and miscellanies with no particular profile. This shows how differently the letter could be read or understood. Taking into account the transmission contexts in manuscripts containing the Letter from Heaven is certainly a path pointing to future research. The aspect of apotropaic use, which has become more important since the late Middle Ages and which then dominates in vernacular versions, where the letter is kept as an amulet, can only be mentioned here.

In this study, an attempt was made to examine the Latin and Greek tradition together, a holistic perspective that has been neglected so far in scholarship. This methodology revealed references and interactions suggesting an East-to-West and West-to-East transmission of the letter. Latin Recension I is related to Greek Recension Alpha 1; Greek Recension Alpha 2 is related to Latin Recension III. Contrary to previous research, Latin Recension II seems to be older than Latin Recension I. Latin Recension II was also transmitted in a wide range of versions and in general more widespread. In contrast, Latin Recension I presents itself rather as a special version of the Carolingian period. Too little attention has been paid so far to the earlier version of the Letter from Heaven, which is—among other manuscripts—attested in an inscription.

Although no definitive answer can be given to the question of the origin of the Letter from Heaven, the end of the sixth century CE is the probable time frame, that is, the time when it was also first attested by Licinianus of Cartagena. Whether it was originally authored in Latin, however, cannot be clearly determined. What speaks for the argument for a Latin origin, apart from the testimony of Licinianus, are the other voices from that time, people who wanted to enforce a stronger observance of Sunday rest by other means (e.g., stories of punitive miracles, ecclesiastical legislation). However, there are also relevant sources from the Greek-speaking world, such as the sermons and the *Diataxis* included here in this volume, that document similar interests. Nevertheless, the orientation toward Rome evident in the earliest Greek (and Armenian) witnesses again argues more for a Western Latin origin. But perhaps the letter was also distributed in both languages from the beginning.

Since other apocryphal and pseudepigraphal writings besides the Letter from Heaven deal with Sunday, they have also been included as comparanda in this volume. The so-called Acts of the Synod of Caesarea bear witness to how the memory of an event—in this case, the Synod of Caesarea at the end of the second century (on the dispute about the date of Easter)—lives on and was creatively adapted to new questions. The text is indirectly related to Sunday, as it treats the question of whether Easter is to be celebrated on a certain date, with a changing day of the week, or always on Sunday. The sermon of Sophronius of Jerusalem, discovered only a few years ago, on the occasion of the circumcision feast of the year 635 CE (which happened to fall on a Sunday), offers a passage from a second-century text (the Dialogue between Jason and Papiscus), where it is hard to distinguish exactly what is actual second-century textual material and what is later expansion. The *Diataxis* is also a dialogue, in this case between the apostles and Christ, on the question of the heavenly reward for the observance of Sunday. The *Visio Pauli* (Sunday rest in hell), the Second Apocryphal Apocalypse of John (weekly rhythm with work and rest), and the Apocalypse of Anastasia (the heavenly woman Sunday complains about disrespect on earth) are other apocryphal apocalypses in which Sunday is a theme. In some manuscripts, the Letter from Heaven and the *Visio Pauli* have even entered into a symbiosis. Since these texts, in addition to others, were also widely used and read, they deserve no less attention than, for example, laws or ecclesiastical canons. Many texts in this volume (the Acts of the Synod of Caesarea; the sermons of Basil, Chrysostom, and Eusebius; the anonymous sermon fragment on Sunday; the *Diataxis*) are based on new editions and are presented here for the first time with annotated translations.

In the introduction, it was pointed out that ancient and late ancient Christian sources for a long time show no particular interest in the further organization of Sunday beyond worship. Not even the rest day legislation of Constantine (transmitted in 321 CE) gained any reception, except for the pause in court activities. Why did no preacher refer to the law while encouraging his congregation to attend worship? Probably because this weekly rest from work was hardly observed at all (except in the law courts), not even in later imperial laws.

In early Christianity, beyond a general expectation of soon parousia of Christ, there were no particularly Christian concepts of time and calendar. A practice of meeting regularly on Sunday soon developed, but this day had no special dignity or sacredness in itself. First of all, a Christian festival calendar with Easter, Ascension, Pentecost, and also Christmas was established. Only then did Sunday gain in importance and a weekly rhythm structure people's lives. Parallel to this, the year itself—remember Dionysius Exiguus's design for calculating the years from Christ's birth for the date of Easter from 529 CE—was also calculated and understood in a Christian way. Just as sacred places were added to Christianity in the form of church buildings and pilgrimage sites, the period of time during which one stayed there was increasingly understood as sacred time. However, this was a process that lasted longer, varied from region to region, and was obviously quite controversial. The sacralization of Sunday was probably the final point in this development, which gained significant momentum only with the disappearance of pagan holidays, either through prohibition or neglect. The texts collected in this volume attempted by various means to establish greater clarity or unambiguity about what significance Sunday had and what behavior it required.

It is difficult to say whether the Letter from Heaven significantly accelerated this process or whether it moved along in the wake of a general development. The legislation in the Merovingian as well as in the Carolingian period (see for Byzantium also the amendment of Leo VI) was likewise dedicated to Sunday worship. But in any case, it was the intention of the letter's author to shake things up. He has resorted to a drastic means, a heavenly letter, which Christ is said to have written personally. The letter wants to cause a kind of divine horror in the reader or listener, and obviously many have reacted to it, not all as negatively as Licinianus of Cartagena. However, the great freedom to rewrite or to augment the text shows an awareness that the message of the letter is to be taken seriously, but not necessarily its claim to be a literal letter from heaven.

Besides the sacralization of time, crisis was also discussed as the occasion and background of the Letter from Heaven. However, it seems to be rather the case that experienced crises could accelerate the recourse to and the spread of the Letter from Heaven, as the text *De plaga* shows. To explain the emergence of Sunday worship with a crisis alone does not explain why the neglect of Sunday worship, of all things, and not other sins was denounced. Therefore, the Christianization of time and calendar seems to have higher relevance than crisis.

The letter primarily calls for rest from work and for worship. The rest from work is not justified by the imperial law, but the Sabbath commandment of the creation story (Gen 2:2–3) and the Decalogue is transferred to Sunday. The exegetical problem—namely, that Sabbath actually is a different day from Sunday—is tacitly ignored; this is not always the case in other texts, such as in the sermons in this volume. It is surprising, however, that the Letters from Heaven are not more specific about what one ought to do on Sunday, especially the Greek versions. The emphasis in the Greek tradition is that Christians are to make time for worship in order to share in the holy fellowship of Christians on earth and in heaven—Sunday is not only the sign of the new covenant for all the baptized, but the Sunday gathering sanctifies and reconciles the Christians who attend it. The absence of Christians from the gathering thus stains the entire community. Therefore, the punishment is pronounced universally for all humankind, whereas the Latin letter is limited to the home or the family. Thus, the character of the day as a day of joy is more in the foreground in the Latin versions, which forbid to perform activities on it that are close to slave labor, just as it is forbidden to fast and kneel in prayer on Sunday. The Letter from Heaven, however, offers not only prohibitions but also recommendations. Thus, it is clear that Christians were definitely called on to do good deeds, especially on Sunday. Therefore, although there are some aspects of Sabbatization of Sunday, this is not an appropriate characterization.

A distinctive and unique feature of the Letter from Heaven is the duration of Sunday from Saturday evening to Monday morning. No matter whether the day begins in the evening, at midnight, or in the morning, the time span of Sunday is covered in all cultures. This could speak for the fact that the Letter from Heaven was indeed universally oriented from the beginning, or transmitted bilingually. Whether this was the actual reason for composing the letter or the reason for the criticism remains questionable—no criticism has survived as to how one could come up with the strange idea of extending Sunday's time span to Monday.

It was pointed out that the Letter from Heaven is part of a development that can hardly be described as Sabbatization of Sunday. Furthermore, one should refrain from using negative value judgments to describe this development as a (regretted) Judaization. It is also out of place to think of a Germanization here. This is true both for the assessment that the newly converted peoples could only be held to a Christian life by means of tougher legislation and threatening backdrops—the whole development is, after all, a new trend and not a special measure for disciplining individual peoples—and for the assertion that (unprovable) Germanic taboo thinking is intruding into Christianity here.

The texts give indications of a Christianization of all areas of life, including time. They are evidence of a sacralization of particular temporal structures and a uniformization and homogenization of the calendar. The different rhythms and holidays of the Roman calendar lost attention; conversely, the Christian days gained importance and became obligatory for all parts of the population. Thus Sunday became piece by piece a vital identity marker of a Christian existence. This was successful—up to the current day. In the wake of the Christian Sunday, the weekly rhythm has continued unbroken from antiquity to the present, a time-honored heritage of antiquity.

B TEXTS AND TRANSLATIONS

1

THE LETTER OF LICINIANUS OF CARTAGENA

Philip Polcar

The earliest evidence for the circulation of a Letter from Heaven is the document presented here: a letter of response written by bishop Licinianus of Cartagena in Spain (ca. 586–ca. 602 CE) in 595 or earlier.[1] The trigger letter was a missive from Ibiza, composed by the island's bishop, Vincentius. Attached was a copy of a version of the Letter from Heaven, which had come to Vincentius in an unknown manner, and he believed it to be a genuine message from Christ. Vincentius consequently followed the instructions given in the letter, as some of the later versions still indicate: he commanded the letter be read from the pulpit to the people of Ibiza and made at least one copy.[2] It was sent to his superior, Licinianus, metropolitan of the province in those times under Byzantine rule, and some 350 kilometers distant. It would seem appropriate for a bishop to request guidance on how to deal with such a matter, but Vincentius had already acted on his own accord. Therefore, Licinianus's reply was harsh. He chastised his colleague rudely and ordered him to destroy the Sunday letter publicly.

Interestingly, only three letters by Licinianus are preserved, but all of them aim to express critique in a lesser or stronger degree. The first one (*Ep.* 1) is directed to Pope Gregory and is quite remarkable. In it Licinianus thanks Gregory for the useful teaching in his *Regula pastoralis* but then expresses certain doubts: some rules might perhaps seem excessively rigorous in the face of human frailty.[3] The second letter (*Ep.* 2) is for a deacon called Epiphanius from an unknown diocese and is considered to have been

1. José Madoz, *Liciniano de Cartagena y sus cartas: Edición crítica y studio histórico*, Estudios Onienses 14 (Madrid: Facultades de Teología y de Filosofía del Colegio Máximo de Oña, 1948), 125.

2. See on this instruction above, p. 141.

3. The letter is taken as an indication for the strong influence the Roman see had on the Hispano-Byzantine church. See Fernando Rodamilans Ramos, "El Primado romano en la

composed in cooperation with Severus, the future bishop of Malaga.[4] It is a refutation of the position of an anonymous "materialistic" bishop, who denied the spirituality of the human soul; the letter emphasizes that angels and human souls must be incorporeal.

The text at hand (*Ep.* 3) treads less carefully in its criticism: Licinianus identifies the Letter from Heaven as a forgery and feels the need to reproach his colleague. Its opening contains some typical opening formulas, which express due respect and summon the connecting love of Christ to indicate fraternal proximity—but it is also insinuated that Licinianus took time off his duties to write this reply (1.1). The second sentence cuts right to the matter: Licinianus is saddened by Vincentius's behavior because the bishop thought the Letter from Heaven was a divine message, and by reading it publicly he had contributed to its prominence.

Then the scene of how the letter was delivered is described (1.3): Licinianus opened and read it in the presence of the bearer, but already after a few sentences he was so infuriated by its content that he tore it apart and threw it to the ground. One should not assume that this truly took place—Licinianus's letter shows that he knew the content of the Letter from Heaven very well and has therefore clearly read it to the end—the scene is merely effective rhetoric.[5] The sentence is, however, quite rude. It expresses Licinianus's dismay about Vincentius's credulity (and implicitly about his simple-mindedness) to have believed in such "rubbish" (*neniae*). Licinianus also cannot hold back a remark on the bad style and bumpy Latin of the Letter from Heaven. This is primarily a slight against the quality of the text, and consequently against Vincentius, who failed to notice or did not question why Christ would compose such deficient Latin. But herein lies also an argument against the Letter from Heaven's claim to be written by Christ.

In addition, Licinianus is not content with delivering a harsh reprimand—he chooses to deliver some valid arguments for why there is no "sound

---

Península Ibérica hasta el siglo X: Un análisis historiográfico," *Espacio, Tiempo y Forma, Serie III, H.ª Medieval* 27 (2014): 419–60, esp. 446; but also that Hispania played a privileged role in ecclesiastical politics of Rome in the Western Roman sphere. See Silvia Acerbi, "El protagonismo de Hispania en la consolidación de la Primacía Petrina: A propósito de dos libros recientes," *Anuaria de historia de la Iglesia* 30 (2021): 215–36, esp. 226.

4. Madoz, *Liciniano*, 17, because no other person of that name can be thought of but the one who in Isidore of Seville, *De viris illustribus* 43 (PL 83:1105A), is called *collega et socius Liciniani episcopi*.

5. The passage should absolutely not be taken at face value, as does Steven van Impe, "Licinian of Cartagena, Letters," 2004, https://tinyurl.com/2j7ecw8s: "Did Licinian destroy a genuine, important early church document? We shall probably never know."

doctrine" (*doctrina sana*) to be found in the letter. First, he grounds the demands of the text in reality: of course, Christians should go to church on Sunday, but if they do not, it is preferable that they work at home instead of going to feasts, where they dance and behave in morally illicit ways.[6] Subsequently, Licinianus opposes the strict rules stemming from Jewish Sabbath observance and therefore disdainfully says that the letter "urges us to behave like Jews" (2.3: *nos iudaizare compellat*)—and that is unacceptable for orthodox Christians.[7] Second, Licinianus argues that the Letter from Heaven should not be counted among biblical Scriptures; it is rather a figment of the devil. The idea may have been triggered by Vincentius himself, who seems to have thought that the Letter from Heaven was to be added to the canon.[8] But Licinianus argues that, except for the Ten Commandments, the holy Scriptures did not come into being as written pieces from heaven but were spoken into the hearts of the prophets and apostles (3.4). Furthermore, there is no need for further divine Scriptures after the Gospels (3.5). They, together with the prophets and the apostles, are "letters from heaven"; Vincentius should look at them instead, and only at them (3.6), as nothing more is forthcoming. This stance is supported with the authority of biblical quotations (4.1f.: Gal 1:9; Matt 11:13).

The final reproach delivered by Licinianus at the end of the letter not only is a command for Vincentius to repent and amend himself, but also offers

6. This implies also that there was indeed free time to be spent on Sunday, at least for some people, so already a kind of Sunday observance was in effect. The argument is similar to a passage in a sermon of Augustine (*Sermo* 9.3 [CCSL 41:109–13 Lambot]), perhaps the model for Licinianus (see below, n. 31). The history of Sunday observance shows that the demand to rest strictly was by no means accepted in those times. See Heil, *From Sun-Day to the Lord's Day*, especially the introduction, 14–26, and the contributions of Meier ("Christian Sunday," 251-73) and Wood ("Hagiography and the Canons," 273-91) in this volume.

7. Perhaps Licinianus argues here in line with the canons of the third Council of Orléans from 538, canon 31 (CCSL 148A:125.281–292 de Clercq): *Quia persuasum est populis die Domineco agi cum caballis aut bubus et ueiculis itinera non debere neque ullam rem ad uictum praeparari uel ad netorem domus uel hominis pertenentem ullatenus exerciri, quae res ad Iudaicam magis quam ad Christeanam obseruantiam pertenere probatur, id statuimus, ut die Dominico, quod ante fieri licuit, liceat.* "Because the people are convinced that on the Lord's Day it is forbidden to go out with horses, or carts, to prepare anything to eat, or to do anything that contributes to the beautification of house or person—all things that are recognized as belonging more to Jewish than to Christian observance—we determine that on the Lord's Day everything that was permitted before is also now permitted." See on this canon also p. 177f.

8. Licinianus says so, though perhaps he is just putting words into Vincentius's mouth; 1.3: *et post prophetarum vaticinia, et Christi evangelia, apostolorumque eius epistolas . . . esse credideris.*

practical advice for how he can limit the damage he has done: Vincentius should perform by a public gesture, by tearing the Letter from Heaven apart, to indicate that he was mistaken and that the letter bears no authority.

Overall, Licinianus's statement is more than a private reproach pinned to his colleague. It is, rather, an official document from the archbishop's see: Vincentius had to act on it. But there is more to it. Late antique letters and letter collections often took on a public dimension.[9] This is most likely true when one looks at Licinianus's epistles 1 and 2. The refutation of the arguments about the materialistic soul brought forth by an anonymous bishop are primarily composed to convince a wider audience that these views are wrong. It is a tractate designed to stop the spread of heretical views. So, Licinianus wanted his letter to be read by a larger group of clerics, intended as a public document from the start, condemning the Letter from Heaven in the hope of halting its circulation. Its widespread tradition shows that Licinianus was only partially successful. The Letter from Heaven drew official attention in the seventh century again.[10]

Though it is safe to say that the version of the Letter from Heaven that Vincentius and Licinianus had at hand is lost, the information one can gather from Licinianus's letter sounds familiar. In the beginning it said that the Lord's Day must be observed (2.1). One must not prepare food, go for a walk, do housework (2.3), nor work in the garden, make a trip, nor, as a woman, spin wool (2.6). Furthermore, it is stated that the Letter from Heaven fell from the heavens onto the altar in the chapel of the apostle Peter (3.6). All these features bear resemblance to Latin Recension II (see above, p. 86).

The Latin text is printed according to the critical edition by José Madoz (1948). His choices in orthography have remained unchanged in most instances.[11] In terms of punctuation I have also mostly followed Madoz's suggestions with minor changes. One instance is to be pointed out: in 3.4 I have changed the semicolon between *delectavit* and *quia* to a comma, as the semicolon broke apart a well-structured sentence.

---

9. See Winrich A. Löhr, "Brief," in *Lexikon der antiken christlichen Literatur*, 3rd ed., ed. Siegmar Döpp and Wilhelm Geerlings (Freiburg: Herder, 2002), 131–32, and Johannes Divjak, "Epistulae," in *Augustinus Lexikon* (Basel: Schwabe, 1996–2002), 2:893–1057.

10. See the introduction on the history of this letter, p. 85f.

11. Madoz gives a summary of the orthographical principles present in manuscript E, such as the use of a *c* instead of a *t* in some instances, for example, *cancione*; see Madoz, *Liciniano*, 78–79.

Madoz has used the following manuscripts:

E = Cod. El Escorial, &. I. 14, s. viii–ix[12]
T = Cod. Toledo, 27.24

Madoz's edition rests mainly on the basis of manuscript E, as T is only a copy of E, but it appears that sometimes T has better variants.[13] For the sake of usability, I have also given the *variae lectiones* from Madoz's apparatus in the commentary. A translation of the letter is available in the public domain, but it is based on the former edition found in the Patrologia Latina, which is quite lacking in comparison to Madoz's.[14] Subsequently, its translation does not give a faithful rendering of the letter's content. My translations of the biblical citations are based on the NRSV.

12. See Guillermo Antolín, *Catálogo de los códices latinos de la Real Biblioteca del Escorial* (Madrid: Helenica, 1910), 2:364–71, esp. 370.

13. See Madoz, *Liciniano*, 76–77.

14. Van Impe, "Licinian of Cartagena, Letters"; PL 72:689–700.

Epistula ad Vincentium episcopum Ebositane insule directa.[15]

[1] (1) Inter varias tribulationum angustias[16] non nos piguit, cogente caritate Christi, hec qualiacumque sunt, ad sanctitatem vestram[17] verba dirigere, insinuantes accepisse nos litteras tuas, et de vestrae sospitatis bono gavisos.[18] (2) sed in id non minime contristati sumus, quod litteras cuiusdam, quas ad nos direxistis, sicut tue indicant littere, susceperis,[19] et de tribunali populis eas feceris annunciari.[20] (3) ego enim mox a te transmissas accepi, in presentia ipsius perlatoris exordium litterarum ipsarum legens, et non patienter ferens nec dignum ducens nenias[21] ipsas perlegere, statim scidi[22] et eas in terram proieci, admirans quod his credulus fueris, et post prophetarum vaticinia, et Christi evangelia, apostolorumque eius epistolas, nescio cuius hominis litteras[23] sub nomine Christi factas, eius esse credideris; ubi nec sermo elegans,[24] nec doctrina sana poterit reperiri.

15. *Epistula ... directa*: Apparently Madoz has copied the following paratext from the manuscripts: *Item epistula cuius supra ad Vincentium episcopum Ebositane insule directa. Contra eos qui credunt epistulas de celo cecidisse in memoriam sancti Petri Romae*. I shortened it for this edition.

16. *varias tribulationum angustias*: A stylish hyperbaton to open the letter; see Augustine, *Civ.* 20.11.28 (CCSL 48:435.14 Dombart/Kalb): *in angustias tribulationis*; Gregory the Great, *Homiliae in Ezechielem, praefatio* 1.5 (CCSL 142:4.7–8 Adriaen): *ab angustiis tribulationum*.

17. *ad sanctitatem*: A title often used to address a fellow bishop from the third century onward, especially frequent in the fifth century; see Mary B. O'Brien, *Titles of Address in Christian Latin Epistolography to 543 AD*, Catholic University of America Patristic Studies 21 (Washington, DC: Catholic University of America Press, 1930), 23, 34, 161, 165.

18. *gavisos*: E has *gavisus*; see Madoz, *Liciniano*, 125.

19. *susceperis*: The choice of word could convey that Vincentius not merely received but also acknowledged the letter as divine. In 1.3 Licinianus uses *accepi*.

20. *de tribunali . . . annunciari*: The *tribunal* denotes a pulpit from which the deacon and other ministers read to the people during liturgical celebrations (Cyprian of Carthage, *Ep.* 39.4.1 [CCSL 3B:190.63–64 Diercks]: *super pulpitum id est super tribunal*; see Madoz, *Liciniano*, 126). Licinianus informs us that Vincentius ordered his clergy to read the Letter from Heaven to the people of Ibiza, as it is commanded in the Letter from Heaven; see above, n. 2. This also indicates that the letter was read in a liturgical context.

21. *nenias*: An expression of disdain and ridicule. Licinianus uses the word also in *Ep.* 1.6 (94–95 Madoz): *miror . . . ut de stellis nenias Originis transferret*.

22. *scidi*: E has *scindi*; see Madoz, *Liciniano*, 126. Though the action is not to be taken literarily, this detail indicates that letters were written on papyrus (not *velum*) at this time and place.

23. *nescio cuius . . . litteras*: Possibly a subtle allusion to Augustine's famous comment on learning Virgil for the most leaned readers; see Augustine, *Conf.* 1.20 (CCSL 27:11.11 Verheijen): *tenere cogebar Aeneae nescio cuius errores*.

24. *legans*: E has *eligans*; see Madoz, *Liciniano*, 126.

A Letter to Vincentius, the Bishop of the Island Ibiza

[1] (1) Among various tribulations and distresses, it has caused us no trouble, urged by the love of Christ, to address these words, for what they're worth, to your holiness, informing you that we have received your letter, and we have rejoiced in your health. (2) However, it has grieved us not to a small degree that you acknowledged the letter of some person, which you have sent to us, as your letter states, and had it read from a pulpit before the populace. (3) For I, as soon as I received it from you, still in the presence of the bearer, read the beginning of the letter, and I did not bear it tolerantly, nor did I think it worthy to finish reading this rubbish; nay, immediately I tore it up and threw it on the ground, astonished that you could believe it, and that you believed this letter of some man, pretending to be written in the name of Christ, was to be classified after the revelations of the prophets, the gospels of Christ, and the epistles of the apostles; in it neither sound language nor sane doctrine can be found.

[2] (1) In principio ipsius epistolae legimus, ut dies dominicus colatur.[25] (2) quis enim Christianus, non propter ipsum diem, sed propter resurrectionem domini nostri Iesu Christi, eo quod in ipso a mortuis resurrexit, reverendissimum non habeat? (3) sed quantum sentio, ideo novus iste praedicator hoc dicit, ut nos iudaizare compellat, ut nullus sibi in eodem die necessaria victus praeparet, aut in eo[26] ambulet. (4) sed hoc quam pessimum sit, sanctitas tua perpendat. (5) utinam populus Christianus, si die ipso[27] ecclesiam non frequentat, aliquod operis faceret, et non saltaret![28] (6) meliusque erat viro hortum facere, iter agere, mulieri colum tenere,[29] et non, ut dicitur, ballare, saltare, et membra a deo bene condita saltando male torquere,[30] et ad excitandam libidinem nugatori<is>[31] cancionibus proclamare.

---

25. *colatur*: The extant versions of the Letter from Heaven mainly use the words *observare* and *custodire* to express the command to observe Sunday rest (see p. 162). Licinianus's use of *colere* could be a deliberate choice, as worshipping a day and abstaining from work is also a pagan practice, similarly phrased in Martin of Braga, *De correctione rusticorum* 18, ed. Claude W. Barlow, *Martini episcopi Bracarensis opera omnia*, Papers and Monographs of the American Academy in Rome 12 (New Haven, CT: Yale University Press, 1950), 202.22–203.2: *nam satis iniquum et turpe est ut illi qui pagani sunt et ignorant fidem Christianum, idola daemonum colentes, diem Iovis aut cuiuslibet daemonis colant et ab opere se abstineant, cum certe nullum diem daemonia nec creassent nec habeant.* Also, Caesarius of Arles, *Sermo* 193.4 (CCSL 104:785.6 Morin): *ista duo luminaria quasi deos colamus.* Though the veneration of saints' feast days is also described by using *colere*: Caesarius, *Sermo* 217.1 (CCSL 104:861.5f. Morin): *Iohannis . . . natalem diem colimus*; Gregory the Great, *Homilia in Evangelia* 35.7 (CCSL 141:327,171 Etaix): *natalem martyris hodierna die colimus.*

26. *in eo*: T has *viam*; see Madoz, *Liciniano*, 127.

27. *die ipso*: E has *diem ipso*; E also adds *ad*; see Madoz, *Liciniano*, 127.

28. *utinam . . . saltare*: The argument resembles a sermon by Augustine, *Sermo* 9.3 (CCSL 41:110.94f. Lambot): *melius enim faceret Iudaeus in agro suo aliquid utile quam in theatro seditiosus exsisteret. et melius feminae eorum die sabbati lanam facerent quam toto die in maenianis suis impudice saltarent.*

29. *hortum . . . tenere*: The version of the Letter from Heaven that Licinianus received prohibited these activities on Sunday. No extant version has this exact list, but Latin Recension II exhibits more similarities; see above, p. 85f. *Lanam facere* describes one of the works considered typical and appropriate for a woman since early Roman times; see Jerome, *Ep.* 107.10 (CSEL 55:300.23 Hilberg): *discat et lanam facere, tenere colum, ponere in gremio calatum, rotare fusum, stamina pollice ducere.*

30. *et non . . . torquere*: This is comparable to Caesarius of Arles, who chastised his flock for not coming to church on feast days (and Sunday): Caesarius of Arles, *Sermo* 55.2 (CCSL 103:242.24–28 Morin): *sunt et alii, qui pro hoc solo desiderant ad natalicia martyrum convenire, ut inebriando, ballando, verba turpia decantando, choros ducendo et diabolico more saltando, et se subvertant, et alios perdant; et qui deberent exercere opus Christi, ministerium conantur implere diaboli.*

31. *nugatoriis cancionibus*: E and T apparently only offered *nugatoribus*; see Madoz, *Liciniano*, 128, but the phrase seems flawed, as *nugator* usually indicates a person. Therefore,

[2] (1) At the beginning of this letter we read that the Lord's Day is to be revered. (2) What Christian does not consider this day a most venerable one—not because of the day itself, but because of the resurrection of our Lord, Jesus Christ, because on this day he rose from the dead? (3) But, I notice, this new preacher tells us so in order to compel us to act like the Jews, that no one may prepare for himself his necessary sustenance, nor may he take a walk on this day. (4) But may your holiness consider, how awful this is. (5) Oh, would that the Christian people, if they do not go to church on that day, would do some work instead of go to dances! (6) Surely it is better for a man to do gardening or to make a journey, if a woman holds the spindle and does not, as they say, dance, jump, and unnaturally twist the God-given limbs while dancing, and bursts out to excite lust with bawdy songs.

I suggest *nugatoriis*, based on Augustine's descriptions of sinful behavior, which may be the basis for Licinianus's choice of words: Augustine, *Enarrat. Ps.* 84.15 (CCSL 39:1175.29f. Dekkers and Fraipont; trans. Maria Boulding, *Expositions of the Psalms. Saint Augustine*, The Works of Saint Augustine 3.18 [New York: New City Press, 2002], 218): *quem delectabant cantica nugatoria et adulterina, delectet hymnum dicere deo* ("worthless and bawdy songs used to afford you pleasure, but now you enjoy singing a hymn to God"). Also, note the use in Augustine, *Sermo* 198 *auctus* 3, ed. Francois Dolbeau, *Collection des Études Augustiniennes: Série Antiquité* 147:368.51: *illa daemonia delectantur canticis vanitatis, delectantur nugatorio strepitu*. The word *cancio* is Proto-Romance (*canción* et al.); see Wilhelm Meyer-Lübke, *Romanisches etymologisches Wörterbuch* (Heidelberg, 1911), s.v. *cantio*.

[3] (1) Absit ergo a sanctitate tua hoc credere, ut epistole nunc nobis mittantur a Christo. (2) sufficiat enim quod locutus est in prophetis, per se ipsum, et per suos apostolos. (3) nam et his non litteras transmittebat e celo, sed Spiritu Sancto eorum corda replebat. (4) exceptis enim decem praeceptis, que in tabulis lapideis mirabiliter data sunt, ad nullum prophetarum aut apostolorum epistole missae sunt de celo. (5) Non igitur credas, que numquam facta leguntur; quod si ea[32] facta essent, post predicationem Evangelii iam necessaria non sunt. (6) Et si forte ipsum nomen novum te delectavit,[33] quia ipsa epistola, sicut simulator scripsit, de celo descendit super altare Christi in memoria sancti Petri apostoli,[34] scito diaboli esse figmentum, et omnem scripturam divinam epistolam aut epistolas esse celestes, et ad nos de celo fuisse transmissas.

[4] (1) Emendet ergo quod temere credidit sanctitas tua, et in praesentia populi ipsam epistolam, si est penes te, rescinde, et hoc te peniteat quod de tribunali[35] eam feceris recitari, beati apostoli sequens doctrinam, quod inter cetera ad Galatas scripsit: si quis evangelizaverit vobis preter id quod accepistis, anathema sit. (2) sed et illud Evangelium: omnis lex et prophete usque ad Iohannem prophetaverunt. (3) deinceps, si qua nova vel inusitata divulgata[36] fuerint, omnino abicienda et detestanda sanctitas tua noverit. (4) ora pro nobis, domine sancte et in Christo charissime frater.[37]

32. *quod si ea*: T has *quae etsi*; see Madoz, *Liciniano*, 128.

33. *delectavit*: E has *delectabit*; see Madoz, *Liciniano*, 128.

34. *in memoria . . . apostoli*: The place in which the letter supposedly was found; *memoria* here means either the altar or the chapel. See Augustine, *Civ.* 1.4.14 (CCSL 47:5.16 Dombart and Kalb): *memoriis nostrorum apostolorum.*

35. *tribunali*: E has *tribunal*; see Madoz, *Liciniano*, 129.

36. *divulgata*: E has *devulgata*; see Madoz, *Liciniano*, 129.

37. *ora . . . frater*: Closing formula.

[3] (1) Let it be far from your holiness to believe that letters are now sent to us by Christ. (2) Let it suffice that he spoke through his prophets, by himself, and through his apostles. (3) Even to them he did not transmit letters from heaven, but he filled their hearts with the Holy Spirit. (4) Except, of course, for the Ten Commandments, which were miraculously given on tablets of stone, no letters were sent from heaven to any prophet or apostle. (5) Therefore, do not believe what was never attested in writing; and if it had indeed happened, it is not needed after the proclamation of the gospel. (6) And if perhaps this new name delights you, because this letter, as the forger writes, came down from heaven to the altar of Christ in the chapel of the holy apostle Peter, know that it is a figment of the devil, and that all the holy scriptures are a heavenly letter or letters and were transmitted to us from heaven.

[4] (1) Let your holiness therefore better himself, since you have believed imprudently, and tear up this letter in the presence of the populace, if it is [still] in your possession, and let it grieve you that you have ordered it to be read from the pulpit, following the teaching of the blessed apostle which he wrote to the Galatians besides others: "If anyone proclaims to you a gospel contrary to what you received, let that one be accursed" (Gal 1:9). (2) But on this also the following gospel: "All the prophets and the law prophesied until John came" (Matt 11:13). (3) If thereupon anything new or unusual is proclaimed, your holiness should know that it must be utterly rejected and despised. (4) Pray for us, holy father and brother most dear in Christ.

2

LETTER FROM HEAVEN—LATIN RECENSION II

According to Vienna, Österreichische Nationalbibliothek Cod. Lat. 1355, fols. 91r–92r

Philip Polcar and Christoph Scheerer

The Latin versions of the Letter from Heaven are grouped into three recensions. This grouping was first established by Robert Priebsch[1] and consequently pursued by Dorothy Haines.[2] Recension II has been, so far, mainly represented by Hippolyte Delehaye's edition of the version preserved in Munich, Bayerische Staatsbibliothek Clm 9550.[3] This chapter offers an alternative: the version preserved in the manuscript Vienna, Österreichische Nationalbibliothek Cod. Lat. 1355 will be provided with a translation and a brief commentary. For a quick overview of the differences between the widely used version of Munich BSB Clm 9550 and of Vienna ÖNB 1355, an apparatus can be found at the end of the chapter, indicating the variations between the two versions in a nutshell.

However, it must be pointed out that versions belonging to Recension II are preserved in a large number of manuscripts.[4] The scope of this study does not permit transcribing them all and including them into the edition and commentary. This subchapter aims to provide the text and its translation of one version of Recension II that has not yet been edited. It may serve as a further stepping stone for future scholars who seek to provide a more complete picture of the texts of Recension II. Nevertheless, an effort will be made to include the already edited versions in the commentary at points of interest. Therefore, as in the subchapter on Recension I, these manuscripts/editions will be referred to as

1. Priebsch, *Letter from Heaven*, 3. See above on research history, p. 36f.

2. See Haines, *Sunday Observance*, 36–37.

3. The text of this manuscript is printed in Delehaye, "Note sur la légende," reprinted in Delehaye, *Mélanges d'Hagiographie*, 155–56.

4. See the list of 46 manuscripts of this recension, pp. 40–42.

comparanda with the following abbreviations, in order to facilitate the use of the commentary; the number 2 indicates that they refer to the text of Recension II:

Mun2 = Munich, Bayerische Staatsbibliothek Clm 9550, fol. 1r (Delehaye)
Ham2 = Hamburg, Bibliothek der Hansestadt, St. Petri-Kirche 30b, fols. 35r–36v[5]
Tod2 = Todi, Perugia (lost)[6]
Par2 = Paris, Bibliothèque National lat. 8508[7]

At least three subversions of Recension II can be identified.[8] One is the version of Munich BSB Clm 9550, folio 1r,[9] which can be found also in, for example, Munich, Bayerische Staatsbibliothek Clm 14673, folios 119v–120r, and Hamburg, Bibliothek der Hansestadt, St. Petri-Kirche 30b, folio 35r–36v.[10] The other is the version provided here from Vienna ÖNB 1355, folios 91r–92r, which is also preserved, for example, in Paris, Bibliothèque National lat. 8508, folios 57v–63r (in margin), and in Todi, Perugia (lost).[11] A very short third version is preserved in London, British Library Add. 30853.[12] Due to the observations made in the introduction (see above, pp. 86–95), it is conceivable that this version may present the text in its most original state.

Furthermore, the manuscripts Vienna, Österreichische Nationalbibliothek Cod. 1878 (s. xii), folios 35v–36v, and Munich, Bayerische Staatsbibliothek Clm 3766 (s. xv), folios 167va–168ra also provide a version of Recension II, but it does not fit in the scheme of the three subversions as just explained. They share the form of the first mentioned subversion (like Munich BSB Clm 9550), including the *incipit* and the lack of the passage 6.3 as well as of the first reference to Peter in 8.1. However, they have many single phrases and minor variant

5. Staphorst, *Hamburgische Kirchengeschichte* 1.3:345–47, reprinted in *Die Handschriften der S. Petri-Kirche Hamburg*, ed. Thilo Brandis (Hamburg: Hauswedell, 1967), 345–47; reprinted also in Röhricht, "Ein 'Brief Christi,'" 440–42.

6. Amaduzzi, *Anecdota litteraria I*, 69–74, reprinted also in Jacques-Paul Migne, *Dictionnaire des apocryphes, ou collection de tous les livres apocryphes relatifs à l'Ancien et au Nouveau Testament* (Paris, 1856-1858), 367–69.

7. Not edited yet; see gallica.bnf.fr/ark:/12148/btv1b9080944s.

8. This is the result of a cursory analysis of the large number of manuscripts containing Recension II. The aim is neither to provide a detailed analysis and classification of all these manuscripts nor to build well-defined groups. Thus, there may be subversions left to be identified.

9. See n. 3.

10. See n. 5.

11. See n. 6.

12. Grégoire, *Les homéliaires du moyen âge*, 161–85, with the text at 226–27. See also Delehaye, "Un exemplaire de la lettre tombée du ciel," 164–69. See also in the introduction the quotations at p. 92f.

readings in common with the second mentioned version (like Vienna ÖNB 1355), including the striking use of the third person in paragraph 4. Therefore, assuming that this is not due to contamination, the text of the Vienna ÖNB 1355 version and the Vienna ÖNB 1878 / Munich BSB Clm 3766 provides a more original text of Recension II than Munich BSB Clm 9550, Munich BSB Clm 14673, and Hamburg St. Petri-Kirche 30b, while Vienna ÖNB 1878 / Munich BSB Clm 3766 are to be regarded as an intermediate between the Vienna ÖNB 1355 version and the Munich BSB Clm 9550 version.

Unlike the versions belonging to the group Latin Recension I, the letters of Latin Recension II do not exhibit a narrative as a prologue. The letters start abruptly by threatening the wrath of God, which will come over humankind in the form of plagues, devastation, and pagan peoples. The phenomena mentioned tend to be rather natural than supernatural. Overall, the language used and the threats uttered aim to imitate the prophetic Old Testament style, similar to Latin Recension I.[13] But in contrast to Latin Recension I, the bearer of the epistle is not the archangel Michael but a bishop named Peter: his testimony is given at the end of the epistle, confirming that the letter is genuine and has been written by the hands of God. The letter refers to Peter twice in a striking manner, first with the phrase *sicut superius dixit* ("as he [i.e., Christ] said above," 5.3), and second by *iuro ego Petrus* . . . ("I, Peter, swear . . ."), which matches the one reference of the other two subversions. However, in the Vienna version nothing can be found to which the "as he said above" (8.1) could refer. Hence, one must assume that a part is missing at the beginning. This is supported by the already mentioned observation that the text of Recension II often starts abruptly, as in Vienna, with *quia*. In addition, in the Vienna version the second reference refers to the apostle Peter and thus to Rome. This suggests that this version as preserved in Vienna is connected to the Greek Recension Alpha 1 by a common predecessor.[14]

Sunday observance is justified in two ways: first, Sunday as the day of resurrection (4.1), and second, by an imprecise counting of the days of creation (4.2f.). The seventh day (Sabbath) is identified with Sunday: Because God rested, Christians should do so as well. The time of rest is also prescribed precisely in 5.1—as in all recensions of the Letter from Heaven: from the ninth hour of the Sabbath until the first hour of the second day (Monday).[15] The prohibitions mentioned—no walking, no business transactions, no household tasks such as cutting hair, washing clothes, or baking bread—bear strong resemblance to Jewish rules for the Sabbath. These rules are the reason Licinianus speaks of *iudaizare* in his reply to Vincentius (2.3).

13. See above, pp. 184–90, and Haines, *Sunday Observance*, 57f.
14. See above on the history of the letter, p. 86f.
15. See above, p. 182f.

Letter from Heaven—Latin Recension II (Cod. Vienna 1355)

[1] (1) In nomine domini nostri Iesu Christi.[16] Incipit epistola de die dominico.

(2) quia nescitis nec timetis[17] eum custodire, propter hoc venit ira dei super vos, et flagella[18] in laboribus, et in pec<udibus>[19] vestris quae vos possidetis. (3) et veniet gens pagana quae corpora vestra teneat in captivitate,[20] pro eo quod non servatis diem sanctum dominicum. (4) ideo ululant super vos lupi rapaces[21] et caligines quae vos in profundum maris demergunt, et avertam faciem meam a vobis et a tabernaculo[22] quod fecerunt manus meae. (5) quaecumque feceritis in ecclesia mea sancta, ego iudicabo, et tradam vos in manus alienas, et exterminabo vos,[23] et submergam, sicut submersi Sodomam et Gomorram quos terra obsorbuit.[24]

16. *in nomine . . . Christi*: Mun2 omits this; see Delehaye, *Mélanges d'Hagiographie*, 156 (hereafter just Mun2 without page).

17. *nescitis nec timetis*: This is strange and maybe due to a transmission error. Par2 provides *quia nec timetis illum custo[dire]*; Tod2 provides *qui nescitis illut timere ne et custodire*. Mun2 omits it.

18. *flagella*: Plagues, like in Gregorius Nazianzenus secundum translationem quam fecit Rufinus, *Homilia* 8.10.3 *De grandinis vastatione* (CSEL 46:247.11 Engelbrecht): *omisi etiam ranas et scinifes et cynomiam et reliqua flagella*.

19. *pecudibus*: The manuscript has *peccatis*, which does not make any sense in this context, but Mun2 and Ham2 provide *pecudibus*.

20. *corpora . . . captivitate*: Mun2 has *alios occidit et alios in captivitatem ducit*.

21. *lupi rapaces*: A phrase describing "false prophets" in Matt 7:15, but also Benjamin in Gen 48:27. It has found broad reception in the works of the Latin church fathers, especially to denounce heretics. It is also attested in Horace, *Epod*. 16.17 (BSGRT 159:20 Shackleton Bailey).

22. *tabernaculo*: Alludes to the tent of meeting (מִשְׁכָּן) from Exodus (25–31; 35–40). In Christian understanding it is a topos for the church; see Augustine, *Enarrat. Ps*. 131.10 (CCSL 38:1916.1–5 Dekkers and Fraipont): *quamquam aliquando dicitur tabernaculum dei domus dei, et domus dei tabernaculum dei, distinctius tamen accipitur, fratres carissimi, tabernaculum ecclesia secundum hoc tempus*.

23. *in manus . . . vos*: Mun2 omits this.

24. *quos . . . obsorbuit*: Mun2 omits this.

Translation

[1] (1) In the name of our Lord Jesus Christ. The letter begins about the Lord's day.

(2) Because you do not know how to observe it, and you are not afraid, the wrath of God comes upon you, and plagues on your works and on your livestock which you possess. (3) And a pagan people shall come which will hold your bodies captive, for the reason that you do not observe the Lord's day. (4) Therefore, ravenous wolves howl at you and [there will be] darkness that drowns you in the depths of the sea, and I will turn my face away from [Ezek 7:22] you and from the tabernacle that my hands have made. (5) And whatever you do in my church, I will judge, and I will deliver you into foreign hands, and I will cast you out and bury you, as I buried Sodom and Gomorrah [see Gen 19:24] which the earth has swallowed.

[2] (1) Et qui ambulaverit in alium locum[25] in die sancto dominico, nisi ad ecclesiam aut in locum sanctorum,[26] aut infirmos visitare aut discordantes ad concordiam veram revocare, et si aliud feceritis, flagello vos diversis flagellis[27] et mittam in vos plagam et conturbationem[28] malam in domos vestras.[29] (2) si quis negotium fecerit in die sancto dominico, ubicumque operatur aliquid,[30] aut capillos aut vestimenta laverit, aut panem coxerit, aut quodcumque fecerit,[31] exterminabo eum et non inveniet benedictionem neque in die neque in nocte,[32] sed maledictionem mittam in domos eius et omnes infirmitates super ipsum et super filios eius.[33] (3) Si quis aut causaverit in die sancto dominico aut detractionem aut contentionem[34] fecerit, aut risum inhonestum aut immoderatum commiserit,[35] mittam in eos omne malum, et deficient et dispergentur.[36]

---

25. *et qui . . . locum*: Mun2 adds to this *aut equitaverit.*

26. *aut in locum sanctorum*: Mun2 has *meam.*

27. *diversis flagellis*: Mun2 and Ham2 have *duris flagellis.*

28. *conturbationem*: "trouble" according to the Vulgate, e.g., Ezra 7:25f.: *angustia superveniente requirent pacem et non erit. conturbatio super conturbationem veniet et auditus super auditum*; Ezra 12:18: *fili hominis panem tuum in conturbatione comede.*

29. *vos plagam . . . vestras*: Mun2 has *vos et domos vestras plagam et conturbationem pessimam.*

30. *ubicumque . . . aliquid*: Ham2 has *aut si aliud in domo suo operatur*; Mun2 has *exterminabo eum, aut si aliquid in domo suo operatur.*

31. *aut quodcumque fecerit*: Ham2 is more extensive here: *aut quicquam inlicite operiss fecerit in die sancto dominico.* Mun2 has *aut aliud quid inliciti operis in die dominico.*

32. *in die . . . nocte*: Mun2 has *hic neque in futuro.*

33. *si quis . . . eius*: The first part mentions labors that are typically done only by either men or women; yet the later part is specifically said for men who are the *patres familias.*

34. *detractionem aut contentionem:* Slander and quarreling; see Augustine, *Ep.* 211 *ad sorores* (CSEL 57:358.4 Goldbacher): *si ergo repullulastis sanum sapere, orate, ne intretis in temptationem, ne iterum in contentiones, emulationes, animositates, dissensiones, detractiones, seditiones, susurrationes*; Augustine, *Serm.* 353 (PL 39:1559): *Agite itaque admoniti sanctae instar infantiae, deponite malitiam, dolum, adulationem et invidiam et detractionem*; *Serm.* 353 (PL 39:1561): *adulatio duplicat linguam: detractio vulnerat famam*; Jerome, *Comm. Isa.* 9.4, ed. Robert Gryson, *Commentaires de Jérôme sur le prophète Isaie: Livres VIII–XI*, VL 30 (Freiburg, 1996), 1030.92: *et haec ipsa tribulatio geminabitur detractione labiorum et blasphemiis persequentium, quibus adversum dei populum rabido ore desaeviunt*; *Regula Pachomii praecepta atque iudicia* 63.3, ed. Amand Boon, *Pachominiana Latina*, Bibliothèque de la Revue d'histoire ecclésiastique 7 (Leuven, 1933), 63.3: *deponamus opera tenebrarum, quae sunt contentiones, detractiones, odia, et tumentis animi superbia.*

35. *aut risum . . . commiserit*: Mun2 and Ham2 have *aut illicitum risum* (Ham2: *visum*) *commiserit.*

36. *deficient et dispergentur*: A threat akin to OT prophetic style; see Lev 26:33: *vos autem dispergam in gentes*; Ezek 22:15.

[2] (1) And whoever walks to another place on the holy Lord's day, except to the church or to a place of the saints, or to visit the sick or to bring the quarreling back to true harmony, and if you do anything else, I <will> hit you with various plagues and I will send a scourge over you, and severe trouble into your houses. (2) If somebody conducts any business on the holy Lord's Day, and wherever they do any work, whether they wash their hair or clothes, or bake bread, whatever they do, I will banish them and they will not find any blessing, neither by day or by night, but I will send curses upon their houses and all kinds of illness upon them and upon their children. (3) If anyone litigates on the holy Lord's day or instigates slander or a quarreling, or commits dishonorable or immoderate laughter, I will send all kinds of evil upon them, and they shall cease to be and they shall be scattered.

[3] (1) Audi, populus incredulitatis[37] et generatio prava atque perversa, quia non vultis credere. (2) pauci sunt dies vestri, cotidie appropinquat vester finis.[38] (3) ego sum patiens super vos. (4) expecto peccatores ut convertantur ad paenitentiam. (5) audite, populi omnes, et videte quod nullus hominum in die dominico operetur.[39]

[4] (1) Surrexit[40] dominus Iesus Christus in ipso die et ascendit in caelum, sedet <ad dexteram> dei patris omnipotentis. (2) in sex diebus fecit dominus omnia et in septimo ab omnibus operibus requievit.[41] (3) ita vos requiescite ab omnibus operibus vestris, tam servi quam liberi, et non aliud faciatis nisi serviatis sacerdotibus vestris.[42]

---

37. *populus incredulitatis*: See Col 3:6: *propter quae venit ira dei super filios incredulitatis.*

38. *cotidie . . . finis*: See Lam 4:18: *conpleti sunt dies nostri quia venit finis noster.*

39. *videte . . . operetur*: Ham2 has *videte, ne quis jurarit in die sancto Dominico.*

40. *surrexit*: Here Christ is spoken of in the third person for the first time in this letter, which is striking for a text that means to imitate a letter written by Christ. It is mostly limited to this fourth paragraph, but at the end of the fifth it happens again, *sicut superius dixit*, a little "trailer," probably inserted by a scribe, as was the fourth paragraph. However, this fits the *incipit* of this version, where it is not stated that Christ himself is the writer of this letter. Also, in the letter itself, Christ never speaks directly, but it seems to be an unspecified divinity speaking, and in 8.2 the throne of God is said to have written this letter, while Christ just approved it.

41. *surrexit . . . requievit*: Ham2 and Mun2 provide a much longer explanation here of why the Lord's Day must be observed.

Ham2: *Ego ipse Christus resurrexi a mortuis tertia die, hoc est, in die sancto Dominico, die veneris, qua debetis jejunare, ad quam ordinavi(t) herbam et oleum comdere et observare vestram vitam, pro qua passus fui, pro vestra ipsa salute et in ipso die resurrectionis mee eripui vos de inferno et de potestate diaboli omne genus quamlibet provocatus. Notum est vobis, quod in sex diebus feci coelum et terram, mare et omnia, que in eis sunt, septimo requievi ab omni opere.*

Mun2: *Ego ipse hac die resurrexi a mortuis, cum passus sum pro vestra omnium salute et in ipso die resurrectionis meae eripui vos de inferno et a potestate diaboli. Quamvis enim in multis me provocetis, notum enim est vobis quia sex diebus creavi caelum et terram, mare et omnia quae in eis sunt; septimo autem requievi ab omni opere.*

42. *faciatis . . . vestris*: Serving the priests appears to be a unique feature of this version so far; Mun2 and Ham2 do not mention them here: *tam servi quam liberi si vultis vitam aut requiem habere mecum.*

[3] (1) Listen, you faithless people, 'you depraved and perverse generation' [Deut 32:5], because you do not want to believe [see John 10:38]. (2) For few are your days, every day your end draws nearer. (3) I am patient with you. (4) I wait for the sinners to turn to penitence. (5) Listen, all peoples, and see to it that nobody works on the Lord's day.

[4] (1) The Lord Jesus Christ rose on this very day and ascended to heaven [see Matt 28:1], and he sits <at the right hand> of God, the almighty father [see Ps 110:1 with 1 Cor 15:25 and Phil 2:8-11]. (2) Within six days the Lord created everything, and on the seventh day he rested from all work [see Gen 1:1-2:3]. (3) Thus, you shall rest as well from all your work, be it slave or free man, and you shall not do anything except serve your priests.

[5] (1) Si enim non custoditis diem sanctum dominicum ab hora nona sabbati usque in horam primam secundae feriae, anathematizabo vos coram patre meo qui est in caelis,[43] et non habeatis partem mecum neque cum angelis meis in saecula saeculorum, amen. (2) amen dico vobis, si non custodieritis diem sanctum dominicum et omnes patres vestr<os>,[44] mittam super vos grandinem in igne et fulgura et coruscationes et tempestates, ut pereant labores vestri. (3) et delebo vineas vestras, nec aqua veniat super vos, nec habundantia,[45] sicut superius dixit.[46]

[6] (1) Date sacerdotibus meis decimas vestras ad ecclesiam et fideliter ostendite.[47] (2) qui ipsa fraudaverit, de omnibus quaecumque manu sua operatur fuerit fraudatus, sive in anima, sive in corpore, et[48] non videbit vitam aeternam vel desiderat videre,[49] et in domo eius nascuntur infantes caeci non audientes neque ambulantes[50] et erit fames in terra Christianorum. (3) o incredule populus, iudicium tibi non reserva, neque secundum hoc condemnabo, si feceritis quae praecipio vobis.[51]

---

43. *qui . . . caelis*: Mun2 omits this.

44. *et omnes . . . vestros*: Mun2 omits this. The manuscript has *vestri*, not *vestros*, but an accusative case seems more likely. However, the meaning of *patres* is unclear: either the heads of family are meant, or this is a vernacular expression and priests are meant (compare Italian *padre*). As a third option, the word could have been *conpatres*, which has been used as "neighbors" elsewhere; see p. 248.

45. *delebo . . . habundantia*: Ham2 has *delebo muros vestros et non dabo vobis pluviam, et ita auferam vobis fructum terre.* Mun2 has *delebo vineas vestras et non dabo vobis pluviam, et auferam a vobis fructus vestros.*

46. *sicut . . . dixit*: this striking third-person reference seems unique to this version; see above, n. 40.

47. *date . . . ostendite*: Mun2 has *Iterum iterumque moneo atque praecipio vobis ut detis mihi decimas iustas et sacerdotibus meis.*

48. *qui . . . et*: Mun2 has *et qui decimam meam defraudaverit.*

49. *vel . . . videre*: Mun2 and Ham2 omit this.

50. *non . . . ambulantes*: Mun2 has *et sine auditu et gressu.*

51. *et erit fames . . . vobis*: Mun2 omits this.

[5] (1) If you do not observe the holy Lord's Day from the ninth hour of the Sabbath to the first hour of the second day, I will curse you before my father who is in heaven [see Matt 6:9], and you shall not partake in me and my angels forever and ever, amen. (2) Truly I say to you, if you do not observe the holy Lord's day and all your fathers, I will send upon you fiery hail, and lightning, and thunderbolts, and tempests, so that your labors will decay. (3) And I will destroy your vineyards, and no water shall come upon you, and no abundance, as he has said above.

[6] (1) Give your tithes to the church into the hands of my priests and present them faithfully. (2) If anyone should cheat [the church] in this matter, he will be cheated out of everything his own hand has made, be it in spirit or body, or he will not see eternal life, though he desires to see it, and in his house children are born blind and deaf and lame and there is hunger in the land of the Christians. (3) O unfaithful people, do not prepare your own judgment, and I will not condemn you like this, if you do what I teach you.

[7] (1) Si custodieritis dominicum diem, aperiam vobis cataractas caeli in omni bono,[52] et multiplicabo labores vestros,[53] et elongabo dies anni vestri,[54] et non erit fames neque conturba<tio>[55] inter gentes,[56] et *stabo ego in vos et vos in me*, ut scietis quia ego sum deus vester et praeter me non est alius. (2) amen, amen dico vobis, si observabitis dominicum diem, omnia mala auferam a vobis. (3) si quis sacerdos[57] epistolam istam non legitur aut[58] populo suo non ostenderit, sive in ecclesia sive in villa, iudicium sustinebit. et istam epistolam legite per dominicos dies, ut credant semper et habeant omnes in memoria.[59] (4) quod si non crediderint in epistolam hanc,[60] anathematizabo illos in saeculum saeculi.

---

52. *cataractas caeli in omni bono*: see Mal 3:10; for the cataracts in a menacing meaning as in the Greek versions, see Gen 7:11; 8:2; 4 Kgs 7:2; Ps 41:8; Isa 24:18; see above, p. 190.

53. *vestros*: Mun2 adds to this *et dabo vobis pacem*.

54. *elongabo . . . vestri*: Lit. "the days of your year," a weird synecdoche, or a confusion.

55. *conturba<tio>*: The manuscript has *conturbabo*. On the word *conturbatio*, see 2.1.

56. *et non . . . gentes*: Mun2 and Ham2 omit this.

57. *si . . . sacerdos*: Mun2 and Ham2 have *praecipio vobis sacerdotibus meis ut unusquisque*.

58. *non legitur aut*: Mun2 omits this.

59. *sive in ecclesia . . . memoria*: Mun2 has *et affirmate illis a me transmissam*.

60. *in epistolam hanc*: Mun2 and Ham2 omit this.

[7] (1) If you observe the Lord's day, I will open for you the cataracts of heaven with every good thing [see Mal 3:10], and I will multiply [the fruits of] your labors, and I will prolong the days of your life, and there will be no hunger, and I will not cause trouble between the peoples, and "I will remain in you and you in me" [John 15:4], as you will know that I am your God and there is no other besides me [see Isa 43:11]. (2) Truly, truly I say to you, if you observe the Lord's Day, I will take away all evils from you. (3) If any bishop does not read this letter or does not show it to his people, whether in the church or in the mansion, he will sustain his judgment. And read this letter on the Lord's days, so that they all believe it always and keep it in mind. (4) If they do not believe this letter, I will curse them for eternity.

[8] (1) Ordinata in throno septimo domini nostri Iesu Christi de praeterito anno in civitate Gaza, ubi sanctus Petrus[61] episcopatum[62] accepit in deo; pax vero dei erat unum quod vos nescitis.[63] (2) Ipse ostendit, qualiter ad aeternam vitam pervenire possitis, <quia non>[64] mentior, quia nichil mandatum est, nisi quod verum est. (3) videte quod superius dixit:[65] (4) Iuro ego Petrus apostolus[66] per dei potestatem, qui fecit caelum et terram et omnia quae eis sunt, et per Iesum Christum filium eius et per sanctam trinitatem et quattuor evangelistas et per duodecim apostolos et per omnes angelos[67] et per beatissimam virginem[68] Mariam et per corpora virginum[69] et per reliquias omnium sanctorum,[70] contestor vobis, homines,[71] quia epistola ista non est formata de manu hominis,[72] sed de throno dei est scripta, et digitis dei[73] transmissa est de

61. *Petrus*: It is not clear who this Peter might be. As Gaza has just been introduced as the city where he obtained his episcopacy, it seems not to be the city of his actual bishop's see. Thus, it is not likely that, for example, Peter the Iberian is meant. In the short version of Latin Recension II in London, British Library Add. 30853, Peter of Nîmes is mentioned, to whom this letter was given at the altar of Baudilus. In Oxford, Merton College 13 (see above, pp. 86, 137–39), one Peter of Antioch is mentioned. In the version of Mun2 and related manuscripts, Peter has no description at all except that he is a bishop. Therefore, the different specifications seem to be later additions by various scribes to add more credibility to the text by inventing some historical detail.

62. *episcopatum*: The *lectio facilior* would be *epistulam*, but the manuscript clearly says *episcopatum*.

63. *pax . . . nescitis*: This sentence is illogical because of the use of the tenses. The *erat* should be *est*.

64. *<quia non>*: The manuscript provides *dum*, which does not make sense. *Quia non* is the reading of Par2; *dico non* is the reading of the Tod2 (Amaduzzi col. 369).

65. *ordinata . . . dixit*: Mun2 and Ham2 omit this.

66. *apostolus*: Of the manuscripts reviewed here, "apostle" is the reading in only Vienna ÖNB 1355. Mun2 and Ham2 have *episcopus indignus*; Tod2 and Par2 have, it appears, *episcopus*.

67. *filium . . . angelos*: Mun2 omits this; Ham2 has *filium ejus et per Spritum Sanctum*.

68. *beatissimam virginem*: Mun2 has *sanctam genetricem*.

69. *et per corpora virginum et*: Mun2 (and Ham2 similar) has *per omnes angelos dei, per omnes patriarchas, prophetas, apostolos, martyres, confessores, virgines*.

70. *sanctorum*: Mun2 adds to this *atque electorum dei*.

71. *contestor . . . homines*: Mun2 and Ham2 omit this.

72. *hominis*: Mun2 and Ham2 add to this *neque scripta*.

73. *sed . . . dei*: Mun2 and Ham2 have *sed est scripta* (Ham2 omits this) *digito dei et domini nostri Ihesu Christi, et est*.

septimo caelo.[74] (5) qualiter diem dominicum sanctum custodire debetis, probante domino nostro Iesu Christo ordinaverit.[75] (6) vivit et regnat deus in saecula saeculorum. Amen.[76]

[8] (1) Decreed from the seventh throne of our Lord, Jesus Christ, in the past year in the city of Gaza, where saint Peter received the episcopacy in God; but the peace of God was the one thing which you do not know. He himself showed how you can attain eternal life, <because> I do <not> lie, because nothing is mandated if it is not true. (3) See what he said above: (4) I, the apostle Peter, swear by the power of God who made heaven and earth and all which is in it [see Exod 20:11; Ps 145:6; Acts 4:24; et al.], and by his son Jesus Christ, and by the holy Trinity and the four evangelists, and by the twelve apostles, and by all angels, and by the most blessed virgin Mary, and by the bodies of the virgins and by the relics of all saints, I bear testimony to you, men, that this letter is not formed by human hands, but is written by the throne of God and transmitted by the fingers of God from the seventh heaven. (5) How you must observe the holy Lord's day, it shall arrange, with the approval of our Lord Jesus Christ. (6) God lives and reigns in all eternity. Amen.

74. *caelo*: Mun2 and Ham2 adds to this *et de throno dei in terram* (*terra* Ham2).

75. *qualiter . . . ordinaverit*: The use of the tenses in this sentence is confusing, yet *ordinaverit* could be meant as an action that is completed in the future (therefore fut. exact.), implying that the letter will be read first.

76. *probante . . . amen*: Mun2 and Ham2 omit this.

Variant readings compared to Munich, Bayerische Staatsbibliothek Clm 9550 (see Delehaye, *Mélanges d'Hagiographie*, 155–56). The lemma is according to Vienna, Österreichische Staatsbibliothek Cod. 1355; the variant readings are according to Munich, BSB Clm 9550.

[1] (1) In . . . Christo *om.* | epistola] de Christo *add.* (2) nec timetis *om.* | eum] illum | peccatis] pecudibus | vos *om.* (3) veniet] venit | corpora . . . captivitate] alios occidit et alios in captivitatem ducit | servatis] observatis | sanctum *om.* (4) ululant] pullulant | demergunt] demergant | avertam] averto (5) quaecumque] et quicquid mali | sancta ecclesia mea *tr.* | in[2] . . . vos *om.* | submergam] vos *add.* | submersi] dimersi | quos . . . obsorbuit *om.*

[2] (1) in[1]] ad | locum] aut equitaverit *add.* | aut[1] . . . sanctorum] meam | discordantes] discordes | veram *om.* | et[2]] quod | aliud] quid *add.* | feceritis flagello] facietis flagellabo | diversis] duris | vos[2]] et domos vestras *add.* | malam . . . vestras] pessimam (2) fecerit] aliquod *add.* | ubicumque . . . aliquid] exterminabo eum, aut si aliquid in domo sua operatur | capillos] tonserit *add.* | quocumque fecerit] aliud quid inliciti operis in die dominico | inveniet] invenient | in die neque in nocte] hic neque in futuro | mittam] inmittam | et omnes] diversas | ipsum] ipsos | eius[2]] eorum (3) aut[1]] proximum | fecerit *om.* | aut[4]] inlicitum *add.* | inhonestum . . . immoderatum *om.* | mittam] inmittam | eos] eum | et deficient et dispergentur] ut deficiat et dispergetur

[3] (1) populus incredulitatis] popule meus incredulus (2) pauci] enim *add.* | vestri dies *tr.* | finis vester *tr.* (4) expecto] quidem *add.* (5) omnes populi *tr.* | homini] iuret | die] sancto *add.* | operetur *om.*

[4] (1)–(2) Surrexit . . . requievit] Ego ipse hac die resurrexi a mortuis, cum passus sum pro vestra omnium salute, et in ipso die resurrectionis meae eripui vos de inferno et a potestate diaboli. (2) quamvis enim in multis me provocetis, notum enim est vobis quia sex diebus creavi caelum et terram, mare et omnia quae in eis sunt; septimo autem requievi ab omni opere. (3) Ita] et *add.* | operibus] et laboribus *add.* | liberi] si vultis vitam aut requiem habere mecum *add.* | et . . . vestris *om.*

[5] (1) Si] Amen dico vobis *praem.* | enim *om.* | custoditis] custodieritis | sanctum diem *tr.* | ab] de | in[1]] ad | coram] cum | qui . . . caelis *om.* | habeatis] habetis (2) amen] iterum | sanctum diem *tr.* | et[1] . . . vestri *om.* | in igne] ignem | et[2-4]] *om.* (3) nec . . . dixit] et non dabo vobis pluviam, et auferam a vobis fructus vestros

[6] (1) Date . . . ostendite] Iterum iterumque moneo atque praecipio vobis ut detis mihi decimas iustas et sacerdotibus meis (2) Qui . . . et[1]] et qui decimam meam defraudaverit | vel . . . videre *om.* | infantes caeci nascuntur *tr.* | non . . . ambulantes] et sine auditu et gressu | et[3] . . . (3) vobis *om.*

[7] (1) Si] Amen dico vobis *praem.* | diem dominicum *tr.* | cataractas] cataracterem | labores] fructus | vestros] et dabo vobis pacem *add.* | anni vestri] annorum vestrorum | et[3] . . . gentes] *om.* | stabo ego] maneo | vos[1]] vobis | scietis] sciatis | deus . . . alius] dominus et non est alius praeter me (2) amen[2]] *om.* | observabitis] custodiatis | diem dominicum *tr.* (3) Si . . . sacerdos] praecipio vobis sacerdotibus meis ut unusquisque | istam epistolam *tr.* | non[1] . . . aut] *om.* | populo . . . ostenderit] ostendat populo suo | sive[1] . . . memoria] et affirmate illis a me transmissam (4) in[1] . . . hanc *om.* | illos] eos usque | saeculi *om.*

[8] (1)–(3) Ordinata . . . dixit *om.* (4) Iuro *om.* | apostolus] episcopus indignus iuro | dei potestatem] maiestatem dei | terram] mare *add.* | quae] in *add.* | et[3] *om.* | filium . . . angelos *om.* | beatissimam virginem] sanctam genetricem | et per corpora virginum et] per omnes angelos dei, per omnes patriarchas, prophetas, apostolos, martyres, confessores, virgines | sanctorum] atque electorum dei *add.* | contestor . . . homines] *om.* | ista epistola *tr.* | formata est *tr.* | de[1] *om.* | hominis] neque scripta *add.* | de[2] . . . dei[2] *om.* | et digitis] digito |dei[3]] et domini nostri Ihesu Christi, et est *add.* | est[3] *om.* | caelo] et de throno dei in terram *add.* (5) sanctum dominicum *tr.* | custodire debetis] observare debeatis | probante . . . (6) Amen *om.*

3

LETTER FROM HEAVEN—STONE INSCRIPTION

Michel-Yves Perrin

Present location: Italy, Brugnato, Museo diocesano. Formerly Piazza (Deiva Marina), Church of S. Maria Assunta, embedded in a wall *in cornu epistulae*, that is, to the left of the altar. During the 1990s, the stone was detached from the wall and stored in the sacristy of the church before being relocated in Brugnato in 2004. The description is based on autopsy by Michel-Yves Perrin on February 21, 2014.[1]

The stone measures 120 cm high by 42.5 cm wide and 13 cm thick. It has clearly been reused. The text on the stone's principal face respects the two holes that pierce through it. The back of the stone shows a central concave structure shaped like a half-cylinder. One can form the hypothesis that the stone originally served as the cover of a water drainage pipe. The original location remains unknown. Rescue excavations carried out in March–April 2005 in the church of Piazza did not identify any traces of occupation before the fourteenth century.

Before the stone was detached, we knew the text only on its principal face, which was published for the first time in 1874 by priest and epigraphist Marcello Remondini (1821–1887).[2] It was only in the 1990s that the left side of the stone was discovered to have a partially mutilated inscription as well. Its right side and the back are anepigraphic.[3] The stone's face is inscribed from the top down to 22 cm from the bottom. A line drawn in two horizontal segments

1. I owe to the generous and enthusiastic welcome given me by the vice-sindaco of Brugnato, Dott. Corrado Fabiani, and Dottoressa Luisa Cascarini, archaeologist working in collaboration with the Soprintendenza per i Beni archeologici della Liguria, and scientist responsible for the Museo diocesano, the privilege of examining the stone in excellent conditions. I thank them warmly.

2. Remondini, *Iscrizioni Medio-evali della Liguria*, 2–4 with pl. 2.

3. Paolo Fiore, "Le epigrafi della chiesa di Santa Maria Assunta a Piazza di Deiva Marina—Note per una prima schedatura," *Ligures* 2 (2004): 13–34.

separates a first text (lines 1-8); its letters are between 3 and 4 cm high, and its last line lines up on the right with a second text, the Letter from Heaven (lines 8-49), whose letters are between 3.5 and 1 cm. Traces of a frame are visible on the right-hand side; some letters had been engraved on this frame.

The first text on the stone's principal face appears in the form of a rubric of a liturgical calendar, a point that has not been remarked until now. The text of the Letter from Heaven contains forty-two lines. On the left side there are two references to a liturgical calendar of the same type as that of the top of the stone's face. The text of the Letter from Heaven is articulated as follows: title, effects of a divine punishment for nonobservance of Sunday rest, examples of nonobservance of Sunday rest and threats, prescriptions, the divine deeds that took place on Sunday.

The chronological assignment of this document depends on the conclusions of the paleographic study of the inscription, given that the original archaeological context is not known and that for the moment the liturgical rubrics that accompany it remain without an identifiable reference. Federico Patetta (1867-1945), an Italian law historian who was a remarkable collector of manuscripts and a first-rate scholar, was able to examine the document in 1906; in 1909 he published an admirable study[4] where, after a minute paleographic analysis, he concluded that the inscription should be dated as belonging to the second half of the seventh or to the eighth century, a date that has since been used by all epigraphists who, under one title or another, have written on this document. In a forthcoming study,[5] the middle of the eighth century will be proposed as a *terminus post quem non*. The letter of Licinianus, bishop of Cartagena, to his colleague Vincentius of Ibiza, at the end of the sixth century,[6] which constitutes the first known and dated mention of a Letter from Heaven, indicates a possible *terminus a quo*.

As such, this inscription, as Patetta had accurately seen, is the first preserved example of the Letter from Heaven, given that the oldest known testimonial manuscripts date from the tenth century. Unfortunately, Patetta's study, which he intended for the "storici di professione," has hardly been known. In fact, this document remained unknown to scholars on Christian apocryphal literature until our communication in Thessaloniki in 2014 at the International Symposium on Christian Apocrypha Literature, Ancient Christian Literature

4. Patetta, "La pretesa lettera," 208-40, 392.

5. Michel-Yves Perrin (with the collaboration of W. Pezé), "Entre apocryphicité, épigraphie et philologie: les plus anciens témoins de la *Lettre tombée du ciel sur le dimanche* (CANT 311)," *Apocrypha* (forthcoming).

6. See on this letter pp. 85-87 and 209-13.

and Ancient Apocryphal Literature (June 26–29);[7] the dissemination of the few studies that previously concern it has not gone beyond the limits of a very small circle of epigraphists and historians, mainly versed in the local or regional history of medieval Liguria.[8]

An in-depth philological and historical study and commentary on this inscription as well on the first witnesses of the "Sunday Letter" will soon be published in *Apocrypha*.[9] According to the typology of the Letter from Heaven, elaborated by Hippolyte Delehaye, Robert Priebsch, and Dorothy Haines[10] and referred to in this volume as well, the text of Piazza clearly belongs to Latin Recension II.

---

7. We then presented our research at a SELAC meeting (Paris, December 18, 2014), at the XVII International Conference on Patristic Studies (Oxford, AIEP, August 10–14, 2015), at the Scuola Alti Studi of the Fondazione San Carlo (Modena, June 7, 2016), at the Société Nationale des Antiquaires de France (Paris, June 15, 2016), at the University of Cagliari as a visiting professor in April 2018, at the international colloquium "From Sun-Day to the Day of the Lord: The Career of a Special Day in Late Antiquity and the Early Middle Ages" (University of Vienna, October 10–12, 2019; organized by Uta Heil), at the University of Bologna at the invitation of Antonio Cacciari on December 12, 2019, and at a meeting of the Swiss French-speaking group of the AELAC in Bex on January 11, 2020, at the invitation of Jean-Daniel Kaestli. During the 2018–2019 academic year we devoted our research seminary at the EPHE to the study of this document. I would like to express my gratitude to all the colleagues and friends who have allowed me to present this research.

8. This document remains unknown to Ross Balzaretti, *Dark Age Liguria: Regional Identity and Power, c. 400–1200*, Studies in Early Medieval History (London: Bloomsbury, 2013), as to Haines, *Sunday Observance*.

9. Perrin, "Entre apocryphicité, épigraphie et philologie."

10. See above, pp. 88–95.

Inscription

[† ?] Incepet epistola | D(omi)ni n(ostri) I(e)h(su)m Chr(ist)i Salu|atoris de celis missa pro die | s(an)c(t)o et glorioso dominico. Amen dico | **u**obis: misi uobis brucus et locusta|[s] qui omnes labores uestrus subduxe[r]|unt; misi pustellas et omnes langori|[s] et non conuersi estis ad diem s(an)c(tu)m do**m**|[i]nicum; misi super uos gentes pag[an]as qui co|[r]pora uestra et filius uestrus vel omne[s | l]abores uestrus possedeant et sub pedis | [e]orum estis cottidie et non agnuscitis; ideo prod|ucam uos [[ad producam vos]] ad profundum maris | [q]uia non obseruastis diem s(an)c(tu)m dominicum; auer|[t]am facie meam a vobis et a tabernaculis quibus | [f]ecit manus mea; et si cufugeretis in eclesia mea | [e]t ego uos indecabo et trada in m(anus) gentium quia non | [o]bseruastis diem [s(an)c(tu)m] *vac.* dominecum et omnium animali[u]|m quatropedium cl*vac.*amantium uoces ad me et ego | [e]as exaudia quia n*vac.*on permisistis requiescere in die | **s**(an)c(t)o dominico nisi ad eclesia cum ueneritis; si quis causam | [a]ud negutium in domo sua fecerit, aut si caput lauauirit, | aut coma toderit, anatima erit illi in generationem et [p]|rogenie; super eus qui *vac.* non costodirent die s(an)c(tu)m | dominicum mittam in d*vac.*[om]o eius famem et mortaletat|em invisibilem glandola cetatam. Si quis autem in die | s(an)c(t)o dominico causa agere uoluerit aut intentionem, | mitta in ipsis pustellas in oculus dolorem ut ceci fia**n**|**t**. Amen dico uobis populus imgredibilis, generatio praua | et peruersa, ut quit non uultis cunuerti ad die s(an)c(t)o do|[m]inicum, nescitis quia multum pacies sum super uos prop|ter electus meus; obdurati estis haec non intelleg|[ent]es; pauperis uoces clamantium ante domus uestr|[as] haec non intellegetis nec exaudiebatis facire mi|[serico]**r**diam et persecuti estis eos bene facientes; su[p|e]r ui[du]as et orfanus opremere nolite. Nullus iuret i|n die s(an)c(t)o [d]ominico. Ame(n) dico uobis: requiescite ab ora no|**na** sabat[i] **u**squ(e) et in tertio die luciscentem. Amen dico | [uo]bis: cruce[fi]xus sum et resurrexi die s(an)c(t)um dominicum | [i]n celis ascin[si] sederem ad dexteram d(e)i patris et r[e]|quieui ab omn**i**[b]us operibus ad quod fici celum et te[r]|am et s(an)c(t)efec**a**[u]**i** hunc die ut omnes requiem abeant | [s]ibe ad superu[s si]be ad inferus.

N.B.: the mutilated letters are in bold; the ligatures are underlined.

Translation

Beginning of the Letter of Our Lord and Savior Jesus Christ sent from Heaven for the most Holy and Glorious Sunday.[11] Amen I say unto you: I have sent you crickets and locusts which have destroyed all the fruit of your labors; I have sent you pustules and sickness, and you have not converted your hearts to the Holy Day of Sunday. I have sent pagans against you to take your bodies and your sons and all the fruits of your labors, and every day you are under their feet and (even so) you have not recognized (your error). Therefore, I shall lead you into the depths of the sea. Because you have not observed the Holy Day of Sunday, I shall turn my face and the sanctuaries I have made with my hands away from you, and if you try to seek refuge in my church, it is I who shall denounce you and turn you over into the hands of the people. Because you have not observed the Holy Day of Sunday, nor heard the cries of the four-legged animals which are lifted up unto me, hear ye, I shall give them my ear, because you have not allowed them to rest on the Holy Day of Sunday, because you have not come to church. If anyone deals with a dispute or other matter in his home or if he washes his head or cuts his hair, he shall be an anathema from generation to generation. On those who do not respect the Holy Day of Sunday, I shall send into their homes hunger and the invisible epidemic hidden[12] under a bubo. If anyone, on the Holy Day of Sunday, wants to begin a dispute or a trial, I shall send them in their eyes pustules and pain such that they will become blind. Amen I say unto you: people of little faith, evil and perverse generation, why will you not convert (your hearts) to the Holy Day of Sunday? Do you not know that I am patient with you for the sake of my Chosen One? You have become hard of heart; you do not hear the cries of the poor that are lifted up before your homes; you do not hear them and you do not listen to them to give them mercy, you have persecuted those who do good. Do not oppress widows and orphans. No one shall swear on the Holy Day of Sunday. Amen I say unto you: take rest from Ninth on Saturday to the dawn of the third day. Amen I say unto you: I was crucified and I rose again on the Holy Day of Sunday to heaven where I am seated at the right hand of (God) the Father and I rested from my labors from the moment I created heaven and earth and I have sanctified this day so that all may enjoy a day of rest, be they in heaven or in hell.

11. I thank very much Dr. Gérard Lorgos for the English adaptation of my own French version.

12. *Cetatam* probably for *celatam* (suggestion of Isabelle Brunetière, CNRS, Sources chrétiennes, Lyons).

4

LETTER FROM HEAVEN—LATIN RECENSION I

According to Vienna, Österreichische Nationalbibliothek Cod. Lat. 1355, fols. 89r–90

Philip Polcar

The Latin versions of the Letter from Heaven are grouped into three recensions, I–III. This grouping was first established by Robert Priebsch[1] and was consequently pursued by Dorothy Haines.[2]

In this book, Latin Recension I will be represented by two versions, both of which are of particular worth (Vienna, Österreichische Nationalbibliothek Cod. Lat. 1355 and, in the chapter below, the manuscript from Tarragona), with a translation, an introduction, and a brief commentary. To avoid bloating, especially in the commentary, most of the manuscripts have been given abbreviations with the number 1 added (except for Tarragona and the Laterana) to indicate that the version belongs to Recension I. These abbreviations are used throughout the chapters concerning the Latin Recensions I and II for the sake of brevity but do not raise the claim to be used as universal sigla for the respective manuscripts. Following manuscripts are known:

Bas1 = Basel B VII 7 (s. x, Basel), fol. 1r[3]
Lon1 = London, British Library, Add. 19.725 (s. x/xi), fols. 87v–88r[4]

1. Priebsch, *Letter from Heaven*, 3.

2. See Dorothy Haines, *Sunday Observance*, 36–37. For a more in-depth discussion of the different recensions, see the introduction.

3. This version was edited by Haines, *Sunday Observance*, 206–7, with a brief introduction. It exhibits only about the final third of the text, which is also quite corrupt but also shows clear similarities to Vie1.

4. See above, p. 39. The manuscript contains more or less the same text as Vie1, only in a worse condition and with a huge lacuna toward the end: paragraphs 7 and 11 are only

Tarr. = Tarragona (Baluzius, now lost[5])
Par1 = Paris, Bibliothèque nationale de France, lat. 12270 (s. xii), fols. 31v–32v[6]
Vie1 = Vienna, Österreichische Nationalbibliothek, 1355 (letter 1 of 2), fols. 89r–90[7]
Gra1 = Universitätsbibliothek 248 (s. xv), fol. 133rb–133va[8]
vers. Later. = versio Laterana[9]

Latin Recension I is represented by the fewest manuscripts.[10] Dating of any of the versions is difficult, especially since they do not (just) represent transmitted works of literature but rather evolving texts that have been redacted by various scribes at different times.[11] Therefore, only the dating of the manuscripts provides a definite *terminus ante quem*. However, the language, as pointed out in more details below, indicates medieval features.

The Vienna manuscript can be considered a somewhat standard version of Latin Recension I, whereas the text of the Tarragona manuscript must be described as a more exotic sample. A common feature of the Latin Recension I is its introductory narrative: the archangel Michael finds or delivers the Letter from Heaven; the place where it happens is the gate Ephraim in Jerusalem.[12] The letter then is sent from one priest to another. These events are followed by a gathering of clerics, who pray and fast; in some versions this takes place in Rome (Vie1, Par1, Lon1, Gra1), while in the Tarragona version the place is unclear.[13]

half extant, and paragraphs 8–10 are missing. Priebsch suggests that a piece of parchment was inserted that is now lost; see Priebsch, *Letter from Heaven*, 5n2. The text of this version was edited by Haines, *Sunday Observance*, 204–5, with a brief introduction.

5. See above, p. 39, and the text below, pp. 270–89.

6. Printed in Delehaye, "Note sur la légende," 181–84; Haines, *Sunday Observance*, 199–201.

7. This manuscript contains two versions; the second one belongs to Recension II and is presented as Vie2 in the chapter above; see pp. 221–35; see also above, p. 50.

8. The version preserved in this manuscript is similar to Vie1. It has not been edited before but is now transcribed and presented as an appendix of this version.

9. The beginning of a version belonging to Latin Recension I is preserved in a letter of Boniface (*Ep.* 59) about a Roman synod at 754 (MGH Epp. Sel. 1:115.23–29 Tangl); see above, p. 97.

10. See also the list of eight manuscripts at p. 39.

11. For a discussion of the dating, see the introduction, pp. 84–133.

12. See also Haines, *Sunday Observance*, 44–45.

13. See about the frames of the Letter from Heaven above, pp. 108, 134–42.

The text of the Vienna manuscript was already edited by Priebsch in 1899 and copied by Haines.[14] Upon inspection of the manuscript it has turned out that Priebsch misread a few words (2.1; 3.1; 3.2; 6.1; see commentary), which were subsequently copied by Haines. These errors are now corrected in the following edition. Additionally, some minor conjectures have been made. The text has been divided into eleven paragraphs with subordinate numbering per sentence (e.g., the sentence *suspiciosa non sit epistola ista* can now be referred to by the number 4.1).

Though the Letter from Heaven has its origin in late antiquity, both Viel and Tarr. are clearly medieval compositions. Their language is stylistically simple and often bumpy, but it can be understood in most cases. The author(s) had only basic Latin learning, and their exposure to Latin literature may have been limited to biblical texts, liturgy, and some sermons, for example, those of Caesarius of Arles. As a consequence of this, and certainly intentionally to some extent, the texts imitate biblical language (more or less successfully). This shows mainly in its paratactical nature and the frequent use of the word *et*, but also in some details, such as the function of *quia*, which, like in the Vulgate, often introduces an indirect statement ("that") in addition to its classical use ("because"). Biblical quotations and clear allusions are rare, but the overall tone of the letter, especially the commands, threats, and promises, resembles the Old Testament prophetic style.[15]

Some more concrete examples for the letter's medieval language will be adduced from Viel, but one would find similar instances in Tarr. The word *ipse* is, for the most part, used just as an article for persons, such as for the priests in the introductory narrative; in one case in reference to the supposed author of the letter himself (Jesus Christ), *ego ipse* (9.2), in which case it seems appropriate to translate as "I myself," and twice in regard to the letter (1.2). The word *iste* serves as a regular demonstrative pronoun without any other connotation, but the *ista epistola* was also used for the sound effect. The word *ille* only appears twice. Furthermore, *apud* or *per* are used in constructions where one would expect *a*/*ab* in Classical Latin; generally, *per* is frequent, indicating the Romance vernacular of the author(s). Once, the medieval conjunction *pro quali* is introducing a relative clause in the sense of *per quod*. The past participle in connection with a present form of *esse* is used to express the passive, as it is common in medieval texts (future: *anathemati eritis*,[16] perfect: *liberati fuistis*). Though there is frequent use of

14. Haines, *Sunday Observance*, 201–3, is a reprint of Priebsch, "Chief Sources," 130–34.

15. See Haines, *Sunday Observance*, 57–58, and above, pp. 184–90.

16. Tarr. uses a corrupt phrasing, *anathema eritis*, but the same is meant.

both future tenses, the present tense also appears with a clear future meaning, maybe due to vernacular influence.[17] This happens mostly in paragraph 8; this section could be the result of a different redactor's work. Last, the gerund in the ablative case is used in a manner where one would expect a present participle or a conditional clause (paragraph 5), also a common feature of medieval Latin.

The offered translation aims at being as precise as possible. Yet it did not seem beneficial to recreate grammatical errors or other stylistic issues, so sometimes the translation is rather *ad sensum*. Should the reader wonder why the English prose appears to be unpleasantly dire at times, may they consider that a faithful rendering should not smooth out all the shortcomings of the Latin original.

The following version (Viel) of the Letter from Heaven claims to be the third and last (8.6; 11.1); therefore, the author(s) knew of at least two other versions, or a later redactor, who knew of two other versions, inserted this statement.[18] However, the letter expresses three main concerns: to observe the Lord's Day, to give the tenth, and to honor the "compaternity of Saint John" (*compatrata de sancto Iohanne*).[19] The latter feature can otherwise only be found in Lon1, Bas1. Furthermore, the word *compatrata* does not appear anywhere else; it is possibly the author's own creation. Thus, one can only assume that he meant to write *compaternitas*. This would make sense if the mentioned Saint John is to be understood as John the Baptist, who is explicitly mentioned later in the letter (7.2). Therefore, *compatrata* probably refers to the spiritual relationship between the baptized and his/her godfather/godmother. It appears that the author did not approve of how the relationship and the resulting obligations, however these might have looked, were handled in his parish. Moreover, John the Baptist's inclusion into the Latin Letter from Heaven may have been inspired by the Greek Recension Alpha, in which he is mentioned, though there he is referred to as the forerunner (Alpha 1, 2.6 and 3.10). The connection between these two versions was discussed in the introduction.

17. To avoid producing completely ungrammatical sentences in English, the word *will* has been added in the translation.

18. This is probably the reason for come copyists to collect two versions in one manuscript; see above, the list on p. 39.

19. Viel, 4.3; 6.2; 7.6; 9.2.

The reason for the strict Sunday observance that the letter demands is given by simply stating that Jesus "was crucified and rose again on the third day" (9.1). Furthermore, it is asserted that the observance was "commanded . . . through scriptures and books" (9.2). The time of the Sunday rest is also specified, "from the ninth hour on the Sabbath until the morning of Monday" (9.4), as in all versions of this letter.[20]

20. For further comparisons to other versions, see p. 182f.

Letter from Heaven—Latin Recension I (Cod. Vienna 1355)

[1] (1) Incipit epistola in nomine trinitatis salvatoris domini Iesu Christi quae de celo in Ierusalem cecidit per Michahelem[21] archangelum. (2) ista epistola est inventa ad portam Effrem[22] per magnum sacerdotem[23] cui nomen Ichor. (3) ipsa epistola fuit relicta ibi et ipsam exemplavit et transmisit ad Ermiam civitatem ad alium sacerdotem nomine Talasium. (4) ipse Talasius transmisit eam de Ebrea civitate ad alium sacerdotem cui nomen Lebonius. (5) et ipse Lebonius transmisit eam ad Capadociam civitatem ad alium sacerdotem nomine Iuram. (6) et ipse Iuras transmisit eam ad Bethaniam civitatem ad alium sacerdotem nomine Marchabeus.[24] (7) et ipse Marchabeus sacerdos transmisit illam epistolam ad montem sancti Michahelis archangeli.[25] (8) et ipsa epistola per voluntatem domini nostri Iesu Christi pervenit ad Romam civitatem ad locum praedestinatum ad sepulcrum sancti Petri et Pauli.

---

21. *per Michahelem*: Tarr. 1.2: *Michaelo ipsam deportavit.*

22. *Effrem*: The northward-facing gate of Ephraim is mentioned in the OT (pre-exile: 2 Kgs 14:13; 2 Chr 25:23; rebuilt by Nehemiah: Neh 12:39). Whether the gate still existed at the time of the letter was probably not of great concern for the author. He aimed at creating authenticity for a Western audience.

23. *per magnum sacerdotem*: Though the manuscript has *magnum*, it can be assumed that *manum sacerdotis* was in the archetype with regard to Lon1, Par1, and vers. Later.: *per manus sacerdotis.*

24. *Ichor . . . Marchabeus*: Almost all the versions of Latin Recension I show a similar list of names. Its variations are due mainly to corruption in transmission. *Ichor* is called *Achor* in Lon1 and Gra1, *Icor* in vers. Later., but *Eros* in Tarr. 1.2. *Ermiam civitatem* is *Erim c.* in Tarr. 1.3, *Armeniam c.* in Par1, Gra1, and in Lon1, *Geremiam c.* in vers. Later. Furthermore, *de Ebrea civitate* is *ad Aebream civitatem* in Lon1, *ad Arabiam c.* in vers. Later. *Lebonius* 1.4–5 appears as *Libonius* (Lon1), *Leobanus* (vers. Later.), *Lebenus* (Gra1), or *Leopas* (Tarr. 1.4–5). Furthermore, *Iuras* is also called *Ioras* (Par1) and *Iuoras* (Lon1). *Bethania* is mentioned in Lon1 and in Par1; it is rendered *Uetfania* in vers. Later. *Marchabeus* is also mentioned as *Machabeus* in Lon1 and Par1.

25. *ad montem . . . archangeli*: Likewise, in Lon1; Par1 is more specific: *ipse transmisit eam ad montem Garganum, ubi est ecclesia sancti Michaelis archangeli*; the redactor of Gra1 thought Michael to be a human saint, not an archangel, 1.7: *ad montem Barganum,*

Translation

[1] (1) It begins the letter, in the name of the trinity of the savior Lord Jesus Christ, that fell down from heaven in Jerusalem by [the action of] the archangel Michael. (2) The letter was found at the gate Ephraim by the great priest called Ichor. (3) The same letter was left there and copied and sent to the city Ermia to another priest called Talasius. (4) Talasius sent it from the city Ebrea to another priest whose name is Lebonius. (5) And Lebonius sent it to the province Cappadocia to another priest called Juras. (6) And Juras sent it to the city Bethania to another priest called Marchabeus. (7) And the priest Marchabeus sent the letter to the mountain of the archangel saint Michael. (8) And the letter came to the city of Rome through the will of our Lord Jesus Christ to its predestined place, to the chapel of saint Peter and Paul.

ubi requiescit sanctus Michael. Monte Sant' Angelo is an Italian town in the Apulia region on the southern slopes of the Gargano. There the Santuario di San Michele Arcangelo was built throughout the seventh and eighth century, its tradition reaching back to the 490s, when the archangel is said to have showed himself to a shepherd in the church's cave. See Lucia Sinisi, "Beyond Rome, The Cult of the Archangel Michael and the Pilgrimage to Apulia," in *England and Rome in the Early Middle Ages: Pilgrimage, Art, and Politics*, ed. Francesca Tinti, Studies in the Early Middle Ages 40 (Turnhout: Brepols, 2014), 43–68; Helen Foxhall Forbes, "Writing on the Wall: Anglo-Saxons at Monte Sant' Angelo sul Gargano (Puglia) and the Spiritual and Social Significance of Graffiti," *Journal of Late Antiquity* 12 (2019): 169-210. The popularity of the place among pilgrims is attested by numerous inscriptions; see also Carlo Carletti, *Iscrizioni murali del Santuario di S. Michele sul Monte Gargano* (Edipuglia: Bari, 1979), and Carlo Alberto Mastrelli, "Le iscrizioni runiche," in *II santuario di S. Michele sul Gargano dal VI al IX secolo*, ed. Carlo Carletti and Giorgio Otranto (Edipuglia: Bari, 1990), 319–32. The medieval foundation legend is called *Apparitio in monte Gargano*, ed. Georg Waitz, in *MGH.SRL* (Hannover: Hahn, 1898), 541–43; see also Giorgio Otranto, "II 'Liber de Apparitione,' il Santuario di San Michele sul Gargano e i Longobardi del Ducato di Benevento," in *Santuari epolitica net mondo antico*, ed. Marta Sordi (Milan: Catholic University Press, 1983), 210–45.

(9) qui erant in civitate, triduanas fecerunt in vigiliis et ieiuniis <et> in orationibus,[26] ut pius deus perdonasset[27] eis auxilium et sensum in corda eorum; pro quali iam ista epistola in Ierusalem et in alias civitates venisset. (10) et per ordinationem domini nostri Iesu Christi invenerunt, quia propter diem sanctum dominicum advenisset.[28]

26. *Triduanas . . . orationibus*: Here, *triduana* is a noun; see 3.1: *triduanam facite*; but: Tarr. 1.4: *et triduanum ieiunium fecerunt in vigiliis et orationibus insistentes*.

27. *ut . . . perdonasset*: The grammar in this sentence is problematic: the *ut* suggests that they prayed the Lord to grant them understanding and help in the future, but the tense of *perdonare* suggests that it had already happened.

28. *et per . . . advenisset*: This sentence is missing in Lon1, which is otherwise very similar.

(9) Those who were in the city held vigils and fasted and prayed for three days that the good God may gift them help and understanding in their hearts; for through his help the letter had already come to Jerusalem and to other cities. (10) And through the arrangement of our Lord, Jesus Christ, they found that it had come because of the holy Lord's Day.

[2] (1) Quia in die sancto dominico sedentes causas iudicantes,[29] iurantes,[30] periurantes, olera in orto colligentes, pecudes mulgentes, molas tornantes, venationes facientes:[31] propter hoc perit mundus et propter hoc venit iudicium dei super populum cunctum praesentem.[32] (2) cognoscite, miserae animae, quia in sex diebus fecit deus coelum et terram, solem et lunam, quattuor evangelistas,[33] mare et omnia quae in eis sunt;[34] praeterea hominem Adam plasmavit de terra.[35] (3) quia in die sancto dominico requievit, et nunc sic debent peccatores et iusti, sicut angeli requiescunt in celo.[36]

---

29. *iudicantes*: Par1, Lon1, and Gra1 have *iudicantes*; Tarr. has *iudicandi*. Priebsch has *indicantes*, but the letters *n* and *u* look very similar in the manuscript, so he misread. The prohibition to judge cases on Sunday goes back to Constantine's legislation, transmitted in Cod. justin. 3.12.2, ed. Paul Krüger, *Corpus iuris civilis 2: Codex Iustinianus* (Berlin: Weidmann, 1906), 127, and in Cod. theod. 2.8.1, ed. Theodor E. Mommsen (Berlin: Weidmann, 1905), 87; see Mitthof, "Christianization of the Empire," with the texts at 57–58. See also above, pp. 3, 19f., 168.

30. *iurantes*: Par1 has an additional, longer passage on swearing added in the second half of the letter (200.56–59 H.): *Ve vobis qui iuramentum mendax diligitis. Nonne intelligitis quod dixerim non iurare omnino, sed sit sermo vester est, est, non, non. Quod autem his habundantius est, a malo est. Pro iuramento crucis peccatores peribunt.*

31. *Quia . . . facientes*: This list of activities goes on in Lon1 (204.14 H.): *focos illuminantes, peccuniam moventes.* On the forbidden activities on Sunday and their subsequent punishment miracles, see pp. 172–82.

32. *populum . . . praesentem*: This strange phrasing may indicate that the author had a situation in mind in which the Letter from Heaven should be read before the gathered populace in such a way as Vincentius of Ibiza had done; see Letter of Licinianus 1.2.

33. *quattuor Evangelistas*: There is an apocryphal tradition in the early medieval (especially Irish) Gospel exegesis that allegorically associates the four evangelists with the four elements; see Ps.-Jerome, *Expositio quatuor Evangeliorum* praefatio (PL 30:532–533A): *Non de duodecim Evangelia recipiantur nisi quatuor, quia totus mundus ex quatuor elementis est, id est caelo, terra, igne, et aqua. Per caelum Iohannes ostenditur quia sicut caelum omnia superat, ita et Iohannes qui dixit* In principio erat verbum. *Per Matthaeum terra, qui dixit* Liber generationis Iesu Christi. *Per Lucam ignis, qui dixit* Nonne cor nostrum ardens erat in nobis. *Per Marcum aqua, qui dixit* Vox clamantis in deserto. *Idem quatuor flumina de uno fonte quatuor euangelistas significat, id est Christum. Fison insufflictio significat Iohannem. Geon velocitas significat Matthaeum. Tigris felicitas significat Marcum. Euphrates fertilitas significat Lucam.*

34. *quia . . . sunt*: Because the sun, moon, and the four evangelists were inserted into the Bible quotation, the final part, *et omnia quae in eis sunt*, does not make that much sense anymore, as the *in eis* refers to the cosmic *trias*, heaven, earth, and sea.

35. *praeterea . . . terra*: In Greek versions, the creation of Adam is adduced as biblical proof for the necessity to venerate Friday, too. Here, however, it is just mentioned to complete the story of creation, and Friday does not appear to be of interest in the Latin recensions, except in Latin Recension III, which seems to have been transferred from the Greek Recension Alpha 2.

36. *sicut . . . celo*: Since angels belong to the heavenly kingdom of God, they also rest like God himself. The torments of hell pause on the Lord's Day, too; see *Visio Pauli*, p. 421.

[2] (1) Because on the holy Lord's Day they sit and judge cases, they swear, they swear false oaths, they collect vegetables in the garden, they milk the cattle, they turn the millstone, they go hunting: Because of this the world is perishing, and because of this the judgment of God is coming over the whole present populace. (2) Understand, miserable souls, that "in six days God made heaven and earth," sun and moon, the four evangelists, "the sea and everything that dwells there" [Exod 20:11]; apart from that he formed the human Adam from the earth. (3) Because he rested on the holy Lord's day, now sinners and righteous men alike must rest, like the angels rest in heaven.

[3] (1) et rogo vos, expurgate vos in vigiliis, in ieiuniis,[37] in orationibus. (2) ad ecclesias meas ambulate, cruces per omnes domos vestras[38] ponite, caput cum cinere spargite,[39] triduanam facite,[40] sicut liberabit vos dominus.[41] (3) miseri populi, arguite vos, dirigite[42] et emite vobis regnum dei, quia cottidie mors ante oculos vestros est.[43]

[4] (1) suspiciosa non sit epistola ista.[44] (2) si bene feceritis, de manu inimici[45] liberati eritis. (3) et mando vobis per epistolam istam: si non emendaveritis et si poenitentiam non egeritis et sanctum diem dominicum et compatratam de sancto Iohanne[46] non observaveritis et decimas[47] non reddideritis, transmitto super vos lapides pendentes ponderibus[48] et aquas calidas usque ad mortem. (4) ego vero dico vobis, quia in isto mense Novembre[49] proximo ventuoso, quia fuit sic,[50] perire debuistis, si deprecatio non esset sanctae Mariae virginis meae et sancti archangeli Michahelis et sancti Petri apostoli mei et sancti Pauli: per eorum orationes liberati fuistis.

37. *in ieiuniis*: Priebsch reads *et ieiuniis*, but the manuscript has *in*. The *in* has an instrumental function here, as sometimes in biblical Latin.

38. *vestras*: Priebsch reads *aras*, but the manuscript clearly says *vestras*.

39. *caput . . . spargite*: A sign of shame and penance in the OT; see the story of the raped Tamar in 2 Sam 13:19: *quae aspergens cinerem capiti suo scissa talari tunica inpositisque manibus super caput suum ibat ingrediens et clamans.*

40. *facite*: Lon1 mentions the Ninevites here, Tarr. in 4.3.

41. *triduanam . . . dominus*: A three-day penitential ritual found in all Letters from Heaven (see p. 140), but here it is part of the admonishments, not of the narrative setting.

42. *dirigite*: Missing in Lon1; Gra1 has it in the form of *dirigit et*.

43. *cottidie . . . est*: Possibly an allusion to one of the instruments of the good works from the Rule of Benedict 4.47: *mortem cotidie ante oculos suspectam habere.*

44. *suspiciosa ... ista*: Lon1 has instead: *et suscipite epistolam istam* (205.25 H.).

45. *inimici*: Haines has *inimica*. Priebsch and the manuscript have *inimici*.

46. *compatratam . . . Iohanne*: The word *compatrata* appears to be very rare. However, due to the connection with saint John, i.e., the Baptist, the spiritual bond between sponsor and baptized person is meant, i.e., the *compaternitas*; see introductory remarks, p. 248.

47. *decimas*: The tithe is a common feature of the Latin recensions.

48. *lapides pendentes ponderibus*: Lon1 has *lapides pensantes pondera quinque* (205.27–28 H.).

49. *Novembre . . . ventuoso*: Haines corrects to *Novembri . . . venturo*, but the latter part does not make much sense in the context, as it is stated that the sinful people should have perished last (*proximo*) November, if not for the intercession of Mary and others.

50. *quia fuit sic*: Lon1 has *qui fuit*.

[3] (1) And I ask you, purify yourselves through vigils, fasts, and prayers. (2) Go to my churches, put crosses throughout all your houses, cast ashes onto your head, do this for three days, so that the Lord will deliver you. (3) Wretched people, blame yourselves, arrange and buy for yourselves the kingdom of God [see Matt 13:44], because every day death is before your eyes.

[4] (1) This letter shall not be suspicious to you. (2) If you do well, you will be freed from the hand of your enemy [see Judge 2:18]. (3) And I command you through this letter: If you do not correct yourselves and do not do penance and observe the holy Lord's day and the compaternity of saint John and do not give the tenth, I will send over you rocks, heavy with weight, and hot water until you die. (4) But I say to you, this last windy November, because it was so, you should have perished, had it not been for the intercession of my holy virgin Mary and saint archangel Michael and saint Peter, my apostle, and saint Paul: through their prayers you were delivered.

[5] (1) et dico vobis: si emendaveritis et si poenitentiam egeritis, dabo vobis frumentum, vindemiam et ligna[51] pomifera, et amplificabo vitam vestram, et vivetis in pace in seculum. (2) dico vobis, populi mei, fides acceptabilis[52] permane<a>t[53] in vobis et gratia[m] dei orando, vigilando, elemosinam dando, actus malos relinquendo, homicidium relaxando, viduis et orphanis adiuvando.[54]

[6] (1) Filius, pater et mater <si> inter se maledictionem tradent, ad penam sunt reversi cum igne ardente[55] et exterminantur. (2) et dico vobis, ad ecclesias meas cum oblacione et luminaribus[56] ambulate et ibi lectiones divinas audiendo manete, ebrietatem fugiendo, maliciam <et> avariciam dimittendo, diem sanctum dominicum et compatratam[57] de sancto Iohanne custodiendo et decimas reddendo. (3) hec diffinicio[58] ante oculos vestros [ut] non sit dimittenda.[59]

51. *ligna*: Biblical use; see Vulg. Gen 1:11: *lignum scientiae boni et mali.*

52. *acceptabilis*: Among the church fathers it is often used in the context of sacrifice, for example, *victima, hostia, sacrificium* (Tertullian, *Adv. Jud.* 5.5 [CCSL 2:1351.43 Kroymann]; Lactantius, *Epit.* 5.3 [CSEL 19:734.13 Brandt]).

53. *permaneat*: The manuscript has *permanent*, which is grammatically problematic.

54. *viduis . . . adiuvando*: Lon1 has the addition: *ut mereatis habere consorcia <omnium sanctorum>.*

55. *ardente*: Priebsch has *ardenti*. Also, the manuscript has *ibi lectiones divinas* (ante corr.) after *ardente*: the scribe made a transposition error, as these words appear in 6.2.

56. *luminaribus*: Lamps according to Vulg. Exod 25:6; possibly candles; see Jerome, *Vigil.* 7 (CCSL 79C:17.21 Feiertag): *per totas orientis ecclesias quando legendum est Evangelium accenduntur luminaria.*

57. *compatratam*: see 4.3.

58. *diffinicio*: I.e., *definitio.*

59. *hec . . . dimittenda*: Lon1 also omits the *ut*, a reading I have chosen to follow. Alternatively, one could add a *ponam* before the *ut*.

[5] (1) And I say to you: If you make amends and if you do penance, I will give you grain, vintage, and fruit-bearing trees, and I will prolong your life, and you will live in peace forever. (2) I say to you, my people, a worthy faith <shall> stay in you and my grace, if you pray to God, hold vigils, give alms, let go of bad deeds, stop murdering, help widows and orphans.

[6] (1) Son, father and mother, if they curse each other, are brought to their punishment with burning fire and they are destroyed. (2) And I say to you, go to my churches with offerings and lamps, and stay there and listen to the divine readings, and flee drunkenness, let go of malice and avarice, observe the holy Lord's day and the compaternity of saint John and give the tenth. (3) This boundary before your eyes shall not be dismissed.

[7] (1) transmisi ad vos ordinationes quae apud me[60] sunt dicte, et non credidistis. (2) coniuro vos, populi mei, per lordanem, ubi mihi sanctus Iohannes baptismum tradidit, cum oleo et crismate unxit me, celum invocavit.[61] (3) per ista sacramenta vos coniuro, scripturam quam transmitto ut credatis et ad ecclesias meas conveniatis et ad sacerdotes meos confessionem faciatis. (4) tendo arcum meum et <mittam sagittas meas super vos>,[62] ut non pereant peccatores sed peccata dimittantur. (5) sed revertimini ad me; recordamini, populi mei, ut animas vestras declaratas accipiat regnum dei. (6) credite vero, quia istam epistolam dominus noster Iesus Christus de vertice celi misit propter diem dominicum et compatratam[63] de sancto Iohanne et propter decimam non redditis.

[8] (1) Amen dico vobis, mitto super vos locustas et brucos qui comedunt fructus vestros, et mitto super vos lupos rapaces et canes malignos qui vos comedunt, et dico vobis, convertam faciem meam a vobis et mittam in tabernaculis vestris omnem maliciam et amaritudinem validissimam.[64] (2) et si <non> fueritis ad ecclesias, ego indurabo[65] et non adiuvabo vos et trado vos in malignantium manus, quia non servatis diem sanctum dominicum. (3) et rogo vos, ut in sancto die dominico caput non lavetis neque comas tondatis. (4) si non custodieritis, anathemati eritis. (5) inmitto in domibus vestris famem et tribulationem. (6) o increduli, quia istam epistolam misi ad vos et noluistis credere, anathemata erit anima vestra, quia mandavi vobis per duas epistolas meas anteriores, ista est tertia.[66] (7) si non observatis diem dominicum, mittam super vos pustulas in faciem, in oculos, in os, in aures, in nares, et in omnia membra, quae vos comedunt usque ad mortem.

---

60. *apud me*: the author means *a me*; see also 8.6.

61. *Iohannes . . . invocavit*: The story is found in Mark 1:9–11. If the author followed it, the word *celum* must be the subject, and it is not John who calls on the heavens; see Mark 1:11: *et vox facta est de caelis*.

62. *mittam . . . vos*: The manuscript has only *aperiam sagitta mea*, but clearly corrupted and/or shortened. Priebsch compares the text to an Anglo-Saxon version, which he believes to be a translation of the Latin. The Old English version exhibits more material here; the Old English also says: "And I flex my bow and I send my arrows over you" (my translation; see Priebsch, "Chief Sources," 132).

63. *compatratam*: The manuscript has *compatrandam*, but this must be an error; *compatratam* is meant, as in 4.3 and 6.2.

64. *convertam . . . validissimam*: The use of the word *tabernacula* in the context of threats and plagues suggest an allusion to Exodus, when the Israelites lived in the desert. On the punishments in more detail, see pp. 184–95. See also the parallels to the inscription and the Latin Recension II, above p. 92f.

65. *indurabo*: Usually the Lord hardens another person's heart, such as Pharaoh's; see Exod 7:3: *sed ego indurabo cor eius*.

66. *quia . . . tertia*: See Bas1 (206.6 H.): *per duas epistolas et ista est tercia*; Par1 (ed. Haines, *Sunday Observance*, 201.75): *ista tertia est, et post illam nulla veniet amplius*; Tarr. does not give a number, 14.4: *iuro vos per epistolam istam quia aliam vobis nunquam mittam*.

[7] (1) I have sent you rules which were spoken by me, and you have not believed. (2) I implore you, my people, by the Jordan, where saint John baptized me, with oil and ointment he anointed me, [and] the heavens spoke. (3) By these sacraments I implore you that you may believe the scripture I send to you and that you may come together in my churches and make confessions to my priests. (4) I flex my bow and <I will send my arrows>, so that sinners must not perish, but sins are forgiven. (5) But return to me; remember, my people, so that the kingdom of God may receive your cleansed souls. (6) But believe that our Lord Jesus Christ has sent this letter from the highest heaven because of the Lord's day and the compaternity of saint John and because of the tenth which you do not give.

[8] (1) Truly, I say to you, I <will> send over you locusts and insects that eat your fruits [see Ps 77:46], and I <will> send over you ravenous wolves and evil dogs that eat you, and I say to you, I will avert my face from you and I will send every evil and bitterness into your tents. (2) And if you won't go to church, I will harden [my heart] and not help you, and I <will> deliver you into the hands of evildoers, because you do not observe the holy Lord's Day. (3) And I ask you, that you do not wash your head on the holy Lord's day nor cut your hair. (4) If you do not heed this, you shall be cursed. (5) I <will> send hunger and tribulation into your houses. (6) O unbelievers, because I have sent this letter to you and you did not want to believe, your souls will be cursed, because I have commanded you through two earlier epistles from me, this is the third one. (7) If you do not observe the Lord's day, I will send blisters into your face, eyes, mouth, ears, noses, and onto every limb, which eat you until you die.

[9] (1) Amen dico vobis, propter vos crucifixus fui et resurrexi die tertio.[67] (2) cognoscite, gentes insipientes, ego ipse mandavi super omnes ecclesias meas per scripturas et libros, ut servetis diem dominicum et compatratam de sancto Iohanne et decimas reddatis, quia Christiani estis.[68] (3) quia pagani non reddunt decimas et me colere nesciunt, quia non sunt similes vobis. (4) amen dico vobis, necessarium est, ut custodiatis diem dominicum et compatratam de sancto Iohanne et decimas reddatis et in die sabbati de hora nona usque lucescente die lune feriatis.[69] (5) si non custodieritis, mitto super vos grandinem et vermes qui comedunt fruges vestras, et monstrabitur et non dabitur,[70] quia decimam non reddetis ad ecclesias.

---

67. *Amen . . . tertio*: Basl (206.10–11 H.) describes the passion of Christ in more detail and mentions that he rose on the holy day (but not on the third): *flagellatus, propter vos spineam coronam accepi et suspensus in ligno et resurrexi diem sanctum dominicum.*

68. *cognoscite . . . estis*: Christian behavior rests on three pillars according to this passage: observing Sunday, giving the tithe, honoring the compaternity (see 4.3); this is contrasted to pagan behavior, as pointed out in the following sentence.

69. *in die . . . feriatis*: On the duration of Sunday, see above, p. 182f. The sentence is very corrupt in Basl (206.17–19 H.) but can be identified by *in die lunis lucisc.*

70. *monstrabitur . . . dabitur*: Literally, "it will be shown but it won't be given," meaning they will see the fruits of their labor grow but will not be allowed to reap them. In Tarr. 11.3 others will be given the benefits: *et aestum gravem in messes et in vineas vestras sive omnes labores vestros, et ad alios demonstrabo, et vobis non dabo, quia decimas vestras, de quantum habuistis, dare noluistis.*

[9] (1) Truly I say to you, because of you I was crucified and rose again on the third day. (2) Understand, foolish peoples, I myself commanded over all my churches through scriptures and books that you shall honor the Lord's day and the compaternity of saint John, and return the tenth, because you are Christians. (3) Because the pagans do not return the tenth and they do not know how to revere me, because they are not like you. (4) Truly I say to you, it is necessary that you observe the Lord's day and the compaternity of saint John, and return the tenth, and from the ninth hour on the Sabbath until the morning of Monday you shall be idle. (5) If you do not heed this, I <will> send over you hail and worms that eat your fruits, and you will see but won't receive, because you do not return the tenth to the churches.

[10] (1) amen dico vobis, <si> colligent mulieres holera in die dominico, mittam super eas serpentes pinnatos qui lacerant mamillas usque in finem.[71] (2) dico vobis, si non custodieritis diem dominicum, erunt infantes nati qui non audiunt neque vident neque ambulant, et sic pereunt.[72]

71. *amen . . . finem*: Many versions of Latin Recension I contain a similar misogynistic passage; see in more detail pp. 195–200. The feathered snakes are a common threat uttered in many versions of the letter (Tarr. 5.3; Bas1, 207.21–23 H.). They also appear in a Vetus Latina version of Isa 14:29 (ed. Roger Gryson, *Esaias*, VL 12 [Freiburg: Herder, 1987], 419): *et de geminibus eorum egredientur serpentes pennati*; in Isa 30:6 they are called *progenies aspidum volantium* (VL [633 G.]). In both cases, the Vulgate version does not mention any feathered serpents, only flying and fiery, as in Deut 8:15: *serpens flatu adurens*, and in another instance fiery—but not flying—in Num 21:6: *misit dominus in populum ignitos serpentes*. Flying serpents also appear in Ovid, *Metam*. 7.350 (BSGRT 158:350 Anderson). The version preserved in Par1 is more extensive (200.60-63 H.): *mulieres autem non colentes diem dominicum et festivitates sanctorum, transmittam super vos serpentes pendentes ad mamillas, sucgentes quasi filius, et puniemini propter castitatem quam non habuistis*. This crude image bears strong resemblance to the *Visio beati Esdrae* 53a (58 W.): *Et vidi alias mulieres per ignes pendentes, et serpentes mamillas earum suggentes*. Here not only the phrase *serpentes mamillas suggentes* appears, but also the participle *pendentes*, yet in another phrasal context. It is not the women who hang (in the fire), but the snakes (but on their breasts). The action expressed by the verb was simply repurposed in the context of the new text. Yet the reasons given for the punishment differ: in the *Visio* the women are said to have killed their children and not fed orphans with their milk. This, however, does not align with the purpose of the Letter from Heaven, so the women's sin had to be connected to Sunday observance as well. Consequently, their sin is the lack of chastity—though not in general, but on the Lord's Day (*non colentes diem dominicum*), a sin already admonished by Caesarius of Arles (e.g., *Serm*. 44.7 [CCSL 103:199f. Morin]). This particular issue is, however, mentioned in the same version of the *Visio beati Esdrae* 10 (50 Wahl): *isti sunt, qui Dominum negaverunt et in die dominica ante missam cum mulieribus peccaverunt*. Here, though, the men are punished for not being chaste on Sundays, but in the Letter from Heaven it is directed toward women in true misogynistic fashion. I owe thanks to my colleague Angela Zielinski Kinney, who identified the *Visio beati Esdrae* as a probable parallel.

72. *erunt . . . pereunt*: Bas1 (207.24–25 H.): *erunt infantes in domibus vestris <qui> non videre nec audire et sic peribunt*. Haines suggests corruption and conjects the *qui*, but the author may have simply produced a vulgar form of the future, *erunt videre, erunt audire*.

[10] (1) Truly I say to you, if women collect vegetables on the Lord's day, I will send over you feathered snakes that will mangle your breasts until the end. (2) I say to you, if you do not observe the Lord's day, children will be born who cannot hear nor see nor walk, and so they die.

[11] (1) ecce iam prophetavi vobis, quia praeter hanc non est ulla.[73] (2) et si mandata mea custodieritis, omnia bona habueritis, et si revertimini ad me. (3) et si sacerdotes aut diaconi aut monachi aut clerici istam epistolam habuerint[74] et non annunciaverint omni populo, anathema erit anima eorum. (4) et qui audierint et non crediderint, anathemati erunt. (5) epistola ista in Ierusalem cecidit[75] et ad sanctum Petrum[76] pervenit (6) et non apud hominem[77] ullum est scripta sed verbo dei dicta et septimo trono transmissa. (7) et certe credatis: si emendare vos nolueritis, parati estis ad mortem. (8) et sciatis, quia in isto mense Novembre[78] proximo ventuoso iram grandissimam volo vobis manifestare. (9) malitiam et amaritudinem transmitto super vos, flammam ignis ardentis et vermes volantes, et certe credatis, quia totus mundus in ruina est positus. (10) et praeter istam epistolam aliam vobis non mittam. (11) et frequentius annuncietis super populum ut omnipotens deus adiuvet illis.

---

73. *praeter hanc*: Sc. *epistulam*. This is supposedly the third letter; see 8.6; *est*: i.e., *erit*.

74. *si . . . habuerint*: Basl (207.26 H.) has *si quis sacerdos aut pontifex <epistolam> habuerint*.

75. *cecidit*: Basl (207.28 H.) adds *ad portas Effraim*.

76. *ad . . . Petrum*: Probably *ad sanctum Petri*; see Parl (199.6 H.): *pervenit ad sepulcum sancti Petri*.

77. *apud hominem*: I.e., *ab homine*; see 5.1.

78. *Novembre . . . ventuoso*: See 4.4. Here *venturo* is possible.

[11] (1) Behold, I have already prophesied to you that after this [letter], there won't be another. (2) And if you heed my commands, you will have all good things, and if you return to me. (3) And if priests or deacons or monks or clerics will come into possession of this epistle and do not announce it to all the people, their soul will be cursed. (4) And those who hear and do not believe will be cursed. (5) This letter fell down in Jerusalem and reached Saint Peter. (6) And it was not written by a man but through the word of God and sent from the seventh throne. (7) And assuredly believe: If you do not want to emend yourselves, you are about to die. (8) And know that in this next windy month of November I want to manifest the greatest wrath against you. (9) I send over you evil and bitterness, flame of burning fire, and flying worms, and assuredly you will believe that the whole world was put to ruin. (10) And after this letter I will not send you another one. (11) And often make it known to the people that the almighty God shall help them.

Graz Universitätsbibliothek 248

Transcription

[1] (1) Incipit epistola dominicalis, quae de caelo in Ierusalem cecidit per Michaelem archangelum. (2) et inventa est ad portam Effeum per manum sacerdotis nomine Achor. (3) Et misit eam ad Armeniam civitatem ad sacerdotem nomine Thalasium. (4) Thalasius vero misit eam ad sacerdotem nomine Lebeneum. (5) Lebeneus vero misit eam ad sacerdotem Iuram. (6) Iuras vero misit eam ad sacerdotem Machabeum. (7) Machabeus vero misit eam ad sacerdotem ad montem Barganum, ubi requiescit sanctus Michael. (8) Et exinde per misericordiam dei venit ad Romam civitatem. (9) Et patres, qui erant in ea civitate, fecerunt triduanum ieiunium in vigiliis, eleemosynis et orationibus, ut pius dominus revelaret per eis, quam causam ista epistola in Ierusalem et alias civitates venisset. (10) Et tunc per revelationem domini nostri Iesu Christi invenerunt, quia venisset propter diem sanctum dominicum.

[2] (1) Quia in die dominico omnes sedentes super modum causantes, iudicantes, iurantes, oleas in horto colligentes, panem facientes, navigantes, negotium exercentes, venationem facientes, pecudes mulentes, molas tornantes, adulteria perpetuentes et alia his similia facientes, propter talia opera perit mundus et propter hoc venit ira dei super cunctum populum. (2) Cognoscite miseri homines, quia deus in sex diebus fecit caelum et terram, mare et omnia, quae in eis sunt; postea hominem Adam de terra plasmavit (3) et certe in die septimo, id est, in die dominico requiescit; sic et nos debemus servare diem sanctum dominicum.

[3] (1) Rogo vos, omnis popule christiane, humiliate in orationibus, in eleemosynis, in vigiliis, et ecclesiam frequentius ambulate et crucem domini super omnem vestram intentionem et operationem ponite. (2) capita vestra cum cinere spargite. (3) miseri populi, arguite vos et dirigit<e> et emite vobis regnum dei, quia cottidiana mors est ante oculos vestros.

[4] (1) Si non bene susceperitis illam epistulam et paenitentiam non agitis et decimas vestras non offeretis, mittam super vos lapides librantes ponda quinque. (2) Ego dico vobis, quod in mense isto in novemberno proximo veniente perire debuissetis, si deprecatio sanctae Mariae non fuisset, Cherubim? et Seraphim deprecatio angelorum sanctorum. (3) Dico autem vobis, si emendaveritis vos, aperiam vobis caracteres caeli et dabo vobis frumentum, vinum et oleum et fructum amborum et amplificabo vitam vestram in saecula.

[5] (1) Dico vobis, populi mei, fidem acceptabilem habete et gratiam dei amate vigilando, orando, eleemosynas dando, viduas et orphanos adiuvando.

(3) Dico vobis, sobrietatem et castitatem amate, deum diligite, regem honorificate, fraternitatem diligite et diem sanctum dominicum omni diligentia custodite etc.

[6] (1) Si autem non observaveritis diem sanctum dominicum, mittam super vos pustulas in faciem vestram, in oculos, in os, in aures et in omnia membra vestra, quae vos comedunt usque ad mortem.

[7] (1) Amen dico vobis, propter vos crucifixus sum et surrexi die dominico. (2) Cognoscite, sapientes, insipientes, ut ego ipse mando super omnes ecclesias per scripturas, ut honoretis diem sanctum dominicum et decimas vestras iuste et quiete detis, quia christiani estis. (3) Et in die sabbato de hora nona usque lucescente die lunae nullum opus servile faciatis et in ecclesia mea nolite loqui, nisi cum deprecationem pro peccatis vestris. (4) Si non emendaveritis, mitto super vos grandinem, bruchus et vermes, ut comedant fructus vestros, et monstrabitur et non dabit<ur>, quia decimas vestras non reddatis ad ecclesias meas.

[8] (1) Amen, amen dico vobis, cum se colligunt mulieres holera in horto in die dominico, mittam super eas serpentes pennatas, ut lacerent mamillas earum usque ad mortem. (2) Dico vobis, si non custodieritis diem sanctum dominicum, erunt infantes nati in domibus vestris, qui non audient et non vident neque ambulant et sic peribunt.

[9] (1) Ecce, iam prophetavi vobis, quia praeter hoc non est aliud, nisi bona habueritis, si revertetis ad me et si habueretis diem sanctum dominicum. (2) Et si quis pontifex aut sacerdos illam epistulam non habuerit et non annunciaverit populo meo, sedens in tenebris usque ad mortem. (3) Haec epistula in Ierusalem cecidit et ad sanctum Petrum pervenit et a nullo homine est scripta, nisi vero domini dicta, et descripta et de septimo throno a deo transmissa. (4) Et certe credatis: Si eam audiere nolueritis, parati estis ad mortem. (5) Et nunc fratres karissimi, frequentius annunciate eam populo meo.

(Transcription of Gra1 by Christoph Scheerer and Philip Polcar)

According to the Tarragona Manuscript, Cathedral Library / Baluzius

The Tarragona manuscript contained a text that belongs to the group of versions called Latin Recension I.[1] As stated above, a common feature of the Latin Recension I is its introductory narrative: The archangel Michael finds or delivers the letter at gate Ephraim in Jerusalem. The letter then is sent from one priest to another up to Rome. It follows a gathering of clerics who pray and fast. However, in the Tarragona version, the place is unclear, but the populace certainly gathers where the letter was found (1.6: *collecti sunt in unum . . . ubi inventa est*), so maybe this implies that the aforementioned gathering of clerics takes place at the gate, too.

The Tarragona version is of particular value to research concerning the Letter from Heaven, as it contains some unique details: the condemnation of pagan rituals at stones, wells, and trees (8.1–3) cannot be found in any other version so far. Thus, Priebsch considers the Tarragona version to be the earliest, but he bolsters his argument with some questionable historical references.[2] In addition, it must also be noted that text contains features that are otherwise only found in versions belonging to Latin Recension II. Haines therefore calls it a "hybrid text."[3] Consequently, the hypothesis must be that the Tarragona version preserved older material that other members of Latin Recension I do not exhibit anymore; yet newer material was added. One can observe that a few topics occur several times throughout the letter: The assertion of authority gained from the creation story in 2.3 is repeated in almost identical words in 7.3f. The threats brought forth in 3.7–9 bear some resemblance of the threats in 6.1 and 7.6f.; the latter ones are otherwise found only in Latin Recension II. These observations could suggest that the Latin Recension II is older and the Latin Recension I was developed only from it (see above, pp. 86–95).

Unfortunately, the only witness of the manuscript is the transcription published by Baluzius in 1677, who presumably inspected the manuscript and associated the text with the Carolingian period.[4] According to Priebsch, the

1. The grouping of the Latin versions was first established by Priebsch, *Letter from Heaven*, 3. It was consequently pursued by Haines, *Sunday Observance*. See above, p. 245f.

2. Priebsch, *Letter from Heaven*, 6–7. Priebsch goes as far as to suggest that the heretic Adalbert, condemned by the Lateran synod in 745, redacted the Tarragona version himself and was responsible for the creation of versions more akin to the other texts of Latin Recension I. This appears to be a rather bold assumption; see above, pp. 95–99.

3. Haines, *Sunday Observance*, 46.

4. Stephanus Baluzius, *Capitularia regum Francorum II*, 1396–99, with the statement at 1396: *aevo, ut videtur, Karoli M. Regis Francorum*.

manuscript was found by Petrus de Marca, archbishop of Paris, in the twelfth century, but it is unclear where Priebsch gets this information from.[5] Baluzius's text was reprinted and slightly adapted by Fabricius.[6] The first modern edition was published postmortem by Priebsch, who copied Baluzius's text and made a few emendations and conjectures. He also found that this version simply states to observe the Lord's Day, whereas other versions specify from when to when.[7]

Translating the letter brought some unexpected pitfalls. Though its Latin is fairly simple, it is not always easy to understand. This is mainly due to heavy corruption but also due to frequent errors and the author's limited capacity to express himself well in Latin.[8] The mode of translation is to a large degree *ad sensum*; it represents what the text supposedly intended to say, as it does not appear to be helpful to recreate grammatical errors or other shortcomings. Yet it was attempted to render the bumpy language to some extent.

---

5. Priebsch, *Letter from Heaven*, 3.

6. Fabricius, *Codex apocryphus Novi Testamenti*, 308–13; see above, p. 34.

7. Priebsch, *Letter from Heaven*, 7.

8. A more detailed analysis of the letter's language is given in the introduction to Viel; see p. 247f.

Letter from Heaven—Latin Recension I (Tarragona)

[1] (1) In nomine domini, incipit epistola salvatoris domini nostri Iesu Christi filii dei, quae in Hierosolymis cecidit.

(2) Michaelo[9] ipsam deportavit, et inventa est ad portam <Efrem>[10] per manus sacerdotis nomine Eros. (3) et ipsa epistola ad Erim civitatem directa est ad alium sacerdotem nomine Leopas. (4) Leopas vero direxit ipsam epistolam ad Cappadociam.[11] (5) et tunc collecti sunt XV episcopi in unum et triduanum ieiunium fecerunt in vigiliis et orationibus insistentes, simulque et omnes presbyteri, diacones, clerici, et omnes populi.[12] (6) tam viris quam mulieribus collecti sunt in unum et ploraverunt, ubi inventa est et a domino directa epistola.

[2](1) Carissimi fratres, audite et auscultate, qualem nobis epistolam direxit dominus e coelo, non tantum nisi ut[13] corrigamus nosmetipsos de omni coecitate huius seculi antequam veniat ira furoris domini super nos, denique non pro aliud nisi sanctum diem dominicum custodiendum et decimas fideles deo reddendum. (2) sicut scriptum est:[14]

---

9. *Michaelo*: Archangel Michael's involvement is a common feature in the letters that belong to Latin Recension I.

10. *Efrem*: The manuscript had *quem*, but already Baluzius emendated to Efrem. For more on the gate, see the commentary in Viel 1.2.

11. *Eros . . . Cappadociam*: The list of names of priests and places through which the letter has passed is cut short in this version. For a comparison of the names, see the commentary on Viel 1.2–6. The name Leopas may bear resemblance to Kleopas (Luke 24:18), but it is rather a garbled form of Lebonius (Viel), Libonius (Lon1), Leobanus (vers. Later.), Lebeneus (Gra1); here and elsewhere he passes the letter on to Cappadocia (Lon1; Viel).

12. *tunc . . . populi*: This usually takes place in Rome; see Viel 1.8–9. In vers. Later. (= Bonifatius, *Ep.* 59 [MGH Epp. sel. 1, 115.23–29 Tangl]) they number 12; in other versions no number is presented.

13. *non tantum nisi ut*: Ignore *nisi* for better understanding; corresponds to *denique non pro aliud nisi*. The bumpy sentence means to express that the following letter is not merely a general admonishment but serves the purpose to impose a strict Sunday observance and giving of the tenth on the Christian people.

14. *sicut scriptum est*: Uncommon use to mark the beginning of the actual letter from heaven.

Translation

[1] (1) In the name of the Lord, the letter of the savior Lord Jesus Christ, the son of God, begins, which has fallen [from heaven] in Jerusalem.

(2) Michael carried it, and it was found at the gate Ephraim by the hand of the priest Eros. (3) And this letter was sent to the city of Erim to another priest named Leopas. (4) Leopas then sent it to Cappadocia. (5) And then fifteen bishops gathered together and fasted for three days, and stayed up in vigils and prayers, likewise the priests, deacons, clerics, and the whole populace. (6) Men and women gathered together and wept where the God-sent letter was found.

[2] (1) Dearest brothers, listen and lend your ears to what kind of letter the Lord has sent us from heaven, not only that we may better ourselves from the blindness of this world before the raging wrath of the Lord comes over us, but also for nothing less than that the holy Lord's day is to be observed and the faithful tenth is to be given to the Lord. (2) So it is written:

[3] (1) Die dominico sedentes in foro et causas iudicandi[15] otiosas;[16] venationes[17] in eodem die non colligere; pecora in eodem die non mulgentes, sed pauperibus vestris aut comparibus non habentes[18] distribuere; boves tuos in eodem die non mittas laborare. (2) propter quod non custodistis diem dom<inicum>, veniat super vos iudicium domini. et propterea lugebunt et . . . generaliter periculum terrae, et captivas animas ducet[19] <in infernum> ubi erit fletus et stridor dentium. (3) nescitis miseri quia <celum>, terram, mare et omnia quae in eis sunt, orna<vi et pos>tea Adam de limo terrae plasmavi et edi<ficavi> . . . bit omnis peccatus in terra donec . . .

15. *iudicandi*: Probably meant to be *iudicantes*, as in Lon1: *in sanctum diem dominicum sedentes et causas iudicantes*; likewise in Vie1 and Gra1.

16. *causas . . . otiosas*: The prosecution of cases, or dissent in general, is sometimes described as tiring, for example, Ambrose, *Tob.* 6.24 (CSEL 32.2:530.11 Schenkl): *otiosa causatio est*; Ambrosius, *Ep.* 9.69.7 (CSEL 82.2:181.66 Zelzer): *iam qui singulorum membrorum officia diligenter expendit, non otiosam causam in hac membri huius portiuncula aestimare poterit.*

17. *venationes . . . colligere*: Here and in other instances the infinitive is used like an imperative/prohibitive.

18. *comparibus non habentes*: I.e., *habentibus*, your neighbors (Matt 19:19), according to *Liber pontificalis ecclesiae Ravennatis* 30 (ninth century; CCCM 199:180.158 Mauskopf Deliyannis): *vade, redde pecuniam compatri tuo*; other versions use the word *compatres* (proto-Romance for Italian *compare* or Spanish *compadre*; see Wilhelm Meyer-Lübke, *Romanisches etymologisches Wörterbuch* [Heidelberg: Winter, 1911], 169).

19. *ducet*: According to Fabricius, Baluzius has *duces*. Since the passage is corrupt it is hard to say which form is correct.

[3] (1) They sit in public squares on the Lord's day and judge idle cases; do not gather hunting parties on that day; do not milk the cattle on that day, but give to your poor and your neighbors who don't have anything. Do not send your cattle to work on this day. (2) Because you do not observe the Lord's day, the judgment of the Lord comes over you. And because of this they will cry and . . . general danger of the earth, and he will lead the captured souls <into hell>, "where there will be wailing and gnashing of teeth" [see Matt 13:42]. (3) Do you not know, wretches, that I have created <heaven>, earth, sea, and all that dwells there, . . . and later I furnished Adam from the clay of the earth [see Gen 2:7] and built . . . will . . . all sin in the world until . . .

[Desunt hic multa][20]

[4] (1) Nihil aliud operantes in die dominico nisi ad ecclesiam concurrere solemnitates domini audire.[21] (2) et post haec, infirmos visitare, mortuos sepelire, tribulantes consolare, discordantes pacificare, crucem Christi in omnibus venerare, deponentes nitidas vestes in saccis et ciliciis et cinere versari, sicut Ninivitae[22] fecerunt, et sic liberati sunt ab ira furoris mei. (3) miseri populi, cur non timetis, ut possitis evadere iram meam? (4) corrigite vos antequam veniat ira mea super vos, et omnes habitantes in terra qui volunt custodire mandata mea et diem sanctum dominicum colere et venerare. (5) ponite, miseri, mortem ante oculos vestros die noctuque,[23] quia nescitis qua hora auferantur a vobis animas vestras et deducantur a diabolo in gehenna ignis, ubi nulla erit requies nisi fletus et ululatus.[24]

20. Unfortunately, Baluzius did not indicate how much is missing, only that there is missing a lot (*multa*).

21. *operantes . . . audire*: The present participle *operantes* is used like a (negated) imperative, the first infinitive (*concurrere*), too; *audire* is an infinitive finalis. In the following sentence (4.2), other infinitives are used as imperatives.

22. *deponentes . . . Ninivitae*: Allusion to Jonah. The king of Nineveh changes his regal clothes in order to do penance, Jonah 3:6: *et pervenit verbum ad regem Nineve et surrexit de solio suo et abiecit vestimentum suum a se et indutus est sacco et sedit in cinere.* The use of two words for sackcloth used here (*saccus et cilicium*) is a mixture of the Vulgate with the Vetus Latina tradition, the latter one popular due to its alliteration, for example, Lucifer Calarithanus, *Quia absentem nemo debet iudicare nec damnara sive De Athanasio* 2.33.17 (CCSL 8:130.18f. Diercks): *abstulit a se stolam suam et circumdedit se cilicium et sedit super cinerem.*

23. See Viel 3.3 and the Rule of Benedict 4.47: *mortem cotidie ante oculos suspectam habere.*

24. *fletus et ululatus*: In the Bible, from an eschatological perspective, weeping or lamentation is envisaged in view of the judgment. This kind of language is alluded to here; see Luke 6:25: *vae vobis qui ridetis nunc quia lugebitis et flebitis*; John 16:30: *amen amen dico vobis quia plorabitis et flebitis.*

[4] (1) Do not do anything else on the Lord's day than come together to listen to the celebrations of the Lord. (2) And after that, visit the sick, bury the dead, console the mourners, make peace among those who fight, honor the cross of Christ in everything, take off your sparkling clothes when in mass, be in sackcloth and ashes like the Ninevites were, and so they were freed from my raging wrath. (3) Wretched people, why do you not fear, so that you may evade my wrath? (4) Better yourselves before my wrath comes over you, and all those who live on earth who want to keep my mandates and observe and revere the holy Lord's day. (5) Put, wretches, death in front of your eyes day and night, because you don't know in which hour you souls shall be taken from you and led into the hell of fire by the devil, where there will be no respite, only wailing and lamentation.

[5] (1) admoneo vos per epistolam istam ut custodiatis omnia, quae dixi vobis. (2) Quod si non custodieritis, mittam super vos lapides calidos ignem et flammam producentes cum magno pondere, qui consumant vos usque ad <mortem> . . . anei[25] qui deglutiant homines, aut velut passer triticum, ita devoret vos infernus. (3) <mittam super v>os[26] serpentes pinnatas[27] malas et pessimas, qui devorent . . . tributio.[28] (4) Si non egeritis poenitentiam et <custodieritis iudici>a in quibus vivitis,[29] vos et filii vestri . . .
[Hic rursum multa desunt][30]

25. *usque ad . . . anei*: One of the most common words with this ending is *extranei*; maybe a pagan people is meant, as in other recensions. But one expects an animal here; see Pal (200.33–34 H.): *mittam . . . in aures bestiolas quas vocant scyniphes venenatas pessimas ad devorandum vos*.

26. *super vos*: Priebsch conjectures *in vos*, but the threat of sending some kind of plague onto humanity is mostly expressed by *super vos* in other versions, for example, Par1: *transmittam super vos serpentes*; Ba1: *mittam super illas serpentes pennatas*; et al.

27. *serpentes pinnatas*: A common threat in many versions of the letter (see p. 264). They appear in a Vetus Latina version of Isa 14:29, according to Jerome (*Esaias*, ed. Roger Gryson, VL 12 [Freiburg: Herder, 1987], 419): *et de geminibus eorum egredientur serpentes pennati*; in Isa 30:6 they are called *progenies aspidum volantium* (Jerome, *Comm. Isa.* [633 G.]). In both cases the Vulgate does not have any flying serpents, only in Deut 8:15: *serpens flatu adurens*; and fiery—but not flying—in Num 21:6: *misit dominus in populum ignitos serpentes*. Flying serpents also appear in Ovid, *Metam.* 7.350 (BSGRT 158:350 Anderson).

28. *tributio*: Though context is missing, maybe *tribulatio* was originally meant, as it is a common word concerning the threats uttered in various versions.

29. *custodierits . . . vivitis*: This conjecture is based on Ezek 20:25: *ergo et ego dedi eis praecepta non bona et iudicia in quibus non vivent*; Baluzius read *-la* after the lacuna, but it may well have been *-ia*. Note also that Baluzius prints *bibitis*, and Fabricius normalizes into *vivitis*, which seems an improvement.

30. Again, Baluzius gives only a vague indication of how much is missing (*multa*).

[5] (1) I admonish you through this epistle that you observe everything that I have told you. (2) If you won't observe it, I will send onto you hot stones with heavy weight, that burn with fire and flame, which will consume you until <you die> . . . which feast upon humans, or like the sparrow the grain, so will hell swallow you. (3) <I will send over> you feathered snakes, bad and very evil, who will swallow . . . (4) If you will not do penance and . . . in which you live, you and your children . . .

[6] (1) Dico vobis, coniuratio fidelis populi, permaneat in vobis gratia mea, qui sum deus vester, vigilando et orando, et eleemosynas faciendo, facta mala relinquendo, homicidia relaxando, viduas et orphanos diligendo, pro peccata vestra semper orando, mala pro malo non reddendo, diem sanctum dominicum custodiendo, compari tuo caritatem et fidem perfectam tependo. (2) si haec feceritis, in regno meo eritis mecum regnaturi in secula seculorum, amen.

[7] (1) Filii parentes non maledicant neque parentes filios, quia maledictio patris et matris eradicat fundamenta domos filiorum. (2) ecce, fideliter iterum dico vobis, ad ecclesias meas cum oblationes frequenter venite. (3) lectiones divinas intento corde audite, ut salvi esse possitis.

[8] (1) qui dissimulaverit ad fontes aut ad arboribus aut ad petra fuerit inventus sacrificare,[31] aut ad sepulcra mortuorum praesumpserit incantare[32] aut in quolibet locis tergere,[33] anathemabo eum, et peribit in inferno inferiori, quia omnis incantator non habebit partem in regno meo. (2) ille tamen qui dimiserit sanctum diem dominicum et non coluerit eum sicut oportet, anathemabo eum. (3) maleficos, divinos, incantatores, auguriatores fugite. (4) ieiunium observate; vestras decimas, de quantum habueritis, in ecclesias meas ponite; estote assidue sine peccato.

---

31. *ad fontes . . . sacrificare*: In pagan tradition, sacrificial rituals were carried out at the mentioned places for similar reasons: springs or well-sources (*fontes*) were seen as places of deities or water spirits. They had healing powers, especially if the water came directly out of the earth, as in the mountains. Sacrifices had to be made to receive healing or fertility (see Richard Hünnerkopf, "Brunnen," in *Handbuch des deutschen Aberglaubens* [Berlin: de Gruyter, 1987], 1:1672–85). Trees (*arbores*) were venerated among all European peoples for various reasons (see Heinrich Marzell, "Baum," in *Handbuch des deutschen Aberglaubens* 1:954–58). Trees were often seen as having a soul; the dead were among the trees; trees were believed to have powers of fertility or even healing; oracles were spoken by the trees. Sacrifices for trees were called *oblationes ad arbores* and are mentioned in old penitentiaries. Stones (*petra*) were venerated for similar reasons: it was believed that stones contain the spirits and souls of the deceased; they performed miracles of healing that were often associated with the cult of the spring (see Karl Olbrich, "Stein I," in *Handbuch des deutschen Aberglaubens* 8:380–90; Richard Hünnerkopf, "Stein II," in *Handbuch des deutschen Aberglaubens* 8:390–402).

32. *ad sepulcra . . . incantare*: Graves were seen as places of not only death and danger but also of healing (Paul Geiger, "Grab," in *Handbuch des deutschen Aberglaubens* 3:1076–82). Spells were chanted in order to heal afflictions of humans and animals, but there were also love or fertility spells.

33. *quolibet locis tergere*: Ungrammatical and semantically unclear. My suggestion is the following: It was believed that one could transfer diseases to trees, stones by

[6] (1) I say to you, the union of my faithful people, for I am your God, my favor will stay upon you through holding vigils and praying, giving alms, letting go of evil deeds, stopping to kill men, loving widows and orphans, always praying for your sins, not repaying evil with evil, observing the Lord's day, warming affection and perfect faith for your neighbor. (2) If you do this, you will reign in my kingdom forever and ever, amen.

[7] (1) Children must not curse their parents, nor parents their children, because the curse of the father and mother uproots the fundament of the houses of the children. (2) See, reliably I say to you again, come often to my churches with offerings. (3) Listen to the divine readings with intent hearts, so that you may be redeemed.

[8] (1) Who secretly goes to the springs or to the trees or stones and is found making sacrifices, or who dares to chant by the graves of the dead or rubs [trees or stones] in any of these places, I will curse them, and they will go down into the deepest hell, because no soothsayer will have a place in my kingdom. (2) But he who neglects the holy Lord's day and does not worship it as required, I will curse them. (3) Stay away from witches, divinators, soothsayers, bird watchers. (4) Observe the fast; put your tenth from what you have into my church; be consistently without sin.

---

touching, brushing, or circling the painful spot (Hünnerkopf, "Stein I," 380–81). More generally it was thought that diseases could be removed by wiping (Hanns Bächtold-Stäubli, "Abwischen," in *Handbuch des deutschen Aberglaubens* 1:150); especially skin diseases and itching, as an "animal" way of getting rid of diseases, which is also done by humans, rubbing against trees, rocks (and walls; Hanns Baechtold-Stäubli, "Abstreifen," in *Handbuch des deutschen Aberglaubens* 1:121). Finally, evil could be washed away by water (Hünnerkopf, "Waschen," in *Handbuch des deutschen Aberglaubens* 9:101–7, here 102). Another solution could be that one must read *pergere* instead of *tergere*; in that case one would expect a prepositional construction with the accusative case (*ad . . . loca*), but the confusion of cases would not be surprising. Fabricius explains the action with only one Latin word, that is, *auguriare* ("to perform divination"), but it is unclear how he came to his conclusion.

[9] (1) Amen dico vobis, si non corrigeritis vosmet ipsos, mittam super vos brucus et locustas,[34] qui comedant fructus vestros, et lupos rapaces qui comedant vos, quia non custodistis diem sanctum dominicum. (2) qui istum non custodierit, maledictus erit. (3) die dominico non lavare vestimenta non caput neque capillos tondere. (4) qui haec fecerit, anathema sit. (5) si custodieritis mandata mea, <non> avertam faciem meam a vobis, et <non> mittam in domibus vestris omnem malitiam et amaritudinem et infirmitatem. (6) si quis tamen in die dominico aut causas voluerit committere vel intentiones facere, aut rixas commiserit, mittam in eis pustellas, accessiones et lang<u>ores, et omne genus infirmitates. (7) et pro eo quod non concurritis ad ecclesias meas, sed magis ad mercimonia vel ad silvam vel otiium, et per plateas sedere, fabulas vanas loquere, et me non timere, et ecclesias meas non venerare, propter hoc tradam vos in fame et in manus gentium (et non pluam super vos) incredulorum paganorum, qui epistolam istam non custodiunt.

---

34. *brucus . . . rapaces*: The same trio of animals as in Viel 8.1: *mitto super vos locustas et brucos qui comedunt fructus vestros et mitto super vos lupos rapaces.*

[9] (1) Truly, I say to you, if you do not correct yourselves, I will send upon you insects and locusts which will eat your harvest, and ravenous wolves which will eat you, because you do not observe the holy Lord's day. (2) He who does not observe it will be cursed. (3) On the Lord's day, do not wash clothes or your head, do not cut your hair. (4) Who does this, will be cursed. (5) If you keep my rules, I will <not> avert my face from you, and I will <not> send into your houses all malice and bitterness and weakness. (6) If someone on the Lord's day still wants to commit causes or make intentions, or starts fights, I will send on them blisters, fever, sickness, and all kinds of illness. (7) And for that you do not come together in my churches, but rather on the markets or in the forest or [take] rest, and sit on the free spaces, talk void stories, and do not fear me, and you do not venerate my churches, because of this I will give you over to hunger and in the hands of the peoples (and I will not rain over you) of the incredulous pagans, those who do not follow this epistle.

[10] (1) Iam enim vobis ante legem meam mandavi, sed minime custodistis diem sanctum dominicum.[35] (2) propterea mittam gladium meum[36] super vos, quia non custodistis haec omnia. (3) amen dico vobis: crucifixus fui propter vos, et resurrexi die dominica, ascendi ad dextram dei, et requiem dedi omnibus die dominico.[37] (4) in ipso feci coelum et terram, solem et lunam, mare et omnia quae in eis sunt.[38] (5) et postea Adam de limo terrae plasmavi, et die<m> dominic<um> sanctificavi,[39] et dedi requiem in ipso ut bene agant, et sine pressure sint, et requiescant per omnia.[40]

35. *legem . . . dominicum*: The *ante* indicates that there was an earlier letter. Consequently, "my law" (*legem meam*) is applied to the Letter from Heaven by the author(s)—a bold statement, as "my/his law" usually refers to the laws received from God through Moses (Luke 2:22; John 7:23; Heb 10:28), or the Bible in general by Christian authors. However, already the Letter from Heaven that was sent to Licinianus might have made this ambitious claim—at least Licinianus says that Vincentius believed it to be so; see Licinianus's Letter 1.3 (see above, p. 214): *admirans quod his credulus fueris, et post prophetarum vaticinia, et Christi evangelia, apostolorumque eius epistolas, nescio cuius hominis litteras sub nomine Christi factas, eius esse credideris.*

36. *gladium meum*: The sword of God is a unique feature.

37. *crucifixus . . . dominico*: This is the theological reason that observance of the Lord's Day is demanded.

38. *in ipso . . . in eis sunt*: According to Gen 1:6–8, God creates heaven and the seas on the second day, that is, Monday. See Viel 2.2: *quia in sex diebus fecit deus coelum et terram, solem et lunam, quattuor evangelistas, mare et omnia quae in eis sunt.*

39. *diem dominicum sanctificavi*: Baluzius printed *die dominico*, but with respect to Gen 2:3, where God sanctifies the seventh day, the accusative case must be meant: *et benedixi diei septimo et sanctificavit illum quia in ipso cessaverat ab omni opere suo quod creavit Deus ut faceret.* See also p. 162.

40. Note that this paragraph contains some repetitions from the corrupt paragraph 3. This may be due to some merging of versions by a redactor.

[10] (1) Thus, I have already before given my law to you, but you do not observe the holy Lord's day at all. (2) Therefore, I will send my sword over you, because you do not observe all this. (3) Verily I say to you, I was crucified because of you, and I have risen on the Lord's day, I rose up to the right of God, and I gave rest to all on the Lord's day. (4) On it I "made heaven and earth" [see Gen 1:1], sun and moon, "the sea and everything which is in them" [see Exod 20:11]. (5) And later I formed Adam from the clay of the earth and sanctified the Lord's day, and I gave rest on it so they may do well and be without pressure, and may rest through all.

[11] (1) sacerdotibus meis praecepi per epistolas et libros, ut legem istam fideliter custodiant, quia pagani sunt in terra qui non custodiunt legem meam. (2) et si non custodieritis omnia quae praecepi vobis, mittam super vos tribulationes et grandines et tempestates et siccitatem, qui exterminet fructum operum vestrorum;[41] et non habebitis partem mecum, neque cum angelis meis, neque cum martyribus meis.[42] (3) amen dico vobis, si non custodieritis sanctum diem dominicum, mittam super vos fame et frigore, et aestum gravem in messes et in vineas vestras sive omnes labores vestros,[43] et ad alios demonstrabo, et vobis non dabo,[44] quia decimas vestras, de quantum habuistis, dare noluistis. (4) inde ad decimum revertatur.[45]

[12] (1) Amen dico vobis, die dominico observate cum omni diligentia, sicut nec ipsas oleras in hortibus vestris die dominico colligatis. (2) si haec feceritis, vos mulieres, mittam super vos serpentes pinnatas qui comedant et percutiant mamillas vestras.[46] (3) amen dico vobis, si non custodieritis sanctum diem dominicum, omnia mala mittam super vos. (4) nam si custodieritis mandata mea et feceritis ea, dabo vobis benedictionem meam et multiplicabo labores[47] vestros usque ad abundantiam et usque ad messem et usque ad vindemiam et pomiferum et totam substantiam,[48] et quaecumque petieritis dabo vobis. (5) amen dico vobis, si non custodieritis mandata mea, omnia mala habebitis, et addam vobis malum super quod habuistis.

---

41. *mittam . . . vestrorum*: This whole paragraph bears some similarities to Latin Recension II, particularly Mun2, Delehaye, *Mélanges d'Hagiographie*, 156: *mittam super vos grandinem, ignem, fulgura, coruscationes, tempestates ut pereant labores vestri*. See p. 236f.

42. *et non . . . meis*: See Mun2 (156 D.): *et non habetis partem mecum neque cum angelis meis in saecula saeculorum, amen*.

43. *aestum . . . vestros*: See Mun2 (156 D.): *et delebo vineas vestras, et non dabo vobis pluviam, et auferam a vobis fructus vestros*.

44. *et ad . . . dabo*: See Viel 9.5: *monstrabitur et non dabitur*, meaning "it will be shown but it won't be given"; but here *ad alios* was added, and thus a different meaning created, if one assumes that *demonstrare* can mean "to give" at least in a colloquial way.

45. *inde . . . revertatur*: The meaning of this sentence is unclear. I suggest that the author ignored that *revertatur* is a deponens and used it to express an impersonal statement; see my translation.

46. *serpentes . . . vestras*: On this misogynistic passage, see pp. 195–200, and Viel, n. 71, for more details.

47. *multiplicabo labor*: Like above in 11.2, it is rather meant that the result of their work will be multiplied (Ezek 30:32: "I will make the fruit of the tree and the produce of the field abundant, so that you may never again suffer the disgrace of famine among the nations.").

48. *multiplicabo . . . substantiam*: The phrasing is bumpy and has been rendered accordingly in English; nonetheless, its meaning is clear: God promises his people that their agricultural work will prosper.

[11] (1) My priests I taught [them] through letters and books that they may observe this law faithfully, because there are pagans on earth who do not observe my law. (2) And if you will not observe all which I have taught you, I will send over you tribulations and hails, and storms and draughts, which will exterminate the fruits of your labor. And you will have no part with me, nor with my angels, nor my martyrs. (3) Truly I say to you, if you will not observe the holy Lord's day, I will send over you famine and frost, and grave heat on your crops and your vineyards or on all your labors, and I will give it to others, and I will not give it to you, because you did not want to give me the tenth of what you had in your possession. (4) Therefore, one shall return to giving the tenth.

[12] (1) Verily I say to you, observe the Lord's day with all diligence, so that you do not collect vegetables in your gardens on the Lord's day. (2) If you do that, you women, I will send over you flying snakes who eat you and pierce through your breasts. (3) Truly I say to you, if you do not observe the holy Lord's day, I will send all calamities over you. (4) Thus, if you observe my mandates and do them, I will give you my blessing and I will multiply your labors into abundance and harvest, and into vintage and fruit-bearing and into all substance, and I will give to you whatever you desire. (5) Truly I say to you, if you do not observe my commands, you will have all bad things, and I will add for you calamities on top of what you have.

[13] (1) Et si fuerint presbyteri aut diaconi, ubicumque invenerint epistolam istam, legant et aperiant illam ad omne populum. (2) frequenter admoneant ut recte dant ab iniquis suis operibus,[49] et omnis qui hoc audierit et non crediderit, anathema sit. (3) ego sum dominus deus vester qui crucifixus fui propter vos, ut custodiatis vosmetipsos per istam epistolam, quae ostensi vobis. (4) suscipite illam et toto corde sine dubio credite et audite frequenter, quia non fuit ab homine scripta neque ab angelo neque ab archangelo, nisi de verbo et de suavitate mea, quia vera est scripta, et a supremo[50] throno submissa fuit, ut credatis.

[14] (1) Et si vos emendare nolueritis, parate vos ad poenam mense Novembrio.[51] (2) sic erit grandis metus super vos, vermis, focus et flamma. (3) quatenus alios comedit vermis, et alios cremet ignis, et +ceterorum+,[52] ut credatis quia mundus iste iudicatus est in grandi ruina. (4) iuro vos per epistolam istam quia aliam vobis nunquam mittam antequam veniat iudicius meus super vos. (5) educ epistolam istam per universum populum denuntiare.

[15] (1) Finit. (2) ut clarus et pius dominus noster Iesus Christus inspirare et liberare dignetur, amen. (3) cui est honor et gloria in secula seculorum, amen.

49. *iniquis suis operibus*: Probably money is meant, as it is called the *mammon iniquitatis* in the Bible.

50. *supremo*: Premio (Fabricius); Gra1 9.3, Vie1 11.6: *septimo*.

51. *mense Novembrio*: In Lon1 it is stated that the recipients of the letter would have already died last November, had Maria and other saints not interceded: *ego vero dico vobis, quia mense iste Novembri proximo qui fuit, perire debuistis si deprecacio fuisset sancte Marie virginis*. This suggests that this version was known to the redactor of Lon1.

52. *ceterorum*: The text is certainly corrupt here.

[13] (1) And if there are priests or deacons, wherever they find this letter, they should open it and read it to the whole populace. (2) They should admonish the people often that they may correctly give from their works of iniquity, and everyone who hears this and does not believe will be cursed. (3) I am the Lord, your God, who was crucified for you so that you may protect yourselves through this letter which I have shown to you. (4) Take it up and believe without doubt with all of your heart, and listen to it often, for it was not written by a human nor by an angel nor archangel, but only by the word, and by my sweetness, because it was truly written and sent from the highest throne, so you may believe.

[14] (1) And if you do not want to make amends, prepare yourself for a punishment in the month of November. (2) Thus, great fear will come over you, worm, fire and flame. (3) For some the worm will eat, and others the flame will burn, and +of others+, so that you may believe this world was sentenced to great destruction. (4) I swear to you by this epistle that I will not send you another one before my judgment will come over you. (5) Bring forth this letter before the whole populace to be read aloud.

[15] (1) The end. (2) May our bright and gentle Lord Jesus deign to inspire and deliver us, amen. (3) To whom there is honor and glory for ever and ever, amen.

5

LETTER FROM HEAVEN—GREEK RECENSION ALPHA

Canan Arıkan-Caba

Manuscripts

The Letter from Heaven in Greek (BHG 812i–s) is preserved in twenty-three manuscripts dating between fourteenth and eighteenth centuries. The long chain of letters reproduced throughout centuries by copyists and redactors precludes a critical edition. As a practical solution, Maximilian Bittner suggests the existence of two traditional families by categorizing them into "Rome recension" and "Jerusalem recension" with respect mainly to the finding story in the prologue of the text.[1] According to his arrangement, manuscripts of the Rome recension are introduced under the group of Alpha.[2] While the original Greek text has not survived, Bittner proposes that the Alpha and Alpha 1 form the earliest of the Oriental tradition, from which the Syriac and the Armenian traditions independently stem. The present study attempts to offer an insight mainly into the Greek Recension Alpha, their structural features, themes, and events along with the translations of Alpha 1 and Alpha 2.

Structural Features

The epistle is set around a frame narrative that encapsulates the main text of the letter and consists of three structural episodes: (1) the title and the finding story by the archbishop of Rome; (2) the letter itself narrated by the hybrid personality of God/Jesus Christ, often fused together; and (3) an epilogue as a final warning and a reassurance on the authenticity of the letter by the

1. Bittner, *Brief Christi*, 7f. See above, pp. 80–82, 108–18, 135f.
2. See the list above, p. 80f.

archbishop of Rome.[3] It incorporates various literary genres such as apocalyptic, apocryphal, prophetic, epistolary, and sermonic.[4] In addition to these, its structure overlaps and features several characteristics of the genre of frame tale (or frame narrative), a popular literary genre of the medieval period that was widely adopted in both Eastern and Western cultures.[5] Defined by Bonnie D. Irwin, a frame tale is "a fictional narrative composed primarily for the purpose of presenting other narratives."[6] Although our epistle does not contain a chain of numerous tales but a letter, it employs the framing device, with the main aim to convince and prime the audience on the credibility and authenticity of the letter. The letter functions as a single tale itself that was multiplied and inserted with different additions and adjustments that would fit in the epistle's overall concept.[7] It was apparently composed by a literate author, probably from the class of clergy who was familiar with a biblical vocabulary.

The episodes 1 and 3 that establish our frame form a literary component in the whole narrative, creating a "letter within a story," and set the scene to emphasize the letter. Its wide circulation and durable popularity result not only from the impact of its "divine" characteristics on its audience, which itself exhorts the readers to copy and circulate the letter, but also from the flexible and adaptable nature of the framing episodes and the core letter, enabling the copyists and compilers to adopt and adjust the letter-telling event, thus textualizing what has become the oral tradition.[8]

The letter with its frame addresses at least two types of audience. The fictional/intratextual audience is depicted as a community of clerics, monastics,

---

3. The structural division was later adopted by the Jerusalem recension, with the archbishop of Rome replaced by the patriarch of Jerusalem, Johannicius; see A. Zielinski Kinney in this volume. See pp. 331–35.

4. Miceli, "Epistle of Christ from Heaven." See also van Esbroeck, "La lettre sur le dimanche," and the introduction, p. 32.

5. The genre can be traced back more than two thousand years in India; see Stuart H. Blackburn, "Domesticating the Cosmos: History and Structure in a Folktale from India," *JAS* 45 (1986): 527–43; see also Bonnie D. Irwin, "What's in a Frame? The Medieval Textualization of Traditional Storytelling," *Oral Tradition* 10 (1995): 27–53, here 29. The most renowned examples of this genre in the Western culture are Boccaccio's *Decameron* and Geoffrey Chaucer's *Canterbury Tales*. See also above, pp. 134–42.

6. Irwin, "What's in a Frame?," 28.

7. The practical intention of the frame and the mysterious finding story can be compared to the modern film technique of "found footage," applied in several horror films, where the opening scenes prime the viewers to believe in the authenticity of the footage; see Peter Turner, *Found Footage Horror Films: A Cognitive Approach* (London: Routledge, 2019), esp. ch. 3, "Priming the Viewer and Mediated Reality," 79–117.

8. Irwin, "What's in a Frame?," 32.

and laypeople who are part of the frame story. The letter is a liturgical text to be performed and recited by a priest at church and a didactic text on everyday morality. The second type of audience, namely, the extratextual, applies both to the listening and the reading audiences from domestic, ecclesiastical, and monastic spheres,[9] to whom moral warnings are addressed through blessings and woes. Although their depiction is not narrated in detail in the found-footage scene, the text illustrates their emotions of fear and astonishment, culminating in an act of crying.[10] This *appeal to emotion* strategy in the narrative might aim at creating a communication between extra- and intratextual audiences that would trigger the emotions of the recipients and provide a potential role model to them.

We cannot prove with certainty whether the epistle was originally composed with this framing narrative or whether it was introduced in the late medieval period. The Latin Recension II, probably the earliest one, lacks such a framing. Therefore, probably the frame was added to the letter after critique of its authenticity was uttered.[11] The earliest manuscript of the epistle containing a finding story, which is in the Latin Recension I, survived in a tenth-/eleventh-century manuscript, but this finding story is structured differently from the later versions in Greek.

Title and the Finding Story

The title itself utters the genre as well as Christ/God as the author and the main concern of the letter. The text is identified with words such as ἐπιστολή and/or πρόσταγμα θέου and λόγος. The main concern of the letter, which is furthermore elaborated and repeatedly emphasized throughout the text, is the observance of the Lord's Day, as stated in the title. The finding story proceeds the title and informs the readers that it is a letter from heaven descended to Rome. While the church where the letter fell in Rome is given as the church of Saint Peter in the Alpha and Alpha 1 versions, the finding place in the Alpha 2 is the church of Saints Peter and Paul.[12]

9. For the distinction between intra- and extratextual audiences in Byzantine literature, see Stavroula Constantinou, *Female Corporeal Performances: Reading the Body in Byzantine Passions and Lives of Holy Women*, Studia Byzantina Upsaliensia 9 (Uppsala: Uppsala University Press, 2005), 20.

10. Alpha 1, 1.7.

11. See above on the history of the letter, pp. 96f., 109f., and the chapter on the frames, pp. 134–42.

12. There is no clear evidence why a church of St. Peter and Paul instead of the church of St. Peter was preferred. Yet it seems to evoke the church of St. Peter and Paul that was built by Justinian before his ascension to the throne in Constantinople alongside the Church of Saints Sergius and Bacchus at place of the former palace of

The scene of the miraculous finding of the letter is similar in the Greek Recension Alpha, with minor divergences where the archbishop is awakened by a voice or a vision, being urged to go to the altar to receive the letter. It is God's voice in the Alpha, whereas in Alpha 1 the apostle Peter and in the Alpha 2 an angel appears to the archbishop.[13] After seeing the letter hanging in the sky above the altar, with fear and astonishment the archbishop summons a community of men and women, lay and clergy, to witness the miracle. The letter descends to the archbishop only after praying and fasting of the community for three days and nights.[14]

The finding story holds an important part of the whole text, as it implies the reception of the letter and reflects emotional reactions of the witnessing people such as horror, astonishment, and fear accompanied with tears, as stated above. In the Alpha 2 the community prays "Kyrie eleison," an often-repeated phrase by the Greek Orthodox.[15] This seems to be a deliberate choice both to convince readers of the authenticity of the letter and to provide a model for how the letter should be revered.

Letter by the Hand of Christ as God

The letter no doubt covers the most essential part of the whole text. It consists of statements of Christ as God on his previous actions, namely, natural catastrophes with references to the Old Testament; his blessings on the world for the people to flourish; and a long list of woes, all of which have in general the purpose to persuade the readers to observe the Lord's Day. It is composed

Hormisdas, where he resided until 527. In a letter of Justinian to Pope Hormisdas, Justinian inquires whether he could send the relics of Saints Peter and Paul to Constantinople on September 2, 519, followed by the positive response from the pope; see *Collectio Avellana* 187.5 (CSEL 35:645 Günther). The church is also counted as one of Justinian's projects in the buildings of Procopius (*De aedificiis* 1.4.1). The palace of Hormisdas named after the Sassanid prince was also assigned to house the non-Chalcedonian refugees by Theodora after the imperial couple moved the Great Palace in 527; see John of Ephesus, *Vitae sanctorum orientalium* 47 (PO 18:676–77); see also Brian Croke, "Justinian, Theodora, and the Church of Saints Sergius and Bacchus," *DOP* 60 (2006): 25–63. On the foundation of the Church of Saints Peter and Paul and Saints Sergius and Bacchus, see also Jonathan Bardill, "The Date, Dedication, and Design of Sts. Sergius and Bacchus," *Journal of Late Antiquity* 10 (2017): 81–86. Note that the epistle was sent to the church of St. Paul in Constantinople in the Syriac Alpha Recension dated to the thirteenth century; see Bittner, 105.

13. Alpha 1, 1.3; Alpha 2, 1.2.

14. See about such miraculous findings above, p. 141f. About the three days' fasting, see p. 140.

15. Alpha 2, 1.4.

in the first-person singular and directly addresses the readers. The Alpha recensions' variations do not follow the same structural sequence but display similarities in the overall scheme.

The beginning of the letter reflects the motives that led to the decision of Christ as God to compose a letter, with references to the people's previous deeds and the response of Christ, allowing him to justify himself and to be more persuasive. The letter recalls the nonobservance of the Lord's Day in the beginning.[16] Additionally, Alpha 2 implies another "first" letter sent by Christ as God, which obviously did not find acceptance and faith, leading him to pen a second letter.[17] The Gospel verse "Heaven and earth will pass away, but my words will never pass away" (Matt 24:35; Luke 21:33; Mark 13:31) is quoted in the Alpha group, as in other Greek recensions.[18] The beginning chapter speaks of natural catastrophes (Exod 9:13–35; 10:1–20) and the goods sent from God as blessings (Joel 2:19; Num 18:12).[19] The letter proceeds to Christ's decision for a complete destruction of humankind and his dissuasion by the Virgin Mary, holy angels, apostles and martyrs, and John the Baptist[20] (he is not mentioned in Alpha 2).

The scene of Christ's having compassion toward humankind through the entreaty of the Virgin and other holy figures is a dramatic and graphic portrayal of the composition known as deesis scene among modern art historians. The deesis (δέησις) stands for entreaty, petititon, supplication and was first coined by Russian art historian Alexander Kirpičnikov in the nineteenth century[21] to refer to the traditional representation of the Virgin and John the Baptist, occasionally accompanied by other saints and angels, standing on either side of Christ. Although a pre-iconoclastic origin of the motif is suspected, clear iconographic evidence is demonstrable from the ninth and tenth centuries.[22] Little is known about which iconographic composition the Byzantines themselves attributed the word;[23] furthermore, the scene does not

16. §2 in both Alpha 1 and Alpha 2.

17. Alpha 2, 2.

18. See pp. 87, 112.

19. Alpha 1, 2; Alpha 2, 3. See p. 188.

20. Alpha 1, 2.5. See also the chapter above about the punishments, pp. 184–95.

21. Alexander Ivanovic Kirpičnikov, "The Deësis in Orient and Occident," *The Journal of the Ministry of Public Instruction* (1893): 1-26.

22. Thomas von Bogyay, "Deesis," *RBK* 1:1178–86.

23. Walter Christopher, "Two Notes on the Deësis," *Revue des Études Byzantines* 26 (1968): 311-36; Christopher, "Further Notes on the Deësis," *Revue des Études Byzantines* 28 (1970): 161-87; Anthony Cutler, "Under the Sign of the Deēsis: On the Question of Representativeness in Medieval Art and Literature," *DOP* 41 (1987): 145–54. See in general Thomas von Bogyay, "Deesis," *LCI* 1 (Freiburg and others: Herder, 1968), 494–99.

have a narrative connotation at all and seems to be a product of Eastern theology. The composition features the intercessory powers of chiefly the Virgin and John the Baptist and clearly illustrates the hierarchical order of the Christian cosmos. The portrayal of this scene in Alpha 1 is remarkable in that it expresses the entreaty exactly with the term δέησις.[24] Moreover, the scene does not only depict the entreaty of the Virgin Mary and John the Baptist but of other holy angels; apostles and martyrs also participate in the appeal, evoking a deesis scene.[25] On the other hand, the parallel compassion scene in Alpha 2 vividly features the entreaty of the multitude of angels falling on their knees at the foot of God for mercy.[26] An iconographic parallel for this scene is found in the apse painting *Christ in Glory* in Pancarlık Church in Cappadocia, dated to the late ninth or early eleventh century. At the center of the composition, Christ is represented seated on his throne and flanked by four winged creatures. The lower register includes representations of three angels facing toward the center, which is labeled on both sides with the inscription "deesis of angels."[27]

A common subject of the letter is to explain the biblical and historical background of the importance of Sunday and Friday for Christians. A summary of the events that took place on both days is presented, beginning with the creation story. In Alpha 1 the letter informs us that God created heaven and earth on the first day. The Sunday events also include Christ's appearance to Abraham near Mamre (Gen 18), his meeting with Moses on Mount Sinai (Exod 19), the annunciation to Mary by the archangel Gabriel (Luke 1:26–38), and the baptism of Christ (Matt 3:13–17; Mark 1:9–11; Luke 3:21–23).[28] Friday is also emphasized as the day of the creation of humankind and the day of crucifixion. In addition, Wednesday along with Friday is introduced as a day on which fasting is commanded. Fasting on Twelve Days, Easter week, and Pentecost is one of the commands included in the Alpha. The letter also clarifies the duration of the Sunday observance, starting from the ninth hour of Sabbath until the dawn of the second day, as in all other versions.[29]

A total rest from all kinds of work is reinforced by imposing a curse. The Alpha and Alpha 2 versions mention that God has given the six days of the week

---

24. Alpha 1, 2.5. The intercession of the Virgin and John the Baptist is rendered in Alpha with the preposition διά; see Bittner 1905, 12.

25. Doula Mouriki, "A Deësis Icon in the Art Museum," *Record of the Art Museum, Princeton University* 27.1 (1968): 13–28, here 16.

26. Alpha 2, 3.5.

27. Anna Sitz, "'Great Fear': Epigraphy and Orality in a Byzantine Apse in Cappadocia, " *Gesta* 56.1 (2017): 5–26, here 14–15.

28. See also pp. 15f., 87, 191 about these Sunday benedictions.

29. About the duration of Sunday, see p. 182f.

to work and Sunday to come to church to pray for the forgiveness of the sins of the six days.[30] To be more specific, attending both the *orthros* at dawn and *vesper* at sundown on Sunday is strictly commanded in these two versions. The letter also encourages commemorating saints in general through celebrating their feasts, which was seen almost as important as observing Sunday.

A common theme that is also introduced in the Alpha recensions within the context of Sunday observance is an analogy between the Hebrews and the Christians in a didactic and accusive manner, blaming the latter, while Hebrews are described as having been loyal to the law of Moses, hence the observance of Sabbath. Still, the main concern is pointed out as "not violating the law," and Alpha 2 explicitly names Sabbath in this regard as the day on which God gave Moses the law on Mount Sinai.

Finally, the letter imposes Sunday observance through threatening with curses and further tragedy that might befall people. A standard scene that is recorded is the threat of sending wild beasts to snatch the breasts of women and sending Ishmaelites, referring to the Arabic tribes, applying an apocalyptic language.[31] Another catastrophe that is the subject of the threats scattered in the letter is potential damage to the harvest and to natural sources by the hand of God, rendered in formulae such as opening the gates of the sky, pouring boiled water, blood, and ash, sending fiery stones, and drying up the water sources.[32] The fear of the anger of God is expressively depicted through the scene in which the people suffering the disasters call out to those who lie in the graves to open the tombs to be hid from the wrath of God.[33] The cursing of the heretical groups such as Bogomils and Cathars in the fifteenth-century manuscript (Alpha) is obviously a later addition to the original text, when these movements were still considered to pose an active threat, rather than being old menaces of the Orthodox Church, which could have been adopted from the Slavic tradition.

An additional predominant subject throughout the letter next to Sunday observance is morality. Moral warnings concerning daily life are frequently dictated in the form of analogy and, more strikingly, through woes. One of the first moral issues referred to is almsgiving and care for widows and orphans. Christians are blamed for not having compassion for widows and

30. See on this topic above, pp. 145, 152, 194.

31. Alpha 1, 4.4; Alpha 2, 4.7. A similar scene about women is described in the seventh-century Apocalypse of Pseudo-Methodius, in which the Ishmaelites attack pregnant women and infants; see Ps.-Methodius, Apocalypsis 11.17. See on the punishment of women pp. 195–200.

32. See, on a positive connotation of the "open sky" in the Latin recensions, p. 190.

33. Alpha 1, 4.7; Alpha 2, 9.2.

orphans and not giving alms,[34] in contrary to pagans, who are also described as simply non-Christian "nations not having the law."

Warnings vary, addressing people from different social classes such as the common people, clergy, and monastics. A certain emphasis is attached to vertical and horizontal relations between different social strata in the society, such as master and slave, parents and children, and neighbors. Hostility and adultery are strictly forbidden at every place of social life, outside and inside the ecclesiastical and monastic spheres, addressing men and women and monks.[35] The letter was intended to spread and reach as many settlements as possible; therefore reproducing and sending it to other settlements was highly encouraged, and this behavior was the subject of blessing from God, whereas priests who do not read the letter at the church are threatened with curses. This duty of spreading and teaching the letter seems to be assigned to the priest.

Rhetorical Devices for Persuasive Speech

It was important for the composer of the letter to persuade the readers first of all to believe in the authenticity of the letter and second to practice the commands in the text. For this, rhetorical devices are employed, particularly a rhetoric of horror, using verbal threats and graphic images. The verbal threats are largely expressed in the form of woes. The woes and warnings are often within themselves divided into two subcategories: (1) those with a simple "woe" (οὐαί) without specifying what the consequences would be, and (2) those with an articulated consequence. The warnings of disasters that carry an apocalyptic evocation can fall into this category, such as opening the skies, sending plague, and sending winged wild beasts to snatch the breasts of women. Cannibalism can be observed as a tool of horror and terror in the Old Testament.[36] Furthermore, curses are employed, which were essential elements of oral culture but also formed persuasive speech not only in the biblical literature but also in the ancient Near East.[37] Curses reminding of the day of judgment (as well as the day for reward) are found in Alpha 1[38] as well as

34. See on this aspect also pp. 8f., 18–21, 168–72.

35. Alpha 1, 7.11–12.

36. Lev 26:29; Deut 28:53–57; 2 Kgs 6:24–31; Isa 9:19f.; 49:26; Jer 19:7–9; Lam 4:10; Ezek 5:10; Zech 11:9.

37. For an extensive work on the phenomenon of curses in the Near East, see Anne Marie Kitz, *Cursed Are You!: The Phenomenology of Cursing in Cuneiform and Hebrew Texts* (University Park: Pennsylvania State University Press, 2014).

38. Alpha 1, 5.2; 7.14.

most vigorous denunciations, such as inheriting the curse of Satan[39] and the curse of Sodom and Gomorrah,[40] and being judged with Judas.[41]

The text aims to evoke fear and terror among readers through the graphic anthropomorphic image of God, featuring the Father and Jesus Christ intertwined as the author. In Alpha 1, God is portrayed as swearing sitting down on a lofty throne.[42] In Alpha 2, we read that God takes an oath by his right hand and by his shoulder.[43] Uplifting a hand was a pictorial expression to reinforce the performance of taking an oath.[44] God's right hand, which is one of the most frequently mentioned body parts of God in the Bible after head and face, in particular expresses the acting power of God to execute his deeds.[45] In another portrayal of God in the letter, God's anger is communicated with the gesture of "turning face away,"[46] which renders the cutting off of any communication. In addition to the visible imagery of God, in the final section of the letter, where the readers are urged to believe in the letter, God is mentioned with his attribute "invisible" (ἀόρατος) to emphasize the horror effect.

Epilogue by the Archbishop of Rome

After the letter written in the first-person singular ends, the narrative continues and takes the readers back to the scene of the archbishop of Rome and the gathered community. The archbishop testifies to the authenticity of the letter and preaches to the community to believe in the letter. The Alpha 1 version contains a short preaching on love and conveys the essential message of the letter, that is, to observe the holy feasts, whereas in the Alpha and Alpha 2 versions an emphasis is given to copying and transferring the letter.

39. Alpha 1, 5.2.

40. Alpha 1, 6.2.

41. Alpha 1, 7.9. The Judas curse was one of the most frequently employed in the medieval era both in the East and in the West. The earliest examples can be found in Christian epitaphs against tomb violators, and the curse was also frequently used at this time in book colophons against book thieves; see Archer Taylor, "Judas Iscariot Curse," *AJP* 43 (1921): 234–52. See pp. 145, 362, 450, 464, 492.

42. Alpha 1, 4.4.

43. Alpha 2, 11.2.

44. Gen 14:22; Deut 32:40; Ezek 36:7; see Andreas Wagner, *God's Body: The Anthropomorphic God in the Old Testament* (London: T&T Clark, 2019), 98; on anthropomorphism and body rhetoric, see also Christoph Markschies, *Gottes Körper: Jüdische, christliche und pagane Gottesvorstellungen in der Antike* (München: Beck, 2016), 43–56.

45. Markschies, *Gottes Körper*, 125.

46. Alpha 1, 4.10. See Ezek 7:22: "I will turn my face away from the people, and robbers will desecrate the place I treasure. They will enter it and will defile it"; Isa 54:8: "In a surge

Thematic distribution list in order after Alpha 1			
	α^1 (Par. gr. 0947 f. 021v–26)	α^2 (Par. gr 929 f. 548–561)	β^1 (see A. Zielinski Kinney in this volume)
Sending barbaric tribes	2.2	3.2	-
Biblical reference: "Heaven and earth will pass away, but my words will not pass away" (Matt 24:35; Luke 21:33; Mark 13:31)	2.3	2.4	2.3
Sending catastrophes, locusts, hailstones, etc.	2.4	3.4	2.5
God's previous blessing to humankind such as grain, wine, olive oil	2.5	3.1	2.10
God decides to destroy humankind but has compassion	2.6	3.5	2.8
Mercy for widows and orphans	2.7		-
Comparison of Christians with the Hebrews, who do not violate the law	2.9	4.1	-
Creation of heaven and earth	3.1	2.1, 12.3	2.1
Creation of Adam and Eve	3.3		-
Crucifixion on Friday	3.4		
Resurrection on Sunday	3.5		4.3
Fasting on Wednesday and Friday	3.6	10.1	7.9
God appears to Abraham (Gen 18)	3.7		4.4
God appears to Moses on Mount Sinai	3.8 (on Lord's Day)	4.1 (on Sabbath)	-
Annunciation by archangel Gabriel	3.9		4.1
Baptism on the Lord's Day	3.10		4.2
Sending wild beasts to snatch the breasts of women	4.4	4.7	-
Duration of Sunday observance from the ninth hour of Sabbath until the dawn of the second day	4.5	6.5, 10.1	7.8

(*Continued*)

of anger, I hid my face from you for a moment, but with everlasting kindness, I will have compassion on you, says the Lord your Redeemer."

(Continued)

Thematic distribution list in order after Alpha 1			
Threat with opening the gates of the skies	4.6	4.6	3.1
Earthquake, pouring ash, and blood in April	4.6		3.2 (June 14)
People crying to the dead to open the tombs to hide from the anger of God	4.7	9.2	3.4-5
Threat of sending Ishmaelites	4.9	4.4	5.6
The curse of Judas and Sodom and Gomorrah	6.2		5.13–14 [9.2—T only]
Woes addressed to monastics	7.10–11		6.13, 15–17
Pouring fiery stones; fire and hail in June		10.2	+

Letter from Heaven—Greek Recension Alpha 1

[1][47] (1) Εἰς τὸ ὄνομα τοῦ πατρὸς καὶ τοῦ υἱοῦ καὶ τοῦ ἁγίου πνεύματος ἀμήν.

(2) λόγος περὶ τῆς ἁγίας καὶ κυρίας κυριακῆς τῶν ἡμερῶν,[48] ἐν ᾗ Χριστὸς ἀνέστη ἐκ νεκρῶν, ὁ κύριος καὶ θεὸς ἡμῶν Ἰησοῦς Χριστός. εὐλόγησον, δέσποτα.[49]

(3) ἐπιστολὴ τοῦ κυρίου καὶ θεοῦ καὶ σωτῆρος ἡμῶν Ἰησοῦ Χριστοῦ πεμφθεῖσα ἐν τῇ παλαιᾷ Ῥώμῃ ἐν τῷ ναῷ τοῦ ἁγίου ἀποστόλου καὶ πρωτοκορυφαίου[50] Πέτρου, ὃν καὶ εἴρηκεν ὁ Χριστός, ὅτι σὺ εἶ Πέτρος καὶ ἐπὶ ταύτην τὴν πέτρα οἰκοδόμισέ μου τὴν ἐκκλησίαν καὶ πύλαι Ἅιδου οὐ κατισχύσουσιν αὐτήν, καὶ δώσω σοι τὰς κλεῖς τῆς βασιλείας τῶν οὐρανῶν, καὶ ὅσα ἂν δέσῃς ἐπὶ τῆς γῆς, ἔσται δεδεμένα ἐν τῷ οὐρανῷ καὶ ὅσα ἂν λύσῃς ἐπὶ τῆς γῆς, ἔσται λελυμέν´ ἐν τῷ οὐρανῷ. (4) ἐγκρεμασθεῖσα δὲ ἡ ἐπιστολὴ αὕτη μέσον τοῦ ναοῦ ἐν τῷ † ἱερῷ. (5) ὤφθη δὲ τῷ ἐπισκόπῳ Ῥώμης κατ´ ὄναρ ὁ μέγας τοῦ κυρίου ἀπόστολος Πέτρος λέγων· ἀνάστα, ὦ ἐπίσκοπε, ἰδὲ τὴν ἄχραντον ἐπιστολὴν τοῦ κυρίου ἡμῶν Ἰησοῦ Χριστοῦ· (6) ὁ δὲ ἀρχιερεὺς ἔντρομος ἀναστὰς καὶ εἰσῆλθεν ἐν τῷ θυσιαστηρίῳ· καὶ ὁρῶν τὴν ἄχραντον[51] ἐπιστολὴν μέσον τοῦ ναοῦ ἐν τῷ ἀέρι καὶ ἐβόησε μετὰ δακρύων· μέγας εἶ, κύριε, καὶ θαυμαστὰ τὰ ἔργα σου, ὅτι ἐφανέρωσε ἡμῶν αὐτὴν τὴν ἐπιστολὴν εἰς ἅπαντα κόσμον.

(7) καὶ προσκαλεσάμενος ἅπαν τὸ πλῆθος τῶν κληρικῶν τῆς μεγάλης ἐκκλησίας, ἱερέων, μοναζόντων, ἀρχόντων, ἀνδρῶν τε καὶ γυναικῶν καὶ παιδίων, καὶ ἐπὶ τρεῖς ἡμέρας καὶ τρεῖς νύκτας μετὰ δακρύων[52] λέγοντες· δεῖξον ἡμῖν, κύριε, τὰ ἐλέη σου τὰ πλούσια τῷ ταπεινῷ καὶ ἀναξίῳ εὐχέτῃ σου· (8) περὶ δὲ ὥρας τρίτης τῆς ἡμέρας[53] κατελθοῦσα ἡ ἄχραντος ἐπιστολὴ εἰς τὰς χεῖρας τοῦ ἀρχιερέως, καὶ προσκυνήσας καὶ ἀσπασάμενος αὐτὴν μετὰ φόβου καὶ τρόμου[54] καὶ ἀνοίξας εὗρε γεγραμμένα ταῦτα· καὶ λέγει·

---

47. §1 Introduction of the epistle.

48. 1.2 ἁγίας καὶ κυρίας κυριακῆς τῶν ἡμερῶν: Uncommon phrase to emphasize the holiness of Sunday.

49. 1.2 ὁ κύριος καὶ θεὸς ἡμῶν Ἰησοῦς εὐλόγησον, δέσποτα: Common introductory prayer to commence religious service.

50. 1.3 πρωτοκορυφαίου: A late Byzantine Greek epithet for the apostle Peter.

51. 1.6 Attribute for Mary, here used for the epistle.

52. 1.7 Three-day penitential prayer; see p. 140.

53. 1.8 περὶ δὲ ὥρας τρίτης τῆς ἡμέρας: nine o'clock a.m.

54. 1.8 μετὰ φόβου καὶ τρόμου: see 1 Cor 7:15, Eph 6:5; Phil 2:12.

Translation

[1] (1) In the name of the Father, and the Son, and the Holy Spirit. Amen.

(2) Teaching concerning the holy Lord's day, the lord of the days, on which Christ, our Lord and God Jesus Christ, rose from the dead. Bless, Lord.

(3) Epistle of our Lord, God and Savior Jesus Christ sent to ancient Rome to the shrine of the holy apostle and first leader Peter, to whom Christ said, "You are Peter, and on this rock I will build my church, and the gates of Hades will not prevail against it and I will give you the keys of the kingdom of heaven, and whatever you bind on earth will be bound in heaven, and whatever you loose on earth will be loosed in heaven" [Matt 16:18f.]. (4) This epistle was suspended in the middle of the shrine at the sanctuary. (5) Peter, the great apostle of the Lord, appeared to the bishop of Rome in a dream saying, "Wake up, bishop, and behold the undefiled letter of our Lord Jesus Christ." (6) The archpriest woke up trembling and went to the altar and seeing the undefiled letter in the middle of the shrine in the air, he cried out with tears: "Great are you, Lord, and so are your miraculous works that revealed this letter to the whole universe" [see Ps 85:10 LXX].

(7) Thereafter, he summoned the whole community of clerics of the great church; priests, monks, and officials, men and women and children. And for three days and nights they uttered with tears, "Show us, Lord, your abundant mercy to your worthless and humble supplicant" [see Ps 84:8 LXX]. (8) Around the third hour of the day the undefiled letter descended to the hands of the archpriest. He bowed, and kissing it with fear and trembling, and after opening the letter he found these written, saying:

[2][55] (1) ἴδετε, ἴδετε, υἱοὶ τῶν ἀνθρώπων, ὅτι ἔδωκα ὑμῖν, ἀλλ´ ὑμεῖς οὐκ ἐτιμήσατε τὴν ἁγίαν κυριακὴν οὐδὲ ἑορτάσατε. (2) καὶ ἀπέστειλα βάρβαρα ἔθνη καὶ ἐξέχεαν τὸ αἷμα ὑμῶν· καὶ ἐποίησα πολλὰ δεινά, καὶ οὐδὲ οὕτω (ἐμετ)ενοήσατε· (3) οὐκ ἠκούσατε τοῦ εὐαγγελίου λέγοντος· ὁ οὐρανὸς καὶ ἡ γῆ παρελεύσονται, οἱ δέ λόγοι μου οὐ μὴ παρέλθωσιν εἰς τὸν αἰῶνα;

(4) ἀπέστειλα ὑμῖν χειμῶνας κὰ παγετοὺς καὶ λοιμοὺς καὶ σεισμοὺς ἐπὶ τῆς γῆς καὶ χάλαζα καὶ ἀ(κ)ρίδας καὶ κάμπας καὶ βροῦχον[56] καὶ ἄλλα πολλὰ διὰ τὴν ἁγίαν κυριακήν, καὶ οὐδὲ(ν) ἐμετανοήσατε·

(5) καὶ ἔδωκα ὑμῖν σῖτον καὶ οἶνον καὶ ἔλαιον καὶ ἄλλον πᾶν ἀγαθόν, καὶ ὅταν ἐχορτάσθητε, τότε πάλιν εἰς τὸ χεῖρον ποιήσατε. (6) καὶ ἠβουλήθην ἀπολέσαι πάντα ἄνθρωπον διὰ τὴν ἁγίαν κυριακήν, καὶ πάλιν εὐσπλαγχνίσθην διὰ τὴν δέησιν τῆς παναχράντου μου μητρὸς[57] καὶ ἁγίων ἀγγέλων[58] καὶ ἀποστόλων καὶ μαρτύρων, ἔτι δὲ καὶ τοῦ προδρόμου καὶ βαπτιστοῦ[59]· ἀπέστρεψαν τὸν θυμόν μου ἀφ´ ὑμῶν.

(7) χῆρες καὶ ὀρφανὰ καὶ πτωχοὶ κράζουσιν ἔμπροσθέν μου καὶ οὐκ ἠλεήσατε αὐτούς· (8) τὰ ἔθνη[60] ἐλεοῦσι, ὑμεῖς δὲ οἱ χριστιανοὶ ἐλεημοσύνην οὐκ ἔχετε. (9) τοῖς Ἑβραίοις νόμον ἔδωκα διὰ Μωυσέως καὶ οὐ παραβαίνουσιν· (10) ὑμῖν δὲ ἔδωκα τὸ ἅγιον εὐαγγέλιον καὶ τὸν νόμον καὶ τὸ βάπτισμά μου καὶ τοῦτο οὐκ ἐφυλάξατε.

55. §2 The actual letter starts.

56. 2.4 χειμῶνας κὰ παγετοὺς καὶ λοιμοὺς καὶ σεισμοὺς ἐπὶ τῆς γῆς καὶ χάλαζα καὶ ἀκρίδας καὶ κάμπας καὶ βροῦχον: Catastrophes with close reference to the ten plagues in Exod 7–10 are one of the common themes in the Greek versions. They are partially mentioned here, supplemented by natural disasters (storms, frosts, earthquakes).

57. 2.6 παναχράντου μου μητρὸς: The figure of the Virgin Mary is accompanied by the epithet *immaculate* in the Alpha group of manuscripts. Mary is portrayed as having an intercessional role between God and people accompanied by holy angels, saints, and John the Baptist (see on the deesis above p. 295f.). Her holiness is furthermore reinforced when God swears an oath by her name to assure the authenticity of the letter. She is otherwise mentioned in the event of Annunciation, which according to the letter took place on a Sunday.

58. 2.6 ἁγίων ἀγγέλων: Holy angels are mentioned along with the Virgin Mary for the compassion of God. In the α[1] and British Library manuscripts, angels are represented as serving alongside with the priests at church.

59. 2.6 τοῦ προδρόμου καὶ βαπτιστοῦ: In addition to the compassion scene, John the Baptist is twice more mentioned in the epistle. The first is the baptism by John, which is one of the listed Sunday benedictions, where John is also depicted as a model of modesty. The second is included in the oath formula, which demonstrates John's high position in the hierarchy of holiness. See also about John in Latin Recension I, p. 238.

60. Comparison with pagans and also with Hebrews in 2.8 and 2.9.

[2] (1) Behold, behold, mankind, what I gave you, but you neither observed the holy Lord's day nor celebrated it. (2) I sent barbaric tribes and poured out your blood [Ps 78:3 LXX], then I performed many disasters, and you did not repent then. (3) Did you not listen to the gospel saying: "Heaven and earth will pass away, but my words will never pass away"? [Matt 24:35; Luke 21:33; Mark 13:31]

(4) I sent you storms, frosts, plagues, and earthquakes to the earth and hail, locusts, grasshoppers and larvae, and many other things for the sake of the holy Lord's day, yet you never repented.

(5) And I gave you grain, wine, olive oil, and many other goods [Num 18:12; Joel 2:19], and whenever you had feasted then you behaved improperly again (6), and I decided to destroy the whole mankind for the sake of holy Lord's day, but still I had compassion due to the entreaty of my wholly immaculate mother, holy angels, apostles, and martyrs, and moreover the Forerunner and Baptist, and they turned my wrath away from you.

(7) Widows, orphans, and the poor cry aloud in front of me, but you did not have any compassion for them. (8) The gentiles have mercy, but you Christians do not have mercy. (9) I gave the Hebrews the law through Moses, and they do not violate it; (10) but to you I gave the holy gospel, the law and my baptism, and you did not observe them.

[3][61] (1) οὐκ οἴδατε, ἄνθρωποι, ὅτι τὸν οὐρανὸν καὶ τὴν γῆν τὴν πρώτην ἡμέραν ἐποίησα καὶ ἀρχὴν ἡμερῶν καὶ χρόνων καὶ λαμπρὰν κυριακὴν[62] καὶ μέγα πάσχα καὶ ἀνάστασιν ἐκάλεσα· (2) καὶ διὰ τοῦτο πᾶς ἄνθρωπος βαπτιζόμενος ὀφείλει τιμᾷ καὶ ἑορτάζῃ καὶ εἰς τὴν ἁγίαν τοῦ θεοῦ ἐκκλησίαν εἰσέρχεται. (3) οὐκ οἴδατε, ὅτι τὴν παρασκευὴν[63] ἐποίησα τὸν πρωτόπλαστον Ἀδὰμ[64] καὶ τὴν Ἔυα· (4) καὶ πάλιν τὴν παρασκευὴν ἐποίησα τὸν σταυρὸν καὶ ὑπέμεινα ταφήν· (5) καὶ τὴν κυριακὴν ἐποίησα ἀνάστασιν διὰ τὴν τοῦ κόσμου σωτηρίαν. (6) διὰ τοῦτο τὰς ἐντολὰς ὑμῖν ἔδωκα, ἵνα τετράδη[65] καὶ παρασκευὴν πᾶς χριστιανὸς νηστεύῃ κρέατος, τυροῦ καὶ ἐλαίου. (7) οὐκ οἴδατε, ὅτι τὴν ἁγίαν κυριακὴν παρῴκησα ἐν τῷ οἴκῳ τοῦ Ἀβραὰμ διὰ τὴν φιλοξενίαν αὐτοῦ, ὅτε καὶ τὸν μόσχον ἔσθισεν εἰς φιλοξενίαν τῆς ἁγίας τριάδος. (8) καὶ κυριακὴν ἐφάνην τῷ Μωυσῇ ἐν τῷ ὄρει τῷ Σινά,[66] καὶ νηστεύσας ἡμέρας τεσσαράκοντα δέδωκα αὐτῷ τὰς θεοχάρακτας πλάκας [ἤγουν τὸν νόμον.] (9) καὶ τὴν ἁγίαν κυριακὴν ἐμήνυσεν ὁ ἀρχάγγελός μου Γαβριὴλ τὸ 'Χαῖρε' [ἤγουν τὸν εὐαγγελισμόν.] (10) καὶ κυριακὴν ἐδεξάμην τὸ βάπτισμα ὑπὸ τοῦ προδρόμου, ἵνα ὑμῖν δώσω τύπον καὶ μὴ ὑψηλόφρονες ἦτε βαπτισθῆναι ὑπὸ ἱερέων πτωχῶν· [μὴ ὑψηλόφρονες ἦτε· μὴ ὑψηλοφρονῆτε ἢ καί τινος πένητος·] (11) ὁ γὰρ Ἰωάννης ὁ ἐμὸς βαπτιστὴς οὐκ εἶχεν, εἰ μὴ τρίχας καμήλου ἐνδεδυμένος, καὶ οὔτε ἄρτον ἔσθιεν οὔτε οἶνον ἔπιεν.

61. §3 Sunday benedictions.

62. 3.1 λαμπρὰν κυριακὴν: The phrase is earliest recorded by John of Damascus (*Oratio in Sabbatum Sanctum* 26.25). The importance of Sunday is underscored with the first day of creation and the day of resurrection (Easter)—interpreted here as the basis for the covenant between God and Christians who are baptized. Further Sunday benedictions follow below.

63. 3.3 παρασκευὴν: In addition to the list of Sunday events, Friday is counted as the day of creation of Adam and Eve, and the day when Christ was crucified and endured the grave, for which reason abstinence from meat and cheese is commanded.

64. 3.3 πρωτόπλαστον Ἀδὰμ: This epithet of Adam is first attested in the Septuagint (Wis 7:1).

65. 3.6 τετράδη: In addition to Friday fasting, which would include abstinence from meat and cheese, Wednesday fasting is also commanded in the epistle, yet unlike Sunday and Friday, the significance of Wednesday is not elaborated in the epistle. Overall, the letter not only encourages the readers to observe Sunday but takes the opportunity to promote the whole rhythm of religious rituals, including weekly cycle and yearly feasts such as Easter and other feasts of the holy saints.

66. 3.8 ἐν τῷ ὄρει τῷ Σινά: In the Greek Recension Apha 2, God appears to Moses on the Sabbath; see below, p. 321.

[3] (1) Do you not know, mankind, that I made both heaven and earth on the first day and I named it "the head of the days and times" [Gen 1:1–5] and "bright Lord's day" and "the great Passover" and "Resurrection." (2) Because of this, each baptized human being is obliged to esteem and celebrate and come to the holy church of God. (3) Do you not know that on Friday I created Adam, the first human being, and Eve? [Gen 1:26f.] (4) And again, on Friday I took my cross and endured the grave (5) and on the Lord's day I gave the resurrection for the salvation of the world. (6) For this reason, I gave you commandments so that the whole Christian community abstains from meat, cheese, and olive oil on Wednesday and Friday. (7) Do you not know that I dwelled at Abraham's house on the Lord's day, owing to his hospitality when he sacrificed the calf for the hospitality of the Holy Trinity? [Gen 18:1–8] (8) I appeared to Moses on the Lord's day on Mount Sinai [Exod 19:3–6], and after he fasted for forty days, I gave him the stone tablets engraved by God [that is to say, the law; Exod 24:18; 34:28], (9) and on the holy Lord's day my archangel Gabriel proclaimed the "Greeting" [in other words, the Annunciation; Luke 1:26–38]. (10) Also on the Lord's day I received baptism from the forerunner [Luke 3:21f.] in order to give you a model so that you may not disdain being baptized by poor priests [may you never be arrogant, or despise someone who is poor], (11) since John who baptized me wore nothing but clothes of camel hair [Mark 1:6] and did not eat meat or drink wine.

[4][67] (1) οὐαὶ τὸν μὴ τιμῶντα τὸν ἑαυτοῦ σύντεκνον καὶ τὰ ἑαυτοῦ τεκνοπαιδία.

(2) οὐαὶ τοὺς σταυροπάτες·[68] (3) οὐκ οἴδατε, ὅτι τὴν ἁγίαν κυριακὴν μέλλω κρῖναι τὴν οἰκουμένην ὅλην καὶ σταθῆναι ἔμπροσθέν μου βασιλεῖς καὶ ἄρχοντες, πλούσιοι καὶ πένητες, γυμνοὶ καὶ ξετραχηλισμένοι.

(4) ὀμνύω κατὰ τοῦ θρόνου μου τοῦ ὑψηλοῦ, ὅτι, ἐὰν μὴ φυλάξετε τὴν ἁγίαν κυριακὴν καὶ τετράδη(ν) καὶ παρασκευὴν καὶ τὰς ἁγίας ἐπισήμους ἑορτάς, πέμψειν ἔχω θηρία ἰοβόλα,[69] ἵνα καταφάγωσι τοὺς μασθοὺς τῶν γυναικῶν, αἵτινες οὐ θηλάζουσι βρέφη μὴ ἔχοντα μητέρων γάλα, καὶ ἁρπάζουσι λύκοι ἄγριοι τὰ τέκνα ὑμῶν.

---

67. §4 Woes and warnings.

68. 4.2 τοὺς σταυροπάτες: A rather late metaphorical term to denote perjurers. A three-year excommunication with a hundred times repentance imposed on those who trample the cross is mentioned by Ps.-Chrysostom, *Epitimia* LXXIII 10.1 (J. B. Pitra, *Spicilegium Solesmense* [Paris: Didot, 1858], 4:461–64). The term was later used to refer to the Photianists, who violated their promises in a ninth-century work against Photius. In the same treatise the term is applied to refer to the Romans who violate their signatures; see Francis Dvornik, *The Photian Schism: History and Legend* (Cambridge: Cambridge University Press, 1948), 216–18; see also Angela Zielinski Kinney, p. 356, n. 88, in this volume.

69. 4.4 θηρία ἰοβόλα: Sending wild beasts is a common apocalyptic warning to be found in the Alpha group.

[4] (1) Woe to the one who does not show respect to his own godparent or his godchildren!

(2) Woe to those who trample the cross! (3) You do not know that on the holy Lord's day I am going to judge the whole world and I am going to make kings and rulers, rich and poor, stand in front of me naked and ruined.

(4) I swear down from my lofty throne, should you not observe the holy Lord's day, Wednesday, and Friday and other notable feasts as well, I will send poisonous wild beasts so that they devour the breasts of women, who will not be able to nurse their infants left without the milk of their mothers, and wild wolves to snatch your children.

(5) ἐπικατάρατός ἐστιν[70] ὁ ἄνθρωπος ὁ μὴ τιμῶν τὴν ἁγίαν κυριακὴν ἀπὸ ὥρας ἐννάτης τοῦ σαββάτου ἕως δευτέρας ἐπιφαυσκούσης,[71] τὰς δὲ τετράδας καὶ παρασκευὰς νηστείαν καὶ ξηροφαγίαν, καὶ δοξάζετέ [μου] τὸ ὄνομά μου τὸ μεγάλον. (6) εἰ δὲ καὶ ταῦτα οὐ μὴ ποιήσετε, οὐ μὴ πέμψω ἄλλην ἐπιστολήν, ἀλλὰ ἀνόξει θέλω τοὺς οὐρανοὺς καὶ βρέξει θέλω πῦρ, χάλαζαν, ὕδωρ καχλάζον, ὅτι οὐ γινώσκει ἄνθρωπος, καὶ ποιήσω σεισμοὺς φοβεροὺς καὶ βρέξω θέλω αἷμα καὶ στάκτη(ν) Ἀπριλλίῳ καὶ ἅπαν σπέρμα, ἀμπελῶνα καὶ φυτὰ ἐξαλείψω καὶ πρόβατα καὶ κτήνη ὑμῶν ἀφανίσω διὰ τὴν ἁγίαν κυριακήν. (7) καὶ πέμψειν ἔχω θηρία πτερωτά, ἵνα φάγωσιν τὰς σάρκας ὑμῶν, ἵνα εἴπητε· ἀνοίγετε τὰ μνημεῖα, οἱ ἀπ' αἰῶνος κεκοιμημένοι, καὶ κρύψατε ἡμᾶς ἀπὸ τὴν ὀργὴν τοῦ παντοκράτορος κυρίου τοῦ θεοῦ[72] (8) καὶ σκοτίσω τὸ φῶς τοῦ ἡλίου καὶ ποιήσω σκότος, καθὼς τὸ ἐποίησα τοῖς Αἰγυπτίοις ποτὲ διὰ Μωυσῆ δούλου μου. (9) καὶ πέμψει θέλω τὸν Ἰσμαηλίτην λαόν,[73] τοῦ δουλεύειν αὐτῶν καὶ κακῷ θανάτῳ καὶ μαχαίρᾳ ἀπολέσεις, καὶ κλαύσετε καὶ μετανοήσετε. (10) καὶ οὕτω ἀποστρέψω τὸ πρόσωπόν μου, τοῦ μὴ ἀκούσειν ὑμᾶς καὶ διὰ τὴν ἁγίαν κυριακήν·

70. 4.5 ἐπικατάρατός ἐστιν: Maledictions are employed as powerful means of dissuasion, especially in the second part of the letter, in which moral principles are imposed. The same formula is widely found not only in the biblical and Christian literature but in the pagan oral culture.

71. See on the duration of Sunday above, p. 182f.

72. 4.7 ἀνοίγετε τὰ μνημεῖα: The complete phrase ἀνοίγετε τὰ μνημεῖα, οἱ ἀπ' αἰῶνος κεκοιμημένοι, καὶ κρύψατε ἡμᾶς ἀπὸ τὴν ὀργὴν τοῦ παντοκράτορος κυρίου τοῦ θεοῦ is given more or less the same as a citation in the Alpha 1, Alpha 2 and London manuscripts. "Opening the tombs" is closely linked to the act of resurrecting dead bodies and may have a biblical reference to Ezek 37:12; Matt 27:52f. However, our letter refers to the phrase paradoxically depicting the tomb as a place of shelter from the natural calamities to describe the despair of the people and the severity of the calamities, that is, God's wrath. See also note 62 at p. 348.

73. 4.9 τὸν Ἰσμαηλίτην λαόν: See Alpha 2, 4.4 below.

(5) Accursed is the one who does not glorify my great name by observing the holy Lord's day starting from the ninth hour of Sabbat until the dawn on Monday and fasting on Wednesday and on Friday eating dry food. (6) If you ever do not do these, I am not going to send another epistle; rather, I will open the heavens [see Isa 24:18; Gen 7:11] and I will pour fire, hail, boiling water, that a human does not know, and I will make dreadful earthquakes and will pour blood and ash in April and I will wipe away all seeds, vineyards, and trees, and will destroy your sheep, flocks, and herds because of the holy Lord's day, (7) and I will send winged beasts to devour your bodies so that you cry aloud: "Open the tombs you've been sleeping, dead from all eternity, and conceal us from the anger of the almighty Lord of God," (8) and I will darken the sunlight and will bring darkness just as I once made to the Egyptians through my servant Moses [Exod 10:21–29], (9) and I will send the Ishmaelites so that they enslave you and kill you by the sword with a terrible death, and you will then weep and repent (10), but I will turn my face away [Ezek 7:22] not to hear you also because of the holy Lord's day.

[5] [74] (1) κακοῦργοι ἄνθρωποι, ψεῦσται, μοῖχοι, ἀντάρται, ἀσεβεῖς, ἀντίδικοι, ἐχθροί, προδόται, ἐπίβουλοι, βλάσφημοι, ὑποκριταί, βδελυκτοί, ψευδοπροφῆται, ἄθεοι, † ὑδὸν νομιαταί, παρακαμπανισταί, † φονοίσκοι, μισότεκνοι, σταυροπάται, πλεόνεκται τοῦ κακοῦ, παρακροαταί, κατάλαλοι, οἱ μισήσαντες τὸ φῶς καὶ σκότος ἀγαπήσαντες, οἱ λέγοντες· τὸν Χριστὸν ἀγαπῶμεν, τὸν δὲ πλησίον ἀτιμάζομεν, καὶ μισούμενοι κατεσθίοντες τοὺς πτωχοὺς † πτωχοὺς τὰς κόπας· (2) ὢ πόσα μετανοήσωσιν οἱ τὰ τοιαῦτα πράττοντες ἐν ἡμέρᾳ κρίσεως· πῶς οὐ μὴ σχισθῇ ἡ γῆ καὶ καταπίῃ ὑμᾶς ζῶντας; ὅτι ἐργάζονται τὰ ἔργα τοῦ διαβόλου καὶ σὺν τῷ σατανᾷ ἀνάθεμα κληρονομήσουσιν, καὶ τὰ τέκνα αὐτῶν ὡς κονιορτὸς ἀφανισθῶσιν ἀπὸ προσώπου τῆς γῆς.

[6][75] (1) μὰ τὴν μητέρα μου τὴν ἄχραντον καὶ τὰ πολυόμματα χερουβὶμ[76] καὶ τὸν Ἰωάννην τὸν βαπτιστήν μου οὐκ ἐγράφη ἡ ἐπιστολὴ αὕτη ἀπὸ ἀνθρώπου, ἀλλὰ ὁλόγραφός ἐστιν ὑπὸ τοῦ ἀοράτου πατρός. (2) εἴ τις κακόφρονος ἤ τις κακόδοξος εὑρεθῇ καὶ εἴπῃ, ὅτι οὐκ ἔστι ἡ ἐπιστολὴ αὕτη ὑπὸ τοῦ θεοῦ, κληρονομήσει τὸ ἀνάθεμα αὐτὸς καὶ ὁ οἶκός του ὡς τὰ Σόδομα καὶ τὰ Γόμορα καὶ εἰς τὸ πῦρ τὸ ἐξώτερον ἀπελεύσεται ἡ ψυχὴ αὐτοῦ, ὅτι οὐ πιστεύει· (3) τὰ ἀδύνατα τοῖς ἀνθρώποις δυνατά εἰσιν παρὰ τῷ θεῷ.

---

74. §5 List of woes on moral aspects.

75. §6 Oath and curse imposed on those who deny the authenticity of the letter.

76. Celestial biblical creature, *cherubim* (a *cherub*, pl. *cherubim*) is used in the epistle with an attached image of holiness along with other holy figures Mary and John the Baptist. In the celestial hierarchy of Ps.-Dionysius Areopagita, cherubim, along with seraphim, are the nearest to God among all (κατὰ τὴν πάντων ὑπερκειμένην ἐγγύτητα περὶ θεὸν); see Ps.-Dionysius Areopagita, *De caelesti hierarchia* 6.2 (PTS 67:26.17 Heil and Ritter).

[5] (1) O Evil-doers, liars, adulterers, revolters, blasphemers, opponents, enemies, traitors, insidious, slanderous, hypocrites, abominable, false prophets, atheists, plotters, false weighers, murderers, haters of your own children, tramplers of the cross, insatiable of the wicked, disobeyers, gossipers, haters of the light and lovers of the darkness, and those who say, "We love Christ, but despise our neighbor," and those who hate and consume the poor, (2) O how much will they repent on the day of judgment who do all these, how does the earth not open up and swallow you alive? Since they do the works of the devil and they will inherit the curse with Satan, and their children will be wiped away like dust from the surface of the earth.

[6] (1) I swear by my immaculate mother, the many-eyed cherubim and by John, my Baptist, this letter was not penned by a human but was entirely composed by the invisible Father. (2) If someone ill-minded or heretic devises and says that "this letter was not written by God," the person and his household will inherit the curse of Sodom and Gomorrah [Deut 29:22f.] and his soul will be thrown into an extreme fire, for he does not have faith. (3) Things which are impossible to humans become possible by the hand of God.

[7][77] (1) οὐαὶ τὸν ἱερέαν ἐκεῖνον τὸν μὴ δεξάμενον [καὶ] ἀναγινώσκειν ταύτην ἔμπροσθεν τοῦ λαοῦ. (2) οὐαὶ αὐτῇ[78] πόλει ἐκείνῃ καὶ τὸν λαὸν ἐκεῖνον τὸν μὴ ἀκούοντα ταύτην ἐξ ὅλης καρδίας· (3) οὐαὶ τὸν ἄνθρωπον τὸν ὑβρίζοντα καὶ ἀτιμάζοντα τὸν ἱερέαν· οὐ γὰρ ὑβρίζει τὸν ἱερέαν, ἀλλὰ τὴν ἐκκλησίαν τοῦ θεοῦ καὶ τὴν πίστιν καὶ τὸ βάπτισμα αὐτοῦ· ὁ γὰρ ἱερεὺς εὔχεται ὑπὲρ πάντας τοῦ λαοῦ, ὑπὲρ τοὺς μισοῦντας καὶ ἀγαπῶντας αὐτόν· (4) οὐαὶ τοῖς ὁμιλοῦσιν ἀλλήλοις ἐν τῇ θείᾳ λειτουργίᾳ καὶ τὸν ἱερέα σκανδαλίζουσι τὸν δεόμενον ὑπὲρ τὰς αὐτῶν ἁμαρτίας· ὁ γὰρ ἱερεὺς καὶ διάκων εὔχεται ὑπὲρ τοῦ ἀρχιερέως καὶ ὑπὲρ τοῦ χριστωνύμου λαοῦ. (5) οὐαὶ τοῖς μὴ τιμῶσιν τὸν ἴδιον σύντεκνον· σταυρὸν Χριστοῦ ἔφερεν ἐν τῷ οἴκῳ σου δεύτερος πατὴρ ἐγένετό σε διὰ τοῦ βαπτίσματος· (6) οὐαὶ τοῖς μὴ πιστεύουσιν τὰς θείας γραφάς· (7) οὐαὶ τοῖς προσεγγίζουσιν οἰκίαν πρὸς οἰκίαν καὶ ἀγρὸν πρὸς ἀγρόν· ἵνα μὴ τὸν πλησίον παραστρώσουσιν· (8) οὐαὶ τοῖς μισθῶν ἐργάτας [οἱ ποιμένες] ἀποστεροῦσιν· (9) οὐαὶ τοὺς δίδοντας τὸ ἀργύριον αὐτῶν ἐπὶ τόκῳ, ὅτι μετὰ τοῦ Ἰούδα κριθήσονται. (10) οὐαὶ τῷ μοναχῷ τῷ μὴ παραμένοντι τῷ μοναστηριῷ καὶ τὴν ἁγίαν τοῦ θεοῦ ἐκκλησίαν· (11) οὐαὶ τῷ μοναχῷ τῷ πορνεύοντι· (12) οὐαὶ τῷ καταλιπότι τὴν ἑαυτοῦ γυναῖκα καὶ ἑτέρᾳ προσκολληθήσεται·

(13) ἐπικατάρατος ὁ ἱερεὺς ἐκεῖνος ὁ μὴ ἀναγινώσκων ταύτην ἔμπροσθεν τῶν ἀνθρώπων, ὅτι κλεῖ τὴν βασιλείαν τοῦ θεοῦ ἔμπροσθεν αὐτῶν καὶ οὔτε αὐτὸς ἔρχεται οὔτε τοὺς βολεύοντας ἐλθεῖν ἀφήνει. (14) εὐλογημένος ὁ ἱερεὺς ὁ ἔχων καὶ ἀναγινώσκων ταύτην ἔμπροσθεν τοῦ λαοῦ καὶ ἀντιγράψῃ αὐτὴν εἰς ἕτεραν πόλιν καὶ χώρας· ἀμὴν λέγω ὑμῖν, εὑρεῖν μισθὸν ἐν τῇ ἡμέρᾳ τῆς κρίσεως καὶ ἄφεσιν ἁμαρτιῶν. (15) οὐαὶ τὸν οἰκοδεσπότην τὸν μὴ ποιοῦντα καρποφορίαν εἰς τὸν οἶκον αὐτοῦ, ὅτι ὡς ξύλον ἄκαρπον ἐν πυρὶ καυθήσεται· (16) οὐαὶ τὸν προφέροντα δῶρα ἐν τῇ ἐκκλησίᾳ καὶ μάχην ἔχοντα μετὰ τῶν πλησίων αὐτοῦ· (17) οὐαὶ τὸν ἱερέαν τὸν λειτουργοῦντα μετὰ μάχης· οὐ γὰρ μόνος λειτουργεῖ καὶ ὑψοῖ τὰ ἅγια, ἀλλὰ οἱ ἄγγελοι συλλειτουργοῦσι μετ᾽ αὐτοῦ.

77. §7 List of woes and blessings. This section starts with the theme of reception of the letter and continues with moral and religious issues addressed to different social classes; lay, clerics, and monastics.

78. 7.2 αὖ τῇ Bittner.

[7] (1) Woe to that priest who does not receive and read this letter in front of the people! (2) Woe to that city and its people who do not listen to it with all their heart! (3) Woe to the person who insults and disrespects the priest, for he does not insult the priest, but the church of God and the faith and his baptism! Since the priest prays on behalf of everyone in the community: on behalf of those who hate him or those who love him. (4) Woe to those who speak to each other during the divine service and offend the priest who invokes for their sins! For the priest and the deacon pray on behalf of the archpriest and on behalf of the people bearing Christ's name. (5) Woe to those who do not respect their godparent! For he carried the cross of Christ into your house, and he became a second father to you through baptism. (6) Woe to those who do not believe in the divine Scriptures! (7) Woe to those who unite one house with another and field with another field to crowd out their neighbor! (8) Woe to those who deprive their laborers of their wages! (9) Woe to those who lend their money at interest! For they will be judged together with Judas. (10) Woe to the monk who does not engage himself to his monastery and the church of the holy God! (11) Woe to the monk who fornicates! (12) Woe to the one who abandons his own wife and has a relationship with another!

(13) Accursed is that priest who does not read this letter in front of the people, for he shuts the kingdom of God in front of them, and neither he himself will enter, nor he lets in those who wish to enter. (14) Blessed is the priest who takes and reads this letter and sends it to another city or other villages. Amen, I assure you that he will find his reward and remission of his sins on the day of judgment. (15) Woe to that housemaster who does not make an offering for his house! Since he will be burned in fire like a dry branch. (16) Woe to the one who brings presents to the holy church while he has a conflict with his neighbors! (17) Woe to the priest who serves while having a conflict! Since he does not serve alone and exalts the holy things, but the angels serve side by side with him.

[8][79] (1) ἐγὼ θεὸς πρῶτος, ἐγὼ καὶ μετὰ ταῦτα καὶ πλὴν ἐμοῦ ἄλλος οὐκ ἔστι.[80] (2) ποῦ φύγητε ἀπὸ προσώπου μου; ἢ ποῦ κρυβήσετε; (3) ἐγὼ ἐξετάζω καρδὶας καὶ νεφροὺς καὶ γινώσκω τοὺς διαλογισμοὺς τῶν ἀνθρώπων καὶ τὰ κρύφια φανερὰ ποιήσω. (4) ἐγὼ διακελεύω, ἵνα πιστῶς ἐξομολογήσεται πνευματικῷ πατρὶ πᾶς ἄνθρωπος ὃ ἔπραξε ἐκ νεότητος αὐτοῦ· αὐτὸς γὰρ ἐδόθη δι' ἐμοῦ καὶ τῆς ἁγίας μου ἐκκλησίας τοῦ λύειν καὶ δεμεῖν τὰ τῶν ἀνθρώπων ἁμαρτήματα. μακάριος ἄνθρωπος ὁ τιμήσας τὴν ἁγίαν κυριακήν· (5) ἐγὼ Χριστὸς εὐλογήσας αὐτὸν καὶ εὐλογημένος ἔσται.

[9][81] (1) ὁ δὲ ἀρχιεπίσκοπος πάπας Ῥώμης εἶπε πρὸς ἅπαντας· ἀδελφοὶ καὶ τέκνα τῆς ἡμῶν ταπεινώσεως, ἀκούσατε, βασιλεῖς καὶ ἄρχοντες, καὶ σύνετε καὶ μάθετε καλὸν ποιεῖν καὶ κρίνετε καὶ δίκαια ἀκούσατε, πατριάρχαι, μητροπολῖται, ἐπίσκοποι, ἡγούμενοι, πνευματικοὶ ἱερεῖς, ἱερομόναχοι, διάκονοι καὶ ἅπας ὁ τοῦ κυρίου χριστώνυμος λαός, καὶ φυλάξατε, ὅπερ ὥρισεν ὁ δεσπότης Χριστὸς διὰ τὴν ἁγίαν κυριακήν, ἵνα εἰς τὸν κόσμον τὸν παρόντα εἰρήνην ἔχετε· (2) χωρὶς τῆς καθαρᾶς ἀγάπης οὐδὲν καλὸν ἔχει ὁ ἄνθρωπος. (3) καθὼς τὰ ἐδέσμετα χωρὶς ἅλας ἄχρητα καὶ ἄνοστά εἰσιν, οὕτως καὶ οἱ ἄνθρωποι χωρὶς τῆς ἀγάπης ἄχρηστοί εἰσιν. (4) διὰ τοῦτο παρακαλῶ· φυλάξετε καὶ τιμήσατε τὴν ἁγίαν κυριακὴν καὶ ἀνάστασιν, ὥσπερ ἐκλήθη, καὶ τὰς ἐπισήμους ἑορτάς, ἵνα εὕρητε ἔλεος ἐν τῇ ἡμέρᾳ τῆς κρίσεως ἐν Χριστῷ Ἰησοῦ τῷ κυρίῳ ἡμῶν, ᾧ ἡ δόξα καὶ τὸ κράτος εἰς τοὺς αἰῶνας ἀμήν.

79. §8 The last section of the epistle where the author expresses himself as God and Christ to leave a lasting impact on the readers of the authenticity of the letter.

80. 8.1 See Isa 44:6: Ἐγὼ πρῶτος καὶ ἐγὼ μετὰ ταῦτα, πλὴν ἐμοῦ οὐκ ἔστιν θεός.

81. §9 Epilogue by the archbishop of Rome as a last reminder and warning to observe Sunday, the main theme of the epistle.

[8] (1) I am God, the first, and I am after all these and there is nobody but me. (2) Where will you escape from my face and where will you hide yourselves? (3) I inspect your hearts and kidneys and I know people's thoughts and make visible what is hidden [Jer 17:10]. (4) I command that the whole mankind shall confess to the spiritual father for what they have done since their youth since he has been appointed by me and by my holy church to untie and tie the sins of people. Blessed is the one who observes the holy Lord's day. (5) I, Christ, blessed it and it will be blessed.

[9] (1) Then the archbishop, the pope of Rome said to all: "Brothers and children of our humility, listen, o kings and rulers, assemble and learn to behave good and judge and listen to the righteous; o patriarchs, metropolitans, bishops, abbots, spiritual priests, hieromonks, deacons and the whole people bearing Christ's name, and observe what exactly Christ, the Lord, appointed because of the holy Lord's day in order that you have peace in the present world. (2) Without pure love, human being has nothing good. (3) Just as the food without salt is useless and tasteless, so are the people worthless without love. (4) For this reason, I beseech you, observe and honor the holy Lord's day and the Resurrection, just as it is called, and the notable festivals, so that you find mercy on the day of Judgment of our Lord Jesus Christ, to whom shall be the glory and might forever and ever. Amen [1 Pet 4:11]."

Greek Recension Alpha 2

[1][82] (1) Ἐπιστολὴ καὶ πρόσταγμα τοῦ κυρίου ἡμῶν Ἰησοῦ Χριστοῦ ἐμφανισθεῖσα ἐν Ῥώμῃ περὶ τῆς ἁγίας κυριακῆς·

(2) ἐπιστολὴ τοῦ κυρίου ἡμῶν Ἰησοῦ Χριστοῦ ἡ κρεμασθεῖσα ἐν τῷ ναῷ τοῦ ἁγίου Πέτρου καὶ Παύλου[83] μετὰ σεισμοῦ καὶ ἀπειλῆς μεγάλης.

(3) ἰδοῦ· ἄγγελος ἐπέστη τῷ ἀρχιερεῖ λέγων· δράμε ἐπὶ το θυσιαστήριον· καὶ βλέπει τὰς θύρας ἀνεῳγμένας καὶ τὴν ἁγίαν ἐπιστολὴν κρεμαμένην ἐπάνω τῆς ἁγίας τραπέζης.

(4) καὶ προσκαλεσάμενος ὁ ἀρχιερεὺς ἅπαν τὸ πλῆθος τοῦ λαοῦ, μοναχοὺς καὶ λαϊκοὺς καὶ πάντας, πρὸς τὸν ναὸν τοῦ ἁγίου Πέτρου, παρακαρτεροῦντες ἐν νηστείᾳ καὶ δέοντες τρεῖς ἡμέρας καὶ τρεῖς νύκτας μετὰ κλαυθμοῦ καὶ ὀδυρμοῦ μεγάλου, καὶ μετὰ τρεῖς ἡμέρας ἥπλωσεν ὁ ἀρχιερεὺς τὸ φελώνιόν του εἰς τὴν ἁγίαν τράπεζα καὶ εὐθέως ἔπεσεν ἐπάνω τῆς ἁγίας τραπέζης μετὰ, Κύριε ἐλέησον΄· καὶ προσκυνήσας εὗρεν γεγραμμένα τοιαῦτα·

[2][84] (1) Οὐκ οἴδατε, ὦ υἱοὶ τῶν ἀνθρώπων, ὅτι ἐγώ εἰμι ὁ ποιήσας τὸν οὐρανὸν καὶ τὴν γῆν καὶ ὑμᾶς πάντας; (2) οὐκ οἴδατε τὴν πρώτην ἐπιστολήν, ἣν ἐπέστειλα πρὸς ὑμᾶς καὶ οὐκ ἐπιστεύσατε, ἵνα αγιάσω ὑμᾶς διὰ τὴν ἡμέραν τῆς ἁγίας κυριακῆς· (3) καὶ οὐκ ἀπέχετε τῶν πονηρῶν ὑμῶν πράξεων. (4) καὶ οὐ νοεῖτε τὰ γεγραμμένα, ὅτι ὁ οὐρανὸς καὶ ἡ γῆ † οὐ μὴ παρέλθωσι;

[3][85] (1) ἔδωκά σας καρπό, σῖτον, οἶνον καὶ ἔλαιον. (2) καὶ διὰ τὴν ἀπιστίαν, τὴν ἔχετε εἰς τὴν ἁγίαν κυριακήν, ἀπέστειλα ὑμᾶς βαρβάρων ἐπιδρομὰς καὶ ἐξέχεαν τὸ αἷμα ὑμῶν καὶ οὐδὲ οὕτως ἐμετανοήσατε. (3) σεισμοὺς καὶ λιμοὺς καὶ συμπτώματα (οὐκ) ὀλίγα ἐποιήσας ὑμᾶς· (4) ἀλλὰ καὶ σκότος καὶ χάλαζα, ἀκρίδας καὶ ἑρπετὰ ἀπέστειλα ὑμᾶς διὰ τὴν ἁγία μου κυριακὴν καὶ οὐ μὴ μετανοήσατε καὶ οὐκ ἐπιστρέψατε ἐκ τῶν πονηρῶν ὑμῶν πράξεων, ἀλλὰ πωρώθησαν αἱ καρδίαι ὑμῶν, τοῦ μὴ εἰσακοῦσαι τῆς φωνῆς μου. (5) καὶ ἠβουλήθην ἀπολέσαι ὑμᾶς ἐκ τῆς γῆς καὶ πάλιν ἐμετεμελήθην, οὐ διὰ ὑμᾶς, ἀλλὰ τὰ πλήθη τῶν ἀγγέλων μου, οἳ προσέπεσαν ὑποπόδιον τῶν ποδῶν μου καὶ ἐδυσώπησαν ὑπὲρ ὑμῶν, τοῦ ἀποστρέψαι τὴν ὀργήν μου ἀφ᾽ ὑμῶν· καὶ ἐλέησα ὑμᾶς· καὶ πάλιν εἰς τὸ χεῖρον προεκόψατε.

---

82. §1 Introduction of the epistle.

83. 1.1 ἐν τῷ ναῷ τοῦ ἁγίου Πέτρου καὶ Παύλου: see n. 12 above.

84. §2 Actual letter starts.

85. §3 Brief history of the previous blessings and catastrophes on the earth.

Translation

[1] (1) Epistle and command of our Lord Jesus Christ concerning the holy Lord's Day which was manifested in Rome.

(2) Epistle of our Lord Jesus Christ which was hung up at the shrine of Saints Peter and Paul together with an earthquake and a great threat.

(3) "Behold," an angel appeared to the archbishop, saying: "Go to the altar and see the gates that have been opened and the holy letter suspended above the holy altar table."

(4) And the archbishop summoned the whole community of people, monastics, laymen, and all the others to the church of Saint Peter, and they fasted and prayed for three days and nights with much weeping and lamenting; and after three days the archbishop unfolded the veil on the holy altar table, and suddenly [it] fell on the holy altar table and, praying the *Kyrie eleison* prayer on his knees, he found these words:

[2] (1) Do you not know, mankind, that I am the one who created heaven and earth and all of you? (2) You did not acknowledge the first letter which I sent to you and did not believe that I am going to bless you on account of the holy Lord's Day (3) and you did not quit your evil deeds. (4) Do you not understand the scriptures stating that heaven and earth will not pass away? [see Matt 24:35 parr.]

[3] (1) I gave you fruit, grain, wine, and olive oil (2) and because of your unfaith in the holy Lord's Day, I sent you barbaric raids and poured forth your blood and still you did not repent. (3) I made to you earthquakes, famine and disasters that are not few. (4) But also, I sent you darkness and hail, locusts and reptiles because of my holy Lord's Day, yet you neither repented nor desisted from your wicked deeds. But your hearts have become too blind to hear my voice, (5) and I decided to destroy you from the earth, but again I felt compassion, not because of you, but due to the multitude of my angels who knelt at my feet and humbled themselves for you to turn my anger away from you, who fell down on their knees at my foot in supplication, and I had mercy for you. Still, you made progress for the worse.

[4][86] (1) Οὐαὶ ὑμᾶς, ἄθλιοι καὶ ἄφρονες· ὅτι τοὺς Ἑβραίους ἔδωκα ἔνταλμα ἐν τῷ ὄρει τῷ Σινὰ διὰ Μωσέως τῷ σαββάτῳ καὶ φυλάττουσιν καὶ οὐ παραβαίνουσιν· (2) ὑμεῖς δὲ διὰ τὸ βάπτισμά μου, ὅ ἔχετε, οὐκ ἐπιβλέπετε τὸν νόμον μου καὶ οὐκ ἐμνήσθητε μίαν ἐντολήν, ἵνα φυλάττετε τὴν ἁγίαν κυριακήν, (3) ὅτι ἐν αὐτῇ τῇ ἡμέρᾳ μέλλω κρῖναι ζῶντας καὶ νεκροὺς καὶ κατακαύσειν αὐτοὺς ὡς κονιορτὸν ὑπὸ ἅλωνος θερινῆς· (4) ἐγὼ λέγω ὑμᾶς· εἴ τις οὐ τιμᾷ τὴν ἁγίαν κυριακὴν καὶ τὰς λοιπάς μου ἑορτὰς καὶ τὰ γεγγραμμένα οὐ φυλάξετε, ἐξαποστελῶ τὸ Ἰσμαηλιτῶν γένος καὶ κακῷ θανάτῳ ἀποθανεῖτε διὰ τὴν ἁγίαν κυριακὴν καὶ τὰς λοίπας μου ἑορτάς· (5) μὰ τὸν βραχίονά μου τὸν ὑψηλὸν τὸν ἐπισκιάζοντα τὴν κεφαλήν μου τὴν ἄχραντον· (6) οὐ μὴ πέμψω ἄλλην ἐπιστολὴν ἐπὶ τῆς γῆς, ἀλλὰ ἀνοίξω ἔχω τοὺς οὐρανοὺς καὶ βρέξω λίθους πυρίνους (7) καὶ πάλιν (πέμψει) ἔχω ἐφ' ὑμᾶς θηρία ἰοβόλα ἔχοντ' ἀετῶν πτέρυγας καὶ ἀντὶ πτερύγων τρίχας γυναικῶν, ἵνα καταφάγωσιν τοὺς μαστοὺς τῶν γυναικῶν καὶ τὰ νήπια (διὰ) τὴν παρακοὴν ὑμῶν καὶ ἐπὶ τοὺς πόδας τῶν βαρβάρων ἀποθανεῖτε· (8) ἐγὼ γάρ εἰμι πάσης ἐξουσίας δεσπότης,

[5][87] (1) καὶ ἐάν τις οὐ μὴ εἰσέλθῃ εἰ(ς) τὴν ἁγίαν ἐκκλησίαν τὴν κυριακὴν μετὰ παντὸς τοῦ λαοῦ αὐτοῦ, ἔστω ἐπικατάρατος καὶ ἀναθεματισμένος, ὡς καὶ ἐδιδάχθητε, ὅτι, ἐὰν ἔχητε ἁμαρτίας ὑπεράνω τῆς κεφαλῆς σας, ἐγὼ ἐξαλείψω αὐτάς· (2) καὶ ἔσται εὐλογημένος ὁ ἔχων τὴν ἐπιστολὴν ταύτην καὶ ἀναγινώσκων αὐτὴν καὶ εἰς ἑτέρους τόπους καὶ πόλεις καὶ χώρας καὶ κάστρα καὶ χωρία· (3) καὶ ποιήσειν ἔχω αὐτὸν κληρονόμον τῆς βασιλείας μου. (4) οὐκ οἴδατε, ὅτι ἐχώρισα τὰς ἓξ ἡμέρας, νὰ ἐργάζεσθε, καὶ τὴν ἁγίαν κυριακήν, τοῦ προσέρχεσθαι εἰς τὴν ἁγίαν τοῦ θεοῦ ἐκκλησίαν καὶ προσευχόμενοι λυτροῦσθαι τῶν ἓξ ἡμερῶν τὰ ἁμαρτήματα; (5) οὐκ οἴδατε, ὅτι, ἂν οὐδὲν βρέξω, οὐ θερίζετε; (6) τὴν θάλασσαν μεταστήσω·τοὺς ποταμοὺς ξηρανῶ· (7) εἰς τὴν γῆν ἐγώ εἰμι, καὶ ποῦ βούλεσθε φυγεῖν ἀπ' ἐμοῦ;

86. §4 The letter proceeds as more emphasis on the importance of Sunday observance is given in this section through comparison with the Hebrews and a reminder of Sunday as the day of final judgment along with warnings.

87. §5 Threats with curse and excommunication regarding the Sunday observance and the reception of the Sunday letter.

[4] (1) Woe to you, wretched and silly; I gave the Hebrews the law on the mount of Sinai through Moses [Exod 24:18; 34:28] on Sabbath, and they obey it and do not violate it; (2) you, however, through my baptism which you had, did not observe my law and did not remember the single command to observe the holy Lord's Day (3) since on that day I will judge the living and the dead and burn you just like chaff on a threshing floor in the summer [Dan 2:35]. (4) I tell you, if anyone does not observe the holy Lord's Day and the other feasts of mine and if you do not obey the scriptures, I will send you the tribe of Ishmaelites so that you die with a bad death because of the holy Lord's Day and my other feasts; (5) I swear on my arm that overshadows my immaculate head, (6) I will not send another letter to the earth, but will open the skies [see Isa 24:18; Gen 7:11] and throw fire stones (7) and I will send upon you again wild beasts which have eagle wings but with women's hair instead of feathers to snatch the breasts of women and your infants because of your disobedience and so that you give your lives at the feet of the barbarians (8) for I am the Lord, who is all-mighty,

[5] (1) and if someone does not come to the holy church together with all his household, he shall be cursed and excommunicated even if you have been told that I will erase your sins above your head. (2) And blessed will be the one who has this letter and reads it and [sends it] to other places and cities and villages and citadels and hamlets (3), and I will make him an heir of my kingdom. (4) Do you not know that I appointed six days for you to work and the holy Lord's Day so that you come to the holy church of God and to pray to wash away the sins of the six days? (5) Do you not know that you harvest not at all if I do not send rain? (6) I will remove the sea, dry out the rivers, (7) the earth is before me, where do you wish to escape from me?

[6][88] (1) οὐαὶ τὸν οἰκοδεσπότην ἐκεῖνον τὸν ὑβρίζοντα τὸν ἱερέαν, οὐχὶ τὸν ἱερέαν, ἀλλὰ τὴν ἁγίαν τοῦ θεοῦ ἐκκλήσιαν· (2) οὐαὶ τὸν οἰκοδεσπότην ἐκεῖνον, ὅπου οὐκ ἔχει μνήμην ἁγίων· (3) οὐαὶ τὴν γυναῖκαν ἐκείνην τὴν ζυμόνοντα τὴν ἰδίαν προσφορὰν μετὰ μάχης· (4) καὶ τὸν πρεσβύτερον τὸν λειτουργοῦντα μετὰ μάχης· πῶς οὐκ ἐμπυρίζεται τὸ στόμα αὐτοῦ; (5) πᾶς οἰκοδεσπότης, ὅς (οὐ) πλησιάζῃ μετὰ τῶν λαῶν αὐτοῦ ἐν ἑσπερινῷ καὶ ὄρθρου εἰς τὴν λειτουργίαν καὶ ἀπὸ ἐννάτης ὥρας τοῦ σαββάτου μέχρι δευτέρας ἐπιφαυσκούσης μετὰ τοῦ λαοῦ αὐτοῦ, (6) καὶ γυμνοὺς περιβάλλῃ, ξένους εἰσαγάγῃ εἰς τὸν οἶκον αὐτοῦ καὶ δόσῃ πεινῶντας τροφήν, οὐ λήψεται μισθὸν βασιλείας ἐν τῷ νῦν αἰῶνι καὶ ἐν τῷ μέλλοντι.

[7][89] (1) καὶ μετὰ τὸ ἀναγνωσθῆναι τὴν ἁγίαν ἐπιστολὴν φωνὴ ἐκ τοῦ οὐρανοῦ ἦλθε λέγουσα· πιστεύσατε τὴν ἁγίαν ἐπιστολὴν ταύτην· (2) καὶ ἐφοβήθημεν πάντες φόβον μέγαν. (3) καὶ πάλιν λέγω ὑμῶν, ὅτι μὰ τὴν μητέρα μου τὴν ἄχραντον καὶ τοὺς ἁγίους μου ἀποστόλους οὐκ ἐγράφη ἡ ἐπιστολὴ αὕτη παρὰ χειρὸς ἀνθρώπου, οὐδὲ πρόσταξις ἀνθρώπου ἐγένετο, ἀλλ᾽ ἔστι ὁλόγραφος ὑπὸ τοῦ ἀοράτου πατρός· (4) καὶ εἴ τις εὑρεθῇ φλύαρος, ὢν κακοῦργος ἢ θεομάχος, καὶ εἴπῃ, ὅτι ἡ ἐπιστολὴ αὕτη οὐκ ἔστιν τοῦ κυρίου ἡμῶν Ἰησοῦ Χριστοῦ, ἀλλὰ προστασίαις ἀνθρώπου ἐγένετο, ὅτι οὗτος κληρονομήσει τὸ ἀνάθεμα εἰς τοὺς αἰῶνας ἀμήν.

[8][90] (1) ὁ δὲ ἀρχιεπίσκοπος Ῥώμης εἶπεν, ὅτι μὰ τὴν δύναμιν τοῦ θεοῦ καὶ τῶν ἁγίων ἀγγέλων καὶ τῆς κυρίας τοῦ κόσμου καὶ τῶν ἁγίων ἀποστόλων καὶ εἰς τοὺς στεφάνους τῶν ἁγίων μαρτύρων οὐκ ἐγράφη ἡ ἐπιστολὴ αὕτη ὑπὸ χειρὸς ἀνθρώπου, ἀλλ᾽ ἔστι ὁλόγραφος ὑπὸ τοῦ ἀοράτου πατρός· (2) καὶ εἴ τις οὐ μὴ πιστεύσῃ αὐτῇ καὶ πέμψῃ εἰς ἕτεραις ἐκκλησίας, ἡ ὀργὴ τοῦ θεοῦ ἔλθῃ ἐπ᾽ αὐτὸν καὶ ἐξολοθρευθείη ἐκ γῆς τὸ μνημόσυνον αὐτοῦ· (3) καὶ εἴ τις ἴδῃ τὴν ἐπιστολὴν ταύτην καὶ οὐ μὴ ἀντιγραψῃ αὐτήν, ἡ ὀργὴ τοῦ θεοῦ εἰς αὐτούς· (4) παρακαλῶ οὖν ὑμᾶς, ἀδελφοί μου, μηδεὶς ἀπιστήσῃ, ἀλλὰ ἐπιστρέψῃ· (5) εἴ τις δὲ παρακούσῃ, παραχρῆμα ἀπολεῖται. (6) ἀλλ᾽ ἐπακούσετε τοῦ κυρίου ἀληθῶς, ἵνα ἐξαλείψῃ ὁ θεὸς πᾶν ἁμάρτημα αὐτῶν, καὶ τύχητε ἐν ἡμέρᾳ κρίσεως.

88. §6 List of woes on moral and social aspects.

89. §7 The actual epistle ends with the scene of the archbishop.

90. §8 The epilogue of the archbishop to ensure the authenticity of the letter along with warnings to convince the crowd to obey the commandments of the letter.

[6] (1) Woe to that housemaster who insults the priest for he does not insult the priest, but the holy church of God. (2) Woe to that master who does not commemorate the saints, (3) woe to that woman who leavens her own bread with hostility (4) and to the priest who serves with hostility; how is not his mouth set on fire? (5) Any housemaster who does not attend the vesper and the morning prayer from the ninth hour of Sabbath until the dawn of the second day for the liturgy with his household (6) and does not clothe the naked and does not welcome guests into his house and give food to the poor, will not receive the reward of the kingdom in the present time and ever.

[7] (1) After the holy letter was read, a voice from the sky reached saying: "Believe in this holy letter!" (2) and we were all frightened with great fear. (3) And I tell you again, I swear on my immaculate mother and my holy apostles, this letter was not penned by a human hand or was not ordained by a human, but was entirely composed by invisible Father, (4) and should someone be a babbler, being wicked or evil, and say that this letter does not belong to our Lord Jesus Christ, but was formed by means of a human, this person will inherit the curse eternally.

[8] (1) Then the archbishop of Rome said: "I swear on the might of God and the holy angels and the Lord of the universe and the holy apostles and on the crowns of the holy martyrs, this letter was not penned by the hand of a human but was entirely written by the invisible Father (2) and if someone does not believe in that and does not send it to other churches, the wrath of God shall come upon him and his memory shall be wiped away from the earth, (3) and if someone sees this letter but does not copy it, God's anger be upon them, as well, (4) therefore I ask you, my brothers, let no one be unfaithful but turn to God; (5) if someone disobeys, he will be destroyed on the spot, (6) but listen to the Lord in earnest so that God eliminates all of their sins and meets them on the day of judgment."

[9][91] (1) Οὐκ οἴδατε, υἱοὶ τῶν ἀνθρώπων κακοῦργοι καὶ ἀνελεήμονες, ψεῦσται, ἄδικοι, κατάφρονες—καταφρονεῖτε τὸν θεὸν καὶ τὰς ἐντολὰς αὐτοῦ, οἱ μισήσαντες τὸ φῶς καὶ ἀγαπήσαντες τὸ σκότος καὶ κατεργαζόμενοι τοὺς ἰδίους γείτονας, ὅπως οὐ μὴ γένη(ται) σεισμοὶς καὶ χάνῃ ἡ γῆ καὶ καταπίῃ ὑμᾶς—(2) ὡς διὰ τὴν ἁγίαν κυριακὴν πέμψω εἰς ὑμᾶς τοιοῦτον φόβον λεόντων, ὅτι ἀναλέγετε· ἀνοίξατε τὰ μνήματα καὶ κρύψατε ἡμᾶς, οἱ ἀπ αἰῶνος κεκοιμημένοι, ὅτι οὐκ ἐφέρομεν τὴν ἀπειλὴν ταύτην καὶ τὸν θυμὸν τοῦ θεοῦ παντοκράτορος. (3) οὐκ οἴδατε, ὅτι τὰ ἔθνη νόμον οὐκ ἔχουσιν, ἀλλὰ φύσιν τὰ τοῦ νόμου ποιοῦσιν, ὑμεῖς δὲ μᾶλλον καὶ τὸ βάπτισμά μου ἔχετε, καὶ τὰ γεγραμμένα οὐ νοεῖτε· (4) ἠθέλησα γὰρ ἀπολέσαι πάντα ἄνθρωπον ἐν νυκτὶ καὶ ἡμέρᾳ καὶ πάλιν ἐσπλαγχνίσθην, οὐχὶ δι᾽ ἐσᾶς, ἀλλὰ διὰ τὴν παράκλησιν τῆς μητρός μου καὶ διὰ τῆς ἁγίας κυριακῆς καὶ τῶν ἁγίων μου ἀγγέλων· (5) ἔπεμψα εἰς ὑμᾶς σεῖσμους καὶ λιμοὺς (καὶ συμ)πτώματα διὰ τὴν ἁγίαν κυριακήν·

[10][92] (1) ἀμὴν ἀμὴν λέγω ὑμῖν, ὅτι, (ἐὰν) οὐ φυλάξητε τὴν ἁγίαν κυριακὴν καὶ τὰς λοιπάς μου ἑορτάς, καὶ ἀπὸ ὥρας ἐννάτης τοῦ σαββάτου νὰ ἀφήνετε τὸ ἐργόχειρον ἕως τῆς δευτέρας ἐπιφαυσκούσης ἡλίου, καὶ τετράδας καὶ παρασκευὰς μετὰ νηστειῶν καὶ λιτανειῶν οὐ ποιῆτε, (2) ἀμὴν λέγω ὑμῖν, ἐὰν οὐ πιστεύσητε τὰ γεγραμμένα, βρέξω ἔχω λίθους πύρινους καὶ πῦρ καὶ χάλαζα, Ἰουνίῳ μηνί, καὶ ὕδωρ πικρὸν εἰς ὅλον τὸν κόσμον καὶ εἰς τὴν ἑνδεκάτην τοῦ Ὀκτωβρίου μηνός, ἵνα καὶ τοὺς ἀγροὺς ὑμῶν ἀφανίσω παντελῶς· (3) ἀλλὰ διὰ τὰ ἄχραντά μου Χερουβίμ, ὅπου ἐδυσώπησαν ὑπὲρ ὑμῶν, ἐμετεμελήθην καὶ ἐφύλαξα ὑμᾶς καὶ ἐγενόμην ἵλεως· (4) καὶ πάλιν ὀμνύω εἰς ὑμᾶς κατὰ τῶν ἁγίων μου ἀγγέλων, ἐὰν μὴ φυλάξητε τὴν ἁγίαν κυριακήν, ἀποστρέψω ἔχω τὸ πρόσωπόν μου ἀφ᾽ ὑμῶν (5) καὶ οὐ μὴ ἐλεήσω ὑμᾶς καὶ ποιήσω ἔχω τὸ φῶς σκότος, ἵνα καταφάγετε ἀλλήλους διὰ τὴν ἁγίαν μου κυριακήν· (6) καὶ ἀποστρέψω τὸ πρόσωπόν μου ἀφ᾽ ὑμῶν καὶ γένηται κλαυθμὸς καὶ ὀδυρμὸς καὶ θρῆνος καὶ πῦρ καὶ συνοχὴ ἐθνῶν, καὶ ού μὴ ἐλεήσω ὑμᾶς.

91. §9 After an interruption of the archbishop's epilogue, the actual letter continues.

92. §10 Warnings reinforced with oaths to observe the Sunday.

[9] (1) You do not know, mankind, wicked and merciless, liars, unjust, scornful—you despise God and his commandments, hating the light and loving the darkness and acting against your own neighbors so that the earthquakes happen and the earth opens up and swallows you in—(2) like this I will send such a fear of lions that you will say, "Open the tombs and hide us, o the dead for long time, for we could not bear this destruction and the wrath of the *Pantocrator.*" (3) Do you not know that the nations fulfill the essence of the law, although they do not have the law? You, however, have even more and my baptism, yet you do not apprehend what is written. (4) Therefore, I wanted to destroy the whole mankind in one night and day, and I had compassion again, not because of you, but because of the intercession of my immaculate mother and for the sake of my holy Lord's Day and my holy angels. (5) I sent you earthquakes and famine and disasters because of the holy Lord's Day.

[10] (1) Amen, amen, I tell you, that if you do not observe the holy Lord's Day and my other feasts and quit your handiwork starting from the ninth hour of Sabbath until the sunrise on the second day and do not spend Wednesday and Friday with fasting and praying, (2) truly I tell you, if you do not believe in the scriptures I will pour fiery stones and fire and hail in the month of June and bitter water to the whole universe and on the eleventh of October to destroy your fields completely. (3) However, because of my immaculate cherubim who convinced me for you, I recanted and preserved you and have become gracious. (4) Yet I swear again to you on my holy angels if you do not observe the holy Lord's Day I will turn my face away [Ezek 7:22] from you (5) and I will not have mercy for you and will make the light darkness in order to make you devour each other because of my holy Lord's Day (6) and I will turn my face away [Ezek 7:22] from you and there shall take place weeping and lamenting and mourning, burning and conflict of nations, but I will not forgive you.

[11][93] (1) Εἰ δὲ ἀκούσατε τῆς φωνῆς μου καὶ τὰ γεγραμμένα φυλάξητε καὶ μετανοήσατε ἐξ ὅλης τῆς καρδίας ὑμῶν, οὐ μὴ ἐγκαταλίπω ὑμᾶς εἰς τὸν αἰῶνα. (2) καὶ πάλιν λέγω ὑμᾶς κατὰ τῆς δεξιᾶς μου χειρὸς καὶ τοὺς βραχίονάς μου τοὺς ὑφηλοὺς καὶ πάντας τοὺς ἁγίους μου· (3) ἐὰν φυλάξητε ὅς΄ ἄν ἀγγέλλω ὑμῖν, οὐ μή σας ἐγκαταλίπω εἰς τὸν αἰῶνα διὰ τὴν ἁγίαν μου κυριακήν· (4) καὶ εἴ τις μεταδιδόναι . . . πτωχῶν, ἐγὼ πληθυνῶ τοὺς καρποὺς αὐτοῦ καὶ τὰ ἀγαθὰ αὐτοῦ ὡς τὰ ἄστρα τοῦ οὐρανοῦ καὶ ὡς τὴν ἄμμον παρὰ τὸ χεῖλος τῆς θαλάσσης, καὶ χρεωστὴς αὐτοῦ γενήσομαι ἐν τῷ νῦν αἰῶνι καὶ ἐν τῷ μέλλοντι καὶ καταστήσω αὐτὸν μετὰ τῶν ἁγίων μου. (5) εἴ τις δὲ δανείσῃ τὸν πλησίον αὐτοῦ καὶ ἀναλάβῃ τόκον, νὰ ἔχῃ τὸ ἀνάθεμα εἰς τοὺς αἰῶνας· (6) καὶ εἴ τις εὑρεθῇ θεομάχος ἢ φλύαρος καὶ ἀπαρνήσεταί μου, κἀγὼ ἀπαρνήσομαι αὐτὸν ἔμπροσθεν τοῦ πατρός μου τοῦ ἐν οὐρανοῖς καὶ τῶν ἁγίων ἀγγέλων· (7) καὶ εἴ τις ἔχῃ ἔχθραν μετά τινος καὶ οὐ μὴ εἰρηνεύσῃ, οὔκ ἔστιν ἄξιος μεταλαβεῖν τοῦ ἀχράντου μου σώματος καὶ τοῦ τιμίου μου αἵματος καὶ ἵνα κἀγὼ διαλύσω αὐτὸν τὰ δεσμὰ τῶν ἁμαρτιῶν αὐτοῦ † ου θρῆνος μετὰ τῶν ἁγίων ἀποστόλων καὶ τὰ στέφανα τῶν ἁγίων μου μαρτύρων.

[12][94] (1) οὐκ ἐγράφη ἡ ἐπιστολὴ αὕτη ὑπὸ ἀνθρώπου τινός, ἀλλ΄ ἰδιόγραφος ἐπέμφθη ἐκ χειρὸς κυρίου. (2) καὶ εὐλογημένος ὁ ἄνθρωπος ἐκεῖνος, ὅπου νὰ πάρῃ τὴν ἐπιστολὴν ταύτην εἰς ἕτερον χάρτην καὶ ἀναγινώσκει αὐτὴν εἰς ἕτερας ἐκκλησίας, καὶ ἂν ἔχῃ ἁμαρτίας ὑπεράνω τῆς κεφαλῆς αὐτοῦ, ἐγὼ ἐξαλείψω αὐτάς. (3) οὐκ οἴδατε, κακοῦργοι ἄνθρωποι, ὅτι τὴν ἁγίαν κυριακὴν ἐποίησα τὸν οὐρανὸν καὶ τὴν γῆν; οὐκ οἴδατε, ὅτι ἐγὼ δίδω καὶ ἐσεῖς καυχᾶσθε; καὶ ἐὰν μὴ δώσω, ποῦ βούλεσθε ζῆν; (4) καὶ πάλιν πῶς φυγεῖν βούλεσθε ἐκ τῶν χειρῶν μου; (5) καὶ εἴ τις φλύαρος εὑρεθῇ ἢ θεομάχος καὶ εἴπῃ, ὅτι ἀνθρωπίνης χειρὸς ἐγένετο ἡ ἐπιστολὴ αὕτη καὶ οὐκ ἔστιν παρὰ θεοῦ, γενήσεται πᾶς ὁ οἶκος αὐτοῦ ἄκληρος καὶ αὐτὸς γίνεται κληρονόμος τοῦ ἀσβέστου πυρὸς εἰς τοὺς ἀπεράντους αἰῶνας· (6) καὶ μακάριος ὁ ἄνθρωπος ἐκεῖνος, ὅστις γράψει τὴν ἐπιστολὴν ταύτην καὶ δώσει αὐτὴν εἰς ἕτερας ἐκκλησίας, ὅτι οὐ μὴ καταισχυνθῇ εἰς τὸν αἰῶνα, ἀλλὰ λήψεται μισθὸν βασιλείας ἐν τῷ νῦν αἰῶνι καὶ ἐν τῷ μέλλοντι. ᾧ ἡ δόξα καὶ τὸ κράτος ἅμα τῷ πατρὶ καὶ τῷ υἱῷ καὶ τῷ ἁγίῳ πνεύματι νῦν καὶ ἀεὶ καὶ εἰς τοὺς αἰῶνας τῶν αἰώνιων ἀμήν.

93. §11 Further warnings regarding Sunday observance and social aspects.

94. §12 Statements on the originality of the letter.

[11] (1) If you listen to my voice and observe the scriptures and repent from the heart, I will not forsake you forever. (2) I tell you again by my right hand and my high shoulders and by all my saints, (3) if you observe, what I announce to you, I will not forsake you forever because of my holy Lord's Day. (4) If someone gives alms to the poor, I will amplify his fruits and his goods, just as much as the stars in the sky and the sand on the sea shore, and I will be his guarantor in the present time and ever and I will place him among my saints. (5) If someone lends to his neighbor and receives interest, he shall have the curse forever, (6) and if someone acts in hostility against me and talks nonsense and denies me, I, too, will deny him in front my Father in heaven and my holy angels (7) and if someone has a hostility with someone and makes no peace, he is not worthy of taking part in my immaculate body and my reverent blood and is not worthy for me to loosen the bonds of his sins. † lament with the holy apostles and the crowns of my holy martyrs.

[12] (1) This letter was not penned by a certain man but was sent from the hand of the Lord as an autograph, (2) and blessed is that human who transfers this letter to another roll and reads it to the other churches; even if he has sins over his head, I will wash them away. (3) Do you not know, wicked humans, that I created heaven and earth on the Lord's Day? Do you not know that I give and you glorify? And If I do not give, where do you think that you are going to live? (4) And again, how can you escape from my hands? (5) And if someone happens to be a babbler and fighter against God and says that this letter was written by a human hand, not by God, all his family will be heirless, and he will be an heir of immortal fire eternally. (6) Blessed is that human whoever writes this letter and gives it to other churches for he will not be disappointed forever but will receive the reward of kingdom in the present time and in the future, to whom shall be glory and might with the Father, Son, and Holy Spirit now and forever and ever. Amen.

6

LETTER FROM HEAVEN—GREEK RECENSION BETA

Angela Zielinski Kinney

Manuscripts and Edition

In the previous chapter, Canan Arıkan-Caba gives a summary of the Greek manuscript tradition for the Letter from Heaven (BHG 812i–s) and presents the older of the two recensions offered in this volume, that is, Greek Recension Alpha, the "Rome recension." This chapter presents the younger "Jerusalem recension," which bears signs of later composition. Maximilian Bittner's study of the Greek manuscripts of the Jerusalem recension assigns the siglum β to a group of texts (the Greek Recension Beta), all of which are related to the Beta text presented by Athanasius Vassiliev.[1] Vassiliev's Beta text stems from the sixteenth-century Codex Roman. Casanatense 481 (olim G. vi. 7), s. xvi, folios 27–37.[2] Bittner prints Beta (β) alongside a parallel text he found, designated as Beta 1 (β_1); linguistically, β_1 is older than β, but the manuscript likewise dates to the sixteenth century: Codex Carpentras (BM) 103 (Omont 36), s. xvi, folios 1–20. Bittner's choice to print Beta and Beta 1 in parallel columns is illuminating in that it shows clearly where there are gaps or expansions in one text or the other. Although Beta 1 is earlier in terms of its orthography and language, Beta sometimes has a fuller text. Canan Arıkan-Caba helpfully transcribed another manuscript (not mentioned by Vassiliev or Bittner) containing a version of the Greek Recension Beta: Codex Tübingen Mb 33, s. xvi, folios 131–137 (=T). The version in this manuscript contains some interesting variations, which have been considered in the following edition and commentary.

1. Bittner, *Brief Christi*, 7-10. See above, p. 81f.

2. Vassiliev, *Anecdota graeco-byzantina*, 28–32.

The work below begins with a brief introduction to the narrative structure of Greek Recension Beta and a prosopographical excursion. This is followed by an edition of the Greek text with apparatus, an English translation of the text, and a commentary on textual and thematic features. The edition here is not intended as a complete critical edition, as the three texts preserve the Letter from Heaven frozen at different moments in time and perhaps in different contexts, as evinced by variations in language as well as additions and deletions. To produce a more comprehensive philological study, much more time and effort would have to be devoted to the texts of the Greek Recension Beta, as well as to other Eastern versions (e.g., those written in Armenian, Slavonic) of the Letter from Heaven; in the end, this would probably still fail to produce a stemma, for reasons discussed at length by Uta Heil.[3] Rather, this edition strives merely to capture the fullest and most comprehensible version of the Greek Recension Beta. The "base" text of the edition is Beta 1, as it preserves older language forms than Beta. The Beta text is used to fill in lacunae from Beta 1, when they exist, and in rare cases, the text of Beta is preferred. If Beta preserves additions to Beta 1, these have generally been included in the main body of the text. To these versions, some readings and additions have been included (in the main body of text or in the apparatus) from the Tübingen manuscript (denoted by the siglum T). Insignificant differences in tenses, wording, and even phrasing among the three versions are not the main focus of this study; rather, the text and apparatus presented here aim to preserve the most complete *content* from the Greek Recension Beta texts.

Structure

Analysis of the content of Greek Recension Beta may be found in the commentary accompanying the text, as many of the general themes do not differ from those of Greek Recension Alpha.[4] However, the structure of Greek Recension Beta is worth discussing briefly here, as it is helpful to situate the letter in its cultural and literary context. Greek Recension Beta is organized according to a framing narrative built on three main structural episodes. As this narrative structure was directly lifted from Greek Recension Alpha, the episodes are basically identical in terms of their function. For Beta these narrative episodes are (1) the letter's authorship is announced, and the discovery of the letter by the patriarch of Jerusalem is described; (2) the content of the letter, delivered by Christ (sometimes amalgamated with God the Father);

3. See Heil, pp. 38, 85, 134–200.
4. See Arikan-Caba, pp. 300f.

and (3) a final epilogue testifying to the authenticity of the letter by the patriarch and exhorting the audience or reader to copy and disseminate the text. The fantastical discovery story leads to the revelation of an ominous divine text. As intriguing as the initial discovery story is, the content of the letter outshines it with harangue and apocalyptic threats, and the miraculous finding story is practically forgotten by the end of the text.

The framing narrative[5] in the Greek Recension Beta underscores the divinity of the letter, connects its discovery to a named or prominent people in the community, and provides a way to import the letter into a liturgical service. Although evidence is lacking as to how often or whether the letter was ever read aloud in the church service, the texts include hallmarks of the liturgy, even referring to important moments in the service (such as the priest's words at the Eucharist, 6.16). The version of the text in the Tübingen manuscript includes a "second epilogue," which has been printed and translated in the following edition. While the initial ending of the letter ended on a formal, liturgical note, the ending of the Tübingen text harks back to the original framing story and emphasizes the emotional reaction of the author (and others present) when the original letter descended. It may be said that the Tübingen text makes a deliberate attempt to connect the exhortations at the end of the Greek Recension Beta to the terrifying, supernatural delivery of the letter at the beginning of the text: if the deeply apocalyptic flavor of the text had not convinced the audience, perhaps a final appeal to human emotion would have an effect.

Prosopography

The finding narrative in Greek Recension Beta names a patriarch of Jerusalem: Iohannicius (Ἰωαννίκιος). A man with this name is listed in the sequence of patriarchs recorded on thirteenth-century diptychs from Jerusalem (in order: Nicephorus I, Iohannicius, Sophronius II, Euthymius),[6] but he is omitted from William of Malmesbury's list of patriarchs in his *De gestis regum Anglorum*, which records only Nicephorus I, Sophronius II, and Euthymius.[7]

---

5. See also the remarks on the frame above, pp. 31, 134–42.

6. Athanasios Papadopoulos-Kerameus, *Ανάλεκτα Ιεροσολυμιτικής Σταχυλογίας* (St. Petersburg: Kirschbaum, 1891), 1:125 (line 24), 139 (line 16), 142 (line 20).

7. William of Malmesbury, *De gestis regum Anglorum*, ed. and trans. R. A. B. Mynors, completed by R. M. Thomson and M. Winterbottom, *William of Malmesbury, Gesta Regum Anglorum*, Oxford Medieval Texts (Oxford: Oxford University Press, 1998), vol. 1, §368: *Theofilus; Niceforus; hic aedificavit ecclesiam sancti Sepulcri quae nunc est, favente*

The diptychs and the work of William of Malmesbury are the only two sources for the order of the Jerusalem patriarchs during the eleventh century. Moreover, there is scant information about these patriarchs; even their dates are uncertain. In 1964 the first recorded seal of Sophronius II was published by Vincent Laurent.[8] Philip Grierson, in his reexamination of the seal, published a study of the dates of Sophronius's patriarchy, revising the dates from "*ante* 1059–*post* 1064" to *post* 1048–1076/83.[9] In this article, Grierson states, "All that we really know of [Sophronius] is that he was patriarch in 1076 and had ceased to be so by 1083."[10] The same is true, sans precise dates,[11] in the case of the elusive Iohannicius in the Jerusalem diptychs, about whom Grierson writes:

> Nothing further is known of this person, who is not mentioned by any other source. It is possible that his name was not that of a patriarch at all but of some benefactor of the church, for the names of such persons seem to have been sometimes inscribed on the diptychs, to ensure their being remembered in the prayers of the faithful, with the consequence that they were accidentally interpolated into episcopal lists when these were copied for record purposes. He may on the other hand have been dropped from William's list either through inadvertence or because of the brevity or unimportance of his pontificate.[12]

It may be argued that the Letter from Heaven provides a piece of evidence that Iohannicius indeed existed and served as a patriarch of Jerusalem. The prominence of Iohannicius in the finding narrative requires the spiritual authority of a patriarch. Only the patriarch is able to move the stone and open it to reveal the heavenly letter. Indeed, the Tübingen manuscript includes a

---

Achim Soldano; Sofronius, in cuius tempore Turchi, Jerosolimam venientes, pugnaverunt cum Saracenis et omnis interfecerunt, et obtinuerunt civitatem; Christiani autem remanserunt ibi sub dominio Turchorum; Euthimius, Simeon. See the commentary by Thomson and Winterbottom, *William of Malmesbury* 2:324.

8. Vincent Laurent, "Un sceau inédit du patriarche de Jérusalem Sophrone II trouvé à Winchester," *The Numismatic Circular* 72 (1964): 49–50.

9. Philip Grierson, "The Dates of Patriarch Sophronius II of Jerusalem (post 1048–1076/83)," *Revue des Études Byzantines* 43 (1985): 231–35. The previous dating (accepted also by Laurent) of Sophronius's time as patriarch is the work of Venance Grumel, *La chronologie*, Traité d'Études byzantines 1 (Paris: Presses Universitaires de France, 1958), 452.

10. Grierson, "Dates of Patriarch Sophronius II," 231.

11. The name does appear in a chronological list, establishing a relative method of dating his office, if he served as patriarch.

12. Grierson, "Dates of Patriarch Sophronius II," 232.

special postscript in Iohannicius's voice, emphasizing how terrifying the miracle was for everyone who viewed it and reminding the audience exactly who opened the stone. Although it is perhaps too much to assume that late medieval or early modern audiences knew the names of the patriarchs during this period, a named patriarch in the context of such a great miracle must have functioned as a stamp of holiness or authenticity for the text; that Iohannicius appears in numerous versions of the Greek Recension Beta is a strong indication that he was indeed a patriarch of Jerusalem.

If Greek Recension Beta is taken as a confirmation of the Jerusalem diptychs that there did exist a patriarch Iohannicius, Grierson's work then provides an approximate date for his time in office: "If Nicephorus was really succeeded by a patriarch named Joannicius, we should have to leave room for his period of office after 1048 [CE]."[13] Thus, approximate dates for Iohannicius's time as patriarch must be post-1048 CE and ante-1076 CE, since William of Malmesbury states definitively that Sophronius was patriarch when the Turks captured Jerusalem in 1076 CE.[14]

I intend to explore the prosopography of Iohannicius and the potential historical ramifications of his prominence in the Letter from Heaven in a future article. For the time being, it suffices to toy with the idea of a historical Iohannicius and a deliberate reference to the milieu of eleventh-century Jerusalem. Could there be, then, any contextual importance for the place and potential dating of the discovery narrative in Greek Recension Beta? One reason to place the letter's descent in the eleventh century may pertain to the political and religious unrest of this century. It would be silly to argue that Jerusalem was ever truly free of conflict, but tensions among followers of Christianity, Islam, and Judaism were especially strong in the eleventh century. From the Muslim conquest in 638 CE until the Crusader conquest in 1099 CE, church structures and monasteries in and around Jerusalem suffered from neglect, looting, and destruction. Raids and conflicts caused renovation work to be abandoned. A decree ordering the demolition of synagogues, monasteries, and churches was issued on October 18, 1009 CE, by the Fatimid caliph al-Ḥākim.[15] Only the

13. Grierson, "Dates of Patriarch Sophronius II," 235.

14. Grierson, "Dates of Patriarch Sophronius II," 234.

15. On the reasons for the destruction of the Church of the Holy Sepulchre, see Jennifer Pruitt, *Building the Caliphate: Construction, Destruction, and Sectarian Identity in Early Fatimid Architecture* (New Haven, CT: Yale University Press, 2020), 106–13. On the restoration of the church, see Robert Ousterhout, "Rebuilding the Temple: Constantine Monomachus and the Holy Sepulchre," *The Journal of the Society of Architectural Historians* 48 (1989): 66–78.

Church of the Nativity in Bethlehem and the Monastery of St. Catherine at Sinai were spared this destruction.[16]

In addition to earthly turmoil, several great natural disasters occurred in the eleventh century. A number of serious earthquakes were documented, including a devastating one in Jerusalem in 1016 CE, as a result of which the Dome of the Rock collapsed and ongoing renovations to the Church of the Holy Sepulchre were destroyed. Although apocalyptic thoughts were a staple of all medieval periods, many astronomical and meteorological events in the eleventh century were interpreted as apocalyptic omens. Indeed, these phenomena—at least in terms of their documentation in the sources—seemed especially prevalent in this time period.[17] One remarkable celestial appearance was a comet in late 1097 CE: "When we approached the city of Heraclea, we saw a certain sign in the sky shining with whitish brilliance, which appeared in the shape of a sword with the point stretching toward the East."[18] This comet is recorded by astronomers from other lands as well.[19] Various chronicles and histories of the Crusades document meteor showers and

---

16. See Denys Pringle, *The Churches of the Crusader Kingdom of Jerusalem: A Corpus*, vol. 1, *A–K (excluding Acre and Jerusalem)* (Cambridge: Cambridge University Press, 1993), 137–56. The reasons for sparing St. Catherine's at Sinai vary; however, there was (and still is) a mosque within the monastery (although the mosque was constructed during the rule of Fatimid king El Amer Bahkam Allah [1101–1130 CE], about a hundred years after the order of al-Hākim).

17. There are a variety of catalogues and texts to consult on this topic, for example, María José Martínez Usó and Francisco J. Marco Castillo, "A Review of the Dall'Olmo Survey of Meteors, Meteor Showers and Meteorites in the Middle Ages from Medieval European Sources," *Journal for the History of Astronomy* 48 (2017): 62–120; and David Cook, "A Survey of Muslim Material on Comets and Meteors," *Journal for the History of Astronomy* 30 (1999): 131–60.

18. Fulcher of Chartres, *Historia Hierosolymitana*, ed. Heinrich Hagenmeyer (Heidelberg, 1913), 203–5: *Vidimus in caelo signum, quoddam, quod alburno splendore fulgens apparuit in modum ensis figuratum, cuspide versus Orientem protento. sed quod futurum promittebat nesciebamus, sed praesentia et futura Domino committebamus.*

19. C/1097 T1 (visible October 2, 1097, until October 25, 1097) according to the work of Gary W. Kronk, *Cometography: Ancient–1799* (Cambridge: Cambridge University Press, 1999), 186–88. Florence of Worcester, *Chronicon ex Chronica* (1118 CE), wrote that the comet was visible for fifteen days from the third of the calends of October. A "broom star" was observed on October 2, 1097, in the Chinese text *Liao shih* (1350 CE); further Chinese texts record more observations about the comet and its appearance on October 6, 1097: *Wen hsien t'ung k'ao* (1308 CE); *Sung shih* (1345 CE); *Hsü Thung Chien Kang Mu* (1476 CE). *Koryo-sa* (1451), a Korean text, records the "broom star" as appearing on October 4, 1097. The Japanese text *Dainihonshi* (1715) records the first observation of the comet on October 8, 1097, stating that on October 25 it moved out of sight. Kronk lists many more testimonia for the comet on p. 188.

strange heavenly appearances, which were interpreted as signs of the last days and reasons to embark on a holy war.

These signs and wonders, along with apocalyptic concerns and the Crusaders' arrival in Jerusalem, may have provided an appropriately ominous backdrop for a narrative in which Christians are urged to distinguish themselves from non-Christians by honoring Sunday as a holy day. The chaos of the eleventh century could have provided a reason and need for the letter: after the ordered destruction of churches and monasteries, a strong collective Christian identity—which could be expressed and exemplified by honoring Sunday instead of Friday or Saturday—is imagined as an ark of stability amid external and internal conflicts.[20] Is it merely coincidence that the recension in which the letter descends to Iohannicius happens to be the only recension wherein this occurs in Bethlehem? As stated earlier, only St. Catherine's Monastery at Mount Sinai and the Church of the Nativity at Bethlehem escaped destruction in the early eleventh century. The Church of the Holy Sepulchre was rebuilt by the middle of the eleventh century and rededicated on July 15, 1049. If the author of the "core text" of Greek Recension Beta knew that the patriarch Iohannicius commenced his service in 1048 CE, he may have chosen to have the letter descend in Bethlehem—a church that was not still undergoing repairs in 1048 CE and a site that remained exceedingly holy after 1099 CE as well. (On the basis of its theological and historical import, the Church of the Nativity was the site of Crusader coronations.) In this case, the Letter's descent in Bethlehem could be defended as a narrative decision made based on an eleventh-century setting. Future work on Greek Recension Beta will include an attempt to make some sense of the various dates mentioned in this recension, in particular September 4, the date on which the letter is said to have descended.

As discussed in the following commentary, there are occasionally hints of a more sophisticated theology in Greek Recension Beta; the metaphorical import of the Word of/as Christ descending in Bethlehem, the birthplace of Jesus (as opposed to a descent to the Holy Sepulchre, traditionally the site of his crucifixion and burial), cannot be ruled out as too lofty. Latin Recension IIIa in fact refers to a descent over the altar of Golgotha (in the Church of the Holy Sepulchre); in Greek Recension Beta, the Letter descends in the Church of the Nativity in Bethlehem, so that both holy sites are represented, albeit in different languages and traditions.

20. On Sunday as an identity marker, see Heil, pp. 152f., 176, 201–205.

Letter from Heaven—Greek Recensions Beta

[1][21] (1) Ἐπιστολὴ τοῦ κυρίου ἡμῶν Ἰησοῦ Χριστοῦ. (2)[22] αὕτη ἡ ἐπιστολὴ ἔπεσεν ἐξ οὐρανοῦ ἐν Ἱερουσαλὴμ τῇ πόλει[23] ἐν μηνὶ Σεπτεμβρίῳ δ'.

(3) πρόλογος καὶ διήγησις τοῦ φοβεροῦ καὶ φρικτοῦ θαύματος τοῦ γενομένου ἐν τῷ λαῷ τῆς Ἱερουσαλήμ.

(4)[24] λίθος ἔπεσεν μικρὸς ἐν Βηθλεὲμ τῇ πόλει, καὶ ὁ λίθος μικρὸς ἦν, τὸ δὲ βάρος φοβερόν. (5) οὐδὲ γὰρ ἴσχυσε τοῦτον κυλῖσαί[25] τις, εἰ μὴ ὁ μακαριώτατος πατριάρχης Ἱεροσολύμων Ἰωαννίκιος[26] σύναξιν ποιήσας μετὰ ἀρχιερέων καὶ ἱερέων καὶ γραμματέων ἡμέρας τρεῖς καὶ νύκτας,[27] καὶ τότε ἐξῆλθε φωνὴ ἐκ

---

21. §1 Introduction and discovery narrative of the letter.

22. 1.2 Only Beta states that the letter descended in Jerusalem in this line. All the versions include a specific date (the fourth day of September).

23. ἐξ οὐρανοῦ ἐν Ἱερουσαλὴμ τῇ πόλει] ἐν Ἱερουσαλὴμ τῇ πόλει **β**; ἐξ οὐρανοῦ **β1 T**

24. 1.4 Bethlehem is the specific city where the letter descended (within the province of Jerusalem). The Church of the Nativity, built over the traditional birthplace of Jesus in Bethlehem, is implied as the location for the letter's descent.

25. κυλῖσαι literally means "to roll." Compound forms of this verb are used in biblical descriptions of the sealing and unsealing of a tomb by rolling a boulder in front of it (Mark 15:46 προσεκύλισεν; 16:3 ἀποκυλίσει; 16:4 ἀποκεκύλισται; Matt 27:60 προσκυλίσας; 28:2 ἀπεκύλισεν; Luke 24:2 ἀποκεκυλισμένον). The patriarch is said to "squeeze" (ἐπίασεν) the stone in Greek Version Gamma, upon which it opens and reveals the letter.

26. Ἰωαννίκιος The name of the patriarch of Jerusalem is given as Ἰωαννίκιος in Beta and manuscript T, but omitted in Beta 1. A man by this name may have been a patriarch of Jerusalem sometime between 1048 and 1072 CE; see the prosopographical excursus preceding this edition and commentary. A certain Iohannicius is listed on diptychs listing the patriarchs of Jerusalem; the diptychs are allegedly from the thirteenth century. The texts of the diptychs may be found in Papadopoulos-Kerameus, *Ἀνάλεκτα Ἱεροσολυμιτικῆς Σταχυλογίας* 1:125 (line 24), 139 (line 16), 142 (line 20). However, Iohannicius is omitted in a list of patriarchs incorporated by William of Malmesbury in his *Gesta regum* (Mynors 1998, 644–47 [cap. 368]). See Amnon Linder, "Christian Communities in Jerusalem," in *The History of Jerusalem: The Early Muslim Period (638–1099)*, ed. Joshua Prawer and Haggai Ben-Shammai (New York: New York University Press, 1996), 160.

μακαριώτατος πατριάρχης Ἱεροσολύμων Ἰωαννίκιος] πατριάρχης Ἱεροσολύμων **β1**; μακαριώτατος πατριάρχης Ἰωαννίκιος **β**; ἐν Ἱεροσολύμων μακαριώτατος πατριάρχης Ἰωαννίκιος **T**

27. ἱερέων καὶ γραμματέων ἡμέρας τρεῖς καὶ νύκτας Beta 1 omits the number of days and nights but adds the scribes. Beta and manuscript T both indicate that the clergy met for three days and nights. The version of T is especially elaborate, adding that Iohannicius

celebrated services with the chief priests, "the elders and the entire people bearing the name of Christ, and he ordered everyone to fast and pray to God and to eat nothing at all for three days and three nights." Within the Beta group, only T mentions fasting and the participation of Christians who are not clerics. In the background of all the Beta recensions is the practice of three-day penitential prayers. This interpretation of the three-day gathering is also pronounced in Greek Recension Alpha 1, 1.7 (see p. 302f.), which bears a certain resemblance to manuscript T, as the clerics pray and fast with laypeople. Notably, as the date of the letter's descent was in September, this cannot have been the Paschal triduum. On the *triduum* in general, see Uta Heil, p. 140.

In the background, especially with regard to Beta 1 and the manuscript T, may be an allusion to Matt 16:21: Ἀπὸ τότε ἤρξατο ‹ὁ› Ἰησοῦς δεικνύειν τοῖς μαθηταῖς αὐτοῦ ὅτι δεῖ αὐτὸν εἰς Ἱεροσόλυμα ἀπελθεῖν καὶ πολλὰ παθεῖν ἀπὸ τῶν πρεσβυτέρων καὶ ἀρχιερέων καὶ γραμματέων καὶ ἀποκτανθῆναι καὶ τῇ τρίτῃ ἡμέρᾳ ἐγερθῆναι ("From that time on, Jesus began to show his disciples that he must go to Jerusalem and undergo great suffering at the hands of the elders and chief priests and scribes and be killed and on the third day be raised"). This verse combines a prophecy made by Jesus, the location of Jerusalem, a community of elders, archpriests, and scribes, and the importance of the third day, all of which are in the various Beta narratives.

On miraculous letters from heaven, see Speyer, *Bücherfunde in der Glaubenswerbung der Antike*, especially the section "Bücher vom Himmel," which discusses heavenly letters contained in stones and meteors (23-42); see also above, p. 141f. The Adoration of the Magi (E-clavis: ECCA 230), an apocryphal text written in Old Turkic, features a tiny but miraculously heavy stone given to the magi by the infant Jesus (ca. 36–46): "For the Magi he broke off a chunk of stone from the corner of the stone cradle, like breaking off bread, and gave (it to them). So the Magi took the stone, but were not able to lift it themselves, and when they loaded it onto a horse, the horse could not lift it either, so they took counsel (together): 'This stone is very heavy! This one chunk of stone, why is the horse, too, unable to lift it for us? It will be impossible for us to carry it!' they said to one another." The magi manage to deposit the stone in a well, whereupon fire rises up to the sky and the men cower in fear. Facsimile, transcription, and German translation of the original text by Friedrich W. K. Müller, "Die Anbetung der Magier, ein christliches Bruchstück," in *Uigurica*, Abhandlungen der Königlich Preußischen Akademie der Wissenschaften, Philosophisch-historische Klasse 2 (Berlin: Akademie der Wissenschaften, 1908), 4–10 and Tafel 1–2. English translation above by Adam Carter Bremer-McCollum, "The Adoration of the Magi: A New Translation and Introduction," in *New Testament Apocrypha: More Noncanonical Scriptures*, ed. Tony Burke (Grand Rapids: Eerdmans, 2020), 2:3–12. The date of the Turkic text can only be roughly estimated; a date around or before 1000 CE is given by Leonardo Olschki, "The Crib of Christ and the Bowl of Buddha," *JAOS* 70 (1950): 161-64, here 161. The Uyghur text has been dated to the eighth century or even earlier. On the Adoration of the Magi in late antique Christianity, see the study by Alexander Markus Schilling, *Die Anbetung der Magier und die Taufe der Sasaniden. Zur Geistesgeschichte des iranischen Christentums in der Spätantike*, CSCO 621, Subsidia 120 (Leuven: Peeters, 2008).

ἱερέων καὶ γραμματέων ἡμέρας τρεῖς καὶ νύκτας] ἱερέων καὶ γραμματέων ἡμέρας γ' καὶ νύκτας γ' **β1**; ἱερέων ἡμέρας τρεῖς καὶ νύκτας **β**; πρεσβυτέρον καὶ πάντος τοῦ χριστονύμου λαοῦ καὶ ἐπρόσταξε πάντας ἵνα ποιησῶσιν νηστίαν καὶ δέησιν πρὸς τὸν θέον καὶ οὐδώλος ἐγευσάντο τρὶς ἡμέρας καὶ τρὶς νύκτας **T**

τοῦ οὐρανοῦ λέγουσα· (6) "λάβε,[28] πατριάρχα, τὸν λίθον μετὰ χειρῶν σου καὶ κύλισον αὐτόν."[29] (7) καὶ λαβὼν ὁ πατρίαρχης τόν λίθον καὶ κυλίσας,[30] εὐθέως[31] ἠνοίχθη ὁ λίθος καὶ εὑρὼν ταῦτα γεγραμμένα·

---

28. λάβε The divine directive to seize (λάβε) the stone is the same as that given to John in Rev 10:8, where he is commanded to take the opened book from the angel: Ὕπαγε, λάβε τὸ βιβλίον ("Go, take the book"); and 10:9, Λάβε καὶ κατάφαγε ("Take and eat"). In the Letter from Heaven, the command to seize the stone is followed immediately by the "opening" of the stone and the revelation of written text. See Augustine, *Conf.* 8.12.29: *Tolle, lege* ("Take, read"), although Augustine receives his revelation via bibliomancy.

29. καὶ κύλισον αὐτόν] *om.* **β T**

30. ἠνοίχθη ὁ λίθος The emergence of the letter from the stone is a parallel to the resurrected Christ emerging from the tomb, which had been sealed with a large stone. In the same way that Christ as incarnate Word exits the sealed tomb, so also the words of the letter written by Christ are sealed in stone and are revealed on the third day of prayer to a worthy recipient (Iohannicius). The "opening" of the stone as if it were a scroll may also be compared to Rev 20:12, where the deceased stand before the great throne for the last judgment. Sealed scrolls are opened at this time to reveal secret information, and the dead are judged according to what is written on the scrolls: καὶ βιβλία ἠνοίχθησαν, καὶ ἄλλο βιβλίον ἠνοίχθη, ὅ ἐστιν τῆς ζωῆς, καὶ ἐκρίθησαν οἱ νεκροὶ ἐκ τῶν γεγραμμένων ἐν τοῖς βιβλίοις κατὰ τὰ ἔργα αὐτῶν. See also the sealed words associated with prophetic revelations, e.g., Isa 29:11: "And the vision of all this has become to you like the words of a book that is sealed. When men give it to one who can read, saying, 'Read this,' he says, 'I cannot, for it is sealed.'"

31. καὶ κυλίσας, εὐθέως] *om.* **β T**

Translation

[1] (1) Epistle of our Lord Jesus Christ. (2) This letter fell from heaven in the city of Jerusalem on the fourth day of the month of September.

(3) Introduction and exposition of the terrifying and awful miracle that occurred among the people of Jerusalem.

(4) In the city of Bethlehem, a small stone fell down, and the stone was small, but its weight was formidable. (5) For no one could budge it except the most blessed patriarch of Jerusalem, Iohannicius, who had held (church) services with the chief priests and priests and scribes for three days and nights. And then a voice came from the heavens, saying, (6) "Seize the stone, patriarch, with your hands and turn it over." (7) And the patriarch seized the stone and turned it over; immediately, the stone was opened and the following letter was found:

[2][32] (1) "Ἴδατε, ἄνθρωποι, ἴδατε, ὅτι ἐγὼ ἐποίησα τὸν οὐρανὸν καὶ τὴν γῆν, τὴν θάλασσαν καὶ πάντα τὰ ἐν αὐτοῖς, καὶ ὑμεῖς καταφρονήσατε ἃ ἐδήλωσα ὑμῖν διὰ τῶν προφητῶν μου καὶ ἀποστόλων μου. (2) καὶ ἔδωκα[33] ὑμῖν διδασκάλους[34] τοῦ ἐλέγχειν τὰς ἁμαρτίαις ὑμῶν ἐπὶ τῆς γῆς. (3) καὶ οὐδὲ οὕτως ἐμετανοήσατε οὐδε τοῦ εὐαγγελίου μου τὰ λόγια ἠκούσατε· 'ὁ οὐρανὸς καὶ ἡ γῆ παρελεύσεται, οἱ δὲ λόγοι μου οὐ μὴ παρέλθωσιν εἰς τὸν αἰῶνα.' (4)[35] καὶ πάλιν ἐπιστολὴν στέλλω πρὸς ἐσᾶς τοὺς ἀνθρώπους, διότι σὰς ἔστειλα τὴν πρώτην ἐπιστολὴν καὶ οὐδὲ οὕτως ἐμετανοήσατε οὐδὲ ἐπιστεύσατε.

32. §2 The text of the letter begins.

33. ὑμῖν διὰ τῶν προφητῶν μου καὶ ἀποστόλων μου. καὶ ἔδωκα] *om.* **B** (lacuna)

34. διδασκάλους] διδασκαλίας ὑπὸ τοῦ παναγίου καὶ ζωαρχίκου πνευμάτος εἰς τὸ ἐλέγχιν ἁμαρτημάτων καὶ ουδώλλως ἐμετανοήσατε οὐδε ἐπειστρέψατε ἀπὸ τὰς ἀνομίαν ἡμῶν. ἀλλὰ μᾶλλον εἰς τὸ χεῖρον ἐπροκόψατε **T**

35. 2.4 This is allegedly the second letter sent from heaven to earth. On the number of letters in various recensions, see Heil, pp. 135f.

[2] (1) "Know, people, know that I created the heavens and the earth, the sea and all that is in them, and you have flippantly regarded the things that I revealed to you through my prophets and my apostles. (2) And I gave you teachers to convict your sins on earth. (3) And yet you still did not repent, nor did you heed the words of my gospel, 'The heavens and the earth will pass away, but my words will not pass away' [Matt 24:35]. (4) Once again I am sending a letter to you people, just as I sent you the first letter, and you did not repent or believe.

(5)[36] καὶ διὰ τοῦτο ἀπέστειλα χειμῶνας πλείστους καὶ παγετοὺς, παραλλαγμοὺς καὶ πῦρ καὶ χάλαζαν καὶ ἀκρίδας καὶ βρούχους[37] καὶ ποταμοὺς ἀτάκτους, καὶ οὐδὲ οὕτως ἐμετανοήσατε οὐδὲ τοῦ εὐαγγελίου μου τὰ λόγια ἠκούσατε· 'γίνεσθε ἀγαθοὶ καὶ ἐλεήμονες, ὅτι κἀγὼ ἀγαθὸς καὶ ἐλεήμων εἰμὶ καὶ εὔσπλαγχνος.'[38] (6)[39] διὰ τοῦτο ἀποστέλλω ἀστραπὴν ἐκ τοῦ οὐρανοῦ, καὶ κατακαύσει πάντα ἄνθρωπον ἐκ νυκτί, ὅταν οὐδεὶς γινώσκῃ, καὶ καύσειν ἔχω τῶν ἀπίστων τὰς[40] καρδίας διὰ τὴν ἁγίαν μου κυριακήν.

36. 2.5 Disastrous natural phenomena and plagues are threatened as retaliation for ignoring God's commandments. The meaning of παραλλαγμούς is unclear: it may mean changes in weather, or perhaps earthquake tremors; the latter is perhaps preferable. The duplicate words for "locusts" strike the reader as strange; it may be more probable that βρούχους is a corruption of βροχή ("rain") in the plural, here meaning "floods." This pairs nicely with the "unruly rivers"; see the list of threats in Latin Recension III, where rivers overflow their banks. However, see the interpretation of *bruchus* in the Latin recensions by Haines, *Sunday Observance*, 184n41. Some of the plagues are those from Exodus: hail (χάλαζαν) is described in Exod 9:18–34, and locusts (ἀκρίδας) in Exod 10:4–19. But there is a distinctly apocalyptic flavor to the text, which can be seen clearly in the parallels from Revelation. Hail and fire correspond to Rev 8:7 (χάλαζα καὶ πῦρ), and violent hailstorms are part of the apocalyptic vision in Rev 11:19 (ἀστραπαὶ καὶ φωναὶ καὶ βρονταὶ καὶ σεισμὸς καὶ χάλαζα μεγάλη / "there were flashes of lightning, rumblings, peals of thunder, an earthquake, and heavy hail"). T in particular seems to draw on Rev 11:19: πλήστους, κέρους **β** ρόντες καὶ ἀστραπὲς καὶ χάλαζα καὶ συμοὺς μεγάλους. See on the punishments in general also pp. 187–90.

37. πλείστους καὶ παγετοὺς, παραλλαγμοὺς καὶ πῦρ καὶ χάλαζαν καὶ ἀκρίδας καὶ βρούχους] πλείστους καὶ παραλλαγμοὺς καὶ πῦρ καὶ χάλαζα(ν) καὶ ἀκρίδας καὶ βρο(ύ)χους **B**; πλήστους, κέρους βρόντες καὶ ἀστραπὲς καὶ χάλαζα καὶ συμοὺς μεγάλους ἐν ὅλῃ τῇ γῇ **T**

38. γίνεσθε ἀγαθοὶ καὶ ἐλεήμονες, ὅτι κἀγὼ ἀγαθὸς καὶ ἐλεήμων εἰμὶ καὶ εὔσπλαγχνος This is not a precise biblical quotation, but it alludes to Luke 6:36 and Matt 5:48.

39. 2.6 See Rev 8:7, where fire burns up a third of the earth (τὸ τρίτον τῆς γῆς κατεκάη).

40. κατακαύσει πάντα ἄνθρωπον ἐκ νυκτὶ, ὅταν οὐδεὶς γινώσκῃ, καὶ καύσειν ἔχω τῶν ἀπίστων τὰς] κατακαῦσαι ἔχω (followed by a significant lacuna) **β**; κατάκαυσιν παντὰς τοὺς μὴ τιμώντας τὴν ἅγιαν μοῦ ἀνάστασιν τὴν κυριακὴν **T**

(5) And for this reason, I sent extremely powerful storms and frosts, (weather?) changes and fire and hail and locusts and the larvae of locusts, and wild rivers, and yet you did not repent or heed the words of my gospel: 'Be good and merciful, since I also am good and merciful and compassionate to you.' (6) For this reason, I am sending lightning from heaven, and it will burn up every human being at night, at a time nobody will know, and I will burn the hearts of the unbelievers for the sake of my holy Lord's day.

(7)[41] καὶ ἠβουλήθηκα ἀπολέσαι πάντα ἄνθρωπον ἀπὸ προσώπου τῆς γῆς διὰ τὴν ἁγίαν μου κυριακήν.[42] (8) καὶ πάλιν ἐσπλαγχνίσθηκα διὰ τὴν πανάχραντόν μου μητέρα[43] καὶ ἀπόστρεψα[44] τὸν θυμόν μου ἀφ' ὑμῶν[45] καὶ διὰ τὰ δάκρυα[46] . . . καὶ[47] ἐπιστρέψατε ὀλίγον. (9) καὶ ἐνέπλησά, ἔδωσά σας καὶ ἔδωκα ὑμῖν πᾶν ἀγαθόν.[48] (10)[49] ἔδωσά σας σῖτον καὶ οἶνον καὶ ἔλαιον,[50] καὶ πᾶν ἀγαθὸν ἐνέπλησα ὑμῖν,[51] καὶ ὅταν ἐχορτάσθητε, πάλιν εἰς τὸ χεῖρον προεκόψατε.[52]

---

41. 2.7–8 Christ already wanted to destroy humankind for neglecting to honor Sunday, but he relents because of the intercession of Mary and her tears. See Greek Recension Alpha 1, 2.4, where Mary is likewise called "immaculate" and serves as the mediator between Christ and humankind. The supernatural and salvific nature of tears (especially female tears) in medieval Christianity is a complex theme. "The Middle Ages were saturated with tears" (Emile M. Cioran, *Tears and Saints* [Chicago: University of Chicago Press, 1995], 29). The Virgin Mary and Mary Magdalene are the most famous people who weep in the NT, and their tears provide a saintly model for a number of medieval women, such as Margery Kempe; see Susan Eberly, "Margery Kempe, St. Mary Magdalene, and Patterns of Contemplation," *The Downside Review* 103 (1989): 209–23. On the efficacy of religious weeping in general as a mediating force, see Piroska Nagy, "Religious Weeping as Ritual in the Medieval West," *Social Analysis: The International Journal of Anthropology* 48 (2004): 119–37. On late medieval understandings of the Virgin's tears and role in mercy, see Eamon Duffy, "Mater Dolorosa, Mater Misericordiae," *NBf* 69 (1988): 210–27. Tears played a special role in emotional displays during the Crusades as well; on this topic see Stephen Spencer, *Emotions in a Crusading Context 1095–1291* (Oxford: Oxford University Press, 2019), 113–72. See also C. Arikan-Caba on weeping in Greek Recension Alpha, though this refers to the recipients of the letter, p. 293.

42. καὶ ἠβουλήθηκα ἀπολέσαι πάντα ἄνθρωπον ἀπὸ προσώπου τῆς γῆς διὰ τὴν ἁγίαν μου κυριακήν.] *om.* **B** (lacuna); καὶ πολάκις ἐβουλήθην τοῦ ἀπόλεσε ἀπὸ προσώπου πασῆς τῆς γῆς πᾶσα ἄνρθωπον διὰ τὴν ἅγιαν κυριακὴν, τὴν ἥμεραν ἀναστάσεως μου **T**

43. καὶ πάλιν ἐσπλαγχνίσθηκα διὰ τὴν πανάχραντόν μου μητέρα] διάδεσιν καὶ παρακάλεσιν τῆς παναχράντου μου μητέρος καὶ τοῦ τιμίου προδρόμου καὶ βαπτίστου μου Ἰωάννου εὐπλαγχνίσθην καὶ **T**

44. ἀπόστρεψα] ἐκράτησα **β**

45. ἀφ' ὑμῶν] *om.* **β**

46. τὰ δάκρυα] νὰ ἴδω **β**

47. καὶ] νὰ **β**

48. καὶ ἐνέπλησά, ἔδωσά σας καὶ ἔδωκα ὑμῖν πᾶν ἀγαθόν.] *om.* **β**

49. 2.10 ἔδωσά σας σῖτον καὶ οἶνον καὶ ἔλαιον A nearly direct quotation of Hos 2:8, ἔδωκα αὐτῇ τὸν σῖτον καὶ τὸν οἶνον καὶ τὸ ἔλαιον ("I gave to her wheat and wine and oil"). The passage in Hosea refers to the unfaithfulness of Israel, represented by Gomer. She was given everything in abundance but made idols for Baal. Beta omits oil and uses later Greek words.

50. σῖτον καὶ οἶνον καὶ ἔλαιον] σιτάρι καὶ κρασὶ **β**

51. ἐνέπλησα ὑμῖν] καὶ ἐχόρτασά σας **β**

52. προεκόψατε] ἐπήγετε **β**

(7) And I wanted to destroy every human being on the face of the earth for the sake of my holy Lord's day. (8) But once more I have been merciful for the sake of my immaculate mother and I have checked my anger toward you because of the tears. . . . and you may repent a little. (9) And I satiated you, I have fed you and I have given you everything good. (10) I have given you bread and wine and oil, and I have filled you with everything good, and after ate your fill, you returned again to your evil practices.

[3] (1)[53] καὶ διὰ τοῦτο[54] λέγω ὑμῖν· οὐ μὴ ἀποστείλω[55] ἄλλην ἐπιστολὴν ἐπὶ τῆς γῆς, ἀλλὰ ἀνοίξειν ἔχω τοὺς καταράκτας τοῦ οὐρανοῦ καὶ βρέξειν ἔχω ὕδωρ καχλάζον Ἀπριλίου ἡμέρᾳ πέ(μ)πτῃ ὥςτε κατακαύσειν[56] πάντας. (2)[57] καὶ βρέξειν ἔχω αἷμα καὶ στάκτην Ἰουνίου δεκατέσσαρεις, ὥστε πολλοὺς θέλω σκοτώσει.[58]

(3)[59] καὶ ἀπολέσω τοὺς ἀμπελῶνας καὶ τὸν σῖτον, ὥσπερ οἴδατε,[60] καὶ ποιήσειν ἔχω τοὺς ποταμοὺς εἰς αἷμα, ὥςτε τά τε κτήνη ὑμῶν ἀπολέσαι.[61]

53. 3.1 The trapdoors of heaven are referenced in Gen 7:11; see also 2 Kgdms 7:2. The date for the punishment of boiling water is set in Greek Beta as the fifth of April. Boiling water sent up on humankind is mentioned in one of Zosimus's dreams representing purgatory: ὕδωρ κοχλάζον (Michèle Mertens, *Les alchimistes grecs*, vol. 4.1, *Zosime de Panopolis. Mémoires authentiques* [Paris: Les Belles Lettres, 1995], 10.3.44–59). On the open doors of heaven, see p. 190f.

54. καὶ διὰ τοῦτο] τότε **β**

55. οὐ μὴ ἀποστείλω] θέλω στέλλειν **β**

56. Ἀπριλίου ἡμέρᾳ πέ(μ)πτῃ ὥςτε κατακαύσειν] Ἀπριλίου ἡμέρᾳ πέ(μ)πτῃ καὶ κατακαύσω **β; ** ὥςτε κατακαύσειν **β1**

57. 3.2 Blood and ashes will rain down on the fourteenth of June. See Ezek 38:22 LXX: καὶ κρινῶ αὐτὸν θανάτῳ καὶ αἵματι καὶ ὑετῷ κατακλύζοντι καὶ λίθοις χαλάζης, καὶ πῦρ καὶ θεῖον βρέξω ἐπ᾽ αὐτὸν ("And I will judge him with pestilence, and blood, and sweeping rain, and hailstones; and I will rain upon him fire and brimstone.").

58. στάκτην Ἰουνίου δεκατέσσαρεις, ὥστε πολλοὺς θέλω σκοτώσει] στάκτην $\mathbf{β}_1$; καὶ βρεχὶν ἔχε Ἰουνίου εἰς τὰς ιδ αἷμα καὶ στάκτην ὥστε πόλου τῶν ἀνθρώπων θανατώσω καὶ ἐνταφιάσω ἐπὶ τῆς γῆς **T**

59. 3.3 See Exod 7:17; Ps 78:44; Rev 11:6; 16:4. The transformation of water into blood is both a plague from Exodus and a feature of Revelation. The destruction of livestock and crops in the Letter from Heaven seems to be a condensed imagined outcome of the plagues in Exod 9 rather than an overt reference to anything in Revelation.

60. καὶ ἀπολέσω τοὺς ἀμπελῶνας καὶ τὸν σῖτον, ὥσπερ οἴδατε] *om.* **β**

61. εἰς αἷμα, ὥςτε τά τε κτήνη ὑμῶν ἀπολέσαι] νὰ γένῃ αἷμα, ὅτε καὶ τὰ κτήνη [ἤγουν τὰ ζῶα] θέλω σκοτώσει **β**

[3] (1) And on account of this, I say to you: I will not send another letter to the earth, but I will open the trap-doors of heaven and I will rain down boiling water on you on the fifth day of April so as to burn everyone up. (2) And I will rain down blood and ashes on the fourteenth of June, so as to plunge many into darkness.

(3) And I will destroy the vineyards and the grain, as you see, and I will turn rivers into blood, so as to destroy your herds.

(4)[62] καὶ ἀπὸ τοῦ φόβου καὶ τρόμου θέλουν βοᾶ[63] πρὸς τοὺς ἀπ' αἰῶνος κεκοιμημένους νεκρούς[64] 'ἀνοίξατε τὰ μνήματα ὑμῶν, οἱ ἀπ' αἰῶνος νεκροί. (5) οὐχ ὑποφέρομεν τὴν ἀπειλὴν τοῦ παντοκράτορος θεοῦ.'[65]

---

62. 3.4 In Job 14:13, Job begs God to give him refuge in Sheol from divine wrath: "O that you would hide me in Sheol, that you would conceal me until your wrath is past, that you would appoint me a set time, and remember me!" A similar motif is found in Isa 26:20, where the people of Judah hide in "closets" from God's anger: "Come, my people, enter your chambers, and shut your doors behind you; hide yourselves for a little while until the wrath is past." The motif of frantically seeking a place to shelter from God's anger culminates in Rev 6:15–17, which incorporates a similar apostrophe to inanimate objects: καὶ οἱ βασιλεῖς τῆς γῆς καὶ οἱ μεγιστᾶνες καὶ οἱ χιλίαρχοι καὶ οἱ πλούσιοι καὶ οἱ ἰσχυροὶ καὶ πᾶς δοῦλος καὶ ἐλεύθερος ἔκρυψαν ἑαυτοὺς εἰς τὰ σπήλαια καὶ εἰς τὰς πέτρας τῶν ὀρέων· καὶ λέγουσιν τοῖς ὄρεσιν καὶ ταῖς πέτραις· Πέσετε ἐφ' ἡμᾶς καὶ κρύψατε ἡμᾶς ἀπὸ προσώπου τοῦ καθημένου ἐπὶ τοῦ θρόνου καὶ ἀπὸ τῆς ὀργῆς τοῦ ἀρνίου, ὅτι ἦλθεν ἡ ἡμέρα ἡ μεγάλη τῆς ὀργῆς αὐτῶν, καὶ τίς δύναται σταθῆναι; ("Then the kings of the earth and the magnates and the generals and the rich and the powerful and everyone, slave and free, hid in the caves and among the rocks of the mountains, calling to the mountains and rocks, 'Fall on us and hide us from the face of the one seated on the throne and from the wrath of the Lamb, for the great day of their wrath has come, and who is able to stand?'") See also p. 310, n. 72.

63. βοᾶ] χράζει ὁ κόσμος **β**

64. ἀπ' αἰῶνος κεκοιμημένους νεκρούς] ἀποθαμένους, νὰ λέγουν **β**

65. τὰ μνήματα ὑμῶν, οἱ ἀπ' αἰῶνος νεκροί. οὐχ ὑποφέρομεν τὴν ἀπειλὴν τοῦ παντοκράτορος θεοῦ.] οἱ τάφοι, καὶ πάρετέ μας μέσα, ὅτι δὲν ἠμποροῦμεν, νὰ ὑποφέρωμεν τὴν ὀργὴν τοῦ θεοῦ. τότε λέγει πάλιν ὁ κύριος **β**

(4) And out of fear and trembling they will cry out to the dead, who have been asleep for ages: 'Open your tombs, you (who) have been dead for ages! (5) We cannot endure the wrath of the all-mighty God.'

[4][66] (1)[67] οὐκ οἴδατε, ἄφρονες καὶ ἀσύνετοι τῇ καρδίᾳ,[68] ὅτι τὴν ἁγίαν κυριακὴν ἐμήνυσα τὸ, 'Χαῖρε κεχαριτωμένη' εἰς τὴν ὑπεραγίαν μου μητέραν μετὰ τοῦ ἀρχαγγέλου Γαβριὴλ εἰς πόλιν Ναζαρέτ;

(2) οὐκ οἴδατε,[69] κακοῦργοι ἄνθρωποι,[70] ὅτι τὴν ἁγίαν κυριακὴν τὸ βάπτισμα ἐδεξάμην ἐν ῥείθροις τοῦ Ἰορδάννου ὑπὸ χειρὸς Ἰωάννου τοῦ βαπτιστοῦ;

(3) οὐκ οἴδατε, ἄφρονες καὶ ἀσύνετοι τῇ καρδίᾳ, ὅτι τὴν ἁγίαν κυριακὴν τὴν ἐμὴν ἀνάστασιν ἐποίησα, ἵνα ἀναστήσω τὸν Ἀδὰμ καὶ τοὺς ἐξ Ἀδάμ;[71]

(4)[72] οὐκ οἴδατε, ἄφρονες καὶ ἀσύνετοι τῇ καρδίᾳ, ὅτι τὴν ἁγίαν κυριακὴν παρῴκησα τὸν Ἀβραὰμ ἐν τῇ δρυῒ τῇ Μα(μ)βρῇ;[73]

(5)[74] οὐκ οἴδατε, παραβάται[75] τῶν ἐντολῶν μου καὶ τῶν θείων μου γραφῶν παραφρονηταί, ὅτι[76] τὴν ἁγίαν μου κυριακὴν μέλλω[ν][77] κρῖναι ζῶντας καὶ νεκρούς;

66. §4 A list of events that have happened (or will happen) on Sunday (Sunday benedictions).

67. 4.1–3 Here NT events (Annunciation, Jesus's baptism by John the Baptist, and the resurrection) are treated.

68. ἄφρονες καὶ ἀσύνετοι τῇ καρδίᾳ] τρελοί **β**

69. οὐκ οἴδατε] ἴδατε **β**

70. ἄνθρωποι] καὶ ἀνόητοι **β**

71. ἀναστήσω τὸν Ἀδὰμ καὶ τοὺς ἐξ Ἀδάμ;]Ἔσωσα τὸν Ἀδὰμ καὶ τοῦ ἐκ Ἀδὰμ καὶ ἠλευθέρωσα αὐτοὺς ἐκ τῶν Ἅδην. **T**

72. 4.4 A sole OT event is alleged to have occurred on Sunday (visit with Abraham, Gen 18:1–15).

73. παρῴκησα τὸν Ἀβραὰμ ἐν τῇ δρυῒ τῇ Μα(μ)βρῇ;] ἐγίνετε **β** (In **β**, Abraham and the oak are mentioned in the previous sentence.)

74. 4.5 The last judgment will occur on Sunday.

75. οὐκ οἴδατε, παραβάται] παραβάται τοῦ νόμου καὶ **β**

76. παραφρονηταί, ὅτι] παραφρονήσατε **β**

77. μου κυριακὴν μέλλω[ν]] κυριακὴν; οὐκ οἴδατε, τὴν ἁγίαν κυριακὴν μέλλω **β**

[4] (1) Do you not know, you brainless ones without intelligence in your minds, that on the holy Lord's day I proclaimed the 'Hail [Mary], full of grace,' to my most holy mother through the archangel Gabriel in the city of Nazareth?

(2) Do you not know, evil-doing people, that on the holy Lord's day I received baptism by the hand of John the Baptist in the streams of the Jordan?

(3) Do you not know, you brainless ones without intelligence in your minds, that I fulfilled my resurrection on the holy Lord's day, so that I could raise up Adam and the descendants of Adam?

(4) Do you not know, you brainless ones without intelligence in your minds, that on the holy Lord's day I dwelt with Abraham in the oak of Mamre?

(5) Do you not know, transgressors of my commandments and those who scorn my holy scriptures, that on the holy Lord's day, I intend to judge the living and the dead?

[5][78] (1)[79] μὰ τὴν μητέρα μου τὴν πανάχραντον καὶ τῶν ἀγγέλων μου τὰ στίφη καὶ ἀρχαγγέλων καὶ τὸν ἅγιον ᾿Ιωάννην τὸν βαπτιστήν.[80] οὐ μὴ ἀποστείλω ἄλλην ἐπιστολὴν ἐπὶ τῆς γῆς, ἀλλὰ ἀποστρέψει ἔχω τὸ φῶς τοῦ ἡλίου εἰς σκότος καὶ τὴν σελήνην εἰς αἷμα, ἵνα κατασφάξητε ἀλλήλους.

(2) καὶ ποιήσειν ἔχω ἐκ τοῦ οὐρανοῦ ἤχους, ἀστράπτων καὶ κτυπῶν. (3) καὶ ἀποστρέψω τὸ πρόσωπόν μου ἀφ᾽ ὑμῶν, ἵνα μὴ[81] ἀκούσω τὸ θρῆνος τῶν ἀπίστων.[82] (4) καὶ οὐ μὴ ἐλεήσω αὐτούς· ἀκούσατε καὶ ὑμεῖς ἡμῶν καὶ οὐ μὴ ἐγκαταλείπω ὑμᾶς.

---

78. §5 Oaths and threats.

79. 5.1 Christ swears by Mary, the angels, the archangels, and John the Baptist. The combination of powerful figures for Christ's oath is reminiscent of late antique and medieval prayers that may also be considered textual charms. See, for example, a sixth- or seventh-century protective amulet written in Greek on papyrus (Vienna, pap. Rainer 5 [13b]): "[In the name of the father] and the son and the holy [spirit, and] our lady, the all-holy mother of god and ever-virgin Mary, and the most saintly forerunner John the Baptist, and the theologian St. John the evangelist, and our saintly fathers the apostles, and all the saints!" Translation by Marvin Meyer in Marvin Meyer and Richard Smith, eds., *Ancient Christian Magic: Coptic Texts of Ritual Power* (San Francisco: HarperCollins, 1994), 41. Another medieval spell from Bulgaria protects against a demon: "in the name of the holy Mother of God, holy John the Baptist, the holy apostles and all the heavenly powers, cherubim and seraphim, in the name of the holy archangels Michael, Gabriel, Uriel, Raphael and all the church saints. . . ." Lead amulet, tenth–eleventh century, trans. Svetlana Tsonkova, "Burnt without Fire: The Illness Demon in Bulgarian Late Medieval Magical Texts," in *The Magical and Sacred Medical World*, ed. Éva Pócs (Newcastle upon Tyne: Cambridge Scholars, 2019), 37–58. See on the deesis above, p. 295f.

The sun becomes black and the moon turns into blood in Rev 6:12: Καὶ εἶδον ὅτε ἤνοιξεν τὴν σφραγῖδα τὴν ἕκτην καὶ σεισμὸς μέγας ἐγένετο καὶ ὁ ἥλιος ἐγένετο μέλας ὡς σάκκος τρίχινος καὶ ἡ σελήνη ὅλη ἐγένετο ὡς αἷμα ("And when I saw [the Lamb] open the sixth seal, there was a great earthquake, and the sun became black like sackcloth made of hair, and the whole moon turned blood red").

80. τὸν ἅγιον ᾿Ιωάννην τὸν βαπτιστήν] τοῦ ἁγίου μου ᾿Ιωάννου τοῦ βαπτιστοῦ **β**

81. μὴ] om. **β**

82. τῶν ἀπίστων] τὸ ἄπαυστον καὶ νὰ μή τους λυπηθῶ, νὰ ἀκούσω τῆς φωνῆς τους **β**

[5] (1) By my mother, who is immaculate, and the hosts of my angels and archangels and the holy John the Baptist, I will not send another letter to earth, but instead I will turn the light of the sun into darkness and the moon into blood, so that you will murder each other.

(2) And I will create loud noises from the heavens, of lightning and thunder. (3) And I will turn my face away [Ezek 7:22] from you, so that I will not hear the laments of the unfaithful. (4) And I will not have pity on them; but as for you, heed me, and I will not abandon you.

. . . if you do not keep the Lord's day: all will die . . .

(5) ὤμοσα[83] καὶ πάλιν ὀμνύω τὴν μητέρα μου τὴν ἄχραντον καὶ τῶν ἁγίων μου ἀποστόλων καὶ προφητῶν·[84] ἐὰν οὐ μὴ φυλάξετε τὴν ἁγίαν[85] κυριακήν, ἐξολοθρεύσω ἔχω ὑμᾶς. (6)[86] καὶ ἀποστείλει θέλω Ἰσμαηλίτας καὶ κακὸν θάνατον παραδῶ ὑμᾶς.[87]

83. ἐλεήσω αὐτούς· ἀκούσατε καὶ ὑμεῖς ἡμῶν καὶ οὐ μὴ ἐγκαταλείπω ὑμᾶς. ὤμοσα] ἐλεήσω. **β**

84. τῶν ἁγίων μου ἀποστόλων καὶ προφητῶν The sentence first (correctly) uses the accusative of the entity by which an oath is sworn but then continues incorrectly with τῶν ἁγίων ἀποστόλων and προφητῶν in the genitive case.

85. ἐὰν οὐ μὴ φυλάξετε τὴν ἁγίαν] ἐὰν μὴ φυλάξετε τὴν ἁγίαν μου **β**

86. 5.6 Christ threatens to send the Ishmaelites as a destructive punishment in Beta 1, just as in Alpha 1, 4.4 and Alpha 2, 4.7. Canan Arikan-Caba mentions the parallel to the apocalypse of Pseudo-Methodius, in which the Ishmaelites attack pregnant women and infants (*Apocalypsis* 11.17), although in Beta 1, the threat is for everyone.

87. καὶ ἀποστείλει θέλω Ἰσμαηλίτας καὶ κακὸν θάνατον παραδῶ ὑμᾶς] καὶ κακὸν θάνατον παραδώσω πάντας **β**

(5) I swore and again I swear by my immaculate mother and my holy apostles and prophets: if you do not observe the holy Lord's day, I will utterly destroy you. (6) And I will dispatch Ishmaelites and sentence you to an evil death:

(7)[88] κακοῦργοι,[89] ψεῦσται, καταλαληταί, μοιχοί, φονευταί, βλάσφημοι, ἅρπαγες, λῃσταί, βδελυκτοί, ψευδοδιδάσκαλοι, ἀσεβεῖς, τυφλοί,[90] ἀντιχριστοί, οἱ τῷ διαβόλῳ ἐλπίζοντες,[91]

---

88. 5.7 A long list of evildoers. The biblical list at Rom 1:29–32 may provide a basis for the catalogue. The list here does not address clerics or monastics in particular but is meant as a general catalogue of evil human beings. Two groups of people are mentioned repeatedly: those who believe or teach heterodoxy and those who do harm to family and close neighbors.

The πνευματομάχοι (literally, "fighters against the Spirit") were also known as the Macedonians after the fourth-century Byzantine bishop Macedonius I; more important was probably Eustathius of Sebaste. The views of the late antique Pneumatomachi can only be reconstructed from polemics against them (e.g., Athanasius of Alexandria, *Epistulae ad Serapionem*; Basilius of Caesarea, *De Spiritu sancto*), as no Pneumatomachian texts have survived. They rejected the divinity of the Spirit and also held that Christ was of a "similar essence" (ὁμοιούσιος) but not of the "same essence" (ὁμοούσιος) as God the Father. See the introduction of Hermann-Josef Sieben in his translation of Basilius, *De spiritu sancto / Über den heiligen Geist*, Fontes Christiani 1 (Freiburg: Herder, 1995). Part of a fifteenth-century fresco in the Church of Saint Herakleidios, the *katholikon* of the monastery of Saint John Lambadistis (Kalopanayiotis, Cyprus), includes the Pneumatomachi specifically in its depiction of the last judgment. An inscription over a group of terrified male faces states: οἱ μὴ ἱερεῖς, οἱ πνευματομάχοι καὶ ἄπιστοι, (οἱ μὴ λέγον)τες τὴν ἀληθείαν, οἱ Ἰουδαῖοι κ(αὶ) Φαρισαῖοι, οἱ βασιλειύς οἱ κακοὶ καὶ τύραννοι ("the false priests, the fighters against the spirit and unbelievers, [those not speaking] the truth, the Jews, the Pharisees, the evil kings, and tyrants"). On this depiction, see Annemarie Weyl Carr, "Paths of Perception in the Last Judgments of Byzantine and Lusignan Cyprus," in *Visibilité et présence de l'image dans l'espace ecclésial: Byzance et Moyen Âge occidental*, ed. Sulamith Brodbeck and Anne-Orange Poilpré (Paris: Sorbonne, 2019), 277–302. Perhaps the enigmatic statement of Jesus in Mark 3:29 (ὃς δ' ἂν βλασφημήσῃ εἰς τὸ πνεῦμα τὸ ἅγιον, οὐκ ἔχει ἄφεσιν εἰς τὸν αἰῶνα, ἀλλὰ ἔνοχός ἐστιν αἰωνίου ἁμαρτήματος, "but whoever blasphemes against the Holy Spirit can never have forgiveness, but is guilty of an eternal sin") is also in the background to this inclusion.

As in the Alpha version (Alpha 1, 4.2; 5.1), σταυροπάται ("those who trample upon the cross") are condemned (see p. 308, 310). This term can mean anyone who disrespects the cross, but it may specifically refer back to the Photian schism (863–867 CE), as the insult is used against Photianists in a ninth-century work (implying that they discredit the cross accompanying their signatures by breaking their promises); see Francis Dvornik, *The Photian Schism: History and Legends* (Cambridge: Cambridge University Press, 1948), 216. This would connect the "cross-tramplers" with other heretical groups listed in the catalogue (false teachers, antichrists, Pneumatomachi).

89. κακοῦργοι] ἄνθρωποι κάκοι, κακοῦργοι **T**

90. λῃσταί, βδελυκτοι, ψευδοδιδάσκαλοι, ἀσεβεῖς, τυφλοί] ὑποκριταί, λῃσταί **β**

91. οἱ τῷ διαβόλῳ ἐλπίζοντες] υἱοὶ τοῦ διαβόλου, παράνομοι **β T**

(7) evil-doers, liars, slanderers, adulterers, murderers, blasphemers, robbers, plunderers, abominable ones, false teachers, impious people, dimwits, antichrists, those who hope in the devil,

πνευματομάχοι, ἀδίδακτοι, παραβάται τῶν ἐντολῶν μου καὶ τῶν θείων μου γραφῶν, παραφρονηταί, μισοσύντεκνοι,[92] μισάδελφοι, σταυροπάται, πλεονέκται, καταδόται,[93] ἀνελεήμονες, κακόφρονοι, κακόζηλοι, οἱ μισήσαντες τὸ φῶς καὶ ἀγαπήσαντες τὸ σκότος,[94] οἱ ἐργαζόμενοι τοὺς ἰδίους γονεῖς καὶ γείτονας διὰ μαγειῶν, ἵνα πτωχεύοντες αὐτούς,[95] καὶ οὐ προσεύχεσθε[96] τὸ ὄνομά μου.

92. μισοσύντεκνοι] συντέκνους **β**

93. καταδόται] ἅρπαγες **β**

94. οἱ μισήσαντες τὸ φῶς καὶ ἀγαπήσαντες τὸ σκότος The biblical allusion is to John 3:19f.

95. οἱ ἐργαζόμενοι τοὺς ἰδίους γονεῖς καὶ γείτονας διὰ μαγειῶν, ἵνα πτωχεύοντες αὐτούς The sophist Libanius of Antioch (314–ca. 393 CE) gave a declamatory speech in which he includes among the abilities of magic workers the ability to inflict poverty (*Declamatio* 41.29, ed. Richard Förster, in *Libanii Opera*, vol. 7, *Declamationes XXXI–LI* [Leipzig: Teubner, 1913], 371–94). Spells for causing someone's economic downfall are discussed by John G. Gager, *Curse Tablets and Binding Spells from the Ancient World* (New York: Oxford University Press, 1992), 151–74; Latin traditions of harming rivals and their businesses are discussed by Daniela Urbanová, *Latin Curse Tablets of the Roman Empire* (Innsbruck: Institut für Sprachen und Literaturen der Universität Innsbruck, 2018). With regard to the Letter from Heaven, the theme of evil people who are especially cruel to their family members and neighbors continues here, as they are targets of these poverty-inducing spells.

96. καὶ γείτονας διὰ μαγειῶν, ἵνα πτωχεύοντες αὐτούς, καὶ οὐ προσεύχεσθε] ἀγαπᾶτε **β**

pneumatomachi, ignorant ones, transgressors against my commandments and my holy scriptures, scorners, those who despise their siblings, those who hate their brothers, those who trample upon the cross, greedy ones, informers, merciless ones, those bearing ill will, evil-minded ones, those who hate the light and love the darkness, those who influence their own parents and neighbors with magic spells so that they become poor, and you who do not worship my name.

(8) καὶ πῶς οὐ[97] μὴ σχισθῇ ἡ γῆ καὶ καταπίῃ ὑμᾶς; (9) ποῖον λόγον ἔχετε ἀποδοῦναι ἐν ἡμέρᾳ κρίσεως;

(10) ἐὰν μὴ ἀρνήσασθε τὰ διαβολικὰ ὑμῶν ἔργα, τὴν ζηλίαν, τὸν φθόνον, τὴν καταλαλίαν, τὴν βλασφημίαν, τὴν καταδοσίαν,[98] τὴν ὑπερηφανίαν, τὴν κλεψίαν, τὴν πορνείαν, τὴν μισαδελφίαν, τὴν μισοσυντεκνίαν[99] καὶ τὰ ὅμοια τούτοις . . .

97. καὶ πῶς οὐ] οὐ **β**
98. τὴν καταδοσίαν] *om.* **β**
99. πορνείαν, τὴν μισαδελφίαν, τὴν μισοσυντεκνίαν] μοιχείαν **β**

(8) And how will the earth not split apart and swallow you up? (9) What case do you have to offer on judgment day?

(10) If you do not deny your works that come from the devil: envy, jealousy, slander, blasphemy, treason, arrogance, theft, fornication, hatred of one's own brother, hatred of one's own siblings, and other things of this sort . . .

(11)[100] καὶ πάλιν ὀμνύω ὑμῖν μὰ τὴν κορυφήν μου τὴν πανάχραντον·[101] οὐκ ἐγράφη ἡ ἐπιστολὴ αὕτη ὑπὸ χειρὸς ἀνθρώπου, ἀλλ' ἔστι ὁλόγραφος ὑπὸ τοῦ ἀοράτου πατρός. (12) εἴ τις δὲ εὑρεθῇ φλύαρος ἢ πνευματομάχος, καὶ φλυαρήσῃ καὶ εἴπῃ ὅτι ὑπὸ χειρὸς ἀνθρώπου ἐγένετο, κληρονομήσῃ τὸ ἀνάθεμα καὶ συναριθμηθῇ μετὰ τῶν κραζόντων: 'ἆρον ἆρον σταύρωσον αὐτόν!'[102]

100. 5.11–14 The first assertion and threats regarding the divine authority of the letter. The Beta versions contain repeated proclamations of this sort.

5.11 ὁλόγραφος ὑπὸ τοῦ ἀοράτου πατρός The letter—allegedly written by Christ—is here said to have been written by the hand of the invisible Father. This "mixture" of Christ with the Father seems to be an intentional doctrinal statement, as it is immediately followed by a threat against any Pneumatomachian who says the letter is written by a human. This is at once an assertion that the letter is divine (since Christ wrote it) and an assertion that Christ is God (since he wrote it and is of the same substance as God). See the mention of the invisible Father followed by the notion that Christ is of the very same substance in Cyril of Alexandria, *Festal Letter* 8.6.2 (CPG 5240.08, dated to 419 CE): ὁρᾷς δὴ πάλιν ὅπως ἡμῖν ἀναμίξας τοῖς θεοπρεπέσιν ἀξιώμασι τὰ τῆς ἀνθρωπότητος ἴδια τὸν αὐτὸν εἶναί φησι καὶ εἰκόνα τοῦ ἀοράτου πατρός· ἀπαύγασμα γάρ ἐστι καὶ χαρακτὴρ τῆς ὑποστάσεως αὐτοῦ ("Indeed you see how, after combining that which is suited to human beings with the qualities suited to God, he tells us that he is one and the same, the image of the invisible Father; for he is the radiance and imprint of his essence"). The Greek edition is by W. H. Burns and P. Évieux, *Cyrille d'Alexandrie. Lettres Festales*, vol. 2, *Lettres 7–11*, SC 392 (Paris: Éditions du Cerf, 1993), 62–112.

101. μὰ τὴν κορυφήν μου τὴν πανάχραντον] κατὰ τὴν κορυφήν μου τὴν ἄχραντον καὶ τὴν μητέρα μου τὴν παναγίαν **β**

102. 5.12 κληρονομήσῃ τὸ ἀνάθεμα καὶ συναριθμηθῇ μετὰ τῶν κραζόντων: "ἆρον ἆρον σταύρωσον αὐτόν." A form of the so-called Judas curse, which in this case omits the name of Judas. However, the "inheritance" of anathema and quotation from John 19:15 cement this as one such example. This curse was often used on gravestones (against those who might violate the tombs) and later was used as a book curse and a curse against thieves. See Archer Taylor, "The Judas Curse," *AJP* 42 (1921): 234–52. For an example of the epigraphic curse and bibliography on its use in antiquity, see G. H. R. Horsley and Stephen Llewelyn, eds., *New Documents Illustrating Early Christianity* (Grand Rapids: Eerdmans, 1997), 1:99–100.

συναριθμηθῇ μετὰ τῶν κραζόντων, ἆρον ἆρον σταύρωσον αὐτόν] τὴν ἀγχώνη(ν) τοῦ 'Ιούδα **β**

(11) And I swear to you again by my immaculate head, this letter has not been written by human hand, but it is wholly the writing of the invisible Father. (12) If there should be found some babbler or *pneumatomachi*, and he talks nonsense and says that it was written by human hand, he shall inherit anathema and be numbered with the blasphemers: 'crucify him, crucify him!' [John 19:5].

(13)[103] καὶ καταστραφήσεται ὁ οἶκος αὐτοῦ ὡς τὰ Σόδομα καὶ τὰ Γόμορα, καὶ δοθήσεται τὸ πνεῦμα αὐτοῦ ἀγγέλοις πονηροῖς ἐν ἡμέρᾳ κρίσεως. (14) λέγω γὰρ ὑμῖν· εὐκοπώτερόν ἐστι Σοδόμοις καὶ Γομόροις σωθῆναι τοὺς μετανοήσαντας τοῖς οὐ μὴ δεξαμένοις[104] τὴν ἐπιστολὴν ταύτην.

---

103. 5.13–14 The curse of Sodom and Gomorrah sometimes accompanies the Judas curse. Gen 18:16–19:29 relates the original story of the destruction of these cities, but 2 Pet 2–3 provides the necessary eschatological context for understanding the reason why they appear here in the Letter from Heaven. A full discussion of Sodom and Gomorrah within 2 Peter is given by Ryan P. Yuza, "Echoes of Sodom and Gomorrah on the Day of the Lord: Intertextuality and Tradition in 2 Peter 3:7–13," *BBR* 24 (2014): 227–45. In relation to the Letter from Heaven, the wicked angels, who will claim the souls of those who blaspheme, are mentioned in 2 Pet 2:4. Furthermore, 2 Pet 2:6 states that the fiery destruction of Sodom and Gomorrah exemplifies the judgment that will come upon the ungodly. But further connections between the Letter from Heaven and the eschatology of 2 Peter have to do with 2 Pet 3, which opens by stating it is the second letter (perhaps this is coincidence) and proceeds to discuss God's perception of time, the promise of the second coming, and, in 2 Pet 3:10, what will happen on the (eschatological) day of the Lord: ἥξει δὲ **ἡμέρα κυρίου** ὡς κλέπτης, ἐν ᾗ οἱ οὐρανοὶ ῥοιζηδὸν παρελεύσονται, στοιχεῖα δὲ καυσούμενα λυθήσεται, καὶ γῆ καὶ τὰ ἐν αὐτῇ ἔργα εὑρεθήσεται ("But the **day of the Lord** will come like a thief, and then the heavens will pass away with a loud noise, and the elements will be destroyed with fire, and the earth and everything that is done on it will be disclosed"). (The final portion of this verse varies in some traditions, but it does not affect the interpretation here.) That the Letter from Heaven threads together the popular, often nonformal Judas curse with a relevant, lofty section of 2 Peter about the eschatological (Sun)day of the Lord via a reference to Sodom and Gomorrah establishes some amount of theological sophistication in the Greek Recension Beta versions of the letter.

One should note that this chapter seems to be a false or premature ending to the Letter from Heaven. Normally, formal appeals to authority and threats to those who deny the authenticity of a text open and/or close a work. It is therefore somewhat strange to encounter this passage in the middle of the epistle. One could speculate that the Beta version is a long letter that could be truncated for certain occasions, although this cannot be definitively proven. At any rate, there is an abrupt stylistic break between these eschatological warnings about believing the epistle, and the list of transgressors in the next chapter.

104. εὐκοπώτερόν ἐστι Σοδόμοις καὶ Γομόροις σωθῆναι τοὺς μετανοήσαντας τοῖς οὐ μὴ δεξαμένοις] μὴ δεξάμενοι **β** (preceded by lacuna)

(13) And his house will be destroyed like those of Sodom and Gomorrah, and his spirit will be given over to the wicked angels on judgment day. (14) For I say to you: it is easier for the repentant sinners in Sodom and Gomorrah to be saved than those who do not accept this letter.

[6][105] (1)[106] οὐαὶ τὸν οἰκοδεσπότην τὸν ὑβρίζοντα τὸν ἱερέα. (2) οὐχὶ[107] ὑβρίζει τὸν ἱερέα, ἀλλὰ τὸν θεὸν ὑβρίζει καὶ ἀτιμάζει, διότι ὁ ἱερεὺς δὲν λειτουργεῖ μοναχός του, ἀλλὰ ἄγγελοι συλλειτουργοῦσιν αὐτὸν καὶ παρακαλεῖ τὸν θεόν διὰ τοὺς ἁμαρτωλούς.[108]

(3) οὐαὶ τοὺς ὑβρίζοντας τὴν ἐκκλησίαν τοῦ θεοῦ.

(4) οὐαὶ τοὺς καταλαλοῦντας τὰ ψεύματα καὶ δὲν λέγουν τὴν ἀλήθειαν τοῦ θεοῦ.[109]

(5) οὐαὶ τὸν δίδοντα τὸ ἀργύριον αὐτοῦ ἐπὶ τόκῳ.[110]

(6) οὐαὶ τοὺς παραζυγιάζοντας.

(7) οὐαὶ τοὺς παραυλακίζοντας.

(8) οὐαὶ τοὺς παραθερίζοντας.[111]

(9) οὐαὶ τοὺς μὴ πιστεύοντας τὴν ἁγίαν τριάδα.

(10) οὐαὶ τοὺς λαλοῦντας τὸ ψεῦδος.[112]

---

105. §6 List of "woe cries" or "woe oracles." On the topic of prophetic woe oracles in OT, see Erhard Gerstenberger, "The Woe-Oracles of the Prophets," *JBL* 81 (1962): 249–63, and Waldemar Janzen, *Mourning Cry and Woe Oracle*, BZAW 125 (Berlin: de Gruyter, 2011).

106. 6.1 The notion of priests working together with angels originates in Judaism. See Mal 2:7, "For the lips of a priest should guard knowledge, and people should seek instruction from his mouth, for he is the messenger(/angel) of the Lord of hosts," and Jubilees 31:14, the blessing of Levi ("And may the Lord cause you and your descendants from among all flesh to approach him to serve in his sanctuary as the angels of the presence and as the holy ones"). This connection is made even more explicit in the Qumran texts; see the Benediction of the Chief Priest (1QS^{b} 4.22–28), where the chief priest is described as like unto the "angel of the presence" who ministers directly to the Lord; this interpretation is discussed by Moshe Weinfeld, *Normative and Sectarian Judaism in the Second Temple Period* (New York: Bloomsbury, 2005), 104–6. On the affinity between priests and angelic beings, see Rachel Elior, *The Three Temples: On the Emergence of Jewish Mysticism* (Liverpool: Liverpool University Press, 2004), 165–200. The concept develops further in late antique Christianity, especially in the East: for example, John Chrysostom describes the priest at the Eucharist as surrounded by angels (*Sac.* 6.4.41–43, 48–49). A Greek edition and German translation of the *De Sacerdotio* ("On the priesthood," CPG 4316) has been published by Michael Fiedrowicz, ed., *Johannes Chrysostomus: De sacerdotio / Über das Priestertum* (Fohren-Linden: Carthusianus, 2013). See also p. 194.

107. οὐαὶ τὸν οἰκοδεσπότην τὸν ὑβρίζοντα τὸν ἱερέα. οὐχὶ] ἀλλ' ἢ ἀποτιμείρα τους ἢ ἐκείνους ὁποῦ ὑβρίζουν τὸν ἱερέαν τους, ὅτι δὲν **β**

108. παρακαλεῖ τὸν θεόν διὰ τοὺς ἁμαρτωλούς] παρακαλοῦν τὸν θεὸν ὑπὲρ ὑμῶν **β**

109. τοὺς καταλαλοῦντας τὰ ψεύματα καὶ δὲν λέγουν τὴν ἀλήθειαν τοῦ θεοῦ] τὸν καταλαλοῦντα τὸν πλησίον αὐτοῦ. οὐαὶ τὸν καταλαλοῦντα τὸν ἴδιον σύντεκνον **β**

110. τὸ ἀργύριον αὐτοῦ ἐπὶ τόκῳ] τὰ ἄσπρα μὲ διάφορον **β**

111. οὐαὶ τοὺς παραυλακίζοντας. οὐαὶ τοὺς παραθερίζοντας] *om.* **β**

112. οὐαὶ τοὺς λαλοῦντας τὸ ψεῦδος] *om.* **β1**

[6](1) Woe to the master of the house who abuses the priest. (2) He does not abuse the priest, but he rather abuses and dishonors God, since the priest does not perform his service alone, but angels work together with him, and he entreats God on behalf of sinners.

(3) Woe to those who abuse the church of God.

(4) Woe to those who spread lies and do not speak the truth of God.

(5) Woe to the one who lends his money at interest.

(6) Woe to those who weigh deceptively.

(7) Woe to those who move land boundaries inappropriately.

(8) Woe to those who harvest unlawfully.

(9) Woe to those who do not believe in the Holy Trinity.

(10) Woe to those who spread lying gossip.

(11)[113] οὐαὶ τοὺς μίγοντας οἶκον μὲ οἶκον, ἵνα ἁρπάζονται τὸν οἶκον τοῦ πλησίου.[114]

(12)[115] οὐαὶ τὸν καταδιδοῦντα δοῦλον εἰς δεσποτείαν.[116]

(13)[117] οὐαὶ τὰς μοναχούς [118] τὰς πορνευούσας.

(14)[119] οὐαὶ τὸν οἰκοδεσπότην[120] τὸν μετὰ μάχ(η)ς ποιοῦντα τὴν προσφορὰν αὐτοῦ.

113. 6.11 Beta curses those who join "house and field," though the meaning is the same. This is a reference to those who deceitfully move boundary posts and the like.

114. οἶκον μὲ οἶκον, ἵνα ἁρπάζονται τὸν οἶκον τοῦ πλησίου] σπίτι καὶ χωράφι **β**

115. 6.12 The meaning of this line is somewhat opaque.

116. τὸν καταδιδοῦντα δοῦλον εἰς δεσποτείαν] ὁποῦ ἁρπάζουν τοῦ γειτόνου του τὸ τίποτες **β**

117. 6.13 The reading of Beta ("monks") has been kept here, but Beta 1 has "nuns."

118. μοναχούς] μοναστρίας **β1**

119. 6.14 Beta has the "mistress of the house." In any case, there is a clear allusion to Acts 5:1–11, the story of Ananias and Sapphira.

120. οἰκοδεσπότην] οἰκοδέσποινα(ν) **β**

(11) Woe to those who join house and house so that they may take possession of their neighbor's living space.

(12) Woe to the one who subjects a slave to the absolute rule of a master.

(13) Woe to monks who fornicate.

(14) Woe to the master of the house who makes an offering with contempt.

(15)[121] οὐαὶ τὸν ἱερέα τὸν μετὰ ἔχ(θ)ρας[122] λειτουργοῦντα. (16) πῶς οὐκ ἐμπυρίζεται τὸ στόμα[123] αὐτοῦ καὶ τὰ χείλη, ὅταν ὑψοῖ τὸν ἅγιον ἄρτον καὶ λέγει· 'πρόσχωμεν τὰ ἅγια τοῖς ἁγίοις';

(17)[124] οὐαὶ τὸν ἱερέα τὸν μὴ δεξάμενον τὴν ἐπιστολὴν ταύτην καὶ προθύμως ἀντιγράφειν[125] καὶ πέμπειν εἰς ἑτέρας πόλεις καὶ χώρας, νὰ ἀναγινώσκεται τὴν ἁγίαν κυριακὴν ἔμπροσθεν δήμου καὶ λαοῦ.[126]

---

121. 6.15–16 The burning of the mouth and lips (or in Beta, the mouth and blood) of a hostile priest during the Eucharistic miracle is an intriguing threat. It may reference certain visions of hell, in which corrupt or heretic clerics are tortured with fire and hot irons.

122. ἔχ(θ)ρας] μάχης **β**

123. στόμα] αἷμα **β**

124. 6.17 Any cleric reading the letter is ordered to make copies and send it to other churches to be read aloud. This is the first indication of Greek Recension Beta's status as a "heavenly chain letter." The line is actually a double threat, as priests must both receive the letter as authentic and pass it along—if they do not, punishment awaits. There is an implication that the clerics ought to produce copies themselves.

125. καὶ προθύμως ἀντιγράφειν καὶ] προθύμως καὶ αὐτὴν γράφει **β**

126. τὴν ἁγίαν κυριακὴν ἔμπροσθεν δήμου καὶ λαοῦ] κάθα κυριακὴν ἔμπροσθεν τῶν ἀνθρώπων **β**

(15) Woe to the priest who performs his service with hostile feelings. (16) How will his mouth and lips not burn when he raises the holy bread and says, 'Let us offer the holy to the holy'?

(17) Woe to the priest who does not accept this letter and eagerly make a copy of it and send it to other cities and lands, so that it can be proclaimed on the holy Lord's day before the city and people.

[7][127] (1)[128] εὐλογημένος δὲ ὁ ἄνθρωπος ἐκεῖνος ὁ ἔχων τὴν ἐπιστολὴν ταύτην καὶ ὑπάγει προθύμως ἀλλαχόθεν καὶ ἀναγινώσκει αὐτήν. (2) ἐὰν ἔχῃ ἁμαρτίας ὑπὲρ τὰς τρίχας τῆς κεφαλῆς του, ἐγὼ ἐξαλείψω αὐτάς.

(3)[129] οὐκ οἴδατε, ἄνθρωποι, ὅτι τὰς ἕξ ἡμέρας ἔδωσα, νὰ ἐργάζεσθε, καὶ τὴν ἁγίαν κυριακήν, ἵνα προσεύχ(εσθ)ε καὶ λυτρωθήσεσθε τῶν ἁμαρτιῶν τῶν ἕξ ἡμερῶν;

(4)[130] οὐκ οἴδατε, κακοῦργοι ἄνθρωποι, ὅτι ἐγὼ ποιῶ[131] καὶ ἐσεῖς καυχᾶσθε; (5) ἐὰν οὐ βρέξω ἐπὶ τὴν γῆν, τί βούλεσθε θερίζειν; (6)[132] οὐκ οἴδατε, ἄφρονες, ὅτι ἐν τῷ οὐρανῷ καὶ ἐν τῇ γῇ ἐγώ εἰμι; (7) καὶ ποῦ βούλεσθε φυγεῖν ἀπ' ἐμοῦ ἢ σωθῆναι;[133]

127. §7 Additional proclamations.

128. 7.1–2 The author (allegedly Christ) promises that merely possessing the letter and reading it will have the effect of cleansing a person from sin.

129. 7.3 Six days are allotted for work, while Sunday is reserved for prayer. The implication is that the prayer undertaken on Sunday has the effect of cleansing the sins incurred during the week. See Ps.-Eusebius of Alexandria, *Hom.* 16 (PG 86.416C): Ἑπτὰ τοίνυν ἡμέρας ἡ ἑβδομὰς ἔχουσα, τὰς ἕξ δέδωκεν ἡμῖν ὁ Θεός, ἐργάζεσθαι, καὶ τὴν μίαν δέδωκεν ἡμῖν, εἰς εὐχὴν καὶ ἀνάπαυσιν καὶ λύσιν κακῶν, καὶ ἵνα, εἴτε ἐν ταῖς ἕξ ἡμέραις ἁμαρτήματα πεποιήκαμεν, ὑπὲρ τούτων ἐν τῇ τῆς κυριακῆς ἡμέρᾳ τῷ Θεῷ ἐξιλασκώμεθα ("Well, the week has seven days, six of which God has given us to work, and one of which he has given us for prayer and rest and deliverance from evil, and so that, if we have committed sins during the six days, we may make atonement for them to God on the Lord's Day"). See the discussion of this homily by Annette von Stockhausen (pp. 444–47) and in the contribution of Uta Heil, "Rest or Work," pp. 145, 152, 194, and the homily at pp. 448–59.

130. 7.4–5 Christ reminds the reader that he enables everything. See Prov 19:21 and Ps 94:11, both of which may be summed up pithily: "Man proposes, God disposes" (see John Pairman Brown, *Israel and Hellas*, BZAW 231 [Berlin: de Gruyter, 1995], 295). The connection between respecting the Lord's Day and God's provision of rain for the harvest is from Lev 26:2–5. The method of argumentation is reminiscent of God's rhetorical flourish in Job 38–41, where the sheer immensity of divine creation and power is displayed with repeated rhetorical questions. Such questions are meant to expose the ignorance and lowly stature of humanity in relation to God, who controls all things.

131. ποιῶ] κάμνω **β**

132. 7.6–7 The force of these lines is twofold: first, Christ is ever-present and controls everything that happens on earth as well as in heaven (the crops and the rain); second, there is no place to hide from him or his wrath, so pleasing him is of utmost importance. See Ps 139:7–9.

133. ἀπ' ἐμοῦ ἢ σωθῆναι] *om.* **β**

[7] (1) And blessed is that person who is in possession of this letter and eagerly brings it from another place and proclaims it. (2) If he should have sins numbering more than the hairs of his head, I will expunge them.

(3) Do you not know, people, that I have granted six days for you to work and the holy Lord's day to pray and be redeemed from your sins of the six days?

(4) Do you not know, evil-doing people, that I do things and you boast? (5) If I do not rain upon the earth, what will you harvest? (6) Do you not know, fools, that I am in heaven and on the earth? (7) And whither will you flee or seek refuge from me?

(8)[134] ἐπικατάρατος ὁ ἄνθρωπος ἐκεῖνος ὁ ἐργαζόμενος ἀπὸ ὥρας ἐννάτης τοῦ σαββάτου ἕως δευτέρας ἐπιφωσκούσης ἡλίου. (9)[135] ἐπικατάρατος ὁ ἄνθρωπος ἐκεῖνος ὁ μὴ διδάσκων τὴν ἁγίαν κυριακήν, τετράδα τε καὶ παρασκευὴν ἀπέχεσθαι οἶνον, ἔλαιον καὶ ἰχθύας νηστεύοντες. (10)[136] καὶ ἐν ἐμοὶ ἀρεστόν ἐστιν ἵνα τιμῶνται αἱ ἡμέραι αὐτῶν.[137]

(11) ἐπικατάρατος ὁ ἄνθρωπος ἐκεῖνος ὁ ταχὺ προγευόμενος τὴν ἁγίαν κυριακήν."

134. 7.8 The precise timespan of Sunday is laid out: the ninth hour of Saturday until the second hour of Monday. Those who work during this time are cursed. On the duration of Sunday, see Heil, pp. 182f.

135. 7.9 This line is incomplete in Beta, but Beta includes an extra proclamation: "Accursed is the man who sleeps with a woman on Sunday." The order to fast from wine, oil, and fish on Wednesday and Friday suggests a xerophagic diet ("dry eating"), which does not permit wine or olive oil to be consumed. It is perhaps notable that two of the three "good gifts" given by Christ to humankind in Beta 2.10 (wheat, wine, and oil, quoting Hos 2:8) should be avoided during the fasting days. On fasting in Byzantium, see Wendy Mayer and Silke Trzcionka, eds., *Feast, Fast or Famine: Food and Drink in Byzantium* (Leiden: Brill, 2017), especially the chapters by Ken Parry, "Vegetarianism in Late Antiquity and Byzantium: The Transmission of a Regimen," 171–88, and Athanasius N. J. Louvaris, "Fast and Abstinence in Byzantium," 189–98. The Latin West and Byzantine East differed wildly in their fasting practices, both in terms of when fasting took place and what was permitted. Much has been published on this topic, but a summary with references is available in Tia M. Kolbaba, *The Byzantine Lists: Errors of the Latins* (Urbana: University of Illinois Press, 2000), 41–43.

136. 7.10 The meaning of this line is unclear. Is it an admonition not to leave church early ("quickly tasting" the Eucharist and then departing)? Or a rebuke to those who eat before the Sunday service?

137. μὴ διδάσχων τὴν ἁγίαν κυριακήν, τετράδα τε καὶ παρασκευὴν ἀπέχεσθαι οἶνον, ἔλαιον καὶ ἰχθύας νηστεύοντες. καὶ ἐν ἐμοὶ ἀρεστόν ἐστιν, ἵνα τιμῶνται αἱ ἡμέραι αὐτῶν] μετὰ γυναικὸς κοιμώμενος τὴν ἁγίαν κυριακὴν . . . οἱ τετράδι καὶ παρασχευῇ νηστεύοντες **β**

(8) Accursed is that person who works from the ninth hour of Saturday until the second (hour) of the dawning day. (9) Accursed is that person who does not preach on the holy Lord's day about the abstention from wine, oil, and fish for the fasts on Wednesday and Friday. (10) It is also pleasing to me that their days be honored.

(11) Accursed is that person who quickly eats on the holy Lord's day."

[8][138] (1)[139] καὶ μετὰ τὸ πληρῶσαι τὴν διδαχὴν ὅ ἀρχιεπίσκοπος, ἦλθε φωνὴ ἐκ τοῦ οὐρανοῦ ἀοράτως καὶ[140] λέγουσα· "μὰ τὴν μητέρα μου τὴν παναγίαν, οὐκ ἐγράφη ἡ ἐπιστολὴ αὕτη ὑπὸ χειρὸς ἀνθρώπου, ἀλλὰ τοῦ πατρὸς τοῦ ἐν οὐρανοῖς. (2)[141] εὐλογημένος ἐστὶν ὁ ἄνθρωπος ἐκεῖνος, ὅπου λαμβάνει τὴν καρποφορὰν[142] τὴν ἁγίαν κυριακὴν σὺν γυναιξὶν καὶ τέκνοις αὐτοῦ καὶ ἔρχεται εἰς τὴν ἐκκλησίαν τοῦ θεοῦ, συλλαμβανόμενοι κηρούς τε καὶ ἔλαιον καὶ λειτουργείας καὶ λαμβάνει τὸν ἅγιον ἄρτον τοῦ Χριστοῦ[143] καὶ φρικτῶν μυστηρίων ἡμῶν. (3) εὐλογῶν εὐλογήσω αὐτόν καὶ πληθύνων πληθυνῶ[144] αὐτὸν καὶ ἔσται εὐλογημένος ἐν τῷ νῦν αἰῶνι[145] καὶ ἐν τῷ μέλλοντι."[146]

138. §8 The archbishop has finished reading out the letter. A voice from heaven confirms the authenticity and authority of the letter. Blessings. Iohannicius adds an epilogue.

139. 8.1 The divine voice swears (again) by the immaculate Virgin Mary.

140. ἀοράτως καὶ] *om.* **β**

141. 8.2 Blessings are promised to the man who comes to church on Sunday with his wife and children. Objects should be brought as well: candles and oil, either to contribute to the lighting of the church service or as offerings. The exhortation to take along the liturgy is somewhat opaque; perhaps this is meant metaphorically. The "mysteries" are mentioned here, giving a subtle connection to the statement in Beta 8.4.

142. ὅπου λαμβάνει τὴν καρποφορὰν] ὁποῦ παγαίνει εἰς τὴν ἐκκλησίαν **β**

143. ἔρχεται εἰς τὴν ἐκκλησίαν τοῦ θεοῦ, συλλαμβανόμενοι κηρούς τε καὶ ἔλαιον καὶ λειτουργείας καὶ λαμβάνει τὸν ἅγιον ἄρτον τοῦ Χριστοῦ] μεταλαμβάνει τῶν θείων **β**

144. εὐλογῶν εὐλογήσω αὐτόν καὶ πληθύνων πληθυνῶ] θέλω τὸν εὐλογήσει καὶ νὰ πληθύνω **β**

145. αἰῶνι] *om.* **β**

146. μέλλοντι] μέλλλοντι **β1** (*sic* Bittner)

[8] (1) After the archbishop had completed the instruction, a voice invisibly rang out from heaven, saying, "By my all-holy mother, this letter was not written by human hand, but by the Father in heaven. (2) Blessed is that person who receives the fruitful, holy Lord's day with his wife and children and comes to the church of God, taking hold of candles and oil and the liturgy, and accepts the holy bread of Christ and of our awe-inducing mysteries. (3) With blessings I will bless him and I will multiply him many times over, and he will be blessed in this age and in the one to come."

(4)[147] ὅθεν κἀγὼ πατριάρχης Ἱεροσολύμων Ἰωαννίκιος ἐμυήθηκα ταῦτα ὑπὸ τοῦ ἁγίου πατρός.[148] (5)[149] καὶ παρακαλῶ ὑμᾶς ὡς τέκνα ἀγαπητά, ὅτι, ἐὰν δὲν ἔχετε, πωλήσατε ἐκ τῶν ὑμῶν πραγμάτων καὶ ἀγοράσατε τὴν ἐπιστολὴν ταύτην. (6)[150] καὶ ὁ ἀγοράσας αὐτὴν ἀγοράσαι τὴν βασιλείαν τοῦ θεοῦ, ᾧ ἡ δόξα καὶ τὸ κράτος,[151] τιμὴ καὶ προσκύνησις, τῷ πατρὶ καὶ τῷ υἱῷ καὶ τῷ ἁγίῳ πνεύματι, νῦν καὶ ἀεὶ, καὶ εἰς τοὺς αἰῶνας τῶν αἰώνων. ἀμήν.[152]

147. 8.4 Iohannicius states that he has been "initiated in these matters" by the Father. The language is slightly gnostic in nature; it is not clear whether the letter is meant or something else.

148. Ἰωαννίκιος ἐμυήθηκα ταῦτα ὑπὸ τοῦ ἁγίου πατρός] ἐμυήθηκα ταῦτα ὑπὸ τοῦ ἁγίου πατρός **β1**; Ἰωαννίκιος ἐμυήθη(ν) ὑπὸ τοῦ ἁγίου πνεύματος **β**; Ἰωαννικίος ἔθηκα ταυτα **T**

149. 8.5 The congregation is exhorted to sell their possessions and purchase the letter, suggesting that copies would have been available. The possibility that a monastic scriptorium could make money from this allegedly salvific letter should be considered. Not only does the letter serve to induce people to attend church, but it could have economic benefits if everyone wants to buy one.

150. 8.6 The preposterous claim that purchasing the letter is equivalent to purchasing the kingdom of heaven resembles the language of indulgences, especially considering the reiteration that the letter itself and its propagation had the power to absolve a vast multitude of sins. The colophon here suggests oral performance (or successfully mimics the liturgy to enhance its apparent authenticity).

151. τοῦ θεοῦ, ᾧ ἡ δόξα καὶ τὸ κράτος] τῶν οὐρανῶν, ᾧ πρέπει πᾶσα δόξα **β**; *om.* **T**

152. τιμὴ καὶ προσκύνησις, τῷ πατρὶ καὶ τῷ υἱῷ καὶ τῷ ἁγίῳ πνεύματι νῦν καὶ ἀεὶ καὶ εἰς τοὺς αἰῶνας τῶν αἰώνων. ἀμήν.] *om.* **T**

(4) I, the patriarch of Jerusalem, Iohannicius, have been initiated in these matters by the holy Father. (5) And I exhort you as my beloved children, that if you possess anything, sell it from your belongings and buy this letter. (6) And the one who buys it will purchase the kingdom of God, to which is due all glory and power, honor and worship, to the Father and to the Son and to the Holy Spirit, now and always, and forever and ever. Amen.

[9][153] (1)[154] καὶ ἡ εὐχὴ καὶ ἡ εὐλογία τῆς ἡμῶν μακαριώτατος ἔσται μετὰ πάντων ἡμῶν, ὅτι πολλὰ ἐκοπίας καὶ ἐτρόμαξα ἐγὼ καὶ ὁ λαὸς τῆς Ἱερουσαλὴμ καὶ Βηθλεὲμ ὅταν ἔπεσεν ὁ φοβερὸς λίθος τοῦ θεοῦ. (2)[155] καὶ εἰ τὶς εὑρέθη καὶ ἀπιστήση τὴν ἐπιστολὴν ταυτήν, κὰν ἀρχιερεὺς κάν τε ἱερεὺς κάν τε διάκονοι κάν τε κληρικὸς τεκάν τε κοσμικοὶ τυγχάνοντες, ἡ γυνὴ ἢ ἡ ἄνδρας, καὶ ἀπιστήση αὐτὴν ἔστω ἀφορισμένος ἀπὸ τοῦ θεοῦ παντοκράτορος καὶ ἀσυγχόρητος καὶ κατηράμενος, καὶ μετὰ θάνατον ἄλυτος καὶ τὸ ἀνάθεμα νὰ κληρονομήση καὶ τὸν τόπον τοῦ Ἰουδα, τοῦ προδότου, ὅτι ἀμήν. (3) ἐν Χριστῷ τῷ Θεῷ ἡμῶν ᾧ ἡ δόξα καὶ τὸ κράτος εἰς τοὺς αἰῶνας τῶν αἰώνων, ἀμήν. (4)[156] κἄγω ὁ πατριάρχης Ἱερυσολύμων ἔθηκα ταῦτα.

(5)[157] ὁ λίθος ἐξ οὐρανοῦ.

153. §9 This additional testimony to the authenticity of the letter and threats against anyone who does not believe it is only included in T.

§4.1–5] *om.* **β1** $_{\beta}$

154. 9.1 The first-person narrative adds an emotional layer that is missing from Beta and Beta 1. The manuscript T emphasizes the human terror the event struck in the hearts of people who were present when the letter descended.

155. 9.2 The "Judas curse" is reiterated.

156. 9.4 Manuscript T claims to be a holograph (or copy thereof), penned by Iohannicius himself.

157. 9.5 Manuscript T includes this bit of text after the letter, when one might expect it before. However, it is not a marginal note.

[9] (1) And our most blessed one will be the prayer and its blessing with us all, because I and the people of Jerusalem and Bethlehem were exceedingly afraid and frightened when the terrible stone of God fell. (2) And if someone should find and not believe this letter, whether it happens to be a chief priest or a priest or a deacon or a member of clergy or a secular person, whether woman or man, may this one in unbelief be excommunicated by God Almighty and unforgiven and accursed and unredeemed after death, and may this person inherit the anathema and the place of Judas, the traitor, amen. (3) In Christ our God be the glory and the power forever and ever, amen. (4) And I, the patriarch of Jerusalem, wrote down these things.

(5) The stone from heaven.

7

LETTER FROM HEAVEN—GREEK RECENSION BETA (LONDON)

BL Add.10073, f. 307–318

Canan Arıkan-Caba

A later version of the Jerusalem recension of the Letter from Heaven is preserved in a manuscript in the British Library, London (BL Add. MS 10073). The text is found in folios 307r–317v, preceded by an epilogue of the scribe in folios 317v–318r. Unlike other versions of the letter, the text in the British Library manuscript stands out, with its prologue of two parts and a colophon of the scribe. Textual divisions, including the colophon of the scribe, prologue, and the final scene in the text in which the patriarch of Jerusalem speaks, are marked with historiated initials and ornamental markers. We present here the prologue and colophon.[1]

First comes the address of the letter, emphasizing the nature of the text as a chain letter that is also within the text strictly commanded to be copied and dispatched to other settlements.[2] This is followed by a prayer consisting of John 1:1 and Psalm 102:19–21, which might indicate the liturgical function of the text. It would be not a coincident decision to choose John 1:1 to commence the letter not only because it is the first verse of the Gospel of John but also because it verbalizes the word *logos*, which is also used as the title for the letter in Alpha 1, λόγος περὶ τῆς ἁγίας καὶ κυρίας κυριακῆς τῶν ἡμερῶν.[3] Furthermore, Psalm

1. A new diplomatic transcription of the so-far unedited text can be found online at the SOLA database.

2. Alpha 1, 7.14; Alpha 2, 8.3.

3. Alpha 1, 1.2. The importance of God's words is also underlined by the biblical reference "Heaven and earth will pass away, but my words will not pass away" (Matt 24:35; Luke 21:33; Mark 13:31), which is found in the Alpha group.

102:19–21 vividly portrays the addressor of the letter, namely, God himself and his explicit address (his sanctuary on high from heaven) from which the letter was sent. This offers a concrete conception of God's physicality with which the readers are encountered throughout the letter.

The epilogue of the patriarch is succeeded by the colophon by a certain Kontakis. The colophon contains praises to God and the name of the scribe. Furthermore, the scribe requests from the readers forgiveness for his potential scribal errors and prayers for himself for the day of judgment.

Letter from Heaven—Greek Recensions Beta (London Add. 10073)

1. Εἰς κατὰ πᾶσαν πόλην καὶ χώραν εὑρισκομένην ἐν Κυρίῳ χριστιανοῖς καὶ ὑπὸ τῆς ἁγίας καὶ ὁμοουσίου καὶ ζωοποίου τριάδος σκεπτομένοις τε καὶ φυλαττομένης ὑπερτίμεις ἁγίοις καὶ τοῖς εἰσαποστόλοις ἀρχιερεῦσι ἡγουμένοις.

. . .

1.2. Ἐν ἀρχὴ ἦν ὁ λόγος καὶ ὁ λόγος ἦν πρὸς τὸν θεὸν καὶ θεὸς ἦν ὁ λόγος. (3) Θεὸς ἐξ οὐρανοῦ ἐπὶ τὴν γῆν ἐπέβλεψε τοῦ ἀκούσαι τοῦ στεναγμοῦ τῶν πεπεδημένων τοῦ λύσαι τοὺς υἱοὺς τῶν τεθανατωμένων τοῦ ἀναγγείλαι ἐν Σιὼν τὸ ὄνομα Κυρίου καὶ τὴν αἴνεσιν αὐτοῦ ἐν Ἱερουσαλήμ.

. . .

19. Δόξα σοι ὁ θεὸς ἡμῶν δόξα σοι Ἰησοῦ τὸ δῶρον *** Πάτερ παρεσφάλημεν ἐκ τείνος τίχεις· ἄνθρωποι μικρὶν ἔσθαι βρωτός καγῶ γε καὶ σφαλμάτων πέπλοις με ἄχρι σφόνδιλον· σύγνωτε τοίνην ἀδελφοὶ καὶ πατέρες ἵνα θεῖον ἐλέον εὕρομεν πάντες ἐν τῇ φοβερᾷ τῇ ἀδεκάστῃ κρίσῃ ἐγράφη παρ᾽ ἐμοῦ ταπεινοῦ καὶ ἀναξίου δούλου οὗτος ἐπίκλη Κοντάκης καὶ ὅσι ἐπὶ χήρας φέρεται εὔχεσται διὰ τὸν Κύριον καὶ μὴ κατάρασται ὅτι ὁ γράφον παραγραφῶν.

Translation

1. To the Christians in every city and village found in the Lord and to the honorable, holy, leading archbishops equal to the apostles who are watched over and guarded by the holy and *homoousios* and lifegiving Trinity.

. . .

1.2 "In the beginning was the Word, and the Word was with God, and the Word was God." (John 1:1) God looked down from heaven to earth, to hear the groans of the prisoners and release the sons of those condemned to death. So, the name of the Lord will be declared in Zion and his praise in Jerusalem. (see Ps 102:19–21)

...

19. Glory to you, our God; glory to you the gift of Jesus [...] Father, (if?) I did a misspelling by any chance. Mankind is exiguous and mortal, and I, too, am indeed full of mistakes up until my nape. Therefore, pardon me, brothers, and fathers so that we may find mercy on the lawful Judgement. This was penned by me, humble and unworthy servant named Kontakis and whoever holds it shall pray for the sake of the Lord and shall not curse the person who has penned the paragraphs (sections).

8

THE SO-CALLED ACTS OF THE COUNCIL OF CAESAREA

Uta Heil and Christoph Scheerer

The so-called Acts of the Council of Caesarea about fasting and the date of Easter are a curious piece and, according to the edition of Bruno Krusch (1880),[1] generally regarded as a forgery of later centuries. The text survived in different versions in manuscripts containing works of Bede, Isidore, and/or computistic texts. There has been no satisfactory edition until now, but a new edition of the two main versions from the earliest manuscripts is published by us in *Zeitschrift für Antikes Christentum* (*ZAC* 26 [2022]: 403–45). Insights from the current work on this edition show that the text does not in fact provide real acts of a council but rather contains reminiscences of a council at the end of the second century, which is mentioned in Eusebius of Caesara in his *Church History* (5.23–25) in his report about the conflict with Quartodecimanians.[2] As Eusebius refers to at least nine letters within this context, parts of the acts may rely on correspondence concerning customs of fasting and the date of Easter. In the following centuries, this text was revised and adapted several times for debates about the date of Easter, as is shown by the fact that there are different versions.

The text in its existing form is presumably incomplete, as it begins with the topic of differing customs of fasting and afterward deals simply with the

1. Bruno Krusch, *Studien zur christlich-mittelalterlichen Chronologie. Der 84jährige Osterzyklus und seine Quellen* (Leipzig: Veit, 1880), 303–10, here 303; in this opinion he follows Johannes van der Hagen, *Observationes in Prosperi Aquitani Chronicum Integrum* (Amsterdam: Johannem Boom, 1733), 329–36.

2. See Alden A. Mosshammer, *The Easter Computus and the Origins of the Christian Era*, OECS (Oxford: Oxford University Press, 2008), 46–48; Wolfram Kinzig, "Quartodezimaner," *RGG* 6:1862f.; Bonnie Blackburn and Leofranc Holford-Strevens, *The Oxford Companion to the Year* (Oxford: Oxford University Press, 1999), 790–94. The debate was about whether Easter could be celebrated on the date of the Jewish Passover, the 14th of Nisan, or whether it was mandatory to choose a Sunday.

date of Easter without applying the result to the question of the correct custom of fasting. The presumably older version,[3] which is in focus here, is strange in some aspects, and there are several transmission errors to be accounted for, as well as some later emendations and additions to be supposed. However, there is no reason not to assume the—maybe early—third century as the period for the original parts of this text. The context of the older version in its existing form seems to be from Gaul of the late fourth or fifth century, as reference is made to the custom of Easter being celebrated on every March 25, independently of the day of the week, which is connected with the custom of Christmas on every December 25.[4] Because linguistic observations lead to the conclusion that this statement is a foreign element in the text, one can assume that this text has been retrieved and revised for a debate about the date of Easter in the late fourth or fifth century in Gaul, since the earlier plea for Sunday against the Quartodecimans could also be applied against an Easter celebration on March 25. Recensio 2, first edited in the print of Johannes Noviomagus in the sixteenth century,[5] shows reworking and emendation in a further, somewhat developed and expanded stage.

The present text can be subdivided into three parts, a *narratio*, a biblical recapitulation of the beginning of the world, and the application of this to the issue of the date of Easter. The biblical references treat three aspects of calculating the date of Easter, namely, the day of the week, the seasonal day, and the day after the new moon.

---

3. In our edition, it is labeled as Recensio 1, in opposition to Bruno Krusch´s "Recension A," i.e., the reprint of Étienne Baluzius, *Nova Collectio Conciliorum* (Paris: Franciscus Muguet, 1683), vol. 1, cols. 13–16, which is already contaminated by the later version, Krusch's "Recension B," which is labeled here as Recensio 2. Either version, Recensio 1 or Recensio 2, can be found in several manuscripts of the late eighth and early ninth century; see below.

4. Several discourses are connected with March 25: There are sources that have calculated the passion of Christ on this date (Tertullian, *Adv. Jud.* 8.18; Hippolytus, *Comm. Dan.* 4.23; Acts of Pilate, prologue; Epiphanius, *Haer.* 50.1.5f.; Ps.-Chrysostom, *De solstitiis et aequinoctiis* [CPL 2277]). Here, however, Easter, that is, the resurrection of Christ, is set on March 25, which is probably oriented to the equinox, as March 25 is the traditional Roman date of the spring equinox (while in the proto-Alexandrian system only March 22 was considered the equinox; in the classical-Alexandrian system from the end of the fourth century March 21). See Mosshammer, *Easter Computus*, 153–57. The Acts presupposes an established Christmas on December 25, which was not common until the end of the fourth century, and also a kind of computational hypothesis according to which the date of Mary's conception on March 25 (nine months before the birth on December 25) corresponds to the date of Jesus's death; see John Chrysostom, *In diem natalem Domini nostri* (PG 49:357f.; 386 CE); Ps.-Chrysostom, *De solstitiis et aequinoctiis*.

5. Johannes Noviomagnus, *Bedae Presbyteris Anglosaxonis . . . opuscula cumplura de temporum ratione . . .* (Cologne: Quentel, 1537), fol. XCIXf.

Regarding Sunday, it is sufficient to present just the passages dealing with the first aspect, the day of the week, leaving aside the aforementioned problems associated with the text(s) as a whole. Thus, there are two passages, from the recapitulation and the application (here as §§1–6 and §§7–23),[6] that shed light on the view of Sunday established probably in the third century at the latest and used as an argument in later debates about Easter, with Gaul in the late fourth or fifth century as the potential context of the text in its existing form.

In detail, the situation described in the *narratio* of Recensio 1 is as follows: Initiated by an inquiry of Victor, bishop of Rome, concerning the customs of fasting and the order of Easter, with the intention of receiving a consistent order from the place where Christ had lived as a man, Theophilus, bishop of Caesarea—and maybe also Jerusalem at this time—convenes a council for this purpose. There, bishops and wise men together discuss the issue. In Recensio 2, in contrast, Victor commands Theophilus to give the order in the East—in the place where Christ lived—to celebrate Easter in the catholic manner, as a measure against Quartodecimanism. Thus, Theophilus convenes the council and in this version presides over it while directing the debate in the interests of Victor.

The first passage (§§1–6) points out that Sunday is the first day created—thus creation started on a Sunday. This is because the Sabbath is the last day that was made, and thus Sunday was necessarily the first.

The second passage (§§7–23) applies the argument of the first passage to the date of Easter. The connection of the creation of the world with Easter shows an implicit understanding of redemption as a new creation, which obviously also affects the parameters of time. The curious wording *elementa* in §9 is translated as "beginnings," meant as a temporal reference besides seasons. In this passage, *tempus* means "season" and also a specific point in time.

However, in the application, Sunday as the day for Easter is actually justified neither by the dichotomy of creation and new creation, nor by Sunday's notable position as the first day, nor by the resurrection, but by other "benedictions." Recensio 1 provides a series of three benedictions: the creation of light, the rescue of Israel at the Red Sea, and a mandate of Moses.[7] Maybe it was the term *tot* (so many) that led the author(s) of Recensio 2 to increase this number of three benedictions to twice that many.[8] They add passages from

6. This numbering differs from how they are set in the edition of the whole text. The text here starts at paragraph 4 in the edition in ZAC.

7. For the latter, see Exod 12:16; Lev 23:7f.; Num 28:18, 25.

8. The version of the manuscript Milan, Biblioteca Ambrosiana H. 150 Inf., fol. 65v, shifts the number six to the holy number seven by inserting the whole passage about Ps 117 from Recensio 1 into the series of benedictions of Recensio 2, albeit without numbering a sixth benediction. Thus, the number seven could also be a mistake.

Psalm 117 LXX, quoted in Recensio 1 afterward (see below), as a distinct benediction, and add further the provision of manna, and last the resurrection. Although Recensio 1 may have a lacuna after the passage quoting Psalm 117 LXX (here §§18–23), the resurrection as benediction would make no sense in Recensio 1, insofar as §10—omitted in Recensio 2—already stated that the resurrection took place on Sunday. This therefore would have been a circular argument. The identification of Sunday as the day of the provision of manna can be found also, and as we know found first, in Origen, *Homily 7.5 in Exodum* 16:4f.: *Ex divinis namque scripturis apparet quod in die dominica primo in terris datum est manna* ("From the divine Scriptures, namely, it is obvious that manna first was given to earth on Sunday").[9] As this conclusion from the biblical text in Exodus is correct but not obvious at first glance, the text of Recensio 2—insofar as this issue here appears to be obvious—implies that this is a somewhat common topos.

The extensive reference to Psalm 117 LXX in Recensio 1 in §§18–23 seems not to fit very well in the context. Yet it can be understood as an explanation of the mandate of Moses because it provides another argument to prove the first day as Sunday. The argument is as follows: The first day is Sunday because the Sabbath is the most recent day—this now simply repeats what has been stated in §6; and Sunday is also the day of the resurrection, as has been stated in §§9–10. Thus, when Psalm 117:24, 27 LXX asserts that the day of the resurrection—which is a Sunday[10]—is constituted as a festive day, and when Moses mandates that the first day, like the most recent day, is a day to be observed, then this first day as a day to be observed—according to the day of the resurrection constituted as a festive day—is to be identified with Sunday.

To summarize, this short text about the order of Easter shows high esteem for Sunday as a notable and benedictory day already at an early stage, maybe around the year 200. It was employed in debates about the date of Easter both in the late fourth or fifth century, the time frame of the text as it has been transmitted, and also later. This high esteem is the reason here for determining Sunday as the only possible day for the festive day of Easter. This may appear trivial, insofar as one could argue that Easter of course must take place on a Sunday because the resurrection took place on the first day of the week.

9. Origen, *Hom. Exod.* 7.5 (GCS 29:211.5–6 Baehrens). The next known reference is Ambrosiaster, *Liber Quaestionum Veteris et Novi Testamenti* 95.3 (CSEL 50:166–170 Souter). See on this exegesis in Origen Stemberger, "Sabbath or Sunday?," 100–104.

10. The connection of Ps 117:24 LXX to Sunday can also be found very often, e.g., in Eusebius, *Comm. Ps.* on Ps 91:5 (PG 23:1173 BD; see on this commentary above, pp. 153–56); Didymus Alexandrinus, *Fr. Ps.* 1081 (PTS 16:276.16–23 Mühlenberg), and Ambrosiaster, *Liber Quaestionum Veteris et Novi Testamenti* 95.3 (see note above). It is possible that Eusebius built this connection on knowledge of this text or on a text related to this one.

However, if things had been that simple, there would have been no need to substantiate this claim with the outstanding properties of Sunday apart from the resurrection, and there would have been no debate about this issue still in the late fourth or fifth century.

The manuscripts for the text of Recensio 1 are:

Bern, Burgerbibliothek Cod. 645 (s. VIII), fols. 72r–74r (= B)
Vaticano, Biblioteca Apostolica Vaticana Reg. lat. 39 (s. IX), fols. 102v, 103v–105v (= S)
Paris, Bibliothèque Nationale lat. 2675 (s. VIII–IX), fols. 78v–82v (= P)
Würzburg, Universitätsbibliothek M. p. th. f. 28 (olim 35; s. VIII), fols. 82r–84r (= W)
Karlsruhe, Badische Landesbibliothek Aug. Perg. 229 (s. IX$^{1/3}$), fols. 12v–16r (= A)
Paris, Bibliothèque Nationale lat. 4860 (s. X), fol. 144r–v (= T)
Barcelona, Biblioteca de la Universitat Ms. 228 (s. X–XI), fols. 89r–91v (= U)
Vaticano, Biblioteca Apostolica Vaticana Pal. lat 277 (s. VIII), fols. 90v–92r (= V)

The manuscripts for the text of Recensio 2 are:

St. Gallen, Stiftsbibliothek Cod. 902 (a. 820–830), pp. 167–69 (= F)
St. Gallen, Stiftsbibliothek Cod. 251 (s. IX), pp. 14–16 (= G)
Cologne, Dombibliothek Cod. 103 (ca. 795 / ca. 819), fols. 190v–192r (= K)
Cologne, Dombibliothek Cod. 102 (s. X), fols. 97r–99r (= L)
London, British Library Cotton Caligula A XV (s. VIII^{2}), fols. 80v–82v (= N)
Vaticano, Biblioteca Apostolica Vaticana Reg. lat. 586, (s. X), fols. 1r–3r (= R)
Bruxelles, Bibliothèque Royale Ms. 10127-44 (a. 750–825), fols. 82v–84r (= M)
Paris, Bibliothèque Nationale lat. 2796 (a. 801–825 / s. IX^{2}), fols. 86r–88r (= Q)

Concerning Recensio 1, manuscripts B, S, and P form a branch (here not labeled specifically), with S and P forming a subbranch of it, as well as A, T,[11] and U (also not labeled specifically). Concerning Recensio 2, manuscripts K, L, and N form a branch (also not labeled specifically) with relations also to R and M that are not entirely clear. The manuscript Milan, Biblioteca Ambrosiana H. 150 Inf. (a. 801–825), on which Krusch based his edition, is a compilation of Recensio 1 and Recensio 2; therefore, it will not be provided in the apparatus. As presumed in the apparatus and mentioned above, there may be a lacuna in Recensio 1 at the end of §23, because a conclusive sentence that embraces the biblical argument is missing when comparing this passage with other biblical quotations and references in the text.

11. This manuscript is very similar to the one Baluzius used.

Acts of Caesarea—Recensio 1

1 Tunc omnes[12] dixerunt: Primum[13] nobis inquirendum est quomodo in principio[14] mundus[15] fuerit[16] factus,[17] et dum[18] hoc fuerit diligentius inuestigatum, tunc poterit ex eo paschalis ordinatio salubriter[19] prouenire.[20]

2 Dixerunt: Quem ergo[21] diem credimus primum[22] creatum in mundum?[23]

3 Dixerunt:[24] Dominicum.[25]

4 Alii[26] dixerunt: Quomodo potestis probare[27] quia[28] primus[29] dominicus fuerit[30] factus?[31]

5 Responderunt dicentes[32] scriptura: Et factum[33] est uespere et[34] mane, dies primus, inde[35] secundus,[36] tertius,[37] quartus, quintus, sextus et[38] septimus, in quo requieuit[39] ab[40] omnibus operibus suis,[41] quem diem sabbatum[42] appellauit.

---

12. *omnes*: *omnis* B.
13. *Primum*: *Primo* V.
14. *in principio*: om. W.
15. *quomodo . . . mundus*: *quando mundus in principio* B.
16. *mundus fuerit*: *fuerit mundus* tr. S.
17. *fuerit factus*: *factus fuisset* V. *factus*: *expl.* V.
18. *dum*: *cum* AT; *ut* U.
19. *salubriter*: expl. B.
20. *prouenire*: *peruenire* S; *praeuenire* P.
21. *Quem ergo*: *ergo quem* tr. ATU.
22. *credimus primum*: *primum credimus* tr. AT. *primum* om. W.
23. *mundum*: *mundo* A.
24. *Quem . . . Dixerunt* om. SP. *Dixerunt*: *Responderunt* ATU.
25. *Dominicum*: *Dominico* SP.
26. *Alii*: *At ille* A; *At illi* TU.
27. *potestis probare*: *potest probari* (*probare* T a.c.) ATU.
28. *quia*: *quod* T.
29. *primus*: *dies* add. SP.
30. *fuerit*: *fuisset* SP. *sit dies* T.
31. *quia . . . factus* om. A.
32. *dicentes*: *dicente* SPAT.
33. *factum*: inc. V.
34. *et*: *factum est* add. SPATU.
35. *inde*: om. V.
36. *secundus*: *et* add. V.
37. *tertius*: *et* add. V.
38. *et*: om. SP.
39. *requieuit*: *requiebit* A; *Deus* add. P.
40. *ab*: *Deus* W(a.c. u.v.).
41. *in . . . suis*: om. V.
42. *diem sabbatum*: *dies sabbato* V.

Translation of Recensio 1

1 Then all said: First, we have to inquire how the world was established at the beginning, and when this has been investigated thoroughly, then the order of Easter can appear from it salutarily.

2 They said: Which day do we believe to be created first in the world?

3 They said: Sunday.

4 Others said: How can it be proven that Sunday was made first?

5 They answered and said, according to the Scriptures: 'And evening and morning were made, the first day' [Gen 1:5], thereafter the second, third, fourth, fifth, sixth [see Gen 1:8, 13, 19, 23, 31], and seventh, on which he rested from all his works, which he called the Sabbath [see Gen 2:2; Exod 20:11].

6 Cum[43] ergo nouissimus sit sabbatus,[44] quis[45] potest[46] esse[47] primus,[48] nisi dominicus?

[. . .]

7 Dixerunt: Sic est.[49] Ergo[50] quomodo creatus fuisset[51] inueniamus.

8 Dixerunt:[52] Die dominico,[53] uernum tempus,[54] in[55] aequinoctium, quod[56] est VIII.[57] Kal. Apr.,[58] luna plena.[59]

9 Dixerunt:[60] Sicut in principio mundus creatus[61] est,[62] et[63] per ipsum tempus[64] et[65] elementa, et[66] per[67] resurrectione dominica[68] redemptus est a peccato.[69]

10 Resurrexit itaque Dominus noster Iesus Christus die dominico, uernum tempus, in aequinoctium,[70] luna plena.

---

43. *Cum*: om. V.
44. *nouissimus . . . sabbatus*: *nouissimum . . . sabbatum* TU.
45. *quis*: *qui* V.
46. *potest*: *poterat* S; *poterit* P.
47. *esse primus*: *primus esse* tr. W.
48. *primus*: *prior* AU.
49. *est*: *uerum* add. ATU; *aliter non est* add. V; expl. V.
50. *Ergo*: *modo* add. A.
51. *creatus fuisset*: *creata fuisse* W; *creatum fuisse* A; *fuisset creatus* tr. T. *fuisset*: *mundum* add. A; *mundus* add. TU.
52. *Dixerunt*: *Responderunt* ATU.
53. *Die dominico*: *Diem dominicum* A; *Die* [!] *dominicum* U.
54. *uernum tempus*: *uerno tempore* T.
55. *in* om. ATU.
56. *aequinoctium quod*: *aequinoctio hoc* T.
57. *VIII*: *CIII* W.
58. *Apr*: *et* add. AT.
59. *Ergo . . . plena* om. SP. *luna plena*: *lunam plenam* A.
60. *Dixerunt*: *Item* praem. SP.
61. *creatus*: *factus* U.
62. *est* om. W.
63. *et* om. ATU.
64. *ipsum tempus*: *ipso tempora* W.
65. *tempus et*: om. SP.
66. *et elementa et: etiam* T; *et elementa* AU.
67. *per* om. SP.
68. *resurrectione dominica*: *resurrectionem dominicam* ATU.
69. *peccato*: *peccatum* W.
70. *uernum tempus . . .aequinoctium*: *uerno tempore . . . aequinoctio* ATU.

6 Thus, if the Sabbath is the most recent, which can be the first, if not Sunday?

[. . .]

7 They said: That is right. Hence, let us embrace how it [the world, C.S.] was created.

8 They said: On Sunday, on the vernal equinox, i.e., on March 25, at the full moon.

9 They said: Like the world was created at the beginning, so also it has been redeemed from sin, at the same season and beginnings, by the resurrection of the Lord.

10 Therefore, our Lord Jesus Christ was resurrected on Sunday, on the vernal equinox, at the full moon.

11 Dixerunt: Ecce,[71] inuestigauimus quomodo[72] factus sit[73] mundus[74] uel[75] a peccato[76] redemtpus.

12 Nunc[77] de obseruatione[78] paschae agendum est. De[79] die dominico, quid uobis uidetur?[80]

13 Responderunt:[81] Nulla ratione sine eo pascha debeat[82] teneri,[83] quia[84] tot et[85] talibus[86] benedictionibus[87] sanctificatus est.

14 Dixerunt: Quibus aut quantis[88] benedictionibus sanctificatus est[89] apertius dicite,[90] ut scire possimus.[91]

15 Dixerunt: Prima illa[92] benedictio[93] quod in ipso tenebrae[94] remotae sunt,[95] lux apparuit.[96]

---

71. *Ecce*: om. W.

72. *quomodo*: *in principio* add. ATU.

73. *sit*: *est* PT.

74. *mundus*: om. A.

75. *uel*: *et* SP; *ut* W.

76. *peccato*: *peccatum* W.

77. *Nunc*: inc. B.

78. *obseruatione*: *obseruationem* BSP.

79. *De* om. P(a.c.).

80. *De . . . uidetur*: *Quo die aut quo* (*quo* om. U) *tempore uel* (*qua* add. A) *luna pascha debeat ordinari* (*ordinare* U) ATU.

81. *Responderunt* ATU; om. BSPW.

82. *debeat*: *debetur* BS; *debet* P.

83. *Nulla . . . teneri*: *Non aliter nisi die dominico* (*pascha faciendum* [*fienda* A u.v.] *est* add. AU) ATU. *teneri*: *tenere* BW.

84. *quia*: *qui* WATU.

85. *et*: *ac* ATU.

86. *talibus*: *alibus* W; *tantis* U.

87. *benedictionibus*: *sic* add. AT.

88. *quantis*: *quantos* A.

89. *Dixerunt . . . est*: om. BSP. *sanctificatus est*: om. AU.

90. *dicite*: *dicere* S.

91. *Dixerunt . . . possimus*: om. T. *possimus*: *possemus* BP.

92. *illa*: *illi* SPW(p.c., a.c. non leg.).

93. *benedictio*: *est* add. ATU.

94. *tenebrae*: *tenere* W(a.c.).

95. *remotae sunt*: *moti sunt* B; *morabantur* SP. *sunt* om. W; *et* add. AU.

96. *lux apparuit* om. T.

11 They said: See, we have investigated how the world was made and has been redeemed from sin.

12 Now we have to deal with the observance of Easter. What do you think about Sunday?

13 They answered: By no means may Easter be kept without this [day, C.S.], because it is sanctified by so many and such benedictions.

14 They said: Say clearly by which and how many benedictions it is sanctified, so we can know it.

15 They said: The first benediction is that the shadows were removed on it, the light appeared.

16 Secunda ei[97] benedictio[98] quod populus[99] Israel[100] ex Aegypto tenebrarum[101]—uelut[102] per baptismum[103] fontis[104]—per mare rubrum[105] de duro seruitio fuerit liberatus.

17 Tertio[106] mandat[107] Moyses ad populum et dicit: Obseruatus[108] sit uobis[109] dies primus et nouissimus, hoc est[110] dominicus et sabbatus.[111]

18 Cum ergo nouissimus sit sabbatus, quis potest esse[112] primus nisi dominicus?[113]

19 Quia[114] CXVII. psalmus totus de passione[115] et de[116] resurrectione[117] cantatur.

20 De passione dicit:[118] Circumdantes[119] circumdederunt me[120] et in[121] nomine Domini uindicaui[122] in eis.[123] Circumdederunt me[124] sicut apes fauum et exarserunt sicut ignis in spinis.[125]

---

97. *ei*: *eius* AU; om. B.
98. *ei benedictio* om. T. *benedictio*: *est* add. AU.
99. *populus*: *populo* U.
100. *Israeliticus* B.
101. *tenebrarum*: *tenebras* A.
102. *uelut*: *ut* BSP; om. U.
103. *baptismum*: *baptismo* S; *baptismi* W.
104. *fontis*: *fontes* SPW.
105. *rubrum*: *rubro* BSP.
106. *Tertio*: *Tertia quia* ATU.
107. *mandat*: *mandati* S.
108. *Obseruatus*: *Obseruatum* BSP.
109. *sit uobis*: *uobis sit* tr. AU.
110. *est*: *dies* add. B.
111. *sabbatus*: *sabbatum* T.
112. *quis . . . esse*: *qui potesse* B.
113. *Cum . . . dominicus* om. ATU.
114. *Quia*: *Qui certissimus* W; *Quarta* praem. ATU.
115. *passione*: *passionem* P(a.c. u.v.).
116. *de* om. W(a.c.) ATU.
117. *passione . . . resurrectione*: *passionem . . . resurrectionem* B. *resurrectione*: *Christi* add. B.
118. (19) *et . . . dicit* om. SP. *dicit*: *Domini* AU; om. T.
119. *Circumdantes*: *canitur* praem. P.
120. *me* om. P.
121. *in* om. S.
122. *uindicaui*: *uindicabor* ATU.
123. *eis*: *uersibus* add. W.
124. *me* om. B.
125. *spinis*: *spini* A.

16 The second benediction upon it is that the people of Israel have been set free from Egypt of the shadows—as by a baptism of water—through the Red Sea from hard bond service.

17 Third, Moses commands the people and says: The first and the most recent day are to be observed by you, i.e., Sunday and the Sabbath [see Exod 12:26; Lev 23:7f.; Num 28:18, 25].

18 Thus, when the most recent is the Sabbath, which can be the first, if not Sunday?

19 Therefore, the 117th psalm as a whole is sung about the passion and the resurrection.

20 About the passion it says: 'They surrounded me all about, and in the name of the Lord I claim justice against them. They surrounded me like bees the comb, and inflamed like fire in thornbushes' [Ps 117:11f. LXX].

21 Et interiectis[126] uersibus: Lapidem quem reprobauerunt aedificantes,[127] hic factus est in[128] caput anguli. Haec[129] de passione.[130]

22 De resurrectione[131] autem dicit:[132] Haec[133] est[134] dies[135] quam[136] fecit Dominus, exultemus et laetemur in ea.[137]

23 Et interiectis[138] uersibus: Constituet[139] diem festum[140] in confrequentationibus[141] usque ad cornu[142] altaris.[143]

126. *interiectis*: *interiectibus* B.

127. *aedificantes* om. BS.

128. *aedificantes . . . in* om. U.

129. *Haec*: *Hac* S(p.c.).

130. *passione*: *confirmat* add. SP.

131. *resurrectione*: *resurrectionem* S.

132. (21) *Haec . . . dicit* om. U. *dicit* om. A.

133. *Haec*: *Hic* BP.

134. *est* om. AT.

135. *dies* om. W.

136. *quam*: *quem* BS.

137. *ea*: *eo* BSP.

138. *interiectis*: *ter iectibus* B(a.c. u.v.); *interiectibus* W.

139. *Constituet*: *Constituit* SP; *Constituite* ATU; *eum* add. W.

140. *festum*: *sollemnem* B(u.v.) ATU.

141. *confrequentationibus*: *condensis* U.

142. *cornu*: *cornum* SW.

143. Possibly there is a lacuna at the end of this passage in Recensio 1, insofar as a conclusive sentence, which can be found after the other biblical quotations in the text or in Recensio 2, is missing here.

21 And after intervening lines: 'The stone which the builders rejected, this is made the head of the corner' [Ps 117:22 LXX]. This is about the passion.

22 About the resurrection, however, it says: 'This is the day which the Lord made, let us exult and rejoice in it' [Ps 117:24 LXX].

23 And after intervening lines: 'He will constitute a festive day to be repeated, up to the horns of the altar' [Ps 117:27 LXX].

Acts of Caesarea—Recensio 2

1 Tunc pariter omnes dixerunt episcopi:[144] Nisi prius, quomodo mundus a principio fuerit,[145] inuestigatus,[146] nihil potest de obseruantia[147] paschae[148] salubriter ordinari.[149]

2 Dixerunt ergo episcopi: Quem diem[150] credimus factum fuisse[151] in mundo[152] primum

3 nisi dominicum diem?[153]

4 Theophilus episcopus dixit: Probate,[154] quod[155] dicitis.

5 Responderunt episcopi secundum scripturae[156] diuinae[157] auctoritatem: Factum est uespere et factum est[158] mane,[159] dies primus, deinde secundus[160] et[161] tertius[162] et[163] quartus[164] et[165] quintus[166] et[167] sextus[168] et[169] septimus,[170] in quo septimo[171] requieuit Deus[172] ab omnibus operibus suis,[173] quem diem[174] sabbatum appellauit.

---

144. *dixerunt episcopi*: *episcopi dixerunt* tr. FGR.
145. *a principio fuerit*: *fuerit a principio* tr. L. *fuerit*: *fuerat* G.
146. *inuestigatus*: *inuestigetur* K(p.c.); *inuestigatum* R; *instructus* MQ.
147. *obseruantia*: *obseruantiae* FGK; *obseruantiam* M.
148. *paschae*: *pascha* F; *pascharum* R.
149. *ordinari*: *ordinare* F(a.c.) R(a.c.).
150. *diem* om. KLNR(a.c.).
151. *fuisse*: om. R.
152. *in mundo*: *mundum* G(a.c.) R(a.c.).
153. *dominicum diem*: *diem dominicum* tr. FGM.
154. *Probate*: *Probates* F(a.c.).
155. *quod*: *quae* Q.
156. *scripturae*: *scripturas* M.
157. *diuinae* om. L.
158. *factum est*: om. FGK(p.c.) LR(p.c.) M.
159. *mane* om. R(a.c.).
160. *secundus*: *duo* R(a.c.).
161. *et* om. G(a.c.) KLN.
162. *tertius*: *tres* R(a.c.).
163. *et* om. GKLN.
164. *quartus*: *quattuor* R(a.c. u.v.).
165. *et* om. GKLN.
166. *quintus*: *quinque* R(a.c.).
167. *et* om. GKLN.
168. *sextus*: *sex* R(a.c.).
169. *et*: *uel* Q; om. KLN.
170. *septimus*: *septem* R(a.c.).
171. *septimo* om. Q.
172. *Deus* om. F(a.c.).
173. *suis*: om. R.
174. *diem*: *dicit* FG.

Translation of Recensio 2

1 Then all bishops said together: If not will be investigated first, how the world was from the beginning, nothing can be ordained salutarily about the observance of Easter.

2 Thus, the bishops said: Which day do we believe to be created first in the world,

3 if not Sunday?

4 Bishop Theophilus said: Prove what you say.

5 The bishops answered according to the authority of the divine Scripture: And evening was made and morning was made, the first day [Gen 1:5], thereafter the second, and third, and fourth, and fifth, and sixth, and seventh [see Gen 1:8, 13, 19, 21, 31; 2:2], on which seventh God rested from all his works, which day he called the Sabbath [see Gen 2:2; Exod 20:11].

6 Ergo, cum[175] nouissimo die[176] signet sabbatum, quis potest[177] esse primus, nisi dominicus dies?

[. . .]

7 Nunc ergo inuestigauimus,[178] quomodo in principio factus fuerit[179] mundus,

8 id est[180] die dominica,[181] uerno[182] tempore, in[183] aequinoctio,[184] quod[185] est VIII. Kal.[186] Apr., luna plena.

9 Per ipsum tantummodo tempus et elementa resurgunt.

10–11 [desunt]

12 Theophilus episcopus[187] dixit: Nunc igitur agendum est de ordinatione, quomodo debeamus pascha tenere.

13 Episcopi dixerunt: Numquid potest dies dominicus praeterire,[188] ut in[189] eo pascha minime celebretur,[190] qui tot et talibus[191] benedictionibus sanctificatus est?[192]

175. *cum*: *di* add. R(a.c. u.v.).
176. *nouissimo die*: *noussimum diem* KLNR; *diem* om. R(a.c.).
177. *potest*: *potes* F; *post est* R(a.c.).
178. *ergo inuestigauimus*: *inuestigauimus ergo* tr. G.
179. *fuerit*: *fuerat* FGN.
180. *est*: *in* add. R.
181. *dominica*: *dominico* KLNR.
182. *uerno*: *uero* K(a.c.).
183. *in* om. FG.
184. *aequinoctio*: *aequitio* G.
185. *quod*: *qui* Q.
186. *Kal.* om. L.
187. *episcopus* om. L.
188. *praeterire*: *praeteriri* KLN(p.c.) R.
189. *in* om. R.
190. *ut . . . celebretur* om. F(a.c.). *celebretur*: *celebraretur* K(a.c.); LN(p.c.).
191. *talibus*: *tali* R(a.c.).
192. (12) *Theophilus . . . est* om. M. *sanctificatus est*: *est sanctificatus* tr. FG.

6 Thus, if the most recent signifies Sabbath, which can be the first, if not Sunday?

[. . .]

7 Now, we found out how the world was created in the beginning,

8 i.e., on Sunday, in spring, on equinox, i.e., on March 25, at the full moon.

9 Merely at this time also the elements resurrect.

10–11 [missing]

12 Bishop Theophilus said: Now we have to deal with the observance of Easter, how we have to keep it.

13 The bishops said: May ever Sunday pass by, so that Easter is not celebrated on it, which is sanctified by so many and such benedictions?

14 Theophilus episcopus[193] dixit: Dicite ergo, quibus et qualibus benedictionibus[194] eum fuisse[195] sanctificatum asseritis,[196] ut scribere[197] possimus.[198]

15 Episcopi dixerunt:[199] Prima illi[200] benedictio est, quod[201] in ipso tenebrae sint[202] remotae et lux apparuit.

16 Secunda est illi[203] benedictio,[204] quod de[205] terra Aegypti uelut de[206] tenebris peccatorum, quasi per fontem baptismi per mare rubrum populus fuerat[207] liberatus.

16a Tertia illi[208] benedictio est, quia[209] in eodem[210] die caelesti cibo[211] manna[212] hominibus datum[213] est.

17–18 Quarta illi[214] benedictio est, quia Moyses mandat ad populum: Sit[215] uobis[216] obseruatus[217] dies primus et[218] nouissimus.

---

193. *episcopus* om. L.
194. *et qualibus benedictionibus* om. R(a.c.).
195. *fuisse*: *esse* L.
196. *asseritis*: *asseritur* F.
197. *scribere*: *scire* R.
198. *possimus*: *possetis* M; *possumus* Q.
199. *Episcopi dixerunt*: *Responderunt episcopi* R.
200. *illi*: *illa* MQ(a.c.).
201. *quod*: *quia* L.
202. *sint*: *sunt* KLNR.
203. *illi*: *illa* M.
204. *est . . . benedictio*: *illi benedictio est* tr. R.
205. *de*: *in eodem R* (a.c. u.v., *eo de* p.c.); om. N.
206. *de*: *ex* R.
207. *fuerat*: *fuisset* KLN; *fuerit* R; *fuisset* iter. L.
208. *illi*: *illa* M.
209. *quia*: *quod* Q.
210. *eodem*: *eadem* N.
211. *caelesti cibo*: *caelestis cibus* LR(p.c.).
212. *manna* om. FG.
213. *datum*: *datus* L.
214. *illi*: *illa* M.
215. *Sit*: *Vt* R.
216. *uobis*: *sit* add. R(p.c.).
217. *obseruatus*: *obseruabilis* R(p.c.).
218. *et* om. FGQ.

14 Bishop Theophilus said: Thus, say by which and what kind of benedictions you assert that it is sanctified, so we can write it down.

15 The bishops said: The first benediction upon it is that the shadows were removed on it and the light appeared.

16 The second benediction upon it is that the people have been set free from Egypt as of the shadows of the sins like by a baptism of water through the Red Sea.

16a The third benediction upon it is that on this day manna as celestial food was given to man.

17–18 The fourth benediction upon it is that Moses commands the people: The first and the most recent day are to be observed by you [see Exod 12:26; Lev 23:7f.; Num 28:18, 25].

19 Quinta[219] illi benedictio[220] est ut in CXVII.[221] Psalmo dicit:[222]

20–21 Circumdederunt[223] me sicut[224] apes fauum,[225] et exarserunt sicut ignis in spinis.

22–23 De resurrectione autem[226] dicit: Haec est dies, quam[227] fecit Dominus, exultemus et laetemur in ea[228] usque ad cornu altaris.

24 Sexta illi[229] benedictio est, quod in ipsa[230] Dominus resurrexit.[231]

25 Vides[232] ergo, quia dies resurrectionis dominicus singulariter in pascha praecepit[233] tenere.[234]

---

219. *Quinta*: *Quintus* R(a.c. u.v.).

220. *benedictio*: *benedicti* M.

221. *CXVII*: *CXVIII* FN.

222. *Psalmo dicit* om. M. *dicit*: *dicitur* Q; om. R.

223. *circumdederunt*: *circumderunt* M.

224. *sicut*: om. R(a.c).

225. *fauum* om. LR.

226. *autem*: om. R; *Domini* add. KLN.

227. *quam*: *quem* R.

228. *ea*: *eo* R(a.c.).

229. *illi*: *illa* M.

230. *ipsa*: *ipso* K(p.c.).

231. *Sexta . . . resurrexit* om. R(a.c., transp. post *25 tenere* p.c.).

232. *Vides*: *Videas* Q(a.c. u.v.).

233. *praecepit*: *praecipit* Q(p.c.).

234. *praecepit tenere*: *teneri praesit* K; *teneri possit* L; *teneri praecepit* NM; *teneri praecipitur* R.

19 The fifth benediction upon it is as the 117th psalm says:

20–21 'They surrounded me like bees the comb, and inflamed like fire in thornbushes' [Ps 117:12 LXX].

22–23 About the resurrection, however, it says: 'This is the day which the Lord made, let us exult and rejoice in it up to the horns of the altar' [Ps 117:24, 27 LXX].

24 The sixth benediction upon it is that on this day the Lord resurrected.

25 Thus, you see that the day of resurrection as a Sunday has prescribed specifically to keep it on Easter.

9

SOPHRONIUS OF JERUSALEM AND DIALOGUE OF JASON AND PAPISCUS

Uta Heil

Sophronius, born around 555 CE in Damascus, was a well-educated monk at the Theodosius monastery in Palestine and became at the old age of about eighty years bishop of Jerusalem (634–638 CE). It was he who had to hand over the city to Caliph Omar in 638 CE to avoid a violent conquest.[1] Sophronius is well-known for his theological engagement against monoenergetism / monotheletism and also composed several hymns.

In a sermon on January 1, 635 CE, a Sunday, he deals with the topic of the weekday, since the circumcision feast fell on a Sunday that year. This sermon, which was only discovered recently, has been handed down in Codex Sinaiticus gr. 1807 (s. xv/xvi) from the Catherine Monastery, and, because of the preceding quotation from his well-known Christmas sermon,[2] is undoubtedly attributable to Sophronius.[3] Therefore, the fragment fits in well with his

1. See John M. Duffy, ed., *Sophronios of Jerusalem: Homilies*, Dumbarton Oaks Medieval Library 64 (Cambridge, MA: Harvard University Press, 2020), here his introduction about his vita (vii–xii); also Elżbieta Szabat, "Sophronios of Jerusalem," in *Prosopography of Greek Rhetors and Sophists of the Roman Empire*, ed. Paweł Janiszewski, Krystyna Stebnicka, and Elżbieta Szabat (Oxford: Oxford University Press, 2015), 341f. Still worth reading is Henry Chadwick, "John Moschus and His Friend Sophronius the Sophist," *JTS* 25 (1974): 41–74.

2. This sermon was preached by Sophronius at the Church of Theotokos—at Christmas 634 CE, Christians were hindered to enter Bethlehem because the Arabs captured this site. Sophronius complains that he and his community are banned "from paradise." His sermon gives several details about the Arab conquest, and he exhorts the congregation to live piously and avoid sins; then they will also be able to rejoice in the downfall of the Saracens.

3. See John M. Duffy, "New Fragments of Sophronius of Jerusalem and Aristo of Pella?," in *Bibel, Byzanz und christlicher Orient, Festschrift St. Gerö*, ed. D. Bumazhnov, Orienalia Lovaniensia analecta 187 (Leuven: Peeters, 2011), 15–28; François Bovon and

other sermons on Christian feast days. In his Christmas sermon, too, Sophronius praises the coincidence of a high feast day with a Sunday, so that there is, so to speak, a double feast. This new fragment of a sermon on the feast of circumcision is reproduced here according to the publication by John M. Duffy in 2011 and after a look of my own into the manuscript.[4]

At the beginning of his sermon, Sophronius reminds the congregation of that very sermon a week earlier. Now what is special about his remarks is that Sophronius claims that the birth and circumcision actually happened on a Sunday at that time of Jesus. To prove this, he quotes from the Dialogue between Jason and Papiscus, which he attributes not to Ariston of Pella but to the apostle Luke. The dialogue tells how the Hebrew Christian Jason convinced the Alexandrian Jew Papiscus by treating the divine plan of salvation and the prophetically foretold messiahship of Jesus, and interpreting some scriptural passages (Gen 1:1; Deut 21:23 = Gal 3:13), and culminates in the decision to baptize Papiscus.

Actually, this dialogue is dated to the second century and is preserved only in fragments and regests, the oldest of which date back to the third century, where it is mostly attributed to Ariston of Pella.[5] It could possibly have served as a source for later anti-Jewish dialogues.

Because of the developed form of the implied creed within this fragment, however, this passage perhaps seems to have undergone some later editing. It presupposes also the idea of Sunday benedictions to emphasize the salvific

---

John M. Duffy, "A New Greek Fragment from Ariston of Pella's Dialogue of Jason and Papiscus," *HTR* 105 (2012): 457–65; Alberto Rigolio, *Christians in Conversation. A Guide to Late Antique Dialogues in Greek and Syriac*, Oxford Studies in Late Antiquity (Oxford: Oxford University Press, 2019), 39–43, and see the collection of testimonies for the dialogue by Harry Tolley, "The Jewish-Christian Dialogue Jason and Papiscus in Light of the Sinaiticus Fragment," *HTR* 114 (2021): 1–26.

4. See the digital version: https://tinyurl.com/4jxuf9sj. The fragment begins at folio 5v, line 2.

5. (Ps.-Cyprian =) Celsus Africanus mentions the dialogue in his letter to Vigilius, *De iudaica incredulitate* 8 (CCSL 3F:485–505 Ciccolini; this is an accompanying letter to a Latin translation of this dialogue); see also Origen, *Cels.* 4.52f. (GCS Orig. IV.1:325. 5-7.15–25 Koetschau). Eusebius of Caesarea reads in Ariston the flight of the Christian community to Pella because of the Jewish war (*Hist. eccl.* 4.6.3). Of interest is a remark by John of Scythopolis (Maximus Confessor), *Scholia in Dionysius Areopagitus, De mystica theologia* 1 (PG 4:421f.; sixth century): he found the mention of seven heavens in the dialogue written by Ariston (ἐν τῇ συγγεγραμμένῃ Ἀρίστωνι τῷ Πελλαί διαλέξει Παπίσκου καὶ Ἰάσονος), but attributed to Luke by Clement of Alexandria in his *Hyp.* 6 (not handed down). As Clement, also Sophronius attributes this dialogue to Luke. Two short remarks can also be found in Jerome: *Qu. hebr. Gen.* (CCSL 72:3.18 de Lagarde) on Gen 1:1; *Comm. Gal.* 2 (CCSL 77A:89f. Raspanti).

relevance of the Lord's Day. These aspects are entered here, so to say, in a formula of faith. This probably explains the duplications (italics); the connection to the Lord's Day is set in small capitals: "ON WHICH also Christ appeared on earth, and because, keeping the commandments and the scriptures, he *suffered*, and after *suffering rose* again, however, again ON HIM *rose* from the dead and appeared to his disciples, that is, the apostles, and ascended into heaven." The passage therefore does not refer all events of salvation history to Sunday, but only where it is explicitly noted: incarnation and resurrection and then also the second coming of Christ. Exactly this is summarized also by Sophronius himself in the last passage. He himself is only lacking the reference to the creation story.

Sunday is such a special day of the week that it overrides all others, especially the Sabbath. Sophronius thus seizes the opportunity, in view of the accidental coincidence of the feast of circumcision with the Lord's Day, to portray the splendor and solemnity of the Lord's Day.

To separate the literary levels, the quotations from Sophronius are indented, and the dialogue fragment quoted by him is indented twice. Not indented are the notes from the excerptor, who apparently collected various passages from the church fathers on the Christian calendar and understanding of time. It would certainly be worthwhile to analyze the entire manuscript itself, but we cannot do that here.

Sophronius of Jerusalem, *Sermon on Circumcision* (fragment)[6]

[5v, line 2] τοῦ αὐτοῦ ἐκ τοῦ β' βιβλίου εἰς τὴν περιτομὴν τοῦ κυρίου ἐν ἁγίᾳ κυριακῇ καταντήσασαν, λόγος ζ', οὗ ἡ ἀρχή "μεγάλα Χριστοῦ τὰ μυστήρια καὶ πάσης ἐκπλήξεως γέμοντα."
καὶ μεθ' ἕτερα·

τῇ πρὸ ταύτης ἁγίᾳ κυριακῇ (μία δὲ σαββάτων αὕτη τὸ παλαιὸν ὠνομάζετο· διὰ γὰρ τὴν ἐν αὐτῇ πραχθεῖσαν ἐκ νεκρῶν τοῦ σωτῆρος ἀνάστασιν κυριακὴ προσφόρως ὠνόμασται· καὶ τῶν ἄλλων γὰρ ἡμερῶν κεκυρίευκεν καὶ κράτος τὸ κατ' αὐτῶν ἐκομίσατο), τὴν τοῦ Χριστοῦ τοῦ θεοῦ καὶ σωτῆρος σωτήριον γέννησιν καὶ τὴν αὐτοῦ φωτοφόρον ἀνάστασιν συνδραμοῦσαν εἰς ταὐτὸν ἑορτάσαμεν. νυνὶ δὲ πάλιν κυριακῆς τῆς μακαρίας ἡ λαμπρότης ἀνέτειλεν, ἄλλην ἡμῖν Χριστοῦ πρᾶξιν μυστικὴν ἑαυτῇ συνεξέλαμψεν, καὶ κοινωνὸν τῆς οἰκείας προόδου πεποίηκεν (οὐκ ἀεὶ μὲν κυριακῆς τὴν προέλευσιν φέρουσαν, νυνὶ δὲ κατὰ τὴν ἑβδοματικὴν τοῦ κύκλου περιφορὰν καταντήσασαν) καὶ φαιδροτέραν ἡμῖν τὴν αὐτῆς ἐνδεικνυμένη λαμπρότητα, διπλῷ φωτὶ τῷ θεικῷ καταστράπτουσα, καὶ τοὺς συνειλεγμένους ἡμᾶς πλουσίως αὐγάζουσα. πολλὰ γὰρ τῆς ἁγίας κυρι[6r]ακῆς ἐστὶν τὰ ἐξαίρετα καὶ ἀξίως καὶ δικαίως παρὰ πάσας τὰς ἡμέρας αὕτη τετίμηται· οὐ μόνον γὰρ ἡμέρα καθέστηκεν Χριστοῦ τοῦ θεοῦ λαμπρᾶς ἀναστάσεως, ἀλλὰ καὶ τῆς αὐτοῦ ἐκ παρθένου τῆς θείας καὶ μόνης ἐπὶ γῆς θεομήτορος θειοτάτης καὶ θαυμαστῆς γεννήσεως. ἐν κυριακῇ γὰρ ἀληθῶς καὶ γεγέννηται, ὅτε καθ' ἡμᾶς ἀπετίκτετο καὶ τῆς ἡμετέρας ἡμῖν σαρκικῆς ἐκοινώνει γενέσεως, τὴν σωτηρίαν ἡμῶν ἐλθὼν πραγματεύσασθαι καὶ θανάτου ἡμᾶς καὶ ἀπωλείας ὠνήσασθαι. καὶ πόθεν τοῦτο φαμέν; ἔστιν γὰρ ἔστιν τοῖς πολλοῖς ἀγνοούμενον καὶ διὰ τοῦτο ξένον φανεῖται λεγόμενον καὶ δεῖται πάντως πιστῆς ἀποδείξεως.

Καὶ μεθ' ἕτερα·[7]

Λουκᾶς οὖν ἡμᾶς ὁ φανότατος ταύτην μυσταγωγεῖ τὴν λαμπροφανῆ καὶ ἐπέραστον εἴδησιν, οὐκ εὐαγγελίῳ τῷ θείῳ ταύτης τυπώσας τὴν μήνυσιν οὐκ ἀποστολικαῖς αὐτὴν ἐγγραψάμενος πράξεσιν, ἀλλ' ἐν ἑτέρῳ αὐτοῦ διαμνημονεύσας συγγράμματι, ὅπερ καὶ χαρακτῆρι διαλογικῷ τεκτηνάμενος Ἰάσωνος ἐπονομάζει καὶ Παπίσκου Διάλογον.[8]

6. Duffy, "New Fragments of Sophronius," 16–18 (see above, n. 3).
7. Tolley presents the fragment from here onward (24f.).
8. On the attribution of the dialogue to Luke, see above, n. 5.

Translation

By the same author, from the second book on the circumcision of the Lord, which happened on the holy Lord's Day, the seventh text, the beginning of which reads, "Great are the mysteries of Christ, and full of all things astonishing."

And after others [Sophronius]:

> On the preceding holy Lord's Day (but it was called the first day of the week in former days, but because of the resurrection of the Savior from the dead which was effected on that day it is primarily called Lord's Day, for it dominates all other days and seized power over them) we celebrated the redemptive birth of Christ, God and Savior, as well as his light-bearing resurrection, which fell on the same day of the week. But now again the splendor of the blessed Lord's Day has risen, another mysterious act of Christ for us has appeared together on it, and happened parallel in the course of time (for it does not always fall on the Lord's Day, but now after the course of the week the passage of time meet) and even more luminous is to us the splendor appearing on this day, dazzling with a double divine light and abundantly irradiating us assembled ones. For the holy Lord's Day has many outstanding aspects and is worthily and rightfully honored above all other days. It is not only the day of the luminous resurrection of Christ as God, but also of his divine and miraculous birth from the divine Virgin, who alone on earth is the Mother of God. For on the Lord's Day he was truly begotten, when he was born like us, and took part in our fleshly birth like us, and came to bring us salvation and to redeem us from death and destruction. And from where do we say this? This is something that is unknown to many, and therefore what is said seems strange and certainly requires trustworthy proof.

And after others [Sophronius]:

> Luke, then, the one thus enlightened, reveals to us this splendid and welcome knowledge, not by giving a hint in the divine Gospel, nor by engraving it in the Acts of the Apostles, but by bringing it to our remembrance in another writing of his, which is composed in the style of a dialogue, and which he called Dialogue of Jason and Papiscus.

Καὶ μετ᾽ ὀλίγα·

> ἐν τούτῳ γοῦν, φησίν, τῷ συγγράμματι, ὡς ἐκ προσώπου Παπίσκου συν[6v] θεὶς τὴν ἐρώτησιν,
>
> > Παπίσκος εἶπεν· ἤθελον μαθεῖν διὰ ποίαν αἰτίαν τὴν μίαν τῶν σαββάτων τιμιωτέραν ἔχετε;
> >
> > Ἰάσων εἶπεν· ταῦτα ὁ θεὸς ἐνετείλατο διὰ τοῦ Μωυσέως λέγων· "ἰδοῦ ἐγὼ ποιῶ τὰ ἔσχατα ὡς τὰ πρῶτα." ἔσχατόν ἐστιν τὸ σάββατον, ἡ δὲ μία τῶν σαββάτων πρώτη· ἐν αὐτῇ γὰρ διὰ λόγου θεοῦ ἡ ἀρχὴ τοῦ παντὸς κόσμου γίνεται, ὡς καὶ ἡ γραφὴ Μωυσέως μηνύει, καθὼς λέγει ὁ θεός· "γενηθήτω φῶς, καὶ ἐγένετο φῶς." ὁ δὲ λόγος ἐξελθὼν ἐκ τοῦ θεοῦ καὶ τὸ φῶς ποιήσας[9] ἦν ὁ Χριστός, ὁ υἱὸς τοῦ θεοῦ δι᾽ οὗ καὶ τὰ λοιπὰ πάντα ἐγένετο.

Καὶ ἕτερα ἀγαθὰ φήσας ἐπάγει λέγων·

> ἔνθεν οὖν γνῶθι, ἄνθρωπε, ὅτι κατὰ πάντα δικαίως τιμῶμεν τὴν μίαν τῶν σαββάτων, ἀρχὴν οὖσαν τῆς πάσης κτίσεως, ὅτι ἐν αὐτῇ ὁ Χριστὸς ἐφανερώθη ἐπὶ τῆς γῆς καὶ ὅτι τηρῶν τὰς ἐντολὰς καὶ τὰς γρφὰς ἔπαθεν, καὶ παθὼν ἀνέστη· ἀνέστη πάλιν ἐν αὐτῇ ἐκ νεκρῶν καὶ ὀφθεὶς τοῖς μαθηταῖς αὐτοῦ, τουτέστιν τοῖς ἀποστόλοις, εἰς οὐρανοὺς ἐπορεύθη· καὶ ὅτι αὕτη ἐστὶν ἡ τῶν αἰώνων ἡμέρα, εἰς ὀγδοάδα πίπτουσα καὶ μέλλουσα ἀνατέλλειν τοῖς δικαίοις ἐν ἀφθαρσίᾳ, ἐν τῇ βασιλείᾳ τοῦ θεοῦ, φῶς αἰώνιον εἰς [7r] τοὺς αἰῶνας, ἀμήν. ἡ γὰρ ἡμέρα ἡ τοῦ σαββάτου πίπτει εἰς κατάπαυσιν διὰ τὸ εἶναι αὐτὴν τῆς ἑβδομάδος. διὰ ταύτην οὖν αἰτίαν ἡμεῖς τὴν μίαν τῶν σαββάτων τιμῶμεν πολλὴν ἡμῖν φέρουσαν ἀγαθῶν παρουσίαν.

Καὶ ταῦτα μὲν Λουκᾶς ὁ Θεσπέσιος τοῦ Ἰάσωνος καὶ Παπίσκου Διάλογον συγγράφων ἐδίδαξεν, ὡς κυριακὴ ἡμέρα <. . .>φεγγὴς καὶ διάσημος καὶ τῶν ἄλλων ἡμερῶν πρώτη τῷ χρόνῳ καθέστηκεν, καὶ τῆς ἐνσάρκου τοῦ Σωτῆρος γεννήσεως ἡμέρα γνωρίζεται καὶ τῆς αὐτοῦ ἐκ νεκρῶν ἀναστάσεως, ὡσαύτως δὲ καὶ τῆς ἀπ᾽ οὐρανῶν αὐτοῦ δευτέρας ἀφίξεως, ἥτις καὶ ἀδιάδοχός ἐστιν καὶ ἀπέραντος, οὔτε εἰς τέλος πώποτε λήγουσα, οὐδὲ ἑτέραν μετ᾽ αὐτὴν παραπέμπουσα πάραδον, καὶ διὰ τοῦτο τὴν ἐξ ἡμῶν τιμὴν καὶ τὸ σέβασμα ὑπὲρ τὰς πολλὰς ἡμέρας κληρώσασα, ὡς μυρίων ἡμῖν ἀγαθῶν παρουσίαν ἀπαρόδευτον τίκτουσα.

---

9. Bovon and Duffy, "New Greek Fragment," translate, "the word which proceeded from God and created the light was Christ" (462), but interpret in a vague manner: "This light is then declared by Ariston to be equivalent to Christ" (464). Tolley translates, "The Logos which came forth from God and made the light was Christ" (25), but overinterprets in this phrase deficient Trinitarian theology (the Logos only came forth from God and is not God himself, 15f.).

And shortly after [Sophronius]:

So in this writing, as I said, by asking the question in the person of Papiscus,

> Papiscus said: I would like to know, for what reason do you consider the first day after the Sabbath more venerable?
>
> Jason said: God commanded this through Moses when he said, "Behold, I make the last things like the first" [*agraphon*, also in Barn. 6.13]. The last is the Sabbath, but the one day after the Sabbath, however, is the first, because at this day, through the Word of God the beginning of the whole world occurred, as indeed the writing of Moses reminds us, as God says, "Let there be light, and there was light" [Gen 1:3]. But the Word who proceeds from God and creates the light was Christ, the Son of God, through whom also the rest of all things came to be [see John 1:1, 3].

And after other good things he continues:

> Therefore, people, recognize that it is justified in every way to honor the first day after the Sabbath, since it is the beginning of all creation, on which also Christ appeared on earth, and because, keeping the commandments and the scriptures, he suffered, and after suffering rose again, however, again on this day he rose from the dead and appeared to his disciples, that is, the apostles, and ascended into heaven, and because this day is the day of the ages, it is falling on the eighth [*ogdoas*[10]] intending to rise for the righteous in incorruption, in the reign of God, as the eternal light for ages, amen. For the day of the Sabbath falls on the rest, for it is the seventh day. For this reason we worship the first day after the Sabbath, for it brings us the great presence of good things.

[Sophronius] And this is taught by the god-inspired Luke, writing the Dialogue between Jason and Papiscus, that the Lord's Day is great, extraordinary and the first in time to precede the other days, and it is known as the day of the incarnation of the Savior and his resurrection from the dead, as well as of his second coming from the heavens, a day without successor and without limit, neither coming to an end once nor being given over to another succeeding day after it, and therefore deserving of honor and veneration from us above all days, since it brings for us unlimited presence of countless good things.[11]

---

10. See Barn. 15.8 for a similar statement.

11. See some parallels with the unknown fragment in Codex Vaticanus gr. 2392, p. 473f.

10

VISIO PAULI 34 OR APOCALYPSE OF PAUL 44

Uta Heil

The (Latin) *Visio Pauli* or (Greek) Apocalypse of Paul (ECCA 818; CANT 325; BHL 6580–6582; BHG 1460) is a revelatory dialogue probably composed at the end of the fourth century at the latest, though it was transmitted in several versions and translations later on.[1] A Latin translation spread from around the fifth century onward. The text describes the afterlife, especially the punishments and the torments of sinners. One passage is of interest here, in which one can read that the damned are granted relief from torment on the Lord's Day.

The *Visio Pauli* was attested by Sozomenus (fifth century), who knew the legend of the finding of the book and questioned its authenticity. He states:

> So the work entitled *Apocalypse of the Apostle Paul*, though unrecognized by the ancients, is still esteemed by most of the monks. Some persons affirm that the book was found during this reign, by divine revelation, in a marble box, buried beneath the soil in the house of Paul at Tarsus in Cilicia. I have been informed that this report is false by Cilix, a presbyter of the church in Tarsus, a man of very advanced age, as is indicated by his gray hairs, who says that no such occurrence is known among them, and wonders if the heretics did not invent the story.[2]

1. See "The Apocalypse of Paul (Visio Pauli)," in *The Apocryphal New Testament: A Collection of Apocryphal Christian Literature in an English Translation*, ed. J. K. Elliott (Oxford: Clarendon, 1993), 616–44, here 616–19, and also the entry in North American Society for the Study of Christian Apocryphal Literature: https://tinyurl.com/3patcay7.

2. Sozomenus, *Hist. eccl.* 7.19.10f. (GCS n.s. 4:331.22–332.1 Hansen; trans. Chester Hartranft in *NPNF*² 2:390): τὴν δὲ νῦν ὡς Ἀποκάλυψιν Παύλου τοῦ ἀποστόλου φερομένην, ἣν οὐδεὶς ἀρχαίων οἶδε, πλεῖστοι μοναχῶν ἐπαινοῦσιν. ἐπὶ ταύτης δὲ τῆς βασιλείας ἰσχυρίζονταί τινες ταύτην ηὑρῆσθαι τὴν βίβλον. λέγουσι γὰρ ἐκ θείας ἐπιφανείας ἐν Ταρσῷ τῆς Κιλικίας κατὰ τὴν οἰκίαν Παύλου μαρμαρίνην λάρνακα ὑπὸ γῆν

Augustine (†430 CE) also criticized this text as a fabrication with the following words:

> Taking advantage of which, there have been some vain individuals, who, with a presumption that betrays the grossest folly, have forged a Revelation of Paul, crammed with all manner of fables, which has been rejected by the orthodox church; affirming it to be that whereof he had said that he was caught up into the third heavens, and there heard unspeakable words "which it is not lawful for a man to utter" (2 Cor 12:2). Nevertheless, the audacity of such might be tolerable, had he said that he heard words which it is not as yet lawful for a man to utter; but when he said, "which it is not lawful for a man to utter," who are they that dare to utter them with such impudence and non-success?[3]

Both descriptions apparently mean the Apocalypse of Paul or *Visio Pauli*, for it invokes Paul's rapture and also starts with a corresponding book-finding legend. The text in both the Greek version and the longer Latin account (see below) actually begins with the following narration of the discovery of the book: During the reign of Emperor Theodosius II, an angel appears at night to a respected man who lives at that time in Tarsus in the house that belonged to St. Paul and tells him to break up the foundations of the house and to publish what he finds there. The man thinks it is a deception. Coming the third time, the angel scourges him and forces him to break up the foundations. He does so and finds a marble box on which it is written that in it are Paul's revelation and the shoes in which he used to walk when he taught the word of God. But he shrinks from opening the box and brings it to a judge, who sends it to the emperor Theodosius,[4] who opens it and sends the text to Jerusalem after making a copy. This frame story introduces the actual text, which recounts Paul's insights into the world beyond.

εὑρεθῆναι καὶ ἐν αὐτῇ τὴν βίβλον εἶναι. ἐρομένῳ δέ μοι περὶ τούτου ψεῦδος ἔφησεν εἶναι Κίλιξ πρεσβύτερος τῆς ἐν Ταρσῷ ἐκκλησίας· γεγονέναι μὲν γὰρ πολλῶν ἐτῶν καὶ ἡ πολιὰ τὸν ἄνδρα ἐδείκνυ· ἔλεγε δὲ μηδὲν τοιοῦτον ἐπίστασθαι παρ' αὐτοῖς συμβάν, θαυμάζειν τε εἰ μὴ τάδε πρὸς αἱρετικῶν ἀναπέπλασται.

3. Augustine, *Tract. Ev. Jo.* 98.8 on John 16:12 (CCSL 36:581.31–21 Willems; trans. James Innes in *NPNF*[1] 7:380): *qua occasione uani quidam apocalypsim pauli, quam sana non recipit ecclesia, nescio quibus fabulis plenam, stultissima praesumtione finxerunt, dicentes hanc esse unde dixerat raptum se fuisse in tertium caelum, et illic audisse ineffabilia uerba quae non licet homini loqui. utcumque illorum tolerabilis esset audacia, si se audisse dixisset quae adhuc non licet homini loqui; cum uero dixerit: quae non licet homini loqui, isti qui sunt qui haec audeant impudenter et infeliciter loqui?*

4. See also the reference to Theodosius in the Apocalypse of Anastasia, p. 497.

One passage of this Latin *Visio Pauli* is of special interest here and is presented below in different versions: By the intercession of the archangel Michael, other angels, and Paul, the damned are granted relief from torment on the Lord's Day. Within the text, this passage forms the conclusion of the description of the punishments of hell before paradise is described. The Greek Apocalypse of Paul, probably the basis for Latin translations, contained this idea of the interruption of the torments on Sunday from the very beginning. Here, it is reported briefly that Christ, at the intercession of Gabriel (not Michael) and Paul, grants rest on the Lord's Day, and all are relieved about it and give thanks.[5] The narrative context makes it clear that this rest from torment on Sunday is not because the agents of torture are granted a day's rest from work, but that the character of Sunday as a day of celebration and joy is not matched by this torment.

Within this context, another passage of Augustine is interesting, although not referring to the *Visio Pauli* directly: just as the happiness of the blessed has no interruption, the torments of those to be punished in hell have also no interruption, even if there might be a temporary (*certis temporum*) mitigation.[6] However, even if Augustine concedes here that God may temporarily alleviate or interrupt the torment, he neither specifies

5. *Visio Pauli* 44 (Greek text from Constantin Tischendorf, *Apocalypses Apocryphae Mosis, Esdrae, Pauli, Iohannis, item Mariae Dormitio* [Leipzig: Mendelssohn, 1866], 63): νῦν δὲ διὰ Γαβριὴλ τὸν ἄγγελον τῆς δικαιοσύνης μου καὶ διὰ Παῦλον τὸν ἀγαπητόν μου δίδωμι ὑμῖν νύκταν καὶ τὴν ἡμέραν τῆς ἁγίας κυριακῆς, ἐν ᾗ ἠγέρθην ἐκ νεκρῶν, εἰς ἀνάπαυσιν. καὶ ἀνεβόησαν πάντες οἱ ἐν ταῖς κολάσεσιν λέγοντες· εὐλογοῦμέν σε, υἱὲ τοῦ θεοῦ τοῦ ζῶντος· βέλτιον ἡμῖν ἡ τοιαύτη ἀνάπαυσις ἢ τὴν ζωὴν ἣν ἐζήσαμεν ἐν τῷ κόσμῳ πολιτευόμενοι. See on the Coptic version of this passage Lautaro Roig Lanzillotta, "The Coptic Apocalypse of Paul in Ms Or 7023," in *The Visio Pauli and the Gnostic Apocalypse of Paul*, ed. Jan N. Bremmer and István Czachesz, Christian Apocrypha 8 (Leuven: Peeters, 2007), 158–97, here 192f. He is preparing a new edition and commentary of the Coptic version, announced for Vigiliae Christianae Supplements in 2023.

6. Augustine, *Ench.* 29.112 (CCSL 46:109.56–58 Evans): *sed poenas damnatorum certis temporum interuallis existiment, si hoc eis placet, aliquatenus mitigari*. See for a more hesitant statement Augustine, *Enarrat. Ps.* 105.2 on Ps 105:1 (CCSL 40:1554.48–52 Dekkers and Fraipont; trans. Maria Boulding in *The Works of Saint Augustine III/19*, 205): *sed tolerabiliorem quosdam excepturos damnationem in quorumdam comparatione legimus; alicuius uero mitigari eam cui est traditus poenam, uel quibusdam interuallis habere aliquam pausam, quis audacter dixerit, quandoquidem unam stillam diues ille non meruit?* "Yet since we read that some will be condemned to a more tolerable damnation than others, who would be so rash as to assert that a punishment assigned to someone can be further mitigated, or interrupted by some kind of respite, when the rich man in hell did not qualify even for a drop of water?" Optimistic also is Prudentius, *Cathemerinon* 5.125–134 (CSEL 61:30 Bergmann), who takes up this idea, possibly borrowed from the *Visio Pauli*; see Sebastian Merkle, "Die Sabbatruhe in der Hölle. Ein Beitrag zur

"temporarily" nor mentions the Lord's Day. See, however, from "this world" the law in *Codex Theodosianus* 9.3.7, which states that prisoners are to be granted relief on Sunday.[7] Therefore, these passages from the *Visio Pauli* testify to the conviction that Sunday is a feast day and a day of joy. A respite from the torments of hell is not granted, after all, because the agents of torment take a break or rest from work but because, out of compassion, relief is to be granted at least on this day of joy. The Lord's Day is also the day on which forgiveness of sins can be requested, and the common and simultaneous prayers of Christians with the apostles and martyrs and angels bring about mitigation of punishment.

On the basis of the new study on the transmission of the Latin versions by Lenka Jiroušková, the general assessment of Theodore Silverstein from 1935[8] that a longer Latin version (which she now divides into L1, L2, and L3 and which is based on seven manuscripts) can be distinguished from a shorter Latin version is correct.[9] While the longer versions report on heaven and hell,[10] the shorter versions concentrate on the description of hell alone, omitting also the above mentioned narration of the discovery in Tarsus. Here, Jiroušková has expanded the inventory of manuscripts up to 102 for the shorter version (and moreover assigns three further manuscripts to an intermediate version).[11] She then deals with this Latin shorter version, which was much more widespread than the longer version, and distinguishes three versions, A, B, and C.[12] In the group of manuscripts that are to be assigned to group B and C, this passage on Sunday rest in hell was even expanded.[13]

Prudentius-Erklärung und zur Geschichte der Apokryphen," *RQ* 9 (1895): 489–505. See also Jewish ideas of a Sabbath rest as long as prayers continue (Gen. Rab. 11.5 and other later evidence): Lévi Israel, "Le repos ṣabbatique des ames damnees," *REJ* 25 (1892): 1–13.

7. See above, p. 19f.

8. See Theodore Silverstein and Anthony Hilhorst, *Apocalypse of Paul: A New Critical Edition of the Three Long Latin Versions*, Cahiers d'Orientalisme 21 (Geneva, 1998), based on the study of Silverstein, *Visio Sancti Pauli. The History of the Apocalypse in Latin Together with Nine Texts* (London, 1935). He reedited M. R. James, *Apocrypha Anecdota: A Collection of Thirteen Apocryphal Books and Fragments*, TS 2/3 (Cambridge: Cambridge University Press, 1893), 11–42.

9. Jiroušková, *Die Visio Pauli.*

10. See the content scheme of Jiroušková, *Die Visio Pauli*, 160.

11. See Jiroušková, *Die Visio Pauli*, 27.

12. See Jiroušková, *Die Visio Pauli*, 163f.; the relevant sections on Sunday rest in hell are at 204, 210, 211–15.

13. See Jiroušková, *Die Visio Pauli*, 263–68, 301–3, listed now as scene 34.

Interestingly, eighteen manuscripts[14] of groups B and C also offer the Letter from Heaven or even connect the *Visio Pauli* with this Letter from Heaven.[15] The connection with the Sunday theme probably also led to the fact that group C even begins with a call for the sanctification of Sunday.[16] Jiroušková's further research result is probably to be corrected in the respect that, in some manuscripts in which the Letter from Heaven is connected with the *Visio Pauli* (C^7; Co; V^3), these passages are rather to be regarded as the independently transmitted list of Sunday benedictions, from which in turn similar passages can be found in the Letter from Heaven.

That this combination of texts is found in various manuscripts of different groups, including three singular manuscripts, suggests that this connection between these two texts occurred several times: Just as the vision of the severe punishment encourages taking Sunday worship seriously, the Letter from Heaven expands the aspects of moral demands. The provenance of the manuscripts indicates that this happened in the German-speaking and Anglo-Norman regions (not in the North French and Lower Lorraine regions of Group A).

In the late Middle Ages (fourteenth century), the so-called Flagellants (*Geißler*) took up both texts again and integrated them into their vernacular sermons—here we also find the combination of both texts, or predominantly the *Visio Pauli* was integrated into the Letter from Heaven.[17]

---

14. From group B: Bx^1 = Bruxelles, Bibl. Royale Albert Ier II 1053 (see p. 45); Co = Collegeville, MN lat. 5 (only Sunday list, see p. 58f.); M^1 = Munich, BSB clm 2625 (before *Visio Pauli*; see p. 92f.); M^3 = Munich, BSB clm 12005 with a short passage from Letter from Heaven in the *Visio Pauli* (see p. 94f.); P^5 = Paris, BN lat. 3343 (see p. 112f.); Pr^1 = Praha, Archiv Hradu N 42 (*Visio Pauli* is part of Letter from Heaven; see p. 117f.); Pr^2 = Praha, Narodni Knihovna III.D.13 (*Visio Pauli* is part of the Letter from Heaven; see p. 118f.); Pr^5 = Praha, Narodni Knihovna XIII.G.18 (*Visio Pauli* is part of Letter from Heaven; see p. 121f.); U^3 = Uppsala, UB C 212 (*Visio Pauli* is part of Letter from Heaven; see p. 131f.); W^2 = Vienna, ÖNB 1629 (Letter from Heaven is part of *Visio Pauli*; see p. 135). From group C: C^7 = Cambridge, St John's College MS F.22 (see p. 54, only Sunday list); L^8 = London, BL Royal 8.F.VI (see p. 81f.); L^{10} = London, BL Royal 11.B.X (next to each other; see p. 83f.); O^5 = Oxford, Merton College MS 13 (next to each other; see p. 106f.). Singular manuscripts also: Be^1 = Berlin, Staatsbibliothek theol. lat. qu. 61 (see p. 40); C^4 = Cambridge, Pembroke College 103 (see p. 51); Ve = Venezia, S.Marco lat. Z. 507 (next to each other; see p. 133f.). In addition V^3 = Vaticana, Ms. Pal. lat. 220 (only Sunday list, see p. 134), a manuscript of transition between the long and short *Visio Pauli*. See Jiroušková, *Die Visio Pauli*, 379–84.

15. See also above on the manuscripts of the Letter from Heaven at pp. 39–44, 53. Mostly in Latin Recension II.

16. E.g. (Jiruošková, *Die Visio Pauli*, 211): *Dies dominicus dies letus, in quo gaudent angeli plus quam in aliis diebus*. See also p. 184.

17. See Jiruošková, *Die Visio Pauli*, 464–68, 491–93. See also above, pp. 124f.

Below, the passages on relief from torment on Sunday are presented in the three versions, A, B, and C, with an English translation by Christoph Scheerer; the Greek version has already been quoted above.[18] The precise duration of Sunday, which becomes recognizable here, is congruent with the provision in the Letter from Heaven.[19]

18. See n. 5.
19. See on p. 182f.

Visio Pauli

Version A (Jiroušková, *Die Visio Pauli*, 204 according to Ba = Barcelona, Archivo de la Catedral de Barcelona, Ms. lat. 28, fols. 118r–119r; s. xii):

Et illi, qui erant in penis, viderunt Michahelem et Paulum et exclamaverunt una voce dicentes: Miserere nobis, Michahel, archangele Christi, et dilectissime Paule, intercedite pro nobis! Scimus enim, quia vestras orationes deus exaudit!

Et ait angelus: Flete et flebo vobiscum et qui mecum sunt, si forte misereatur vobis deus et donet vobis refrigerium. Audientes autem hec, qui erant in penis, exclamaverunt omnes una voce dicentes: Miserere nobis, fili dei!

Et exaudivit eos dominus Ihesus Christus et dixit eis: Propter pietatem meam et propter Michahelis archangeli et Pauli apostoli et aliorum sanctorum et propter orationes fratrum nostrorum, qui sunt in mundo, damus vobis indulgentiam omnibus dominicis diebus.

Version A (Jiroušková, *Die Visio Pauli*, 538 according to Bx^2 = Bruxelles, Bibliothèque Royale Albert Ier, 4774–4779 [Van den Gheyn Nr. 1367], fols. 120vb–122ra; s. xiii):[20]

Et peccatores, qui erant in penis, exclamaverunt una voce, cum vidissent Micaelem et Paulum cum eo dicentes: Miserere nostri, domine, filii dei vivi!

Et oraverunt Michael et Paulus ad deum pro illis, et pro illorum oratione et misericordia omnipotentis dei optinuerunt refrigerium noctis et diei dominice.

Siquidem quando vadit anima de corpore, primo ad orientem, deinde ad Iherusalem, deinde ad domum, quam edificavit Adam, deinde ad Iordanem, deinde ad templum Salomonis, deinde ad Bethleem Iuda, deinde ad montem Oliveti, deinde ascendit scalam ad superna, ubi conveniunt ei quatuor milia angelorum et archangelorum de tartaris preliantes circa anima hominis. Deinde venit ad Ierusalem celestem in septem diebus et die VII. iudicatur in conspectu troni, prout gessit sive bonum sive malum et alia multa, que non licebat homini loqui.

20. Compared to the version above, where the prayers are embellished in verbatim speech, here the events are reported more briefly. The following passage offered here describes the ascent of a soul to heavenly judgment: after a journey to the Holy Land with

Translation

And they, who were in punishment, saw Michael and Paul and cried out with one voice: Have mercy upon us, Michael, archangel of Christ, and most beloved Paul, stand up for us! For we know that God answers your prayers!

And the angel said: Cry, and I, and who are with me will cry with you, if God might like to have mercy on you and grants you refrigeration. But when they, who were in punishment, heard that, they all cried out with one voice: Have mercy upon us, son of God!

And the Lord Jesus Christ answered their prayer and said to them: Due to my charity and due to [the charity of] the archangel Michael and the apostle Paul and other saints and due to the prayers of our brothers who are in the world, we grant you relief on every Sunday.

And the sinners, who were in punishment, cried out with one voice as they saw Michael and Paul with him, and said: Have mercy upon us, Lord, son of the living God!

And Michael and Paul prayed to God for them, and by their prayer and by the mercy of the almighty God, they obtained refrigeration during the night and day of Sunday.

But when the soul goes away from the body, [it goes] first to the East, then to Jerusalem, then to the house which built Adam, then to the Jordan, then to the temple of Salomon, then to Bethlehem in Judah, then to the Mount of Olives, then it climbs the stairs upwards, where four thousand angels and archangels from the nether world meet with it, and they fight about the soul of man. Then it comes to celestial Jerusalem for seven days and on the seventh it is judged before the throne according to whether it has donc good or cvil and many other things about which man is not permitted to speak.

---

several stations, the soul remains for seven days, that is, one week, in the heavenly Jerusalem with the subsequent judgment on the seventh day. No explicit day of the week is mentioned, but the idea of the eschatological judgment on the Lord's Day has certainly influenced the depiction of the heavenly soul's journey with this seven-day sojourn in heavenly Jerusalem. See variants of further manuscripts from version A in Jiroušková, *Die Visio Pauli*, 538f.

Version B (Jiroušková, *Die Visio Pauli*, 210f., according to St = Stuttgart, Württembergische Landesbibliothek, HB I 74, fols. 62v–64v; s. xiii: 3. third):[21]

Et ecce movebatur celum et filius dei descendebat de celo et diadema in capite suo.

Et iterum clamabant omnes anime in tormentis posite: Miserere, domine, miserere nobis! Prosit nobis adventus tuus, domine!

Quibus dominus dixit: Quare estis in pena? Et cur postulatis a me requiem, cum nichil boni fecistis? Quid passi estis propter me? Crucifixus sum pro vobis, lancea perforatus, clavis fixus et mortuus sum pro vobis; vos non redemi auro nec argento, sed meo corpore proprio. Dedi me in mortem, ut viveretis. Et vos semper iniqui fuistis, fures, avari, superbi, invidi, mendaces, cupidi, terrenis actibus semper inhesistis et non celestibus.

Et iterum clamabant: Miserere nobis, Michahel, et tu Paule, dulcissime domini, interpella pro nobis!

Et ait Michahel: Nunc flete et ego et Paulus una cum omnibus angelis flebimus vobiscum. Et ait Paulus: Misereatur vestri deus et propitius sit vobis, ut det vobis refrigerium. Audientes hec, qui erant in penis, clamabant una voce: Miserere nobis, fili David!

Et dixit iterum Christus: Quid boni fecistis?

Prostravit se Michahel et Paulus et omnes angeli ante filium dei, ut requiem in die dominico haberent anime.

Et ait Christus: Nunc propter Michahelem et Paulum, dilectum meum, et angelos meos et propter omnes fratres meos, qui offerunt oblationes in terra pro vivis ac defunctis, et maxime pro mea misericordia do vobis requiem omnibus, qui estis in penis, nocte diei dominice usque in perpetuum de hora nona sabbati usque ad secundam feriam hora prima.

21. This version is more elaborate, with longer dialogues, which expands on Christ's response in the style of Matt 25 and also contains a dialogue between the damned and the archangel Michael. See variants of further manuscripts of version B in Jiroušková, *Die Visio Pauli*, 628–45.

Translation

And see, heaven moved and the son of God descended from heaven and had a diadem on his head. And once more, all souls which are put in torment cried: Have mercy, Lord, have mercy upon us! Your advent, Lord, shall benefit us!

The Lord said to them: Why are you in pain? And why do you postulate rest from me, albeit you have done nothing good? What have you suffered for me? I have been crucified for you, perforated by a lance, fixed by nails, and died for you; I have redeemed you neither by gold nor by silver but by my own body. I gave me to death for you can live. But you have been iniquitous all the time, thieves, niggards, proud boys, enviers, liars, voluptuaries, all the time you stuck to terrestrial and not celestial acts.

They cried once more: Have mercy upon us, Michael, and you, Paul, most sweet of the Lord, appeal for us!

And Michael said: Now cry, and I and Paul together with all angels will cry with you. And Paul said: May God have mercy upon you and be well-disposed to you, so that he gives you refrigeration. When they, who were in punishment, heard that, the all cried with one voice: Have mercy upon us, son of David!

And once more Christ said: What good have you done?

Michael prostrated himself and Paul and all angels before the son of God so that the souls might have rest on Sunday.

And Christ said: Now, due to Michael and Paul, my beloved, and my angels, and due to all my brothers who give oblations on earth for the living and the dead, and mostly by my mercy, I give rest to all of you who are in punishment from the night of Sunday for ever from the ninth hour of Sabbath until the first hour of the second day.

Version C (Jiroušková, *Die Visio Pauli*, 215f., according to C^5 = Cambridge, Pembroke College, MS. 258, fols. 52ra–53ra, s. xiii ex.):[22]

Et tunc Paulus vidit celum subito moveri et filium dei descendentem de celo et diadema in capite eius. Et tunc clamaverunt una voce, qui erant in inferno, dicentes: Miserere nobis, filii dei excelsi!

Et vox audita est super omnes dicens: Quare non fecistis bonum? Ut quid postulatis a me benediccionem vel requiem? Ego crucifixus fui pro vobis, lancea perforatus, clavis confixus, acetum cum felle mixtum dedistis mihi bibere; ego pro vobis dedi me ipsum in mortem, ut vivetis mecum. Et vos mendaces fuistis et fures et avari et invidi et superbi et maledicti nec quecqua bona fecistis nec penitenciam nec ieiunium nec elemosinam.

Post hec prostravit se Michael et Paulus et milia milium angelorum ante filium dei et petierunt, ut requiem haberent in die dominico omnes, qui erant in inferno.

Et ait dominus: Propter Michaelem et Paulum, maxime propter meam bonitatem dabo eiis requiem ab hora nona sabbati usque ad primam horam secunde ferie.[23]

22. See variants of further manuscripts of version C in Jiroušková, *Die Visio Pauli*, 821–43.

23. Interestingly, the exact length of the Lord's Day is given here, in the same form as it is found in the Letter from Heaven—an influence of this text into this tradition can be assumed, since this time indication is unique. See p. 182f.

And then Paul saw that heaven suddenly moved and the son of God descended from heaven and had a diadem on his head. And then they who were in the inferno cried with one voice and said: Have mercy upon us, son of the exalted God.

And a voice was heard that said upon all: Why did you no good? What for do you postulate benediction or rest from me? I have been crucified for you, perforated by a lance, fixed with nails, you gave me vinegar mixed with bile to drink; I gave myself for you to death for you live with me. But you were liars and thieves and niggards and enviers and proud boys and maledicted, you did not anything good neither penance nor fasting nor charity.

After that Michael prostrated himself and Paul and thousands of angels before the son of god and requested that all who were in the inferno have rest on Sunday.

And the Lord said: Due to Michael and Paul, mostly due to my goodness, I will give them rest from the ninth our of Sabbath until the first hour of the second day.

Variant of the Long Latin Recension (according to Paris, BN Nouv. acq. lat. 1631, s. viii; from James, *Apocrypha Anecdota*, 36; see also Silverstein and Hilhorst, *Apocalypse of Paul*, 162):[24]

Nunc uero, propter Michaelum archangelum testamenti mei, et qui cum ipso sunt angeli, et propter Paulum delectissimum meum, quem nolo contristare, propter fratres uestros qui sunt in mundo et offerunt oblaciones, et propter filios uestros, quoniam sunt in his praecepta mea, et magis propter meam ipsius bonitatem,—in die enim qua resurrexi a mortuis, dono uobis omnibus qui estis in penis noctem et diem refrigerium in perpetuum.

Et exclamauerunt omnes et dixerunt: Benedicimus te, filius dei, quia donasti nobis noctem et diem refeccionem. Melius est enim nobis refrigerium die unius super omne tempus uite nostre quod fuimus super terram: et si manifeste cognouisemus quoniam propositus hic est qui peccant, aliut laboris nihil omnino operati essemus, nihil negociati fuisemus et nullam iniquitatem fecissemus: quod opus fuit nobis nasum in mundo? hic enim superbia nostra comprehensa est que ascendit de ore nostro aduersus proximum, molestia ac nimiae angustie nostrae et lacrime et uermes qui sub nos sunt, ec magis peiora nobis sunt quam pene que decinemus (†) nos.

Haec illis loquentibus irati sunt aeis angeli maligni et penarum, dicentes: Usque quo plorastis et suspirastis? non enim abuistis misericordiam. Est enim aec iudicium dei qui non fecit misericordiam. Anc autem magnam percepistis gratiam nocte et die dominice refrigerium propter Paulum dilectissimum dei qui descendit ad uos.

24. In this version, the transgression of the sinners is narrated through self-accusation, which in turn entails a rebuke from the angels of punishment, who reprove the self-pity of the punished. The insight that sinners would not have worked or traded (*aliut laboris nihil omnino operati essemus, nihil negociati fuisemus*) is probably to be referred to the Lord's Day, even though this is not mentioned. However, it is similar to the accusations of Sunday work in the Latin versions of the Letter from Heaven; see p. 164f.

Translation

But now, due to Michael, the archangel of my covenant, and the angels who are with him, and due to Paul, my most beloved, whom I would not grieve, due to your brethren who are in the world and offer oblations, and due to your children, because my commandments are in them, and still more for my own goodness, namely, on the day I am risen from the dead, I grant all of you who are in punishment refrigeration for a night and a day for ever.

And all cried out and said: We praise you, Son of God, because you have given us recreation for a night and a day. For better for us is the refrigeration of this day than all the time of our life that we have been on earth. And if we had known for sure that this place is appointed for those who sin, we would have done nothing than work at all, would have done no business, and would have committed no inequity. Why was it necessary for us to be born in this world? For here our pride is grasped, which ascended from our mouth against the neighbor. Annoyance and our too great narrowness and tears and worms that are among us, that is far worse for us than the punishments that detain us.

When they had said that, the angels which are evil and for the punishments became angry with them and said: How long have you wept and sighed? For you have not had mercy: for this is the judgment of God upon whom had not had mercy. But this great mercy you have received: refrigeration at night and on the day of Sunday, due to Paul, the most beloved of God, who descended to you.

11

THREE PSEUDEPIGRAPHAL SUNDAY HOMILIES

Annette von Stockhausen

A Homily "Today, My Beloved, I'd Like to Praise the Day of the Lord" (CPG 2955 und 4869 [= urn:cts:pta:pta0040.pta001])

The text transmitted as "Sermon on the Holy Day of the Lord by Our Holy Father Basilius Archbishop of Caesarea in Cappadocia" (version A) or as "Sermon on the Holy Day of the Lord by Our Holy Father John Chrysostom, Archbishop of Constantinople" (version B) was neither written by Basil of Caesarea nor by John Chrysostom but is rather of other and probably even later origin.[1]

As already the two different attributions show, the homily exists in two versions: while it is difficult (for now) to demonstrate clear evidence, version A (attributed to Basilius of Caesarea = CPG 2955) seems to be closer to the original at least in its composition, if not in its wording, than version B (attributed to John Chrysostom = CPG 4869), although the manuscript evidence for version B is older than that for version Λ.

Version A is attested by five manuscripts: Scorialensis Ψ.II.20 (Diktyon 15226),[2] s. xiii, folios 124v–126r (= E); Parisinus Suppl. gr. 1255 (Diktyon 53919), s. xiii–xiv, folios 52v–53v (= S); Parisinus gr. 1034 (Diktyon 50627),

1. I can only provide preliminary observations and reflections here. The transcriptions of the manuscripts and the critical edition(s) of this previously unedited text are published in the Patristic Text Archive at https://pta.bbaw.de/text/urn:cts:pta:pta0040.pta001. Below I will provide a reading text and a translation of version A.

2. This manuscript also transmits CPG 5525 "A Question and Answer about Sunday"; see p. 444.

s. xv, folios 305v–309v (= P);[3] Athous Xenophontos 53 (Diktyon 30342),[4] s. xvii, folios 40v–42r; Iraklio Archaiologiko Mouseio 5 (Diktyon 32833), s. xvi, folios 301r–304v.[5]

Version B is only attested by one manuscript, Londinensis Add. 36753 (Diktyon 39136), s. xii, folios 221r–225r (= L). Version B differs from version A mainly in rephrasing of sentences and in transpositions of textual passages that seem to have caused some incoherence.

The anonymous author composed a rhetorically ornamented text. In addition to the many, even small, biblical allusions, it is characterized by a figurative language that situates the text in an urban milieu within a rural setting. The homily is a witness to the "Sabbatization" of Sunday: Any kind of work is forbidden on Sunday. Besides, going to church on Sunday is perceived as mandatory. The author begins (§1) with his thesis formulated as a series of rhetorical questions. Whoever does not honor Sunday transgresses the eternal boundaries that God has set and dissolves the law. On Sunday, one should not be concerned about physical well-being but about the kingdom of God. That's why on Sunday you don't go to the field or the vineyard but to church. It is about spiritual work and it is about repentance, which is made clear by the author when the example of the publican from the Gospels is given. Sunday is not about money and profit but about spiritual goods (§2). And that is because the Lord has set Sunday apart and sanctified it. Therefore, it is about praise and sanctification, as human praise is countered by divine love for humankind and human prudence by communion with God. That's why it is necessary to dedicate one day of the week to God and to refrain from workday occupation.

The following section (§3) is then devoted to the question which of these days of rest from work is to be kept, that of the Jews (Sabbath), that of the gentiles (Thursday), or that of the Christians (Sunday). As the Christian is Christian and not a Jew nor a gentile, he needs to keep Sunday;

3. This manuscript also transmits the homily CPG 4848 "Hear, All Brothers Christians"; see p. 460.

4. This manuscript also transmits CPG 5525 "A Question and Answer about Sunday"; see p. 446.

5. I was not able to see this manuscript. According to the museum, this manuscript does not exist. All my efforts to locate its current place failed.

otherwise he acts impiously. Whoever works seven days a week (§4) transgresses the law (Deut 5:13); that is, Sunday rest is justified by the Sabbath command; the Sabbath legislation is transferred to Sunday. See on this topic pp. 144–61. The social component of rest is also emphasized by the fact that granting rest to the farm animals and the servants is connected with the rest the landowner receives in the last judgment. The rest of the animals is further emphasized by the following relatively detailed reference to Balaam's donkey and the Balaam story, which also adds an anti-Jewish and antipagan note. The cautionary example is meant to serve as a warning to the listeners and lead them onto the right path.

In the following section (§5), the author returns to his topic: One should not transgress the commandment of the Lord by working on Sunday. But the thesis is now formulated even more steeply, and Sunday is, as it were, made absolute. For the author now continues: "On this day hang heaven and earth"—clearly Matthew 22:40 is echoed here, only that now not everything hangs on the double commandment of love, but on Sunday. This absolutization of Sunday is also made clear by the two following allusions, to Matthew 5:19 and to 1 Corinthians 5:6. Further biblical examples then illustrate the negative consequences that can result from disregarding one little thing such as not working on Sunday. This (§6) brings the author back to his admonition: on Sunday one must go to church, and on Sunday there is no work to be done: there is no school, no military, no exercise of state power (jurisdiction). Rather, Sunday is the day of the week that is eagerly awaited, as is explained once again in a pictorial way.

Text (Version A)

§ 1 Βούλομαι σήμερον, ἀγαπητοί, τὴν κυριακὴν ἐγκωμιάσαι ἡμέραν τὴν ὑπὸ πολλῶν μὲν τιμωμένην, ὑπὸ πολλῶν δὲ ὑβριζομένην, μᾶλλον δὲ τὴν ὑπὸ θεοῦ τιμωμένην, ὑπὸ δὲ τῶν ἀνθρώπων ὑβριζομένην. διὰ τί ὑβρίζεις, ὦ ἄνθρωπε, τὴν ὑπὸ θεοῦ τιμωμένην; διατί παρέρχῃ ὅρους αἰωνίους, οὓς ἔθετο ὁ θεός; διατί λύεις αὐτοῦ τοὺς νόμους; ἐξεδύσω τὸν παλαιὸν ἄνθρωπον καὶ τὰς πράξεις αὐτοῦ· διὰ τί αὐτὸν ἐνδύσασθαι σπεύδεις; ἔργασαι οὖν ἐν τῇ κυριακῇ ἡμέρᾳ οὐ τὰ τῆς κοιλίας, ἀλλὰ τῆς βασιλείας τῆς οὐρανίου· μὴ εἰσέρχου ἐν αὐτῇ εἰς χώραν ἢ εἰς ἀμπελῶνας, ἀλλὰ τρέχε ἐν αὐτῇ εἰς ἐκκλησίας καὶ εἰς μαρτύρια· μὴ σπείρῃς ἐν αὐτῇ σπέρματα γήινα, ἀλλ᾽ ἔργασαι ἐν αὐτῇ ἔργα πνευματικά. μὴ τυπτήσῃς ἐν αὐτῇ βοῦν ἀροτριοῦντα, ἀλλὰ τύπτησον ἐν αὐτῇ εὐχόμενος τὴν ψυχήν· μίμησαι τὸν τελώνην ἐκεῖνον τὸν τυπτήσαντα ‹τὴν› καρδίαν ἑαυτοῦ καὶ ἀνοίξαντα θύραν φιλανθρωπίας, τὸν ἀνελθόντα εἰς τὸ ἱερὸν ἁμαρτωλὸν καὶ κατελθόντα δὲ δικαιωμένον, τὸν ἀνελθόντα τετραυματισμένον καὶ κατελθόντα τεθεραπευμένον· ἀνῆλθε φορῶν ἁμαρτίας καὶ κατῆλθεν ἐνδεδυμένος δικαιοσύνην, ἀνῆλθε μεμελανωμένος ὡς κόραξ καὶ κατῆλθε λευκὸς ὡς περιστερά, ἀνῆλθε λυπούμενος εἰς τὸ ἱερὸν καὶ κατῆλθεν εἰς τὸν ἴδιον οἶκον χαιρόμενος.

§ 2 κίνησον οὖν καὶ αὐτός, ἀγαπητέ, τὰς χεῖρας σου ἐν τῇ κυριακῇ ἡμέρᾳ, οὐχ ἵνα σαρκικὰ συνάξῃς χρήματα, ἀλλ᾽ ἵνα πνευματικὰ θερίσῃς ἀγαθά. ηὐλόγησεν γὰρ ὁ θεὸς τὴν ἡμέραν τῆς κυριακῆς καὶ ἡγίασεν αὐτήν· εὐλογίας οὖν χρῄζει οὐχὶ ἐργασίας, ἁγιωσύνης δεῖται οὐχὶ ἐπιθυμίας. εὐλόγησον αὐτὴν διὰ τῆς ὑμνῳδίας, ἵνα ὁ θεὸς εὐλογήσῃ σε. ἁγίασον αὐτὴν διὰ τῆς σωφροσύνης, ἵνα ἁγιάσῃ σε διὰ τῆς κοινωνίας· μίαν ἡμέραν ὀφείλεις ἀργῆσαι διὰ τὸν θεόν, ἀγαπητέ, κατὰ πᾶσαν ἑβδομάδα.

§ 3 ποίαν ἐξ αὐτῶν θέλεις ἀργῆσαι, εἰπέ μοι, τὴν τῶν ἰουδαίων ἢ τὴν τῶν ἑλλήνων ἢ τῶν χριστιανῶν; τρία τάγματα εἰσὶν ἐν τῷ κόσμῳ· ἰουδαίων, ἑλλήνων, χριστιανῶν. ἰουδαῖοι ἀργοῦσιν ἐν τῷ σαββάτῳ· ἕλληνες ἀργοῦσιν ἐν τῇ πέμπτῃ· χριστιανοὶ ἀργοῦσιν ἐν τῇ κυριακῇ. μετὰ ποίων οὖν τούτων θέλεις ἀργῆσαι, εἰπέ μοι; μετὰ ἰουδαίων; ἀλλ᾽ οὐκ εἶ περιτετμημένος· μετὰ ἑλλήνων; ἀλλ᾽ οὐκ εἶ εἰδωλολάτρης· ἐκεῖνοι ἀσεβεῖς ὄντες, ἀγαπητέ, τὰς ἑαυτῶν ἀργοῦσιν ἡμέρας· καὶ σὺ χριστιανὸς ὢν τὴν ἑαυτοῦ καταφρονεῖς ἡμέραν; πεῖσον τὸν ἕλληνα ἐργάζεσθαι ἐν τῇ πέμπτῃ καὶ ἡσυχάσω· πεῖσον τὸν ἰουδαῖον ἐργάζεσθαι ἐν σαββάτῳ καὶ οὐ λαλῶ· ἐκεῖνοι παρὰ γνώμην θεοῦ τὰς ἑαυτῶν ἀργοῦσιν ἡμέρας· πολλῷ οὖν μᾶλλον ἡμεῖς οἱ κατὰ γνώμην θεοῦ ποιεῖν τοῦτο ὀφείλομεν.

Translation (Version A)

§1 Today, my beloved, I'd like to praise the day of the Lord, which is honored by many, but also maltreated by many, which rather is honored by God, but maltreated by man. Why, o man, do you maltreat the day honored by God? Why do you transgress eternal boundaries that God set? Why do you break his laws? You took off the old man and his actions. Why do you hasten to take it on (again)? Now don't do in the day of the Lord that of your belly, but that of the heavenly kingdom. Do not enter the countryside or the vineyards on it, but come quickly to the churches and the martyria on it! Do not sow earthly seeds on it, but produce spiritual deeds on it. Do not beat a ploughing cow on it, but pray and beat your soul on it. Mimic that collector of tolls who beat his heart and opened the door of clemency, who went up to the temple as sinner and came down as righteous, who went up wounded and came down healed. He went up carrying sins and came down clothed in righteousness, he went up black like a raven and came down white like a dove, he went up to the temple distressed and came down into his own house joyfully.

§2 Now move also yourself, beloved, your hands on the day of the Lord, not that you collect fleshly money, but that you harvest spiritual goods. For God blessed the day of the Lord and sanctified it.[6] Therefore, he wants praise and not work, he asks for sanctity, not for desire. Praise it by singing hymns, so that God may bless you. Sanctify it through prudence, that he sanctifies you through communion. You have to stop to work one day for God, beloved, each week.

§3 Which day of those do you want not to work, tell me, the day of the Jews or that of the Greek or that of the Christians? For there are three groups in the world: Jews, Greeks, and Christians. The Jews do not work on the Sabbath, the Greeks do not work on Thursday, the Christians do not work on the day of the Lord. With which of those then do you want not to work, tell me? With the Jews? But you are not circumcised. With the Greeks? But you are no idolater. Those, although they are impious, beloved, do not work on their days. And you being Christian despise your day? Persuade the Greek to work on Thursday and I will shut up. Persuade the Jew to work on the Sabbath and I won't say anything. Those keep their days against the wish of God; therefore, to a much greater extent, we living according to God's will owe to do that.

6. P has an addition: "the seventh day according to the old law; now, he praised and sanctified and praised instead of that day the holy day of the Lord, as in it all the goods came into being: the annunciations, the birth, the holy and life-giving and gladdening resurrection and all the other things that were mentioned before; and on this day he should come again to judge the living and the dead."

§ 4 παρανομεῖς οὖν, ἀγαπητέ, ἐὰν τὰς ἑπτὰ ἡμέρας ἐργάσῃ· καὶ ὅτι παρανομία ἐστί, μαρτυρεῖ ὁ θεὸς διδάσκων· *ἐν ταῖς ἓξ ἡμέραις ποιήσεις, φησί, τὰ ἔργα σου·* ἐν δὲ τῇ ἑβδόμῃ οὐ ποιήσεις πᾶν ἔργον· ἀναπαύσεως γὰρ ἐστὶν λογικῶν τε καὶ ἀλόγων· ἀναπαυέτω ἐν αὐτῇ, ἀγαπητέ, ὁ βοῦς σου καὶ ὁ παῖς σου καὶ ἡ παιδίσκη σου καὶ ὁ ὄνος σου καὶ οἱ μίσθιοί σου· δὸς αὐτοῖς ἐν τῇ κυριακῇ ἀνάπαυσιν, ἵνα ἀναπαύῃ ἐν τῇ μεγάλῃ ἡμέρᾳ τῆς ἀναστάσεως· εὐλογήσει βοῦς σου καὶ ἡ ὄνος σου τὸν δώσαντα αὐτοῖς τὴν κυριακὴν εἰς ἀνάπαυσιν· καὶ ὅτι λαλεῖ τὰ ἄλογα ζῷα, ὅτε θέλει ὁ θεός, βαρεῖται τὸν Βαλαὰμ βαστάξασα ἡ ὄνος· τί με τύπτεις, φησίν, ἀδίκως; ἄγγελον ὁρῶ ἑστῶτα ἐν τῇ ὁδῷ κατέχοντα μάχαιραν δίστομον· κατελθὼν προσκύνησον, φησίν, μή ποτε σφαγῶμεν ἀμφότεροι. ἐλάλησεν ἡ ὄνος, ἵνα ἡ συναγωγὴ σιωπήσῃ· ἀνεώχθη τὸ στόμα τῆς ὄνου, ἵνα τὸ στόμα τῶν ἰουδαίων καὶ αἱρετικῶν ἐμφραγῇ· *ἐνεφράγη γάρ φησι στόμα λαλοῦντων ἄδικα.* ἐλάλησεν ἡ ὄνος, ἐπειδὴ ἀδίκως ἐτύπτετο· μὴ τυπτήσῃς τὸν βοῦν σου ἐργαζόμενον ἐν τῇ κυριακῇ, ἵνα μὴ στραφεὶς εἴπῃ πρός σέ· τί με τύπτεις; οὐκ ἔξεστί σοι ἐργάζεσθαι σήμερον. ἀλλὰ τάχα αἰδὼς ἔχετε ταῦτά μου λέγοντος, ἀγαπητοί· ‹εἰ› μὴ ἔχετε αἰδώς, . . .[7]. εἰ γὰρ καὶ αὐστηρὰ τὰ φάρμακα, ἀλλ᾽ ὠφέλιμα εἰς θεραπείαν· εἰ καὶ ὀξεία τὰ σίδηρα, ἀλλὰ τὰ σεσηπότα ἀποκόπτει μέλη· αὐστηρὸς καὶ τῷ παιδίῳ ὁ διδάσκαλος, ἀλλὰ παρ᾽ αὐτοῦ κτᾶται σοφίαν· φοβερὸς καὶ τῷ ἀθλητῇ ὁ ἀντίπαλος, ἀλλὰ διὰ τούτου λαμβάνει στέφανον καὶ βραβεῖον· σκληρὰ φαίνεται καὶ τοῖς ἀκροαταῖς τὰ διδάγματα, ἀλλὰ διὰ τούτων ὁδηγοῦνται πρὸς τὴν ἀλήθειαν.

7. Some text is missing here.

§4 So you transgress the law, beloved, if you work the seven days. And that it is a transgression of law, God confirms by teaching: 'On the six days you will do, he says, your works' [Deut 5:15]. But on the seventh you will do no work at all. The day of the Lord is a day of rest. It is a day of rest from work by the reasonable and by the unreasoning: Your cattle, your male and female servants, your ass, and your tenants should rest on it, beloved. Grant them rest on the day of the Lord [see Deut 5:14], that you may rest on the great day of resurrection.[8] Your cattle and your ass will praise the one who granted them the day of the Lord to rest. And as the speechless animals speak, if God wills, therefore the ass that carried Balaam complains: Why do you beat me, it says, unjustly? I see an angel standing on the road with a two-edged dagger. Get down and do reverence to him, he says, that we possibly may not both get killed [see Num 22:25–28]. The ass talked that the synagogue gets silent. The mouth of the ass was opened that the mouth of the Jews and the heretics gets blocked. 'For the mouth of those speaking unjust words, it says, were blocked' [Ps 62:12 LXX]. The ass spoke, since it was beaten unjustly. Do not beat your cattle that works on the day of the Lord, that it may not turn around and then say to you: Why do you beat me? You are not allowed to work today! Perhaps you have respect for me, if I say that, beloved! If you have no respect, [. . .]. For even if the remedy is bitter, it is still beneficial for the treatment. Even if the iron is sharp, it cuts off the putrid limbs. The teacher is harsh to the child, too, but from him it receives wisdom. Likewise the opponent is awe-inspiring for the athlete, but through him he receives the crown of victory and the prize. So the teachings appear hard to the hearers, but they are guided by them to the truth.

8. P: "judgment."

§ 5 μὴ οὖν παραβῇς ἐντολὴν θεοῦ διὰ τὸ ἐργάσασθαι ἐν τῇ κυριακῇ ἡμέρᾳ. μὴ καταφρόνει ταύτης τῆς ἐντολῆς· ἐν αὐτῇ γὰρ κρέμαται ὁ οὐρανὸς καὶ ἡ γῆ· καὶ μὴ λύσῃς μίαν τῶν ἐντολῶν· πήρωσις γὰρ ἀπὸ μέρους τῷ Ἰσραὴλ γέγονε. μὴ καταφρόνει τῆς μικρᾶς ζύμης· *μικρὰ γάρ* φησιν *ζύμη ὅλον τὸ φύραμα ζυμοῖ*· μικρὰ ἐφάνη, ἀγαπητέ, καὶ τῷ Ἀδὰμ ἡ βρῶσις τοῦ ξύλου, ἀλλ' ἐξέδυσεν αὐτὸν τῆς μεγάλης ἐκείνης δόξης· ἄλλος τίς πάλιν, ἵνα ἅψηται ἀκαίρως τῆς κιβωτοῦ, ἀπέθανεν ἀώρως· ἄλλος τις πάλιν κρύψας γλῶσσαν χρυσὴν μικρὰν μετὰ τῶν ἑαυτοῦ ἐνεπρήσθη· ἄλλος τις πάλιν, ἵνα γεύσηται ἀκαίρως τῶν θυσιῶν, ἀπεξηράνθη ἡ χεὶρ αὐτοῦ· ἄλλοι πάλιν δύο, ἵνα ἀκαίρως προσενέγκωσι θυμιατήρια, ὑπὸ τῆς γῆς κατεπόθησαν· ἠνοίχθη γάρ φησιν ἡ γῆ καὶ κατέπιε Δαθὰν καὶ Ἀβείρων· ἵνα δὲ τὸ ἴδιον πληρώσουσιν ἔργον, ἐβράδυναν· διὰ τοῦτο οὐκ ἐδέχθη αὐτῶν ἡ θυσία.

§ 6 παράμεινον οὖν, ἀγαπητέ, ἐν τῇ ἁγίᾳ κυριακῇ τῇ ἐκκλησίᾳ. μάθε, πῶς πτωχεύουσιν αἱ σχολαὶ τῶν παιδίων ἐν τῇ ἡμέρᾳ τῆς κυριακῆς· μάθε, πῶς ἡσυχάζουσιν αἱ συναγωγαὶ τῶν στρατιωτῶν ἐν τῇ κυριακῇ· μάθε, πῶς πενθοῦσιν οἱ θρόνοι τῶν ἀρχόντων ἐν τῇ κυριακῇ· κἀκείνων μὲν πενθοῦσιν οἱ θρόνοι, τοῦ Χριστοῦ δὲ λάμπει ὁ θρόνος. οὐδεὶς βλέπει παῖδα τεταμένον ὑπὸ διδασκάλων ἐν τῇ ἡμέρᾳ τῇ κυριακῇ· οὐδεὶς ὁρᾷ τινὰ τυπτόμενον ὑπὸ χιλιάρχου ἐν τῇ ἡμέρᾳ τῆς κυριακῆς· οὐδεὶς εὑρίσκει καταδεδικασμένον ἐν τῇ ἁγίᾳ κυριακῇ. ἐκδέχονται πάντες τὴν κυριακήν, ὡς ἐκδέχονται οἱ ἐν φυλακαῖς τὴν ἀπόλυσιν, ὡς μόσχοι ἐν πάλοις δεδεμένοι· ἐκδέχονται πάντες τὴν κυριακήν, ὡς ἐκδέχονται αἱ σχολαὶ τῶν παίδων τὴν ἀπόλυσιν· ἐκδέχονται πάντες τὴν κυριακήν, ὡς ἐκδέχονται τὰ ἀρνία ἐν ταῖς μάνδραις τὴν ἀπόλυσιν· ἐκδέχονται πάντες τὴν κυριακήν, ὡς ἐκδέχονται οἱ νεκροὶ τὴν ἀνάστασιν. μετὰ χαρᾶς οὖν καὶ ἀγαλλιάσεως τὴν ἡμέραν, ἀγαπητοί, τῆς κυριακῆς φυλάξωμεν προσφέροντες ἐν αὐτῇ θυσίαν ζῶσαν ἁγίαν, ἔργα δικαιοσύνης, καρποὺς φιλοπτωχίας, εὐχάς, ἀναγνώσεις δοξάζοντες πατέρα καὶ υἱὸν καὶ ἅγιον πνεῦμα, τὴν μίαν βασιλείαν καὶ θεότητα, νῦν καὶ ἀεὶ καὶ εἰς τοὺς αἰῶνας τῶν αἰώνων. ἀμήν.

§5 Therefore, do not transgress the commandment of God by working on the day of the Lord! Do not despise that commandment! For on that commandment heaven and earth hang [see Matt 22:40]. And do not unfasten one of the commandments [see Matt 5:19]! For blindness afflicted in part Israel. Do not despise the small leaven. For it says, 'that a little leaven leavens all the lump' [1 Cor 5:6; Gal 5:9]. Also the eating from the tree seemed small to Adam, beloved, but it got him out of that great glory [see Gen 3]. Another one in turn died untimely, because he took hold of the ark at the wrong time [see 2 Sam 6:6–7; 1 Chr 13:10]. Again another one concealed a small golden tongue under his belongings and was burned [see Josh 7:21–25]. Again another one, because he took food from the sacrifice at the wrong time, his hand withered [see ?]. Again two others, because they used censers at the wrong time, were swallowed by the earth. For the earth opened, it says, and swallowed Dathan and Abiron. Because they performed their own work, they were delayed. That's why their sacrifice was not accepted [see Num 16].

§6 Therefore, stay, beloved, on the holy day of the Lord in the church! Learn, how the schools of children are begging on the day of the Lord! Learn, how the assemblies of the soldiers rest on the Lord's day! Learn, how the thrones of the rulers mourn on the Lord's day! The thrones of those mourn, but the throne of Christ shines. Nobody sees a child stretched out by teachers on the day of the Lord. Nobody sees someone beaten by the tribune on the day of the Lord. Nobody finds someone condemned on the holy day of the Lord. Everybody waits for the day of the Lord, like those on watch wait for the detachment, like the calves bound to stakes. Everybody waits for the day of the Lord, like the schools of the children wait for the release. Everybody waits for the day of the Lord, like the lambs wait in their pen for the release. Everybody waits for the day of the Lord, like the dead wait for the resurrection. Therefore, let us keep with joy and exaltation, beloved, the day of the Lord and let us bring on it a living holy sacrifice, deeds of righteousness, fruits of love for the poor, prayers, readings, and let us praise the Father and the Son and the Holy Ghost, the one kingdom and divinity, now and for ever and into all eternity. Amen.

A "Question and Answer about Sunday" (CPG 5525 = urn:cts:pta:pta0030.pta016)

Annette von Stockhausen

The text transmitted as Homily 16 by "Eusebius Alexandrinus" (= CPG 5525 = BHG 635c and 635d)[1] is no homily but rather a *quaestio et responsio* that is put into a narrative framework: after the liturgy on Sunday a bishop Eusebius answers to the question of a man (in most versions named Alexander) who asks him why Sunday as a day of rest from work is to be observed.[2] This text, therefore, is another attestation to the "Sabbatization" of Sunday.

According to my preliminary study on the transmission of this text, it is transmitted in several versions:[3]

Version A is attributed to Eusebius in the title[4] and in the *incipit*. Eusebius has the attribute μακάριος and in some late manuscripts is identified as (arch-) bishop of Alexandria. The incipit is Μετὰ τὴν ἀπόλυσιν τῆς ἐκκλησίας. This version is transmitted in the following manuscripts: Vaticanus gr. 1633 (= Diktyon 68264), s. x–xi, folios 341v–343r; Scorialensis Υ. II. 09 (= Diktyon 15477), s. xi, folios 203v–206; Oxoniensis Bodleianus Roe 17 (= Diktyon 48399), s. xii, folios 203v–206v; Vaticanus Palatinus gr. 68 (= Diktyon 65801), s. xiii, folios 33v–37r; Vindobonensis hist. gr. 63 (= Diktyon 70940), a. 1319, folios 39v–42v; Berolinensis (Krakow) gr. 4° 46 (= Diktyon 9215), s. xvi, folios 78r–81v; Scorialensis Υ. II. 04 (= Diktyon 15472), s. xvi, folios 331r–334r;

1. Ps.-Eusebius "Alexandrinus" has already been the subject of some research; Rémi Gounelle, "Les éditions de la Collectio sermonum d'Eusèbe d'Alexandrie," *AnBoll* 127 (2009): 249–72, provides an overview of the earlier research and editions. BHG 635d is my version C, while BHG 635c is partially my version A, B, and D.

2. I can only provide preliminary observations and reflections here, based on the preparative work on 12 manuscripts out of 30 manuscripts known; see https://pinakes.irht.cnrs.fr/notices/oeuvre/12440/ (three of the manuscripts mentioned in the Pinakes database, Ambrosianus D 92 sup., Vaticanus gr. 840, and Vaticanus gr. 1190 provide only excerpts). The transcriptions of the manuscripts and the critical edition(s) of this text will be published in the Patristic Text Archive at https://pta.bbaw.de/text/urn:cts:pta:pta0030.pta016. Below I will provide a reading text and a translation of version A according to Janus's edition (see n. 5) with minor corrections.

3. As the collation of the manuscripts is not yet finished, the following statements are to be handled with caution, as they are mainly based on the titles and the *incipia*. Also, interdependence between the versions is an option that needs to be checked.

4. One manuscript in this series (Codex Vaticanus gr. 1633) has no title.

Vatopedinus 13 (= Diktyon 18160), s. xvi, folios 196v–197v; Parisinus suppl. gr. 407 (= Diktyon 53152), a. 1592, folios 216v–219v. This version was edited according to the codices Oxoniensis Bodleianus Roe 17 and Vaticanus Palatinus gr. 68 (and with Latin translation) in Johann Wilhelm Janus,[5] 1–10 (reprinted by Andrea Gallandi,[6] 252–55, and in PG 86.1:413–21).

There are obviously several otherwise closely related versions dependent from version A. I have been able to identify six tentative variations so far (subsumed under "B"):[7]

Version B1 is attributed to Eusebius, archbishop of Alexandria, but has a beginning different from version A and is characterized by some transpositions; it begins with Καθεζομένου του ἐν ἁγίοις πατρὸς ἡμῶν εὐσεβείου ἀρχιεπισκόπου ἀλεξανδρείας ἐν ἡμέρα τῆς ἁγίας κυριακῆς μετὰ τὴν ἀπόλυσιν τῆς ἐκκλησίας. It is transmitted by Codex Vindobonensis hist. gr. 67 (= Diktyon 70944), s. xiii, folios 90v–95v.

Version B2 is attributed to Eusebius in the title (Λόγος τοῦ μακαρίου εὐσεβίου) but identifies this Eusebius as Eusebius of Rome in the text. The *incipit* of the text differs from version A by removing the setting before the church after the service on Sunday and begins with ἐν ἡμέρα κυριακῆς· καθεζουμένου τοῦ μακαρίου εὐσεβείου τοῦ ἐπισκόπου (πάπα) ῥώμης. This version is transmitted in Codex Hierosolymitanus Panagiou Taphou 39 (= Diktyon 35276), s. xii, folios 158v–159v, and the late Codex Parisinus gr. 947 (= Diktyon 50536), a. 1574, folios 107v–109v. The variants in the text in Codex Parisinus gr. 947 were annotated by F. Nau,[8] 414sq. in the footnotes of his (partial) edition of Codex Parisinus gr. 929 (belonging to version D!).

Version B3 is different from version B2 already in the title attributed to Eusebius of Rome (Τοῦ ἐν ἁγίοις πατρὸς ἡμῶν εὐσεβίου πάπα ῥώμοις λόγως) but identifies Eusebius as Eusebius, archbishop of Alexandria, in the text and has also the *incipit*, as in version A.[9] This version is transmitted in Codex Scorialensis Ψ. II. 20 (= Diktyon 15226), s. xiii, folios 126r–128r.

---

5. Johann Wilhelm Janus, ed., *Τοῦ μακαρίου Εὐσεβίου ἐπισκόπου (Ἀλεξανδρείας) λόγος περὶ τῆς ἡμέρας κυριακῆς. B. Eusebii episcopi vulgo Alexandrini oratio de die dominico* (Lipsiae: Gleditsch, 1720).

6. Andrea Gallandi, *Bibliotheca veterum Patrum antiquorumque scriptorum ecclesiasticorum* (Venezia: Hieron, 1772).

7. The numbering and sequence provided is at the moment no argument for age or for the status of reworking.

8. "Notes sur diverses Homélies pseudépigraphiques, sur les oeuvres attribuées a Eusèbe d'Alexandrie et sur un nouveau manuscrit de la chaine contra severianos," *Revue de l'Orient chrétien* 13 (1908): 406–35.

9. Μετὰ τὴν ἀπόλυσιν τῆς ἐκκλησίας προκαθεζομένου του ἐν ἁγίοις πατρὸς ἡμῶν εὐσεβείου ἀρχιεπισκόπου ἀλεξανδρείας ἐν ἡμέρα κυριακῆς, ἀνήρ τις ὀνόματι ἀλέξανδρος

Version B4 is attributed to Eusebius (Τοῦ ὁσίου πατρὸς ἡμῶν εὐσεβίου) in the title and mentions Eusebius as Alexandrian bishop in the *incipit*, which is as in version A. This version is attested by a codex at Xenophontos monastery on Mount Athos, no. 53 (= Diktyon 30342), s. xvii, folios 34v–40r.

Version B5 is attributed to John Chrysostom in the title but has Eusebius (τοῦ μακαριωτάτου ἐπισκόπου Εὐσεβίου) in the beginning of the text. The *incipit* is as in version A. This version is transmitted in Codex Parisinus gr. 1468 (= Diktyon 51085), s. xi, folios 229v–232v.[10]

Version B6 is attributed to Eusebius of Nicomedia in the title and has the *incipit* as version A.[11] This version is transmitted in Codex Hierosolymitanus Hagiou Saba 373 (= Diktyon 34629), s. xvi, folios 210r–217v.

Besides these B versions there are two more versions, which seem more remote from version A in their transmission and are therefore named C and D:

Version C (= BHG 635d) is attributed to Leontius in the title.[12] The *incipit* mentions Eusebius, while the questioner Alexander becomes King Alexander.[13] The beginning of the text is otherwise comparable to version A (and B). This version is transmitted in Codex Parisinus gr. 769 (= Diktyon 50353), s. xiii–xiv, folios 180r–184r. The text according to this manuscript was edited in Nau,[14] 415–20.

Version D is attributed to John Chrysostom in the title. In the text Eusebius and Alexander as persons are not called by name, but we have a bishop and his parishioner, that is, the setting is generalized: "A pious man came to his bishop."[15] This version is transmitted in the late manuscripts Parisinus gr. 929 (= Diktyon 50518), s. xv, pages 532–47; Scorialensis Ω. II. 7 (= Diktyon

ὁ δι αὐτοῦ ἐπιστρέψας πρὸς κν τον θν ἡμῶν προσελθὼν λέγει αὐτῶ· δέομαι σου κε· τίνος ἕνεκεν ἡμῖν ἐστιν ἐπάνάγκαις φυλάσσειν τὴν ἡμέραν τῆς κυριακῆς.

10. This version was translated into German by Theodor Zahn, "Eine altkirchliche Rede über die Sonntagsruhe nebst Untersuchungen über ihren Verfasser," *Zeitschrift für kirchliche Wissenschaft und kirchliches Leben* 5 (1884): 516–34.

11. This manuscript is currently known to me only thanks to the catalogue of Athanasios Papadopoulos-Kerameus, *ΙΕΡΟΣΟΛΥΜΙΤΙΚΗ ΒΙΒΛΙΟΘΗΚΗ Ἤτοι Κατάλογος Τῶν Ἐν Ταῖς Βιβλιοθήκαις Τοῦ . . . Ὀρθοδόξου Πατριαρχικοῦ Θρόνου Τῶν Ἱεροσολύμων . . . Ἀποκειμένων Ἑλληνικῶν Κωδίκων* (Sankt-Peterburg, 1894), 498; therefore I do not know the full wording of the *incipit*.

12. Λόγος τοῦ μακαρίου λεοντίου. Probably the attribution to an author other than Eusebius is caused by the fact that the exemplar of the transmitting manuscript (or its exemplar) had no title.

13. Μετὰ τὴν ἀπόλυσιν τῆς ἁγίας κυριακῆς, προκαθίσαντος τοῦ μακαρίου Εὐσεβείου, προσελθὼν Ἀλέξανδρος ὁ βασιλεὺς, λέγει αὐτῷ.

14. "Notes" (see n. 8).

15. Προσελθῶν της (!) ἀνὴρ εὐλαβὴς, τῷ ἐπισκόπῳ αὐτοῦ παρεκάλει αὐτὸν λέγων· μετὰ τὴν ἀπόλυσιν τῆς ἁγίας ἐκκλήσιας· ἐν ἡμέρα κυριακῆς (the *incipit* according to Codex Parisinus gr. 929).

15073), s. xvi med., folios 147r–150v; Parisinus gr. 390 (= Diktyon 49963), s. xvi, folios 59r–65v. The first few lines of the text in Codex Parisinus gr. 929 were edited by Nau,[16] 414sq.

The text is also translated into Latin, Syriac, Armenian, Georgian, and Paleo-Slavonic.[17]

Apart from the titles and the beginnings, there are major differences between the versions of this text in length and in points made. Version A is as follows: From the start and fitting to the narrative framework after the liturgy, the Lord's Day is connected with Christ and the Last Supper. The celebration of the Lord's Day ensures the remembrance (ἀνάμνησις) as announced in the Last Supper. Also, Sunday is connected to creation and resurrection. In §2 the characteristics of the biblical Sabbath are transferred to Sunday. The aim of Sunday is rest from work (ἀνάπαυσις), prayer (εὐχή), and forgiveness of sins or repentance (λύσις κακῶν). Especially the last point is very closely connected with the celebration of the Eucharist on Sunday: only with a pure soul may one partake of the Eucharist. Furthermore, the church must not be left before the Eucharist; patience (ὑπομονή) is needed here, otherwise the fate of Judas, who also left the Last Supper early and then fell into the hands of the devil, is threatened. In §3 the importance of rest is emphasized: no work is to be done; Sunday is the day for prayer. No work, however, means not only abstinence from physical labor but also from bad deeds, namely, hanging out on the main street with amusements such as music and dancing. The attractions of the street are then rhetorically emphasized against what is to be experienced in worship, the wild goings-on in the street with theater, music, and dance are contrasted with the solemn celebration of worship in the church. Section 4 extends this critique of worldly behavior to the administration of justice on Sunday and focuses especially on the administration of justice by bishops who prefer to do that instead of holding the liturgy at the appointed (morning) hour. The author also criticizes the fact that people do not go to the Eucharist sober or in good conscience. Once again it is emphasized that Sunday is not for playing the kithara, dancing, administering justice, swearing, taking oaths, but for prayer, the removal of evils, repentance, salvation, rest also for servants. The audience is obviously an urban public from all social strata. In §5 the author turns to the masters and exhorts them to treat their servants in a manner appropriate to Sunday. Therefore, rest is again emphasized: the masters are not to use Sunday for helping the poor through their servants, as this will deprive the servants of their rest and will thus not at all cause salvation for the masters. The text ends (§6) with a brief conclusion and a doxology that fits more to a homily than to an answer to a question.

16. "Notes" (see n. 8).

17. See the entry in the Clavis Clavium database at https://clavis.brepols.net/clacla/OA/Details.aspx?id=2813A8E487CF426B9E45AE2339EC2C7E.

Text (Version A)[18]

Τοῦ μακαρίου Εὐσεβείου ἐπισκόπου (Ἀλεξανδρείας) λόγος περὶ τῆς ἡμέρας κυριακῆς

§1 Μετὰ τὴν ἀπόλυσιν τῆς ἐκκλησίας, ἐν ἡμέρᾳ τῆς ἁγίας κυριακῆς, καθεζομένου τοῦ μακαρίου Εὐσεβίου τοῦ ἐπισκόπου προσελθὼν ὁ Ἀλέξανδρος λέγει αὐτῷ· δέομαί σου, κύριέ μου, τίνος ἕνεκεν ἡμῖν ἐστιν ἀναγκαῖον φυλάττειν τὴν κυριακὴν καὶ μὴ ἐργάζεσθαι, καὶ ποῖον κέρδος ἔχομεν μὴ ἐργαζόμενοι; Ὁ δὲ μακάριος ἤρξατο λέγειν· ἄκουσον, τέκνον, καὶ ἐρῶ σοι, τίνος χάριν παραδέδοται τὸ φυλάσσειν ἡμᾶς τὴν κυριακὴν καὶ μὴ ἐργάζεσθαι. Ὅτε παρέδωκεν ὁ κύριος τὸ μυστήριον τοῖς μαθηταῖς, *λαβὼν τὸν ἄρτον, εὐλόγησεν, καὶ κλάσας ἔδωκε τοῖς μαθηταῖς αὐτοῦ, λέγων, λάβετε, φάγετε,* τοῦτό μού *ἐστι τὸ σῶμα, τὸ ὑπὲρ ὑμῶν κλώμενον, εἰς ἄφεσιν ἁμαρτιῶν.* Ὁμοίως *καὶ τὸ ποτήριον δέδωκεν αὐτοῖς λέγων· πίετε ἐξ αὐτοῦ πάντες, τοῦτο ἐστὶ τὸ αἷμα μοῦ, τὸ τῆς καινῆς διαθήκης, τὸ ὑπὲρ ὑμῶν, καὶ πολλῶν, ἐκχυνόμενον, εἰς ἄφεσιν ἁμαρτιῶν, τοῦτο ποιεῖτε εἰς τὴν ἐμὴν ἀνάμνησίν φησι.* Ἀνάμνησις τοίνυν τοῦ κυρίου ἐστὶν ἡ τῆς κυριακῆς ἁγία ἡμέρα. Διὰ γὰρ τοῦτο καὶ κυριακὴ ἐκλήθη, ὡς κυρία τῶν ἡμερῶν. Πρὸ γὰρ τοῦ δεσποτικοῦ πάθους οὐκ ἐλέγετο κυριακή, ἀλλὰ πρώτη ἡμέρα. Ἐν ταύτῃ τῇ ἡμέρᾳ τὴν ἀπαρχὴν τῆς κοσμοποιΐας ἤρξατο ὁ κύριος. καὶ ἐν αὐτῇ τῇ ἡμέρᾳ τὴν ἀπαρχὴν τῆς ἀναστάσεως ἐδωρήσατο τῷ κόσμῳ, ἐν ταύτῃ τῇ ἡμέρᾳ, ὡς ἔφημεν, καὶ τῶν ἁγίων μυστηρίων ἐκέλευσεν ἐπιτελεῖσθαι. ἀρχὴ οὖν πάσης ἀγαθοσύνης γέγονεν ὑμῖν ἡ τοιαύτη ἡμέρα, ἀρχὴ κτίσεως κόσμου, ἀρχὴ ἀναστάσεως, ἀρχὴ ἑβδομάδος. τρεῖς ἀρχὰς ἔχουσα ἡ ἡμέρα αὕτη, τριάδος τῆς ὑπεραγίας τὴν ἀρχὴν ὑποφαίνει.

18. The segmentation of the text is introduced by Gallandi, *Bibliotheca veterum Patrum antiquorumque scriptorum ecclesiasticorum* (see n. 6).

Translation (Version A)

Speech by the blessed bishop Eusebius (of Alexandria) on the day of the Lord.

§1 After the release from church on the holy day of the Lord, while the blessed bishop Eusebius sat down, Alexander came forward and asked him: "I beg you, my Lord, why is it necessary to keep the day of the Lord and not to work? And what kind of gain do we have, if we do not work?" The blessed opened his mouth and said: "Hear, child, and I will tell you, why it is taught to us to keep the day of the Lord and not to work. When the Lord taught his disciples the mystery (of Eucharist), he took the bread, blessed it and breaking it gave it to his disciples and said: 'Take, eat, this is my body, which is broken for you, for remission of sins.' Likewise he also gave them the cup and said: 'You all, drink from it, this is my blood of the new covenant, which is poured out for you, the many, for remission of sins. Do that for my remembrance,' he says [see 1 Cor 11:23–26; Matt 26:26–29 par.]. Therefore, the holy day of the Lord is remembrance. That's why it is called day of the Lord, as it is lord over the days. For before the passion of the Lord, it was not called Lord's day, but first day. On that day the Lord began the first-fruits of the creation.[19] And on exactly that day he gave the world the first-fruit of the resurrection, on that day, as we said, he also ordered the holy mysteries to be performed. Now, we have the beginning of all goodness on such a day, the beginning of the creation of the world, the beginning of the resurrection, the beginning of the week. Three beginnings has that day, it dawns the beginning of the most-holy trinity.

19. In the text, τῆς ἀναστάσεως, ἤγουν τῆς κοσμοποιΐας, "of the resurrection or of the creation," is printed. It seems that "or of the creation" is a marginal correction that has entered the text. *Creation* should be the correct word here; *resurrection* is an error, as it is mentioned (again) in the following sentence. I have therefore deleted "of the resurrection or" and kept "creation."

§2 Ἑπτὰ τοίνυν ἡμέρας ἡ ἑβδομὰς ἔχουσα, τὰς ἓξ δέδωκεν ἡμῖν ὁ Θεὸς ἐργάζεσθαι, καὶ τὴν μίαν δέδωκεν ἡμῖν εἰς εὐχὴν καὶ ἀνάπαυσιν, καὶ λύσιν κακῶν, καὶ ἵνα, εἴτε ἐν ταῖς ἓξ ἡμέραις ἁμαρτήματα πεποιήκαμεν, ὑπὲρ τούτων ἐν τῇ τῆς κυριακῆς ἡμέρᾳ τῷ Θεῷ ἐξιλασκώμεθα. Ὄρθρισον οὖν ἐν τῇ τοῦ Θεοῦ ἐκκλησίᾳ, πρόσελθε τῷ δεσπότῃ, ἐξομολόγησαι αὐτῷ τὰ ἁμαρτήματά σου, μετανόησον ἐν εὐχῇ καὶ καρδίᾳ συντετριμμένῃ, παράμεινον ἐν τῇ θείᾳ καὶ ἱερᾷ λειτουργίᾳ, πλήρωσόν σου τὴν εὐχήν, μηδαμῶς πρὸ τῆς ἀπολύσεως ἐξερχόμενος. Ἴδε σοῦ τὸν δεσπότην μελιζόμενον, καὶ διαδιδόμενον, καὶ μὴ δαπανώμενον. καὶ εἰ μὲν ἔχεις καθαρόν σου τὸ συνειδός, πρόσελθε, καὶ κοινώνησον τοῦ σώματος, καὶ αἵματος τοῦ κυρίου. εἰ δὲ κατακρίνει σὲ τὸ συνειδὸς ἐν πονηροῖς καὶ ἀτόποις ἔργοις, τὴν μὲν κοινωνίαν παραίτησαι, μέχρις ἂν διορθώσῃ ἑαυτὴν διὰ μετανοίας, τὴν δὲ εὐχὴν παράμεινον, καὶ μὴ ἐξέλθῃς τῆς ἐκκλησίας, ἐὰν μὴ ἀπολυθῇς. Μνήσθητι Ἰούδα τοῦ προδότου. ἐκείνου γὰρ ἀρχὴ τῆς ἀπωλείας τὸ μὴ παραμεῖναι μετὰ πάντων ἐν τῇ εὐχῇ γέγονε. λαβὼν δὲ φησὶν τὸν ἄρτον, πρῶτος πάντων ἐξῆλθεν, καὶ εὐθέως εἰσῆλθεν εἰς αὐτὸν ὁ Σατανᾶς, καὶ ἐσπούδασεν εἰς τὸ προδοῦναι τὸν κύριον. Ἐὰν οὖν πρὸ τῆς ἀπολύσεως ἐξέλθῃς, μιμητὴς γέγονας τοῦ Ἰούδα. Μὴ τοίνυν διὰ βραχεῖαν ὥραν μέλλεις μετὰ τοῦ Ἰούδα κατακρίνεσθαι; οὐδὲν σὲ βλάπτει ἡ παραμονή. οὐ χιόνας ἔχει ἡ ἐκκλησία ἔνδον, οὐ πῦρ, οὐχ ἕτερον κολαστήριον οὐδέν, ἀλλ' ἢ μόνον ὑπομονῆς ἐστι χρεία ῥοπῆς μιᾶς, καὶ ἀπήρτισταί σου ἡ εὐχή.

§2 Well, seven days has the week, God gave us six days to work, and he gave us one for prayer, rest, and deliverance from evil and that we may make atonement for them before God on the day of the Lord, if we did sinful actions during the six days. Get up before dawn in the church of God, come to the Lord, confess him your sins, repent in prayer and with a contrite heart, stay in the divine and holy liturgy, complete your prayer and never leave before the release! Look, how your Lord is cut in pieces and distributed and is not eaten up! And if you have a good conscience, come forward and take part in the body and the blood of the Lord! But if your conscience condemns you for bad and foul deeds, decline the community until you amend yourself in repentance, but stay for the prayer and do not leave the church, if you are not released. Remind yourself of Judas the traitor! The beginning of his destruction was that he did not stay with the others praying. When he (Jesus), it says, took the bread, he (Judas) as first of all left and at once Satan entered him, and he eagerly betrayed the Lord [see John 13:26f.]. Now, if you leave before the release, you impersonate Judas. Certainly, you do not want to get judged with Judas because of a little time! Staying doesn't hurt you. The church has no snow inside, no fire, no other thing tormenting you, but only a small amount of patience is needed and your prayer is perfect.

§3 Δι᾿ οὐδὲν δ᾿ ἕτερον φυλάττομεν τὴν ἡμέραν τῆς κυριακῆς, ἀλλ᾿ ἵνα τοῦ ἔργου ἀπεχόμεθα, καὶ τῇ εὐχῇ σχολάσωμεν· εἰ δὲ τοῦ ἔργου ἀπέχεις, εἰς τὴν ἐκκλησίαν δὲ οὐκ εἰσέρχῃ, οὐδὲν ἐκέρδανας. τοὐναντίον μὲν οὖν οὐ μικρῶς ἑαυτὸν κατέβλαψας. Πολλοὶ δὲ ἐκδέχονται τὴν κυριακήν, ἀλλ᾿ οὐκ ἑνὶ σκοπῷ πάντες. Οἱ δὲ φοβούμενοι τὸν Θεὸν ἐκδέχονται τὴν κυριακὴν, ἵνα τὴν εὐχὴν τῷ Θεῷ ἀναπέμψωσι, καὶ τοῦ τιμίου σώματος καὶ αἵματος ἀπολαύσωσιν· οἱ δὲ ῥᾴθυμοι καὶ ἀμελεῖς ἐκδέχονται τὴν κυριακὴν, ἵνα τοῦ ἔργου ἀπεχόμενοι τοῖς κακοῖς σχολάσωσι. καὶ ὅτι οὐ ψεύδομαι, μαρτυρεῖ τὰ πράγματα. ἔξελθε ἐν τῇ μέσῃ ἐν ἄλλῃ ἡμέρᾳ, καὶ οὐδὲν εὑρήσεις. ἔξελθε ἐν τῇ ἡμέρᾳ τῆς κυριακῆς, καὶ εὑρήσεις τοὺς μὲν κιθαρίζοντας, ἄλλους ἐπικροτοῦντας καὶ ὀρχουμένους, ἄλλους καθεζομένους, καὶ σκώπτοντας τὸν πλησίον, καὶ λοιδοροῦντας, ἄλλους παλαίοντας, ἑτέρους διαπληκτιζομένους πρὸς ἀλλήλους, ἄλλους ἐπὶ κακῷ διανεύοντας, καὶ εἴ που κιθάρα καὶ ὄρχησις, ἐκεῖ πάντες τρέχουσι. Καλεῖ εἰς τὴν ἐκκλησίαν ὁ κήρυξ, καὶ πάντες ὄκνον προβάλλονται, καὶ ἀδυναμίαν. Γέγονε κιθάρας ἦχος ἢ αὐλοῦ, ἢ κρότος ὀρχήσεως, καὶ πάντες, ὡς ὑπόπτεροι, ἐκεῖ προφθάνουσι. Τί θεωροῦσιν οἱ ἐρχόμενοι εἰς τὴν ἐκκλησίαν; ἐγώ σοι λέγω, τὸν δεσπότην χριστὸν ἐπὶ τῆς ἱερᾶς τραπέζης ἀνακείμενον, τῶν σεραφὶμ τὸν τρισάγιον ὕμνον ᾀδομένων, πνεύματος ἁγίου παρουσίαν καὶ ἐπιφοίτησιν, τὸν προφήτην καὶ βασιλέα Δαβὶδ κελαδούμενον, τὸν εὐλογημένον ἀπόστολον Παῦλον, τὴν οἰκείαν ἐνηχοῦντα διδασκαλίαν ταῖς τῶν ἁπάντων ἀκοαῖς, τὸν τῶν ἀγγέλων ὕμνον, τὸ ἀκατάπαυστον ἀλληλούϊα, εὐαγγελικὰς φωνάς, δεσποτικὰ παραγγέλματα, τὴν τῶν ὁσίων ἐπισκόπων καὶ πρεσβυτέρων νουθεσίαν τε καὶ παραίνεσιν, ὅλα πνευματικά, ὅλα οὐράνια, ὅλα σωτηρίας καὶ βασιλείας πρόξενα. Ταῦτα ἀκούει, ταῦτα ὁρᾷ ὁ εἰς τὴν ἐκκλησίαν ἐρχόμενος. Τί θεωροῦσιν οἱ εἰς τὰ θέατρα τρέχοντες; γυναῖκας πορνευομένας, ᾄσματα διαβολικά, φωνὰς αἰσχρότητος πλήρεις, καὶ ἀταξίας, γυναῖκας ὀρχουμένας, μᾶλλον δὲ δαιμονιζομένας. Τί γὰρ καὶ ποιεῖ ἡ ὀρχουμένη; οὐδὲν ἕτερον, ἀλλ᾿ ἢ αὐθαιρέτως δαιμονίζεται. ὁμοίως δὲ καὶ ὁ κιθαρῳδός, ὥσπερ τις δαίμων, τῷ ξύλῳ προσμάχεται. Ταῦτα τὰ θεάματα τῶν θεάτρων ὅλα δαιμονικά, ὅλα ἀπωλείας πρόξενα, ὅλα δαιμονίων ἐπιτηδεύματα. διὰ τοῦτο καὶ ὁ μισθὸς αὐτῶν πονηρός. Τοιοῦτον ἦν τὸ συμπόσιον τοῦ Ἡρώδου, καὶ εἰσελθοῦσα ἡ Ἡρωδιὰς ὠρχήσατο, καὶ τὴν κεφαλὴν Ἰωάννου τοῦ βαπτιστοῦ ἀπέτεμε, καὶ τὰ καταχθόνια τοῦ ᾄδου ἐκληρονόμησεν. Οἱ οὖν τὴν ἐκείνης ἀγαπῶντες κακότεχνον ὄρχησιν, μετ᾿ αὐτῆς ἔχουσι τὴν μερίδα, καὶ τὴν κατάκρισιν.

§3 We keep the day of the Lord only to stay away from work and to have opportunity to pray. But if you stay away from work and do not go to church, you gain nothing. To the contrary, you hurt yourself greatly. Many wait for the day of the Lord, but not all for the same end. Those who have fear for God wait for the day of the Lord, that they may send their prayer to God and enjoy the dear body and blood. But the careless and the negligent wait for the day of the Lord that they may stay away from work and spend their time with bad people. And what happened gives evidence that I do not lie: Go to the main street on any day and you will find nobody. Go on the day of the Lord and you will find some playing the lyre, others beating and dancing, others sitting and joking with their neighbor and scolding, others wrestling, others wrangling with each other, others nodding to bad things, and if somewhere there is a lyre and a dance, then all run. The announcer calls to the church and all display hesitation and inability. A sound of the lyre or of the flute or a beat of dancing is produced, and all come there very fast as if they had wings. What do those who come to church look at? I say it to you: the Lord Christ offered on the holy table while the Seraphim sing the three-holy hymn, the Holy Spirit's arrival and visit, the prophet and king David celebrating, the praised apostle Paul, who resonates his teaching in the ears of everybody, the hymn of the angels, the never-ending hallelujah, the evangelical voices, the Lord's commandments, the admonition and counsel of the holy bishops and presbyters, all spirituals, all heavenly things, all relief of salvation and kingdom. Who comes to the church hears that and sees that. What see those who run to the theater? Prostitutes, devilish songs, voices full of filth and anarchy, women dancing, or rather being possessed by a demon. For what does the female dancer? It's nothing other than that she is voluntarily possessed by a demon. Equally the lyre-player assaults his wooden instrument like a demon. All those spectacles of the theater are demonic, all are causing destruction, all are amusements of demons. That's why their reward is good-for-nothing. Such was the banquet of Herod. As Herodias entered, she danced and cut off the head of John the Baptist [see Matt 14:1–10 par.], and (then) she inherited the Hades under the earth. Now, those who loved her lascivious dance have their share and their condemnation with her.

§4 Ἀρκέσθητι οὖν, ἀγαπητέ, ἐν ταῖς ἓξ ἡμέραις εἰς τὰ βιωτικὰ πράγματα ἀσχολούμενος, καὶ παῦσαι κακοπραγίας ἐν τῇ ἡμέρᾳ τῆς κυριακῆς. Οἶδα πολλοὺς πρὸς ἀλλήλους πράγματα ἔχοντας καὶ φιλονεικοῦντας, λέγοντας· ἔρχεται ἡ κυριακὴ, καὶ τὴν δίκην λέγομεν. Ἄθλιε καὶ ταλαίπωρε, εὔξασθαι προσετάγης τῇ κυριακῇ, οὐχὶ δὲ καὶ δικαστήρια συνιστᾶν; ἔρχεται οὖν ἡ κυριακή, καὶ ὁ ἔχων τὴν δίκην, ὅλην τὴν νύκτα ἐκείνῳ σκέπτεται κατὰ τοῦ πλησίον αὐτοῦ, καὶ ὅτε ὁ ὄρθρος ἀνατείλῃ, ὁπλίζεται κατ' αὐτοῦ. Συνήθεια δὲ αὕτη κεκράτηκε παρὰ τοῖς πολλοῖς, ἵνα, ὅτε ἀπὸ τῆς ἐκκλησίας ἐξέλθωσι, προκάθηνται ἔξω, καὶ πρῶτος πολλάκις ὁ πρεσβύτερος τοῦτο ποιεῖ, καὶ προβάλλουσι πρὸς ἀλλήλους πράγματα, διαπληκτισμοὺς, ὕβρεις, λοιδορίας, καὶ ὅσα τοιαῦτα, καὶ τὰ τούτων χείρονα. εἶτα πάλιν εἰσέρχονται εἰς τὴν ἐκκλησίαν, καὶ ἀλλήλους ὑποβλέπονται ὥσπερ θηρία τρίζοντες τοὺς ὀδόντας αὐτῶν. οὐαὶ δὲ τῷ πρεσβυτέρῳ τῷ τὰ τοιαῦτα κινοῦντι ἢ δικάζοντι ἐν ἡμέρᾳ κυριακῆς, καὶ μὴ ἀποδιδόντι τῷ κυρίῳ τὰς εὐχὰς ἐν τῇ τεταγμένῃ ὥρᾳ. ἐὰν δὲ καὶ πρὸ τῆς ἀπολύσεως γεύσηταί τις τῶν λαϊκῶν, μεγάλης κρίσεως καὶ τιμωρίας ἔνοχός ἐστιν. ἐὰν δὲ καὶ γευσάμενος κοινωνήσῃ τοῖς μυστηρίοις, μετὰ τοῦ προδότου Ἰούδα ἡ μερὶς αὐτοῦ ἐστιν. Πολλοὺς οἶδα ἐν τῇ τοῦ ἁγίου πάσχα ἡμέρᾳ γευσαμένους καὶ κοινωνήσαντας, καὶ οὐαὶ τῇ ψυχῇ αὐτῶν, καὶ μάλιστα, εἰ ἐν ἡλικίᾳ τελείᾳ ὦσι, ὅτι ἀντὶ τοῦ λύειν τὰ ἁμαρτήματα, μᾶλλον ἐπιφορτίζουσι ταῦτα. Ἀλλὰ καὶ ὁ πονηρὰ ἔργα ἑαυτῷ συνειδὼς καὶ πρὶν ἢ ταῦτα διὰ τῆς μετανοίας ἀπονίψασθαι κοινωνῶν, τῆς αὐτῆς ἐστι κατακρίσεως. ὅσῳ γὰρ μείζων ἐστὶν ἡ ἡμέρα, μείζων ἐστὶ καὶ ἡ ἁμαρτία. Ὅσοι δὲ καὶ ἀνέγκλητοι ὑπάρχουσιν, ὀφείλουσι καρτερεῖν μέχρι τῆς ἀπολύσεως καὶ οὕτω κοινωνεῖν. οὐαὶ τοῖς ἐν τῇ κυριακῇ κιθαρίζουσιν, ἢ ὀρχουμένοις, ἢ δικαζομένοις, ἢ δικάζουσιν, ἢ ἐργαζομένοις, ἢ ὀμνύουσιν, ἢ ὁρκίζουσιν, ὅτι ἐν πυρὶ ἀσβέστῳ κατακριθήσονται, καὶ τὸ μέρος αὐτῶν μετὰ τῶν ὑποκριτῶν ἐστιν. αὕτη γὰρ ἡ ἡμέρα εἰς εὐχὴν καὶ λύσιν κακῶν ἐδόθη ἡμῖν, εἰς μετάνοιαν καὶ σωτηρίαν, εἰς ἀνάπαυσιν μισθίων καὶ δούλων.

§4 Now, be content, my beloved, to work on six days for your business and to cease wrongdoings on the day of the Lord. I know many who have troubles with each other and are fighting and say: 'The day of the Lord comes and we have a trial.' Oh wretched and miserable man! You are ordered to pray on the day of the Lord, not to organize courts of justice! Now the day of the Lord comes and the one who has a trial premeditates the whole night what he has against his neighbor and when the sunrise comes he arms himself against him. This custom is custom with most people that they sit outside when they leave the church and often the presbyter acts like that in the first place, and then they throw affairs at each other, disputes, insolences, reproaches, and such things and even worse things than that. Then they reenter the church and look angrily on each other like wild animals that creak with their teeth. Woe to the presbyter who sets such things in motion or sits in judgment on the day of the Lord and does not give his prayers to the Lord at the set hour! But if someone tastes from the common things before the release, he is liable to great judgment and punishment. And if he had tasted and has communion in the mysteries, then his part is that of the traitor Judas [see Matt 27:5; John 17:12; Acts 1:18–20]. I know many who tasted and took part on the day of the holy Pascha and woe to their soul, even more, if they are in adult age, that they instead of releasing their sins load even more on themselves. But also who has acknowledged bad deeds to himself and has had communion before he wiped them off through repentance is liable to the same judgment. For the bigger the day the bigger the sin. And those who are not without blame need to be strong until the release and need to have communion in that way. Woe to those who play lyre on the day of the Lord or dance or get judged or sit as judges or work or take an oath or make one swear, that they will be condemned to inextinguishable fire and their part is with the hypocrites. For that day was given to us for prayer and for atonement of evil, for repentance and for salvation, for rest of hired laborers and of servants.

§5 *Αὕτη γὰρ ἡ ἡμέρα, ἣν ἐποίησεν ὁ κύριος, ἀγαλλιασώμεθα, καὶ εὐφρανθῶμεν ἐν αὐτῇ.* εὐφρανθῶμεν δὲ οὐ κραιπάλῃ καὶ μέθῃ σκοτούμενοι, ἀλλ' ἐν τῇ μελέτῃ τῶν θείων γραφῶν ἐντρυφῶντες. Ἔδωκεν ἡμῖν ὁ Θεὸς ταύτην τὴν ἡμέραν, ἐν ᾗ ἤρξατο ποιῆσαι τὸν κόσμον, ἐν ᾗ τὸ τοῦ θανάτου κράτος κατέλυσε, καὶ ἐπωνόμασε ταύτην κυριακήν, ἵνα καὶ ἐξ αὐτοῦ τοῦ ὀνόματος τῆς ἡμέρας αἰδεσθέντες φυλάξωμεν τὰς ἐντολὰς τοῦ κυρίου. Εἰσέρχεται μίσθιος εἰς τὸν οἶκόν σου, καὶ ὑποτίθησιν ἑαυτὸν τοῖς ἔργοις σου, καὶ ἐν ταῖς ἓξ ἡμέραις οὐ τολμᾷ ἀνανεῦσαι καὶ ἰδεῖν τὸν ἥλιον, πόθεν ἦλθεν, καὶ ποῦ ὑπάγει, ἀλλὰ κατακοπτόμενος ἐν τοῖς ἔργοις σοῦ συντρίβεται καὶ συγκλαίεται ὁ οἴκτιστος, ἐν ἱδρῶτί τε καὶ καμάτῳ, καὶ οὐδαμῶς συγχωρεῖται οὔτε ἀνανεῦσαι, οὔτε ἀναπαύεσθαι, καθάπερ ἔφημεν, ἀλλ' ἢ μόνον ἐκδέχεται τὴν κυριακὴν, ἵνα κἂν τὸν κονιορτὸν ἀπὸ τοῦ σώματος αὐτοῦ ἀποτινάξηται, καὶ οὐ συγχωρεῖς αὐτῷ πολλάκις. καὶ ποίαν ἀπολογίαν ἕξεις, εἰπέ μοι. Εἰσί τινες οἱ χάριν εὐποιΐας δῆθεν ἐν τῇ ἡμέρᾳ τῆς κυριακῆς λέγοντες, δεῦτε, σήμερον βοηθήσωμεν τοῖς πένησιν ἐν τοῖς ἔργοις αὐτῶν, καὶ οὐκ οἴδασιν, ὅτι ἐξ ὧν βούλονται ἀγαθοποιῆσαι, πλέον ἐξαμαρτάνουσι. θέλεις βοηθῆσαι τοῖς πένησι, μὴ κλέψῃς τοῦ Θεοῦ τὴν ἡμέραν, ἀλλὰ τὴν σὴν παράσχου τοῖς πένησιν ἐργασίαν, ἐξ ὧν ἔλαβες τοῦ ἐργάζεσθαι, ὅτε τὰ σὰ ἔργα ὀφείλουσι γενέσθαι. τότε μετάδος βοηθείας τοῖς πένησιν. Ὅτε δὲ οἱ δοῦλοί σου, καὶ οἱ μίσθιοι, καὶ οἱ βόες ἀναπαύεσθαι ὀφείλουσιν, ἀποστερεῖς αὐτῶν τὴν ἀνάπαυσιν, καὶ τοῖς πένησι δίδως. οἶδεν ὁ Θεός, τίνος ὁ κάματος. μὴ παρέλθῃς τὴν ἐντολὴν τοῦ κυρίου, μὴ κλέψῃς τὴν ἡμέραν αὐτοῦ, μὴ ἀποστερήσῃς τοῖς δούλοις καὶ τοῖς μισθίοις σου τὴν ἀνάπαυσιν, μὴ χωρισθῇς τῆς εὐχῆς, μὴ ἀποστῇς τῆς ἐκκλησίας. οὐδὲν γὰρ τῆς ἐκκλησίας ἀνώτερον, τοῦ οὐρανοῦ ὑψηλοτέρα ἐστὶν, τοῦ ἡλίου λαμπρωτέρα, τῆς σελήνης, καὶ τῶν ἄστρων φωτεινοτέρα, τοῦ κόσμου ὅλου ἐντιμοτέρα. Οἶδα πολλούς, ὅτι παρέρχεται ἡ ἑβδομὰς ὁλόκληρος, καὶ οὐκ εἰσέρχονται εἰς τὴν ἐκκλησίαν, πολλάκις δὲ καὶ μὲν ὅλως. ἐὰν δὲ ἐπέλθῃ αὐτοῖς κακόν τι, διὰ τὴν κακοπραγίαν αὐτῶν, ἐπαιτιῶνται τὸν Θεὸν, καὶ οὐκ ἑαυτούς, λέγοντες· διὰ τί συνεχώρησεν ὁ Θεὸς τοῦτο γενέσθαι; καὶ οὐκ οἴδασιν, ὅτι ὅσον ἀπὸ τῆς ἐκκλησίας αὐτοὶ μακρύνονται, καὶ ὁ Θεὸς ἐξ αὐτῶν, καθὼς καὶ ὁ προφήτης φησίν· *οἱ μακρύνοντες ἀπὸ σοῦ, ἀπολοῦνται.*

§5 "For that is the day that the Lord had made. Let us praise and rejoice in it!" [Ps 117:24 LXX] Let us rejoice not befuddled by intoxication and drunkenness, but delighted in the declamation of the divine scriptures! God gave us that day, on which he began to make the world, in which he destroyed the power of death, and he called it the day of the Lord, that beginning with the name of the day itself we respect and keep the commandments of the Lord. A hired laborer goes in his house and dedicates himself to his work and on six days he does not dare to look up and see the sun, where it comes from and where it goes to, but weary in your works the lamentable shatters and weeps, in sweat and in pains, and never is it granted to him to look up or to take a rest, as we said, but he only waits for the day of the Lord, that, if anything, the dirt is shaken off his body, and often you do not even concede him that. And which defense will you have, tell me! Of course, there are some who out of beneficence will say on the day of the Lord: Come here, today let's help the poor in their work! And who do not know that since they want to do good they sin even more. If you want to help the poor, do not steal the day of God, but give your earnings to the poor, from which you have your revenue. When they are obliged to do your work, then give help to the poor! But when your slaves and your hired laborers and your cattle are obliged to rest, then you take away their rest and give it to the poor. God knows whose work it is! Do not transgress the commandment of the Lord, do not steal his day, do not deprive your slaves and your hired laborers from their rest, do not get separated from the prayer, do not stay away from the church! For nothing is higher than the church, the church is higher than the heaven and brighter than the sun and clearer than the moon and the stars and more valuable than the whole world. I know many who do not enter the church the whole week, often even entirely. And when something bad happens to them because of their ill doing, they accuse God and not themselves and say: 'Why has God allowed that to happen?' And they do not know that as far as they put themselves away from the church as far away is also God from them, as also the prophet says: 'Those far away from you perish' [Ps 72:27 LXX].

§6 Ἀρκεῖ τάχα ταῦτα, ἀγαπητοί, πρὸς νουθεσίαν καὶ φόβον πολλῶν. Εἰ γὰρ ταῦτα οὐκ ἀρκεῖ, καὶ πείθει τοὺς ἀκούοντας, οὐδὲ τὰ πλείονα τούτων ἀκούσονται. φρονίμῳ γὰρ, φησίν, ἀνδρὶ εἷς λόγος αὐτάρκης, μωρῷ δὲ ἐξηγούμενος οὐ πείσεις τὴν καρδίαν αὐτοῦ ἕως θανάτου. Θέλεις μὴ ἐπελθεῖν σοι κακὸν; τὴν κυριακὴν μὴ ὑβρίσῃς, τῶν πονηρῶν ἔργων ἀπόστηθι, τῇ εὐχῇ σχόλασον, τὸ στόμα σου ἀπὸ αἰσχρολογίας κατάπαυσον, μετὰ ἀνδρῶν εὐλαβῶν συναθροίσθητι, καὶ σὺν αὐτοῖς τῷ Θεῷ εὐχαρίστησον, δοξολογίαν ἀνάπεμψον. αὕτη γὰρ ἡ ἡμέρα, πολλαχῶς εἴρηται, εἰς τὴν εὐχὴν καὶ ἀνάπαυσιν ἐδόθη σοι. *αὕτη οὖν ἡ ἡμέρα, ἣν ἐποίησεν ὁ κύριος, ἀγαλλιασώμεθα καὶ εὐφρανθῶμεν ἐν αὐτῇ*, καὶ τῷ ἐν αὐτῇ ἀναστάντι δόξαν ἀναπέμψωμεν σὺν τῷ πατρὶ καὶ τῷ ἁγίῳ πνεύματι, νῦν, ἀεὶ, καὶ εἰς τοὺς αἰῶνας τῶν αἰώνων. Ἀμήν.

§6 That probably will suffice, my brothers, as warning and for the fear of most people. For if that does not suffice and persuade those hearing, then they will also not hear which is greater than that. For it says: 'For the sensible man one word is sufficient, but even if you explain at length to the foolish, you will not persuade his heart until death.'[20] You want no evil to come upon you? Do not abuse the day of the Lord, keep away from bad deeds, devote yourself to prayer, stop your mouth to use foul language, get together with pious men, and thank God together with them, and send up praise! For in many ways it is said that that day was given you for prayer and for rest. 'This, really, is the day that the Lord had made. Let us praise and rejoice in it!' [Ps 117:24 LXX]. And let us send up honor to the one risen on it together with the Father and the Holy Spirit, now, ever and in all eternity! Amen."

20. Proverb? Also quoted by Ps.-Gregentios of Taphar, *Dialexis* 4 (724, 983f. Berger).

A Homily "Hear, All Brothers Christians, What the Prophets Say" (CPG 4848 = urn:cts:pta:pta0039.pta001)

Annette von Stockhausen

The text transmitted as "Parenetic Sermon[1] by Our Holy Father John Chrysostom, Archbishop of Constantinople, on the Holy Day of the Lord" is definitely falsely attributed to John Chrysostom and rather of late (Byzantine) origin.[2] In its extant form the text is also very unbalanced, and it is therefore difficult to imagine it at all as a speech to an audience. Nevertheless, it reflects how Sunday was understood and what kind of behavior was expected on Sunday at a certain time in history.[3]

The text exists in (at least) two versions.[4] Probably also due to the composition of the text, that is, the many repetitions, both versions are in a poor state of transmission and in several places hard to understand.

Version A is preserved in Codex Parisinus gr. 1034 (Diktyon 50627),[5] s. xv, folios 296r–305r (= P).

Version B is preserved in Codex Bodleianus Holkham gr. 22 (Diktyon 48090), s. xv/xvi, folios 466r–470v (= O) and in Codex Marcianus gr. II 90 (Diktyon 70252), s. xvi inc., folios 24r–26v (= M) and its copy or rather close relative Codex Vaticanus gr. 659 (Diktyon 67290), s. xvi, folios 205r–208v (= V).[6]

1. So in version A; version B has "Sermon of Benefit for the Soul."

2. The earliest manuscripts (see below) are from the fifteenth century.

3. I can provide only preliminary observations here. The transcriptions of the manuscripts and the critical edition(s) of this previously unedited text are published in the Patristic Text Archive at https://pta.bbaw.de/text/urn:cts:pta:pta0039.pta001; below I provide a reading text and a translation of version A.

4. Not all manuscripts could be consulted. Not accessible were the late manuscripts Ankara, Türk Tarih Kurumu 27 (Diktyon 699), s. xviii; Mytilene, Μονὴ ἁγίου Ἰωάννου τοῦ Θεολόγου Ὑψηλοῦ, 25 (Diktyon 45290), s. xvii; Venice, Biblioteca del Seminario Patriarcale 196 (Diktyon 69471), s. xvii, and the earlier manuscript St. Petersburg, RNB Ф. № 906 (Gr.) 572 (Diktyon 57644), s. xv. According to the Pinakes database (https://pinakes.irht.cnrs.fr/notices/oeuvre/2438/), at least the manuscript from Ankara differs from the other manuscripts consulted both at the beginning and at the end, so that another, albeit very late, version could possibly exist in this manuscript.

5. This manuscript also transmits the homily CPG 2955 "Today, my Beloved, . . ."; see p. 435f.

6. Both manuscripts M and V share the homilies of fifteenth-century Cretan monk Neilos-Nathanael Bertos. Bertos also authored a homily on Sunday (*Sermo* 11) that obviously uses our text and is known to him as a text by John Chrysostom; see Bjarne Schartau, *Nathanaelis Berti Monachi sermones quattuordecim*, Cahiers de l'Institut du Moyen-Âge Grec et Latin 12 (Copenhagen, 1974) (https://cimagl.saxo.ku.dk/download/12/12Schartau11-85.pdf), 44–48, here 44.9–13.

Version B is distinguished from version A by some extensions of the text, which make this version appear to be a later expansion of the other; but it is also possible that version A is a shortened form of version B. Both versions show a late linguistic form in the manuscripts.[7] This probably is due not only to the lack of an older, "better" manuscript tradition but also to a late date of origin of both versions, respective of the original text and its revision.[8] Being extant in more than one manuscript, version B shows quite a few additions and/or omissions, which might be transmission errors caused by the repetitious composition but might also be additions added by the respective scribe or reuser of the homily.

The text consists for the most part of two monotonously constructed series about the one who honors Sunday (§2) and the one who does not honor Sunday (§3–5) and about the consequences of both behaviors. In the beginning of the text (§1) Sunday is connected with biblical events: on Sunday the Annunciation of Mary, the appearance of God to Moses in the bush, the resurrection, and the incarnation took place. Sunday is the new Sabbath. It becomes clear that Sunday draws more and more salvation-historical events to itself and thus becomes the weekly repeating crystallization point of salvation history. Probably in analogy to the theology of icons, the veneration of Sunday is referred to God as creator of Sunday and not to Sunday as a day. In §4, a small insertion in the negative series, the necessity of attending church on Sunday is emphasized. In the enumeration of negative consequences, he who does not keep Sunday is finally also associated with barbarians and Jews and the devil and thus is ultimately excluded from Christianity. In §6 it is emphasized that whoever is at odds with others must not take part in the Eucharist, and in §7 it is also made clear that worship takes place on the Sabbath and on Sunday and that going to church is expected. At the end of the text, ending quite abruptly, emphasis is put on conversion and repentance and on the consequences of right and wrong behavior on Sunday.

7. For example, με is used for μετά, να for ἵνα. In various places, the accusative is used instead of the expected dative. And we find verb forms such as ἤλθασι. Besides, orthographic uncertainties due to itacism are also found throughout all manuscripts.

8. Manuscript P (Parisinus gr. 1034) does *not* exhibit these orthographic and linguistic peculiarities in the transmission of the homily CPG 2955, so that the peculiarities mentioned are more likely due to the respective textual source than to the scribe of the manuscript.

Text (Version A)

§1 Ἀκούσατε, ἀδελφοὶ πάντες οἱ χριστιανοί, τί λέγουσιν οἱ προφῆται· ‹*σχολάσατε καὶ γνῶτε*› *ὅτι ἐγώ εἰμι ὁ θεός*, καὶ πάλιν λέγει· *αὕτη ἡ ἡμέρα ἣν ἐποίησεν ὁ κύριος· ἀγαλλιασώμεθα καὶ εὐφρανθῶμεν ἐν αὐτῇ*· ὅτι τὴν ἁγίαν κυριακὴν εὐηγγελίσατο ὁ ἀρχάγγελος Γαβριὴλ τὴν θεοτόκον τὴν σύλληψιν· καὶ τὴν ἁγίαν κυριακὴν ὤφθη ὁ θεὸς τῷ Μωυσῇ ἐν τῇ βάτῳ· καὶ τὴν ἁγίαν κυριακὴν ἐδέξατο τὸ βάπτισμα ἐκ χειρὸς τοῦ προδρόμου καὶ τὴν ἁγίαν κυριακὴν ἐποίησεν ὁ κύριος τὴν ἀνάστασιν καὶ τὴν ἁγίαν κυριακὴν μέλλει ὁ κύριος τοῦ κρίναι τὸν κόσμον ὅλον· καὶ πρὸ τοῦ να καταβῇ ὁ κύριος ἐπὶ τῆς γῆς ἡ ἁγία κυριακὴ πρώτη ἡμέρα ἐλέγετο· ὁ Μωυσῆς παρέδωκεν τοῖς ἑβραίοις τὸ σάββατον καὶ φυλάττουσιν αὐτὸ καὶ οὐ παραβαίνουσιν· ἀφ' οὗ δὲ κατέβη ὁ κύριος ἐπὶ τῆς γῆς, ἐπλήρωσε τὸν παλαιὸν νόμον ‹καὶ παρέδωκε ἡμᾶς τὴν νέαν διαθήκην, ἵνα› φυλάττομεν αὐτήν· ὥσπερ οὖν ἔστιν ὁ κύριος ἐν τῷ κόσμῳ, οὕτως καὶ ἡ ἁγία κυριακὴ εἰς τὰς ἡμέρας ὅλας τῆς ἑβδομάδος.

§2 καὶ ὅστις τιμᾷ τὴν ἁγίαν κυριακήν, τὸν θεὸν τιμᾷ, ὅτι ὁ κύριος ἐστὶν ἡ κυριακή· ὁ τιμῶν τὴν ἁγίαν κυριακὴν τοῦ παραδείσου οἰκητὴς γίνεται· ὁ τιμῶν τὴν ἁγίαν κυριακὴν τῶν ἀγγέλων γίνεται συνόμιλος· ὁ τιμῶν αὐτὴν μετὰ τοὺς μάρτυρας ἀγάλλεται· ὁ τιμὼν αὐτὴν εὐλογημένος ἐστὶν ὁ οἶκος αὐτοῦ καὶ πάντα τὰ ἐνεργήματα αὐτοῦ· ὁ τιμῶν αὐτὴν φίλος τοῦ θεοῦ γίνεται· ὁ τιμῶν αὐτὴν ὁ κύριος τιμᾷ αὐτὸν καὶ δίδωσι ὁ θεὸς εἰς αὐτὸν πλῆθος σίτου καὶ οἴνου καὶ ἐλαίου· καὶ εὐλογήμενος ἐστὶν ὁ ἄνθρωπος ἐκεῖνος ὁ τιμῶν τὴν ἁγίαν κυριακὴν καὶ τὰ πάντα αὐτοῦ εὐλογημένα εἰσίν· ὁ τιμῶν αὐτὴν μέγαν φίλον ἔχει τὸν θεόν· καὶ ὁ τιμῶν αὐτὴν κληρονόμος γίνεται τῆς βασιλείας τῶν οὐρανῶν· καὶ τί εἴπω· οὐκ ἔστιν ἄλλη μεγαλοτέρα καὶ τιμιωτέρα τῆς ἁγίας κυριακῆς, ὅτι ὑψηλοτέρα καὶ τιμιωτέρα καὶ μεγαλοτέρα ὑπάρχει τῶν οὐρανῶν.

§3 ἀκούσατε, ἀδελφοί, τί ὄφελος ἔχει ὁ τιμῶν αὐτήν. ὁ δὲ μὴ τιμῶν αὐτὴν τὴν ἁγίαν κυριακὴν ἐχθρὸς τοῦ θεοῦ εὑρίσκεται· ὁ μὴ τιμῶν αὐτὴν οὐκ ἔχει μέρος εἰς τὸν παράδεισον· ὁ μὴ τιμῶν αὐτὴν οὐκ ἔστι φίλος τῶν ἁγίων· ὁ μὴ τιμῶν αὐτὴν μὴ σιτῶν ἐστὶ θεῷ καὶ ἀνθρώποις· ὁ μὴ τιμῶν αὐτὴν τὸν διάβολον ἔχει φίλον καὶ τὸν θεὸν ἀντίδικον· ὁ μὴ τιμῶν αὐτὴν φίλος δαιμόνων ὑπάρχει· ὁ μὴ τιμῶν αὐτὴν οὐκ ἔχει μέρος ἐν τῇ ἐκκλησίᾳ· ὁ μὴ τιμῶν αὐτὴν ἐπικατάρατος ἐστὶν ὁ οἶκος αὐτοῦ καὶ τὰ ἔργα αὐτοῦ· ὁ μὴ τιμῶν αὐτὴν πολὺ ἐμπόδιος γίνεται εἰς αὐτόν· ὁ μὴ τιμῶν αὐτὴν οὐκ ἔχει τι ὄφελος εἰς τὴν ψυχὴν αὐτοῦ.

Translation (Version A)

§1 Hear, all brothers Christians, what the prophets say: 'Study and learn that I am God' [Ps 45:11 LXX], and again it says: 'This is the day the Lord made. Let us praise and rejoice in it' [Ps 117:24 LXX]; that on the holy day of the Lord the archangel Gabriel announced to the Mother of God the conception [see Luke 1:26–33], that on the holy day of the Lord God appeared to Moses in the bush [see Exod 3:2]. And on the holy day of the Lord he received the baptism from the hand of the forerunner [see Luke 3:21] and on the holy day of the Lord the Lord made the resurrection [see Matt 28:1–6] and on the holy day of the Lord the Lord will judge the whole world [see Matt 25:31–46]. And before the Lord went down to earth, the holy day of the Lord was called first day. Moses gave the Hebrews the Sabbath and they keep it and do not transgress it. But since the Lord came down to earth, he fulfilled the old law and gave us the new testament that we keep it; therefore, as the Lord is in the world, so the holy day of the Lord in regard to all days of the week.

§2 And whoever honors the holy day of the Lord, honors God, as the Lord is the day of the Lord. Who honors the holy day of the Lord becomes an inhabitant of the paradise. Who honors the holy day of the Lord lives with the angels. Who honors it is glorified together with the martyrs. Who honors it his house and all his actions are praised. Who honors it becomes a friend of God. Who honors it the Lord honors him and God gives him a great amount of grain and of wine and of oil. And that man is praised who honors the holy day of the Lord, and all his belongings are praised. Who honors it has God as a mighty friend. And who honors it becomes heir to the kingdom of heavens. And what should I say? There is no other day of greater meaning and honor than the day of the Lord, as it is higher and of more honor and greater than the heavens.

§3 Hear, brothers, what good has who honors it! Who does not honor the holy day of the Lord is found as enemy of God. Who does not honor it has no part in paradise. Who does not honor it is no friend of the saints. Who does not honor it is not fed by God and man. Who does not honor it has the devil himself as friend and God as adversary. Who does not honor it is friend of demons. Who does not honor it has no part in the church. Who does not honor it is cursed, his house and his works. Who does not honor it, much will be in his way. Who does not honor it has no advantage for his soul.

§4 καὶ εἴ τις ἀκούσῃ τὸ σήμαντρον τοῦ σαββάτου καὶ τῆς ἁγίας κυριακῆς καὶ οὐκ ἔρχεται εἰς τὴν ἐκκλησίαν χωρὶς να ἔχει ἀσθένειαν μεγάλην, ὅσα ἔργα ἐργάζεται, ἐπικατάρατα εἰσίν· ἐν γὰρ τῇ ἁγίᾳ κυριακῇ οὐκ ἔχει ἄνθρωπος ἐξουσίαν κἂν τοῦ περιπατεῖν, καθὼς λέγει ὁ ἀπόστολος· μηδεὶς περιπατεῖ ἐν δόλῳ, μηδεὶς δικάζεται, μηδεὶς μνησικακεῖται· ἀλλὰ εἰσέρχεσθαι εἰς τὴν ἐκκλησίαν μετὰ καθαροῦ συνειδότος, ἵνα λάβῃ μισθὸν ἐκ θεοῦ καὶ ζωὴν αἰώνιον.

§5 ὁ μὴ τιμῶν τὴν ἁγίαν κυριακὴν οὐκ ἔχει μέρος μετὰ τοὺς ἀποστόλους, οὐκ ἔχει μέ‹ρος μετὰ› τοὺς ὁσίους· ὁ μὴ τιμῶν αὐτὴν ποτὲ ἀγαθὸν πρᾶξαι οὐ δύναται εἰς τὴν καρδίαν αὐτοῦ· ὁ μὴ τιμῶν αὐτὴν φίλους ἔχει τοὺς ἰουδαίους, ὅτι αὐτοὶ ποτὲ οὐκ ὀνομάζου‹σι›ν τὴν ἁγίαν κυριακήν.

§6 εἴ τις εἰσέρχεται τὴν ἁγίαν κυριακὴν ἐν τῇ ἐκκλησίᾳ καὶ ἔχει ἔχθραν με τὸν σύντεκνον αὐτοῦ ἢ μετὰ ἄλλον χριστιανόν, ἐπικατάρατος ἐστίν. καὶ ἐὰν λάβῃ δῶρον ἢ ἁγίαν δωρεάν· ὥσπερ να λάβῃ τίς πῦρ καὶ βάλλῃ αὐτὸ ἐν τῇ ἅλωνι αὐτοῦ πεπλησμένην οὖσαν πᾶσαν τὴν γεωργίαν αὐτοῦ καὶ κατακαύσει καὶ ἀπολέσει αὐτήν, οὕτως καὶ ὁ τὴν ἁγίαν δωρεὰν λαμβάνων ἀνάξιως φλογίζῃ καὶ τὴν ψυχὴν καὶ τὸ σώμα.

§7 καὶ εἴ τις οὐκ ἔρχεται τὴν ἁγίαν κυριακὴν εἰς τὴν ἐκκλησίαν, ἄνδρες τε καὶ γυναῖκες, ἱερεῖς, μοναχοί, διάκονοι, μικροί τε καὶ μεγάλοι, με τὸν ἀντικείμενον ἔχουσι τὸ μέρος, ὅτι τὰ χορεύματα καὶ τὰ συνεργήματα εἰσὶ τοῦ διαβόλου· εἴ τις εἰστήκει εἰς τὴν ἐκκλησίαν καὶ ὁμιλεῖ ἢ φλυαρεῖ τὰ μὴ δέοντα, να τὸν ἐκβάλλουσιν ἔξω ἐκ τοῦ ναοῦ, να ποιεῖ καὶ μετανοίας ρʹ· διὰ τί λέγεται ἐκκλησία; διὰ τὸ κλεῖν τὰς ἁμαρτίας τῶν ἀνθρώπων. ἠκούσατε, ὅτι ἦλθασι τινὲς ἄνθρωποι δύο εἰς τὴν ἐκκλησίαν να προσεύξονται· εἶχεν δὲ ὁ εἷς καθαρὰν καρδίαν καὶ ὁ ἄλλος εἶχε κακήν· ἀνέβη δὲ τοῦ ἑνὸς ἡ πρòσευχὴ εἰς τὸν θεὸν καὶ ἐπήκουσεν αὐτοῦ, ἀνέβη δὲ καὶ τοῦ μαχομένου ἡ προσευχὴ εἰς τὸν θεὸν καὶ οὐ προσεδέχθη αὐτὴν ὁ θεός, ἀλλὰ ἀπέστειλεν ἄγγελον ἀνελεήμονα καὶ ἐπάταξε τὸν ἄνθρωπον ἐκεῖνον καὶ τὸν οἶκον αὐτοῦ καὶ πάντα, ὅσα εἶχεν, ἐνέπρησεν αὐτά· καὶ λέγει ὁ ἄγγελος πρὸς αὐτόν· διὰ τί οὐκ εἶχες καθαρὰν καρδίαν καὶ συνήδεισιν; ὕπαγε, ὡς ἔπραττες, οὕτως ἀπολάμβανε. οὐκ οἶδας, ἐλεηνὲ ἄνθρωπε, ὅτι ὁ ἔχων κακίαν κατά τινος καὶ οὐ διαλλαχθῇ ἐχθρὸς τοῦ θεοῦ ἐστὶ; ἐὰν βάλῃ τίς ἄνθρωπος πῦρ εἰς τὸν κόλπον αὐτοῦ καὶ οὐχὶ ἐκκαύσει τὰ ἱμάτια αὐτοῦ, οὕτως καὶ ὁ ἔχων κακίαν καὶ λάβῃ δῶρον καίῃ ὅλον τὸ σῶμα αὐτοῦ. τῷ δὲ θεῷ ἡμῶν πρέπει δόξα εἰς τοὺς αἰῶνας τῶν αἰῶνων, ἀμήν.

§4 And if someone hears the *semantron* on Saturday or on the day of the Lord and does not go to church—unless he has a severe disease—whatever work he does, it is cursed. On the holy day of the Lord, man has no permission, not even to go for a walk, as the apostle says: nobody should walk around cunningly [see Rom 13:13], nobody should go to law, nobody should bear malice, but go to church with a clean conscience, so that he may receive reward by God and eternal life.

§5 Who does not honor the holy day of the Lord has no part with the apostles, has no part with the pious. Who does not honor it can never do any good in his heart. Who does not honor it has the Jews as friends, because they do not even know the holy day of the Lord.

§6 If somebody enters the church on the holy day of the Lord and has a grudge with his fellow child or with another Christian, then he is cursed. And should he take a gratitude or a holy gift: as if someone takes fire and throws it in his barn, while it is filled with all his agricultural products, and burns it down and destroys it, so he sets on fire his soul and his body who takes the holy gift unworthy.

§7 And if somebody does not enter the church on the holy day of the Lord, men and women, priests, monks, deacons, small and great, they have their part with the adversary, because their dances and their help is of the devil. If one stands in the church and talks or gossips things not needed, they should expel him from church, so that he may repent a hundred times. Why is it called church? Because it calls the sins of man. You have heard that two people went to church to pray. One had a clean heart and the other an evil. The prayer of the one ascended to god and he gave his ear to him, also the prayer of the fighting one ascended to God and God did not accept it, but sent a merciless angel and struck that man and his house and burned everything he had. And the angel said to him: Why didn't you have a clean heart and conscience? Off with you, as you did you receive! Don't you know, wretched man, that who has an evil against someone and was not reconciled is an enemy of God. If someone throws fire in his lap and does not burn his clothes, so also who has an evil and takes a gift burns his whole body. Glory be to our God in all eternities, Amen.

12

FOUR NAMES FOR SUNDAY (FROM CODEX VATICANUS GRAECUS 2392)

Renate Burri

During the course of an experimental research project, carried out in the Vatican Apostolic Library in 2020/2021, I came across a short text about Sunday or, more literally, about the Lord's Day, which discusses four different names for this day.[1] The manuscript presenting this text, Codex Vaticanus graecus 2392 (Diktyon no. 69023), is neither particularly old nor in any way outstanding in material, paleographical, or decorative regard. It belongs to a part of the collections of Greek manuscripts of the Vatican Library that is not recorded in printed catalogues yet, not made accessible yet through digitization, and mainly still understudied. To date no other manuscript is known to me that provides the same text, nor did I find this text attested anywhere in printed or digital form.[2]

This contribution presents the unknown text accompanied by an English translation, offers possible explanations for its origin and meaning, and looks at its textual witness as to better understand the text's path of transmission as far as is reconstructable.[3]

1. The project was titled "In the Name of the Rose: Searching for Unknown, Lost, and Forgotten Greek Manuscripts and Texts." It was funded by the program Spark of the Swiss National Science Foundation. More information on the project is available at https://tinyurl.com/3sd2u852.

2. Except for rare and mere mentions of its existence in Vat. gr. 2392, the most detailed in Eustathii Antiocheni, Patris Nicaeni, Opera quae supersunt omnia, ed. José H. Declerck, CCSG 51 (Turnhout: Brepols, 2002), XLI, where the title, the incipit, and the explicit of the text are given.

3. Uta Heil not only contributed the second section, on the text's background, but also helped to considerably improve the text's English translation with various suggestions and references to the Bible. I wish to thank her for her expertise and for inviting me to present this text in this volume. I am also very grateful to Elisabeth Schiffer for her

1. The Text

The text appears at the very end of Vat. gr. 2392 and covers only three pages (fols. 88v–89v). The title of the text, Περὶ τῆς κυριακῆς ἡμέρας ("About the Lord's Day"), is situated in the upper margin of folio 88v, written in the copyist's hand. The text itself starts in the first line of the same folio. The numbering in the margins also stems from the main copyist.

The short text presents four different names for the Lord's Day: this day can be called the first day, the Lord's Day, the eighth day, or day one. Each name is followed by an explanation of its reason and/or origin. All names and explanations go back to antiquity.

At the end of this contribution, I give a diplomatic transcription and an English translation of the text. In the transcription, a single vertical dash indicates a line break, a double vertical dash a page break. I reproduce hyphenation and accentuation as they occur in the manuscript. The same is true for punctuation, except a few omissions and unifications I have made.[4] The translation is mine; citations from the Bible follow the electronic edition of the New English Translation of the Septuagint (NETS) for the Old Testament and the English Standard Version (ESV) for the New Testament. Additions and explanations to the translated text are given in brackets. My sincere thanks goes out to Uta Heil and Elisabeth Schiffer for their advice on the translation and intertextuality.

2. The Text's Possible Background(s) (by Uta Heil)

This text is perhaps a part of a sermon now lost. The explanations for the four names for Sunday are in accordance with the counting of the days within the Jewish week: Sunday is the first, ruling, eighth, and one.[5] Maybe the text generally dealt with the names of the days of the week and discussed the names of the planetary gods. This, of course, remains speculative, since the "day of

---

precious remarks on the translation and for pointing out helpful bibliography from which this article profited substantially.

4. The "strongest" intervention from my side in this regard is the deletion of a comma and the interpretation of an apostrophe not as indicating a number but for eliding a vowel. In the manuscript, the sentence in question reads Λέγεται καὶ ὀγδοὰς, ὅτι μετὰ τὸ πλη-|ρωθῆναι τοῦτον τὸν θ΄, ἕβδομον αἰ-|ῶνα τὸν παρόντα, ἄρξεται ὁ ὄγδο-|ος. (The signs I have adapted in the transcription at the end of this contribution are underlined.)

5. A useful overview of this topic is provided by Gerhard Podskalsky, "Ruhestand oder Vollendung? Zur Symbolik des achten Tages in der griechisch-byzantinischen Theologie," in *Fest und Alltag in Byzanz*, ed. Günter Prinzing and Dieter Simon (München: Beck, 1990), 157–66 (notes on 216–19).

the sun" is not listed as another possibility of designation.[6] The reflections on the Lord's Day as the eighth day with eschatological meaning occur already in the Epistle of Barnabas of the second century.[7] The day is equated with an era, since according to Psalm 90:4, one thousand years can be described as one day, and the duration of the world is analogized with the creation week, so that either after six thousand years the seventh era or, as in the text here in millenniarist thinking, after seven thousand years, the end sets in as the eighth era.[8] Another possible reason could have been that the author wanted to emphasize that Sunday is not a fasting day, because it is explicitly stated that fasting may only begin on the second day of the week, that is, on Monday. Since one of the preceding texts in the manuscript is the *Physiologus* (see below), it could perhaps have been the reflection on the names of the day and their symbolic meaning that prompted the inclusion of this text in the manuscript. Unusual is the designation of the Lord's Day as "day one," which can only be justified by an isolated exegesis of Genesis 1:5b.

3. The Manuscript

Vat. gr. 2392, so far the only witness for the text about the four names for Sunday, consists of two independent units, of which the first is a paginated printed edition of Francisco de Torres's *Epistola scripta ad quendam in Germania Theologum, contra Ubiquistas Arianistas*,[9] on pages ‹1›–26.[10] I will not further elaborate on this edited text here. The second unit is the proper manuscript. It consists of eighty-nine folios. Their numbering—in this unit not as pagination but as foliation—starts again from 1 on the recto of the first folio, the folio numbers being located in the upper outer corner of the recto pages and written in pencil.

Two blocks can be distinguished. The first block (fols. 1–81) contains four patristic texts, namely, the so-called tribiblos, consisting of Origen's *De engastrimytho*, Eustathius of Antioch's *De engastrimytho contra Origenem*, and

6. As for the Christian discourse on the names of the weekdays, see Anderson, "Christianizing the Planetary Week."

7. See Stemberger, "Sabbath or Sunday," 97–100.

8. See Klaus Fitschen, "Chiliasmus. Alte Kirche," in *Religion in Geschichte und Gegenwart* (accessed online May 22, 2023). See also Andrew Sharf, "The Eighth Day of the Week," in *ΚΑΘΗΓΗΤΡΙΑ: Essays Presented to Joan Hussey for Her 80th Birthday* (Camberley, UK: Porphyrogenitus, 1988), 27–50, here 40–47.

9. Franciscus Torrianus, *Epistola scripta ad quendam in Germania Theologum, contra Ubiquistas Arianistas* (Ingolstadii: Ex Officina typographica Dauidis Sartorij, 1583).

10. On the first page of the edition's text there is no printed page number.

Gregory of Nyssa's *Epistula de Pythonissa ad Theodosium episcopum*, combined with Zeno's *Henotikon*. The combination of these four texts in a manuscript is not uncommon. They even appear in three manuscripts copied by the same scribe who has copied Vat. gr. 2392, Ioannes Sagktamauras (on this copyist see below).[11]

The other, much shorter block, a single quaternion (fols. 82–89), exhibits excerpts from the famous anonymous text *Physiologus* (fols. 82r–87r, top),[12] a short text about the Theotokos's genealogy, titled ἡ γενεαλογία τῆς θ(εοτό)κου | ἐστὶν οὕτως ("The Theotokos's genealogy is as follows") (fols. 87r, bottom–88r),[13] and finally the text about the four names for Sunday presented below (fols. 88v–89v).

The whole manuscript unit is copied by the extremely prolific scribe Ioannes Sagktamauras (Italianized Giovanni Santamaura). Born in Nicosia (Cyprus) in 1539, he sought refuge in Italy in 1572, fleeing from the Ottoman invasion and conquest of Cyprus in 1570/1571. Sagktamauras's presence in Italy is attested first in Messina, then in Calabria, in Naples, and finally in Rome (there from ca. mid-1582). He became the "personal" scribe of Italian cardinal Guglielmo Sirleto (1514–1585). Sagktamauras died in Rome in 1614.[14]

Sagktamauras is said to have copied this manuscript for Spanish theologian José Esteve (Giuseppe Stefano Valentini, 1550–1603),[15] who probably

11. The manuscripts in question are New Haven (CT), Yale University Library, Beinecke Rare Book and Manuscript Library, MS 288 (diktyon no. 46528); London, British Library, Burney MS 53 (diktyon no. 39323); Rome, Biblioteca Vallicelliana, MS R 26 (gr. 125) (diktyon no. 56383).

12. The excerpts are not subsumed under a common title. Instead, each excerpt exhibits its own title. They deal with the elephant, the pelican, the long-eared owl, the eagle, the turtle, the partridge, and the unicorn.

13. This text has close analogies with text no. XVIIIb in Franz Diekamp, *Hippolytos von Theben. Texte und Untersuchungen* (Münster: Aschendorff, 1989), 50f.

14. On Sagktamauras's life, see Giuseppe De Gregorio and Domenico Surace, "Giovanni Santamaura. Copista al servizio del Cardinale Guglielmo Sirleto," in *Il "sapientissimo calabro." Guglielmo Sirleto nel V centenario della sua nascita (1514–2014). Problemi, ricerche, prospettive*, ed. Benedetto Clausi and Santo Lucà (Rome: Università degli Studi di Roma "Tor Vergata," 2018), 495–531, here 497–500. On Sagktamauras as copyist, see Ernst Gamillscheg, Dieter Harlfinger, and Herbert Hunger, eds., *Repertorium der griechischen Kopisten 800–1600*, 3 vols. (Vienna: Verlag der Österreichischen Akademie der Wissenschaften, 1981–97), vol. 1A, no. 179; vol. 2A, no. 238; vol. 3A, no. 299. For a sample of Sagktamauras's hand, see vol. 1C, plate 179.

15. Salvatore Lilla, *I manoscritti Vaticani greci. Lineamenti di una storia del fondo* (Città del Vaticano: Biblioteca Apostolica Vaticana, 2004), 111; De Gregorio and Surace, "Giovanni Santamaura," 509n38.

commissioned it during his stay in Rome, which preceded his appointment as bishop of Vieste (Apulia) in March 1586.[16] This seems to be confirmed by a Latin note written in the lower margin of folio 1r, saying *1584. Ex Bibliotheca Josephi Stephani Valentinj. 18 Julias.*

On the other hand, a subscription at the end of folio 89v of Vat. gr. 2392, subsequent to the text about the four names for Sunday, attests, beyond paleographical evidence, the identity of Sagktamauras as copyist: Ἐγὼ Ἰω(άννης) Σάνκτα μαύρας ἐγράψα *[sic]*; thereunder, in two lines, ταῦτα πάντα εὑρικὼς ἔν τισι βι-|βλίοις πεπαλαιωμένοις, ἐν Κα-|λαβρίᾳ μετέγραψα. Again there under, but from another hand (which seems to be identical with the hand that wrote the Latin note on fol. 1r) *1584*. This same other hand also seems to have added the last word of the first line of the subscription (ἐγράψα *[sic]*).[17] The subscription therefore says (excluding the added word ἐγράψα), "I, Ioannes Sankta mauras, having found all this in some old books, have copied in Calabria."

The subscription has been misunderstood for a long time, leading to the opinion that the manuscript as a whole had been copied in Calabria in 1584. This would have been in conflict not only with Sagktamauras's biographical data but also with the information given in the Latin note on folio 1r, which clearly points to Rome as the much more plausible place of production of the manuscript, especially against the background of the year mentioned.

But first, since the last quire (fols. 82–89) is codicologically independent of the rest of the manuscript, the subscription strictly speaking only refers to the excerpts from the *Physiologus*, the Theotokos's genealogy, and About the Lord's Day.[18] It is worth mentioning that the manuscripts Paris, Bibliothèque nationale de France, *grec* 3067 (diktyon no. 52712), fols. 68r–69r, and Vatican City, Vatican Library, Vat. gr. 1130 (diktyon no. 67761), from fol. 44v onwards, contain the very same excerpts of the *Physiologus* as Vat. gr. 2392 does, and in

16. José M. Floristán, "Epístola literaria de Camillo Peruschi Isidoro, Rector del estudio de Roma, al patriarca ecuménico Metrófanes III (1569)," *Rivista di studi bizantini e neoellenici* 40 (2003): 171–207, here 173–75.

17. See De Gregorio and Surace, "Giovanni Santamaura," 520n80.

18. For the same reason it would not really help to know the role of Vat. gr. 2392 in the Stemma codicum of the tribiblos and the *Henotikon*. Anyway, Hadwiga Hörner does not mention Vat. gr. 2392 in her edition of Gregory of Nyssa's *Epistula de Pythonissa ad Theodosium episcopum* (in *Gregorii Nysseni Opera dogmatica minora*, ed. Kenneth Downing et al., vol. 2, GNO 3.2 [Leiden: Brill, 1987]), probably simply because this textual witness was unknown to her. At least for Eustathius of Antioch's *De engastrimytho contra Origenem*, José H. Declerck, *Eustathii Antiocheni . . . Opera . . . omnia*, XLIV regards Vat. gr. 2392 as an apograph of Rome, Biblioteca Vallicelliana, MS R 26 (gr. 125) (diktyon no. 56383) and as a "brother" of Vatican City, Vatican Library, Vat. gr. 1073 (diktyon no. 67704) and London, British Library, Burney MS 53 (diktyon no. 39323), two other direct copies of the manuscript in the Vallicelliana Library (ibid.). In all the manuscripts mentioned in this note here, the tribiblos was copied by Sagktamauras.

each case the excerpts are in the hand of Sagktamauras.[19] In the manuscript from Paris, the excerpts are followed by the Theotokos's genealogy (fols. 69r/v), also in Sagktamauras's hand, exactly as in Vat. gr. 2392, but the text About the Lord's Day does not occur in the manuscript. Second, the subscription nowadays is interpreted differently: Sagktamauras found the textual material in Calabria, where he transcribed it from old books during his stay there, but the manuscript itself, that is, folios 82–89, was most likely copied in Rome, probably shortly before the date 1584 was written into the manuscript by another hand.[20] The very same place and date of production is in all probability and in accordance with the Latin note on folio 1r also good for the bulk of the manuscript, that is, folios 1–81.

To cut a long story short, the origin of the text about the four names for Sunday remains widely in the dark. Sagktamauras found the *Vorlage* for its copy probably in Calabria, as the subscription reports. The presence of Greek in southern Italy, including Calabria, was due to the centuries-long Byzantine rule in these areas until the eleventh century. The Greek language and culture continued to flourish in the ex-Byzantine Italian regions far beyond this time, but since Sagktamauras explicitly speaks of old books in which he found the texts copied in the last quire of Vat. gr. 2392, his *Vorlage* might well have originated from a period when the territory was indeed still under Byzantine rule.[21]

It is theoretically not excluded that the print and the last quire were not yet part of the manuscript when it belonged to José Esteve, although the activity of the hand that added the Latin note on folio 1r and intervened in the subscription on folio 89v suggests rather that at least the two blocks of the manuscript already formed a unit at that time and that its commissioner was a reader of the text about the four names for Sunday.

19. See *Physiologus*, ed. Francesco Sbordone (Hildesheim: Olms, 1991 = second edition of Rome, 1936), XXXIII, and Declerck, *Eustathii Antiocheni...Opera...omnia*, XLn58. For the identification of Sagktamauras's hand see Hunger et al., *Repertorium*, vol. 3A, no. 299 (Vat. gr. 1130) and Henri Omont, *Inventaire sommaire des manuscrits grecs de la Bibliothèque nationale*, vol. 3 (Paris: Picard, 1888), 102 (Paris. gr. 3067). I have currently no access to information about the exact contents of Vat. gr. 1130.

20. Downing et al., *Gregorii Nysseni Opera dogmatica minora*.

21. See on these cultural contacts, promoting the Letter from Heaven, also pp. 84–133. Maybe a hot scent for identifying a possible Calabrian *Vorlage* for (parts of) Vat. gr. 2392 is codex Milan, Ambrosian Library, A 82 inf., copied by Sagktamauras. This manuscript contains an *Oration on Palm Sunday* which is copied from a manuscript that Sagktamauras found in San Lorenzo di Tucco in Calabria in 1573. Sagktamauras used the Ambrosian manuscript as a *Vorlage* when he copied the *Oration on Palm Sunday* in Vat. gr. 1130, Paris. gr. 3067, and Vatican City, Vatican Library, Ottobonianus graecus 60 (see Cesare Pasini, "Giovanni Santa Maura e la Biblioteca Ambrosiana," *Rivista di Studi bizantini e neolellenici* N.S. 42 [2005]: 223–281, here 234). As we have seen, the first two manuscripts also share

[fol. 88v] Περὶ τῆς κυριακῆς ἡμέρας

Τετραχῶς εὑρίσκομ(εν) τὸ ὄνομα τῆς | κυριακῆς ἡμέρας.

πρῶτον μ(ὲν) | [in marg. exteriore: α′.] λέγεται, πρώτη· ὅτι ταύτην τὴν ἡ-|μέραν ἐποίησε πρώτην τῶν ἄλλων | ἡμερῶν ὁ θ(εό)ς:–

[in marg. exteriore: β′] Λέγεται δὲ καὶ κυριακή, διὰ τὸ οὐ | μόνον εἶναι ταύτην τὴν ἡμέραν πρώ-|την καὶ κυρίαν πάντων τῶν ἡμε-|ρῶν, ἀλλὰ καὶ ἐν ταύτῃ τῇ ἡμέ-|ρᾳ ἀνέστη ἐκ τῶν νεκρῶν ὁ κ(ύριο)ς. | διὰ τοῦτο καὶ τὴν τεσσαρακονθήμε-|ρον ἀπὸ δευτέρας ἡμέρας ἀρχό-|μεθα νηστεύειν, καθὼς καὶ ὁ | δεσπότης ἤρξατο. καὶ ἐν τῇ κυ-|ριακῇ ἀνέστη:–

Καὶ ἐν ταύτῃ τῇ ἡμέρᾳ κατῆλθε | τὸ πνεῦμα τὸ ἅγιον ἐπὶ τοὺς ἁ-|γίους ἀποστόλους φανὲν ἐν εἴδει πυ-|ρίνων γλωσσῶν φωτίζον αὐτοὺς | πᾶσαν σοφίαν καὶ σύνεσιν· εἰς || [fol. 89r] τὸ κηρύξαι καὶ ἐπιστρέψαι τὰ ἔθνη εἰς | τὴν ὀρθόδοξον πίστιν τῶν χριστιανῶν. | ἵνα πληρωθῇ τὸ ῥηθὲν διὰ τοῦ προ-|φήτου λέγοντος εἰς πᾶσαν τὴν γῆν | ἐξῆλθεν ὁ φθόγγος αὐτῶν, καὶ εἰς | τὰ πέρατα τῆς οἰκουμένης τὰ ῥή-|ματα αὐτῶν:–

[in marg. interiore: γ′,] Λέγεται καὶ ὀγδοάς, ὅτι μετὰ τὸ πλη-|ρωθῆναι τοῦτον τὸν θ' ἔβδομον αἰ-|ῶνα τὸν παρόντα, ἄρξεται ὁ ὄγδο-|ος. ὥστε ἀρχὴν μὲν ἔχουσι τὰ τῆς | αὐτοῦ ἀνατολῆς, κατάληξιν δὲ οὐχί. | ἐν ταύτῃ τῇ ἡμέρᾳ ἐλεύσεται κ(ύριο)ς | ἐξ οὐ(ρα)νοῦ μετὰ δόξης, κρίναι *[sic]* ζῶν-|τας καὶ νεκρούς:–

[in marg. interiore: δ′.] Λέγεται καὶ μία, διὰ τὸ μὴ ἀνατεῖλαι | ἑτέραν ἡμέραν ἀντ' αὐτῆς. εἰς τοῦτο γὰρ | ἐπιβλέπων ὁ μακάριος μωϋσῆς λέ-|γει· καὶ ἐγένετο ἑσπέρα, καὶ ἐγέ-|νετο πρωῒ ἡμέρα μία:–|| [fol. 89v]

Ἑσπέραν δεικνύει τὴν κατάληξιν τοῦδε | τοῦ παρόντος αἰῶνος, διὰ τοῦτο ἐπω-|νόμασεν αὐτὴν ὁ Μωϋσῆς, μίαν, | ὅτι ἀνατολὴν γὰρ ἕξει, ἀλλ' ἀνέσπερον | καὶ ἀκατάληκτον· εἰς τοῦτο γὰρ ἔχει | αὕτη ἡ ἡμέρα ταῦτα τὰ τέσσαρα | ὀνόματα.

α′. πρῶτον μ(ὲν), πρώτη·
β′, δεύτερον, – κυριακή·
γ′,– τρίτον, – ὀγδοάς.
δ′,– μία:–

texts with Vat. gr. 2392. Could the Calabrian *Vorlage* for some texts of the Ambrosian mansucript also have been the Vorlage for (parts of) Vat. gr. 2392? Howsoever, the exact relationships among all these manuscripts first still need further and deeper study.

About the Lord's Day

We find the name of the Lord's Day to be fourfold.

(1) First, it is called "first [*scil.* day]," because God made this day as the first of the other days [see Gen 1:5].

(2) But it is also called [*scil.* Day] "of the Lord," for the reason that this day is not only the first and head of all the days, but also that on this day the Lord has risen from the dead. For this reason, we also start fasting for forty days from the second day [*scil.* Monday] on,[22] as has started also the Lord. And on the Lord's Day he has risen.

And on that day the Holy Spirit has come down on the holy apostles, having appeared in a form of fire tongues,[23] illuminating them with all wisdom and comprehension [see Acts 2:2–4],[24] so as to proclaim and to turn the peoples towards the right faith of Christians [see Acts 2:7–11], "in order to fulfill what was spoken by the prophet, saying" [Matt 21:4b][25] "their sound went out to all the earth, and to the ends of the world their utterances" [Ps 18:5 LXX].[26]

(3) It is also called "eighth [*scil.* day]," because after the completion also of the seventh age, the current one, the eighth will begin. Therefore, the parts of its dawn have a beginning, but no ending. On that day the Lord will come from heaven with glory "to judge the living and the dead" [1 Pet 4:5b].[27]

(4) It is also called [*scil.* day] "one," because it does not bring forth another day instead of it. Looking at this, blessed Moses says: "And it came to be evening and it came to be morning, day one" [Gen 1:5b].

It shows evening as the end of this current age, that is why Moses has given as a name to it [*scil.* day] one, because it will have dawn, but no evening and no end. For this reason, this day has these four names.

First, "first."
Second, "of the Lord."
Third, "eighth."
"One."

---

22. As for fasting before Easter, see also the Acts of Caesarea, p. 388, 481.

23. See also Acts 2:3 (γλῶσσαι ὡσεὶ πυρός, "tongues as of fire"). The whole formula "in a form of fire tongues" is not biblical but was often used by Christian authors from the third through the eighteenth/nineteenth centuries. In this passage, our text shares the longest textual coincidence with the *Menologion* of Emperor Basil II ("the Holy Spirit has come down [. . .] in a form of fire tongues"; see PG 117:116f.).

24. Ps.-Dionysius the Areopagite, Div. nom. 7.1 ("with all wisdom and comprehension").

25. See also the fulfillment notes in the Gospel of Matthew, such as Matt 1:17–23; et al.

26. Ps 18:5 LXX is quoted by the apostle Paul in Rom 10:18b.

27. See Acts 10:42.

13

DIATAXIS—INSTRUCTIONS OF THE TWELVE APOSTLES

Uta Heil and Ioannis Grossmann

The *Diataxis* of the Holy Apostles (BHG 812a–e) presents a conversation between Jesus Christ and his disciples after Jesus ascended to heaven from the Mount of Olives and the disciples themselves fasted in the Valley of Jehoshaphat for forty days while reflecting on human transgressions and possible penances (§1), and then experienced an ecstasy (§2). At first an angel appeared to them, but the third disciple Andrew recognized Christ in person, who then revealed himself completely (§7). Therefore, the *Diataxis* presents questions and answers between the twelve disciples, including Paul, and Christ.

It consists of two parts connected by a transition (§30), in each of which six disciples have a chance to speak; only Bartholomew asks a second question in the second part (§31). The topics of the first part (§§1–29) are fasting and praying on Wednesday and Friday, and honoring Sunday through communion, observing sexual abstinence, and rest, all of which is necessary for attaining the kingdom of heaven. In the second part (§§31–55), which is left out here, Christ expounds on the seven heavens (§§32–34), the creation of Adam and the fall of the devil (§§37–41), the sins of men (§ 43–45), and their punishments in hell (§§47–53). The text ends with the command to the apostles to teach all nations (§55). Already in the transition (§30) between the two parts of the *Diataxis*, the apostles are commissioned to record and disseminate in written books the mysteries about which Christ will now speak (§30).[1]

The *Diataxis* has been handed down in a second version (*Didaskalia*). The fundamental difference is that the second part of the *Diataxis* (§§31–55), which contains the description of the seven heavens (§§32–34) and especially the controversial story about the devil's fall (§§39–41), was replaced by a long

1. See on this text, which is seldom studied, Baun, *Tales from Another Byzantium*, 360–63, 453.

series of woes. Already in the *Diataxis*, woes are interspersed in four places, interrupting the narrative (§§6, 13, 18, 24–29). Thematically, the woes of the second part of the *Didaskalia* were adapted to the first part of the *Diataxis* by taking material from it: responsibility of priests (§§23, 26, 48, 49), value of the Scriptures (§§13, 18, 26, 28), Sunday observance (§§12, 13, 16, 18, 29), and communion (§§23, 27).

The reason for the deletion of the second part of the *Diataxis* seems to be due to the apocryphal story about the devil contained there (§§37–41). The text relates that after the creation of Adam, God called on the angels to worship Adam (προσκυνήσατε), the work of his hands, to which Gabriel and Michael complied with their hosts (§§37–38). Samuel, however, resisted, since he is made of fire and thus is above Adam, who was made of clay, and on top of that put himself on a par with God (§39). This enraged God, who then ordered Gabriel to hurl Samuel down into the underworld, where he now ended up as Satanael with his hosts, all of whom became demons (§§40–41). This variant of the devil's fall is encountered in some other texts, often in briefer allusion (Life of Adam and Eve; Apocalypse of Sedrach; Questions of Bartholomew; Treasure Cave; Jesus' Dialogue with the Devil,[2] also in Installation of the Archangel Michael[3]) and can also be found in the Qur'an.[4]

2. Life of Adam and Eve 12–16 (after the devil seduces Eve in paradise, he tells her his own story—in Latin: Wilhelm Meyer, ed., *Vita Adae et Evae*, ABAW.PP 14 [Munich: Bavarian Academy, 1878], 185–250, here 225.65–226.93 and 246; repr. in Albert-Marie Denis, ed., *Concordance latine des pseudépigraphes d'Ancien Testament*, Corpus Christianorum Thesaurus Patrum Latinorum Supplement [Turnhout: Brepols, 1993], 545–48; in Armenian: Michael E. Stone, ed., *The Penitence of Adam*, CSCO 430, Scriptores Arm. 14 (Leuven: Peeters, 1981], 4); Apocalypse of Sedrach 5.2–3 (Otto Wahl, ed., *Apocalypsis Sedrach*, PVTG 4 [Leiden: Brill, 1977], 39); Questions of Bartholomew 4.52–56 (as part of a dialogue between Bartholomew and the devil; see Christoph Markschies, ed., "Die Fragen des Bartholomäus," in *Antike christliche Apokryphen in deutscher Übersetzung*, vol. 1, *Evangelien und Verwandtes*, ed. Christoph Markschies and Jens Schröter [Tübingen: Mohr Siebeck, 2012], 801–5); Cave of Treasures 3 (as a retelling of the biblical story—in Syriac: Su-Min Ri, ed., *La Caverne des Trésors*, CSCO 486, Scriptores Syri 207 [Leuven: Peeters, 1987], 20–27); Jesus' Dialogue with the Devil 3 (in Greek A); 4 (in Slavonic R1 und R2; see Robert Casey and A. Thomson, "A Dialogue between Christ and Devil," *JTS* 6 [1955]: 49–65, here 51.49–51, 56, 59).

3. Installation of the Archangel Michael 3 (C. Detlef G. Müller, ed., *Die Bücher der Einsetzung der Erzengel Michael und Gabriel*, CSCO 225–26, Scriptores Copt. 31–32 [Leuven: Peeters, 1962], 31:10.27; 11.25–12.32, 13.35; translation in 32:13.11–16.2). See also C. Detlef G. Müller, *Die Engellehre der koptischen Kirche. Untersuchungen zur Geschichte der christlichen Frömmigkeit in Ägypten* (Wiesbaden: Harrassowitz, 1959), 187–208; Jan Dochhorn, *Apokalypse des Mose. Text, Übersetzung, Kommentar*, TSAJ 106 (Tübingen: Mohr Siebeck, 2005), 52 with n. 39.

4. Johannes Pedersen, "Adam," in *Encyclopaedia of Islam*, 2nd ed. (Leiden: Brill, 2012), 1:176–78.

However, this version was rejected in other writings as heretical.[5] Obviously, this was sufficient reason to delete the passage. The debate about the devil's origin therefore makes it likely that the *Diataxis* was written in the sixth century, when the first clear criticism of this story of the devil can also be traced, and then revised into the version of the *Didaskalia*.

A prominent theme of the *Diataxis* is the days of the week. Andrew, as the third apostle, asks about the power of the seven days of the week. In the Savior's response, the different valence of the days of the week is justified by details from the history of creation: The Lord's Day surpasses all other days; it is the first day in order and in importance, since God created heaven and earth on it (Gen 1:1). God had placed it at the head of his works and days (§11). Therefore, it is to be kept from the ninth hour of the Sabbath onward. Furthermore, Wednesday and Friday are singled out as fasting days. In the subsequent woe, the prohibition of work on the Lord's Day is pronounced.

The following question of James also ties in with the question about the days of the week and asks about the reward for fasting on Wednesday and Friday. The answer again describes the special value of Wednesday and Friday as well as the Lord's Day, this time with a reference to the heavenly mysteries: the soul will meet in heaven the aforementioned days in person, who will greet them with joy.[6] The Lord's Day will be outstandingly grandly decorated with eight brightly robed angels and himself like the daughter of Zion in the middle.

---

5. Ps.-Athanasius, *Quaestiones ad Antiochum ducem*, quaestio 10 (PG 28:604C): a critique is presented to this devil's fall story: "When and why did the devil fall? Indeed, some say that because he refused to worship Adam, he fell because of that." This is rejected as words of foolish people, because the devil was expelled because he made himself equal to God (Isa 14:13f.). Anastasius Sinaita, *Quaestiones et responsiones* 80 (CCSG 59:131.1–7 Richard and Munitiz): According to Anastasius Sinaita, the idea that Satan fell because he did not want to worship Adam is a fairy tale believed by pagans and Arabs (i.e., Muslims). He justifies this by saying that according to the prophets, Satan was rejected by God because of his pride even before Adam was created. In *Palea Historica* (189 Vassiliev) this story is rejected as heretical in one sentence: "But some say that he was thrown out because he did not worship the man formed by God; and anathema on those who speak such!" The reason given is, "Man was created on the sixth day, but the adversary fell on the fourth day!" Also in the sermon on the archangel Michael of Egyptian bishop John of Parallos (end of the sixth century) such a critique can be found (A. van Lantschoot, "Fragments coptes d'une homélie de Jean de Parallos contre les livres héretiques," in *Miscellanea Giovanni Mercati 1: Bibbia—Letteratura christiana antica*, Studi e testi 121 [Vatican City, 1946], 296–326, here 318 [fol. 62b.5–25], 326 translation); see also Müller, *Engellehre*, 166f.

6. This can be read also in the Apocalypse of Anastasia; see p. 498f. Here, however, the angels are friendly celestial beings, whereas in the Apocalypse of Anastasia they appear as disgruntled beings who complain about humans.

Further details (except the prohibition to work) on how actually the Sunday is to be preserved, the author does not relate. From the answer to Thomas's question (§21), the following aspects still become clear, which are connected with Sunday and the Sunday liturgy: a cleric must attend to his liturgical duties and not turn away from the church and turn to "shameful gain" (§21); a deacon may not marry a second time (§23; also §51); a priest may not live in fornication and a second marriage (§23; also §52); those who wish to receive communion may not have been with a woman on the previous day (§§27; 29; also §49).

There are some connections with the Greek versions of the Letter from Heaven, which also deals with Wednesday and Friday fasting and Sunday worship, as well as parallels to the Greek homilies presented here, especially to the homily of Pseudo-Eusebius of Alexandria on Sunday worship, which support a dating of this text around 600 CE.

The text of the *Diataxis* of the Holy Apostles is available in two Parisian manuscripts (sigles D and E) from the fifteenth and sixteenth centuries, which reproduce a version that is very corrupt in some places but uniform. Interestingly, the Codex Parisinus gr. 929 also contains the Greek Letter from Heaven.[7] For the partial reconstruction of these passages, textual witnesses of the other, later version written under the title *Didaskalia* of Our Lord Jesus Christ as well as the tradition of the Slavic translation[8] was consulted.

Diataxis

D Codex Parisinus graecus 929 (fifteenth century), 480–501 (Nau Sigle A)
E Codex Parisinus graecus 390 (sixteenth century), fols. 37v–46r

Didaskalia[9]

Shortened, but close to *Diataxis* (DE)

C Codex Ambrosianus gr. M 15 sup. (MB 506) (fifteenth century), fols. 212r–216r (up to §18)

---

7. See p. 80 (Greek Recension Alpha).

8. Johannes Reinhart, "Славянский перевод апокрифа Didascalia Domini / Откровение святым апостолам (BHG 812a-e)," *Studia Ceranea* 4 (2014): 151–60 (based on five manuscripts).

9. Further manuscripts are (B) Bodl. Rawlinson G 4 (Misc. 142) (s. xvi), fols. 123v–132v; (F) Athens, IEE [Histor. Museum] 39 (s. xvi), fols. 89r–94r, up to §22; (G) Athens, EBE [National Library of Greece] 1021 (a. 1517/8), fols. 145v–157r; (K) Athos, Koutloumousiou 176 (a. 1438/9), fols. 126v–132r. A new critical edition of the second version is still demanded. See also Aurelio de Santos Otero, *Die handschriftliche Überlieferung der altslavischen Apokryphen*, PTS 23 (Berlin: De Gruyter, 1981), 2:233–36.

Further older manuscripts

A Codex Ambrosianus gr. G. 63 sup. (MB 405) (1000 CE), fols. 174v–176v (up to §22)

V Codex Vaticanus gr. 2072 (eleventh century), fols. 178v–182v (Nau Sigle B)

In 1907 François Nau published a critical edition of this text;[10] however, he merged the Codex Parisinus gr. 929 (D, in Nau sigle A) with Codex Vaticanus gr. 2072 (in Nau sigle B), therefore mixing the *Diataxis* with the *Didaskalia*, thus creating a text of the *Diataxis* that never existed. The former edition of the *Didaskalia* by Krasnosel'cev[11] transmits the singular version of the probably burned manuscript Athos, St Andrew Skete 96. Jagič based his edition of the *Didaskalia* on Codex Patmiacus 379.[12] The text presented here with translation is based on a new edition of the version *Diataxis*, established by Uta Heil and Ioannis Grossmann.

10. François Nau, "Une Didascalie de notre-Seigneur Jésus-Christ (ou: Constitutions des saints apôtres)," *ROC* 12 (1907): 230–54 (with French translation).

11. N. F. Krasnosel'cev, *Addenda к изданию А. Васильева: «Anecdota graeco-byzantina» (Москва, 1893)*, Летопись историко-филологического общества при Императорском Новороссийском Университете 7: Византийское отделение 4 (Odessa 1899), 182–88.

12. I. Victor Jagič, *Отчет о тридцать третьем присуждении наград графа Уварова*, Приложение к LXX-му тому Записок Императорской Академии Наук 3 (St. Petersburg, 1892), 272–75.

Διάταξις τῶν ἁγίων ἀποστόλων

1 Ἐν ταῖς ἡμέραις ἐκείναις, μετὰ τὸ ἀναληφθῆναι τὸν Κύριον ἡμῶν Ἰησοῦν Χριστὸν εἰς τὸ ὄρος τῶν ἐλαιῶν, κατῆλθαν οἱ δώδεκα μαθηταὶ αὐτοῦ ἐν τῇ κοιλάδι τοῦ Ἰωσαφάτ καὶ ἐνεθυμήθη εἷς ἕκαστος[13] αὐτῶν περὶ τῆς γενεᾶς τῶν ἀπίστων ἀνθρώπων, κεφάλαια ἑκάστου πταίσματα, πῶς πταίουσιν οἱ ἄνθρωποι, ἵνα γνῶσιν τί μέλλουσιν ἐργάζεσθαι πρὸς συγχώρισιν τῶν παραπτωμάτων.

2 ποιήσαντες δὲ ἡμέρας σαράκοντα ἐν τῇ κοιλάδι νηστεύοντες καὶ προσευχόμενοι, ἐγένετο δὲ ἐπ᾿ αὐτοῖς[14] ἔκστασις ἡμέρας[15] ἐπιφαύσις παρασκευῆς· καὶ είστήκεισαν ἐνώπιον τοῦ Θεοῦ τῶν ἀγγέλων ἐν ἐσθήσεσιν λευκῶν καὶ λέγουσιν αὐτοῖς· θαρσεῖτε οἱ πολλὰ κοπιάσαντες καὶ προσευχόμενοι·

3 ἀναστὰς δὲ Πέτρος· εἶπεν πρὸς αὐτόν· Κύριε, θεωρῶ τὸ πρόσωπόν σου ὡς τὸ πρόσωπον τοῦ διδασκάλου μου τοῦ ἀναληφθέντος εἰς τοὺς οὐρανούς ἐξαστράπτοντα, καὶ φόβος μὲ συνέχει σφόδρα· νῦν δὲ ἐρωτῶ σε, ὁ δοῦλος σου ἐνώπιόν σου περὶ τῶν σαράκοντα ἡμερῶν τῶν πρὸ τοῦ πάσχα· Κύριε, ἀποκάληψόν μοι τὸν μισθὸν αὐτῶν· ἵνα κἀγὼ ἀναγγείλω τοῖς υἱοῖς τῶν ἀνθρώπων.

4 λέγει ὁ ἄγγελος τῷ Πέτρῳ· ὁ μισθὸς τῶν σαράκοντα[16] ἡμερῶν πολὺς ἐστὶν τοῖς νηστεύουσιν αὐτὴν εἰλικρινῶς καὶ ἀμέμπτως, καὶ τὰς εὐχαριστίας τῷ Θεῷ ἀναπέμπουσιν καὶ προσκαρτεροῦντες ταῖς ἁγίαις τοῦ Θεοῦ ἐκκλησίαις ἐν προσευχαῖς καὶ δεήσεσιν. λέγει γὰρ ὁ ψαλμὸς τοῦ Δαυίδ· μακάριοι οἱ ἐξερευνοῦντες τὰ μαρτύρια αὐτοῦ· ἐν ὅλῃ καρδίᾳ[17] ἐκζητῆσουσιν αὐτά[18]· ὅστις γὰρ ἐὰν[19] ἔχει ἁμαρτίαν ὡσεὶ ἄμμον τῆς θαλλάσσης καὶ νηστεύει τὴν ἁγίαν σαρακοστὴν μεταδιδῶν πτωχοῖς τὴν καθημερινὴν τροφήν, μακαρίσουσιν αὐτὸν[20] πᾶσαι αἱ γενεαί· ἄγγελοι δὲ παρειστήκεισαν ἐνώπιον αὐτῶν ἐξαλείφοντες τὸ χειρόγραφον τῶν ἁμαρτιῶν αὐτῶν·

13. Conj. Nau, εἰς ἕκαστον in DE.

14. ἐπ᾿ αὐτοῖς om. in E.

15. δέκα add AV B C.

16. σαράκοντα ἡμέρες means the fasting for 40 days (σαρακοστή).

17. αὐτοῦ add in D.

18. Ps 117:2 LXX: μακάριοι οἱ ἐξερευνῶντες τὰ μαρτύρια αὐτοῦ· ἐν ὅλῃ καρδίᾳ ἐκζητήσουσιν αὐτόν.

19. Left out in D.

20. This in version AV, αὐτὴν in DE.

Instruction of the Holy Apostles

1 In those days, after our Lord Jesus Christ was taken up on the Mount of Olives [see Acts 1:4-12], his twelve disciples[21] went down into the Valley Jehoshaphat,[22] and each one of them reflected about the generation of unbelievers, and about the chief faults of each one, in what ways men commit faults, that they might know what they could do for the forgiveness of faults.

2 Now when they had spent forty days in the valley fasting and praying,[23] there came upon them an ecstasy at daybreak on Friday; and they stood before the white-robed angels of God [see Acts 1:10]; and they (the angels) say to them: "Be undaunted, you much afflicted and praying ones!"

3 Then Peter arose and said to him: "Lord, I see your face shining like the face of my teacher who was taken up into the heavens, and great fear seizes me. But now I ask you, your servant before you, about the forty days before the Passover. Lord, reveal to me the reward of those (days), so that I too may proclaim it to the sons of men!"

4 The angel says to Peter: "The reward of the forty days is great for those who fast honestly and blamelessly during that time, who send up prayers of thanksgiving to God and persevere in the holy churches of God with prayers and supplications. For the Psalm of David says: 'Blessed are those who search out his testimonies, who seek them with all their heart' [Ps 117:2 LXX]. For

21. In fact, twelve apostles appear in the *Diataxis*: Peter, Paul, Andrew, James, Bartholomew, Thomas, John, Philip, Luke, Matthew, Mark, Thaddaeus. Because of the naming of Thaddaeus and the absence of Judas, the list seems to be oriented more to Mark 3:16-19 than to Luke 6:14-16 and Acts 1:13, 26. In addition, Simon is missing, and only one James appears; this makes it possible to include the apostle Paul next to the Gospel lists of Luke and Mark, although historically Paul does not belong to the twelve disciples but was called only after the resurrection of Christ (1 Cor 15:8f.). Already in the *Epistula Apostolorum* 31 from the second century (C. Detlef G. Müller, "Die *Epistula Apostolorum*," in Markschies and Schröter, *Antike christliche Apokryphen*, 1:1062-92, here 1081), Paul is added as an apostle; in lists such as in Ps.-Chrysostom, *Hom. in XII Apostolos* (PG 59:495), Paul is simply listed among the twelve apostles; on the classification of the apostle Paul among the Twelve, see Dietrich-Alex Koch, "Zwölferkreis," *RGG* 8:1956-58.

22. The valley of Jehoshaphat, according to Joel 4:2-12 the place of the last judgment, lies between Jerusalem and the Mount of Olives. Since Eusebius, *Onomastikon* (GCS Eusebius Werke 3.1:118.18f. Klostermann) it is identified with the Kidron Valley.

23. The forty days of prayer and fasting takes up the forty-day fast of Jesus (Matt 4:2 par.), as well as the forty-day gathering of Jesus with the disciples (Acts 1:3). Here, however, with the exception of the feast of Pentecost, a forty-day fast of the apostles after the ascension is described. If, however, one adds to the sentence "Then an ecstasy came over them" with "of ten days" according to the version *Didaskalia*, one actually arrives at a Friday, since ascension falls on a Thursday.

5 προσελθῶν λέγει καὶ ὁ Παῦλος· ἐπερωτῶ περὶ τῶν πόρνων· καὶ ἀρσενοκοιτῶν.

. . .

8 τότε λέγει Ἀνδρέας· Κύριε, δεῖξον μοι τὴν δύναμιν τῶν ἑπτὰ ἡμερῶν τῆς ἑβδομάδος· ἐν ποίᾳ δόξῃ παρειστήκεισάν σοι;

everyone, if he has sins like the sand of the sea, fasts the holy forty days, giving daily bread to the poor, all generations will call him blessed. For angels stand before them and wipe away the record of their sins."[24]

5 Then Paul comes and says: "I am asking about fornicators and adulterers" [see 1 Cor 6:9; 1 Tim 1:10].[25]

. . .

8 Then Andrew says: "Lord, show me the power of the seven days of the week, in what glory they stand before you."

24. See on this topic Claudia Rapp, "Safe-Conducts to Heaven: Holy Men, Mediation and the Role of Writing," in *Transformations of Late Antiquity. Essays for Peter Brown*, ed. Philip Rousseau and Manolis Papoutsakis (Farnham, UK: Routledge, 2009), 187-203.

25. Their punishment is inextinguishable fire, fiery river, and the sleepless worm—this passage is left out here.

9 ἀπεκρίθη Κύριος καὶ εἶπεν τῷ Ἀνδρέᾳ· ὥσπερ ἀστὴρ ἀστέρων διαφέρει ἐν <φωτὶ οὕτως καὶ ἡμέρα ἡμέρας διαφέρει ἐν>[26] δόξῃ· πρῶτον ἐποίησεν ὁ Θεὸς τὸν οὐρανὸν καὶ τὴν γὴν καὶ, ὁμοίως, πάντων μειζωτέρα ηὑρέθη ἡ ἁγία κυριακή· διὰ τί κυριακὴν ἐκάλεσεν λοιπῶν;[27]

10 ἐποίησεν ὁ Θεὸς τοὺς δύο φωστῆρας τοὺς μεγάλους· εἰς διακόσμησιν τῆς ἡμέρας καὶ τῆς νυκτός· τὸν μέγαν ἐκάλεσεν ἥλιον· καὶ ποικύλως κεκοσμημένος, ἀερικοῖς δρόμοις ἐλαυνόμενος ὑπὸ ἅρματος πυρὸς, ἀκτίνας ἐκπέμπων τὴν ἡμέραν τελείως εἰσβαπτίζεται· ὁμοίως δὲ καὶ ἡ σελήνη τὴν νύκταν ἐκτελεῖ[28]· τὴν δὲ τετάρτην ἡμέραν εἰς ἔργα[29] δικαιοσύνης καὶ νηστείας·

11 τὴν δὲ πέμπτην[30] εἰς διαχώρησιν γῆς καὶ ὕδατος· τὴν ἕκτην δὲ κτίσιν ἀνθρώπων καὶ κτηνῶν καὶ ἑρπετῶν· τὴν δὲ ἑβδόμην κατέπαυσεν ὁ Θεὸς ἀπὸ πασῶν τῶν ἔργων αὐτοῦ [Gen 2:2]. καὶ ἔθηκεν εἰς κεφαλὴν τῶν ἔργων αὐτοῦ καὶ ἡμερῶν <τὴν> ἁγίαν κυριακήν·

12 διὰ τοῦτο μακάριος ἐστὶν ὁ ἄνθρωπος ὁ φυλάσσων τὴν ἡμέραν τῆς τετράδης καὶ τῆς παρασκευῆς· ἐξαίρετος δὲ καὶ τὴν ἁγίαν κυριακὴν ἀπὸ ὥρας ἐννάτης τοῦ σαββάτου· ἵνα ἐπαίρῃ τὸν λαὸν αὐτοῦ καὶ ὑπάγῃ εἰς τὴν ἐκκλησίαν·

13 οὐαὶ τοῖς παρακούουσιν τῶν θείων γραφῶν·
οὐαὶ τοῖς ἐργαζομένοις τὴν ἁγίαν κυριακήν·
οὐαὶ τοῖς παραδίκοις ὅτι οὐκ ἔχουσιν ἄνεσιν. ·

26. Added according to some manuscripts (AV) of version *Didaskalia*.

27. See Ps.-Eusebius Alexandrinus: διὰ γὰρ τοῦτο καὶ κυριακὴ ἐκλήθη (see p. 448), perhaps the decisive reference text for this *Diataxis*.

28. ἐκστελεῖ in D.

29. ἔργον in E.

30. Corrected, πέπτην in DE.

9 The Lord answered and said to Andrew: "Just as a star differs from other stars <in luminosity, so a day differs from other days> in glory. First God created heaven and earth [Gen 1:1], and accordingly the holy Lord's Day was adjugded greater than all. Why is it called Lord's Day otherwise?

10 "God created the two great stars of light to adorn the day and the night [Gen 1:16].[31] The great one he called Sun, and it is colorfully adorned, is pulled by a chariot of fire [see 2 Sam 2:11; 6:17] on heavenly orbits, and by emitting rays, it completely immerses in the day. Similarly, the moon also completes the night. So the fourth day is for the works of righteousness and fasting.

11 "The fifth day is for the separation of earth and water.[32] The sixth day is for the creation of man and herds and creeping things [see Gen 1:24–31]. But on the seventh day God rested from all his works [Gen 2:2]. And he set at the head of his works and days the holy Lord's Day.

12 "Therefore blessed is the man that keeps the fourth and sixth day, but chosen is he that keeps the Lord's day from the ninth hour of the sabbath, to fetch[33] his people, and to bring them into the church.

13 "Woe to those who despise the divine Scriptures!

"Woe to those who work on the holy Lord's Day!

"Woe to those who disregard the laws, for they have no forgiveness!"

31. The author jumps here to the events of the fourth day of creation; the second and the third day of the creation history are skipped.

32. Actually the topic of the second day.

33. ἐπαίρω in the late meaning "to fetch, bring," vgl. LBG 1.549a, s.v. ἐπαίρω; Lampe 506b, s.v. ἐπαίρω B.

14 προσελθῶν καὶ ὁ Ἰάκωβος· ἐπερώτησεν λέγων· Κύριε, τί ὁ μισθὸς τῆς τετράδης[34] καὶ τῆς παρασκευῆς;

15 λέγει ὁ Σωτήρ· μακάριος ἐστὶν ὁ ἐν τῇ[35] πίστει φυλάττων αὐτάς· ὅτι αὐτόν[36] μετὰ τὸ βληθῆναι ἐκ τοῦ σκολιοῦ βίου· καὶ ἀπελθῶν εἰς προσκύνησιν τοῦ ἀχράντου θρόνου· ὑπὸ ἀγγέλων· καὶ ἐν τῷ εἰσιέναι τὴν ψυχὴν αὐτοῦ ἐν τῷ οὐρανῷ· ὑπαντοῦσιν αὐτὸν αἱ ἡμέραι τετράδη[37] καὶ παρασκευῆ μετὰ χαρᾶς λέγουσαι· χαῖρου φίλε ἡμῶν· ὁ καὶ πολλὰ κοπιάσας ἐπὶ τῆς γῆς· νηστείαις καὶ ἀγρυπνίαις δεῶμενος τῷ Θεῷ· καὶ ὅλον σου τὸν οἶκον κωλύων ἀπὸ πάσης σχολῆς[38] τῶν γηίνων[39]· νῦν δὲ χαίρου καὶ εὐφραίνου ἐν παραδείσῳ.

16 καὶ λαλούντων αὐτῶν, ἔρχεται καὶ ἡ ἁγία κυριακὴ μετὰ ὀκτὼ ἀγγέλων λαμπροφώρων· καὶ αὐτὴ μέσον κεκοσμημένη ὡς θυγάτηρ Σιῶν· μαρτυροῦσα τὴν ψυχὴν καὶ ἀσπαζομένη καὶ λέγουσα τοῖς ὀκτὼ ἀγγέλοις τοῖς ἐν αὐτῇ· δεύτε ἴδετε ψυχὴν δικαίαν, ἥτις[40] μώλωπας οὐκ ἔχει, ἥτις[41] καλῶς ἀγωνησαμένη ἐπὶ τῆς γῆς· καὶ ἐφύλαξεν ἑαυτὴν[42] ἀπὸ πάσης ἐνεργίας[43] τοῦ διαβόλου· τότε χαίρουσιν <ἐπ'>[44] αὐτὴν οἱ ἄγγελοι καὶ πᾶσαι αἱ δυνάμεις τῶν οὐρανῶν· τότε διασπαζώμενοι τὴν ψυχὴν τὴν καλῶς πολιτευσαμένην· τοῦτος δέ ἐστιν ὁ μισθὸς τῶν τὴν ἁγίαν κυριακὴν φυλαξάντων· καὶ τὴν τετραδοπαρασκευὴν[45] νηστευσάντων·

34. τετράδι in E.
35. Added in D.
36. αὐτὲς DE (modern Greek) instead of αὐτὰς.
37. τετράδι DE.
38. χολῆς E.
39. πύκνων Nau; ἀπὸ – γηίνων, "from any occupation with earthly things."
40. εἰς τις in D.
41. Corrected; εἴ τις in DE.
42. αὐτὴν D.
43. ἐργίας D.
44. Added according to C.
45. μὴ added in E.

14 James also came near and asked the following question: "Lord, what is the reward for Wednesday and Friday?"

15 The Savior says: "Blessed is he who keeps them in faith, for immediately after he is cast out of the perverse life and departs with the help of angels to worship the spotless throne, the fourth and sixth days meet him as his soul enters heaven, saying delightedly: 'Hail, our friend, who labored much on earth, praying to God with fasting and watchfulness, and keeping all your house from all occupation with earthly things. But now be glad and rejoice in paradise.'

16 "And while they speak, the holy Lord's Day also comes together with eight bright-robed angels and he in the midst adorned like the daughter of Zion.[46] He bears witness to the soul and greets it, saying to the eight angels with him, 'Behold a righteous soul, which has no blemish, which has fought well on earth and has kept itself from all activity of the devil.' Then the angels and all the powers of heaven rejoice over it and greet the soul that has walked well. This, then, is the reward for those who have kept the holy Lord's Day and fasted on Wednesday and Friday."

---

46. Later on in the text (§33), Zion is located in the fourth and paradise in the fifth heaven, and (§34) the spotless throne is located in the seventh heaven. There, however, in the description of the seven heavens, the personified days are missing. These inconsistencies point to the composite character of this text. For the personification of Wednesday, Friday, and the Lord's Day, see also the Apocalypse of Anastasia, p. 498f.

18 οὐαὶ τοῖς μὴ ἀκούουσιν τῶν θείων γραφῶν·

οὐαὶ τοῖς ἐργαζομένοις τὴν ἁγίαν κυριακὴν ἀπὸ παντὸς ἔργου· ὅτι οὐκ ἔχουσιν ἔλεος[47] εἰς τὸν αἰῶναν·

. . .

27 οὐαὶ τοῖς λαμβάνουσιν τὴν ἁγίαν κοινωνίαν καὶ τὴν ἡμέραν ἐκεῖνην μετὰ γυναικὸς συγγενόμενοι ἢ μαχόμενοι ἢ ψευδόμενοι ἢ ὀμνύοντες ἢ γελόντες[48] ἢ λέγοντές[49] τι κακόν· οὗτοι εἰς γεένναν τοῦ[50] πυρὸς ἀπέρχονται·[51]

28 οὐαὶ τοῖς μὴ πιστεύουσιν τῶν θείων γραφῶν·

29 οὐαὶ τοῖς μὴ φυλάσσουσιν τὴν νύκταν τῆς ἁγίας κυριακῆς ἀπὸ πασῶν τῶν ἐπιθυμιῶν·

47. ἔλος in D.

48. Left out in E.

49. εἴ added in DE.

50. Left out in E.

51. οὐαὶ τοῖς μὴ φυλάσσουσιν added in D.

18 "Woe to those who do not listen to the divine scriptures!

"Woe to those who do not abstain from all work on the holy Lord's Day, for they will have no mercy for eternity!"

. . .

27 "Woe to those who receive holy communion and on that day come together with a woman, or fight, or lie, or swear, or laugh, or speak evil, these will descend into the hell of fire!

28 "Woe to those who do not believe in the divine scriptures!

29 "Woe to those who do not keep the night of the holy Lord's Day from all concupiscence!"

. . .

14

THE SECOND APOCRYPHAL APOCALYPSE OF JOHN

Uta Heil

The Second Apocryphal Apocalypse of John (*Apocalypsis Iohannis apocrypha altera*; ECCA 107; CANT 332; BHG 922i; CPG 4755),[1] also attributed as Apocalypse of John Chrysostom to the namesake John Chrysostom, offers questions from John the theologian to the Savior he has approached, with the Savior's answers, about several sins, which include disregard for Sunday, further at length about church liturgy, and ends with a demand for respect for priests, baptism, and mercy. The disregard for the preservation of Sunday as the third sin thus leads to an explanation of the liturgy and its symbolism.

In genre, the text resembles the *Diataxis* / *Didaskalia* of the Apostles or also the *Testamentum Domini*,[2] so it can also be described as a noneschatological dialogue of revelation, and like the *Diataxis* of the Apostles, can probably be dated to the end of the sixth century.

1. Nikolai F. Krasnosel'cev, *Addenda "Anecdota Graeco-Byzantina"* (Odessa: Ekonomicheskaa Tipografia, 1898), 98–101; François Nau, "Une deuxieme apocalypse apocryphe grecque de Saint Jean," *RB* 11 (1914): 209–21; repr. with English translation in John M. Court, *The Book of Revelation and the Johannine Apocalyptic Tradition*, JSNTSup 190 (Sheffield: Sheffield Academic, 2000), 67–103; also in Rebecca Draughon, Jeannie Sellick, and Janet E. Spittler, "2 Apocryphal Apocalypse of John: A New Translation and Introduction," in *New Testament Apocrypha: More Noncanonical Scriptures*, ed. Tony Burke (Grand Rapids: Eerdmans, 2020), 2:399–422. See also the entry in North American Society for the Study of Christian Apocryphal Literature, https://tinyurl.com/8erm5bev.

2. See p. 475. See also Péter Tóth, "New Wine in Old Wineskin: Byzantine Reuses of the Apocryphal Revelation Dialogue," in *Dialogues and Debates from Late Antiquity to Late Byzantium*, ed. Averil Cameron and Niels Gaul (New York: Routledge, 2017), 77–93.

The text is transmitted in five manuscripts; a new edition is a desideratum, since Krasnosel'cev transcribed only one manuscript from the Athos Monastery, and Nau's 1914 study offers the text only on the basis of Codex Parisinus gr. 947. However, this manuscript is relevant in that it offers both a version of the Letter from Heaven (Greek Recension Alpha) and the Sunday sermon of Ps.-Eusebius of Alexandria.[3] The manuscripts are:

Codex Mount Athos, Hagiou Andreou, 96, fols. 78r–81v (sixteenth century), destroyed, but available in edition by Krasnosel'cev
Codex Parisinus gr. 947, fols. 276v–280v (sixteenth century, edited by Nau)
Codex Bibl. Nazionale Marciana gr. II.106, fols. 22v–25v (sixteenth century)
Codex Bibl. Nazionale Marciana gr. III.012 (Venice), fols. 412–413v (fifteenth century)
Codex Hagiou Nikanoros 127 (Hellas, Zaborda), fols. 186v–189 (seventeenth century)
Codex Monē tēs Hagias Aikaterinēs (Sinai), MΓ 66 and MΓ 69 (eighth/ninth century)

Presented here is the passage dealing with the third sin, the disregarding of Sunday worship, and John's subsequent question with Christ's answer to it. The text is taken from Nau's edition, and the translation is by John M. Court.[4]

The sentence "This is the third sin: if one relaxes from work during the six weekdays, and avoids his grindstone and his business affairs until Sunday" indirectly presupposes the commanded rest from work, since an upside-down attitude is described here, so to speak: someone rests for six days and saves his work for the Lord's Day. The condemnation like Judas[5] is not surprising for this text, which carries an anti-Jewish tone. The passage offers the conviction, documented elsewhere,[6] that Sunday is for the forgiveness of sins—therefore, the person who does not observe Sunday sins in two ways: he commits a sin and at the same time misses the opportunity for the forgiveness of sins.

The description of the beginning of the Lord's Day with the ninth hour of the Sabbath corresponds to the idea of the Letter from Heaven and also the

3. See at pp. 80, 444f.

4. Court, *Book of Revelation, 75, 77.* Nau reproduced the orthography of the late Byzantine manuscript and is also copied here.

5. See also at pp. 145, 299, 362, 450, 464.

6. See pp. 145, 152, 194.

Visio Pauli, however, without extending Sunday up to Monday morning.[7] Sunday worship, including rest from work, is strictly commanded, clearly expressed with the last sentence on this subject: "Whoever says that he loves God, and does not honor Sunday, is a liar." In the context of this apocalypse, this is the prelude to further questions and answers about the liturgy, which of course are related to Sunday.

7. See p. 182f.

Apocalypse of John

1 Προσελθὸν Ἰωάννης ὁ θεολόγος τῷ κυρίῳ ἡμῶν Ἰησοῦ Χριστῷ, εἶπεν· Κύριε, ὑπέ μοι πόσε ἀμαρτίαι ἡστίν, καὶ πεία ἀμαρτία ἀσυγχώριτος ἐστὶν τοῖς ἀνθρώποις.

. . .

4 Τρίτη ἁμαρτία ἐστίν. ἐὰν τὴς τὰς ἕξ ἡμέρας ἀναπαύση τὸν κάματον αὐτοῦ, καὶ φυλάττη τὸν μίλον αὐτοῦ, καὶ τὰς ἀποκρίσης αὐτοῦ ἕως τῆς κυριάκῆς· πῶς κρίνη αὐτὸν ὁ Θεός· ὀς τὸν Ἰοῦδαν τὸν προδότην.

5 Ὁ δὲ Ἰωάννης ἠρώτησεν τῷ Κυρίῳ λέγων· Εἶπέ μοι καὶ περὶ τῆς ἁγίας κυριάκῆς.

6 Ὁ δὲ Κύριος εἶπεν· Ἄκουσον δήκεε Ἰωάννη· Κυριάκῆ ὁ Κύριος, καὶ ὁ Κύριος κιριάκή. Ὁ τημῶν τὴν ἁγίαν κυριάκήν, τὴμὰ αὐτὸν ὁ Κύριος ἐνόπιον ἀγγέλων καὶ ἀνθρωπών.

7 Ὁ τημὸν τὴν κυριάκὴν μετὰ παντὸς τοῦ οἶκου αὐτοῦ, ἀπὸ ὥρας θʹ τοῦ σαμβάτου ἀφήεὶ τὸ ἔργον αὐτοῦ, καὶ ὑπάγι εἰς τὴν ἐκλησίαν καὶ εὐχαρίστι τῷ Θεῷ, καὶ εἰς τὴν θείαν λυτουργίαν τὸ αὐτὸ τρόπω, καὶ ἐσπέρας τῆς ἁγίας κυριάκῆς, λυτροῦτε τῶν ἓξ ἡμερῶν τὰ πταῖσματα, εὐλογῆ αὐτὸν ὁ Θεὸς ὡς τὸν Ἀβραάμ, εὐλογῆ τὸν οἶκον αὐτοῦ, καὶ τοὺς καμάτους αὐτοῦ.

8 Ὁ δὲ Ἰωάννης εἶπεν· Ἐᾶν τις τὰς ἕξ ἡμέρας νηστεύων καὶ προσεὔχεται, τὴν ἁγίαν κυρἰάκὴν οὐ τὴμά, τί μηστὸν λύψεται;

9 Ἄκουσον, δίκαιε Ἰωάννη· τὸν δρόμον ὅλον τῆς ἡμέρας ἐᾶν βόσκει τις τὰ πρόβατα αὐτοῦ καὶ τὴνικτα (τὴν νύκτα) οὐκ ἀποκλῆσι αὐτά, τί ὄφελος;

10 Οὕτω ἔσται καὶ ὁ νυστεύων προσευχόμενος, τὴν ἁγίαν κυριάκὴν οὐ τιμὰ τὴν καλὴν ὁμολογὶαν· καὶ ὤστις λέγει ὅτι ἀγαπὰ τὸν Θεὸν, καὶ τὴν ἁγίαν κυριάκὴν οὐ τιμά, ψεύστοις ἐστίν.

Translation

1 John the theologian approached our Lord Jesus Christ and said: "Lord, tell me how many sins there are, and what kind of sin is unforgivable for human beings."

. . .

4 "This is the third sin: if one relaxes from work during the six weekdays, and avoids his grindstone and his business affairs until Sunday. How does God judge him? Like Judas the betrayer."

5 John asked the Lord: "Tell me also about Sunday, the holy day of the Lord."

6 The Lord said: "Listen, righteous John, Sunday is the Lord and the Lord Sunday. The Lord honors, before angels and men, the man who honors Sunday. 7 The man who honors Sunday with his whole household, leaves work at the ninth hour on Saturday, goes to church and gives thanks to God, and similarly goes to the divine liturgy, and on Saturday evening cleanses himself from the sins of six days, this man is the one God blesses like Abraham, blesses his house, and his labors."

8 John said: "If someone fasts and prays for the six weekdays, but does not honor Sunday, what punishment will he receive?"

9 "Listen, righteous John: if someone feeds his sheep throughout the day, but doesn't shut them up at night, what good is it?

10 "So will he be who fasts and prays, but does not honor holy Sunday and the good confession. Whoever says that he loves God, and does not honor Sunday, is a liar."

15

THE APOCALYPSE OF ANASTASIA

Uta Heil

The Apocalypse of Anastasia (BHG 1868–70) is, like its model, the *Visio Pauli* or Apocalypse of Paul,[1] a revelation that describes a kind of rapture experience or heavenly journey of an earthly person: heaven and hell are passed through, their inhabitants are observed, and the rewards of the exemplary believers and punishments of the sinners are described. In this case, it is a nun named Anastasia who undergoes a kind of near-death experience and during these three days undertakes a journey to the overworld and underworld. However, the Apocalypse of Anastasia does not only serve to convey an idea of the afterlife but envisages to adress ethical norms in this way.[2]

The text dates itself (§3) incongruently to the time of an emperor named Theodosius (Theodosius I, 379-395? Theodosius II, 408-450? Theodosius III, 715-717?), and also in the year 6015 from creation (*anno mundi* = 507 CE according to Byzantine creation era 5508 BCE?; = 523 CE according to Alexandrian creation era 5492 BC?), or to 505 *anno Domini* in one manuscript tradition, on a March 25, the Feast of Annunciation (§6). The dates have more symbolic value, on the one hand suggesting great age, recalling an important emperor's name, and at the same time emphasizing the lasting relevance of the revelation. With the naming of 6,015 years after the creation, the time of the world era of six thousand years since creation is actually exceeded[3]—the

1. See above, p. 419.

2. Baun, *Tales from Another Byzantium*, is the latest thorough and excellent study on this text. See also her article "Taboo or Gift?"

3. The indication of the years according to cosmic time is based on the idea of being able to calculate the time since the beginning of creation: since the world was created in six days (Gen 1), and since God counts one day as a thousand years (1 Pet 3:8 = Ps 90:4), a total time of six thousand years is assumed (see also p. 469). Different calculations, how many years had elapsed up to the birth of Christ, lead to different datings. When finally the limit of six thousand years was clearly exceeded and the dating of Christ's birth became increasingly accepted, the respective one thousand years were interpreted only as

Naherwartung becomes here a steady *Jenseitserwartung*. However, it is still to be considered that the text itself was probably written between the ninth and eleventh century, so that, in comparison to this date, again a high age is claimed. Thus probably also a mirror of the past is to be held up to the present at that time. As Jane Baun states: "Anastasia's vision taking place in the sixth century would not preclude her viewing the consequences of tenth-century events, since in the eternal abiding of the Other World, one is not limited by one's own time frame or historical consciousness."[4]

Two versions of the text have survived, one by Codex Parisinus graecus 1631 (s. xv) and Codex Ambrosianus A 56 superior (a. 1542 CE) and Oxford, Bodleiana MS Selden supra 9 (a. 1340 CE), one by Codex Panormitanus III.B.25 (s. xv/xvi). The following text is based on the edition by Rudolf Homburg and the additions of Jane Baun. The translation is also taken from her publication.[5]

The Apocalypse of Anastasia addresses Sunday in a variety of ways. It begins by describing the exemplary ascetic lifestyle of the nun Anastasia (§4), who ate only measured portions of bread and water during the week, following a weekly meal plan.[6] An asceticism in a weekly rhythm is thus presented here.

Furthermore, next to the heavenly throne before which Abraham sits, Anastasia sees four women representing Mary and the three days of the week, Wednesday, Friday, and Sunday (§§14; 25). Thus, a similar idea as in the *Diataxis* of the Apostles[7] is encountered. In this vision, these women are surrounded by many children—they are those whom Herod had executed—and the four women bring accusations against sinners before God. The female

---

a symbolic number. See Alden A. Mosshammer, *The Easter Computus and the Origins of the Christian Era*, OECS (Oxford: Oxford University Press, 2011), 27–30, 278–316 on the origins of the Byzantine era.

4. Baun, *Tales from Another Byzantium*, 221. On the chronological problems and their possible interpretations, see 215–22.

5. Rudolf Homburg, *Apocalypsis Anastasiae, ad trium codicum auctoritatem Panormitani Ambrosiani Parisini* (Leipzig: Teubner, 1903), 5.10–6.6 (text below), 12.1–14.2 (text below), and 20.4–21.5 (text below); translation Baun, *Tales from Another Byzantium*, 403, 405f., 408. At 59–67 she informs about the manuscripts and their scribes.

6. Apocalypse of Anastasia 4 (1.15–18 Homburg; translation Baun, *Tales from Another Byzantium*, 401): πάσας δὲ τὰς ἡμέρας διετέλει ἐν τῇ ἀσκήσει τῶν θείων γραφῶν καὶ τὰς μνείας τῶν ἁγίων ἐπιτελοῦσα, μὴ γευσαμένη μήτε ἑψητοῦ μήτε ἐλαίου, ἀλλὰ ἀπὸ κυριακῆς ἕως κυριακῆς ἤσθιεν ἄρτου καὶ ὕδατος εὐτάκτως μεμετρημένου. "She preserved all her days in the study of the Holy Scriptures, and observed the commemorations of the angels. She tasted neither cooked food nor food prepared with oil, but from Sunday to Sunday she would eat bread and water, measured out in well-ordered fashion."

7. See above, pp. 477, 486f.

figures are thus personified weekdays as celestial figures and symbolize each the specific topic of the weekday. Accordingly, they appear here as relentless accusers against the sinners or against the sins that relate to the days of the week. Since it is a question here of the complaint against sins, the personified days of the week appear rather as angry figures, while in the *Diataxis* of the Apostles they welcome in a positive sense the soul cordially who observed Sunday.[8] Mary, the God-bearer, as the fourth female figure, on the other hand, appears as an intercessor and is apparently still able to avert the destruction of the "works of God" through her supplication. Thus, heavenly figures appear here comparable to the Letter from Heaven.[9] The sin now associated with Sunday, unsurprisingly, is work. As in the Letter from Heaven, Sunday rest is demanded from the ninth hour of the Sabbath until the next dawn as in the Letter from Heaven,[10] and a curse is pronounced against those who do not observe it. Perhaps the author of the Apocalypse of Anastasia had used a version of the Letter from Heaven as a model, or at least as a source of inspiration.[11]

Another aspect is addressed a little later (§33): priests are accused of having sexual intercourse with their wives on the Lord's Day. On the one hand, it is interesting how naturally the marriage of a priest is presupposed and no celibate life demanded. On the other hand, the special holiness of the day is emphasized by required sexual abstinence. This second aspect is also found in texts from the Latin West and reflects a growing tendency of the time to prohibit sexual intercourse on holidays.[12]

8. See p. 486f.

9. See Baun, *Tales from Another Byzantium*, 271-87, on Mary as intercessor. On the Letter from Heaven, see pp. 187–89.

10. See above, p. 182f.

11. See also Baun, *Tales from Another Byzantium*, 346-50.

12. See on further sins, Baun, *Tales from Another Byzantium*, 328f. (overview).

Apocalypse of Anastasia

. . .

14 Καὶ εἰς τὰ νήπια ἵσταντο γυναῖκες τέσσαρες. Καὶ ἠρώτησα τὸν ἄγγελον καὶ εἶπέ μοι· ἡ μία ἐστὶν ἡ ἁγία θεοτόκος καὶ ἡ ἄλλη ἡ ἁγία Κυριακὴ καὶ ἡ ἑτέρα ἡ ἁγία Τετράδη καὶ ἡ ἁγία Παρασκευή, καὶ ἐγκαλοῦσιν τὸν θεὸν διὰ τὰς ἁμαρτίας, ἃς ποιοῦσιν οἱ ἄνθρωποι ἐπὶ τῆς γῆς καὶ μολύνουσιν αὐτάς. ἡ δὲ ἁγία θεοτόκος παρακαλεῖ καὶ δυσωπεῖ τὸν θεὸν λέγουσα· δέσποτα, ἐλέησον τὸ πλάσμα τῶν χειρῶν σου καὶ τὸν κόσμον σου καὶ μὴ ἀπολέσῃς αὐτούς.

. . .

25 Τότε κρατήσας ὁ ἄγγελος τῆς δεξιᾶς μου χειρὸς ἀνήγαγέν με εἰς τὸν θρόνον, ὅπου παρειστήκεσαν αἱ τάξεις τῶν ἀγγέλων· καὶ εἶδον πάλιν τὰς πρώτας γυναῖκας αὐτὰς ἐγκαλούσας τὸν θεόν, καὶ ἐδέοντο καὶ ἔλεγον· δέσποτα, καταπόντισον τοὺς ἀπίστους καὶ ἀνελεήμονας, ὅτι οὐ δύναμαι τὰς αἰσχρὰς αὐτῶν πράξεις ὑπενεγκεῖν. ἰδοὺ γάρ, ἀπὸ ὥρας ἐννάτης τοῦ σαββάτου ἕως δευτέρας ἐπιφωσκούσης ἐργάζονται τὰ ἔργα τῶν χειρῶν αὐτῶν, μὴ τιμῶντες τὴν ἡμέραν τῆς ἀναστάσεώς σου. ἐξάπτουσιν τοὺς κλιβάνους αὐτῶν καὶ τὰς ὁδοὺς αὐτῶν ἀπέρχονται καὶ ἄλλα χειρῶν ἔργα ἐργάζονται. Καὶ καταπόντισον αὐτούς, ὅτι ἀναβαίνουσιν αἱ κακίαι αὐτῶν πρός με καὶ καταισχύνουν μου τὸ πρόσωπον, καὶ ἵσταμαι ἐνώπιόν σου κατῃσχυμμένη. Καὶ ἦλθεν φωνὴ λέγουσα· ἐπικατάρατος ὁ οἶκος ἐκεῖνος, ὅστις ἀπὸ ὥρας ἐννάτης τοῦ σαββάτου ἕως δευτέρας ἐπιφωσκούσης ἡλίου ἔργου ἅψηται, ὅτι αὐτὸν ἀναμένει τὸ πῦρ τὸ αἰώνιον, καὶ ἐπὶ τῆς γῆς αὐτὸν οὐκ εὐλογήσω.

26 Ἡ δὲ ἁγία Παρασκευὴ καὶ ἡ ἁγία Τετράδη παρίστανται καὶ αὐταὶ τῷ θεῷ λέγουσαι ὅτι· ἐν ταῖς ἡμέραις ἡμῶν ἐσθίουσι κρέας καὶ τυρὸν καὶ μίγνυνται μετὰ τὰς γυναῖκας αὐτῶν καὶ μολύνουσιν ἡμᾶς. Καὶ ἦλθεν φωνὴ λέγουσα· ἐπικατάρατος ὁ λάρυγξ ἐκεῖνος ὁ ἐσθίων κρέας καὶ τυρὸν ἐν τετραδοπαρασκευῇ, εἰ μὴ ἐν τῇ ἑβδομάδι τοῦ πάσχα καὶ τῶν δώδεκα ἡμερῶν καὶ τὴν πεντηκοστήν. τὰς δε λοιπὰς φύλαττε καὶ ἐγκρατεύου. Μηδὲ μνείαν ἁγίων διαλύσῃς, ὦ ἄνθρωπε, εἰ μὴ λειτουργήσῃς καὶ κοινωνήσῃς· εἰ δὲ μήτε, τὸ πῦρ τὸ αἰώνιον κληρονομήσεις.

. . .

Translation

. . .

14 And among the infants were standing four women. I asked the angel, and he said to me, "The one is the holy Theotokos, and the other, holy Sunday, and the others holy Wednesday and holy Friday, and they bring suit to God on account of the sins which people do upon the earth, defiling them. But the holy Theotokos entreats and beseeches God, saying, 'Master, have mercy on the creation of your hands, and on your world, and do not destroy them.'"

. . .

25 Then the angel, taking hold of my right hand, led me up to the throne, where the ranks of the angels stood by. And I saw again those same first women, and they were bringing suit to God. [Holy Sunday, her countenance luminous, also was beseeching God, saying,][13] "Master, wash the faithless and merciless ones into the sea, for I am not able to endure their shameful deeds. For behold: from the ninth hour of the Sabbath until the second drawing towards dawn, they work the works of their hands, not honoring the day of your resurrection. They light their ovens and go away into their streets and work other works of [their] hands. So wash them into the sea, since their vices mount up to you and my countenance is thoroughly disgraced, and I stand before you thoroughly disgraced." And there came a voice saying, "Cursed is that house which from the ninth hour of Saturday until the second dawning of the sun engages in work, for the eternal fire awaits it, and I will not bless it upon the earth."

26 Holy Friday and holy Wednesday present themselves and are saying to God: "On our days they eat meat and cheese, and copulate with their wives, and defile us." And there came a voice saying, "Cursed is that throat, the one that eats meat and cheese on Wednesday and Friday, save in the Paschal week, and during the twelve days,[14] and during Pentecost. Keep the remainder and abstain. Nor should you break your fast for the commemorations of the saints, o man, until you have participated in the liturgy and received Communion. But if not, you shall inherit eternal fire."

. . .

13. Only in Codex Ambrosianus.

14. Twelve days before Lent. See Baun, *Tales from Another Byzantium*, 328, 350–52.

. . .

33 καὶ πάλιν ἔδειξέν μοι ὁ ἄγγελος ἄλλην κόλασιν λεγομένην ἑπτάλοφον ἔχοντα καμίνους ἀναριθμήτους· ἐπάνω δὲ ἔχων σκεπασμένας τὰς θυρίδας. ἐξ αὐτῶν δὲ ἐξήρχετο ἄχνη καὶ πῦρ καὶ βροντισμὸς τῆς φλογός. Καὶ ἐν αὐτῷ εἶδον πλῆθος ἀνθρώπων πολλῶν εἰσιόντων ἐν αὐτῷ. καὶ λέγει μοι ὁ ἄγγελος· οὗτοί εἰσιν οἱ πρεσβύτεροι οἱ δίγαμοι, οἱ μετὰ ἔχθρας εἰσίοντες εἰς ναὸν κυρίου καὶ τὴν ἁγίαν λειτουργίαν ἐκτελοῦντες· ἱερεῖς οἱ ἀνάγοντες τοὺς ἀνθρώπους εἰς κριτήριον, καὶ ἱερεὺς ὁ συγγενόμενος μετὰ τῆς γυναικὸς αὐτοῦ τῇ ἁγίᾳ κυριακῇ ἢ ἑτέρᾳ ἑορτῇ, ἱερεὺς ὁ ἔχων γυναῖκαν κρυπτήν, ἱερεὺς ὁ μὴ ἐτάζων τὸν λαὸν αὐτοῦ ἐν τῇ ἁγίᾳ κοινωνίᾳ λέγων· "μὴ ἔκλεψας; μὴ ἐπόρνευσας; μὴ ἔχθραν ἔχεις μετά τινος; μὴ ἐσυκοφάντησας κατὰ τὸν πλησίον σου;" ἱερεὺς λαβὼν δῶρα καὶ κρύπτων γυναῖκα πόρνην; ἱερεὺς ὁ καινόδοξος.

. . .

. . .

33 And again the angel showed me yet another punishment, called *Heptalophos*, which has innumerable ovens—but on top, it has covered entrances. From them there came out foam and fire and a thundering of the flame. And in it I saw a multitude of many persons inside it. And the angel said to me, "These are the twice-married priests, those who go into the Lord's temple with enmity and serve the Holy Liturgy; the priests who take people to court, and the priest who copulates with his wife on the holy Lord's Day or on other feasts; the priest who has a hidden woman, the priest who does not examine his people at the Holy Communion, saying, 'Have you stolen? Have you fornicated? Have you harbored enmity against anyone? Have you borne false witness against your neighbor?'; the priest who takes bribes and hides a woman prostitute, the priest who has new-fangled opinions."

. . .

C LITERATURE

Selected Bibliography

Alikin, Valeriy A. *The Earliest History of the Christian Gathering: Origin, Development and Content of the Christian Gatherings in the First to Third Centuries.* VCSup 102. Leiden: Brill, 2010.

Allen, Edward. "How Did the Jewish Sabbath Become the Christian Sunday? A Review of the Reviews of Bacchiocchi's 'From Sabbath to Sunday.'" *AUSS* 53 (2015): 337–53.

Amaduzzi, Johannes Christoph. *Anecdota litteraria ex mss codicibus eruta I.* Rome: Anton Fulgonium, 1773.

Anderson, Mark. "Christianizing the Planetary Week and Globalizing the Seven-Day Cycle." *Studies in Late Antiquity* 3 (2019): 128–91.

Auffarth, Christoph. "Wie kann man von Heiligkeit in der Antike sprechen? Heiligkeit in religionswissenschaftlicher Perspektive." In *Heilige, Heiliges und Heiligkeit in spätantiken Religionskulturen*, edited by Peter Gemeinhardt, 1-34. RVV 61. Berlin: de Gruyter, 2012.

Bacchiocchi, Samuele. *Du Sabbat au Dimanche: Une recherche historique sur les origins du Dimanche chrétienne.* Paris: P. Lethielleux, 1984.

Backus, Irena. "Lettre du Jésus-Christ sur le Dimanche." In *Écrits apocryphes chrétiens*, edited by François Bovon and Pierre Geoltrain, 2:1101–19. Bibliothèque de la Pléiade 516. Paris: Gallimard, 2005.

Baechtold-Stäubli, Hanns. "Sonntagsbrief." In *Handwörterbuch des deutschen Aberglaubens* 8:99–103. Berlin: de Gruyter, 1936.

Baluzius, Étienne. *Capitularia regum Francorum II.* Paris: Franz Muguet, 1677.

Bauckham, Richard. "The Lord's Day." In *From Sabbath to Lord's Day: A Biblical, Historical and Theological Investigation*, edited by Donald A. Carson, 222-50. Grand Rapids: Zondervan, 1982.

———. "Sabbath and Sunday in the Medieval Church in the West." In *From Sabbath to Lord's Day: A Biblical, Historical and Theological Investigation*, edited by Donald A. Carson, 300-309. Grand Rapids: Zondervan, 1982.

———. "Sabbath and Sunday in the Post-apostolic Church." In *From Sabbath to Lord's Day: A Biblical, Historical and Theological Investigation*, edited by Donald A. Carson, 252-98. Grand Rapids: Zondervan, 1982.

Baun, Jane. "Taboo or Gift? The Lord's Day in Byzantium." In *The Use and Abuse of Time in Christian History*, edited by Robert N. Swanson, 45-56. Suffolk: Boydell, 2002.

———. *Tales from Another Byzantium: Celestial Journey and Local Community in the Medieval Greek Apocrypha*. Cambridge: Cambridge University Press, 2007.

Beckerath, Jürgen V. "Zeiteinteilung, -messung." In *Lexikon der Ägyptologie*, edited by Wolfgang Helck, 6:1371f. Wiesbaden: Harrassowitz, 1986.

Benente, Fabrizio, ed. *Santa Maria di Piazza: Culto, territorio e popolamento al crocevia di una chiesa millenaria*. Bordighera: Quadernia della Tigullia, 2002.

Beskow, Per. *Strange Tales about Jesus: A Survey of Unfamiliar Gospels*. Philadelphia: Fortress, 1983.

Bittner, Maximilian. *Der vom Himmel gefallene Brief Christi in seinen morgenländischen Versionen und Rezensionen*. Denkschriften der Kaiserlichen Akademie der Wissenschaften, Philosophisch-Historische Classe 51.1. Vienna: Alfred Hölder, 1905.

Bradshaw, Paul F., and Maxwell E. Johnson, eds. *The Origins of Feasts, Fasts and Seasons in Early Christianity*. Collegeville, MN: Liturgical Press, 2011.

Buchinger, Harald. "Sunday Celebration in the Early Church. A Review of Basic Structures, Characteristic Elements, and Significant Developments." In *From Sun-Day to the Lord's Day. The Cultural History of Sunday in Late Antiquity and the Early Middle Ages*, edited by Uta Heil, 401-33. CELAMA 39. Turnhout: Brepols, 2022.

Bultrighini, Ilaria. "Theōn Hemerai: Astrology, the Planetary Week, and the Cult of the Seven Planets in the Graeco-Roman World." In *Religion and Education in the Ancient Greek World*, edited by Irene Salvo and Tanja Susanne Scheer, 217-39. Tübingen: Mohr Siebeck, 2021.

———. "Thursday (*Dies Iovis*) in the Later Roman Empire." *Papers of the British School at Rome* 86 (2018): 61-84.

Bultrighini, Ilaria, and Sacha Stern. "The Seven-Day-Week in the Roman Empire: Origins, Standardization, and Diffusion." In *Calendars in the Making: The Origins of Calendars from the Roman Empire to the Later Middle Ages*, edited by Sacha Stern, 10-79. Time, Astronomy, and Calendars 10. Leiden: Brill, 2021.

Carson, Donald A., ed. *From Sabbath to Lord's Day: A Biblical, Historical and Theological Investigation*. Grand Rapids: Zondervan, 1982.

Delehaye, Hippolyte. "Note sur la légende de la Lettre du Christ tombée du ciel." *Bulletin de l'Académie royale de Belgique, Classe des Lettres* 37 (1899): 171–213. Reprinted in Hippolyte Delehaye, *Mélanges d'Hagiographie grecque et latine*, 150–78. SHG 42. Brussels: Société des Bollandistes, 1966.

———. "Un exemplaire de la letter tombée du ciel." *RSR* 18 (1928): 164-69.

Dieterich, Albrecht. "Himmelsbriefe." In *Kleine Schriften*, 234–42. Leipzig: B. G. Teubner, 1911.

———. "Weitere Beobachtungen zu den Himmelsbriefen." In *Kleine Schriften*, 243–51. Leipzig: B. G. Teubner, 1911.

Divjak, Johannes. "Epistulae." In *Augustinus Lexikon*, edited by Cornelius Mayer, 2:893-1057. Basel: Schwabe, 1996-2002.

Doering, Lutz. "The Notion of *mela'khah* in Tosefta Shabbat." In: *Tosefta Studies: Manuscripts, Traditions, and Topics*, edited by Lutz Doering and Daniel Schumann, 93–107. Münster: LIT, 2021.

———. "Sabbat." *RAC* 29:226-33.

Dölger, Franz J. "Die Planetenwoche der griechisch-römischen Antike und der christliche Sonntag." *Antike und Christentum* 6 (1950): 228–38.

Drecoll, Volker Henning. "Not Every Sunday Is the Same. Observations on the Development of the 'Sunday Propria' in the Liturgies of the Old Gallican Rite in the Early Middle Ages." In *From Sun-Day to the Lord's Day: The Cultural History of Sunday in Late Antiquity and the Early Middle Ages*, edited by Uta Heil, 435-52. CELAMA 39. Turnhout: Brepols, 2022.

Dumaine, Henri. "Dimanche." In *Dictionnaire d'archéologie chrétienne et de liturgie* 4.1:858–994. Paris: Letouzey, 1920.

Durst, Michael. "Remarks on Sunday in the Early Church." In *From Sun-Day to the Lord's Day: The Cultural History of Sunday in Late Antiquity and the Early Middle Ages*, edited by Uta Heil, 373-400. CELAMA 39. Turnhout: Brepols, 2022.

———. "Sonntag." *RAC* 30:849-76.

Erbetta, Mario. *Gli Apocrifi del Nuovo Testamento*. Vol. 3, *Lettere e apocalissi, versione e commento*. Turin: Marietti, 1969.

Esbroeck, Michel van. "La lettre sur le Dimanche, descendue du ciel." *AnBoll* 107 (1989): 267–84.

Fabricius, Johannes Alberto. *Codex apocryphus Noui Testamenti I*. Hamburg: Schiller & Kisner, 1719.

Fowler, W. Warde. *The Roman Festivals of the Period of the Republic*. Piscataway, NJ: Gorgias, 2004.

Goldhill, Simon. *The Christian Invention of Time: Temporality and the Literature of Late Antiquity*. Greek Culture in the Roman World. Cambridge: Cambridge University Press, 2022.

González, Justo L. *A Brief History of Sunday: From the New Testament to the New Creation*. Grand Rapids: Eerdmans, 2017.

Goodspeed, Edgar J. *Strange New Gospels*. Chicago: University of Chicago Press, 1931.

Graf, Fritz. *Der Lauf des rollenden Jahres. Zeit und Kalender in Rom*. Lectio Teubneriana 6. Stuttgart: Teubner, 1997.

Graf, Georg. "Der vom Himmel gefallene Brief Christi (nach Cod. Monac. Arab. 1067)." *ZS* 6 (1928): 10–23.

Graumann, Thomas. "In Search for Synodical Activities on Sundays." In *From Sun-Day to the Lord's Day: The Cultural History of Sunday in Late Antiquity and the*

Early Middle Ages, edited by Uta Heil, 143–86. CELAMA 39. Turnhout: Brepols, 2022.

Grégoire, Réginald. *Les homéliaires du moyen âge, inventaire et analyse des manuscrits.* Rerum Ecclesiasticarum Documenta, Series Maior, Fontes 6. Rome: Herder, 1966.

Grund, Alexandra. *Die Entstehung des Sabbats. Seine Bedeutung für Israels Zeitkonzept und Erinnerungskultur.* FAT. Tübingen: Mohr Siebeck, 2011.

Haines, Dorothy. *Sunday Observance and the Sunday Letter in Anglo-Saxon England.* Anglo-Saxon Texts. Cambridge: Brewer, 2010.

Hall, Isaac H. "The Letter of Holy Sunday: Syriac Text and Translation." *JAOS* 15 (1893): 121–37.

Heil, Uta. "Ein Sonntag in Cividale. Bemerkungen zum *Concilium Foroiuliense* (Cividale) im Jahr 796." In *Frömmigkeit. Historische, systematische und praktische Perspektiven*, edited by Uta Heil and Annette Schellenberg, 91–109. Wiener Jahrbuch für Theologie 11. Göttingen: Vandenhoeck & Ruprecht and Vienna University Press, 2016.

———, ed. *From Sun-Day to the Lord's Day: The Cultural History of Sunday in Late Antiquity and the Early Middle Ages.* CELAMA 39. Turnhout: Brepols, 2022.

———. "Ignatios von Antiochia und der Herrentag." In *Die Briefe des Ignatios von Antiochia: Motive, Strategien, Kontexte*, edited by Thomas Johann Bauer and Peter von Möllendorff, 201–27. Millennium Studies 72. Berlin: de Gruyter, 2018.

Heil, Uta, and Fritz Mitthof. "Missachtung der Sonntagsruhe als Kapitalverbrechen." In *From Sun-Day to the Lord's Day: The Cultural History of Sunday in Late Antiquity and the Early Middle Ages*, edited by Uta Heil, 75–92. CELAMA 39. Turnhout: Brepols, 2022.

Hohmann, Hanns. "Gerichtsreden." In *Historisches Wörterbuch der Rhetorik*, edited by Gert Ueding, 3:770–815. Basel: Schwabe, 1996.

Huber, Hans. *Geist und Buchstabe der Sonntagsruhe. Eine historisch-theologische Untersuchung über das Verbot von knechtlicher Arbeit von der Urkirche bis auf Thomas von Aquin.* Studia Theologiae moralis et pastoralis 4. Salzburg: Otto Müller, 1958.

Jiroušková, Lenka. *Die Visio Pauli. Wege und Wandlungen einer orientalischen Apokryphe im lateinischen Mittelalter unter Einschluss der alttschechischen und deutschsprachigen Textzeugen.* Mittellateinische Studien und Texte 34. Leiden: Brill, 2006.

Jungmann, Josef. "Die Heiligung des Sonntags im Frühchristentum und im Mittelalter." In *Der Tag des Herrn. Die Heiligung des Sonntags im Wandel der Zeit*, edited by Hermann Peichl, 59–75. Vienna: Herder, 1958.

Kadish, Gerald E. "Time." In *The Oxford Encyclopedia of Ancient Egypt*, edited by Donald B. Redford, 405–9. Oxford: Oxford University Press, 2001.

Kinzig, Wolfram. "Sunday Observance. Norm and Norm Deviation in Late Antiquity." In *From Sun-Day to the Lord's Day: The Cultural History of Sunday in Late*

Antiquity and the Early Middle Ages, edited by Uta Heil, 319-72. CELAMA 39. Turnhout: Brepols, 2022.

Kretzenbacher, Leopold. "Sveta Nedelja - Santa Domenica - Die hl. Frau Sonntag. Südslawische Bild- und Wortüberlieferungen zur Allegorie-Personifikation der Sonntagsheiligung mit Arbeitstabu." *Die Welt der Slaven. Halbjahresschrift für Slavistik* 27 (1982): 106-30.

Malay, Hasan. "A New Inscription from Anaia: Greek Translation of Codex Theod. 2.8.18 (on Stopping Litigation on Sunday)." *Epigraphica Anatolica* 53 (2020): 173–77.

McReavy, Lawrence Leslie. "The Sunday Repose from Labour. An Historico-Theological Examination." *ETL* 12 (1935): 291-323.

Meier, Mischa. "The Christian Sunday in the Sixth Century: The Sunday Discourse in Politics." In *From Sun-Day to the Lord's Day: The Cultural History of Sunday in Late Antiquity and the Early Middle Ages*, edited by Uta Heil, 251-72. CELAMA 39. Turnhout: Brepols, 2022.

Miceli, Calogero A. "The Epistle of Christ from Heaven: A New Translation and Introduction." In *New Testament Apocrypha: More Noncanonical Scriptures*, edited by Tony Burke and Brent Landau, 1:455–63. Grand Rapids: Eerdmans, 2016.

Mitthof, Fritz. "Christianization of the Empire or Power Struggle with Licinius." In *From Sun-Day to the Lord's Day: The Cultural History of Sunday in Late Antiquity and the Early Middle Ages*, edited by Uta Heil, 27-74. CELAMA 39. Turnhout: Brepols, 2022.

Morin, Germain. "A propos du travail du P. Delehaye sur la letter du Christ tombée du ciel." *RBén* 16 (1899): 217.

———. "Sermo de dominica observatione. Une ancienne adaption latine d'un sermon attribué à Eusèbe d'Alexandrie." *RBén* 24 (1907): 530–34.

Müller, Andreas. "Sunday in Palestinian Monasticism." In *From Sun-Day to the Lord's Day: The Cultural History of Sunday in Late Antiquity and the Early Middle Ages*, edited by Uta Heil, 233-49. CELAMA 39. Turnhout: Brepols, 2022.

Nicolai, Karl. "Feiertage und Werktage im römischen Leben, besonders in der Zeit der ausgehenden Republik und in der frühen Kaiserzeit." *Saeculum* 14 (1963): 194-220.

Palmer, Nigel F. "Himmelsbrief." *TRE* 15:344–46.

Patetta, Federico. "Una pretesa lettera di Gesù Cristo in un'iscrizione ligure dell'alto medio evo." 1907. In *Storia di Genova dalle origini al tempo nostro 2: Genova nel basso impero e nell'alto medioevo*, edited by Ubaldo Formenti, 282-308. Milan: Garzanti, 1941.

Pietri, Charles. "Le temps de la semaine à Rome et dans l'Italie chrétienne (IVe–VIe siècle)." In *Le temps chrétien de la fin de l'antiquité au moyen âge, IIIe–XIIIe siècles*, 63–97. Paris: Éditions du Centre National de la Recherche Scientifique, 1984.

Priebsch, Robert. "The Chief Sources of Some Anglo-Saxon Homilies." *Otia Merseiana* 1 (1899): 129–47.

———. *Diu vrône botschaft ze der Christenheit. Untersuchungen und Text.* Grazer Studien zur deutschen Philologie 2. Graz: Styria, 1895.

———. "John Audelay's 'Poem on the Observance of Sunday.'" In *An English Miscellany Presented to Dr. Furnivall in Honour of His Seventy-Fifth Birthday*, 397–407. Oxford: Clarendon, 1901.

———. *Letter from Heaven on the Observance of the Lord's Day.* Medium Aevum 5.3. Oxford: Blackwell, 1936.

Puk, Alexander. *Das römische Spielewesen in der Spätantike.* Millennium Studies 48. Berlin: de Gruyter, 2014.

Rakotoniaina, Marie-Ange. "Redefining the Sabbath Rest in the Sermons of Augustine: Of Heart, (Re)Quies, and Time." In *From Sun-Day to the Lord's Day: The Cultural History of Sunday in Late Antiquity and the Early Middle Ages*, edited by Uta Heil, 113-41. CELAMA 39. Turnhout: Brepols, 2022.

Remijsen, Sofie. "Business as Usual? Sunday Activities in Aphrodito [Egypt, Sixth to Eighth Century]." In *From Sun-Day to the Lord's Day: The Cultural History of Sunday in Late Antiquity and the Early Middle Ages*, edited by Uta Heil, 143-86. CELAMA 39. Turnhout: Brepols, 2022.

Remondini, Marcello. *Iscrizioni medioevali della Liguria.* Atti della Società Ligure di Stodia Patris 12. Genova: Tipografia del R. I. de Sorde-Muti, 1874.

Renoir, Ernest. "Christ (Lettre du) tombée du ciel." In *Dictionnaire d'archéologie chrétienne et de liturgie* 3:1534–46. Paris: Letouzey, 1913.

Rivière, Ernest-M. "La Lettre du Christ tombée du ciel: le manuscrit 208 de Toulouse." *Revue de questions historiques* 79 = n.s. 35 (1906): 600–605.

Röhricht, Reinhold. "Ein 'Brief Christi.'" *ZKG* 11 (1890): 440–42, 619.

Rordorf, Willy. *Der Sonntag: Geschichte des Ruhe- und Gottesdiensttages im ältesten Christentum.* Abhandlungen zur Theologie des Alten und Neuen Testaments 43. Zürich: Zwingli-Verlag, 1962. ET: *The Sunday: The History of the Day of Rest and Worship in the Earliest Centuries of the Christian Church.* London: SCM Press, 1968.

———, ed. *Sabbat und Sonntag in der Alten Kirche.* Traditio Christiana 2. Zürich: Theologischer Verlag, 1972.

Rouwhorst, Gerard. "The Reception of the Jewish Sabbath in Early Christianity." In *Christian Feast and Festival: The Dynamics of Western Liturgy and Culture*, ed. Paul Post et al., 223-66. Liturgia Condenda 12. Leuven: Peeters, 2002.

Rugo, Pietro. *Le iscrizioni die sec. VI–VII–VIII esistenti in Italia 5: La Neustria.* Padua: Bertoncello, 1980.

Rüpke, Jörg. *The Roman Calendar from Numa to Constantine: Time, History, and the Fasti.* Translated by David M. B. Richardson. Oxford: Wiley, 2011.

———. "Sakralisierung von Zeit in Rom und Italien. Produktionsstrategien und Aneignung von Heiligkeit." In *Heilige, Heiliges und Heiligkeit in spätantiken*

Religionskulturen, edited by Peter Gemeinhardt, 231-47. RVV 61. Berlin: de Gruyter, 2012.

Sachot, M. "Homilie B. christlich." *RAC* 16:155-75.

Salzman, Michele Renée. "Pagan and Christian Notions of the Week in the Fourth Century C.E. Western Roman Empire." In *Time and Temporality in the Ancient World*, edited by Ralph M. Rosen; 185–211. Philadelphia: University of Pennsylvania Press, 2004.

Santos Otero, Aurelio de. "Der apokryphe sogenannte Sonntagsbrief." StPatr 3 (1961): 290–96.

———. "Epistola de die dominica." In *Die handschriftliche Überlieferung der altslavischen Apokryphen* 1:158–69. Berlin: de Gruyter, 1969.

———. "La carte del Domingo." In *Los Evangelios Apócrifos. Colección de textos griegos y latinos, versión crítica, estudios introductorios y comentarios*, 664–76. BAC 148. Madrid: Editorial Catolica, 1963.

Scheibelreiter, Georg. "Sonntagsarbeit und Strafwunder. Beobachtungen zu hagiographischen Quellen der Merowingerzeit." In *Der Tag des Herrn. Kulturgeschichte des Sonntags*, 175-86. Vienna: Herder, 1998.

Schmitz, Wilhelm. "Nochmals ein vom Himmel gefallener Brief und ein Segen gegen Gift." *Neues Archiv* 23 (1898): 762–63.

———. "Tironische Miscellen." *Neues Archiv* 15 (1890): 602–5.

Schneider, Johannes. "Brief." *RAC* 2:564-85.

Schnell, Bernhard. "Himmelsbrief." In *Die deutsche Literatur des Mittelalters. Verfasserlexikon, 2. Auflage*, 4:28–33. Berlin: de Gruyter, 1983.

Schürer, Emil. "Die siebentägige Woche im Gebrauch der christlichen Kirche der ersten Jahrhunderte." *ZNW* 6 (1905): 1–66.

Scullard, H. H. *Festivals and Ceremonies of the Roman Republic*. London: Thames & Hudson, 1981.

Speyer, Wolfgang. *Bücherfunde in der Glaubenswerbung der Antike*. Hypomnemata 24. Göttingen: Vandenhoeck & Ruprecht, 1970.

Staphorst, Nicolaus. *Hamburgische Kirchengeschichte*. Vol. 1.3, *Darinnen die im II. Bande übrig gelassene Beilagen, und mittelst derselben Urkunden und Nachrichten von denen Kirchen S. Catharinae, S. Nicolai, S. Petri, wie auch von denen Memorien im Dom gegeben werden*. Hamburg: Felginer, 1727.

Stemberger, Günter. "Sabbath or Sunday? Rabbis and Church Fathers in Dialogue." In *From Sun-Day to the Lord's Day: The Cultural History of Sunday in Late Antiquity and the Early Middle Ages*, edited by Uta Heil, 97-111. CELAMA 39. Turnhout: Brepols, 2022.

Stübe, Rudolf. *Der Himmelsbrief. Ein Beitrag zur allgemeinen Religionsgeschichte*. Tübingen: Mohr, 1918.

Thomas, Wilhelm. *Der Sonntag im frühen Mittelalter mit Berücksichtigung der Entstehungsgeschichte des christlichen Dekalogs dargestellt*. Das Heilige und die Form 6. Göttingen: Vandenhoeck & Ruprecht, 1929.

Tosi, Michele. "I monaci colombaniani del sev. VII portano un rinnovamento agricolo-religiose nella fascia littorale Ligure." *Archivum Bobiense* 14/15 (1991/93): 36–42.

Vassiliev, Athanasius. *Anecdota graeco-byzantina I.* Moscow: Universitätsverlag, 1893.

Weinreich, Otto. "Antike Himmelsbriefe." *AR* 10 (1907): 566–67.

Wood, Ian. "Hagiography and the Canons on Sunday Work." In *From Sun-Day to the Lord's Day: The Cultural History of Sunday in Late Antiquity and the Early Middle Ages*, edited by Uta Heil, 273-91. CELAMA 39. Turnhout: Brepols, 2022.

Index of Sources

Works presented in this volume (the Letter from Heaven in its different recensions) are only referred to outside the respective chapter, without giving exact passages.

About the Lord's Day / Four Names for Sunday 28
Acts of John
44 173
86 173
Acts of Philipp
133–136 173
Acts of Pilate
prologue 388
Acts of the Council of Caesarea 4, 24f., 202f., 474
Adoration of the Magi 337
Alfonso Buenhombre
Epistola ad Rabbi Isaac 60f., 63
Ambrosiaster
Liber quaestionum Veteris et Novi Testamenti
29 16
84 16
95 16
95.3 390
112 16
Ambrosius
De Tobia
6.24 274
Letters
9.69.7 274
Anastasius Sinaita
Disputatio adversus Judaeos 52
Questiones et responsiones
80 477
Palea historica
189 Vassiliev 477
Annales Disibodi
ad a. 1096 118
Annales Magdeburgenses
ad a. 1096 118
Annales Roselveldensis
ad a. 1096 118
Annalista Saxo
ad a. 1096 118
Anselmus Cantuariensis
De miseria humanae conditionis 61
Apocalipsis Goliae 67f.
Apocalypse of Anastasia 30, 130, 149, 182, 203, 420, 477, 487
Apocalypse of Ezra
5.2f. 198
Apocalypse of Maria 82
Apocalypse of Paul. *See Visio Pauli*
Apocalypse of Peter 198f.
8.4 198
Apocalypse of Sedrach
5.2-3 476
Apocalypse of Thomas 64
Apostolic constitutions 13
2.47.1–2 169
8.4.3 13
8.47 129
8.47.64 129
8.47.90 129
Arnobius Iunior
Commentarii in Psalmos
91 159
Athanasius of Alexandria
Epistulae ad Serapionem 356

Augustine
Confessiones
1.20 214
8.12.29 338
De civitate Dei
1.4.14 218
20.11.28 214
Enchiridion
29.112 421
Enarrationes in Psalmos
84.15 217
91.2 159
105.2 421
131.10 224
In John tractatus
98.8 420
Letters
211 226
Sermones
9.3 211, 216
198 auctus 3 217
353 226

Barnabas, Letter of 144, 469
6.13 417
15.8 3, 417
Basil of Caesarea 26, 203, 435
De Spiritu sancto 356
Basil II
Menologion 474
Benediction of the Chief Priest (1QS[b])
4.22–28 366
Bernardus Claravallensis
Locus ex "De perfectione vitae contemplativae" 62
Boniface
Letters 95, 133
57 95
59 95–97, 246, 272
60 95f.
62 95
77 95

Caesarius of Arles 175f.
Sermones 247
44.7 199, 264
55.2 216
193.4 216
217.1 216

Calendar of Philocalus 6
Catechesis celtica 48f.
Cave of treasures
3 476
Celsus Africanus (Ps.-Cyprian)
De iudaica incredulitate
8 412
Certa miracula de dedicatione ecclesiae 61
Canones Hippolyti 13
Cassiodorus
Expositio Psalmorum
91.1 159f.
Charlemagne
Admonitio generalis 38, 89, 95, 102, 104, 133
76 [78] 102
79 [81] 102
Chronicle of St. Maxentius in Poitiers
ad a. 1110 120
Chronicle of Fritsche Closener 125
pp. 111–116 125
Chrysostom see John Chrysostom
Clement of Alexandria
Eclogae propheticae
48.1–49.1 198
Excerpta ex Theodot
63 4
Hypotyposes
6 412
Stromateis
5.14.106.2–4 4
Codex Justinianus 126f.
1.4.3 20
1.4.9 20
1.4.22 20
3.12.2 254
3.12.9 20
Codex Theodosianus 3, 126f.
1.4.7–8 169
1.27.1 169
1.27.2 169
2.8.1 254
2.8.18 170
2.8.20 20
2.8.25 20
9.3.7 19, 422
15.5.2 20
15.5.5 20

Collatio copiosa de indulgentiis 51
Collectio Avellana
187.5 294
Commentarius in Apocalypsim 67
Commonitorium de casis die vel monasteriis 108
Corpus documentorum inquisitionis haereticae pravitatis Neerlandicae
vol. 3, no. 71 125
Cyprian of Carthage 192
Letters
39.4.1 214
Cyril of Alexandria
Festal Letter
8.6.2 362

De arte loquendi et tacendi 72f.
De Antichristo 66f.
De clericis 69
De confessione 74–76
De custodia et studio conscientiae 61
De decem praeceptis et plagis Aegyptiacis 72f.
De die sabbato 56
De expulsione Ade et Eve de paradiso / Vita Adae et Evae 50f., 57, 64f., 476
12–16 476
De extremo tempore 66
De indulgentiis 76
De inicio annorum ante tempora Christi. De iudicio Antichristi 67
De institutione novitiorum 69
De iudicio extremo bonus tractatulus 61
De matrimonio 72
De miraculis faciendis 72
De originali peccato et de fine mundi 72f.
De plaga que facta est/fuit in Hierusalem 54, 72, 95, 104, 106f., 110f., 117, 126, 133, 149, 192, 204
9–12 106
22–28 106
27 107
De potencia racionali 72
De septem peccatis capitalibus 75
De septem seris 66
De septem virtutibus turturis sive beatae virginis 79
De sexta feria ... De sabbato 72f.
De victoria Christi contra Antichristum 61
De vita et moribus clericorum suorum 69
Defensor of Ligugé
Liber scintillarum 55
Denariis triginta deum vendidit Galilaeus 59
De xv signis ante diem iudicii 66f.
Dialogue of Jason and Papiscus 25, 87, 203
Diataxis and Didaskalia of Jesus Christ / the Holy Apostles 28–30, 87, 148f., 181, 202f., 491, 498f.
Didache
14.1 3
Didymus Alexandrinus
Fragmenta in Psalmos
1081 390
Dionysius Exiguus 203
Disputatio Christiani cum Judaeo 60
Dionysius of Corinth
Letter to Soter of Rome. See Eusebius of Caesarea. *Church history* 4.23.11

Eckehard
Chronicon universale 119
Hierosolymita
36.4 119
Einhard
Vita Caroli
16 107
27 107
Epiphanius
Panarion / Adversus haereses
50.1.5f. 388
Epistola Abgari cum Christi responso 65, 142
Epistola ad Rabbi Isaac de religione judaica et christiana see Alfonso Buenhombre
Epistola Apostolorum
31 481
Evangelium Nicodemi 64f.
Eusebius of Caesarea 153–160
Church history 153
3.27 3
4.6.3 412
4.23.11 3
4.26.2 4

5.23–25 24, 387
6.38 142
10.4 157
Commentary on the Psalms 144, 153f.
91 158–160
91.1165D 154
91.1168BC 155
91.1168C 155
91.1169B 155
91.1169C 155
91.1169D 155
91.1172A 156
91.1172D 157
91.1173BD 390
Commentarii in Isaiam
1.16 157
Onomastikon
118,18f. Klostermann 481
Vita Constantini 153
3.25 157
3.35–43 157
4.41.2 157
4.44.2 157
4.59 157
4.60.4 157
4.70.2 157
Eustathius of Antioch
De engastrimytho contra Origenem 469, 471
Examinatio haereticorum atque infidelium et rebellium contra fidem 61
Exemplum de Antichristo 67, 72f.
Exemplum de miraculo de corpore Christi 73
Excerpta de erroribus Judaeorum in Thalmut quos transtulit Theobaldus supprior ord. praedicat 59

Florence of Worcester
Chronicon ex chronica 334
Formula confessionis 75f.
Formula confitendi 75
Fulcher of Chartres
Historia Hierosolymitana
203–205 334

Gelasius of Rome
Letters
14.11 16
15.3 16
16.3 16
41 16
Genesis Rabbah
11.5 422
Gennadius of Massilia
De ecclesiasticis dogmatibus 50
Godfrey of Viterbo
Speculum regum 62
Gospel of Peter
35 3
50 3
Gospel of Ps.-Matthew 64f.
Gospel of Ps.-Thomas 64
Gregory of Nazianz secundum translationem quam fecit Rufinus
Homilies
8.10.3 224
Gregory of Nyssa 158f.
Epistula de Pythonissa ad Theodosium episcopum 470f.
In inscriptiones Psalmorum
43 158
Gregory of Tours 86, 173, 176f.
Historia Francorum
10.30 173, 178
Liber in gloria martyrum
15 173
Liber vitae patrum
7.5 173
15.3 173
Vita Juliani
11 174, 178
Vita Martini
2.13 173
2.24 173, 178
3.3 173
3.7 173f., 178
3.29 173, 178
3.31 173
3.45 173
3.55 173
3.56 173
4.45 173
Gregory the Great 22f., 144, 209
Homilia in Evangelia
35.7 216
Homiliae in Ezechielem
praefatio 1.5 214
Registrum epistularum
9.1 23

13.1 22f.
Regula pastoralis 209

Heinrich von Langenstein
Tractatus de confessione 51
Helmoldus
Chronica Slavorum
ad a. 1096 118
Hilary of Poitiers 159
Tractatus super Psalmos
91 159
Hippolytus
In Danielem
4.23 388
Philosophumena
9.13 142
Homily "De misera vita seculi" 61
Homily "De vanitate saeculi" 61
Homily "Veneranda/o est nobis . . ." [Sunday homily] 53, 61f.
Honorius of Autun
Elucidarium 71
Horace
Epodos
16.17 224
Hugh of Saint Cher
Speculum ecclesiae 55f., 69–71
Hugo of Reutlingen
Chronica metrificata 125

Ignatius of Antioch
Letter to the Magnesians
9.1 3
Ildefons of Toledo 91
Installation of the Archangel Michael
3 476
Irenaeus of Lyon
Adversus haereses
3.22.4 200
Isidore of Seville 91
De ecclesiasticis officiis
1.24.1–25.4 91
De viris illustribus
43 210

Jean Gerson
Tractatus de condicionibus confessionis, absolucionis, excommunicacionis et penitencie iniunccionis 51
Jerome 9f.
Adversus Vigilantium
7 258
Commentarii in Galatas
2 412
2.4.10–11 10
Commentarii in Isaiam
9.4 226
Letters
107.10 216
Quaestionum hebraicarum liber in Genesim
on Gen 1:1 412
Tractatus XXI in Psalmos
91.1 160
Jesus' dialogue with the Devil
3 476
4 476
Johannes Geuss
Sermo de igne conflagrationis 61
John Chrysostom 26, 28, 149, 171, 435, 446, 460, 491
De baptismo Christi et de epiphania
1 8f.
De eleemosyna
3 19
De sacerdotio
6.4.41–43, 48–49 366
In diem natalem Domini nostri 388
In epistulam i ad Corinthios homilia
43.1 18
In Matthaeum homilia
5.1 9
John Lydus 127
John Malalas 127
John of Damascus
Oratio in sabbatum sanctum
26.25 306
John of Ephesus
Vitae sanctorum orientalium
47 294
John of Parallos
Sermon on the archangel Michael 477
John of Scythopolis (Maximus Confessor)
Scholia in Dionysius Areopagitus, De mystica theologia
1 412
John Zonaras 130

Julian of Toledo
Prognosticorum futuri saeculi libri tres 49
3.14 91
Jubilees 167
2:29 167
2:29f. 167
31:14 366
50:8–12 167
50:12 168
Justin Martyr 144
First apology
45 173
67 3, 18
67.5–7 171
67.8 16
Dialogue with Tryphon
24.1 3
41.4 3
100 200
138.1 3

Lactantius
Epitome divinarum institutionum
5.3 258
Lectiones de dedicatione ecclesiae 56, 77
Letter of Barnabas see *Barnabas, Letter of*
Letter of Heaven
Latin Recension I 31, 34–37, 39, 44, 46, 48–52, 57, 79, 84–86, 89, 91, 94–99, 102f., 108f., 119, 133, 135–137, 139f., 162–166, 170, 172, 182, 185–187, 189f., 194–197, 199, 202, 221, 223, 293, 297, 304, 342
Latin Recension II 31, 34–36, 40–42, 44, 46f., 50, 52–79, 84–86, 90–95, 99, 103, 108, 110, 126, 133, 135–139f., 162–166, 170, 172, 182, 184, 185–187, 189f., 194f., 197, 202, 212, 216, 246, 254, 256, 260, 286, 293, 297, 342, 423
Latin Recension IIa 31, 37, 42, 46, 84, 120f., 133, 140, 16f., 170, 172, 194, 197, 254, 256, 297, 342
Latin Recension III 31, 35f., 42–44, 48, 52, 83f., 87, 103, 110, 112–118, 120, 124f., 133, 140, 162f., 170, 172, 182, 194, 197, 202, 254, 256, 297, 342
Latin Recension IIIa 31, 37, 43f., 52, 84, 121, 133, 140, 162, 170, 172, 194, 197, 254, 256, 297, 335, 342
Greek Recension Alpha 1 31–36, 52, 80f., 82–86, 91, 95, 108–112, 130, 133, 135f., 138–141, 150–152, 162, 166, 182, 184, 188–190, 194–197, 199, 202, 223, 248, 329f., 337, 344, 478, 492
Greek Recension Alpha 2 31f., 35–36, 52, 80f., 83–87, 91, 95, 103, 108, 110–116, 120, 130, 133, 135f., 138–141, 150–152, 162, 166, 182, 184, 188–190, 194–197, 199, 202, 254, 306, 329f., 478, 492
Greek Recension Beta 1 31f., 35, 52, 81f., 83–85, 111, 118–120, 130, 133, 135f., 139–141, 150–152, 162, 166, 182, 184, 188–190, 192, 194f., 197
Greek Recension Beta 2 31f., 34f., 52, 81f., 83–85, 111, 118–120, 130, 133, 135f., 139–141, 150–152, 162, 166, 182, 184, 188–190, 192, 194f., 197
Greek Recension Gamma 31f., 36, 52, 82–85, 111, 133, 139–141, 150–152, 162, 166, 184, 190, 194f., 197
Letter of Licinianus of Cartagena see Licinianus of Cartagena
Leo the Great 11f., 101, 138
Letters
6 11f.
6.6 12
9 13–16
10 16f.
Sermons
41.1 17
Leo (Emperor) VI.
Novels
54 127f., 131f.
Lex Alamannorum
38 103
Lex Baiuvariorum
7.4 103
Lex Frisonum
18 103
Libellus de peccatorum agnitione, seu inquisitione, seu facienda confessione 51, 75
Liber de gestis sanctorum patrum miracula 50
Liber de ordine creaturarum 49
Liber pastoralis 69
Liber pontificalis ecclesiae Ravennatis
30 274

Libanius of Antioch
Declamatio
41.29 358
Licinianus of Cartagena
Letters
1 209
1.6 214
2 209
3 31, 34, 36, 38, 84–87, 90, 94, 133, 164, 166, 181f., 202f., 223, 240, 254, 284
Lucifer Calarithanus
Quia absentem nemo debet iudicare nec damnara sive De Athanasio
2.33.17 276
Lumen confessorum 75

Manipulus curatorum 69
Manuale confessorum 75
Martin of Braga 173
De correctione rusticorum
18 177, 216
Martyrium Polycarpi
9.2 173
Melito of Sardis see Eusebius of Caesarea. *Church history* 4.23.12
Michel le Syrien
Chronique
12.3 107
Midrash Aseret Hadibrot
Pesiq. Rab. 14 150
Minucius Felix
Octavius
9 4
31 4
Modus confitendi 75

Neilos-Nathanael Bertos
Sermo 11 460
Nicholas of Lyra
Responsio ad quendam Iudaeum 59f.
Nicholas III Grammatikos 130
Nicolaus von Dinkelsbühl
De confessione 51
Expositio de oratione dominica 55
Sermones super passione Christi 61
Nota salutares effectus, quos operatur paenitentia 61
Notula de dignitate diei dominicae 61

Origen
Commentary on the psalms 159
Contra Celsum
4.52f. 412
De engastrimytho 469
Homilies in Exodum
7.5 16, 390
Ovid
Metamorphoses
7.350 264, 278

Passio of Perpetua and Felicitas
18.8 173
Peregrinus de Oppeln
Sermones de tempore et sanctis 54
Peter Ceffons of Clairvaux
Epistola Luciferi 67f., 70–73
Peter Pictor
De vita Pilati 65
Petrus of Alexandria (I.)
De paschate ad Tricentium
15 129
Physiologus 469–472
Pirmin
Scarapsus / Dicta Pirmini 89, 99–101
23 100f.
Pliny the Younger
Letters
10.96.7 4
Poenitentiale Merseburgensea 89
Procopius
De aedificiis
1.4.1 294
Prudentius
Cathemerinon
5.125-134 421
Ps.-Athanasius of Alexandria
Expositiones in Psalmos
404 158
Homilia de semente 160f.
1.1–3 161
9.1 161
14.5f. 161
Quaestiones ad Antiochum ducem
Questio 10 477
Ps.-Augustin
De dignitate sacerdotum 69–71
Sermo app. 254 75
Sermo app. 393 75

Ps.-Basilius / Ps.-Chrysostom
Homily "Today, My Beloved, I'd Like to Praise the Day of the Lord" 26f., 149, 171, 203, 460
Ps.-Chrysostomos
De solstitiis et aequinoctiis 388
Epitimia LXXIII
10.1 308
Homilia in XII Apostolos
495 481
Homily "Hear, All Brothers Christians, What the Prophet Says" 28, 147f., 171, 203, 436
Ps.-Cyprianus
Liber de XII abusionibus seculi 49
Ps.-Cyril of Alexandria / Ps.-Diodorus of Tarsus
In Psalmum 91
1225 158
Ps.-Dionysius Areopagita
De caelesti hierarchia
6.2 312
De divinis nominibus
7.1 474
Ps.-Eusebius of Alexandria
Sermo de die dominica / Homily 16 see Question and Answer about Sunday
Ps.-Gregentios of Taphar
Dialexis
4 459
Ps.-Jerome
Expositio quatuor Evangeliorum praefatio 532–533A 254
Ps.-Jesse of Amiens
Epistola de baptismo 50
Ps.-John
First apocryphal apocalypse 80
Second Apocryphal Apocalypse 29, 203
Ps.-Methodius
Revelationes / Apocalypse 80
11.17 197, 297, 354
Ps.-Thomas von Aquin
Expositio super oratione dominicali 55
Pupilla oculi 69

Question and Answer about Sunday 27, 80, 91, 128, 144–146, 149, 203, 372, 484, 492
Quaestio de sollemniter paenitentibus 75
Questions of Bartholomew
4.52–56 476
Quaestiones super officium missae 69
Quattuor incommoda in servitio dei 70
Quodvultdeus
Contra Iudaeos, paganos et Arianos 59, 64

Raymond of Penyafort
Summa de poenitentia 51, 75
Regula Pachomii praecepta atque iudicia
63.3 226
Regulae et instructiones ecclesiastice sacerdotum 50
Responsio ad quemdam judaeum ex verbis evangelii secundum Matthaeum contra Christum nequitur arguentem 59–61
Rimbert
Vita Ansgarii
37 173
Roger de Hoveden
Chronicle of the history of England 35, 43f., 121, 133
Romanus Melodus 127
Rule of Benedict
4.47 256, 276

Sermo de communi vita clericorum 69
Sermo de die dominica 54
Sermo de quatuor impedimentis confessionis 74
Sermo de novo sacerdote 69f., 73
Sermo de uno confessore 76
Sermo synodalis de emendatione morum et cleri 70
Sermones de Beata Maria Virgine 78f.
Sermones de dedicatione 56f., 77
Sermones de sanctis 54, 70, 73
Sermones de tempore 58, 73
Severus of Antioch 127
Sibyllae vaticinantes de Christo 61, 63f.
Sigebert of Gembloux
Chronica sive chronographia universalis
ad a. 1033 118
Somniale Danielis 59
Sophronius of Jerusalem
Sermon on circumcision 25, 30, 87, 202f.
Sermon on Christmas 25, 411f.

Sozomenus
Historia ecclesiastica
7.19.10f. 419
Speculum sacerdotum 69
Stella clericorum 69–73
Stephen the Younger
Passio XX monachorum Sabaitarum 107
Summa poenitentiae / de poenitentia / poenitentialis 52, 74f.
Syriac Didaskalia
11 169

Tertullian
About flight in persecutions
4.1 4
Ad nationes
1.13 4
Ad Scapulam
3.4f. 173
Adversus Judaeos
5.5 258
8.18 388
Apology
16.11 4
39 4
De carne Christi
17 200
De corona
3.3f. 4
De cultu feminarum
1 200
On fasting
15.2 4
On idolatry
14.7 4
Testamentum Domini 13, 29, 491
Theobald of Sézanne
Pharetra fidei contra Iudaeos 60
Reprobatio Talmot Iudeorum 59f.
Theodore Balsamon 130f.
Responsa ad interrogationes canonicae Marci 130f.
51 (53) 131
Theodore of Canterbury
Poenitentiale
11.1 89
Theodoret of Cyrus
Commentarii in Psalmorum
1616f. 158f.
Theotokos's genealogy 470–472
Thomas a Kempis
De imitatione Christi 61
Tractatu[lu]s de confessione 74, 76
Tractatus breves argumenti theologici 50
Tractatus de christiana religione 61
Tractatus de indulgenciis 51
Tractatus de peccato 51
Tractatus de poenitentia et confessione 76
Tractatus super Magnificat 79
Traditio apostolica
2 13
Transitus Mariae 65

Ut dies dominicus districte custodiatur, hanc epistolam scripsit Christus 61

Venantius Fortunatus 177
Vita Germani Parisiensis 177
14 173
16 173
35 173
49 173
50 173
51 173
58 173
Versus de recto servitio Christi 70
Versus de signis iudicii ultimi 52
Vindicta salvatoris 59, 63, 65
Visio beati Esdrae
10 264
53f. 198f.
53a 264
Visio Pauli 20f., 25f., 39f., 42f., 53, 66–68, 93, 126, 137, 141, 182, 203, 254, 493, 497
Visio Philiberti 67
Vita Adae et Evae see De expulsione Ade et Eve
Vita Audoini episcopi Rotomagensis
9 173
Vita beati Maurilii 173
Vita Genovefae
37 174f.
54 174f.
Vita of Rusticola of Arles 175
Vita sancti Arnulfi
28 173

William of Malmesbury
De gestis regum Anglorum
1.368 331–333, 336

Zeno
Henotikon 470f.

Zosime de Panopolis
Mémoires authentiques
10.3.44-59 346

Papyri
Oxyrhynchos
LIV 3759 168
XLVIII 3407 168
Vienna
Rainer 5 (13b) 352

Inscriptions
CIL 4121. in CIL 3.2. 523 Mommsen. or HD064415 7
CIL 2.5181 = ILS 6891 21

Councils/Synods/Canons
Apostolic Canons (s. IV)
8.47.64 129
8.47.90 129
Arles (a. 813)
can. 16 102
Chalôn (a. 813)
can. 50 103
Carthage (a. 419)
can. 64 (Greek) / 61 (Latin) 129f.
Ephesus (a. 431) 200
Frankfurt (a. 794)
can. 21 102f.
Friuli (a. 796)
can. 13 102
Gangra (s. IV)
can. 18 129
Macon (a. 585) 36
can. 1 179–181
Mainz (a. 813)
can. 37 103
Nicaea (a. 325)
can. 20 129
Orléans (a. 511)
can. 27 140
Orléans (a. 538) 179
can. 31 169, 177f., 211
Orléans (a. 549)
can. 20 20
Paris (a. 829)
can. 50 102f., 111f.
Reims (a. 813)
can. 35 102
Rome (a. 826)
can. 9 102f.
can. 30 103
Soisson (a. 744)
can. 2 95
can. 7 95
Tarragona (a. 516)
can. 4 169
Tours (a. 813)
can. 40 103
Trullo (a. 691/692)
can. 55 129
can. 90 129

Index of Biblical Passages

Old Testament

Gen
1:1–2:3 229
1 146, 497
1:1–5 307
1:1 29, 285, 412, 477, 485
1:3–5 183
1:3 417
1:5 392f., 403, 469, 474
1:6–8 284
1:8, 13, 19, 23, 31 392f., 403
1:11 258
1:16 485
1:24–31 485
1:26f. 307
2:1–3 143
2:2 392f., 403, 485
2:2f. 154, 204
2:3 284
2:7 275
3 26, 443
7:11 191, 232, 311, 321, 346
8:2 191, 232
14:22 299
18 109, 296, 300
18:1–15 350
18:1–8 307
18:16–19:29 364
19:24 189, 225
48:27 224

Exod 260, 346
3:2 463
7–10 189, 304
7:3 260
7:17 346
9 346
9:13–35 188, 295
9:18–34 342
10:1–20 188, 295
10:4–19 342
10:21–29 311
12:16f. 100
12:16 389
12:26 398f., 407
16 26
16:5 143, 167, 390
16:29 143
19 296
19:3–6 307
20 142
20:8–11 143
20:11 162, 235, 255, 285, 392f., 403
20:12 146
23:12 143
24:18 307, 321
25–31; 35–40 224
25:6 258
31:13–17 143
31:18 57
32:19 57
34:1 57
34:21 143, 167
34:28 307, 321
35:2f. 143
35:3 167

Lev
16–26 143
19:3, 30 143
23:3 160
23:7f. 143, 389, 398f., 407

23:7f., 21, 25, 35f. 143
23:32 111, 183
24:8f. 143
26:2–5 372
26:29 298
26:33 226

Num
15:32 167
16 26, 443
18:12 295, 305
21:6 197, 264, 278
21:8 197
22:25–28 26, 149f., 441
28:18, 25 389, 398f., 407

Deut
4:2 141
5:13 26, 149, 437
5:14 441
5:15 441
8:15 264, 278
13:1 141
21:23 412
28:53–57 298
29:22f. 313
32:5 229
32:40 299

Josh
7:16–26 26
7:21–25 443

Judges
2:18 257

2 Sam
2:11 485
6 26
6:6f. 443
6:17 485
13:19 256

2 Kgs
6:24–31 298
7:2 191, 232, 346
14:13 250
18:4 197
22f. 142

1 Chr
13:10 443

2 Chr
25:23 250

Ezra
7:25f. 226
12:18 226

Neh
9:14 143
10:32 143
12:39 250
13:15–22 143

Job
14:13 348
38–41 372

Psalms
5 156
6 143
11–13 156
11 143
18:5 (LXX) 474
23 143
37 143
41–43 156
41:8 191, 232
45 156
45:11 28, 463
47 143, 156
58–59 156
62:12 (LXX) 441
68 156
68:3 (LXX) 90
72:27 (LXX) 457
73 156
77:46 261
78:3 (LXX) 305
78:44 346
84:8 (LXX) 303
85:10 (LXX) 138, 303
89 156
90 156
90:4 469, 497
91 143, 154, 156–161
92 143, 156

93 143, 156
94 156
94:10f. (LXX) 154
94:11 (LXX) = 95:11 146, 159
94:11 372
102:19–21 383f., 386
110:1 229
117 (LXX) 390, 398f.
117:2 (LXX) 480f.
117:11f. (LXX) 398f.
117:12 408f.
117:22 (LXX) 400f.
117:24 (LXX) = 118:24 27f., 100, 390, 400f., 457, 459, 463
117:24, 27 (LXX) 390, 408f.
117:27 (LXX) 400f.
139:7–9 372
145:6 235

Prov
19:21 372

Isa
1:13 143, 155
1:11–15 156f.
8 190
9:19f. 298
14:13f. 477
14:29 197, 264, 278
24:18 191, 232, 311, 321
26:20 348
29 190
29:11 338
30:6 197, 264, 278
43:11 233
44:6 316
49:26 298
54:8 299
58:13 167

Jer
17:10 317
17:17–29 143
17:21f. 167
17:24 23
19:7–9 298

Lam
4:10 298
4:18 228

Ezek
1:1 191
3:1–3 142
5:10 298
7:22 225, 299, 311, 325, 353
20:25 278
22:15 226
30:32 286
36:7 299
37:12 310
38:22 189, 346

Hos
2:8 344, 374
2:13 143

Joel
2:19 295, 305
4:2–12 481

Amos 32, 184
6:3 155
7:1–6 189
8:5 143

Jonah
3:6 276

Zech
11:9 298

Mal
2:7 366
3:10 190, 232f.

Wis
7:1 306

Dan
2:35 321

New Testament

Matt 474
1:17–23 474
3:13–17 296
3:16 191

4:2 par. 481
5:19 437, 443
5:23f. 170
5:33–37 140
5:48 342
6:9 231
7:15 224
11:13 211, 219
12:5–7 143
12:8 143
12:11f. 143
13:42 275
13:44 257
14:1–10 par. 453
16:18f. 135, 138f., 303
16:21 337
19:19 274
21:4b 474
22:40 437, 443
24 parr. 32
24:19 197
24:35 32, 87, 112f., 117f., 184, 295, 300, 305, 319, 341, 383
25 33, 184, 428
25:16 20
25:31–46 463
26:26–29 par. 449
26:26 145
27:5 455
27:52f. 310
27:60 336
28:1–6 463
28:1 229
28:2 336

Mark
1:6 307
1:9–11 260, 296
1:11 260
2:23–28 143
2:28 143
3:1–5 143
3:16–19 481
3:29 356
11 173
13:31 122, 295, 300, 305, 319, 383
15:46 336
16:3 336
16:4 336

Luke
1 173
1:26–38 296, 307
1:26–33 463
2:22 284
3:21–23 296
3:21f. 307
3:21 463
6:1–5 161
6:5 143
6:6–11 161
6:14–16 481
6:25 276
6:36 342
13:15f. 143
14:5 143
21:33 295, 300, 305, 319, 383
22:19 27
24:2 336
24:18 272

John
1:1 383, 386
1:1, 3 417
1:51 191
3:19f. 358
7:22f. 143
7:23 284
10:1–17 142
10:38 229
13:26f. 451
15:4 233
16:30 276
17:12 455
19:5 363
19:15 362
20:22f. 15

Acts
1:3 481
1:4–12 481
1:10 481
1:13, 26 481
1:18–20 455
2:2–4 474

2:3 474
2:7–11 474
5 173
5:1–11 368
7:58f. 143
4:24 235
9:9–19 140
10:11 191
10:42 474
13 173
13:2f. 14
20:7 3

Rom
1:29–32 356
10:18b 474
13:13 147, 465

1 Cor
5:6 437, 443
6:9 483
7:15 302
10:9 197
11:23–26 449
15:8f. 481
15:25 229
16:2 3

2 Cor
12:2f. 26
12:2 420
5:17 146

Gal 28, 147
1:8f. 147
1:9 211, 218f.
3:13 412
4:10f. 9
5:9 443

Eph
6:5 302

Phil
2:8–11 229
2:12 302

Col
3:6 228

1 Tim
1:10 483

Heb
4:3 146
10:28 284

1 Pet
3:8 497
4:5b 474
4:11 317

2 Pet 364
2–3 364
2:4 364
2:6 189, 364
3 364
3:7–13 364
3:10 364

Rev 346
1:10 3
6:12 352
6:15–17 348
8:7–9, 15 189
8:7 342
10:1–11 142
10:8 338
10:9 338
11:6 346
11:19 191, 342
12:13–19 197
16:4 346
19:11 191
20:12 338

Index of Modern Authors

Acerbi, Silvia 210
Adam, Barbara 5
Alikin, Valeriy 4
Allen, Edward 4
Allen, Paul 171
Allen, Pauline 32
Amaduzzi, Johannes 34, 40, 44, 52, 94, 163, 164, 165, 185, 186, 222, 234
Anastos, Milton V. 128
Anderson, Gary A. 200
Anderson, Mark 5, 148, 469
Angheben, Marcello 149
Antolín, Guillermo 213
Arfuch, Diego A. 12
Auffarth, Christoph 193

Bacchiocchi, Samuele 4
Bächtold-Stäubli, Hanns 281
Backus, Irena 33, 37, 80
Baechtold, Hanns 33
Baluzius, Étienne 34, 36, 39, 44, 98, 99, 103, 162, 163, 164, 165, 185, 186, 246, 270, 272, 274, 276, 278, 284, 388, 391
Balzaretti, Ross 241
Bandt, Cordula 156
Bardill, Jonathan 294
Barré, Henri 65
Bauckham, Richard 4, 49, 144, 153, 177
Baumann, Notker 197
Baun, Jane 128, 130, 131, 149, 191, 475, 497, 498, 499, 501
Beckerath, Jürgen von 183
Belzer, Jack 183
Benente, Fabricio 88
Bergdolt, Klaus 124
Berger, Jan 95
Beskow, Per 33
Bieberstein, Klaus 107
Bittner, Maximilian 35, 36, 80, 81, 82, 83, 109, 150, 151, 152, 291, 294, 296, 314, 329, 376
Blackburn, Bonnie 387
Blackburn, Stuart H. 292
Blake, Robert P. 107
Bogyay, Thomas von 295
Borgolte, Michael 107
Borresen, Kari E. 200
Boulding, Maria 217
Bovon, François 25, 411, 416
Bradshaw, Paul F. 4, 11, 13, 153
Brändle, Rudolf 8
Bremer-McCollum, Adam Carter 337
Bremmer, Jan M. 172
Brennecke, Hanns Christof 157
Bronwen, Neil 138
Buchholz, Dennis D. 198
Buchinger, Harald 4, 140, 183, 176
Bultrighini, Ilaria 5, 6, 143, 149, 176

Cappozzo, Valerio 59
Carletti, Carlo 251
Carmichael, Casey 153
Carson, Donald A. 4
Castillo, Francisco J. Marco 334
Chadwick, Henry 411
Christopher, Walter 295
Cioran, Emile M. 344
Claude, Dietrich 87
Clauss, Manfred 7
Closs, August 124
Constantinou, Stavroula 293
Cook, David 334
Copeland Klepper, Deeana 60
Croke, Brian 294

Cunningham, Mary B. 32
Curti, Carmelo 154
Cutler, Anthony 295

Deeg, Alexander 32
Del Prete, Leone 41, 47
Delehaye, Hippolyte 35, 36, 37, 40, 90, 121, 124, 162, 221, 222, 224, 236, 241, 246, 286
Diekamp, Franz 470
Dieterich, Albrecht 33
Dihle, Albrecht 212
Divjak, Johannes 6, 32, 212
Doering, Lutz 143, 153, 167
Dolbeau, Francois 217
Dölger, Franz J. 5
Döpp, Siegmar 212
Dörries, Heinrich 131
Drecoll, Volker H. 4
Duensing, Hugo 198
Duffy, Eamon 344
Duffy, John M. 25, 411, 412, 414, 416
Dumaine, Henri 5, 183
Dupont, Anthony 32
Durst, Michael 4, 153
Dvornik, Francis 308, 356

Eberly, Susan 344
Effenberger, Arne 149
Elias, Norbert 5
Elior, Rachel 366
Elliott, J. K. 419
Erbetta, Mario 33
Esbroeck, Michel van 37, 292

Fagan, Garrett G. 21
Fengren, Gary B. 171
Fiore, Paolo 239
Fitschen, Klaus 469
Fowler, W. Warde 194
Foxhall Forbes, Helen 251
Frenschkowski, Marco 192

Gager, John G. 358
Gamillscheg, Ernst 470
Garstad, Benjamin 197
Geerlings, Wilhelm 13
Geiger, Paul 280
Gemeinhardt, Peter 139, 193
Georges, Tobias 171
Gerstenberger, Erhard 366
Glorieux, Palémon 51, 60
Goetz, Hans-Werner 173
Goldhill, Simon 193
González, Justo L. 4
Goodspeed, Edgar J. 33
Gosselin, Edward A. 60
Gounelle, Rémi 444
Graf, Fritz 194
Graf, Georg 36
Graumann, Thomas 5, 170
Graus, Frantisek 124
Greenslade, Stanley L. 12
Grégoire, Réginald 37, 40, 90, 93, 222
Gregorio, Giuseppe de 470, 471
Grierson, Philip 332, 333
Grossmann, Jannis 29
Grounds, Duard 172
Grumel, Venance 332
Grumel, Victor 131, 183
Grund, Alexandra 153

Häfele, Wolfgang 22
Hahn, Ferdinand 138
Haines, Dorothy 34, 37, 39, 42, 46, 49, 54, 86, 91, 112, 121, 153, 163, 176, 196, 199, 221, 223, 241, 245, 246, 247, 256, 260, 264, 270, 342
Hall, Isaac H. 35
Hanneken, Todd R. 167
Harlfinger, Dieter 470
Harnack, Adolf von 172
Harper, Kyle 192
Hartmann, Carmen Cardelle de 60
Hartmann, Wilfried 103, 130, 131
Hauswald, Eckhard 100
Heil, Uta 4, 103, 167, 211, 372
Heinzelmann, Martin 17
Helgeland, John 7
Hen, Yitzhak 55
Heyden, Katharina 193
Hieke, Thomas 198
Hill, George Francis 63
Hoffmann, Paul 138
Hohmann, Hanns 32
Holford-Strevens, Leofranc 387
Hollerich, Michael J. 154
Huber, Hans 4
Hübner, Arthur 124

Humfress, Caroline 169
Hunger, Herbert 470, 472
Hünnerkopf, Richard 280, 281

Impe, Steven van 210, 213
Irwin, Bonnie D. 137, 292

Jagič, I. Victor 479
Janzen, Waldemar 366
Jiroušková, Lenka 39, 40, 41, 42, 43, 46, 53, 66, 124, 422, 423, 426, 427, 428, 430
Johnson, M. D. 65
Johnson, Maxwell E. 4, 13, 153
Jungmann, Josef 176

Kadish, Gerald E. 183
Kessler, Herbert L. 149
Kinzig, Wolfram 89, 172, 181, 192, 199, 387
Kirpičnikov, Alexander Ivanovic 295
Kitz, Anne Marie 298
Koch, Dietrich-Alex 481
Kolbaba, Tia M. 374
Krasnoseltsev, Nicolai F. 492
Krause, Karin 149
Kretzenbacher, Leopold 149
Kronk, Gary W. 334
Krüger, Jürgen 119
Krusch, Bruno 387, 388, 391

Lambert, David 140
Langgärtner, Georg 17
Lanzillotta, Lautaro Roig 421
Latowsky, Anne 107
Laurent, Vincent 332
Laux, John 95
Leemans, Johan 11
Lees, Clare 54
Leppin, Hartmut 7
Leyerle, Blake 18, 171
Liebeschuetz, J. H. W. G. 8
Lilla, Salvatore 470
Linder, Amnon 54, 104, 106, 107, 336
Llewelyn, Stephen R. 168, 362
Löhr, Winrich A. 7, 89, 190
Louvaris, Athanasius N. J. 374

Madoz, José 209, 210, 212, 213, 214, 216, 218
Magoulias, Harry J. 20
Maier, Bernhard 98
Malay, Hasan 170
Markschies, Christoph 13, 22, 149, 299, 476, 481
Martínez Usó, Maria José 334
Marzell, Heinrich 280
Mastrelli, Carlo Alberto 251
Mayer, Wendy 374
McCormick, Michael 108
McKitterick, Rosamund 103
McNally, Robert E. 39
McNamara, Jo Anne 175
McNamara, Martin, MSC 49
McReavy, Leslie Lawrence 176
Meier, Mischa 4, 127, 172, 176, 191, 192, 194, 211
Merkelbach, Reinhold 197
Merkle, Sebastian 421
Mertens, Michéle 346
Meyer-Lübke, Wilhelm 217, 274
Meyer, Marvin 352
Meyer, Mati 199
Meyer, Wendy 171
Miceli, Calgore A. 34, 80, 292
Michels, Thomas 11
Mitthof, Fritz 3, 153, 169, 170, 254
Mölich, Georg 121
Moorhead, John 87
Morin, Germain 90, 91
Mosshammer, Alden A. 387, 388, 498
Mouriki, Doula 296
Müller, Andreas 4, 5, 172
Müller, C. Detlef G. 476, 477, 481
Müller, Friedrich W. K. 337
Murdoch, Brian 51

Nagy, Piroska 344
Nathan, Geoffrey S. 140
Nau, Francois 29, 445, 446, 447, 478, 479, 480, 486, 491, 492
Nicolai, Karl 168
Nirenberg, David 144
Noethlichs, Karl L. 7
Nußbaum, Norbert 121

O'Brien, Mary B. 214
Oberste, Jörg 121
Ocker, Christopher 51
Olbrich, Karl 280

Olschki, Leonardo 337
Otranto, Giorgio 251
Ousterhout, Robert 333

Pairman Brown, John 372
Palmer, Nigel F. 33
Papadopoulos-Kerameus, Athanasios 21, 107, 331, 336, 446
Parry, Ken 374
Patetta, Federico 88, 240
Pedersen, Johannes 476
Pelle, Stephen 54
Pennington, Kenneth 130, 131
Perisandi, Maroula 130
Pernot, Hubert 82
Phelan, Owen M. 100
Phillips, Edward L. 13
Podskalsky, Gerhard 468
Porter, Stanley E. 32
Powell, Kathryn 49
Powell, Susan 41, 47
Pratsch, Thomas 22
Predel, Gregor 11
Priebsch, Robert 36, 37, 39, 41, 42, 43, 112, 119, 221, 241, 245, 246, 247, 254, 256, 258, 270, 271, 278
Prinzivalli, Emanuela 200
Pruitt, Jennifer 333
Puk, Alexander 7, 152

Raby, Frederic James Edward 68
Rakotoniaina, Marie-Ange 144, 153, 159
Ramos, Fernando Rodamilans 209
Rapp, Claudia 483
Rauchegger, Andreas 141
Rebenich, Stefan 10
Reinhardt, Klaus 60
Reinhart, Johannes 478
Remijsen, Sofie 5
Remondini, Marcello 88, 239
Renoir, Ernest 33
Ricker, Venumdat C. 107
Rigolio, Alberto 412
Rist, Josef 12
Ritter, Adolf Martin 18
Rivers, Theodore J. 90
Riviére, Ernest-Maria 36, 43, 113, 114, 115, 116, 117, 120
Rodríguez, Félix 169
Röhricht, Reinhold 35, 41, 43, 121, 222
Rordorf, Willy 4, 11, 153
Rouwhorst, Gerard 144
Rubel, Alexander 98
Rugo, Pietro 88
Rüpke, Jörg 5, 193
Russel, Jeffrey B. 95
Russell, James C. 98

Sachot, M. 32
Salzman, Michele Renée 5
Santos Otero, Aurelio de 33, 80, 478
Schabel, Chris 59
Schäfer, Peter 144
Schäferdieck, Knut 89
Scheibelreiter, Georg 176
Schilling, Alexander Markus 337
Schmitz, Wilhelm 39
Schneider, Johannes 32
Schnell, Bernhard 33
Schürer, Emil 5
Scragg, Donald 49
Scullard, H. H. 194
Sharf, Andrew 469
Sieben, Hermann-Josef 356
Sinisi, Lucia 251
Siquans, Agnethe 200
Sirks, Adriaan J. B. 169
Sitz, Anna 296
Smith, Richard 352
Soulen, R. Kendall 146
Spencer, Stephen 344
Speyer, Wolfgang 33, 141, 337
Staphorst, Nicolaus 34, 35, 41, 222
Stemberger, Günter 144, 390, 369
Stern, Sacha 5, 6, 80, 143
Stockhausen, Annette von 161
Stübe, Rudolf 36, 124
Stumpf, Augustinus 125
Surace, Domenico 470, 471
Szabat, Elzbieta 411

Tabboni, Simonetta 5
Tatarzyński, Richardus 54
Taylor, Archer 299, 362
Theobald, Michael 18
Thomas, A. 476
Thomas, Wilhelm 4
Thomson, R. M. 331, 332

Tolley, Harry 412, 414, 416
Tosi, Michele 88, 89
Tóth, Péter 491
Trzcionka, Silke 374
Tsonkova, Svetlana 352
Tumanov, Vladimir 200
Turner, Peter 292

Ulrich, Jörg 171

VanderKam, James C. 167
Vassiliev, Athanasius 35, 36, 80, 81, 83, 329
Villani, Barbara 153

Wagner, Andreas 299
Walker, Becky 171
Weinfeld, Moshe 366
Weinreich, Otto 33, 142
Wessel, Susan 11, 138
Weyl Carr, Annemarie 356
Whitelock, Dorothy 112
Wilmart, André 48
Winterbottom, M. 331, 332
Wischmeyer, Wolfgang 6
Wolkenhauser, Anja 182
Wolter-von dem Knesebeck, Harald 121
Wood, Ian 172, 175, 177, 211
Wright, Charles D. 49
Würth, Ingrid 124, 125

Yuza, Ryan P. 364

Zahn, Theodor 446
Zeddies, Nicole 95
Zweck, Jordan 112